D0450090

THE WORLD AT WAR
1939–1945

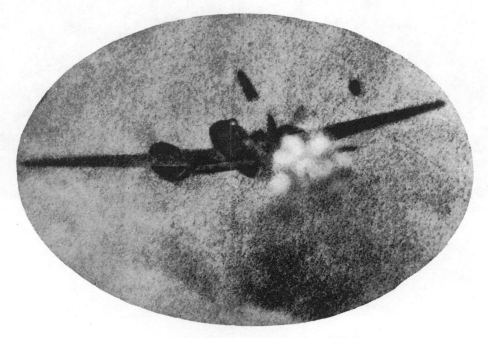

PIECES FLYING FROM A STRICKEN HEINKEL "III" AS FIRE SPREADS, CAUSED BY THE DEVASTATING MACHINE-GUN FIRE OF
ITS PURSUER: A STILL FROM A FILM TAKEN BY A BRITISH FIGHTER.

THE GUARDIAN OF FRENCH LIBERTIES: AN INFANTRY DETACHMENT IN THE FÊTE NATIONALE PARADE, WHEN ALL WERE IMPRESSED BY THE OBVIOUS FIGHTING EFFICIENCY OF THE FRENCH ARMY.

THE WORLD AT WAR 1939–1945

INTRODUCTION BY

JOHN KEEGAN

Foreword by James Bishop
Editor-in-Chief, The Illustrated London News

DOUBLEDAY CANADA LIMITED
TORONTO

PUBLISHER'S NOTE

The World at War is a distillation of 364 issues of *The Illustrated London News* published between the years 1939–1945. It provides a balanced view of this momentous period of history, concentrating essentially on the events, places and people of consequence but also including insights into the social history of the period.

   We would like to acknowledge the contribution in this work of Ben Mackworth-Praed who has selected the material to go in and singlehandedly knitted the many strands together into a coherent whole, so that it represents the story in the exact style of *The Illustrated London News* of the time.

   We would finally like to thank James Bishop, Editor-in-Chief, *The Illustrated London News*, for his encouragement and to Elaine Hart, Librarian of *The Illustrated London News* Picture Archive, for her co-operation.

This edition published in Canada by
Doubleday Canada Limited
105 Bond Street
Ontario
M5B 1Y3

By arrangement with Studio Editions Limited, London

Published by Studio Editions Limited
with the permission of *The Illustrated London News*

Copyright © Studio Editions Limited 1991

ISBN 0-385-25270-6

Printed and bound in Hong Kong.

Canadian Cataloguing in Publication Data

Main entry under title:

The World at War 1939–1945

Fascimiles from the Illustrated London News.
Includes bibliographical references.
ISBN 0-385-25270-6

1. World War, 1939–1945 – Sources. I. Bishop,
James (James D.).

D735.W67 1990   940.53   C90-093734-3

CONTENTS

FOREWORD

THE BIG THREE: THE LEADERS OF THE THREE MAIN ALLIED POWERS DURING THEIR FIRST JOINT CONFERENCE IN TEHERAN IN NOVEMBER 1943. LEFT TO RIGHT: MARSHAL STALIN, PRESIDENT ROOSEVELT AND MR CHURCHILL WITH SOME OF THEIR CIVILIAN ADVISORS.

FOREWORD

Wars have been an almost continuous preoccupation of *The Illustrated London News* (*ILN*). The founder, Herbert Ingram, gave the magazine its name because it was the first publication regularly to carry illustrations, and because he wanted it always to include news from London. In fact London's cosmopolitan character ensured that the news was often international, and the turbulent nature of the last century and a half meant that news has frequently been about wars, revolutions or colonial upheavals. Few years have passed without the *ILN* having to report on the progress of some kind of conflict. It covered ten small wars during its first ten years, and this baptism of fire was quickly followed by the larger Crimean War, by which time the magazine was well enough established to be able to send six war artists to the front.

In the early days there were no photographs, and even when Roger Fenton began sending photographs back from the Crimea they had to be translated into wood engravings before they could be printed in the *ILN*. The half-tone block came a generation, and a few more wars, later; its arrival paved the way for the popular press, and remained the chief method of illustration for newspapers and magazines in both world wars of the twentieth century.

The *ILN* used photographs from many sources to cover the Second World War, as this volume shows, but it maintained the tradition of using war artists as well. Their work complemented that of the photographers and correspondents, giving an extra dimension to the *ILN*'s memorable coverage of these important years.

JAMES BISHOP
Editor-in-chief
The Illustrated London News
March 1990

THE PRICE OF WAR – A CITY OVERWHELMED: AN AERIAL VIEW OF BERLIN SHOWING (LEFT) THE RUINS OF THE REICHSTAG AND THE SHELLS OF GUTTED BUILDINGS.

INTRODUCTION

Like many others who grew up in the Second World War, I remember *The Illustrated London News* as part of my childhood. Its photographic coverage of the war was unique in its excellence and breadth, while what would today be called its 'graphics' were superior to anything else available. There were the lively topographical maps by G.F. Morrell; and, wholly fascinating to a child, the wonderfully clear and explanatory drawings by G.H. Davies. The distinctive G.H. Davies colophon in the corner of a drawing was a guarantee of hours of pleasure. He was an artist who seemed to have an instinctive understanding of how to prepare a cutaway diagram of a ship or an aeroplane in a way that would rivet the attention of a child – but no doubt also that of the adult reader for which it was intended. Looking back over Davies' work today I find it as fascinating now as I did then, and not only for the period charm of his style and annotations.

My parents did not take *The Illustrated London News* (*ILN*), a good reason for visiting neighbours who did, but for a Christmas present in 1941 they gave me a collected edition of the *ILN*'s photographs – and G.H. Davies' drawings – of the world's warships. I literally wore the book to pieces over the next months, so that when I came across its dog-eared remains many years later I threw it away, now to my great regret. Much of what I know of Second World War naval affairs derives from the hours spent with it by the fireside on winter afternoons, and, even though its pages were eventually criss-crossed with sellotape, I should like to have kept it as a reminder of how I learnt what I did all those years ago.

HOLIDAY-MAKERS ASSIST IN FILLING SANDBAGS ON AN EAST COAST BEACH IN SEPTEMBER 1939: IT WAS NECESSARY TO FILL SOME 60,000 SANDBAGS TO PROTECT HOSPITALS AND SO FORTH AT THIS SEASIDE RESORT. SAND AND VOLUNTEERS WERE CONVENIENTLY AT HAND.

The Illustrated London News has always been a magnificent source for historians, as well as a gripping record of passing events for the ordinary reader. The particular nature of its lay-out is an arresting reminder to historians of the conjunction of events, causing such reactions as 'Did the loss of the airship *Hindenburg*, the coronation of George VI and Stalin's purge of the Red Army *all* happen in mid-1937?'. The reminder of such conjunctions is highly stimulating to the historical process, and all the more so when the *ILN* is the agent because of its remarkably eclectic coverage of events. *Life* may be remembered for the quality of its photographs; the *ILN* should be respected for its policy of recording events in any particular week from every corner of the globe. Its photographic standards were in any case high; but its picture selection policy made it, in the era of the world wars, a journal of record of the photographic news image probably without parallel among competitors.

The *ILN* had established an altogether admirable reputation before 1939 as a calm but telling source of warning about the danger that the dictators offered to the democracies. It was not, unlike *The Times*, an appeasement paper. Though its tone was

THE UNHOLY ALLIANCE OF NAZI AND BOLSHEVIK: GERMAN SOLDIERS MEET THE CREW OF A RUSSIAN ARMOURED CAR IN CENTRAL POLAND. IDEOLOGICAL DIFFERENCES HAVE APPARENTLY BEEN SUNK AT THE PROSPECT OF SHARING THE COUNTRY BETWEEN THEM.

always unemotional and apparently dispassionate, it left its readers in no doubt, both by its choice of illustrations and its cool but incisive captioning, that Hitler, Mussolini and the Japanese military – of whose aggression in China it was a relentless chronicler – were men who threatened the peace of the world. When war broke out, therefore, it was not a paper saddled with a burden of explaining its position to its readers. Its pictures had told the story: that the dictatorships were preparing for war, that the democracies had followed them reluctantly, that Britain in particular was ill-prepared and that the experience of war when it at last came was likely to prove grim.

The *ILN* may be forgiven a certain patriotic uncriticality in its portrayal of British equipment and armed forces at the war's outbreak, much of which was in any case a consequence of official policy in the recaptioning of photographs released to the Press, a policy designed to boost the morale of both our own people and that of neutrals and potential allies. Aircraft and ships which we know today to have been obsolete or ill-conceived in initial design, were described as the equivalents of German equipment far superior in quality. There was a similar equation of British and, initially, French fighting units with those of the enemy. Once combat was joined, however, the inequality of the two sides was revealed all too starkly by events, and the *ILN* moderated the tone of its captioning, in which, even as a schoolboy, I sometimes detected a certain tongue-in-cheek attitude: the deadpan comment that 'The Sultan of Oman, ruling over 83,000 square miles and 550,000 inhabitants, has offered his assistance', cannot greatly have stirred British hearts, even in the uncertain days of September 1939. From Dunkirk onwards the *ILN* told it as it was, not simply because the pictures it reproduced ruled out any monkeying with the facts.

The war which the *ILN* set out to report – as it had reported all Britain's wars since the Sikh wars of the 1840s – began badly for the alliance to which it belonged, though without immediate harm to the people of the United Kingdom, or those of its Commonwealth and Empire whom the *ILN* kept so constantly on its pages. The *ILN* had closely followed Hitler's moves to strengthen the German hold on the Free City of Danzig, an ethnic German enclave in the territory of Poland. When the German fleet began its attack from Danzig on September 1, 1939, the magazine printed extensive photographs of the fighting. It also covered the wider campaign in Poland in great detail, reporting both the advance of the German troops in overwhelming strength on Warsaw and the Red Army's 'stab in the back'. Extensive coverage of the Soviet Union had been a distinctive feature of the magazine in the inter-war years.

The collapse of the brave Polish army after three weeks of fighting ushered in what was to become known from an American correspondent's despatch, as 'the Phoney War'. Hitler brought

ANOTHER VICTIM OF UNRESTRICTED MINE-WARFARE: THE 10,000-TON UNION CASTLE STEAMSHIP "DUNBAR CASTLE" SUNK ON JANUARY 9, 1940, AFTER BEING MINED OFF THE SOUTH-EAST COAST OF ENGLAND. SHE WAS NOT UNDER CONVOY WHEN THE DISASTER OCCURRED.

back the Wehrmacht to the West but, at loggerheads with his generals over strategy, did not open an autumn campaign – or a winter one. The U-boats attacked shipping on the high seas, as did German surface raiders; the largest of them, the *Graf Spee*, was caught and disabled British cruisers in the Battle of the River Plate on December 13, a drama of which the *ILN* made a great deal. The opposed air forces scarcely fought each other, however, since there was a mutual embargo on bombing cities, not broken until the height of the Battle of Britain in the following year; and the armies seemed frozen in stalemate. The most significant factor in the military situation in the West during the Phoney War seemed the Maginot Line, which the *ILN* illustrated and described in detail.

Hitler's unprovoked invasion of Denmark and Norway in April 1940 disturbed the torpor of the Phoney War, though it was a less dramatic campaign than the Russo-Finnish War of December 1939 to March 1940, in which the Western Powers had almost intervened on Finland's side. Then, on May 10, 1940, the first of 'the sixty days that overthrew the West', the Wehrmacht launched the great offensive against the French, the British Expeditionary Force, and the neutral Belgian and Dutch armies. Within three days the German army had crossed the Meuse, the only large water obstacle in its path, and begun the panzer drive across the plains of northern France which was to bring the German forces to the Channel on May 19. The Maginot Line, whose underground forts the *ILN* had illustrated so extensively, was simply by-passed. The Belgian army, which fought stoutly as long as it could, was encircled. With it also the BEF and the mobile divisions of the French army were cut off in a pocket progressively constricted by the Wehrmacht and centring on the small port of Dunkirk. From Dunkirk and the nearby beaches, the BEF was rescued, together with 200,000 French soldiers, by destroyers of the Royal Navy and the armada of 'little ships', in the miraculous 'nine days' of the Dunkirk evacuation from May

PARIS MELANCHOLY IN DEFEAT: THE PLACE DE L'OPÉRA, NORMALLY ONE OF THE BUSIEST SPOTS IN THE CITY, WITH A SOLITARY HAND-CART ITS ONLY TRAFFIC.

27 to June 4. The escape of the BEF was celebrated by the British as a sort of triumph, to the great disapproval of Winston Churchill, Prime Minister since May 10, who sombrely reminded the House of Commons that 'wars are not won by evacuations'. There was no vestige of triumph for the French in what remained of the campaign. On June 17 their new head of government, Marshal Pétain, announced that he was seeking an armistice, and on June 25 it came into effect. The terms were deeply humiliating. The greater part of France was to be occupied, in the south-east by Mussolini's Italians, who had entered the campaign just before it ended. The French army was to be reduced to a shadow. The French navy was to be exiled to North Africa. Only the colonies and the 'free zone' were to remain under the control of Pétain's government, based at the little spa town of Vichy.

'The Battle of France is over', Churchill had announced to the House of Commons at the close of Dunkirk. 'I expect that the Battle of Britain is about to begin'. Hitler's failure to trap and destroy the BEF in France had cheated him of victory over Great Britain and he now turned to invasion plans. Invasion, however, could only succeed if the Royal Air Force could be swept from the skies over the Channel which his invasion fleet must negotiate. During July the Luftwaffe began to test its strength against Britain's air defences, which included the Chain Home radar stations built just before the war. On August 13, Eagle Day, it opened the Battle of Britain in earnest.

TRACK AND PLATFORM BOTH UTILISED BY SHELTERERS AT ALDWYCH TUBE STATION. TRAINS BETWEEN ALDWYCH AND HOLBORN WERE SUSPENDED TO PROVIDE A DORMITORY FOR LONDONERS.

The Battle was to last until the end of September and fell into two distinct phases. For the first three weeks the Luftwaffe tried to defeat the RAF by attacking its bases; when that strategy failed it turned, on September 7, to attacking London. 'The first day of the bombing', as East Enders called it, left London's docks aflame and the destruction caused a worldwide sensation. It was the first great aerial assault on a large city, repeated again on December 29, by night, and for the third time on December 10, 1941. Most of the intervening nights had brought German bombers to London, but also to the major provincial centres, some of which, like Coventry and Bristol, had suffered appallingly. The scenes which the German bombers left filled page after page of the *ILN*, many of the pictures being of historical landmarks – the chamber of the House of Commons, Wren churches, City livery halls – all gaping from fire and explosion.

May 10, the anniversary of Hitler's attack in the West, proved the last night of what Londoners had come to call the Blitz, because the Luftwaffe was then being deployed for his next surge of conquest – Operations Margarita in the Balkans and Barbarossa against Russia. In the autumn of 1940 Hitler had conducted an energetic diplomatic offensive in the Balkans which had brought Hungary, Romania and eventually Bulgaria within his Tripartite Pact. Only Greece and Yugoslavia had proved resistant. Greece, at war with Italy, had actually invited the British to base forces on its soil, an extension of their campaign against Italy in the

Western Desert which was in itself a humiliation for the Italo-German Axis. When, at the end of March 1941 a pro-Axis government in Yugoslavia was overthrown by a military coup, Hitler decided to solve his Balkan problem by overrunning Yugoslavia and Greece. Despite British intervention, the brave Greek army was overwhelmed in less than a month of fighting; the Yugoslav army collapsed in a few days.

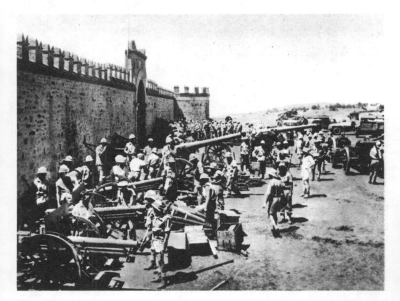

THE LIBERATION OF ABYSSINIA: ITALIAN GUNS AND EQUIPMENT CAPTURED BY SOUTH AFRICANS AT FORT MEGA, ITALIAN SOMALILAND ON FEBRUARY 20, 1940, WHERE MANY PRISONERS WERE ALSO TAKEN.

On June 22, 1941 the Wehrmacht was deployed to invade Russia. Stalin, whose rise to power the *ILN* had documented in great detail, was unprepared for the danger of invasion. As a co-signatory with Hitler of the Molotov-Ribbentrop non-aggression pact of August 22, 1939, he believed that the territorial agreement then negotiated satisfied the ambitions of both parties. Whatever the more distant future might hold, his policy was based on the assumption that Hitler would not attack Russia. His

THE BLITZ RETURNS TO LONDON OVERNIGHT AND IN EARLY MORNING OF MARCH 20, 1941: A MOTHER SMILES AMID THE RUINS, ALL THAT REMAINS OF A TYPICAL WORKING-CLASS HOME.

military dispositions, in consequence, were quite unsuited to a strong defence, and the Wehrmacht, in the opening stages of Barbarossa, broke through the new Russian frontier – 200 miles further to the west than that of 1939 – on the widest scale.

The Red Army was almost destroyed in the Wehrmacht's opening moves. The three German army groups, North, Centre and South, devoured the enemy in great gulps, sending the tanks ahead to throw strong pincers around the enemy and then allowing the infantry to catch up and complete the envelopments. At Minsk and Smolensk, on Napoleon's road to Moscow, Russian soldiers were encircled in hundreds of thousands. Army Group North meanwhile advanced along the Baltic coast to besiege Leningrad, while in the Ukraine Army Group South drove across the great steppe towards Kiev. After six weeks the advance halted. Hitler and his generals had fallen into a disagreement about strategy, the Führer wanting to complete the capture of Kiev and Leningrad before resuming the advance on Moscow, his panzer leaders wanting to end the campaign by a swift strike at the capital.

HOW THE NAZIS TOOK CRETE: FULLY EQUIPPED GERMAN PARATROOPS, IMMEDIATELY AFTER LANDING, UNLOADING FROM A JUNKERS MACHINE MOTOR-CYCLES AND SIDECARS, BY MEANS OF WHICH AID WAS RUSHED TO HARD-PRESSED UNITS.

The dispute took six weeks to resolve and, though the Führer eventually had his way, the outcome was to prove disastrous to the success of Barbarossa. The shift of panzer forces towards Kiev resulted in the largest encirclement the Wehrmacht had yet achieved, with nearly a million Russian soldiers falling into its hands. By the time the tanks had been redeployed to strike for Moscow, however, the summer was already drawing in; and when the German vanguards reached the capital's outskirts in early December the German troops were exhausted, the Russian winter had set in hard and Stalin had assembled a counter-attack army.

The *ILN*'s coverage of the Russian campaign had been hampered by the secretiveness of the Stalinist regime, compounded understandably by the dimensions of the catastrophe Russia had undergone between June and December 1941. The magazine had filled its pages by way of compensation with news from the Western Desert, not all of which had been good. The Western Desert Force, later renamed the Eighth Army, had won a great victory over the Italians at the end of 1940; shortly afterwards the Italians had also been defeated in Ethiopia. But during 1941, when the dashing young German general Erwin Rommel had appeared in Libya at the head of the Afrika Korps, the British had been forced back to the borders of Egypt. Under Auchinleck the Eighth Army had succeeded in recovering most of the ground lost, but had then been repulsed when Rommel got his second wind. At the beginning of 1942 the Afrika Korps was once again entrenched on the Egyptian border.

In retrospect, however, we are enabled to see that the German effort to win victory had reached crisis point at the beginning of 1942. The outcome of the war in the Desert was balanced on a knife's edge, while in Russia the Red Army had won its first victory when Stalin's counter-attack force, brought from Siberia to Moscow in the autumn of 1941, had repelled the Wehrmacht from the capital. The menace to the Allies now took on a different form. As Germany's offensive lost impetus, it was taken up by the Japanese who, on December 7, 1941, launched their surprise attack against the American fleet at Pearl Harbor.

JAPAN'S SUCCESSES IN BURMA: JAPANESE TANK TROOPS CROSSING A TEMPORARY BRIDGE BUILT TO REPLACE ONE DESTROYED BY RETREATING BRITISH FORCES.

The beginning of the Pacific war brought the editors of the *ILN* a plethora of dramatic photographs, almost all conveying bad news. The magazine had always extensively covered naval affairs. Between December 1941 and June 1942 its pages were filled week after week with pictures of famous American and British warships sunk, sometimes pictures of the sinkings themselves. Five American battleships were sunk at Pearl Harbor on December 7, although only the loss of two was admitted at the time; three days later HMS *Prince of Wales* and *Repulse* were sunk by Japanese aircraft off Malaya. In February the brave Dutch Admiral Karel Doorman led his fleet of Dutch, British, Australian and American ships to heroic defeat in the Battle of the Java Sea; and in April Nagumo, the visitor of Pearl Harbor, raided as far as Ceylon, sinking the carrier *Hermes* and three other British ships. In these six months the Royal Navy and the RAN lost two capital ships, a carrier, numerous destroyers and four cruisers, including two of the beautiful County class which the *ILN* had featured so often from pre-war reviews of the fleet.

On land the humiliation was extreme. Hong Kong was overrun on Christmas Day, 1941, after a brave but hopeless defence. Malaya fell to a brilliant Japanese offensive, which culminated in the shameful surrender of Singapore on February 15. America's last strongholds in the Philippines, the Bataan peninsula and Corregider Island, were surrendered after heroic resistance in April and early May. By then most of Burma and the whole of the Dutch East Indies had fallen into Japanese hands. At the beginning of June, Japan controlled almost the whole of the South-East Asian and Pacific island zone it had set out to conquer only seven months before.

Then, in mid-1942, the tide began to turn for the Allies. In May the Japanese suffered a setback in the Battle of the Coral Sea when they attempted to win control of the waters which would give them access to northern Australia. It was not a clear victory for the American fleet; the battle of Midway, June 4, unquestionably was. In ten dramatic minutes American carrier aircraft sank three of Nagumo's carriers, the heart of his Pearl Harbor striking force, a loss from which the Japanese navy was never to recover. Nor was its strategy to recover; Japan's war plan depended for success on seizing an island perimeter in the western Pacific.

FOUR ENGINED HANDLEY PAGE "HALIFAX" HEAVY BOMBERS NEARING COMPLETION. TO SPEED PRODUCTION EACH MACHINE IS MADE UP FROM A LARGE NUMBER OF SUB-ASSEMBLIES, THE WINGS FOR EXAMPLE BEING MADE IN FIVE PARTS, SO THAT CONSTRUCTION CAN BE DIVIDED UP AMONG THE LARGEST POSSIBLE NUMBER OF OPERATIVES.

Some gaps still remained in the perimeter before Midway was fought. Afterwards they could not be closed, and presented the United States Navy with the points of entry by which it fought its way back to eventual victory.

The summer of 1942 also saw a shift of fortunes in the war in Europe. After the spring thaw the Wehrmacht had recovered from its setback outside Moscow and resumed its advance into south Russia, towards Stalingrad. Once again vast pockets of Russian soldiers had been encircled and devoured. On this leg of his march of conquest, however, Hitler overreached himself. His objective was the Russian oil centre in the Caucasus, possession of which would make him strategically self-sufficient. By attempting to seize the oil-bearing regions and at the same time fight a decisive battle at Stalingrad, he dissipated his force, was obliged to withdraw from the Caucasus and then found that he could not disengage from Stalingrad. There a German force of twenty divisions was encircled by a Russian counter-offensive in November and eventually forced to surrender, after sustaining a brutal siege, on February 1, 1943.

The *ILN* was able to cover the Stalingrad saga in detail, since the Russians freely distributed pictures of their first great victory. It also had western victories to cover, however, for in October 1942 the Eighth Army, commanded by Montgomery, had defeated Rommel at Alamein, while in November an Anglo-American army had landed in French North Africa. These successes culminated in the defeat of the Afrika Korps and its Italian allies in Tunisia in May, 1943, opening the way for an Allied invasion of Italy, via Sicily, in September.

While the armies of Hitler's enemies were grappling with the Wehrmacht, the western air forces had begun a direct attack on the cities of the Reich. During 1941 the RAF had opened a bombing offensive, but with little effect. In 1942 Bomber Command's new chief, 'Bomber' Harris had inaugurated thousand-bomber raids, and during 1943 the RAF and the US Eighth Air Force began a combined bomber offensive which inflicted catastrophic damage on one German city after another, the British bombing by night, the Americans by day. The development of a long-range escort fighter, the P-41 Mustang, allowed the Eighth Air Force to penetrate deep into German territory during daylight hours. The *ILN*, thanks particularly to G.H. Davies, had always closely documented developments in air warfare and its readers were kept closely abreast of the characteristics of such key instruments of air warfare during this period such as the American B-17 Flying Fortress, the RAF Lancaster, Halifax and Stirling bombers and the German Fw 190 and Me 110 night fighters which attempted to counter their intrusions into Reich airspace.

The most dramatic event on the established ground fronts during 1944 was the fall of Rome, captured by Allied troops after their breakthrough of German positions in Italy on June 5, 1944. Next day began the operation for which *ILN* readers had waited four years, the return of British – together with American –

troops to France in a great amphibious invasion. D-Day, June 6, 1944, was mounted with a plethora of the equipment which the magazine delighted in describing (although in this case not at the time): landing-craft of many types, floating harbours, swimming tanks and massed glider and parachute forces. Allied war leaders, particularly Churchill, had feared heavy losses on the Normandy beaches. Thanks to the specialised equipment employed, and a brilliant deception plan which misled the Germans as to the true landing place, D-Day itself cost the invasion armies only a fraction of the casualties anticipated.

The battle of Normandy, however, was to develop into a bloody campaign, for the allies and even more so for the Germans. On June 22, moreover, the Russians opened in White Russia a great offensive, Operation Bagration, which led to the

A FIFTEEN-MILE STREAM OF FORTRESSES PASSING OVER BERLIN IN THE FIRST MAJOR DAY AIR BATTLE OF MARCH 6, 1944: ALLIED LOSSES AMOUNTED TO 68 BOMBERS AND 11 FIGHTERS, BUT THEY SHOT DOWN 176 ENEMY FIGHTERS. ON MARCH 8, 38 BOMBERS AND 16 FIGHTERS WERE LOST, BUT 125 ENEMY FIGHTERS WERE SHOT DOWN. IN THE THIRD RAID, ON MARCH 9, NOT ONE ENEMY FIGHTER CHALLENGED THE U.S. AIR FORCE.

destruction of Army Group Centre. In six weeks the front – which they had advanced the previous year across the Ukraine, following their great victory at Kursk – was pushed deep into Poland, from which the frontier of the Reich itself henceforward lay under direct threat.

In August the allies broke out of Normandy and began their own advance to Germany's western frontier, driving the broken remnants of the German defenders before them. A Franco-American force landed simultaneously in the South of France and advanced up the Rhone valley. By mid-September the whole of France, most of Belgium and part of Holland had been liberated and it seemed that Germany was about to be invaded from west as well as east before winter set in.

Then the Germans staged a recovery. Despite the swelling power of the strategic bombing offensive, despite a plummeting fall in the output of war material, despite the loss of territory from which much of its essential resources were drawn, despite an assassination attempt by German army officers against Hitler himself, the Wehrmacht beat off an Anglo-American airborne assault on the Rhine, manned its western frontier defences, closed the yawning gap left by the destruction of Army Group Centre, stabilised a line in northern Italy, blocked the advance of the Red Army into the Balkans and raised new armies for the defence. Not merely for the defence: throughout the winter of 1944 London was kept under attack by V-2 rockets, successors to the flying bombs which had done such damage in the summer; and in December Hitler launched a great ground offensive in the Ardennes that drove a vast 'bulge' in the American line and

threatened Antwerp. The Ardennes offensive, however, proved Germany's last gasp. With the onset of spring weather, the western and Red armies resumed their offensive, broke across the Rhine and the Oder and began to fight battles of annihilation on German soil. At the beginning of April Berlin came under threat. Hitler, with his empire crumbling about him, announced his determination to remain within the capital, and there, on April 30, with Russian shells falling in the garden of the Reich Chancellery above his bunker, he committed suicide. Eight days later his successor, Admiral Doenitz, instituted the ceasefire which brought the European war to an end.

Japan continued to fight, though the home islands were now vulnerable to air attack from American bases established on the islands of Saipan, Iwo Jima and Okinawa. Mac Arthur's South-West Pacific Command having recaptured the Philippines, while Nimitz's fleet had broken open Japan's island perimeter in the Central Pacific, and the United States Army, Navy and Marine Corps - spearhead of the island fighting – were ready to invade Japan. The operation, codenamed Olympia, was one from which the American leaders shrank even more fearfully than Churchill had from D-Day. The conventional wisdom was that it would cost 'a million casualties' – and that despite the state of semi-starvation into which the Japanese had fallen, their merchant fleet sunk and their industry staggering to a halt.

At the last moment the great scientific innovation of the war, the atomic bomb, intervened to make invasion unnecessary. Proved at test in July, its use as a weapon received the assent of the new American president, Truman, immediately afterwards and the only two working examples were dropped on Hiroshima and Nagasaki on August 6 and 9, 1945. The Japanese government at once recognised that the war could not be continued, and the Emperor Hirohito, in a broadcast which transmitted the imperial voice to his people for the first time in history, conceded surrender.

The aftermath of the war provided the *ILN* with a superfluity of the material it had always preferred to publish – scenes of great ceremony, as surrenders were formally signed, of great formal events, such as the trials of the war criminals which began to unfold in 1946, and of great moment, like the inauguration of post-war governments and of the United Nations. There was also a vast gallery of portraits of new leaders and heroes to present to its readership, from guerrilla chiefs like Tito to apostles of world government like Trygve Lie. Never again, however, would there be a series of world events so dramatic or so universal in scope as those the *ILN* had covered in the Second World War. It had risen magnificently to the reporting challenge the war had presented, and the record it left will remain an unparalleled source of interest and information as long as the war is studied.

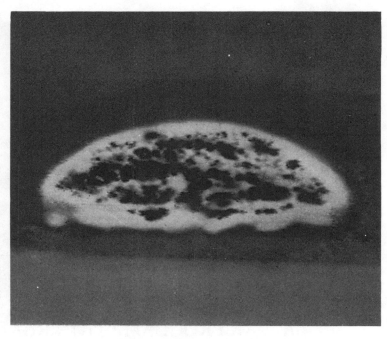

THE FIRST ATOM BOMB EXPLODES. A PHOTOGRAPH TAKEN WITH A SPECIAL CAMERA FROM A DISTANCE OF ABOUT SIX MILES AT THE TEST EXPLOSION AT ALAMOGORDO AIR BASE IN NEW MEXICO ON JULY 16, 1945.

THE ILLUSTRATED LONDON NEWS

A WAR PROCLAMATION READ WITH HISTORIC CEREMONY

The state of war which was broadcast to the nation on Sunday received a further ratification in an official proclamation made in front of the Royal Exchange in the centre of the City. The proclamation was read by Mr. W. J. Boston, Salt-bearer and acting Common Crier.

The proclamation covered matters of contraband – arms and ammunition, fuel of all kinds, all means of communication, and of transportation (including animals), coin, bullion, currency, evidences of debt, metal materials, food, forage and clothing.

1939

*The Polish Crisis — The Russo-German Non-Aggression Pact —
Poland prepares — Germany invades Poland — Britain and her
Empire and France declare War on Germany — Russia invades Poland
— Warsaw falls to the Germans — Polish resistance ends — Poland
partitioned — Russia forces Treaties on Baltic States — The Battle of
the Atlantic begins — Prime Minister Calinescu of Rumania assassinated — women volunteers in England — Polish Government in exile
formed — Germany's indiscriminate mine laying — British Expeditionary Force arrives in France — Munich bomb attack fails to kill Hitler
— Russia invades Finland — the Winter War — USA adds "Cash and
Carry" Clause to the Neutrality Act — the Battle of the River Plate:
British sink "Admiral Graf Spee" — King George VI visits France —
first Empire troops arrive in England.*

DANZIG IN THE SHADOW OF THE NAZI SWASTIKA:
THE CLASH OF POLISH AND GERMAN INTERESTS IN EUROPE'S STORM-CENTRE

UNIFORMED NAZIS MARCHING THROUGH THE STREETS OF THE FREE CITY – APPARENTLY AN EVENT SO COMMON IN DANZIG THAT ONLY ONE WINDOW CONTAINS AN ONLOOKER

HERR FORSTER PRESENTING COLOURS TO THE DANZIG HEIMWEHR COMMANDER, COLONEL GORTE (WHO WEARS A UNIFORM REMINISCENT OF THE NAZI SCHUTZSTAFFEL) AT A PARADE WHICH REVEALED THE CORPS' PRESENT STRENGTH AT ABOUT TWO THOUSAND.

THE LEADER OF POLAND AT A CRITICAL POINT IN HER HISTORY: MARSHAL SMIGLY RYDZ, INSPECTOR GENERAL OF THE ARMED FORCES WITH HIS WIFE, ON THE TERRACE OF THEIR HOME IN WARSAW.

THE LEAGUE HIGH COMMISSIONER FOR DANZIG SINCE 1937: DR KARL BURCKHARDT (LEFT) TALKING TO A NAZI OFFICIAL; THE APPOINTMENT OF DR. BURCKHARDT, A SWISS, LASTS TILL 1940.

On April 28 Herr Hitler replied to the message which President Roosevelt sent to him and Signor Mussolini, on April 15, outlining measures for establishing peace in Europe, before the Reichstag, in the Kroll Opera House, Berlin. The Führer stated that Germany knew nothing of any "threat" to other nations and was prepared to give each of the States named by Mr. Roosevelt an assurance of the kind desired,

A GERMAN NAVAL TRAINING SHIP ARRIVES AT DANZIG AT A FATEFUL HOUR: THE "SCHLESWIG-HOLSTEIN", WHICH IS ARMED WITH 11-IN. GUNS, ENTERING THE HARBOUR ON AUGUST 25.

provided that the States concerned wished it and made Germany appropriate proposals. He denied that all international troubles could be solved at the conference table and stated that at all times in the future German negotiators would have behind them the armed strength of the German nation. Herr Hitler announced that he had denounced the ten-year pact of non-aggression with Poland, signed in January 1934, as he considered the Anglo-Polish Agreement was a regular alliance directed exclusively against Germany, and had also denounced the Anglo-German Naval Agreement of June 1935, by which Germany accepted a limitation of the total tonnage of her Fleet to 35 per cent. of the aggregate tonnage of the naval forces of the British Empire.

The substance of the proposals made by Herr Hitler to Poland in his Reichstag speech were: the return of Danzig; a road and railway line through the "Corridor possessing the same extra-territorial status for Germany as the Corridor itself has for Poland". He said he has proposed: to recognise all Polish economic rights in Danzig; to ensure for Poland a Free Harbour in Danzig of any size; to accept as permanent the present boundaries between Germany and Poland; conclude a twenty-five year non-aggression pact with Poland and to have the "independence of the Slovak State guaranteed by Germany, Poland and Hungary jointly – which means in practice the renunciation of any unilateral German hegemony in this territory".

The Polish Government denied knowledge of the last two proposals. It did not "reject" the others: it submitted alternatives as a basis for discussion: (1) to negotiate concerning the question of a substitute for the Commissioner of the League of Nations (at Danzig) and (2) to consider facilities for the transit traffic through the Corridor. As the Führer himself suggested, the Czecho-Slovak situation of a year ago might be recalled. And, it may justly be pondered, of what use is a fresh pact, even of twenty-five years, when the existing agreement is denounced on so flimsy a pretext as the Anglo-Polish mutual guarantees? Polish counter-demands are foreshadowed which include a Polish Protectorate over Danzig.

Recently agitation has again come to the fore, a German coup, indeed, in early July being thought possible by many political observers. Polish Navy Week culminated on June 29 in national demonstrations throughout the country under the slogan "We will not be forced from the sea". On the same day Lord Halifax, speaking at the Royal Institute of International Affairs, emphasised Britain's Continental commitments. "We have assumed obligations", he said, "and are prepared to assume more, with full understanding of their consequences." In Danzig itself, Nazi military preparations were taking place, in the shape of armed "tourists" from the Reich with "Heimwehr" marked on their sleeves; the formation of a Nazi "Free Corps" in which it was reported that all young Danzigers between the ages of fifteen and twenty-five were ordered to enlist, with July 6 as the day by which enrolment had to be completed; and the pouring in from East Prussia of arms, including tanks and heavy guns.

Poland, however, refused to be provoked into rash action. Thus the Government informed the Danzig Senate that they saw no objection to the German cruiser "Konigsberg" visiting Danzig on August 25; and a similar line was reported to be taken over Herr Hitler's projected visit to the Free City on or about July 20. Danzig for long has been one of the "danger spots of Europe" and on more than one occasion it has seemed that the danger could no longer be tided over. But such speeches as that on July 2 of the Free City's Nazi Gauleiter, Herr Forster, when he declared that "Danzigers and all Germans in Great Germany have drawn the conclusion that there is nothing for it but to accept the standpoint of force adopted by Britain and her allies", do not materially help in the finding of a peaceful solution.

THE HEIMWEHR, OR "S.S. HOME DEFENCE CORPS", IS A BODY RECENTLY CREATED OSTENSIBLY FOR THE DEFENCE OF DANZIG AND ALLEGEDLY FROM THE LOCAL MALE POPULATION, BUT IS BELIEVED TO BE ALMOST WHOLLY MANNED BY GERMANS INTRODUCED INTO THE FREE CITY AS "TOURISTS".

Herr Forster returned on August 9 after conferring with Herr Hitler at Berchtesgaden, and the following day made a typical speech in which he attacked England, France and Poland. "Danzig is not English, not French, and not Polish" he said; and "the hour of liberation is at hand . . . our Motherland and our Fuhrer, Adolf Hitler, are determined to support us."

POLAND SHOWING THE "CORRIDOR" BETWEEN POMERANIA AND EAST PRUSSIA, GDYNIA, THE ONLY PORT OVER WHICH POLAND POSSESSES SOVEREIGNTY, AND DANZIG, BY THE VERSAILLES TREATY A UNIT OF THE POLISH CUSTOMS ADMINISTRATION.

A REVERSAL OF POLICY: THE ASTONISHING RUSSO-GERMAN PACT.

SIGNING THE WORLD-STAGGERING PACT: RUSSO-GERMAN SMILES IN MOSCOW

The laborious and protracted negotiations for a defensive anti-aggression Pact between Britain, France and the U.S.S.R. have, since the sudden eclipse of M. Litvinoff been carried on on the Soviet side by the new Commissar for Foreign Affairs, M. Molotov, who is also Chairman of the Council of People's Commissars of the U.S.S.R.

British and French military, naval and air missions arrived on August 11 at the "October Terminus" at Moscow, having travelled from Leningrad in the Soviet crack train "Red Arrow." A sumptuous banquet was given in honour of the Anglo-French missions that evening by the Commission for Defence, at which Marshal Voroshiloff toasted the British and French Services. August 12 was the weekly Soviet "free day"; but Marshal Voroshiloff insisted that work should commence at once; and the beginnings of the talks were reported to be held in a most cordial atmosphere.

The announcement that Herr von Ribbentrop, the German Foreign Minister, would visit Moscow to conclude a pact of non-aggression with the Soviet Government, was made on August 21. It is hard to find a case where two important nations, endeavouring to make an agreement with a third nation, are suddenly informed that a fourth party has negotiated a definite pact at the same time, having entered, as it were, by a secret door; in this case, of the Kremlin. Such was, however, the news which burst upon Europe on the morning of Tuesday, August 22.

On August 22 the British and French Ambassadors were in conference with M. Molotoff, Soviet Prime Minister and Foreign Commissar, and it was believed that they asked for an explanation of the developments regarding the Russo-German pact in view of the fact that the Anglo-French-Soviet conversations are still in progress and staff talks

THE RESIGNATION OF THE SOVIET FOREIGN MINISTER: M. LITVI-NOFF (RIGHT) WITH HIS SUCCESSOR, M. MOLOTOFF (LEFT), AND M. STALIN.

are being held. It will be recalled that a Russo-German trade pact was signed in Berlin on August 19, whereby the Soviet will supply raw materials in exchange for "high-grade manufactured goods."

Herr von Ribbentrop, German Foreign Minister, arrived in Moscow by air at 1 p.m. on August 23. He was met at the airport by the Assistant Commissar for Foreign Affairs and a number of other high Soviet officials, German and Italian diplomatists. The absence of Japanese representatives was noted. The Swastika Flag was displayed next to the Red Flag on this occasion. An ironical touch was lent to the proceedings by the fact that Herr von Ribbentrop stayed at the former Austrian Legation, almost next door to the house occupied by the British and French Military Missions. The German-Russian non-Aggression Pact was signed in the presence of M. Stalin that evening. The clauses of this document are now widely known and it is unnecessary for us to detail them here. Particular attention has been drawn to Article 4, by which the two Powers bind themselves not to join "any other group of Powers directly or indirectly if directed against one of the two". Herr von Ribbentrop spent the next morning sight-seeing in Moscow and then left by air for Germany.

The news of the project for a non-aggression Pact between Germany and Soviet Russia resulted in intense activity in Whitehall. Mr. Chamberlain had already returned to London in view of the deterioration of the international situation. On August 21 he saw Lord Halifax and also Mr. Greenwood, the acting Leader of the Opposition. Mr. Hore-Belisha hurried back from the South of France, stopping in Paris for consulta-

THE ANGLO-FRENCH MISSIONS ON ARRIVAL AT THE OCTOBER RAILWAY TERMINUS, MOSCOW, (LEFT) GENERAL DOUMENC, THE FRENCH LEADER, AND (RIGHT) ADMIRAL-SIR REGINALD PLUNKETT-ERNLE-ERLE-DRAX.

A SMILING GROUP AFTER THE SIGNING OF THE NON-AGGRESSION PACT BETWEEN FASCIST GERMANY AND COMMUNIST RUSSIA: HERR VON RIBBENTROP, M. STALIN AND M. MOLOTOFF.

tions with the French authorities, and concluding his journey by air. On August 22 Mr. Chamberlain took his usual morning walk before 10 o'clock, and Mrs. Chamberlain accompanied him. Callers at No. 10 that morning included Sir Kingsley Wood, Secretary of State for Air, Sir John Simon, and Dr. Kordt, the German Charge d'Affaires in London. Mr. S.M. Bruce, High Commissioner for Australia had an interview with the Premier. A Cabinet meeting began at 3 p.m. A communiqué issued afterwards included the statement that a non-aggression Pact between Germany and Russia would in no way affect our obligations to Poland; and that Parliament would be summoned and asked to pass the Emergency Powers (Defence) Bill.

In some quarters it is believed that the whole diplomatic balance of Europe will be altered by the pact. Should Germany feel justified by what she considers a diplomatic triumph in making an attempt to seize Danzig, it would undoubtedly lead to the gravest consequences.

POLAND PREPARES: HER "WAR POTENTIAL" AND TRENCH-DIGGING IN WARSAW

POLAND'S IMPRESSIVE HORSED CAVALRY – EQUIPPED WITH SWORDS, LANCES AND MACHINE-GUNS: AN ARMY WHICH HAS GREATER MOBILITY IN DIFFICULT TERRAIN THAN MECHANISED FORCES BESIDES BEING ABLE TO LIVE ON THE COUNTRY.

STRENUOUS WORK IN WHICH ALL CLASSES WILLINGLY JOINED: MEN, WOMEN AND CHILDREN DIGGING TRENCHES IN AN OPEN SPACE IN WARSAW TO PROVIDE SHELTER FROM RAIDING GERMAN AIRCRAFT.

The passing of Slovakia and Moravia under German control has seriously modified the strategical situation of Poland. None the less, the Carpathians provide strong protection for her south-west frontier – which, indeed, enjoys better natural protection than any other of her frontiers.

Poland's ability to remain firm over the Danzig question rests on her vast resources of man-power which enable her to rank as the fifth military power in the world. To-day 66 per cent. of the population are under thirty years of age, and with a total of only 34,000,000, Poland can mobilise an army larger than that of France. The strength of the standing army in 1938 was 18,738 officers and 255,150 other ranks, and on a war footing, it could easily be increased to 2,000,000 men. Poland has 3,000,000 trained reserves and could

ultimately mobilise a force of 6,000,000 men for service in the army. Recently she has strengthened her mechanised forces and is now producing tanks and armoured cars for her army, whose excellent quality and high performance is widely recognised. The terrain, however, present difficulties to mechanised and motorised forces and an invader would find his way barred by lakes, woods and marshes, leaving him open to attack by the Polish cavalry which has been extensively developed and is probably the best in Europe. The horsemen are equipped with rifles, bayonets, swords, and lances, and are provided with light machine-guns; while horse artillery and horse-drawn anti-tank and anti-aircraft guns operate with them. Poland possesses 3,950,000 horses classed as fit for military service.

THE GERMAN ATTACK ON POLAND:
RUTHLESS BOMBINGS AND OTHER SCENES FROM THE POLISH FRONT.

THE RACK OF BATTLE-SMOKE ON THE POLISH FRONT – HORSE-DRAWN GERMAN ARTILLERY ADVANC-
ING THROUGH A BURNING POLISH VILLAGE.

GERMAN ADVANCE-GUARDS, IN CAR AND ON MOTOR-CYCLES, PASSING THROUGH A VILLAGE STILL
BLAZING FROM HEAVY BOMBARDMENT.

Few campaigns have been begun with immediate advantages so overwhelming as those possessed by Germany when she launched her attack on Poland. Time, strategic situation, material and numbers were all on her side. She had the advantage of time, first, because she could count on a certain delay before Great Britain and France even declared war; secondly, because her western defences freed her from the risk of any serious ground attack on that flank for a considerable period; thirdly, because she was fully mobilised, while the Polish forces in the interior were not, though those in the western part of the country were.

Her strategic situation as regards Poland is at once proclaimed by the map. All was cut and dried for her favourite strategy of envelopment. To the south she outflanked her victim from Slovakia, to the north from East Prussia. From the west she was faced by huge, open plains, ideal for the movement of cross-country vehicles. Even the weather was on her side; for the summer had been unusually dry, so that the roads, few and poor as they are, were at their best for the purpose of withstanding heavy traffic. In material, she disposed of a superiority of probably four to one in aircraft; she had an enormous superiority in armoured fighting vehicles, and a considerable superiority in artillery. In actual numbers she had not sufficient strength to command success against such fine troops as the Polish, had other things been equal; perhaps three to two. But other things were not equal.

THE GERMAN LINES OF ADVANCE: A PLAN DESIGNED TO ENTRAP
THE POLES ROUND WARSAW.

This is how she opened the *Blitzkreig*. From East Prussia she launched an assault southward. She did not, it would appear, dispose of more than ten divisions in this isolated territory, and their attack by itself would have been fruitless. But, simultaneously she thrust across the Corridor from Pomerania, overran it, opened up land communication with East Prussia, and continued the drive in the direction of Warsaw. The Poznan salient she neglected; indeed, the Poles won a local success in this quarter, and reached for a moment the soil of the Reich. From the direction of Breslau came the main onslaught, in which most of her motorised and mechanised divisions were employed with terrific effect. Further south still, she thrust in Silesia, into that area of coal and iron, of intense industry, which contained the life-blood of Poland. This thrust was accompanied by another across the Beskiden and Tatra ranges of the Carpathians.

A BODY OF POLISH TROOPS PRACTISING WITH THEIR GAS-MASKS
BEFORE RESUMING THE MARCH.

USED BY GERMANY AS A PRETEXT FOR BOMBING OPEN TOWNS:
ALLEGED POLISH "FRANC-TIRRURS".

POLISH DEMOLITIONS HAVE KEPT GERMAN ENGINEERS WORKING
FEVERISHLY: THE RUINS OF A BRIDGE.

MUD – ONE OF THE THINGS MOST FEARED BY THE GERMAN
PLANNERS OF A "LIGHTNING WAR".

PATHETIC HUMAN SALVAGE AND INHUMAN DESTRUCTION:
HOUSEHOLD GOODS, INCLUDING A LAMP AND A SHOE, SAVED
FROM A GERMAN AIR RAID ON WARSAW.

THE CULMINATION OF THE GERMAN CAMPAIGN IN CENTRAL POLAND:
INFANTRY ADVANCING IN THE OUTSKIRTS OF WARSAW.

This concentric attack might have been met with a measure of success by the mobile and determined defence, but for one factor – the power of her air forces. They not only enabled the German ground forces to move with complete freedom, but also blinded and crippled the Polish. Communications were shattered by constant bombing; counter-attacks were detected in assembly areas and broken up before they could develop; all troop movements had to be confined to the hours of darkness. Polish artillery was instantly engaged by German, ranged by aircraft, whereas German battery positions could not be identified. Low-flying aeroplanes, using machine-guns as well as bombs, preceded and covered the advance of fighting vehicles and of infantry. Back-area bombing spread disorganisation in the rear. It must be added that, whereas, in the first stage, the German aircraft made some attempt to concentrate on military objectives – though even then the bombers, when engaged with anti-aircraft fire, were apt to drop their bombs quickly into the nearest built-up area and then make off – there seems to be no doubt that since then deliberate attacks have been made upon the civilian population.

**HIS MAJESTY THE KING SPEAKS
TO HIS PEOPLE**
Sunday, Sept. 3, 1939

**THE PRIME MINISTER ANNOUNCES
A STATE OF WAR**
Sunday, Sept. 3, 1939

**M. EDOUARD DALADIER, PRIME
MINISTER OF FRANCE**
Sunday, Sept. 3, 1939

"Sir, that was a final Note. No such undertaking was received by the time stipulated, and consequently this country is now at war with Germany.

"I am in a position to inform this House that, according to arrangements made between the British and French Governments, the French Ambassador in Berlin is at this moment making a similar demarche, also accompanied by a definite time-limit.

"The House has already been made aware of our plans, and, as I said the other day, we are ready.

"It is a sad day for all of us. For none is it sadder than for me. Everything that I have worked for, everything that I had hoped for, everything that I believed in during my public life has crashed into ruins this morning.

"There is only one thing left for me, and that is to devote what strength and powers I have to forwarding the victory of the cause for which we have to sacrifice so much.

"I cannot tell what part I may be allowed to play myself, but I trust I may live to see the day when Hitlerism has been destroyed and a restored and liberated Europe has been re-established." (Cheers.)

"In this grave hour, perhaps the most fateful in our history, I send to every household of my peoples, both at home and overseas, this message. . . . For the second time in the lives of most of us we are at war. . . . For we are called, with our Allies, to meet the challenge of a principle which, . . . stripped of all disguise, is surely the mere primitive doctrine that might is right: and if this principle were established throughout the world, the freedom of our own country and of the whole British Commonwealth of Nations would be in danger.

But far more than this the peoples of the world would be kept in bondage of fear, and all hopes of settled peace and of the security of justice and liberty among nations would be ended. . . .

It is to this high purpose that I now call my people at home and my peoples across the seas, who will make our cause their own.

I ask them to stand calm, firm and united in this time of trial. The task will be hard. There may be dark days ahead, and war can no longer be confined to the battlefield. But we can only do the right as we see the right, and reverently commit our cause to God.

If one and all we keep resolutely faithful to it, ready for whatever service or sacrifice it may demand, then, with God's help, we shall prevail.

May He bless and keep us all."

"Time presses. France and Britain will not stand by at the destruction of a friendly people. The aggression against Poland is a new enterprise of violence against Britain and France. It is not a question of German-Polish conflict. It is a question of a new attempt by the Hitler dictatorship at the domination of Europe and the world.

"A France which would allow this aggression to be carried out would soon be scorned, isolated, discredited, helpless and before long delivered over to the most formidable of onslaughts.

"After the repudiation of the guarantees given to Austria, Czechoslovakia and Poland, the aggressors would turn against France."

"On our honour, we have no hate for any people of the world, and if we shirked our duty it would be only a precarious peace. We should be no more than a wretched people reduced to defeat and servitude.

"When our soldiers are rejoining their regiments none of them has in his heart any hate for the German people. But all are ready to do their duty. Peace-loving as they are, they are ready to defend the dignity and existence of their country, which is at stake."

WAR DECLARED 11 a.m.   WAR DECLARED 5 p.m.

BRITAIN'S WAR CABINET OF NINE – ANNOUNCED ON THE FIRST DAY OF THE WAR – TOGETHER WITH THE HOME SECRETARY, THE DOMINIONS MINISTER, AND THE CABINET SECRETARY, WHO ALSO HAVE ACCESS TO THE MEETINGS.

THE POSSIBILITY OF THE REPEAL OF THE U.S. ARMS EMBARGO: THE SENATE FOREIGN RELATIONS COMMITTEE CONSIDERING THE ADMINISTRATION'S PROPOSED NEW NEUTRALITY LEGISLATION.

Britain's War Cabinet of nine, on the lines of the War Cabinet set up in December 1916, was announced on the night of September 3, the first day of the war. Our photograph shows (back row, left to right) Sir John Anderson, Home Secretary and Minister of Home Security; Lord Hankey, Minister Without Portfolio; Mr. Hore-Belisha, Secretary of State for War; Mr. Churchill, First Lord of the Admiralty; Sir Kingsley Wood, Secretary of State for Air; Mr. Anthony Eden, Secretary of State for Dominion Affairs and Sir Edward Bridges, the Secretary of the Cabinet. In the front row (left to right) are: Lord Halifax, Secretary of State for Foreign Affairs; Sir John Simon, Chancellor of the Exchequer, Mr. Chamberlain, Sir Samuel Hoare, Lord Privy Seal; and Admiral of the Fleet Lord Chatfield, Minister for Coordination of Defence. Sir John Anderson and Mr. Eden are not actual members of the War Cabinet, but have access to the meetings; as does Sir Edward Bridges, the Secretary of the Cabinet.

The repeal of the arms embargo was the chief provision of the U.S. Administration's new Neutrality legislation, which was submitted to the Senate Foreign Relations Committee on September 25 by Senator Key Pittman, the chairman, who is seen above at the far end of the table. The other members of the committee in our photograph are (left to right around the table, beginning from the far side): Senators Guy M. Gillette; Bennett Champ Clark; Henrik Shipste; Wallace H. White; Arthur H. Vandenberg; Robert M. Lafollette; Arthur Capper; Hiram W. Johnson; William E. Borah; Key Pittman (chairman); Walter F. George; Robert F. Wagner; Tom Connally; Elbert D. Thomas; Theodore F. Green; Lewis B. Schwellenback; and Claude Pepper. The first round in the fight was won on October 10, when a suggestion to split the Bill into two parts was defeated by 65 votes to 26. The firm speeches of Mr. Chamberlain and M. Daladier in response to Herr Hitler's "peace overtures" are reported to have won many to the ranks of those seeking the repeal.

POLAND STABBED IN THE BACK: THE RED ARMY ADVANCES.

RUSSIAN TROOPS ENTERING VILNA AFTER THE DECLARATION BY THE SOVIET GOVERNMENT OF THE "DISINTEGRATION" OF THE POLISH STATE – THE FIRST TELEPHOTO TRANSMITTED TO LONDON SINCE THE OUTBREAK OF WAR.

THE SOVIET INVASION OF EASTERN POLAND, OSTENSIBLY TO PROTECT RUSSIAN MINORITIES IN THE WESTERN UKRAINE AND WESTERN BELORUSSIA: A RED ARMY TANK PASSING THROUGH A STREET IN RAKOV.

SOME OF THE "BLOOD-RELATIONS LIVING ON POLISH TERRITORY" WHICH THE RUSSIAN GOVERNMENT DEEMED IT THEIR "SACRED DUTY" TO PROTECT: PEASANTS AT GRODETSK GREETING RED ARMY TANKS.

EVIDENCE OF THE RAPID SOVIETISATION OF EASTERN POLAND, WHERE A MILLION PORTRAITS OF STALIN ARE SAID TO HAVE BEEN DISTRIBUTED: RED ARMY SOLDIERS DISTRIBUTING MOSCOW NEWSPAPERS TO PEASANTS.

THE FOURTH PARTITION OF POLAND: THE RUSSIAN PLENIPOTENTIARY, BOROWENSKI, STUDYING A MAP WITH GERMAN OFFICERS, AT BREST LITOVSK, WHERE GERMAN AND RUSSIAN TROOPS MET ON SEPTEMBER 18.

UNSMILINGLY ENTERING HIS ARMOURED CAR: THE RUSSIAN COMMANDER, BOROWENSKI, LEAVING BREST LITOVSK AFTER AGREEING UPON THE LINE OF DEMARCATION, WITH EQUALLY UNSMILING GERMAN OFFICERS.

After mobilising the strength of the Red Army up to the significant and formidable total of four million men, the Russian Government announced on September 17 that it had directed the High Command of the Red Army to order the troops to cross the frontier "and take under their protection the life and property of the population of Western Ukraine and Western White Russia" which formed part of pre-war Russia. The reason advanced was that the Polish Government had disintegrated and no longer showed any sign of life, and the Moscow authorities were at pains to explain to the British, French and neutral Ambassadors that it was not an act of war.

Russian troops crossed the Polish frontier along its whole length on September 17. In a note handed to the Polish Ambassador in Moscow the Russian Government stated that, owing to the "disintegration" of the Polish State, they felt it their "sacred duty" to protect their blood relations living on Polish territory.

Vilna, in northern Poland, was occupied without resistance on September 18, German and Russian troops

meeting on the same day at Brest Litovsk, the place where Germany imposed a crushing peace treaty on Russia in 1917. Everywhere propagandist Soviet aircraft preceded the troops, dropping leaflets in Ukrainian and Russian. The occupation was carried out by two armies commanded by Generals Kovoloff and Timoshenko.

The reports which reached Moscow all tended to show that the Russians, in their advance into Poland, met little resistance except from some few detachments of the ordinary frontier guards who hastily manned the trenches at a few points. The regular Polish armies were all facing in the opposite direction. This singularly simplified the task of the very considerable Russian forces.

Motorised columns rattled through the empty countryside at a great rate, covering in some cases as much as 40 miles each day to keep their appointment with the victorious German armies and complete the "fourth partition" of Poland.

POLAND CRUSHED BY TWO INVADERS: THE TRAGEDY OF WARSAW

IN THE OUTSKIRTS AND SUBURBS OF WARSAW: GERMAN INFANTRY ADVANCING BEHIND A TANK.

MOVING EVIDENCE OF THE DESPERATE HEROISM WITH WHICH THE POPULATION OF WARSAW DEFENDED THEIR BELOVED CAPITAL: STREET BARRICADES HASTILY THROWN UP IN A SUBURB OF THE CITY – AN ENEMY PHOTOGRAPH.

A Warsaw defence communiqué received in Paris on September 25 first officially revealed to the world the appalling loss of life and the havoc caused by the German bombardment of the Polish capital. In Warsaw, it was stated, "there are no longer any buildings where there have not been victims, or which remain intact. Most houses, and especially the public buildings, are in ruins. As a result of the bombardment of the last twenty-four hours about 100 fires have broken out, and in the same space of time there have been several thousand victims among the civil population."

A "Times" Special Correspondent stated on September 26 that the intensity of the artillery and air bombardment of the Polish capital was further increased on September 25–6, apparently with the determination to reduce the city on the left bank of the Vistula "to heaps of ruins." In explanation of these ruthless methods the German Command announced that the defenders had forced them to resort to cruel measures because they "obstinately refused to listen to reason or to recognise the futility of resistance."

Warsaw, which sustained appalling casualties from German air and land bombardment, only capitulated on September 29, after the destruction of half the city. In view of the tremendous German forces, this was one of the most heroic resistances in history. The wounded numbered 16,000 soldiers and 20,000 civillians.

UNDER THE NAZI HEEL IN POLAND: SERFDOM — AND "VICTORY PARADES."

FORCED LABOUR UNDER THEIR NAZI GUARDS – POLISH PRISONERS BEING MARCHED TO WORK IN THE FIELDS, ESCORTED BY GERMAN SOLDIERS.

ELOQUENT OF THE MISERY OF THE PEOPLE OF POLAND: A COLUMN OF REFUGEES PLODDING ALONG A ROAD OVER AN APPARENTLY LIMITLESS PLAIN.

THE FÜHRER REVIEWING HIS TROOPS IN WARSAW ON OCTOBER 5. ADMITTED GERMAN LOSSES INCLUDED 10,000 DEAD; ACTUAL FIGURES OF 90,000 WERE REPORTED.

The pictures on this page show the conqueror and his army in Warsaw, serfdom reigning in the countryside, and peasants terrified by German inquisitors. But though the last remnant of the Polish Army surrendered on October 6, according to the German High Command, resistance still continues in Poland. This appears from the recent article in the "B.Z. am Mittag," published under the heading "German Police in Poland." The article states that the Gestapo in Poland are compelled to have their revolvers ready on their desks; when they go out they have to be protected by machine-gun squads. Sabotage is revealed to be extensive. "The Poles," remarks the writer, "are masters of guerilla warfare."

For their conquest of Poland, the German admitted losses are 10,572 killed, 30,333 wounded, 3400 missing. According, however, to the Zurich "Arbeiter Zeitung," real losses, compiled by the Nazi War Ministry, were 91,278 dead, and over 140,000 wounded.

UNHOLY ALLIANCE: THE CARVE-UP OF POLAND BETWEEN NAZI AND BOLSHEVIK. GERMANY SURRENDERS VAST INTERESTS TO RUSSIA IN THE BALTIC.

The final frontier demarcation line in Poland as provided for the German-Russian agreement signed in Leningrad by the Foreign Ministers of Germany and Soviet Russia respectively on September 29, begins at the southernmost part of Lithuania from whence it runs in a general westerly direction to the north of Augustowo as far as the frontier of Germany, and follows the frontier as far as the River Pissa; and then, through Ostrolenka and along the Bug to Sokal, and along the upper San. About 80 per cent of the Polish oil-wells go to the Soviet.

FORCIBLE EMIGRATION OF BALTIC GERMANS: PATHETIC GROUPS ON THE QUAYSIDES AT RIGA

ENJOYING A JOKE WITH STALIN ON THE "CARVE-UP" OF POLAND, WHICH WAS DESCRIBED BY MR. CHURCHILL AS A MEASURE "CLEARLY NECESSARY FOR THE SAFETY OF RUSSIA AGAINST THE NAZI MENACE": M. STALIN HEARTILY PATS RIBBENTROP ON THE BACK, WHILE M. MOLOTOFF READS OVER THE TERMS.

Hitler has paid a tremendous price for his agreement with Russia, and Stalin has gained almost as much by hard bargaining as Germany did with the sacrifice of lives and *matériel*. The Soviet advance to the Baltic began with the signing of a pact with Esthonia, giving the Russians the right to naval and air bases in that country. Then M. Munters, the Latvian Foreign Minister, went to Moscow; with the Lithuanian Minister hard on his heels. Latvia accepted a pact on October 5, giving the Soviet bases at Libau and Windau. On October 7 it was announced in Moscow that Russia had asked Finland to send a negotiator to Moscow. Dr. Paasikivi saw M. Molotov in Moscow on October 11, but meanwhile the Finnish Government set about strengthening their defences and taking precautions against air raids. Perhaps the most amazing development of all was the German decision to repatriate Germans living in the Baltic States. This, of course, represents a complete reversal of Nazi policy, which has long held up the Baltic shore as one of the most sacred areas of German "cultural expansion." Not surprisingly there were widespread rumours of discontent in Germany at this cynical bargaining.

A CHILD VICTIM OF AS CRIMINAL A DEED AS THE SINKING OF THE "LUSITANIA": A LITTLE BOY FROM THE "ATHENIA" CARRIED ASHORE AT GALWAY.

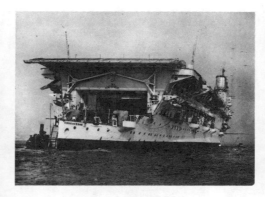

PROVIDING A GOOD IDEA OF THE WIDTH OF THE FLIGHT DECK ON THE LOST VESSEL: A STERN VIEW OF H.M.S. "COURAGEOUS."

SCANNING THE FIRST LISTS OF SURVIVORS FROM THE "ROYAL OAK": A SCENE IN A NAVAL PORT ON THE SOUTH COAST ON OCTOBER 15.

At 11 p.m. on September 3 S.S. "Athenia" was torpedoed and sunk 250 miles off the Donegal coast. "Such action," stated the Ministry of Information, "is in direct contravention of the rules regarding submarine warfare by which Germany is bound. These rules . . . lay down clearly that no merchant ship may be sunk without warning." The majority of the crew, numbering 320, and the 1400 passengers were saved; but some deaths were reported caused by the explosion and by drowning.

More than anything, the idea of the sufferings of the children in the

"Athenia" horrified people in every civilised country in the world. Anguished passengers told of how they lost sight of their families below decks when the lights went out, and of sons and daughters who were never seen again. Even more dreadful was the experience of those who were forced to look on while their children drowned before their eyes, or saw them drifting away in lifeboats as they themselves stood on the decks of rescuing ships.

The definitive account of the torpedoing of the "Courageous" was given by Mr. Churchill in the House of Commons on September 20. He stated that the ship had on board 1202 officers and men at the time – that is, somewhat less than her full complement, as she had embarked a reduced number of aircraft. The lists of survivors published by the Admiralty included nearly 700 names. Warm tributes have been paid to the heroism of Captain Makeig-Jones, who was in command of the "Courageous." Survivors saw that very gallant officer standing on the bridge as the ship sank, saluting the ensign. The submarine which fired

the torpedo was set upon by the screening vessels, and Mr. Churchill said there was every reason to suppose that she had been sent to the bottom.

On October 14 the Royal Navy sustained the second loss of a capital ship since the commencement of the war in the sinking by U-boat action at 1.30 a.m. of H.M.S. "Royal Oak" (29,150 tons) while at anchor in Scapa Flow. The "Royal Oak" was lying at the extreme end of the harbour; and therefore many lives – upwards of 800 – were lost before rescue could be organised.

THE WAR AT SEA: DEBITS AND CREDITS ON THE ALLIES "ACCOUNT".

A U-BOAT SUNK BY DESTROYERS: A UNIQUE PHOTOGRAPH, SHOWING A MAN ON THE CONNING-TOWER, WHICH IS BARELY AWASH, AND TWO MORE IN THE WATER.

THE ROYAL NAVY OBSERVES THE TRADITIONAL CHIVALRY OF THE SEA: GERMAN SUBMARINE SURVIVORS IN THE DESTROYER WHICH RESCUED THEM.

THE SUBMARINE THAT LET THE "BREMEN" GO, BUT TORPEDOED A U-BOAT AND TWO GERMAN CRUISERS, RETURNS TO PORT: COMMANDER BICKFORD, OF THE "SALMON".

The photograph above is claimed to be the first taken of the actual destruction of a U-boat since the war began. A description of the action runs: "Sound detectors gave the destroyers their clue. Depth-charges

were dropped and found their mark. Desperately the U-boat dived deeper and deeper, but at last was forced to the surface, where it was immediately fired upon by the destroyers' guns."

During the first month of the war, Mr. Churchill pointed out in his broadcast of October 1, "we captured by our efficient contraband control 150,000 tons more German merchandise – food, oil, minerals, and other commodities – for our own benefit than we have lost by all the U-boat sinkings put together." The total, for the first five weeks of the war, amounted to 315,000 tons.

Great satisfaction was also felt at the failure of the German air-attacks on a British convoy in the North Sea on October 21; since, although it was universally recognised that the Navy could protect merchant-ships from submarine attack, there was no experience to go upon in assessing the vulnerability of convoys to bombing.

Five officers and thirty-eight members of the crew of a U-boat who had been taken prisoner were landed at a Scottish port on December 3. They were brought in by two destroyers, and their reception showed that whatever the feelings in this country towards the Nazi leaders, there is no hatred towards the German people. When the prisoners went down the gangway they were good-humouredly cheered by the British sailors who lined the decks and rails of the warships.

In any case, no U-boat can have equalled the bag of the "Salmon," which returned home after torpedoing a submarine and two cruisers in the course of a single cruise; while the feat of Lieut-Commander Phillips of the "Ursula" in getting into the mouth of the Elbe, and sinking a cruiser of the "Koln" class, screened by six destroyers, fully equalled in daring that of the U-boat commander who penetrated Scapa Flow to sink the "Royal Oak." Of the contrast between the strict

adherence of the British submarine service to the laws of the sea, even at risk to themselves, and the brutalities committed by the U-boats, there is no need to speak. It is only necessary to recall that the "Salmon" had the "Bremen" at her mercy, but let her go when it was clear that it was impossible to sink her without endangering the safety of her non-combatant crew.

THE LIEUT -COMMANDER IN CHARGE OF A SEARCH PARTY LOOKING FOR CONTRABAND EXAMINING GRAIN IN THE HOLD, AFTER APOLOGISING TO THE NEUTRAL CAPTAIN FOR THE DELAY CAUSED.

A TYPE OF VESSEL WHICH IS PROTECTING MERCHANT CONVOYS FROM AIR AND UNDER-WATER RAIDERS: CRUISERS OF THE "SOUTHAMPTON" CLASS WITH ALL THEIR A.-A. GUNS AT THE READY.

M. CALINESCU ASSASSINATED

M. ARMAND CALINESCU, THE SECOND RUMANIAN PREMIER TO BE MURDERED BY THE IRON GUARD, AN ORGANISATION MODELLED ON NAZI LINES.

On September 24 M. Armand Calinescu, the Rumanian Premier, was assassinated by members of the Iron Guard. M. Calinescu was returning home by car. At the Dimbovitza Bridge, Bucharest, a car intentionally collided with M. Calinescu's; another car drove up; and a group of young men leapt out and opened fire. A peasant cart had been drawn across the road as a partial and additional barricade. M. Calinescu was hit by seventeen bullets, which entered his chest in a straight line. His bodyguard was killed; the chauffeur injured. The assassins then drove to the Bucharest Radio, and shot and wounded the doorkeeper. Inside the building one of them seized the microphone and broadcast the murder; only his first words were heard, an engineer switching off the apparatus. Twenty minutes later the police entered and overpowered the assassins. Next day, after a reconstruction of the crime, they were shot in full view of the public. M. Calinescu – Rumania's "Man of Steel" – had ruthlessly suppressed the Iron Guard, which was pro-Fascist and violently anti-Semitic. In 1933 M. Duca, then Rumanian Premier, was also assassinated by the Iron Guard.

NON-STOP REVIEW HAS BEGUN AGAIN AT THE WINDMILL THEATRE: REHEARSING A TOPICAL ITEM IN WHICH TIN HATS AND GAS-MASKS APPEAR.

THE FEMININE TOUCH

AMBULANCE DRIVERS IN FUR COAT AND GAS-MASK: AN ADVANCED RECRUIT ON A PRACTICE DRIVE.

A MIGHTY SWING WITH THE SHOVEL: BEFORE FILLING A SAND-BAG, THE HARD EARTH MUST FIRST BE BROKEN UP.

THE BEGINNING OF POLAND'S RE-BIRTH

A POLISH GOVERNMENT, FORMED IN PARIS: (R. TO L.) COLONEL ADAM KOC, MINISTER OF FINANCE, M. STRONKI, VICE-PRESIDENT OF THE COUNCIL, RACZKIEWICZ, THE PRESIDENT, GENERAL SIKORSKI, THE PRIME MINISTER AND WAR MINISTER, AND M. ZALESKI, FOREIGN MINISTER.

THE FORMATION OF A POLISH ARMY ON FRENCH SOIL: THE TROOPS BEING REVIEWED BY GENERAL DENAIN.

HITLER'S "SECRET WEAPON"? MAGNETIC OR NON-CONTACT MINES, LAID BY 'PLANE AND U-BOAT.

HOW MAGNETIC OR NON-CONTACT MINES SINK SHIPS

The new Nazi frightfulness campaign, expressed in the enemy propaganda boast that "to travel to England will be to travel to death," may be said to have opened with the sinking on November 18 by a German mine off the East Coast of the Dutch liner "Simon Bolivar" (8309 tons), with the loss of 86 lives. Immediately following on this barbarity five more ships were sunk in similar circumstances wholly attributable to Germany's ruthless contravention of international law.

Whether or not the magnetic mine is Hitler's "secret weapon," the possibilities of a non-contact mine have long been known to Admiralties, and its design is familiar to experts. Magnetic mines, having neither cable, winch, nor sinker, can be laid from the air as well as by U-boat. Now every metal structure, such as a ship, is surrounded by a magnetic field, and though feeble, this area of electric force is sufficient to attract the sensitive needle of the mine. This operates the detonator and explodes the mine. The explosion drives a "hole" in the surrounding water (as does a depth-charge) and the pressure bursts open the plates of the ship – the mine itself never coming in direct contact with her. The principal increased danger of magnetic mines, as opposed to ordinary mines, is that, being unmoored, ordinary minesweeping devices do not touch them.

THE WOMEN'S LAND ARMY IN ACTION: MEMBERS OF THE LAND ARMY FOLLOWING THE TRACTOR-DRAWN POTATO-DIGGER, GATHERING UP THE PRODUCE BEFORE IT CAN BE AFFECTED BY THE FROSTS.

THE NEW "CONTEMPTIBLE" ARMY LEARNS TO "PARLEY-VOO": "SHOULDER TO SHOULDER WITH OUR FRENCH ALLIES": THE NEW B.E.F.

SOME OF THE 1939 BRITISH FIELD FORCE PRIOR TO THEIR DEPARTURE FOR FRANCE.

HISTORY REPEATS ITSELF ON THE SHORES OF THE CHANNEL: BRITISH UNITS DISEMBARKING AT A FRENCH PORT WHICH WELCOMED THEIR PREDECESSORS IN THE PREVIOUS WAR.

FRANCE WELCOMES HER ALLIES: LEFT: GRAPES FOR TOMMIES IN A VILLAGE STREET. CENTRE: A LIFT FROM A FRIENDLY FRENCH FARMER. RIGHT: A FRENCH SENTRY PRESENTS ARMS AS A BRITISH DETACHMENT MARCHES IN TO TAKE OVER.

HITLER MISSES DEATH BY 15 MINUTES: THE MUNICH BOMB EXPLOSION.

WORKING ONE OF THE FRENCH GUNS WHICH ARE POUNDING THE SIEGFRIED DEFENCES.

MR. L. HORE-BELISHA, SECRETARY OF STATE FOR WAR, AND THE COMMANDER-IN-CHIEF, LORD GORT, TOUR THE BRITISH LINES.

If any comfort is to be derived from the renewed hostilities on the Western Front after a lapse of twenty-five years it is surely to be found in the fact that the fighting is now taking place for the first time since the Napoleonic era, not on French but on German soil, where it may quite well remain for the "duration," and that, on the assurance of the High Military Commands, there is to be no wastage of human life.

As these pictures amply testify, if the personnel of the new British Expeditionary Force to France is totally different from that of 25 years ago, the spirit animating the men reveals itself as unflinchingly cheerful as it always was in the last war. Certainly the Tommies shown above, so good-humouredly leaving home to face the perils of modern war on the new Western Front, have good reason for coolness and confidence, for they are better equipped and prepared for active service than were the handful of divisions which crossed the Channel under the command of Sir John French; and there is a further reason for confidence in the Maginot Line, which was, of course, non-existent in those shattering first weeks of the German invasion of France and Belgium in 1914.

The War Minister has just completed a visit to the Forces in France. He is seen, (*Left*) with General Lord Gort, the British Commander-in-Chief, and other officers (note the high-ranking officer on the right, attired in a Tommy's "battle dress" uniform, with only his epaulettes to denote his rank).

WHERE HITLER WAS NEARLY ASSASSINATED: THE WRECKAGE IN THE MUNICH BURGERBRÄUKELLER AFTER THE BOMB EXPLOSION WHICH OCCURRED 15 MINUTES AFTER HE HAD LEFT THE BUILDING, DURING THE ANNIVERSARY CELEBRATIONS OF THE 1923 PUTSCH, ON NOVEMBER 8.

Eight persons were said to have lost their lives, including two members of Hitler's personal bodyguard, and sixty-three to have been injured by the explosion of a time-bomb in the Bürgerbräukeller in Munich on November 8 during celebrations, at which Herr Hitler and other Nazi leaders were present, of the sixteenth anniversary of the abortive 1923 *putsch*. It was a pure chance, due to the fact that Hitler was anxious to return to Berlin as early as possible, that he was not in the hall when the explosion took place. On previous occasions, such as the 1936 celebrations he had been in the habit of beginning his speech about 8.30 and speaking for about an hour and a half. But on November 8 he began earlier than usual and spoke for less than an hour. Rewards totalling £45,000 were offered for the discovery of the perpetrators and hundreds of arrests were made. Neutral observers found the best explanation of this extremely well-laid plot in dissensions in the Nazi party itself.

THE WAR IN FINLAND'S SNOW-BOUND FORESTS:
WITH THE FINNISH ARMY IN THEIR GALLANT FIGHT AGAINST RUSSIA.

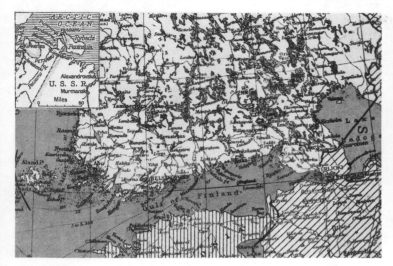

A MAP SHOWING THE KARELIAN ISTHMUS; FINLAND'S BALTIC PORTS; AND (INSET) THE NORTHERN FRONTIER, WITH PETSAMO AND THE RYBACHI PENINSULA.

FINLAND MOBILISED: FINNISH CAVALRY ON THEIR STURDY LITTLE PONIES. THE FINNISH ARMY INCLUDES ONE CAVALRY BRIGADE; WHILE RUSSIA, OF COURSE, HAS ENORMOUS CAVALRY FORCES.

The Soviet invasion of Finland, which began on the morning of November 30, followed Russian accusations over a border shooting incident on November 26. In this, the Russians stated that three privates and one officer were killed, seven shells being fired. The Finns denied that the shells were fired from their side, and maintained that they were Russian shells from Russian guns.

The attack was heralded by air raids. Among the towns reported to have been attacked were Helsinki, Viborg, Lahti, and Enso, where a hospital was totally destroyed. On land Soviet troops operating on the northern frontier captured Petsamo, but the town was later retaken after hand-to-hand fighting in the dark. Terijoki, a port some ten miles from the Soviet frontier, was bombarded from the sea and then occupied by Russian troops. It is now the seat of a puppet "Government" of Finland set up by the U.S.S.R. At Suojarvi, on the east front, the Finnish troops repulsed the enemy with great loss. At sea warships of the Soviet Navy bombarded Hango and were answered by the fixed defences. One destroyer was reported to have been sunk, another damaged, and the new cruiser "Kirov" had to be towed to Tallinn for repairs.

LIKE A WEIRD MONASTIC ORDER: FINNISH SKI-TROOPS GLIDING THROUGH THE SNOW-CARPETED FOREST.

THE ART OF WINTER WARFARE: WHITE-CLOAKED MACHINE-GUNNERS TAKING ADVANTAGE OF NATURAL COVER.

FROZEN SOLID AS THEY FELL – RUSSIAN TROOPS MACHINE-GUNNED BY A FINNISH PATROL.

A CONVOY HALTED FOR THE NIGHT CAUGHT BY THE FINNS DURING THE KEMIJAERVI COUNTER-OFFENSIVE.

PART OF A MASS BOMBING RAID ON VIBORG CARRIED OUT ON CHRISTMAS DAY.

A RUSSIAN TANK, OF WHICH AT LEAST 200 ARE REPORTED TO HAVE BEEN CAPTURED OR DESTROYED.

The Russian attack on Finland appeared to fall into four divisions: operations in the Gulf of Finland, including the occupation of the Finnish islands there and bombing attacks on large towns; the "southern sector" – that is, the areas north-south of Lake Ladoga, where there was heavy fighting; the "central sector," of which very little was heard at first though probably the most important area strategically – a Soviet thrust towards Meaborg might cut Finland in two; and the "northern sector," where there was heavy fighting in the neighbourhood of Petsamo.

By December 19, the situation in Central Finland appeared very critical. Advancing past Salla, the Russians had reached Kemijaervi, after taking Kursu, 65 miles from the frontier. Kemijaervi is the northernmost Finnish railhead; the Russians were threatening the Finnish communications. But on December 22 came news that the Finns had checked the advance. A two-day counter-attack struck at the Russian flank as they were attempting to cross the Kemi River, and the Russians were thrown back twenty miles, leaving behind them tanks, lorries, guns and horses. Some of the Finnish forces ski-ed sixty miles in a single run from Kemijaervi and attacked on both Russian flanks. Finns moving in silence encircled a Russian encampment, putting a convoy out of action with hand-grenades and attacking the Russians with automatic pistols and machine-guns. As the heroism and phenomenal successes of the Finnish Army remain unaltered, the Red leaders are apparently attempting to break the resistance of the civil population of Finland by ruthless bombardment from the air – in flagrant contravention, of course, of their recent explicit undertaking in response to the humane appeal of the President of the United States. On Sunday, December 31, Bolshevik aircraft raided eleven Finnish towns with incendiary and high-explosive bombs, in some places afterwards diving down and sweeping the streets with machine-gun bullets; while on December 21, a fleet of a hundred and fifty Soviet bombers roamed over the whole of Southern Finland, incidentally gutting the Central State Institution for the Blind in Helsinki, and various hospital buildings. On New Year's Eve, more than 300 bombs were dropped at Vaasa, and several open squares were ploughed up by high explosive. Groups of as many as forty aeroplanes were seen over some towns in Southern Finland.

More, perhaps, than any pictures from the front in Finland which we have so far published do the bare facts bring home the full heroism and splendour of the Finn Army's triumph against even greater odds than faced the old British "Contemptibles" in 1914. During the five weeks and more that the unacknowledged Russo-Finnish war has been raging, no fewer than eight Russian Army divisions have been stopped on the Karelian Isthmus, while a total of seven more Russian divisions has been thrown back at every vital point on the 750-mile Eastern Front. The Soviet losses in dead and wounded are reliably reported to exceed 100,000 men, in comparison with which the Finnish casualties have been very small. "The Finns," to quote Mr. Garvin, "have adapted Nature's principle of protective coloration. Amid the snow they wear white. To Russian eyes they seem to come suddenly out of the waste like ghosts. These ghosts are anything but wraiths of dead men. They are only dead-shots."

THE UNITED STATES TO ALLOW "CASH AND CARRY" ARMS SALES

U.S. 'PLANES FOR ENGLAND, DISMANTLED AND HOISTED ON TO BARGES AT NEW YORK.

The United States' revised Neutrality Act which removes the embargo on the export of war material and allows belligerents to buy arms on a "cash and carry" basis, was adopted by the Senate and the House of Representatives on November 3. On the following day the President signed the Act at a simple ceremony in the White House and it then became law. There were no speeches or statements, but the importance of the measure was emphasised by the presence of Congress leaders and State Department chiefs.

Following the repeal of the Arms Embargo, belligerents are allowed to take munitions of war out of the U.S.A. in their own ships; which, in effect, means that the Western Allies may profit by the great development of the American aircraft industry while the Nazis may not, since the Allies have command of the sea.

PRESIDENT ROOSEVELT SIGNING THE REVISED "CASH AND CARRY" NEUTRALITY ACT ON NOVEMBER 4; THE SIMPLE CEREMONY IN THE WHITE HOUSE.

THE BATTLE OF THE RIVER PLATE: THE END OF THE "ADMIRAL GRAF SPEE".

ONE OF THE TWO LIGHT-CRUISERS, WHICH "FOUGHT LIKE TERRIERS": H.M.S. "ACHILLES" (7030 TONS.)

"THE CRUISERS MADE A GALLANT FIGHT – WHEN PEOPLE FIGHT LIKE THAT PERSONAL ENMITY IS LOST": CAPTAIN HANS LANGSDORFF, BEFORE HE SHOT HIMSELF.

THE WAGNERIAN FINISH: THE "GRAF SPEE" SUBSIDING LIKE A BURNING PYRE IN A REDDENING SUNSET.

WITH TOPMASTS GONE, AND HOLES COVERED BY FRESH PAINT, THE "EXETER" AT DRAKE'S "HOME PORT."

THE MELANCHOLY MONUMENT OF NAZI NAVAL IMPOTENCE, REARED BY HITLER IN THE PLATE ESTUARY: THE WRECK OF THE "ADMIRAL GRAF SPEE".

THE VICTORS OF THE RIVER PLATE MARCHING THROUGH LONDON ON THEIR WAY TO THE GUILDHALL LUNCHEON.

On December 13 three British cruisers, H.M.S. "Exeter," "Achilles," and "Ajax," met the powerful 10,000-ton German battle-ship and commerce-raider, "Admiral Graf Spee," and drove her, in a severely damaged condition, into Montevideo harbour, outside of which she scuttled herself on December 17 rather than face certain destruction at sea. One of the best accounts of this great battle came from the commander of the defeated vessel himself, Captain Langsdorff, who gave unstinted praise to the "incredibly audacity" of the attacking cruisers, which did not hesitate to close with the "Graf Spee" and smother her with shells from a distance of no more than a mile. The captain told the port authorities at Montevideo that he saw the cruiser "Exeter" about 6 a.m. on December 13 in the distance, off the Brazilian coast. As he was short of fuel he attempted to slip away to the south. Suddenly, however, there appeared in his way the "Ajax" and the "Achilles," which, being faster than the "Admiral Graf Spee," manoeuvred so as to force the enemy battleship between them and the Uraguayan coast, thus placing him "between the devil and the deep blue sea." Thereupon he opened fire on the "Exeter" with his 11-in. guns, and she replied with her 8-in. guns. "Ajax" and "Achilles" were still too far away to get into action with their 6-in. guns, and before they could get up he had severely damaged the "Exeter." When the other cruisers did get within range of him, however, they inflicted "enormous damage," he said, holing the bow of the "Graf Spee" and battering the control tower.

"They aimed effectively," Captain Langsdorff drily observed.

Taking an extrordinary risk, the "Ajax" and "Achilles" crossed through a smoke screen which one of them had laid and got within a mile of the "Admiral Graf Spee," scoring effective hits on both sides of the ship.

Five officers and fifty-six ratings of the cruiser "Exeter" lost their lives in the action with the "Admiral Graf Spee," and three officers and twenty ratings were wounded. The ship's normal complement numbers 600. The "Exeter" bore the brunt of the early stages of the battle, gallantly returning the "Admiral Graf Spee's" fire, shot for shot, until only one 8-in. gun could be fired, and that by hand. The steering-gear became damaged; for 45 minutes Captain F. S. Bell conned the ship from the after-control position, using a boat's compass. Through a chain of ten sailors, orders were conveyed to the after-steering wheel and the engine-room, until the ship fell out of the action.

Considering the disparity in gun-power of the ships, the British casualty lists were low, almost incredibly low. In theory, just one well-placed salvo from the Germans' 11-in. guns was needed to put each of the cruisers out of action in turn, and sink her with the loss of every soul on board; but in actual fact, although the "Exeter" was somewhat severely handled, the little "Ajax" and "Achilles" escaped with but four men killed in one and seven in the other – in spite of the great daring of their attacks.

THE KING'S VISIT TO THE BRITISH AND FRENCH ARMIES IN FRANCE.

GREAT EAGERNESS WAS DISPLAYED BY THE FRENCH PRESS THAT THE KING SHOULD VISIT THE FRENCH AS WELL AS THE BRITISH ARMY: HIS MAJESTY SALUTING A GUARD OF HONOUR IN A FRENCH SECTOR.

HIS MAJESTY WITH MAJOR-GENERAL SIR ALAN BROOKE DURING AN INSPECTION OF HIS ARMY IN FRANCE.

The King's visit to the Western Front took place twenty-five years after the first of the visits paid by his father, King George., to the B.E.F. in France in 1914. In the course of his tour, he visited troops of all arms, went right up into the line, and also spent two days with the French Army. The King's tour of the Maginot Line was made in the company of General Gamelin, Commander-in-Chief of the Allied Armies. The King saw the fortifications and inspected units of the R.A.F. and British troops in contact with the enemy there. In the course of his tour of the Army zones in France the King had lunch with the President of the French Republic and M. Daladier on December 7. The lunch took place at the invitation of his Majesty and was given at a restaurant in a town behind the lines. The meal was a simple one and there was no special ceremony.

THE COMING OF THE CANADIANS.

THE FIRST CONTINGENT OF THE DOMINION FORCES STEPPING ASHORE. TREMENDOUS ENTHUSIASM PREVAILS. THE FORCE IS NOW COMPLETING ITS TRAINING IN ENGLAND.

"AUSTRALIA WILL BE THERE!" THE MEN AND THE ARMS OF THE SECOND A.I.F.

SIX THOUSAND STALWART "DIGGERS" OF THE SECOND AUSTRALIAN EXPEDITIONARY FORCE SWINGING DOWN MARTIN PLACE, SYDNEY, ON THEIR LAST PARADE BEFORE SAILING.

AUSTRALIA'S ANSWER TO NAZI-ISM.

THE FIRST AUSTRALIAN AIR CONTINGENT LANDS IN ENGLAND. THE MEN ARE ALREADY FULLY TRAINED AND ARE STARTING ACTIVE SERVICE WITH THE BRITISH COASTAL COMMAND.

ADMIRAL BYRD RETURNS TO THE ANTARCTIC: A U.S. EXPEDITION.

A GIGANTIC "SNOW-CRUISER" FOR USE IN THE ANTARCTIC WASTES BY THE THIRD BYRD EXPEDITION, TAKEN APART TO ENABLE IT TO BE SHIPPED: SHOWING THE TAIL SECTION – TO BE RE-WELDED AT THE DESTINATION – CUT AWAY BEFORE DESPATCH, AND ESKIMO SLED-DOGS IN THE FOREGROUND.

THE 27-TON POLAR "SNOW-CRUISER," DESIGNED BY DR. THOMAS POULTER FOR ADMIRAL BYRD; AND COSTING OVER £30,000: A DIAGRAM SHOWING THE ELABORATE INTERIOR EQUIPMENT AND THE AEROPLANE CARRIED.

Commissioned by the U.S. Government to claim for the United States an unspecified land lying within the Western Hemisphere – regarded as having, apart from mineral and meterological advantages, great potential value as a site for air bases – Admiral Byrd, accompanied by about seventy men, has sailed on a long-projected third voyage to Antarctica, to establish two other bases, in addition to Little America, on the Bay of Whales. The First Byrd Expedition to Antarctica took place in 1928–30. He made the first flight to the South Pole in 1929. Twenty-two men will be left at each base, with provisions for a year, after which reliefs will take place. Among the equipment is the "snow-cruiser" illustrated here. The view is officially held that the claiming and settlement of Antarctic territory is fully within the sphere of the Monroe Doctrine, islands in the Pacific and Polar regions having always been understood to be exceptions to the theoretical position taken up by the United States that she does not seek additional territory.

THE ILLUSTRATED LONDON NEWS

THE ONLY THING THAT AFFORDS HARASSED NEUTRALS SAFETY FROM NAZI BRUTALITY IN EUROPEAN WATERS: A BRITISH CONVOY – MOVING IN ORDERED FORMATION UNDER NAVAL ESCORT.

There is no doubt that the safest place afloat – at any rate, in European waters – is in an Allied convoy. In his broadcast speech on 30 March 1940 Mr. Churchill said that "only one in 800 neutral ships which have resorted to our protection has been sunk." According to figures issued by the Admiralty, out of 12,816 British, Allied and neutral ships convoyed, only 28 have been lost. These remarkable figures lend indisputable proof to the success of the system, and, as the authorities state, there is little wonder that the neutrals show an increasing desire to be given Allied escort. This photograph was taken on board a collier off the East Coast. Ships' lifeboats are swung out for instant use, while escorting warships are busy dashing up and down the line keeping a sharp look-out.

1940

Minesweeping — U.S. aircraft arrive — First German bomber shot down — The "Altmark" incident — Finland signs treaty with Russia — Natural defences of Holland and Rumania — Hitler and Mussolini meet on the Brenner Pass — German Raid on Scapa Flow — Wartime fashion and a film — The Nazi invasion of Denmark and Norway — The first and second Battles of Narvik — Germany invades Holland, Belgium and Luxembourg — Winston Churchill becomes Prime Minister — Rotterdam devastated — Holland capitulates — The drive to the Channel ports — The RAF in action — Local defence volunteers in Britain — The Belgian King surrenders his army — The defence of Calais — The miracle of Dunkirk — The German onslaught on the Weygand Line — Allies capture Narvik — Allies withdrawn from Norway — Norwegian army surrenders — Paris bombed — Paris abandoned — Italy declares war on France and Great Britain — The Collapse of the French Army — Evacuation of remaining Allied troops — French armistices with Germany and Italy signed — Channel Islands occupied by Germans — Iceland and Faroes occupied by Allies — United States waive neutrality regulations — Aliens interned in Britain — Russia annexes Bessarabia and the Balkan Republics — Royal Navy destroys French fleet at Oran — Britain prepares for invasion — Italy attacks the Sudan, and Egypt takes British Somaliland — Japanese forces enter French Indo-China — First mass air raids on Britain — The Battle of Britain begins — Berlin raided — The London blitz — The Royal Navy attacks the Italian fleet in the Mediterranean — Germany, Italy and Japan sign the Tripartite Pact — Britain reopens the Burma Road — Germany occupies Rumania — Italy invades Greece and is heavily repulsed — Hitler's talks with Franco, Pétain and Molotov — Coventry bombed — Abortive Italian air raid on Britain — The "Jervis Bay" incident — British sink three Italian battleships in Taranto harbour — Heavy German air raids on British towns — Eighth Army advances out of Egypt — Battles of Sidi Barrani and Sollum.

A PERILOUS BUT UNSPECTACULAR TASK – MINESWEEPERS AT WORK.

LEFT: LOWERING AN "OROPESA" FLOAT – THESE TORPEDO-SHAPED INSTRUMENTS KEEP THE "SWEEPS" AT THE REQUIRED DISTANCE FROM THE SHIP, WHILE THE "OTTER", THE LADDER-LIKE DEVICE FITTED BENEATH THE "OROPESA" FLOAT AT THE END OF THE SWEEP WIRE, KEEPS IT AT THE REQUIRED DEPTH. A FLOTILLA OF A RECENT TYPE OF MINESWEEPER OFF THE BRITISH COAST. THESE LITTLE VESSELS HAVE A SPEED OF SOME 16 TO 17 KNOTS, WHICH IS AMPLE FOR THEIR TYPE OF WORK.

The menace of mines, to neutral as well as to Allied shipping, was cruelly and vividly brought home by the recent sinking of eight ships in rapid succession, five of them being neutrals. Sweeping consists in "sweeps," kept at the requisite distance from the ship by the "oropesa" floats, and at the requisite depth by the "otter" (both these appliances are illustrated above). Attached to the sweeps are strong cutters whose serrated jaws cut through the cable which moors the mine. Brought to the surface, the mine is disposed of by rifle fire: the bullets do not explode the mine, but pierce its shell, and the mine sinks, waterlogged.

The mine-sweeper's main dangers are manifold, the most serious being that of the mines themselves. As well as mines laid against naval or merchant shipping, mines are specially laid at a shallower depth against the mine-sweepers – 214 being thus sunk in the last war – while in this war the mine-sweeper "Mastiff" was announced lost on November 21 by striking a mine off the East coast.

HANDLING DEATH ON EAST COAST BEACHES: THE MENACE OF THE STRANDED MINE.

LASSOING, NOT BRONCOS, BUT A MINE STRANDED ON THE BRITISH COAST. ONCE ASHORE THE MINE WILL BE MADE HARMLESS.

As soon as the horned mine is successfully lassoed, a party of naval men start hauling it ashore. It may be a foreigner, but often it is a British mine, broken from its sinker mooring. Considerable risks have to be taken by mine experts, though the apparent danger of lassoing a horn, and thus causing an explosion, is remote. Mines should, on breaking their moorings, automatically become harmless.

U.S. AIRCRAFT FOR BRITAIN.

THE STREAM OF AMERICAN PLANES BEGINS TO ARRIVE AT VARIOUS BRITISH PORTS.

For some time the newspapers have been giving particulars of the orders placed by this country with American aeroplane manufacturers. It is good to learn that these orders are now materialising. Among the latest arrivals are the American Lockheeds, one of which is here seen swaying on the crane as it is being conveyed to the quayside. Both engines were carefully shielded against winter weather in the Atlantic. The main wing spans are, of course, detached during the period of transport and added later when the whole aircraft is properly overhauled and fitted out for service.

WOMEN DO THEIR BIT.

WOMEN PILOTS TO DELIVER 'PLANES TO THE R.A.F. FROM THE FACTORIES: THE WOMEN'S SECTION OF THE AIR TRANSPORT AUXILIARY.

The Women's Section of the Air Transport Auxiliary, comprising eight young women of exceptional flying skill and experience, under a First Officer, have recently been officially engaged to deliver new aeroplanes from the factory to storage depots in England. Above they are seen in flying kit on a flying-field near London. They have mostly been engaged in commercial flying, many have trained pilots up to the exacting "B" standard. The youngest is twenty-two.

FIRST GERMAN PLANE ON BRITISH SOIL.

A GERMAN BOMBER CRASHED ON THE LAMMERMUIR HILLS.

British fighter pilots spoke with admiration of the "fine achievement" of the pilot of the German aircraft forced down at Humbie, East Lothian, Scotland, last October 28, after his machine had been riddled with bullets in the air east of Dalkeith by Royal Air Force fighters and he himself had received a number of wounds. He held on, nevertheless, and managed to pancake his machine safely among the heather on a hillside, after going through a wall and crashing in a hollow. The machine carried a crew of four, and when the pilot staggered from the aircraft, assisted by his unwounded navigator, he said in excellent English to a policeman who had appeared: "We surrender as prisoners of the war. Please see to my gunners in the back of the aircraft." When, however, investigation was made, the men were found to be dead. Every part of the German aircraft bore traces of devastating machine-gun fire, and even the two metal propellers were drilled with holes. According to "The Times" aeronautical correspondent, the German bomber was a Heinkel 111 K, of a recent short-nosed model.

A WHITE AND BITTER WINTER ON THE WESTERN FRONT.

INDIAN FILE IN THE SNOW: A FRENCH PATROL SETTING OUT – THEIR FIGURES DARK AGAINST THE WHITE TRACERY.

BRITISH SOLDIERS, WEARING WHITE SUITS OVER THEIR KHAKI UNIFORMS, LINING A SUNKEN ROADWAY IN FRANCE.

Snow and frost lend these photographs of British and French activities on the Western Front a picturesque but no less grim aspect. This year snow fell unusually heavily in the district between the Rhine and the Moselle: and the bleak downs and scattered villages of Lorraine, and the forests and ridges of the lower Vosges experienced severe winter conditions. At one time as much as 25 degrees of frost was registered. (In parenthesis, it might be added that on the Petsamo front in Finland operations have been conducted with a temperature of 41 degrees below zero.) Once the snow stopped falling on the Western Front aerial reconnaissance began again. Grounded machines were covered with tarpaulins to prevent freezing up, and in some cases housed in tents built specially round them. Apart from aerial reconnaissance, the main activity on the Western Front, as we go to press, continues to be that of patrols. Since the New Year these patrols are now being increasingly carried out by daylight.

A HYDRO-ELECTRIC INSTALLATION INGENIOUSLY IMPROVISED FROM ODDS AND ENDS – INCLUDING AN OLD BICYCLE-WHEEL AND HOME-MADE MILL-WHEEL "PADDLES" – BY ALPINE CHASSEURS TO IMPROVE THEIR CAMPING AMENITIES.

A FORMIDABLE SURFACE STRONGHOLD IN THE GREATEST DEFENSIVE SYSTEM EVER DEVISED: THE MAGINOT LINE.

EXCEPTIONALLY DEEP AND NARROW AND COVERED WITH BARBED WIRE TO FRUSTRATE SUDDEN ATTACK: AN ELABORATE COMMUNICATION TRENCH, WINDING THROUGH A SNOW-COVERED LANDSCAPE.

A remarkable photograph from which it is possible to gain an even more powerful general idea of the extraordinary range and complexity of this, the mightiest and most effective chain of interconnected fortresses, which the mind of man has devised. Work on the Maginot Line was begun in 1925 by that far-seeing French Minister of War – a *poilu* in the trenches in the Great War – M. André Maginot, who, by this prevision of France's necessity, has bequeathed his name to posterity as surely as did ever Hadrian (by a less secure title) by his wall, or Offa by his dyke. The Premier has reminded those who find in the prevailing state of military inactivity on the land a fruitful source of boredom that the art of war consists in bringing the greatest pressure to bear on the enemy at a stategic point at the right moment. Therefore the prolonged period of inaction is being utilised by the French Army as well as by our own Field Force in consolidating its strength and state of preparedness, in order to be in instant readiness for action when the vital time arrives. "Silent as yet, or almost," ran a recent message from the "Daily Telegraph" representative with the French Army, "but tremendous in power as in purpose, here stands the mighty army which forms, together with the British and French Navies, the guardian of the liberties of Western Europe and of the hopes of all the free peoples in the world." The recent spell of cold weather, when the thermometer in the war zone fell to minus 20, 25, and even 28 centigrade – representing 36, 45 and 50 degrees F. of frost – made the earth like rock. Food that was sent hot from the field kitchens at battalion headquarters was cold by the time it reached the outposts, while the soldier's *pinard*, the welcome daily wine ration sometimes arrived "in solid blocks." The "Daily Telegraph" correspondent observed that it all recalled the great frost of 1917: an observation that prompts reflection on the very great advance that has been made in the "standard of living" of the *poilu* between that year of sinister memory and now.

THE RESCUE OF BRITISH PRISONERS FROM THE GERMAN SHIP "ALTMARK".

VIENNA AND PRAGUE "BOMBED" WITH LEAFLETS.

WHEN THE KING ACTED AS A TEMPORARY TICKET COLLECTOR.

THE "ALTMARK'S" STERN HELD IN THE ICE AT THE EDGE OF THE JOSING FIORD.

HOW THE R.A.F. CARRIES ON ITS PROPAGANDA WAR: PLACING LEAFLETS IN THE CHUTE OF A BOMBER.

AN ASTONISHED N.C.O ON LEAVE FROM FRANCE HAS HIS PASS TORN OUT AT THE RAILWAY BARRIER BY HIS SOVEREIGN.

The "Altmark", bound south from Bergen, had been "inspected" by the Norwegian authorities, who had failed to notice that there were over 300 British prisoners on board captured by the "Admiral Graf Spee". Accompanying the "Altmark" were two Norwegian torpedo boats. The same afternoon (Friday, February 16) appeared on the scene a British destroyer. Captain Vian of H.M.S. "Cossack" stated to the Norwegian commander that there were British prisoners on the "Altmark". This was denied. Captain Vian suggested a joint conference and examination at Bergen. This proposal was refused. The "Cossack" retired, but on later instructions forced her way through ice to the "Altmark". The "Altmark" was boarded and a scrambling fight took place. The "Graf Spee" guard fled across the ice to the shore and fired from their positions. The prisoners were rapidly transferred to the "Cossack".

The most daring Allied reconnaissance flight of the war took place on the night of January 12, when Royal Air Force pilots, flying for nine hours and covering well over a thousand miles of enemy territory, flew over Vienna, Prague, and Eastern Germany. They nowhere met with any resistance, and all returned undamaged. "Vienna was easily recognisable because of the river," said one of the pilots. "We circled the city and let fall our leaflets, wishing them luck."

This photograph, taken inside one of the Royal Air Force machines engaged in reconnaissance and leaflet raids over Prague, Vienna, and "Gross Deutschland," shows a member of the crew putting Ministry of Information leaflets printed in German into the chute of the aircraft.

An incident, entertaining, but all the same typical of the sincere interest taken by the King in the conditions and the life of the troops, occurred during his Majesty's visit to the coast on March 14 to inspect the work of the Dover Patrol. After presenting medals for gallantry to a number of seamen and warrant officers, the King stood for some time beside the ticket-collector at a South Coast port, watching officers and men of the British Expeditionary Force arriving on leave. Most men, however, were so excited at being on British soil that they failed to recognise his Majesty, who was wearing the undress uniform of Admiral of the Fleet. When, however, he took the place of the permanent officer for a few moments and tore out the necessary pass from a homecoming corporal's leave voucher-book, the glance of blank amazement which he received from the warrior greatly entertained his Majesty.

THE EPIC OF FINLAND: THE BATTLE FOR VIBORG – A MONTH OF RUSSIAN ATTACK.

A RELIC OF THE CRIMEA? – A CAPTURED COACH, INCONGRUOUSLY SURMOUNTED BY A CUMBERSOME AERIAL, USED AS A SOVIET ARMY WIRELESS WAGON.

At Lake Kianta and Suomusalmi the Finns turned back the greatly superior numbers in two actions constituting a "little Tannenberg." The Finns, like the Germans in East Prussia, were faced by a double invasion; like the Germans they took advantage of the bad co-operation of the two Russian columns to defeat first one in detail; then to annihilate the second. "The Times" correspondent's description was graphic. "About four miles from Suomusalmi, at a bend of the road I came upon a sight I never wish to see again: the main battle-scene. A wrecked Russian tank had held up a mechanised battalion, and as the long column had telescoped behind, the Finns had advanced from the flanks and poured a deadly fire into the Russians. The result was visible over a four-mile stretch of road, in one vast junk heap. . . . The Red commander Colonel Vinogradoff, disappeared on the second day of the battle." One is reminded of Samsonoff, the Russian general who shot himself in the forests after Tannenberg.

FIELD-MARSHAL MANNERHEIM, SUPREME HEAD OF THE FINNISH FORCES (FOREGROUND), WITH (L. TO R.) GENERALS OHQUIST, ÖSTERMANN AND OESCH – THE "THREE Os" OF FINLAND'S HIGH COMMAND.

During the last war Field-Marshal Mannerheim fought under the Tsar on the Eastern front. Also on the Eastern front, but under Kaiser Wilhelm II., fought 2000 Finns – in the 27th Royal Prussian Jäger Battalion. Among these 2000 were the three men, the three Os', who to-day are the Field-Marshal's closest collaborators in a strategy which has often been spectacularly successful.

A FINNISH CHURCH BURNING FIERCELY FROM A RUSSIAN IN-CENDIARY BOMB – PERHAPS RELEASED FROM A "MOLOTOV BREADBASKET."

The struggle of the Soviets for Finland began with intensive force on February 1. Day after day masses of Russian troops were hurled against the front positions of the Mannerheim Line. Following the advances came a general retirement to new defensive positions. No concessions had been made to the enemy's wild expenditure of men and munitions. Scores of tanks were either captured or destroyed. Finnish Red Cross hospitals, Swedish field ambulances, and country churches and monasteries have been repeatedly bombed. Most of the bombs were dropped from "Molotov's breadbasket" – a hollow cylinder with a propeller on the end and fitted with a thousand small incendiary bombs and shrapnel bombs, which cause the greatest havoc when released.

THE EFFECT OF FROST ON HOLLAND'S DEFENCES: NEW OBSTACLES FOR AN INVADER; SOLDIERS ON SKATES.

ANOTHER EXAMPLE OF THE HELP OF SEMI-THAWED ICE: AN ARMOURED CAR MAKES NO HEADWAY ONCE THE ICE BREAKS.

At the moment of writing, the Low Countries appear to be in as grave a danger of Nazi invasion as they were reported to be in November. All leave has been cancelled in the Dutch Army – as it has been in the B.E.F. Meanwhile official circles in Holland emphasize that the measures taken are of a purely precautionary nature. Germany is reported, however, to have 1,000,000 men concentrated along the Dutch frontier; and a form of the Von Schlieffen plan of 1913 is suggested to be approved by the Führer. (The Schlieffen plan was that of invading Holland as well as Belgium). Opinions differ as to whether ice would help the invader. Certainly thawing ice would seem no better than marshy ground for motorised transport. The possibility, moreover, of Belgium or Holland standing aside should Germany invade one of

THEIR SPEED AND MOBILITY FAR ABOVE THAT OF ORDINARY INFANTRY: A SECTION ADVANCING RAPIDLY ON SKATES DURING RECENT DUTCH MANOEUVRES.

them singly appears much more remote than in November.

In modern systems of strategic resistance to the threat of sudden unprovoked aggression, national defences based on natural resources are proving of the utmost importance. In Finland the snow and the forests have proved invaluable allies. The Dutch are relying on the network of waterways in Holland to hold up indefinitely any German thrust. In Rumania an ingenious second line defensive system has been devised, by means of which a long chain of frontier canals would, in the event of sudden attack, be filled with oil by subterranean pipes and set alight, thus forming an impassable "river of fire" for hundreds of miles.

"RIVERS OF FIRE" TO GUARD RUMANIA: CANALS TO BE FILLED WITH OIL.

RUMANIA'S SECOND LINE OF DEFENCE, WHICH MIGHT BECOME A "RIVER OF FIRE" HUNDREDS OF MILES LONG.

One of the above illustrations shows work in progress on these fuel-oil canals along the frontiers of Bessarabia and Bukowina, where the enigmatic attitude of Stalin, and the assault on Finland, have impelled Rumania to undertake extra defensive measures to ensure her protection from Red imperialistic ambition. At the present time a hundred thousand Rumanians are said to be at work behind the frontier all along the north of Bessarabia and the Bukowina, the defensive work being hastened on in time for its planned completion by April 1 next. In addition to the fuel-oil canals, which are camouflaged to form anti-tank traps – the natural defence system of Rumania – a formidable wall of concrete has been constructed, the sections being joined by iron barriers which in case of need can be electrified.

HOW A CRUEL PEACE AFFECTED FINNISH HOMES: A WINTER MIGRATION – WHEN 500,000 CHOSE EXILE RATHER THAN SOVIET RULE.

LEFT: WHEN THE STUNNING NEWS OF THE CESSION OF THE KARELIAN ISTHMUS BROKE UPON THE FINNS, A GREAT TREK BEGAN OF BOTH THE ARMY AND THE INHABITANTS OF THE DISTRICT WHICH HAD BEEN SO COURAGEOUSLY DEFENDED. LONG PROCESSIONS OF HORSED SLEIGHS PROCEEDED NORTHWARDS, BEARING GOODS OF ALL KINDS, ACCOMPANIED BY MANY PEOPLE ON FOOT. RIGHT: MEN OF THE FINNISH FORCES TRAMPING THROUGH THE SNOW WHEN THEY LEFT VIIPURI AFTER THE SIGNING OF THE RUSSO-FINNISH PEACE AGREEMENT.

"A NORMAL MANIFESTATION OF THE AXIS": THE TWO DICTATORS MEET IN AN ARMOURED TRAIN ON THE BRENNER. MUSSOLINI SAYING GOOD-BYE TO HITLER, WHO IS BY THE WINDOW OF HIS ARMOURED TRAIN.

The first meeting since Munich of the two dictators took place on March 19 at Brenner station, in the armoured train of Signor Mussolini, and lasted two and a half hours. They were seen to remove their overcoats, and then the curtains were closely drawn. The Italian Press was at pains to stress the fact that nothing spectacular was afoot. "It belongs to the normal manifestations of the Axis. The German Press, on the other hand, tried desperately to exploit the propaganda value of the meeting.

TWO PARTICIPANTS IN THE ABORTIVE RAID ON SCAPA FLOW, WHICH BROUGHT DOWN ON SYLT DEVASTATING R.A.F. REPRISALS: "LIEUT. PHILIPPS" (LEFT) AND "LIEUT. MAGNUSSEN."

A twenty-seven-year-old civilian James Isbister – the first British civilian to be killed in the present war – lost his life when the fleeing German bombers, after their abortive attack on warships anchored in Scapa Flow, unloaded their bombs on farms and cottages in the village of Bridge of Waith at dusk on March 16. About fourteen enemy aircraft reached the objective, and among a considerable number of bombs dropped, one hit a warship, which, however suffered only minor damage, injuries being sustained by seven sailors. Seven people were also wounded in Bridge of Waith. It was suggested that the raid was timed to impress Signor Mussolini on the eve of his meeting with Hitler at Brennero.

Despite the death of a civilian it is clear that the Nazis are still anxious to avoid the indiscriminate bombing of civilians and the inevitable reprisals which would open up an orgy of destruction. The danger always is that an "accident" involving civilian death will one day not be accepted as such. Meanwhile, one more proof is clearly supplied as of the stupidity of curiosity. There is one rule and one only. If you have no shelter, go into the centre of your house under the highest storey, keep away from the windows, and deny to yourself and your children the "war experience" you crave.

THE MEN WHO CARRIED OUT THE RAID ON SYLT: R.A.F. OFFICERS AND SERGEANTS CELEBRATE THEIR SUCCESS ON RETURNING TO THE STATION MESS.

Last week was remarkable for the first attack by the R.A.F. on a German aerodrome. It was a swift answer to the German attack on the Orkneys, when a civilian was killed. The raid began on Tuesday night and continued into Wednesday morning. The definite objective was of the air base in the district of Hornum on Sylt. The pilots had no light task, as they encountered intense anti-aircraft fire from Sylt and the neighbouring islands. Direct hits were obtained on hangars, seaplane slopes, oil tanks and a railway jetty. All machines returned save one.

A WAR NEWSLETTER

FRENCH GOVERNMENT CHANGES. – With our experience in the past twenty years of French Cabinet making we could not but deplore the fall of M. Daladier and the uneasy start of M. Reynaud's Government. But let us always remember that France is never so strong as in time of trouble. The French may be fierce and bitter political partisans, but they are fierce and bitter patriots when threatened from outside. Let us remember that M. Daladier's fall was due not to discontent with the war, but to discontent with the absence of war. Where is the immediate remedy? If the Finnish debacle brought matters of discontent to a head, what could a stronger French policy have achieved to prevent that debacle? Admit that Sweden's part was decisive. Admit that Sweden loathes Nazism and Fascism and would have welcomed a victorious and intact Finland. Sweden's weakness was due to Sweden's terror of Germany. What was wanting in Allied policy in the past six months which has increased that fear and lowered the stock of Allied military effectiveness in neutral eyes? Only one thing has been wanting. The launching of a major land offensive either on the Western Front or elsewhere.

CONDUCT OF MODERN WAR. – This is an afterthought on the affairs of Scapa and Sylt and any other war episodes that have followed them. The more I think of them, the more I rub my eyes and wonder if I am dreaming. The conduct of this war is so totally different to that of any which has preceded it. Surprises we have had in plenty. Nothing has gone as forecast, but no one even dimly conceived the possible development of the *showmanship* of the war To what extent does the development of broadcasting account for it? The naked truth is that both sides at present are much more concerned with the propaganda campaign than with the war of lethal weapons. The affairs of Scapa and Sylt were war episodes, minor Zeebrugges: their results are war *facts* which need no words. And what do we find? Each side neglects the *actions* and is concerned solely with the impression it can produce in neutral eyes of the effects, minimised or exaggerated, of these actions. It is not war but showmanship, pure and simple (or impure and very slick). The cinema rights, the broadcasting rights, must be safe guarded before military action can be planned. This is indeed a Hollywood war run mad. The heroes of a raid on land or by air are hurried to the B.B.C. headquarters to be shown off to a gaping public like queens of beauty on a seaside pier. Prisoners are taken, not to prison camps, but to the microphone to keep the ring of watchers amused. Wounded men,

too, go to the microphone before the dressing station. In this modern warfare the war of arms takes second place, the war of paper and propaganda and rival showmanship is the big thing. The courage of our fighting men needs no showmanship. The heroes of past war kept silence, but their exploits were never forgotten. Is this the meaning of a "people's war" – that the people must be kept constantly amused by showmanship, that the bloody business must be made a peep show?

M. REYNAUD'S CALL: BRITAIN'S ANSWER? – I don't know, after reading M. Reynaud's broadcast speech, whether it was wishful thinking that guided many British newspapers to declare that he had declared for total warfare. At least we believe that M. Reynaud came to power because of a deep-seated desire to end the hesitation and be done with idle words. Some of us believe that the bulk of this country, also loathing war and all its hideous implications, wishes to be done with words. Six months of propaganda warfare have begun to affect our morale, ever so little, but none the less perceptibly. If it be so, our Government also falls to be reconstituted. The weak spots in our Government must be removed. We must have the best available men to safeguard our food, run our transport, equip our armies, defend our shores, extend our trade, and conserve our resources. In any sort of war, whether *vi et armis* or a war of words, it is, and has been, intolerable that the Government should include portfolio-holders who, when they raise their voices on any subject across the ether or in the House, instantly lower our morale, excite our irritation. Such Ministers may be endurable in peace. In war they are dangerous and intolerable.

LORD HAW HAW. – Several correspondents have written to me about Lord Haw Haw and his broadcasts. Some spill bitter words and condemn those who turn on the tap of his poisoned trickles. I don't take that view. I have not often heard him. Indeed the wireless gives me more pain and boredom than recreation. But Lord Haw Haw is by no means one of the big curses of the accursed little box. Like most Englishmen, I have not yet lost so much confidence and pride in my race as no longer to enjoy immensely hearing a foreigner or a traitor blackening our national character. I infinitely prefer Lord Haw Haw to most of our "Front Bench" orators who give me the jim-jams and megrims. Lord Haw Haw is a lost soul who is working off in Purgatory the gross and petty sins of a small mind and an enlarged ego and he is doing the business very much to my satisfaction.

SLOGANS FOR CHATTERERS: WOOLLEN WORDS OF WISDOM EMBROIDERED ON HATS FOR ALL TO MARK AND LEARN.

Fashion is lending a hand in the campaign against enemy agents. The need for caution is emphasised in embroidery on hat-bands, scarves, and veils, similar to those of the Frenchwomen who started the idea.

"GONE WITH THE WIND" – THE LONG-AWAITED FILM WHICH WILL HAVE THREE PREMIÈRE SHOWINGS IN LONDON ON APRIL 18.

The Technicolor film production of Margaret Mitchell's best-selling novel, is due to be presented at the Palace, the Empire, and the Ritz. There was wide speculation as to the final choice for the role of Scarlett O'Hara. After many trials the part was given to Vivien Leigh.

PRESIDENT ROOSEVELT'S ENVOY-AT-LARGE SEES THE FIRST LORD: MR SUMNER WELLES WITH MR. CHURCHILL AND THE AMERICAN AMBASSADOR, MR. KENNEDY.

Mr. Sumner Welles, after visits to Rome, Berlin, and Paris, reached London on March 11, to round off his impressions of Europe at War. After lunch with the American Ambassador, Mr. Welles had an audience with the King at Buckingham Palace. He then went on to No. 10, Downing Street, where he was received by the Prime Minister, with Lord Halifax, Foreign Secretary, in attendance. He then had a long day of interviews in London on March 12.

"ERSATZ" HORSES COMPENSATING FOR THE GERMAN PETROL SHORTAGE, REAL HORSES BEING COMMANDEERED: PLOUGHING BY ELEPHANTS IN A FIELD NEAR HAMBURG.

The pachydermatous method of ploughing shown in this photograph suggests the straits to which German farmers have been put by the petrol shortage and the commandeering of horses. The field being ploughed by these "Ersatz" horses is near Hamburg: it seems probable, then, that the elephants came from Hamburg's famous zoo, of which Baedeker puts the elephant house first, as its most interesting point.

THE ATTEMPT TO PUT TWO MILLION ADDITIONAL ACRES UNDER THE PLOUGH BEFORE THE END OF MARCH: FARMING BY FLOODLIGHT.

Until recently the lighting restrictions made night work on farms very difficult. The Government has now, however, relaxed these restrictions for tractors, which, in fact, go better at night, in the gigantic effort to put two million additional acres under the plough before the end of March. The photograph reproduced above shows farming by floodlight in progress on Mr. Lloyd George's farm at Churt, Surrey. Soon 60,000 tractors will be working.

GERMANY INVADES NORWAY AND DENMARK: THE END OF THE PHONEY WAR?

THE NAZI INVASION OF NORWAY: OSLO BETRAYED.

NAZI SOLDIERS WITH AN ANTI-AIRCRAFT GUN IN AN OCCUPIED TOWN IN NORWAY: THE EXPRESSION OF THE YOUTH ON THE LEFT IS ELOQUENT OF HIS THOUGHTS.

A first-hand account of the German occupation of Oslo on April 9 appeared in the "Daily Telegraph" on April 16. "Between midnight and noon Norway's capital, all her principal seaports, and her most strategic coastal defences fell into German hands like overripe plums. The Norwegian people have no conception of how this tragedy could have happened . . . Norway's capital and great seaports were not captured by armed force, but with unparalleled speed by means of a conspiracy which must undoubtedly rank among the most audacious and most perfectly oiled political plots of the century. By bribery and infiltration on the part of Nazi agents, and by treason on the part of highly placed Norwegian officials, the German dictatorship built its Trojan horse." Describing the entry of the invading troops, the correspondent said "The German column marched steadily nearer . . . It required only six to seven minutes to march past . . . Norway's capital of nearly 300,000 inhabitants was being occupied by a German force of approximately 1500 men."

GERMANY INVADES DENMARK BY LAND, SEA AND AIR.

A STUDY IN ARROGANCE AND RESIGNATION, WITH WAR AND PEACE HEADGEAR STRONGLY CONTRASTED: A GERMAN COLUMN ENTERING A DANISH TOWN.

Hitler's invasion of Denmark came as a shock even to a world inured to such gestures of "protection," although, as Mr. Churchill pointed out, "Denmark had special reasons for apprehension, not only because she was the nearest and weakest of Germany's neighbours, but because she had a recent treaty with Germany, which guaranteed her from all molestation." It is reported that the German organisation within the city made Copenhagen's capture in four hours possible. While motorised and armoured units crossed the frontier troops were landed at five points on the Danish islands. Troops were landed by warship and armoured train, and one civil train was utilised as a "Trojan Horse." An ultimatum was given to the Government. They and King Christian had an hour to decide whether to give in or be bombed. More than fifty Nazi aeroplanes wheeled over the city. A lone Danish military 'plane', with suicidal courage, took off to give battle and was driven down by machine-gun bullets.

WHY GERMANY HAS INVADED SCANDINAVIA AND DENMARK.

THE LATEST ONSLAUGHT OF GERMANY UPON HER LITTLE NEIGHBOURS SHOWN IN GEOGRAPHIC FORM.

The strategic situation in Scandinavia was summed up in "The Times": "The most effective contribution sea-power can make to a rapid decision is to deprive the enemy of supplies of essential materials. Among these iron ore is one of the two most vital to Germany. Most imports, and those most valuable for war purposes, come from Sweden; part is shipped through Lulea and other Baltic ports, but a larger part through the Norwegian port of Narvik.

NARVIK, THE FIRST NAZI STRONGHOLD IN NORWAY TO BE ATTACKED.

THE NORWEGIAN PRO-NAZI LEADER WHOSE NAME BECAME IN A NIGHT A SYNONYM FOR "TRAITOR": MAJOR VIKDUN QUISLING. FOR A FEW DAYS PREMIER OF THE "NATIONAL GOVERNMENT" FORMED BY THE GERMANS.

On his resignation, Major Quisling said he would be "Commissioner of Demobilisation" in the new administration. "We should all be profoundly grateful to Major Quisling," said "The Times", "he has added a new word to the English language."

WHAT THE "HARDY" MEN SAW AS THEY WATCHED THE SECOND ATTACK ON NARVIK FROM BALLANGEN SCHOOL-HOUSE: THE "WARSPITE" STEAMS UP, PRECEDED BY DESTROYERS. TWO SIGNAL LAMPS CAN BE SEEN FLASHING ON HER BRIDGE.

ABANDONED, WITH HER GUNS AND TORPEDO-TUBES LEFT TRAINED TO PORT, THIS GERMAN DESTROYER OF THE LARGE 1811-TON TYPE WAS PHOTOGRAPHED AS SHE DRIFTED HELPLESSLY, LISTING TO STARBOARD, AND ON FIRE FORWARD.

NORWAY'S HEROIC KING HAAKON – WHO PRONOUNCED "THE NORWEGIAN GOVERNMENT CAN NEGOTIATE ON NO BASIS BUT THE REMOVAL OF THE GERMAN TROOPS FROM THE COUNTRY."

German aircraft evidently have orders to attack the King of Norway personally, as they have been bombing each successive place he stays in. He told a Swedish journalist "I must stay in my country as long as there remains a single inch of Norwegian soil."

Last week saw almost continuous naval actions in the area of Narvik, the port from which Swedish ore has been pouring southwards. Early on April 8 the 1345-ton destroyer H.M.S. "Glow-worm" fought single-handed at point-blank range against two german destroyers and the 10,000 ton German cruiser "Hipper." Burning and severely damaged, she turned in a last gesture of defiance and rammed her largest enemy, a heroic action which earned a posthumous V.C. for her captain, Lt. Cdr. Roofe. Then at day-break on April 9 the British battle-cruiser H.M.S. "Renown" (32,000 tons) met the German battleship "Scharnhorst" (26,000 tons) together with "a cruiser of the Hipper class" [after the war discovered to have been the "Scharnhorsts" sister-ship "Gneiserau"] in very dirty weather off the rock-bound coast. The "Renown" scored three hits on the "Scharnhorst" [actually the "Gneiserau"] at 18,000 yards but the Germans escaped into the murk.

At dawn on April 10 five British destroyers entered Narvik Fiord itself, and engaged first five, then five more, German destroyers of the lastest and largest type. Two German destroyers and six merchant ships were sunk. Three more destroyers were reported heavily damaged. H.M.S. "Hunter" was sunk and H.M.S. "Hardy" so severely damaged that she had to run ashore, where the survivors of her crew were hidden by Norwegian patriots. Her commander, Captain Warburton-Lee, the flotilla leader, was also awarded a posthumous V.C. Finally on April 13 the British battleship H.M.S. "Warspite" led a flotilla of nine destroyers up the Ofoten Fiord until they came in sight of the surviving eight German destroyers. Four appear to have been rapidly sunk where they lay; the others attempted a vain flight up the Rombaks Fiord, a cul-de-sac, up which they were pursued and all sunk, without British loss.

THE CLIMAX OF AN EPIC OF SEA POWER: THE B.E.F. LANDS IN NORWAY WITHOUT A SINGLE CASUALTY.

SOME OF THE FAMOUS FRENCH *CHASSEUR ALPIN* TROOPS, WHO SAILED WITH THEIR ST. BERNARD DOGS TO NORWAY.

HOW THE NAVY PROTECTED THE TRANSPORT OF BRITISH TROOPS TO NORWAY: BOATDRILL IN A LINER, WITH ONE OF THE GUARDIAN DESTROYERS PASSING ALONGSIDE.

A NORWEGIAN SOLDIER RELOADING HIS RIFLE BEHIND A BARRI-CADE. THE NORWEGIANS WERE SEVERELY HANDICAPPED BY LACK OF AMMUNITION.

A GERMAN TANK ON A MOUNTAIN ROAD IN NORWAY, WITH A FALLEN PINE-TREE BEHIND. MOTORISED ENEMY DETACHMENTS MADE RAPID ADVANCES UP THE GUDBRANDS VALLEY.

"The German forces will see to it that no Englishman or Frenchman shows his nose in Norway or Denmark for the rest of the war." Thus Ribbentrop on April 9.

From various reports it seems certain that landings have been made at some five or six points along the Norwegian coast, and that these landings have been carried out without any loss of life or any kind of mishap. One landing was evidently at Andalsnes, at the head of the famous Romsdal Fiord, to the south of Trondheim, where the Germans are established in some strength, and another at Namsos to the north, where the British were able to join with the Norwegian forces stationed at Steinkjer. There is no certainty about a landing at Laerdal, on the Sogne Fiord, though it seems very probable. A mountain road from this point leads to Lake Mjosa, north of Oslo, where fighting has been taking place. Landings have been made to the north of Narvik, and British forces are definitely stated to be at various points on Narvik Bay. The gallant Norwegian troops, in any event less well equipped than the German forces, suffered from the additional handicap that, owing to the start Germany obtained through internal treachery, they were in many places unable to mobilise properly and obtain their arms and ammunition. But when Allied help arrived they proved their worth. Naturally, they have perfect knowledge of the terrain. The Norwegian New Year's defence budget of nearly £20,000,000 included an allocation of £8,000,000 for extraordinary military measures "to safeguard neutrality." It is a sad thought that so many of these measures should have been invalidated by traitors in their

midst. Addressing his men recently in an Order of the Day, General Ruge, Commander-in-Chief of the Norwegian Army, said: "As defenders of the soil of the Fatherland, you have now for two weeks done what your duty commands . . . Although we have up to now been powerless against many of the war methods of the enemy, you have gained the respect of the world. I thank you all."

The Nazi air strength, with the bases they seized by their surprise invasion, has been their strongest weapon. Their bombers have, till the last few days, had it all their own way, able to dive low to get direct hits, and to machine-gun the towns, villages, and defending troops. Now that the British have obtained a temporary air base on a frozen lake, the German bombers have received a check and are no longer so active.

Trondheim remains the chief centre of the battlefront, where the result will be most critical. The Allies had hoped to cut the town off entirely, but the German air superiority has checked this, and the German armies from Oslo are now making desperate efforts to relieve the town, marching troops up the two great valleys of Osterdal and Gudbrandsdal to crush the Allied forces. Planes have carried troops, the large Hansa planes bringing fifty men at a time, but little has arrived by sea. The Nazis have no compunction about destroying Norwegian towns and villages, whereas the Allies are reluctant to bomb anything but military objectives and have not bombed the city of Trondheim with the severity shown by the Germans at Namsos and Steinkjer. These two places have been completely destroyed, all the houses burnt, and the civilians rendered homeless.

UNDAUNTED ALLIED TROOPS RETURN FROM THE FIGHTING IN NORWAY.

A LOW-ALTITUDE PHOTOGRAPH OF FOUR NAZI "H.E.115" SEA-PLANES, TAKEN FROM A ROYAL AIR FORCE MACHINE IN THE COURSE OF ACTUAL OPERATIONS.

THE NAZI LUFTWAFFE REPEATS IN NORWAY ITS COWARDLY CRIMES: WITH THE SHELLS OF A FEW HOUSES STILL STANDING, THE STREETS OF THE ONCE-PROSPEROUS LITTLE PORT OF NAM-SOS QUICKLY REDUCED TO A DEVASTATED AREA.

AN INTERNATIONAL TRIO PHOTOGRAPHED ON BOARD A BRITISH WARSHIP JUST AFTER RE-EMBARKATION AT NAMSOS. (FROM LEFT TO RIGHT) FRENCHMAN, ENGLISHMAN, NORWEGIAN.

After a brief period in which the German bombers held undisputed sway in the air over Norway, the R.A.F. has been asserting itself in no uncertain fashion and has been supplying the aid which is absolutely necessary in all modern military operations. At the week-end the presence of British fighting planes was immediately felt by the backing away or disappearance in many cases of the once so-dashing Nazi bombers.

The Nazis however, held the head of Beitstad fjord, where the two roads from Namsos meet. The Norwegian mountain fortress of Hegra surrendered on May 5, after holding out for more than three weeks. The withdrawal of all Allied troops south of Trondheim was announced by the Premier on May 2, and the evacuation of Namsos by the War Office the following day.

THE WAR WITH NAZI GERMANY: THE CRISIS HAS COME.
HOLLAND OPENS THE DYKES: THE ALLIES RUSH TO BELGIUM'S AID.

On May 10, Holland was invaded by German troops at 3 a.m. When the war storm broke on the Low Countries, the Dutch troops were standing by the first water defence along the Yssel River, it having been recognised that the N.E. provinces would have to be surrendered. At Arnhem the Yssel appears to have been crossed, together with the Maas, farther to the south. At the same time a determined attempt on The Hague and Rotterdam was made by parachute troops. German troop-carrying planes landed on the long sandy beach stretching north from Scheveningen bathing resort, which lies in close proximity to The Hague. The R.A.F. promptly intervened by attacking the German troop-carrying planes. Bombers and fighters dived to 50 ft. and smashed plane after plane. The Dutch destroyer "Jan Van Gelder" assisted from the sea and Dutch ground troops held off the attackers.

At 8 a.m. appeal for assistance was sent to Allies who replied, within 30 minutes, that they would bring all help in their power. At Rotterdam, Germans alighted from Dornier flying-boats at 5 a.m.- landing troops seized bridges without difficulty, and secured the Stock Exchange and Waalhaven Aerodrome, a few miles from the city. By 3 p.m. the R.A.F. had made a fierce attack on the aerodrome, obtaining great success on the German troop-carriers.

THE FRENCH ARMY ADVANCES IN LUXEMBOURG: FRENCH TANKS SHUTTERED DOWN FOR INSTANT ACTION DASH TO MEET THE ONCOMING GERMANS AND STEM THE ADVANCE. FOR HOUR AFTER HOUR THE STREAM OF WAR MACHINES RUMBLED THROUGH TOWN AND VILLAGE, MECHANISATION PROVING ITS VALUE TO THE HILT DURING THESE FIRST ANXIOUS MOMENTS.

A BRITISH GUN CROSSES THE FRONTIER INTO BELGIUM: VEHICLES OF ALL TYPES TOOK PART IN THE DASH: NEVER IN THE WORLD'S HISTORY HAS AN ARMY GONE INTO ACTION QUICKER, OR MORE FULLY EQUIPPED, THAN THE BRITISH AND FRENCH FORCES.

With every respect for the sanctity of international usage, the British and French Armies did not advance into Belgium or Luxembourg until after the Germans had violated the Eastern frontiers. The active preparations of the enemy were known, but no forward movement was made until the situation warranted it. As the Allied forces advanced at the gallop across the frontiers the Belgian troops saw for the first time the might of the British and French forces – many of the tanks, guns and other weapons still being on the Secret List, and therefore never before seen by our Allies.

ON THE BRIDGE: MR. WINSTON CHURCHILL, A DESCENDANT OF THE GREAT MARLBOROUGH, SEEN HERE ON THE BRIDGE OF A DESTROYER DURING HIS RECENT VISIT TO A NORTHERN PORT, NOW BECOMES PRIME MINISTER AND MINISTER OF DEFENCE.

THE MAN OF THE HOUR MR. CHURCHILL'S CABINET: AN ALL-PARTY MINISTRY.

THE WAR CABINET.

Prime Minister and Minister of Defence,
MR. WINSTON CHURCHILL.
Lord President of the Council,
MR. NEVILLE CHAMBERLAIN.
Foreign Secretary,
VISCOUNT HALIFAX.
Lord Privy Seal,
MR. C. R. ATTLEE.
Minister without Portfolio,
MR. ARTHUR GREENWOOD.

OTHER NEW MINISTERS.

First Lord of the Admiralty,
MR. A. V. ALEXANDER.
Secretary for War,
MR. ANTHONY EDEN.
Secretary for Air,
SIR ARCHIBALD SINCLAIR.
Lord Chancellor,
SIR JOHN SIMON.
Chancellor of the Exchequer,
SIR KINGSLEY WOOD.
Home Secretary,
SIR JOHN ANDERSON.
Colonial Secretary,
LORD LLOYD.
President of the Board of Trade,
SIR ANDREW DUNCAN.

Minister of Supply,
MR. HERBERT MORRISON.
Minister of Information,
MR. DUFF COOPER.
Minister of Labour and Minister of National Service,
MR. ERNEST BEVIN.
Secretary of India and for Burma
MR. L. S. AMERY.
Minister of Health,
MR. MALCOLM MACDONALD.
Minister of Food,
LORD WOOLTON.
Dominions Secretary,
VISCOUNT CALDECOTE.
Secretary for Scotland,
MR. ERNEST BROWN.
Minister for Aircraft Production,
LORD BEAVERBROOK.
President, Board of Education,
MR. H. RAMSBOTHAM.
Minister of Agriculture,
MR. ROBERT HUDSON.
Minister of Transport,
SIR JOHN REITH.
Minister of Shipping,
MR. RONALD CROSS.
Minister of Economic Warfare,
MR. HUGH DALTON.

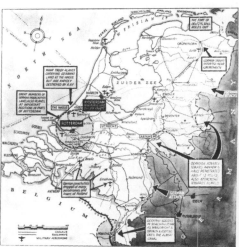

THE GERMAN THRUST AGAINST HOLLAND: THE FIRST MAIN ATTACKS SHOWN.

Announcing the formation of a Government "representing the united and inflexible resolve of the nation to prosecute the war with Germany to a victorious conclusion," Mr. Churchill stated that it was the evident wish and will of Parliament and the nation that it should be conceived on the broadest possible basis and include all parties.

DUTCH ROYAL REFUGEES.

THE DUTCH ROYAL FAMILY ESCAPE THE NAZI GANGSTERS: PRINCE BERNHARD HELPING TO CARRY HIS YOUNGEST DAUGHTER IN A GAS-PROOF COT ON ARRIVAL IN ENGLAND.

Shiploads of refugees from the Low Countries have been arriving in England. Nearly all of them had stories to tell of German parachute troops and spies, the sinister collaboration of the Fifth Column, and attacks with bombs, machine-guns, and magnetic mines on the ships which brought them to England.

THE HORROR OF ROTTERDAM.

THE WHITE "SCAR" IS THE TWO SQUARE MILES OF THE HEART OF ROTTERDAM, BOMBED TO DESTRUCTION ON MAY 14. THE CITY WAS THEN WITHOUT ANTI-AIRCRAFT DEFENCES.

On May 14 the Germans, angered by the prolonged armed resistance put up by the Dutch, decided to finish it by ruthless destruction at Rotterdam. For three hours the unprotected open city, without anti-aircraft defences, was subjected to a hail of heavy bombs, systematically rained upon it by scores of German dive-bombers.

THE DUTCH ARMY SURRENDERS.

GENERAL H. G. WINKELMAN, COMMANDER-IN-CHIEF OF THE NETHERLANDS ARMY, WHO, ON MAY 14, ORDERED "THE TROOPS CONCERNED" TO CEASE FIGHTING, EXCEPT IN ZEELAND, TO SAVE THE CIVIL POPULATION AND FURTHER SACRIFICE OF LIFE.

In a broadcast he declared that ultimately the Netherlands would rise again as a free nation. The Dutch Foreign Minister revealed the following day that the Army had lost one quarter of its total of 40,000 men in resisting the invader.

HOMES WRECKED BY NAZI BOMBS IN BELGIUM, HOLLAND AND FRANCE.
THE PITIFUL TREK FROM THE NAZIS IN BELGIUM.

A STREET DEMOLISHED BY BOMBS: REFUGEES, CARRYING HUR-
RIEDLY GATHERED BELONGINGS, THREAD THEIR WAY THROUGH
THE DEBRIS. MANY WERE BURIED BENEATH BLAZING RUINS.

A PITIFUL "CARAVAN OF SORROW," GREEK-LIKE IN ITS POIGNANT
TRAGEDY: MOTHERS OF NEWLY-DEVASTATED LOUVAIN FLEEING
FROM THEIR WRECKED HOMES.

ANOTHER PATHETIC SCENE: A MOTHER ATTEMPTING TO FIND A
WAY TO SAFETY WITH HER THREE YOUNG CHILDREN DURING
THE BOMBING OF AN OPEN TOWN.

AN OLD BELGIAN WOMAN BEING LED AWAY FROM HER WRECKED
HOME BY A BRITISH SOLDIER.

MANY GROUPS OF NUNS APPEARED IN THE LONG LINES OF THE HOMELESS. SEVERAL OF THE OLDER SISTERS, INCLUDING THE AGED
MOTHER SUPERIOR, HAD HAD TO BE LEFT BEHIND AS THEY WERE UNABLE TO TRAVEL.

The trek from the German invader set out from various places, growing in volume as time progressed. The urge to move away from the very presence of the Hun affected all grades of society. Peasants with their farm carts passed in dusty procession with generations of the same family, grandmère, nursing a little girl, while mothers and daughters clung to parcels. Bicycles innumerable, old cabs in the melancholy procession. Then a group of better-class children, neatly dressed, and all helping with bundles and blankets. "I passed many thousands of refugees," writes one correspondent. "When planes flew overhead a few raised tired eyes to see whether it was friend or foe. The distant grumble of the heavy guns from the great battle raging only a few miles away left them equally unmoved as they walked like automata. Almost all their wordly belongings had been abandoned. Even those owning carts carried no furniture. I saw one woman trudging along carrying nothing but a babe in arms."

THE BATTLE FOR SEDAN.

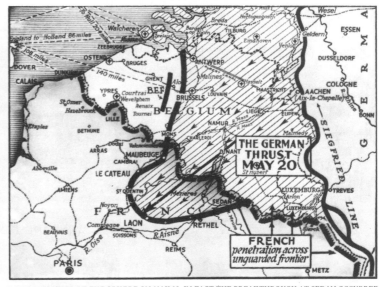

GERMAN FIGHTING VEHICLES PASSING THROUGH A FRONTIER ROAD-BLOCK ON THEIR ADVANCE.
ONCE THE LOCAL DEFENDERS HAD BEEN KILLED, SUCH OBSTACLES CAN BE SURMOUNTED.

A MAP PUBLISHED BY *THE SPHERE* ON MAY 25: IN FACT THE BREAKTHROUGH AT SEDAN OCCURRED
ON MAY 14 NOT 20. BY MAY 20 THE GERMANS HAD ALREADY REACHED THE CHANNEL COAST.

THE ARDENNE GATE WHICH WAS LEFT OPEN.

On May 14 a massed German tank attack broke through the French line without warning, the tanks emerging from the deep valleys of the Belgian Ardennes country. The first news of this attack was published on Tuesday of last week, when it was evident that the Nazi main thrust was to be made against France and in a section of the frontier which was only lightly held.

The stream of massed German tanks, although gallantly met by French resistance appeared in such numbers that they were able to fan out down every road and lane.

As soon as the German tanks had broken down the local resistance infantry began to follow, in order to consolidate the positions won. The French infantry endeavoured to stem the attack.

The concentration of such a huge mass of tanks here was a puzzle to military critics. It is very difficult country. The Semois River twists and turns and a few roads penetrate thickly-wooded heights, and they do not all lead immediately to the objective of the Sedan bridge. It was not until Saturday morning that the *Daily Telegraph* in a message from Paris stated that "the Belgian General Staff, which was in charge of the Ardennes sector east of the Meuse, did not believe it possible that such a hilly and thickly wooded country could be crossed by an invader so speedily and so easily."

"TANKS OPEN THE WAY" IS THE GERMAN DESCRIPTION OF THIS
PHOTOGRAPH, WHICH STATES THAT THE INFANTRY ARE HERE
SEEN, WAITING TO FOLLOW UP.

THE GERMANS HAVE ALSO USED RUBBER BOATS TO FORM PON-
TOON BRIDGES. SUCH A BRIDGE SEEN ON THE RIGHT, CAN SUP-
PORT A MOTOR CAR AS WELL AS HORSE DRAWN TRANSPORT.

THE WAR WITH NAZI GERMANY: THE DRIVE TO THE CHANNEL PORTS.

BLOWING UP BRIDGES AS THE GERMAN TANKS CROSSED BELGIUM.

Uncertainty as to the exact moment when bridges should have been blown up led in many cases to the enemy pouring in his armoured attack, but in this case the B.E.F. blew up a Belgian bridge with timely effect.

A TANK DRIVER CHEWS A BABY'S TEAT TO EASE THE STRAIN OF THE ROUGH GOING WHEN PROCEEDING TO AN ACTION POSITION.

British and German tanks fought in the main street of Arras – familiar to the B.E.F. in the last war – while violent house-to-house fighting took place in the crooked streets of the old town, now reported to be seriously damaged. Most of the town was destroyed during the last war. The Hôtel de Ville, with its Gothic façade, the Cathedral and the Abbaye de St. Vaast were among the ruins.

A BRITISH GUN TEAM, AFTER BLAZING AWAY AT AN ENEMY BOTH IN THE FORM OF TANKS AND INFANTRY.

"At some places the Germans have launched infantry in such masses that our men have become physically fatigued with the effort of continually firing. . . . Their faces black with a week's beard and dust caked on sweating skin, they are still grinning, still ready to make another stand. They have shown supreme courage and endurance," writes "Eye-witness" with the British Army in France.

THE ALLIED ARMIES FIGHT TOGETHER IN BELGIUM: ALL ACCOUNTS BEAR WITNESS TO THE DOGGED RESISTANCE BEING PUT UP BY THE BELGIAN ARMY. THE RECORD OF THE FORTS OF LIÈGE AND NAMUR IS A STIRRING WITNESS TO THE SPIRIT MOVING THE BELGIAN ARMY OF 1940.

DIAGRAM 2

SITUATION OF B.E.F. 23TH MAY, 1940.

British Line
Allied Line
British Troops.
Allied Troops.
German Panzer Divisions

A DIAGRAM OF THE SITUATION ON MAY 23, WHEN THE LINE OF THE ESCAUT WAS ABANDONED. THE KING OF THE BELGIANS, WITH "EVIDENT RELUCTANCE," AGREED TO WITHDRAW TO THE LINE OF THE YSER. THE ENEMY HAD WIDENED THE GAP BETWEEN THE BRITISH AND FRENCH ARMIES.

It is now clear that the Allies did not contemplate marching any considerable force into Holland in an attempt to stem the German invasion. Their plan was to wheel left into Belgium from the point where the Meuse enters Belgian territory near Givet. They then took up positions on the principal Belgian line of defence, which followed the Meuse down to Namur, then crossed the plateau of Gembloux to the Dyle and so on to the neighbourhood of Antwerp. The French were to occupy the southern portion of this line, the British, generally speaking, the centre, and the Belgians the left. If the Belgians maintained their positions further forward and held the Albert Canal, well and good; if, on the other hand, the Belgians were driven out of the Ardennes and the Albert Canal were turned, there would be good reason to hope that the German onslaught could be checked on the line described. The plan was put into effect, without serious interference.

Meanwhile, the first phase of the German plan was the obvious one which every serious commentator recognised at once. It was to force a way through south of the Dutch water defences to the coast, thus separating the Dutch and Belgian Armies, and then putting the former out of action. This part of the programme was accomplished much sooner than had been thought possible by a combination of various methods: "Quislings" who seized bridges and sluices after, in many cases, murdering the guardians, parachute troops who took possession of nodal points, forces landed from troop-carrying aircraft, who arrived in strength sufficient to attack whole cities, and the threat of unlimited bombing of the civil population.

What is much more interesting is the development of the second phase. It appears certain that the enemy

knew the Allied plan and that, far from desiring to prevent its being put into operation, he actually encouraged it. He limited his bombing to what he considered would be the minimum necessary in order to prevent the Allies from smelling a rat. After he had turned the line of the Albert Canal he launched no more than what appear to have been containing attacks anywhere north of Namur. He had got a large Allied force where he wanted it, and was now free to turn to the second phase. In this he was powerfully aided by the slackness and inefficiency which M. Reynaud has revealed in scathing terms, though we must give him credit for knowing which troops were designated to hold the Meuse south of Namur. He rushed mechanised forces and bridging material with amazing speed through Luxemburg, which he had seized without opposition as a preliminary step, and through the Ardennes, where the Belgian resistance seems to have been very speedily overwhelmed. The huge *massif* which the French forces on the Meuse looked upon as a barrier served the Germans as a covered approach. Next the Germans launched a series of assaults on the line of the Meuse, secured a number of bridge-heads, and poured their tanks across the river. The co-operation of their low-flying aircraft and dive-bombers broke down the French resistance, and for a time the armoured columns met with little opposition. Worse still, a gap appeared between the British and French, and through this gap the German mechanised columns swept to capture Cambrai, Arras, and Amiens.

Such was the second phase of the German programme: the capture of the Channel ports and the separation of the British and Belgians, with certain French forces, from the main French Army.

THE R.A.F. IN ACTION.

WHEN A DORNIER AEROPLANE WAS SHOT DOWN IN FRANCE: ITS CREW OF FIVE WERE ARRESTED BY ONE ENGLISHMAN!

Mr. George Muir is an Englishman living in France, the keeper of a British War Graves Cemetery. When this Dornier crashed near his cemetery, as the result of an attack by R.A.F. fighters, Mr. Muir found the crew – fully armed – walking away from the wreckage. With great bravery he called on them to hand over their arms, which in this case were revolvers – and they did! Mr. Muir then handed over his captives to the French authorities, to join the many scores of enemy pilots now in prisoner of war camps behind the lines. In our picture Allied officers are seen inspecting the wreckage of the aeroplane.

WEYGAND TAKES COMMAND.

"THE MAN WHO NEVER KNEW DEFEAT"

MARSHAL PÉTAIN RETURNS TO FRANCE.

General Weygand, the new French Generalissimo, was Chief of Staff and right hand man of Marshal Foch, who brought victory to Allied arms in 1918. His record is an impressive one: apart from his contributions in the last war, he defeated the Bolsheviks within a month when they were actually at the gates of Warsaw. He is seventy three years of age. Eighty-four years old, Petain has been called back from Spain, where he was serving as French Ambassador, to act as vice Premier of France. It was he who commanded the French Army at Verdun and held up the Germans until they were smashed. Afterwards, until the age of seventy five, he was Inspector General of the French Army and helped to map out the famous Maginot Line.

LOCAL DEFENCE VOLUNTEERS.

THE LOCAL DEFENCE VOLUNTEER FORCE TURNS OUT "TO DEFEND TOWNS AND VILLAGES WHEN OCCASION ARISES."

Police stations everywhere have been besieged by men of all ages and types eager to serve in response to the recent broadcast call of the Secretary of State for War for volunteers to deal with any Germans who may attempt parachute landings in Britain. One of the first to offer his service to the corps was the Bishop of Chelmsford, who warned the public some months ago of this danger. A large number of early applicants were members of rifle clubs. The uniform of the Local Defence Volunteer Force, as it is called, will be a two-piece garment of khaki denim which may be worn over civilian underclothing.

THE KING WHO SURRENDERED HIS COUNTRY.

KING LEOPOLD III OF THE BELGIANS WHO CAPITULATED TO THE GERMANS ON MAY 28.

At 4 a.m. on Tuesday of this week (May 28) there took place one of the most astonishing events in recorded military history. With two of his allies occupying positions of great gravity, in Western Belgium and Northern France, King Leopold of the Belgians made approaches to the German Army Command with a view to the surrender of his Army. By four o'clock the Belgian Army laid down its arms and ceased to protect the left flank of the British Expeditionary Force, which was occupying the central portion of the Allied Line to the north of the Arras Bapaume gap. M. Reynaud, in a broadcast on Tuesday at 8.30 a.m., could scarcely veil his feelings at the defection of the King who but a few days before had appealed for Allied help. "It is a fact without precedent in history."

Speaking in the House of Commons the Prime Minister said: "I have no intention of suggesting to the House that we ought at this moment to attempt to pass judgment on the action of the King of the Belgians in his capacity as Commander-in-Chief of the Belgian Army."

On May 30 a Cabinet meeting of Belgian Ministers held in France approved the text of a decree stating that "In the name of the Belgian people, in pursuance of Article 32 of the Constitution and in view of the fact that the King is in the power of the invader, the Ministers, met together in Council, declare that it is impossible for the King to reign."

THE DEFENDER OF CALAIS.

BRIGADIER CLAUDE NICHOLSON, WHOSE ACTION SAVED THE B.E.F. IN FLANDERS.

AN ORIGINAL PLAN OF VAUBAN'S DAY, SHOWING RAMPARTS USED IN THE HEROIC DEFENCE BY A BRITISH BRIGADE.

The name of the commander who led and inspired the gallant defence was revealed by General Sir Hubert Gough. "His 'No' to the German demand to surrender is an example and inspiration to all of us." The troops under his command were units of the Rifle Brigade, a battalion of the 60th Rifles, a battalion of Queen Victoria's Rifles, and a battalion of 4000 men. Brigadier Nicholson was captured.

BOULOGNE'S GREAT STORY.

THE EVACUATION OF BOULOGNE UNDER FIERCE SHELL-FIRE ON MAY 24 – TAKEN BY THE LIGHT OF A BURSTING SHELL: A BRITISH DESTROYER GOING OUT STERN FIRST, ON FIRE BUT WITH ALL HER GUNS IN ACTION, AND ANOTHER DESTROYER COMING IN TO THE JETTY TO EMBARK TROOPS.

In a week of stirring deeds the great evacuation from Dunkirk is apt to overshadow everything else. We must not, however, let go unrecorded the brilliant work of the Navy and a demolition party.

A combined party of seamen, Royal Marines, and small detachments of Royal Engineers was rushed across the Channel, reaching the main jetty at Boulogne in the morning of May 24. The naval party was landed to hold the railway station, fit demolition charges, and "earmark" bridges, trains, lock-gates and everything which should be destroyed when the time came. Owing to the position of the Germans all around the town, it had been impossible to send field guns or other assistance. Consequently, the troops could not hold out indefinitely against the enemy's armoured vehicles. Small parties of Germans were already coming down streets on the outskirts of the town. The destroyer bringing the naval demolition party had already left under orders. She was relieved by another, which, in turn, was relieved by a third. Naval and military officials conferred and soon came to the conclusion that the town could not be held. Demolition of all the bridges and important points was decided upon and small parties of seamen went out with parcels of explosives. The enemy was closing in.

"THE MIRACLE OF DELIVERANCE": THE EVACUATION FROM DUNKIRK.

THE EVACUATION OF BRITISH TROOPS FROM THE BEACHES ROUND DUNKIRK: EMBARKATION PARTIES MAKING THEIR WAY INTO THE WATER UNDISTURBED BY GERMAN AIR OR ARTILLERY ACTION.

STANDING ROOM ONLY ON THE DECK OF A BRITISH DESTROYER.

"ANYTHING CAPABLE OF KEEPING AFLOAT AND CARRYING TROOPS ACROSS THE CHANNEL".

THE EMBARKATION AS IT APPEARED FROM THE BEACH.

The troops remained scattered about the sand-dunes until the moment came for embarkation, when they went down to the beach in batches, every sort of small craft was used to get them off.

As the days wore on, the stream of soldiers reaching Dunkirk increased in volume especially when the French forces began to arrive. It was necessary to clear the air for the protection of these masses. More R.A.F. fighters poured over to the beaches and, says Mr. Churchill, "our Air Force decisively defeated the main strength of the enemy Air Force."

A tribute to the indomitable fight put up by the British Expeditionary Force and their French comrades in the epic retreat to Dunkirk and the defence of its perimeter was provided by (of all places) Berlin on June 3, when a German radio announcer declared: "We must admit that the British fighters were magnificent." That this is nothing less than full truth is borne out by Captain Cyril Falls in his article this week. "Remember," he emphasises, "that not all the skill and courage of the Navy, and the French warships which so gallantly assisted it, not all the devotion of the Mercantile Marine, not all the supremacy of the Royal Air Force could have saved these troops from destruction if they had not fought like lions at bay." When a rearguard position was abandoned, and its defenders slipped away, the oncoming enemy found that they had passed through another line, which was held every whit as stoutly. Innumerable fiercely fought rearguard actions have cost the Germans heavy losses.

The "New York Herald-Tribune," in a comment which summed up the tremendous impression created in America by the successful

EVERY KIND OF CRAFT, DOWN TO THE CARLEY RESCUE FLOATS

EVERY KIND OF CRAFT, DOWN TO THE CARLEY RESCUE FLOATS CARRIED BY WARSHIPS, WAS UTILISED.

UNQUENCHABLE –
THE POILU, WITH THE TORN CLOTHES, CIGARETTE IN LIPS, UNSHAVEN CHIN, WAS ONE OF THE HEROIC ARMY WHICH HELD UP THE GERMAN ADVANCE LONG ENOUGH TO ALLOW 335,000 BRITISH AND FRENCH TROOPS TO LEAVE FOR SAFETY. WHAT CAN HITLER'S ARMIES DO WHEN MEN OF SUCH UNCONQUERABLE COURAGE FACE THEM?

evacuation of the British Expeditionary Force in Flanders, wrote: "A defeat sustained with such fortitude is not a disaster. These are soldiers of civilisation losing their own dire battle, but, in so doing, enrolling themselves imperishably among those who will yet save by their suffering everything which makes civilised life of value." General Lord Gort, V.C., Commander-in-Chief of the "New Contemptibles," only left Flanders when four-fifths of his army were evacuated, in obedience to a direct order from the Government. He said, on arriving in England on June 1: "The next time victory will be with us."

THE GERMAN ONSLAUGHT ON THE WEYGAND LINE
THE LAST PHASE OF THE FRENCH ARMY'S FIGHT.

CUT OFF ON THE SOMME: A BRITISH LORRY CRASHES THROUGH A BARRICADED ROAD ON ITS WAY TO ULTIMATE FREEDOM.

FRENCH INFANTRY MARCHING TOWARDS A GUARD POST IN THE BATTLE ZONE. TROOPS HAVE BEEN OCCUPYING ALL KINDS OF NATURAL STRONG POINTS DURING THE WEEK.

A GERMAN MOTOR-CYCLIST SPEEDING PAST THE PITIFUL WRECK-AGE OF A FRENCH CONVOY OF REFUGEES.

Refugees cumbering the roads were a constant cause of disorganisation during the fighting in France; and often seriously hampered the operations of their own side. Instructions issued by the Home Office on what to do in case of invasion lay it down as a first principle that no one should move until ordered to do so. "During the day's tour," wrote a "Manchester Guardian" correspondent, "I must have passed a hundred thousand refugees streaming away from the German advance."

The Weygand Line had as its front the Somme, the Oise, the Aillette canal and river and the Aisne. These natural obstacles were not as effective as one might have expected, for the very dry season had reduced the volume of all these streams and rivers. Forty German divisions and some 2,000 tanks, it is estimated, were thrown against this line.

The main lines of the German attack which opened with great ferocity on June 5 are indicated by black arrows on the first map the most westerly being that towards the River Bresle, and the most easterly in the neighbourhood of Pontavert, on the River Aisne. Facing these German thrusts are indicated a number of French strong points. They are indicated here in order to convey an impression of the nature of the resistance which is being made to the German attack. Passing eastwards there was a violent assault across the Somme between Aumale and Noyon. Advanced forces in the Amiens and Peronne districts were later withdrawn to smooth out a big salient. Eastward of Noyon, the enemy succeeded in crossing the area south of Ham. The Aillette Canal and the famous ridge of the Chemin des Dames were swarmed over and the German forces appeared on the banks of the Aisne.

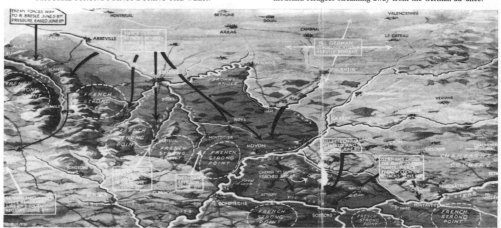

A PANORAMIC VIEW OF THE WEYGAND LINE WHERE THE FRENCH RESISTED THE INITIAL ONSLAUGHT OF THE GERMANS ON JUNE 5.

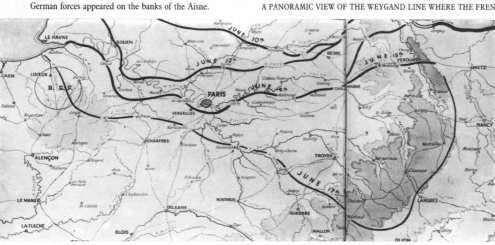

THE TIDE OF BATTLE BETWEEN JUNE 10 AND JUNE 17 WHEN THE FRENCH ARMY RETREATED TO THE LINE OF THE LOIRE.

THE BREAK-THROUGH AT AUMALE did not appear to be as serious as after events proved it to be. The infiltration of tanks was not apparently promptly arrested and the stream grew, more or less along the lines here indicated. The numerous pontoon bridges erected by the enemy were broken from time to time, but so determined was he to gain his objectives by a given date that bridgeheads were formed at two places and the flow of mechanised units began on the south shore of the Seine. The wider advance to the river followed the Aumale thrust a day or so later.

The black lines on the second map indicate the successive advances of the enemy from the Soissons Line of June 10 through the line of June 12 in front of Paris, to the line of June 14 when Paris was surrendered with Versailles. The gap of the week-end did not reveal much change, and it was not until Monday morning that the vulnerable position of the French Army became obvious. Lack of reserves appeared to be the reason for the inability of the French to stop the forward rush of the enemy armoured divisions. The line of June 17 stretched down to the Burgundy area of Auxerre and Avallon. On the east the German thrust was turning the Maginot Line by way of the famous Verdun fortress.

BOMB ATTACKS ON THE RED CROSS.

THE NAZI WAR ON THE HELPLESS AND WOUNDED: THE WRECK-AGE OF A FRENCH HOSPITAL TRAIN BOMBED BY ENEMY AIRMEN.

GERMAN BOMBS ON PARIS: FUTILE AND PROMPTLY AVENGED.

DÉBRIS OF BUILDINGS HIT BY BOMBS. MUNICH AND RHINELAND TOWNS WERE PROMPTLY BOMBED AS A REPRISAL.

THE "LANCASTRIA" SINKS IN 30 MINUTES.

SURVIVORS FROM THE "LANCASTRIA" CLIMBING ABOARD ANOTHER SHIP FROM THE TRAWLER WHICH RESCUED THEM.

The stark and ruthless character of the present German offensive is no more unmistakably revealed than in the deliberate attacks carried out by Nazi airmen on hospitals, hospital trains and ambulances, despite their conspicuous markings. A message from Paris of May 26 stated that the committee directing the American volunteer ambulance service on the French front had ordered the obliteration of the Red Cross sign on their vehicles. "All our drivers agree," the announcement declared, "that the Red Cross only attracts attention of German pilots. It no longer protects our men, and we are removing it in their interests." Hospital ships clearly marked with huge Red Crosses have also been deliberately bombed and machine-gunned by Nazi airmen, both in Norwegian and French ports.

Paris experienced its first real air raid on June 3. For over an hour waves of bombers, amounting to at least 150, accompanied by fighters (which would have been impossible from bases situated in Germany), attacked the south-west of Paris and numerous suburbs with 100-lb. and 200-lb. bombs. They were aimed, it was said, at military objectives, but as the bombers were flying very high the bombs fell haphazard. At 30,000 feet accuracy was sacrificed for safety from anti-aircraft fire. The guns were firing for about twenty minutes. At least twenty-five Nazi 'planes were shot down. 254 people were killed and 652 wounded. The raiders used the new German siren bomb, which makes a weird whistling noise as it drops, its object being to terrify the public and start panic, in which, of course, it failed entirely.

The "Lancastria," in peacetime a well-known pleasure-cruise liner, was bombed and sunk off St. Nazaire on the afternoon of June 17. The exact number of those on board is not known; it was probably about 5000, of whom some 2500 were saved. Most of the passengers were British soldiers, but there were also on board some 600 R.A.F. officers and men. The "Lancastria" was lying about five miles off shore, embarking troops which came out in tugs and tenders. It was also learned in London on June 14 that about six thousand men belonging to a British division operating north of Le Havre had been made prisoners at St. Valery-en-Caux, by German forces by whom they had been surrounded. The weather was entirely against rescue, it was stated, there being a heavy fog on the night of the proposed evacuation.

ITALY DECLARES WAR ON FRANCE AND GREAT BRITAIN.

A GANGSTER'S GIFT FOR MUSSOLINI: AN ARMOURED TRAIN FROM HITLER.

On June 10 Italy declared war on France and Britain.
If the addition to our enemies of a nation of forty-five millions increases the perils of a critical situation, the position of the new aggressor herself is vulnerable in the extreme. Writing in the "Sunday Express" recently, Sir Ronald Storrs pointed out that Italy is virtually an island, with over 5000 miles of assailable coastline, subject to blockade from both ends of the Mediterranean for many necessities she cannot herself produce – notably oil. All her west coast bases become subject to fierce bombing from Toulon and Corsica, and in the Mediterranean she is ringed round by foes, from Greece, Turkey, Syria, Palestine, Egypt, Tunis, Algiers and Morocco, while she likewise faces the hostility of all Islam.

THE COLLAPSE OF FRANCE: THE LAST DAYS IN BORDEAUX.

THE DEFENDER OF VERDUN – MARSHAL PÉTAIN.

MR CHURCHILL WHO MADE M. REYNAUD THE OFFER.

By June 16, the French Cabinet at Bordeaux was believed to be considering whether the French armies could continue the struggle against Germany, though a categorical denial had been issued the day before to the rumour that France was contemplating a separate peace. It was confidently asserted in London that France and Britain were pledged to each other to continue the war to the end. A message from President Roosevelt, promising all possible help with munitions, and a message from Mr. Churchill were received by M. Reynaud's Government. Mr Churchill had suggested constitutional union and common citizenship. Late in the evening it was learnt that M. Reynaud had resigned and the aged Marshal Pétain had become Prime Minister.

THE TRAGIC STORY OF FRENCH AVIATION.

OFF ON PATROL: AN R.A.F. PILOT, STANDING ON THE WING OF A POTEZ, WISHES LUCK TO THE FRENCH PILOT.

Rather naturally we in this country are interested in the reasons for the collapse of the French Army and Government. One point on which all soldiers seem to agree is that the first great break-through by the Germans succeeded largely because of their tactical use of aeroplanes. They sent over masses of dive-bombers which performed in front of their tanks the same function as General Horne's creeping artillery barrage performed for our infantry in the last war. The dive-bombers beat the infantry into the ground. And now the soldiers want to know why the French Air Force, the *Armée de l'Air*, allowed it to happen. The answer is that they never had enough aeroplanes. Under the *Front Populaire*, production practically ceased.

BRINGING THE CURTAIN DOWN ON A NATIONAL TRAGEDY: FRANCE'S HUMILIATION: HOW HITLER STAGED THE COMPIÈGNE ARMISTICE.

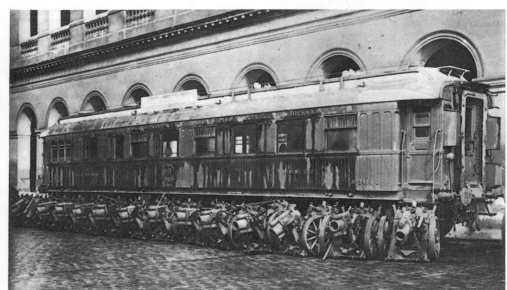

THE SETTING FOR THE HUMILIATION OF FRANCE ON JUNE 21: MARSHAL FOCH'S DINING-CAR WHERE HITLER, AFTER "WADING THROUGH THE BLOOD OF A MILLION MEN, WOMEN AND CHILDREN," DICTATED HIS ARMISTICE TERMS.

THE GERMANS PREPARE THE STAGE FOR THE SIGNING OF THE ARMISTICE WITH FRANCE AT COMPIÈGNE.

The Government which was to hand France over to her enemies was formed under Marshal Pétain on June 16. General Weygand became Minister of National Defence, General Colson Minister for War, Admiral Darlan Minister of the Navy, and M. Baudouin Minister for Foreign Affairs. Hitler summoned the French representatives to hear his terms on June 21. He received them in Marshal Foch's railway-coach, where the Armistice was signed in 1918, at the same spot in the forest at Compiègne.

The terms stated that for the security of German interests, territory north and west of the following line was to be occupied: Geneva-Dole, Chalons-sur-Saone, Paray le Monial, Moulins, Bourges, Vierzon, thence to 20 kilometres east of Tours, thence south parallel to Angoulème railway to Mont de Marsan and St. Jean Pied de Port. The areas not yet occupied in this territory were to be occupied immediately. All ports, permanent fortifications, and naval building yards were to be left in their present state.

FACING THE FUTURE. BY CYRIL FALLS.

When on June 17, Marshal Pétain announced that he had asked for a cessation of hostilities, he advised his troops that "resistance must cease". The phrase was disastrous. To tell troops who are fighting in adverse circumstances that resistance must come to an end before it is known what terms the victorious enemy will impose, and while it is certain he will continue his attack, is a grave error. Certainly our own troops – what has been described as "the Second B.E.F." – were placed in needless peril by this speech, and it has not been due to Marshal Pétain that we have been able to bring them off. The Poles, who fought most gallantly and never lost their morale, have likewise nothing for which to thank him. On top of all this has come the Franco-German Armistice, which places France virtually in the position of a belligerent against the ally to whom her faith was pledged and to whom she had solemnly sworn never to conclude a separate peace. The occupation of the western coast of France, the occupation of the whole country down to a line from Tours to Geneva, the demobilisation and disarmament of the French Army, the surrender of all arms and munitions, the promise to prevent any forces leaving the country or any material being sent to Great Britain, the prohibition against shipping leaving French ports and the undertaking to recall ships at sea, the handing over of all ports and stocks of supplies, the silencing of wireless stations, the facilitation of trade between Germany and Italy, the surrender of all German prisoners of war, while more than one and a half million French prisoners remain in captivity, the promise to recall and intern the French naval Fleet – these are conditions which render France the passive but effective ally of the two dictator States in their efforts to crush this country and liberty. It is an entirely unconstitutional decision, taken without the assent of the French Senate and Chamber by a body of defeatists behind whom stand pro-Nazis and pro-Fascists. If it be said that there was no alternative, the answer is that other conquered countries have found one, and in so doing have preserved their honour. The Government could have retired to Morocco or Algeria, and by this time have transported an army of hundreds of thousands to reinforce that already stationed in those provinces.

THE DISMEMBERMENT OF FRANCE BY THE ARMISTICE.

THE FINAL HUMILIATION: THE DELEGATES OF THE BORDEAUX GOVERNMENT SEEK AN ARMISTICE WITH ITALY.

NARVIK TOWN CAPTURED.

BUILDINGS BURNING IN THE NARVIK AREA PRIOR TO THE FALL
OF THE TOWN ON MAY 28: INSTEAD OF PROVING THE FORTRESS
THEY HAD HOPED, NARVIK HAS TURNED OUT TO BE A TRAP FOR
THE GERMAN FORCES.

A joint Admiralty and War Office communiqué issued on May 29
stated that Narvik had been captured the previous night by Allied
forces, and that Fagerness and Forneset were also in our hands. The
description enclosed with this photograph, which reached us from a
Surgeon-Lieutenant on board a British battleship, mentioned that the
port possessed great natural advantages for the defenders.
The story of the gangster methods employed by the Nazis in the
capture of Narvik in April was revealed after the arrest, on the ground
of Nazi sympathies, of Colonel Sundlo, Commander of the Norwegian
forces there. The Port Commander was held indirectly responsible for
the loss of two Norwegian warships, with the loss of 350 lives. These
ships had been assigned to help the land forces. Instead of being sent
out into Ofot Fjord to intercept the German naval units when the alarm
was given, the warships were ordered to remain stationary. When the
Germans landed, a well-directed force, supported by accurately aimed
artillery, could have held the town. Instead, the troops were ordered
not to shoot, but to give way, and once the Germans had control of the
centre of the town, the main road, the railway bridge, and the station,
further resistance was useless. Thus the capture of Narvik was due to a
combination of surprise and assistance from within. A further proof
that German troops had arrived before the Allied minefield was laid was
provided by a British captain who got his ship away before the invasion.
He said: "One day we saw men coming up out of a ship's ventilation
shaft, but it never struck us then that they had men down below. We
also noticed the ships moving about the harbour a good deal. Now the
whole plot has been made clear."

BRITAIN TAKES OVER THE FAROES.

YOUTHFUL FAROYANS HAVE VISIBLE PROOF OF THEIR PROTEC-
TION BY THE BRITISH: THE GUARD OF ROYAL MARINES PARADING
IN THORSHAVN, CAPITAL OF THE FAROE ISLANDS.

The Faroes, a lonely group of islands situated half-way between the
Shetlands and Iceland, are a possession of Denmark which the British
Government undertook to protect when Germany invaded their parent
country. The capital, Thorshavn, is a little town of steep, narrow
streets and gardens, built on the northern island of Streymoy, above a
good roadstead protected on north, east and west. The inhabitants
often wear the knee-breeches and buckled shoes of another century,
and deal in fish and eider ducks' feathers among other things. There are
twenty-two islands, though not all are inhabited. The language is a
form of old Norse, like Icelandic.

THE OCCUPATION OF ICELAND.

FOUR O'CLOCK A.M. IN THE COLD GREY OF EARLY DAWN THE
LANDING PARTIES MUSTER ON THE DECK OF THE BATTLESHIP TO
LAND AT REYKJAVIK.

FAR FROM RESENTING THE OCCUPATION, THE TOWN BAND OF
REYKJAVIK TURNS OUT TO GREET THE FORCE OF OCCUPATION IN
PROPER MARTIAL STYLE.

IN THE GERMAN CONSULATE – A BRITISH OFFICER GOES
THROUGH THE GERMAN RECORDS BEFORE A BUST OF HITLER.

Not for 130 years, since 1809, had soldiers been seen in Iceland, for
there is no Iceland army or navy. But as soon as Denmark was invaded
foreign troops were expected to appear, and the Icelanders wondered
whether the Germans or British would be the first to arrive. Although
naturally they would have preferred to remain as they were, it did seem
that they preferred a British occupation to a German one. And the
Prime Minister of Iceland was able to reassure the people as to the
British intentions in a broadcast.
In the days that followed, the British troops settled themselves in and
fortified their positions against a possible German invasion. And many
Germans, several of whom were Nazi agents, were taken prisoner and
kept under guard. The immediate object had been achieved. Iceland
was occupied and protected against German invasion.
Canadian troops are now announced to have landed in Iceland and to
have occupied the island, to guard against invasion by Germany.

SOVIET RUSSIA'S NEW PROVINCES.

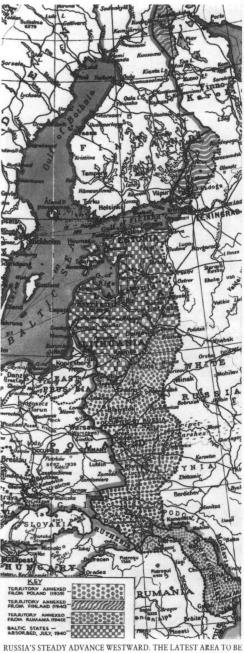

KEY
TERRITORY ANNEXED
FROM POLAND (1939)
TERRITORY ANNEXED
FROM FINLAND (1940)
TERRITORY ANNEXED
FROM RUMANIA (1940)
BALTIC STATES –
ABSORBED, JULY, 1940

RUSSIA'S STEADY ADVANCE WESTWARD. THE LATEST AREA TO BE
OCCUPIED IS THAT OF THE THREE LITTLE BALTIC STATES OF
LATVIA, LITHUANIA AND ESTHONIA.

On June 28, after an attempt to negotiate had been rejected by the
Soviets, the Rumanian Government accepted the Soviet demand to
evacuate the ceded areas in Bessarabia and Bukovina in four days. The
Rumanian Government had been reshuffled to meet the new situation.
Serious clashes occurred between the Russian troops advancing into
Bessarabia and the retiring Rumanian forces. The Russians, using
parachute troops and air transports carrying machine-guns and motor-
cycles, occupied the ceded provinces two and a half days in advance of
their time-table.
These two provinces have been claimed as definitely Russian, though
for centuries Bessarabia was part of the Rumanian principality of
Moldavia, only being annexed to Russia in 1812.

AMERICA'S AID FOR BRITAIN.

A METHOD OF AMERICAN AIRCRAFT DELIVERY MADE NECESSARY
BY NEUTRALITY REGULATIONS, WHICH HAVE NOW BEEN
WAIVED: A LOCKHEED BOMBER BEING TOWED INTO CANADA.

It was announced on June 17 that a new ruling had been endorsed by
the State Department in the United States whereby American 'planes
bought for Britain could be flown direct to Canada, or even to the
British Isles, instead of delivery being made at the Canadian border.
The ruling declared that border stops were no longer necessary and that
the legal title to the 'plane would be automatically transferred "as the
machine flies across the border."

THE LATE AIR-MARSHAL BALBO.

KILLED IN AN UNEXPLAINED AEROPLANE CRASH: MARSHAL
BALBO, MUSSOLINI'S ANTI-GERMAN RIVAL.

Mystery surrounds the death of Marshal Balbo. His flying exploits
before the war had made him a well-known figure, so popular with the
Italians that Mussolini found it necessary to remove him as far as
possible from the public eye. The Italian official announcement states
that he was "killed in battle" while flying over Tobruk, the Libyan
naval base. Careful investigation has shown that no large machine such
as that described was either seen or attacked by the R.A.F.

ALIENS INTERNED IN ENGLAND.

THE INTERNMENT OF ENEMY ALIENS IN ENGLAND – NOW AN
URGENT SECURITY MEASURE: MEN MARCHING TO A CAMP IN A
NORTHERN TOWN, UNDER GUARD.

A round-up of enemy aliens took place throughout the Eastern coastal
area of the United Kingdom, from the Isle of Wight to the Moray Firth,
on May 12. It included all German and Austrian men between the ages
of sixteen and sixty, excepting the invalid or infirm. No German or
Austrian is now allowed to enter this area without the express
permission of the Secretary of State. Special restrictions for all male
aliens under the age of sixty living in this area were also announced.

THE LAST EVACUATIONS FROM FRANCE.

THE CHANNEL ISLANDS UNDER THE SWASTIKA: A GERMAN PROPAGANDA PHOTOGRAPH SHOWING THE "CAPTURE" OF JERSEY.

FINAL EMBARKATIONS AT ST. JEAN DE LUZ, IN THE BAY OF BISCAY: THE CANADIAN DESTROYER *FRASER*, BEFORE SHE WAS LOST IN COLLISION "IN FACE OF THE ENEMY". FISHING BOATS ARE STANDING BY FULL OF REFUGEES WAITING TO GET ABOARD THE STEAMER *BARON NAIRN*, FROM WHICH THE PICTURE WAS TAKEN. THE *BARON NAIRN* WAS THE LAST SHIP TO TAKE BRITISH SUBJECTS AND OTHER ALLIED REFUGEES FROM ST. JEAN DE LUZ.

FRENCH FORCES, LEAVING BREST FOR ENGLAND, WATCH A BLAZE CAUSED BY THE EXPLOSIVE AND PETROL STORES THEY HAD BLOWN UP.

Despite the fact that the Home Office announced last Friday that in view of the German occupation of the part of France close to the Channel Islands, it was decided to demilitarise the islands, the Germans raided them that night, killing and wounding a number of people. Fortunately, almost the entire civil population had already left. The enemy have now occupied Jersey and Guernsey, and all communication has been cut. According to the German official news agency, the occupation was the result of a *coup* by the air force. In actual fact, of course, there could have been no resistance, owing to the withdrawal of all armed forces. The islands, the nearest of which is 90 miles from the English coast, will be of no economic value to Germany.

It was on June 21 that the German high Command announced the taking of Brest. The Allied troops, after fighting strenuously for continuous days and nights, withdrew from the French naval base in Brittany, in the face of overwhelming odds. After making an heroic stand, everything that could have been of use to the enemy was destroyed. Brest is one of the most important French naval bases on the Atlantic. During the World War it became the port of disembarkation for the American Army fighting in France, and since 1918 it has become increasingly important as a calling port for Transatlantic liners and a leading naval centre. It is interesting to note that Brest was in English hands from 1342 to 1397.

FRENCH WARSHIPS IN BRITISH PORTS – FIGHTING FOR A FREE FRANCE.

TWO FRENCH DESTROYERS IN HOME WATERS. THE GOVERNMENT AT VICHY ANNOUNCED THAT FRENCH PERSONS FIGHTING FOR A FREE FRANCE WITH THE BRITISH FORCES SHALL BE LIABLE TO PENALTIES RANGING FROM HARD LABOUR TO DEATH.

FRANCE STILL FIGHTS ON – BASTILLE DAY CELEBRATED IN LONDON: GENERAL DE GAULLE, INSPECTING THE FRENCH VOLUNTEER LEGION LAST SUNDAY WHEN THEY CELEBRATED *LE QUATORZE JUILLET* AND THE FALL OF THE BASTILLE.

CARRYING OUT THE PREMIER'S PROMISE THAT ALL FRENCH TROOPS EXCEPTING THOSE WHO HAD VOLUNTEERED TO FOLLOW GENERAL DE GAULLE, WOULD BE REPATRIATED: SENEGALESE SOLDIERS AT A WEST COUNTRY PORT.

On July 3 the greater part of the French Fleet was taken under our control or called upon to comply with our requirements. Two battleships, two light cruisers, some submarines (including the "Surcouf," aboard which a misunderstanding resulted in the only casualties of the whole operation in home waters), eight destroyers, with approximately 200 smaller but extremely useful mine-sweeping and anti-submarine craft were boarded after brief notice had been given wherever possible to their captains. The French sailors in the main cheerfully accepted the end of a period of uncertainty, and 800 or 900 have expressed an ardent desire to continue the war and had asked for British nationality. The British Government are granting this without prejudice to the

other Frenchmen, numbered by thousands, who prefer to fight on with us as Frenchmen. All the rest are being repatriated to France, as are all French troops in the country except those who volunteered to follow General de Gaulle. Several French submarines also joined us independently and their services have been accepted. The first French ship had arrived at Plymouth on June 19 – two days after the capitulation of France. She received a tumultuous welcome from thousands of people on the foreshore. The outwitted Axis Powers were forced to come out in their true colours, and repudiated that part of the Armistice whereby they agreed not to use French ships in the war and to demilitarise the French naval bases.

SCENE OF A TRAGIC NAVAL ACTION: ORAN AND MERS-EL-KEBIR.

THE LEADER IN THE MELANCHOLY ACTION AT ORAN: VICE-ADMIRAL SIR JAMES SOMERVILLE.

THE "STRASBOURG," SISTER-SHIP OF THE "DUNKERQUE," WHICH GOT AWAY FROM ORAN, PROBABLY TO TOULON, THOUGH HIT BY A TORPEDO FROM ONE OF OUR AIRCRAFT.

DRIVEN ASHORE AND DAMAGED IN A SHORT TIME IN THE "MELANCHOLY ACTION" AT ORAN; AND, LATER, BOMBED BY BRITISH AEROPLANES: THE FRENCH BATTLE-CRUISER "DUNKERQUE."

AN INSTRUMENT OF THE BORDEAUX GOVERNMENT: ADMIRAL GENSOUL, WHO REFUSED ALL OF OUR PROFERRED ALTERNATIVES AT ORAN.

The problem of the war which had been uppermost in everyone's mind was answered when the Prime Minister spoke on July 4, and the need for the previous silence was explained. The most strenuous efforts had been made by the Government to avoid the painful, but ultimately inevitable, use of force against a former ally to prevent the transfer of the balance of naval power that would have been of the gravest menace to the future development of the war.

Captain Holland, formerly Naval Attaché in Paris, had waited upon Admiral Gensoul with a document demanding that the French Fleet, then at Mers-el-Kebir and Oran, should act in accordance with three alternatives – one of which was to take his ships to the West Indies or America. All the honourable alternatives being refused, Admiral Somerville, who had already arrived with a British battle squadron – and who ironically had distinguished himself at Dunkirk by rescuing 100,000 Frenchmen – had to attack the French ships to prevent their falling under German or Italian control.

The battleship "Dunkerque" was heavily damaged and run ashore and was then hit by our bombers, and the battleship "Bretagne" and the seaplane carrier "Commandant Teste" sunk. The battleship "Strasbourg" managed to escape, but was torpedoed and so badly damaged that she will be out of commission for some time to come. Some small ships got away from North African ports; another battleship, the "Provence," was

heavily damaged in the engagement. At Alexandria, one battleship, four cruisers, three of them 8-in. gun vessels, and a number of small ships chose to remain under British control. In British ports are more than 200 French vessels including two battleships, two light cruisers, some submarines and eight destroyers.

It was "a bitter road," said the First Lord on July 5, "from the glorious co-operation of two navies at Dunkirk to the melancholy action at Oran."

It is not often that the House of Commons is so deeply moved as it was after the Prime Minister's speech, describing the heartrending events concerning the French Navy and emphasising Britain's determination to fight on in the "supreme hour" to which she has been called. While Parliament stood and demonstrated its approval, Mr. Churchill sat with his elbows on his knees, his chin cupped in his hands, visibly moved.

The First Lord of the Admiralty, Mr. A. V. Alexander, told the House on July 9 that the Navy had also prevented the new 35,000-ton French battleship "Richelieu" from falling into the enemy's hands. A two-fold attack was made on her while lying at Dakar. A ship's boat was sent into the harbour with depth-charges, which, with great daring, were dropped close to the stern, in order to damage the propellers and steering-gear. The main attack came afterwards from aircraft of the Fleet Air Arm, which were successful with their torpedoes, a number of which hit the battleship.

THE DEFENCE OF BRITAIN: THE THREAT OF AIR-BORNE INVASION.

A GERMAN PARACHUTISTS' MACHINE-GUN POST IN HOLLAND: A PHOTOGRAPH CAPTURED IN ONE OF THEIR OWN CAMERAS.

WHAT A GLIDER LOOKS LIKE AT NIGHT: THE EXAGGERATED WIDTH OF WING IN COMPARISON TO THE LENGTH OF FUSELAGE IS CHARACTERISTIC.

GERMAN BARGES: A COLLECTION OF LARGE-CAPACITY VESSELS – SUCH AS ARE BEING ADAPTED BY THE GERMAN MILITARY AUTHORITIES FOR POSSIBLE USE AGAINST ENGLAND.

The above picture was taken from films found in the cameras of German parachutists captured in Holland and now prisoners of war in England. Parachutists in uniform are not likely to be seen singly or in twos and threes – they usually appear in groups, dropping from 'planes at very low altitudes, usually from 300 ft., thus ensuring accuracy. An aeroplane carries up to 30 parachutists, and 12 of these can be dropped in 10 seconds. The men, arriving in groups, at once split into active units of six or eight, to carry out their work. During the jump the man carries very little: weapons are dropped separately in containers made of metal or wood, cylindrical or six-sided in shape and open all along the length. Every parachutist carries a revolver at his belt.

From the ground a large glider, such as might be employed for troop-carrying, would be readily distinguishable from the ordinary troop-carrying German aeroplane by the great span of its wings in relation to the length of the body. For some years the Russian Army has been experimenting with a new method of infantry air transport, which the Swedish Press has not been slow to suggest might possibly be used for enemy operations against these islands. This is the use of air "troop-trains" of gliders, towed by high-powered aircraft and each containing six to eight fully-equipped infantrymen ready for immediate action on landing.

Reports had been coming in of the intended use by Germany of towed gliders in attacks on this country. The advantage would be to increase the capacity of a troop-carrier by perhaps 75 per cent., but this would mean a sacrifice in speed, range and defensive power.

The passing river steamer gives an idea of the great size of these barges, which could each transport great numbers of men, and cope with heavy guns or tanks. As ships, they are, however, unwieldy in a seaway for which they are not designed and terribly vulnerable to action from the air or by light naval craft. If they got into choppy weather their speed might be reduced to as low as two knots, and towing them would cease to be a practical operation, though some of them are self-propelling. These drawbacks do not apply to Dutch and Danish coasting craft, of which the German High Command has presumably collected all the German transport organisation can spare.

Göering, in a characteristically savage announcement, remarked a short time ago that Germany had more than one "secret weapon", besides the magnetic mine which the Admiralty has now succeeded in mastering. "Flame-throwing" tanks and gliders were reported to have played a part in the capture of the Belgian fort of Eben Eymael, near Liège, while the use of parachute troops on a large scale for the first time in history enabled the enemy to drop "cells" of Nazi aerial soldiers right in the central districts of Rotterdam, Amsterdam, The Hague and elsewhere, many of them disguised in Dutch uniforms, or dressed (fantastic as it seems) as women, gardeners, and clergymen. Describing the capture of the aerodrome at Rotterdam, an article sent to the "Corriere della Sera" by its correspondent in Germany, stated: "A squadron of German 'planes flew over the site, which had been carefully studied beforehand, at a distance of about two miles from the aerodrome. The troop-carriers came down low. The parachute used opens automatically when the man

jumps. Each parachute takes ten seconds to come to ground. At the end of ten minutes a troop of about one hundred men, well armed, sets itself in good order and marches forward. Soon they are at the entrance to the aerodrome. At the same moment the 'planes which have brought the troops bomb and machine-gun the landing-ground . . . The aerodrome is seized. The 'plane on which is the commanding officer announces the success of the enterprise to another squadron of troop-carriers. This brings the 'landing-troops.' The troop-carriers now descend on to the conquered aerodrome. Eight hundred men land in half an hour." Writing in the "Evening News" Brigadier-General C. F. Aspinall-Oglander declared: "There can no longer be any doubt that in the new form of tactical penetration by means of parachute jumpers supported by troops in carrier 'planes, the Germans have adopted and are continuing to perfect a highly dangerous operation of war, the potentialities of which are taking the world by surprise."

WIDESPREAD COUNTER-MEASURES EMPLOYED TO STOP AIR- OR SEA-BORNE TROOPS.

A REMINDER OF THE TIMES SET AGAINST THE PEACEFUL BACKGROUND OF CHURCH AND RIVER: A TYPE OF CONCRETE ROADBLOCK, BARRING A BRIDGE TO AN ENEMY'S PASSAGE.

DERELICT CARS THAT HAVE NOT YET OUTLIVED THEIR USEFULNESS ACT AS MEASURES AGAINST HOSTILE TROOP-LANDINGS.

The prospect of the invasion of England was referred to by Mr. Churchill on June 19. "I expect," he said "that the 'Battle of Britain' is about to begin. Upon this battle depends the survival of the Christian civilisation. Let us therefore address ourselves to our duty, so bear ourselves that if the British Commonwealth and Empire lasts for a thousand years, men will still say, 'This was their finest hour . . . ' "

THE FIRST OFFICIAL "CAVALRY TROOP" OF THE HOME GUARD AS THE LDV IS NOW CALLED: TWO EXMOOR FARMERS SCAN THE DIFFICULT AND BROKEN COUNTRYSIDE.

"WE SHALL FIGHT ON THE BEACHES . . . " MR. CHURCHILL SEES THE MEANING GIVEN TO HIS WORDS.

HOME GUARDS PRACTISE BLOWING UP TANKS: GUERILLA WARFARE AT OSTERLEY PARK.

THE PRIME MINISTER PAYS A SURPRISE VISIT TO THE NORTH-EAST: MR. CHURCHILL AT A GUN EMPLACEMENT DURING A RECENT TOUR OF COASTAL FORTIFICATIONS AND DEFENCE WORKS.

MR. CHURCHILL HOLDS A "TOMMY" GUN AND ADJUSTS THE MAGAZINE DRUM. THOUSANDS ARE NOW BEING DELIVERED TO THIS COUNTRY.

The Prime Minister, escorted by soldier motor-cyclists and accompanied by General L. H. Ismay, Military Secretary to the War Cabinet, Commander Thompson, Flag Officer to the Board of Admiralty, and other Service chiefs, paid a surprise visit to the North-East on July 31 to inspect coastal fortifications and defence works. Mr. Churchill motored slowly along the coast, occasionally leaving his car to inspect some particular section of the defences or a squad of soldiers on parade. He found both men and defences very much on the alert. The Prime Minister also visited a North-East England shipyard and, addressing the workers who gathered round him said that the country urgently needed the craft they were building: that theirs was a most essential work, and thanked them for their great effort.

THE DUCE'S RECKLESS BID TO RECREATE ROME'S AFRICAN EMPIRE.

WATCHING ABYSSINIA FROM THE SUDAN: THE ATTACK ON BRITISH SOMALILAND

THE EMPEROR HAILE SELASSIE RE- TURNS TO AFRICA – HE WAS REPORTED TO HAVE REACHED KHAR TOUM.

On July 13, the Government of the Emperor Haile Selassie was recognised by the British Government as the lawful Government of Abyssinia, with the promise of independence when victory is achieved.

The British forces on the Sudan frontier consist almost entirely of Sudanese troops. They are well supplied with ample food, and can get munitions along the railway, while the Italians, occupying Kassala, are harassed by growing difficulties of supplies. As the rainy season lasts until mid-September their position is not a very enviable one.

By advancing on Kassala the Italians hoped to forestall a British advance. The fighting round Gallabat has been with a similar object in view, but the largest operation of this kind was in British Somaliland.

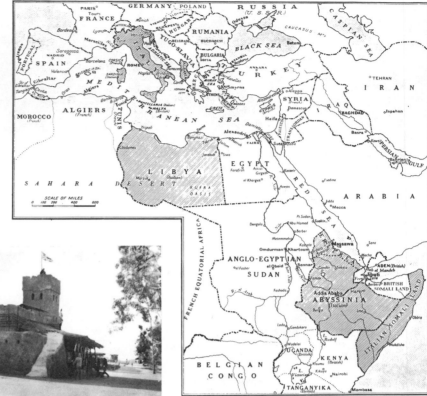

CLOSE TO THE GREAT SCREES OF JEBEL KASSALA: DOMES OF BLACK GRANITE RISE ABOVE THE SLOPING SCREE, WHICH ITA- LIAN OUTPOSTS CLIMBED TO WATCH BRITISH MOVEMENTS.

THE SCENE OF A HEROIC RESISTANCE AGAINST A "PROPAGANDA" OFFENSIVE: THE LITTLE BRITISH FORT AT MOYALE, ON THE KENYA-ABYSSINIA BORDER.

WITH ITALY JOINING THE CONFLICT, THE ROYAL NAVY HAS RETURNED TO THE MEDITERRANEAN AND THE RAF HAS BEEN ACTIVE OVER LIBYA AND ABYSSINIA.

WAR ON THE AFRICAN SEABOARD: ITALY'S ADVANCE INTO EGYPT.

SOLDIERS OF AN ADVANCE UNIT OF THE ITALIAN INVADING FORCES, CLAD IN LONG, THICK PANTS AND HEAVY BOOTS, WITH MOTORISED EQUIPMENT ON THE MARCH UNDER A BURNING DESERT SUN.

EGYPTIAN MEHARIST WARRIORS, THE RITUAL SCARS UPON THEIR CHEEKS GIVING THEM A VERY FEROCIOUS LOOK. READY TO JOIN BRITISH AND EMPIRE TROOPS FOR THE DEFENCE OF EGYPT.

WITH THE 5000-YEAR-OLD PYRAMID-TOMBS OF CHEOPS, KEPHREN AND MYCER- INUS IN THE BACKGROUND, BREN-GUN CARRIERS OF THE INDIAN FORCE RECENTLY IN EGYPT.

Italy's declaration of war on the Allies gave an immense impetus to Egyptian defence measures, the Premier, Aly Maher Pasha, announcing the immediate formation of a force of reservists.

As we write, there is no war between Italy and Egypt, and our ally will not be rushed into any premature decision by skirmishes in the Western Desert, which have little significance for Egypt itself. Broadcasting in London on August 27, Hafez Afifi Pasha, the first Egyptian Ambassador to London declared that for many years Italy had been planning offensive measure. "Egypt is a country enjoying the full rights of independence, having its own brave army to defend its freedom. The interests of Egypt and Britain are interwoven. It is a great mistake to believe that if Italy should attack Egypt her only reason would be the presence of British forces. Italy wishes to restore the ancient Roman Empire."

Two Italian mechanised columns, pushing forward into Egypt from the Libyan frontier, occupied on September 16 the village of Sidi Barrani, lying about 35 miles east of Buqbuq. The "News Chronicle" reminded its readers that it was the British intention to meet the enemy upon ground of our own choosing, some 150 miles inside Egyptian territory.

For unknown reasons, after the occupation of Sidi Barrani, Marshal Graziani's forces came to a halt. It may be that the Italian commander is awaiting further orders from Rome as a result of the Brenner meeting between Mussolini and Hitler, or it may be that the Navy commands the road along the coast, British and Empire forces are massed in opposition over the whole 300-mile stretch to the Nile, and the R.A.F. has already been reinforced by men and machines from home.

CHINA'S STAND AGAINST JAPAN: THREATENED INDO-CHINA AND THE FATEFUL BURMA HIGHWAY.

A GORGE ON THE RAILWAY GOING TO YUNNAN.

THE RAILWAY FROM FRENCH INDO-CHINA TO YUNNAN AND THE LASHIO-YUNNAN HIGH- WAY THAT LEADS ON TO CHUNG KING.

SUSPENSION BRIDGE SOMEWHERE ON THE BURMA HIGHWAY.

Passage of war materials to General Chiang kai-Shek has been the focus of recent Japanese diplomacy. The Pétain Government agreed to cease supplies and has replaced the defiant General Catroux with Admiral Necoux: Japanese demands for the facilities to land 60,000 troops and the use of airports were only initially resisted. This threat to Indo-China is thought in Washington to portend a further advance into Thailand from whence to launch aerial attacks on Singapore and the Malay Peninsula. Anti-American feeling in Japan – a trade treaty not renewed, an "open door" policy insisted upon in China – can only have been increased by President Roosevelt's decision to place an embargo on the export of iron and steel. Despite demands that no further British arms and munitions should enter China via the Burma-Yunnan road or through Hong Kong territory, it is reported that the Burma road will re-open on October 17. As it happens, no British supplies have been making China by any route for a long time, all such materials being from America or Russia.

THE FIRST NAZI MASS AIR RAIDS ON BRITAIN:
NON-COMBATANT VICTIMS, AND THE PRICE EXACTED BY THE DEFENDERS.

A LINE OF WRECKED HOUSES WHERE NINE PEOPLE WERE KILLED. ONE OF THE LESSONS OF THE FIRST RAIDS WAS THE RELATIVE IMMUNITY OF PEOPLE WHO TOOK SHELTER PROMPTLY.

FIGHTER PILOTS RUSHING OUT TO THEIR MACHINES FOLLOWING A WARNING FROM HEADQUARTERS.

A GERMAN BOMBER WHICH CRASHED INTO THE SEA AFTER NARROWLY MISSING A HOTEL IN AN EAST COAST TOWN. THE RAIDS DEMONSTRATED THE EFFICIENCY OF OUR DEFENCES.

The first large-scale German raids on Britain cannot have given the *Luftwaffe* much encouragement. Probably they were in the nature of rehearsals. But they showed the effectiveness of our anti-aircraft fire and of our standing patrols of fighters in comparison with those met by our bombers over Germany; and also it would seem the lack of training of the German bomber crews in nightflying. At least seven German bombers were brought down in the raid on June 18, in which about a hundred machines took part, and many German airmen were made prisoners in Norfolk, Suffolk, Essex and Kent. Twelve civilians, including five children, were killed and at least thirty injured. The Air Ministry announced that several R.A.F. aerodromes were attacked without success. Three German bombers were shot down by "Spitfire" pilots during raids on England, Scotland and South Wales on the night of June 19 and the early morning following. The casualties were eight dead and about sixty injured. There were further raids on Eastern England on the night of June 21. One interesting point about these raids was that it was subsequently announced that two further German machines had been destroyed by running into barrage balloons, thus demonstrating the effectiveness of this form of protection; another was the effectiveness of the protection of Anderson steel shelters where these had been properly erected.

AN "APPEAL TO REASON" BY THE "HOMICIDAL LUNATIC" OF BERCHTESGADEN! – HITLER'S LEAFLETS BEING EXAMINED WITH AMUSEMENT BY A.R.P. WARDENS.

AFTER THE FIERCEST AIR BATTLE TO BE FOUGHT OVER BRITAIN – WHEN 17 NAZIS WERE SHOT DOWN IN 30 MINUTES: A BRITISH FIGHTER-PILOT, BACK FROM DEFENDING DOVER (LEFT), SHOWS WHERE A BULLET GRAZED HIS HELMET; WHILE OTHERS (RIGHT) RELAX IN THE SUN.

Hitler unwittingly benefited the Red Cross through this leaflet raid, when thousands were dropped in North-Eastern England. The enterprising villagers collected them and sold them on behalf of charities. The leaflets contained a translation of Hitler's previous Reichstag speech, which most people had already seen in the papers.

On July 29 Britain experienced her biggest raid of the war when eighty enemy aeroplanes concentrated in an attack on Dover Harbour. The result was disaster for Germany – the R.A.F. not only beat off the attack but brought down seventeen of the enemy at a loss to our own forces of just one aeroplane. This was the first mass raid on a land objective, and that it should have failed so signally is, let us hope, an augury for the future.

493 GERMAN AEROPLANES BROUGHT DOWN IN ONE WEEK.

A JUNKERS "88" SHOT DOWN ON AUGUST 12.

FIGHTING HIS BATTLE OVER AGAIN: AN R.A.F. SERGEANT-PILOT DESCRIBES TO A FLIGHT-LIEUTENANT THE MANŒUVRES HE USED IN SHOOTING DOWN A NAZI.

THE WRECK OF ONE OF AUGUST 16'S SEVENTY-FIVE CASUALTIES.

The thousandth German warplane to be "smacked down" – in the vivid words of a young Air Force pilot – since June 18 was sent crashing into the English Channel on August 22; and as we go to press the victory score is steadily mounting. The wildly inaccurate German initial reports have been corrected by the careful calculations of our own Air Ministry, and opinion is unanimous in praise of the stupendous feat performed by the Air Force in defeating the greatest and most venomous air onslaught in the history of war. "It is possible," declared "The Times" on August 24, "that we do not even yet realise the extent of our victory," while on August 20 Lord Halifax said the fate of modern civilisation depended on pilots, their average age perhaps twenty-three, "whose courage and skill was saving the world and earning the world's admiration."

THE FIRST BOMBING OF CENTRAL LONDON: THE ROYAL AIR FORCE IN BERLIN.

THE OLD BAILEY'S DOMES SILHOUETTED AGAINST THE GLOW OF FIRE CAUSED BY A LONE RAIDER ON AUGUST 24. THE BRIGHT BLAZE WAS DUE TO THE FIRING OF A WAX-DUMMY WAREHOUSE.

THE R.A.F. LEAVE A "VISITING-CARD" IN CENTRAL BERLIN: THE CRATER FORMED BY A BRITISH BOMB RAILED OFF IN THE UNTER DEN LINDEN – THE BRANDENBURG GATE BEYOND.

CREWS WHO TOOK PART IN A BERLIN RAID GROUPED BEFORE ONE OF THEIR BOMBERS. THE NAZIS HAVE REPEATEDLY TOLD THEIR PEOPLE THAT BERLIN WAS TOO WELL DEFENDED TO BE BOMBED.

Enemy bombs fell in Central London for the first time in the war on the night of August 24. Both high-explosive and incendiary bombs were used. The largest fire was caused by a screaming bomb which fell in the City. A warehouse containing wax dummies was set on fire and the flames rose 150 ft. in the air and vividly illumined the sky.

A despatch published in the "New York Post," on September 29, from its Berlin correspondent, stated: "I have just been through a genuine, unadulterated air raid on Berlin. The R.A.F. have been here before, but never on such a persistent and big-time scale. The crescendo of bombs and anti-aircraft and ground fire, accompanied by parachute flares and searchlights in action, would have done credit to your New York Fair." Even the iron censorship of the Nazi Propaganda Ministry has been unable to circumvent confirmation of the extensive damage caused by the recent RAF raids on Britain.

THE "REPRISALS" BOMBING OF LONDON, SEPTEMBER 7–9.

"BURNING FURIOUSLY WITH A GLOW WHICH COULD BE SEEN MORE THAN A DOZEN MILES FROM LONDON": THE POOL OF LONDON ILLUMINATED ON THE MEMORABLE NIGHT OF SEPTEMBER 7–8.

SHARING LONDON'S LOT: THEIR MAJESTIES INSPECTING THE DAMAGE TO BUCKINGHAM PALACE AFTER THE EXPLODING OF THE DELAYED-ACTION BOMB ON SEPTEMBER 10.

In the first of the heaviest German air attacks yet made on England, the mass attack on London on the night of September 7–8, no fewer than a quarter (totalling 103 machines) of the raiding force was destroyed by our defences, with a consequent loss to the enemy in personnel of something like 250 skilled airmen. "It was impossible to miss those we aimed at," said one "Hurricane" squadron leader after the raid, "there seemed oceans of them." Dockland and the industrial areas in the East End received considerable attention from the enemy, who later resorted to indiscriminate bombing of purely residential quarters of the Metropolis. "Bombers came in from different directions, guided by the flames over East London," reported a "Times" special correspondent. "Near at hand they turned night into day, and even bright searchlights were made to look pale. All over the London sky the searchlights stabbed and flashed, picking out the raiders for the A.-A. guns. Still more light was contributed by the flashes of the guns and the exploding bombs."

THE PLOTTINGS OF HITLER AND GOERING.

THE ENEMY OF ALL FREE PEOPLES STUDIES HIS WAR PLANS: A GROUP AT HITLER'S HEADQUARTERS "ON THE WESTERN FRONT."

At the Führer's headquarters on the Western Front, Adolf Hitler has explained to him the manner in which England is being attacked by Field-Marshal Keitel (right). Looking on are Major Deide (holding paper) and General Jodl. Although Marshal Graziani was in Rome at the time of the Brenner meeting between Hitler and Mussolini, Field-Marshal Keitel attended part of the conversations, which were "held in the Axis spirit."

SO NEAR AND YET SO FAR: FIELD-MARSHAL GOERING (FIRST FROM RIGHT) STUDYING A MAP OF GREAT BRITAIN.

Goering is seen with some of the *Luftwaffe*'s chief officers. Air Force General Jeschonnek, Chief of the General Staff, is on the left; between him and Goering is Air Force General Loerzer. The abortive air attacks against this country have cost Germany dear. During September over 1000 machines and probably 3000 airmen were lost.

THE AIR ASSAULT ON BRITAIN.

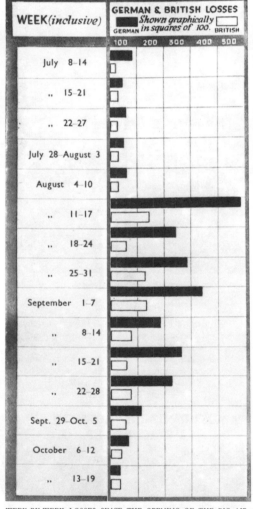

WEEK (inclusive)	GERMAN & BRITISH LOSSES Shown graphically in squares of 100. GERMAN ■ BRITISH □
July 8–14	
„ 15–21	
„ 22–27	
July 28–August 3	
August 4–10	
„ 11–17	
„ 18–24	
„ 25–31	
September 1–7	
„ 8–14	
„ 15–21	
„ 22–28	
Sept. 29–Oct. 5	
October 6–12	
„ 13–19	

WEEK-BY-WEEK LOSSES SINCE THE OPENING OF THE BIG AIR ATTACKS ON BRITAIN IN JULY.

We give here, in a graphic presentation, a summary of the German losses in both bombers and fighters since the real air attack on Britain was started in July. These figures only show the results of daytime fighting. In sum, the enemy has lost – since July 8 up to October 19 – a total of 2,570 aircraft (and his *best* aircraft).

HOW THE RAIDERS ARE FOLLOWED.

THE WATCHERS OF THE OBSERVER CORPS AND SIGNALLERS OF THE A.A. DEFENCES CHECK ON THE ENEMY'S MOVEMENTS.

Although one of the least known branches of our defensive organisations, the Observer Corps is a vitally important unit of our defence. Day and night its members keep constant watch, reporting to the Control Room all aeroplane movements, friendly or enemy. From here all centres and Fighter Command are kept informed.

ATTACKING HITLER'S "INVASION PORTS".

A SECTION OF DUNKIRK HARBOUR: INVASION BARGES CAN BE SEEN IN RANKS ON EITHER SIDE OF THE CENTRE QUAY, WITH A NUMBER SCATTERED AND DAMAGED NEAR THE ENTRANCE.

Hitler's having ordered large formations to the ports facing England, ready for an invasion, and accumulated large quantities of stores and valuable transport there, presented the R.A.F. with an opportunity of inflicting terrific damage on the Germans.

Since the German Air Force began the main attack on Great Britain nearly three months ago, on August 11, the enemy has chopped and changed his tactics many times in an effort to beat down the Royal Air Force and penetrate our defences.

In its previous campaigns the *Luftwaffe* had smashed all opposition by the very weight of its attack. The German High Command believed that the same tactics would batter down our defences and open the way for invasion. In that belief they reckoned without the Fighter Command of the R.A.F.

First in big waves almost unescorted, then in even bigger waves with steadily increasing escorts, the German bombers were hounded on to the attack. The losses were colossal. From August 11 to October 5 the enemy lost nearly 1,200 bombers, 1,000 fighters and 5,200 men, compared with the British losses of 600 fighters and 300 men in repelling the attacks. Then the *Luftwaffe* acknowledged its defeat – its failure to smash the R.A.F. – and turned over to the new tactics of the fighter-bomber to upset morale. In acknowledging that defeat the enemy turned over to its serious bombing by night and left the daylight hours to the fast bomb-carrying fighter on its errands of tip and run.

The first stage of the attack began on July 8 in a series of attacks on shipping in the Channel. The battle of the blockade raged for a month over the Channel and the Channel ports, culminating in a great attack on shipping on August 8 when the *Luftwaffe* lost sixty aeroplanes to the sixteen of the R.A.F.

The first great attack on Great Britain itself began on August 11. Some 400 enemy aeroplanes began the assault against Dover and Portland. That day sixty-seven German aeroplanes were lost. Thereafter the attack developed against British fighter aerodromes along the South Coast in an effort to knock out the R.A.F. By the end of that first week the German Air Force had lost 495 aeroplanes – 281 bombers and 214 fighters. The R.A.F. lost 115 fighters.

The battle continued in the following weeks, as everyone will remember.

WAR IN THE MEDITERRANEAN: ITALIAN LOSSES.

THE ITALIANS REFUSE TO FIGHT.

THE SCENE ON DECK WHEN AN ITALIAN BATTLESHIP WAS HIT AT LONG RANGE BY HER BRITISH PURSUERS ON JULY 9, SHOWING SAILORS HOSING THE BURNING ANTI-AIRCRAFT GUN PLATFORM.

"Reports established that . . . British light cruisers met with an enemy cruiser force, which retired immediately on coming within extreme range of our supporting battleships. The enemy was pursued until the British Fleet was in sight of land, and though our forces remained to offer battle until the evening despite a succession of bombing attacks by large forces of Italian aircraft, the enemy did not offer to renew the action. The British convoys to which they were acting as a covering force have now arrived at their destination in safety."

THE "SYDNEY" AND THE "COLLEONI".

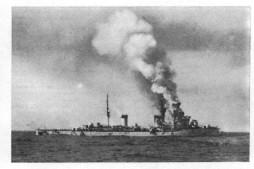

THE END OF THE "SYDNEY'S" FIGHT WITH THE "BARTOLOMEO COLLEONI," PROUDLY CLAIMED BY THE ITALIANS TO BE THE "FASTEST CRUISER AFLOAT": HER BOW BLOWN OFF.

The enemy was first sighted by destroyers, the 'Sydney' arriving in support about an hour later. The enemy altered course and endeavoured to escape. Our forces, however, made a determined attack, and fire from the 'Sydney' caused vital hits on the 'Colleoni,' which reduced speed, enabling our destroyers to complete her destruction. The second cruiser 'Giovanni delle Bande Nere,' was chased and hit but her superior speed saved her from a similar fate. Our forces rescued 545 men from the 'Colleoni' and were bombed by the Italian Air Force.

LATEST VICTIM OF H.M.S. "AJAX".

A DIRECT HIT ON THE AFTER-MAGAZINE OF THE "ARTIGLIERE." AS H.M.S "YORK'S" FIRST SHELL IS FIRED TO SINK H.M.S "AJAX'S" VICTIM.

A huge pillar of smoke rising from the explosion which marked the end of the "Artigliere" after she had been crippled by H.M.S. "Ajax". When H.M.S. "York" came up with her and after the destroyer towing her had made off, her crew at once began to abandon ship. Our forces allowed half an hour's grace before sinking her and dropped boats and rafts for the survivors. A message was broadcast on the commercial wavelength of the Italian stations, giving the position of the survivors, a message that compromised the position of the British forces.

GOERING'S SAVAGERY: "MILITARY OBJECTIVES" BOMBED IN LONDON.

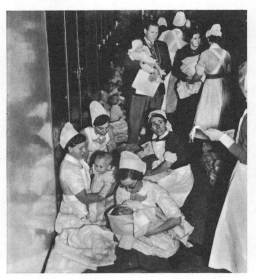

BABIES BEING PUT TO SLEEP AT GREAT ORMONDE STREET CHILDREN'S HOSPITAL, WHILE AIRMEN, WHO RECEIVE IRON CROSSES FOR RAIDING ENGLAND, SCATTER AIMLESS DESTRUCTION.

Two of Field-Marshal Goering's most savage and futile blows in the indiscriminate night bombing of London struck two hospitals in the centre of the Metropolis, which both received direct hits. One was a hospital for maternity cases, the other was the famous Hospital for Sick Children in Great Ormonde Street, Bloomsbury, which has 326 beds. A bomb hit the roof of the hospital and shattered it, blowing out every pane of glass from scores of windows and causing a fire on the top floor.

SIR CHRISTOPHER WREN'S MASTERPIECE DAMAGED BY A NAZI BOMB: THE HIGH ALTAR OF ST. PAUL'S CATHEDRAL DESTROYED BY FALLEN MASONRY.

The High Altar of St. Paul's Cathedral was destroyed by great blocks of masonry which fell when a Nazi bomb exploded on the choir roof during a recent raid. The bomb penetrated the roof at the eastern end of the cathedral, making a rectangular hole 20 ft. by 10 ft., and tons of masonry crashed directly on to the High Altar, dating from 1888, and smashed it to the ground, the Cross, the candles, and the altar ornaments being also crushed.

THE LONE PERFORMER OF A PERILOUS DUTY: A MEMBER OF LONDON'S GALLANT FIRE SERVICES FIGHTING A BOMB FIRE FROM HIS HAZARDOUS PERCH ON A FIRE-FIGHTING LADDER.

The services, faced with their long-awaited test, acquit themselves in a manner beyond praise. The burden of dealing with intense, indiscriminate raids fell not least on the London Fire Brigade and the A.F.S., who were faced with an enormous task on such nights as that of September 7. Royal recognition of the wonderful work, not only of the men, but of the women, of the fire services is revealed in the visit of the King to London Fire Brigade headquarters on October 16.

THE U.S. DESTROYERS ARRIVE: BASES LEASED TO THE U.S.

THE TRANSFER OF THE AMERICAN DESTROYERS OF WHICH SCORES ARE SEEN LAID UP HERE, IS OF TREMENDOUS IMPORTANCE TO BRITAIN AND DEMOCRACY.

The first flotilla of the American destroyers which have been handed over to the Royal Navy in exchange for the leasing of certain bases arrived in British waters on September 28, after an uneventful voyage across the Atlantic. New names, of towns existing in both Britain and the United States, have already been assigned to some of the fifty U.S. destroyers acquired by the Admiralty, though the old names of notable American personalities have not yet been removed from those that have arrived carrying the British crews who took them over in Canada.

"A MOST DASTARDLY ACT": THE SUNK EVACUEE SHIP.

FIVE OF THE SIX BOYS WHO WERE RESCUED WHEN THE "CITY OF BENARES" BOAT WAS FOUND FAR OUT IN THE ATLANTIC.

When the *City of Benares* was torpedoed it was announced that eighty-five children perished. This number can now be reduced by six owing to the rescue of a boat-load of forty-six survivors, among whom were six boys in the evacuation party. The first rescue was by a British warship, after the survivors had been adrift for twenty-four hours. The second rescue was also by a British warship, with which a Sunderland flying-boat got into touch. After having been adrift in the Atlantic for eight days the boys rapidly recovered and enjoyed their ride on the backs of sailors from the warship to the waiting train.

SIGNING THE GERMAN-ITALIAN-JAPANESE PACT.

THE NEW MILITARY ALLIANCE BETWEEN GERMANY, ITALY AND JAPAN. THE SCENE AT THE SIGNING OF THE PACT IN BERLIN ON SEPTEMBER 27.

Our picture shows the German Foreign Minister Ribbentrop reading the declaration at the ceremony of the signing of the ten-year Pact between Germany, Italy and Japan in Berlin on September 27, "to assist one another . . . if one of the high contracting parties should be attacked by a Power not at present involved." The figures, seated l. to r., are M. Saburo Kurusu, the Japanese Ambassador; Count Ciano, Hitler, and Ribbentrop (standing).

As regards the pact itself, Germany and Japan have so far spoken with rather different voices.

CHINA'S LIFE-LINE TO THE SEA: THE BURMA ROAD REOPENS.

BUILT IN THE EARLY FIFTEENTH CENTURY BY CHINESE OFFI-CIALS: ALL ALONG THE BURMA ROAD EVIDENCES OF EARLY CHINESE BRIDGE-BUILDING ARE EVIDENT TO THE TRAVELLER. THIS BRIDGE, STILL USABLE, IS SUPPORTED ON IRON CHAINS.

After remaining closed for the three worst months of the year when traffic is at a minimum, the Burma-Yunnan Road was reopened at midnight on Thursday, October 17.

The first lorry was reported to have crossed the border seven minutes after midnight, and sixty more followed shortly afterwards, the van-guard of a fleet of lorries which were waiting to take all kinds of stores to Kunming and on to Chungking, the Chinese capital.

GENERAL DE GAULLE AT DAKAR, THE VITAL PORT, AND DUALA.

GENERAL DE GAULLE, WITH HIS OFFICERS, DECIDING NOT TO CAUSE BLOODSHED BY ATTEMPTING TO FORCE A DECISION BY WEIGHT OF ARMS AGAINST HIS COMPATRIOTS.

In anticipation of German attempts to gain control of the port, General de Gaulle, with a Free French Force and accompanied by a British naval squadron, arrived off Dakar on September 23. He sent interme-diaries to meet officials loyal to Vichy in an effort to persuade them that the cause of France was not lost. His efforts were unsuccessful. General de Gaulle then went to Duala, capital of the Cameroons, where he was warmly welcomed by the Governor, Colonel Leclerc.

GERMANY STRIDES (ACROSS HUNGARY) INTO THE BALKAN RING.

RUMANIA'S RICHEST OIL WELLS AT MORENI. GERMAN TROOPS ENTERED RUMANIA ON OCTOBER 7 TO GUARD THE OILFIELDS AGAINST ALLEGED SABOTAGE, FOR WHICH THEY HAVE TOR-TURED BRITISH SUBJECTS.

The great desire of the Balkan States at the opening of the war against Germany was to remain neutral and to save their people from the horrors of war. But they could not settle their differences among themselves to form a united front against aggression.

Rumania, at the beginning of this year, appeared to be solidly behind King Carol, who was prepared to defend the frontiers of this greatly-enlarged country. The army was said to be ready to meet any aggression, while the great Ditch was made to hinder any sudden advance. All the time Germany was increasing her pressure upon the Rumanian Government.

In March, King Carol found it necessary to restore the Iron Guard, whose organisation he had broken up. It was so obvious that Rumania might be attacked that the Allies begged the Government, via the B.B.C., not to delay in asking for help. This was on May 1, before Hitler's invasion of Holland and Belgium, and at that time there were large Allied forces in the Near East ready to prevent any attack upon Rumania. No response was made to the appeal.

After France was surrendered in June, Russia made her demand for Bessarabia and Bukovina, to which Rumania, with no friends now to help her, was obliged to yield.

On July 1, under Nazi insistence, the Anglo-French guarantee of her frontiers was officially renounced, and later in the month, Rumania sent representatives to pay a visit of respectful homage to Hitler.

August brought the Bulgarian claims to the forefront, and again Rumania had to submit, agreeing, on the 18th, to the surrender of the Dobrudja.

Talks began with Hungary concerning Transylvania, but without success. Hungary wanted everything she had lost at Versailles. When the talks broke down both parties were summoned hurriedly to Vienna on August 28, where Hitler and Mussolini decided the matter for them. The delegates were not allowed the opportunity of putting forward their own views.

Rumania gave way, submitting to the loss of more than half of Transylvania. In return she got the promise of the guarantee of her frontiers by both of the Axis powers.

GREECE ATTACKED BY ITALY: THE GREEKS VICTORIOUS.

KORITZA, THE LARGEST TOWN IN ALBANIA, ESTIMATED POPULATION 30,000, LIES A FEW MILES FROM THE MACEDONIAN FRONTIER, AND WAS USED AS THEIR NORTHERN BASE BY THE ITALIANS.

GENERAL ALEXANDER PAPAGOS, WHO HAS BEEN APPOINTED COMMANDER-IN-CHIEF AND EN-TRUSTED WITH THE DEFENCE OF HIS COUNTRY.

Growing tension between Italy and Greece, as the result of Axis threats, culminated on Monday, October 28, at 3 a.m. with an Italian ultima-tum demanding the immediate surrender of certain strategic points to be used against Britain. Three hours later Italian troops were reported to have crossed the Albanian frontier. For some time past Italy has massed over a dozen divisions on this frontier, but the few roads into Greece are unsuited to mechanised forces and already snow is reported on the Albanian mountains. If Italy can quickly overcome Greece – who at once was granted aid by Britain – it would give her practical command of the Ægean Sea and Dardanelles, with the use of Greek aerodromes at Syra and Delos, affording an easy "hop" between Greek airfields and seaplane bases at Phaleron Bay, Salonika, and Lavrion, to the Dodecanese Islands, thus threatening Syria with the possibility of air-borne troops. With the Corinth Canal also in her hands Italy could conveniently pass into the Ægean by sea.

"The hour has come to fight for the independence of Greece, for her integrity, for her honour," General Metaxas declared in a proclamation issued to the Greek nation early on the morning of October 28, after the violation of the frontier by Italian troops.

In a message to his people on the day of the Italian invasion, King George II of the Hellenes said: "In this moment I am sure all Greeks will do their duty to the end, as it is written in the glorious history of Greece. The whole nation is ready to fight as one man till the final victory." King George of Greece has assumed the supreme leadership of his army, navy and air force.

On the southern front, from the toe of Albania, the Italians moved forward with caution to the Kalamas River, being opposed by nothing more than fluid Greek outposts. In the air the campaign opened with attacks on Patras, at the entrance to the Gulf of Corinth, followed by comparatively small-scale attacks on Corinth and Piræus, several on Salonika, one on Candia, the capital of Crete, and one on Larissa. The Italian Navy was inactive, probably owing to fear of British move-ments, and two Greek destroyers, which boldly steamed out of the Gulf of Corinth to fire on troops of the Italian right flank, were able to pursue their task without molestation. Meanwhile the Greeks were given an invaluable respite in which to proceed with their mobilisation, and as long ago as Thursday, Oct. 31, it was reported from Athens that fresh troops had been moved up to relieve the small covering forces which had hitherto been opposing the leisurely Italian advance.

BRITISH FORCES NOW KNOWN TO BE FIGHTING ON GREEK SOIL: THE BISHOP OF CANEA BLESSING BREN CARRIERS AND LIGHT TANKS AS THEY PASSED THROUGH A TOWN OF GREECE.

EVZONES, THE "GUARDS" OF THE GREEK ARMY: (LEFT) WEARING THEIR FAMOUS PEACETIME WHITE *FUSTANELLA* KILTS AND *TSAROUCHIA* (MOUNTAIN SHOES), WITH POMPONS AND (RIGHT) IN BATTLE DRESS WITH BRITISH HELMETS.

BRITISH AND GREEK SOLDIERS FRATERNISE: HELMETS APART, GREEK EQUIPMENT CLOSELY RESEMBLES THAT OF THE BRITISH ARMY BEFORE THE INTRODUCTION OF "BATTLE DRESS".

A REMARKABLE PICTURE SHOWING ITALIAN TROOPS FLEEING FROM THE ADVANCING GREEKS AND FRANTICALLY URGING ON A MULE-DRAWN WAGON. THE STATE OF THE GROUND SHOWS THE CONDITIONS THE RETREATING ARMY HAD TO FACE.

Further south, the Italians attacked in considerably greater strength in the coast zone, quickly forced their way to the Kalamas River, established bridgeheads beyond it, were counter-attacked and driven back, and then mounted a heavier attack, which drove the Greeks back. The Greek command withdrew its forces on the coast to another river, the Acheron, and thence to a steep ridge running northward to the upper waters of the Kalamas. Meanwhile the Greeks boldly accepted the opportunities afforded by the Italian dispositions. They crossed the Albanian frontier west of Koritza, and, after sharp fighting, established themselves on the Morova Planina, whence they looked down upon the town, which is the Italian advanced base in this region. In the air the Italians also displayed less vigour than had been expected of them. The little Greek Air Force has acted boldly and pluckily. The R.A.F. has gone into action and has carried out effective raids on bases in Italy and Albania, including the ports of Brindisi and Valona.

From November 4, when British Air Force units first set foot in Crete, there opened up a new chapter in the war against the Axis Powers. The landing of R.A.F. personnel on the mainland of Greece, and their subsequent feats in the battles in Albania, together with the constant bombing of Italian ports and communications, have played an enormous part in the Greek successes of which our Allies are fully cognisant.

The fall of Koritza towards the end of November marked a definite victory for the Greeks; the Italian advanced G.H.Q. was vacated by the enemy with loss of 1,500 officers and men, numbers of tanks, guns, and impedimenta, some of which is now being used by the Greeks (using ammunition captured in Libya by the British force there). A further advance to Pogradets, close to Lake Ochrida, was made up the road to Elbasan. Moscopole, a position 12 miles to the west of Koritza, was also occupied.

GERMAN DIPLOMACY: HITLER MEETS FRANCO, PÉTAIN AND MOLOTOV.

AN ENCOUNTER WHICH FAILED TO ACHIEVE THE RESULTS HOPED FOR BY THE AXIS: GENERAL FRANCO'S MEETING WITH HITLER ON OCTOBER 24.

Hitler, in pursuance of his plans to circumvent Britain in the Mediterranean, where his grandiose schemes stretched from Gibraltar to Syria, met General Franco in a small station decorated with the swastika and Spanish flags. The meeting was described as most cordial. The upshot of it was kept secret.

THE VICHY CABINET IN SESSION WHEN THE FÜHRER'S TERMS FOR "FRENCH CO-OPERATION" WERE DISCUSSED: AFTER MARSHAL PÉTAIN'S MEETING WITH HITLER.

The photograph shows (l. to r.) Gen. Huntziger (War), Raphael Alibert (Justice), Marshal Pétain, Paul Baudouin (formerly Foreign Affairs), Caziot (Agriculture), Marcel Peyrouton (Interior), Pierre Laval (Vice-Premier and Foreign Affairs), Yves Bouthillier (Finance) and René Bettin (Industrial Production).

ANOTHER MEETING IN THE GERMAN DIPLOMATIC OFFENSIVE WHICH FELL SHORT OF THE HOPED-FOR RESULTS: M. MOLOTOV IN CONFERENCE WITH HITLER.

M. Molotov, the Soviet Premier and Foreign Commissar, left Berlin for Moscow on November 14 after a two-day visit during which he had two conferences with Hitler and several meetings with Ribbentrop. Above he is seen with Hitler. The meeting was held with all the pomp beloved of the Nazis, but no results have yet become apparent.

Hitler's meetings with General Franco and with Marshal Pétain were certainly not lacking in dramatic atmosphere and they have given rise to speculation. There was first of all a suggestion that some form of peace proposal might be coming from Madrid as a result of Señor Suñer's visit to Germany. When he replaced as Foreign Minister a colleague considered more friendly to us than he himself was thought to be, it was further suggested that Señor Suñer had assumed this office because, if Spain decided not to march with Germany, it would look like a personal setback for him and a check to the Falange unless the direction of foreign policy were in his hands. This was before Hitler's visit to France and the Spanish frontier, which seemed to put a different complexion upon affairs; because such a project would not appear to require a meeting with the Caudillo and would not directly concern Marshal Pétain. For the moment the favourite theory was that, as regards France, Hitler was preparing some form of co-operation.

"AID FOR BRITAIN": ONE SLOGAN BY U.S. RIVAL PRESIDENTIAL CANDIDATES.

PRESIDENT FOR THE THIRD TIME – THE FIRST OCCASION IN AMERICAN HISTORY: FRANKLIN DELANO ROOSEVELT.

Although, amid the many cares of office, President Roosevelt did not attempt the electioneering activities of his younger opponent Mr. Wendell Willkie, his comparatively few public speeches attracted equal attention. At Cleveland, Ohio, the President aroused great enthusiasm by explaining that the true reason he was running for a third term was because "there is a great storm raging now" throughout the world.

ITALY'S ARMISTICE DAY DÉBÂCLE – 13 BOMBERS LOST IN FIRST RAID.

NOVEMBER 11, ARMISTICE DAY, SAW THE DESTRUCTION OF THIRTEEN ITALIAN 'PLANES – ON THEIR FIRST DAY ATTACK ON ENGLAND. THIS "C.R.42" FIGHTER WAS BROUGHT DOWN AT ORFORD, SUFFOLK.

The Italian Air Force, who made their first daylight foray on Britain on November 11, will have cause to remember for long their celebration of Armistice Day. Some 80 machines, bombers and fighters, flying from 10,000 to 12,000 ft., in an attack on a convoy off the Thames Estuary, were intercepted by "Hurricanes," fighters intending to make acquaintance with the Duce's Air Force. Within a few minutes, eight bombers (six "Capronis" and two "Piaggis") were shot down, seven in the sea and one on land in Suffolk. The rest dropped their bombs in the sea and fled. The "Hurricanes" then attacked the Italian fighters, and within 15 minutes brought down five, one of them rammed by a zealous "Hurricane" pilot who had expended all his ammunition.

THE SAVAGERY AT COVENTRY.

ALL THAT REMAINS OF COVENTRY CATHEDRAL AFTER THE NAZI ONSLAUGHT – THE TOWER AND TALL SPIRE, 303 FEET IN HEIGHT, THE PRIDE OF THE CITY, STILL STANDING.

We have all heard of how German dive-bombers wiped out the town of Guernica in Spain and deliberately wrecked the cities of Warsaw and Rotterdam, killing right and left and wreaking such havoc as to make civilisation gasp. The same methods have now been used against Britain. During the night of Thursday, November 14, 2,000 high explosive bombs and thousands of incendiaries were showered on the City of Coventry. 250 people are known to be killed, and about 800 seriously injured. The city itself consists of masses of rubble – Cathedral, famous public buildings, cinemas, shops and houses have all been obliterated, and in places it was almost impossible to tell which was roadway and which were buildings. According to one report, no fewer than 1,000 buildings have been damaged, among them factories, schools, hospitals, the post office, police station, and hundreds of red-brick villas. This destruction was carried out by the dive-bombers, once the pride of the inhuman *Luftwaffe*, which, however, can now only be used under cover of darkness. The boasts of the Germans over the radio concerning this wanton display of typical brutality were soon answered by the R.A.F. Large forces twice attacked the city of Hamburg and wrought terrific destruction there.

THE HERO OF CONVOY HX84: CAPTAIN FEGEN OF THE "JERVIS BAY".

CAPTAIN E. S. FOGARTY FEGEN, R.N., THE "JERVIS BAY'S" COMMANDER, WHO HAS BEEN AWARDED A POSTHUMOUS V.C.

As the result of his heroic action in going straight for the far more powerfully armed raider, at least 33 out of 38 ships in the convoy were able to escape. "It was glorious. Never shall I forget the gallantry of the British captain, sailing forward to meet the enemy," Captain Sven Olander, master of the Swedish freighter which turned back to rescue survivors, declared when landing in Canada the sixty-five members of the eighteen-year-old, 14,164-ton armed merchant cruiser's crew.

THE SCRAP-IRON CAMPAIGN: THE GERMAN VERSION.

FIELD-MARSHAL GÖERING RESPLENDENT IN WHITE TUNIC SEES A BUST OF HIMSELF AND ONE OF HIS FÜHRER IN A COLLECTION OF SCRAP IRON CONTRIBUTED BY THE PEOPLE OF GERMANY.

Meanwhile in Britain under the ægis of the Iron and Steel Control Board, a nation-wide campaign for the collection of scrap-iron and steel has already brought an immense quantity of waste metal to the yards of British steel-works for intensive production of high-grade steel needed to reinforce and to replenish munitions of war for the fighting Services. This is in addition to the huge quantities of metal realised by the collection of iron railings, etc., in public parks. It was estimated that railings in London alone would yield between three and four thousand tons of metal, and that over a thousand tons could be salvaged from Hyde Park without touching the boundary railings. An encouraging response has also been made to Lord Beaverbrook's appeal for the collection of aluminium pots and pans – the "Saucepans into Spitfires" campaign.

When the Minister of Aircraft Production told housewives that their pots and pans were virgin aluminium he was more than 99.2 per cent. correct. The first 50,000 kitchen utensils collected in response to his appeal have now gone into the furnaces – and have come out as 10 tons of pure aluminium, worth £1,100.

MR. EDEN AGAIN FOREIGN SECRETARY: M. LAVAL LEAVES VICHY GOVT.

M. PIERRE LAVAL
whom Marshal Pétain has relieved of his office. M. Pierre Flandin, who now has the Foreign Affairs portfolio, is "better fitted to pursue a policy of *rapprochement* between France and Germany."

THE RIGHT HON. ANTHONY EDEN, M.C., M.P.,
who returns as Secretary of State for Foreign Affairs – a portfolio which he gave up in 1938, when he resigned from Mr. Chamberlain's Government.

MR. CHARLES CHAPLIN
As Charlie, the great dictator: one of the first pictures in his new film *The Great Dictator* which is calculated to make Hitler and his bell-boy Mussolini rage at its satirical humour.

THE RIGHT HON. VISCOUNT HALIFAX, K.G.,
is taking up the British Ambassadorship in Washington. The "New York Times," stated: "The British Government have paid us a compliment."

MR. NEVILLE CHAMBERLAIN
who died on Saturday, November 9. Last week it was reported that he was seriously ill, and on Saturday in the evening he died at Highfield Park, near Basingstoke, at the age of seventy-one.

THE ATTACK ON TARANTO HARBOUR: ITALY'S RUN-AWAY NAVY.

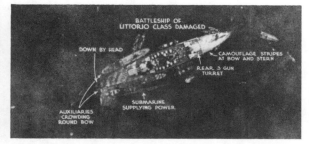

A 23,622-TON BATTLESHIP OF THE CAVOUR CLASS BEACHED ON THE EAST SHORE OF THE OUTER HARBOUR.

THE INNER HARBOUR AT TARANTO AFTER THE BRITISH ATTACK.

A LITTORIO CLASS BATTLESHIP IN THE OUTER HARBOUR AFTER SHE HAD BEEN CRIPPLED BY THE TORPEDO ATTACK.

On the night of November 11, as the Prime Minister announced to a cheering House of Commons, units of the Fleet Air Arm attacked the Italian Fleet lying, as they believed, snugly behind their shore defences. Although the Italian communiqué only admitted that one warship had been severely damaged, the Admiralty official communiqué of November 15 made it evident from reconnaissance that three battleships were thoroughly crippled. Efforts were being made to salve the battleship of the "Littorio" class of 1937, of which there are four in all and two of the "Cavour" class of four battleships (reconstructed 1933–39; 23,622 tons, with ten to twelve 6-in. and twelve 4.7-in. guns). She was seen to have had her forecastle under water and a heavy list to starboard. It was ascertained that two of the "Cavour" class were aground, one beached, and netted for protection, the other lying heeled over to starboard, with only the forward part of her upper works above water. The pilot of a reconnaissance aircraft reported that four other shapes lay under water.

NAZI TOTAL WAR: GERMANY'S LATEST "MILITARY OBJECTIVES"!

MANCHESTER'S WORST AIR RAID OF THE WAR: A VIEW TAKEN FROM THE HIGH ALTAR IN MANCHESTER CATHEDRAL.

BRISTOL'S LANDMARKS DESTROYED BY NAZI VANDALS: THE TEMPLE CHURCH GUTTED BY INDISCRIMINATE BOMBING.

SCENE OF THE CITY OF LONDON'S MOST PRINCELY ENTERTAINMENTS PRESIDED OVER BY LORD MAYORS FOR NEARLY 450 YEARS.

A very large number of 'planes took part in the first long and most severe raid Manchester has experienced, on December 23. The drone of engines was practically continuous.

It is estimated that about 100 'planes took part in a raid on this West of England town last week. As usual, the bombing was apparently aimless and much damage was done to dwelling-houses and shops.

The Guildhall, historic and ancient centre of the City of London's proud past, was reduced to a mass of smoking ruins after the Germans' wanton fire raids on Sunday, December 29.

BRITISH FORCES LAUNCH MAJOR ATTACK ON ITALY'S LIBYAN ARMIES: THE BATTLE OF SIDI BARRANI.

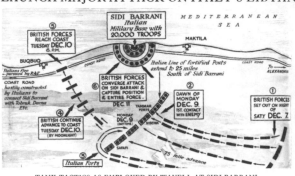

MARSHAL GRAZIANI: AN UNCONVENTIONAL PHOTOGRAPH

TANK TACTICS AS EMPLOYED BY WAVELL AT SIDI BARRANI.

A STRIKING PICTURE OF CHEERFUL-LOOKING LIBYAN PRISONERS RESTING.

Three months ago, following the defection of France, the British troops in Egypt were forced to retreat before Marshal Graziani's forces, which were greatly superior in number to our own. Had Graziani continued his drive east the British situation might well have become serious.

The diagrammatic exposition of the highly mechanised "Army of the Nile" – or the armoured spearhead of that Army – illustrates the main points of attack, and indicates the method whereby General Wavell's brilliant attack on Sidi Barrani was launched.

The latest official estimate of Italian prisoners captured by General Wavell's troops on December 11 is 35,949, including 1704 officers, while a Cairo communiqué dated December 23 stated that several thousand more were still awaiting return from the forward camps.

THE ILLUSTRATED LONDON NEWS

THE MEN WHO FOUGHT AT BARDIA: THE CREW OF A BRITISH TANK BEFORE THE ASSAULT.

After swift and smashing blows delivered by our forces on land, sea and in the air, Bardia fell on the afternoon of January 5. The defensive works of the town, constructed by the Italians over a period of four years, had been confidently declared to be well-nigh impregnable, but the illusion was quickly shattered by General Wavell's army. Apart from the vast number of prisoners and booty captured, the effect of this victory on Axis propaganda was notable: for instance, after it had fallen, the Italian "bastion" suddenly became – according to Rome Radio – "only a group of houses round a creek."

This picture, one of a series of official photographs just arrived in this country from the Western Desert, was taken on Christmas morning in front of Bardia. The men standing before their tank are eating a Christmas pudding "made of biscuits, prunes, marmalade and rum." They have been fighting in the desert since the war began, and actually took part in the final assaults on Bardia. Contrary to popular conception, the weather in the Western Desert at this time of the year can be very bitter – heavy rain and intense cold alternating with sandstorms: hence the general unkempt appearance of this hard-bitten crew! The tanks have played a very decisive part in the Libyan operations; their weight and numbers, together with their clever tactical handling, appeared to confound the Italians completely.

1941

Eighth Army captures Cyrenaica; reaches El Agheila — British Somaliland regained — Germany sends Rommel and Afrika Korps to aid Italians — USA signs Lend-Lease Act — British send troops to aid Greece — Rommel drives 8th Army back to Egypt; besieges Tobruk — Bulgaria joins Axis — Germany signs Pact with Yugoslav Government; repudiated by King — Germany occupies Yugoslavia and Greece — Italy driven out of Eritrea & Ethiopia — Germany invades Crete — Pro-Axis revolt in Iraq suppressed — German battleship "Bismarck" sunk — Hitler's deputy Hess flies to Britain — British and Free French seize Syria from Vichy — Germany makes surprise attack on Russia — Great Britain and Russia sign Mutual Aid pact; US extends Lend-Lease to USSR — Vichy French surrender Southern Indo-China to Japanese — US freezes Japanese assets in USA; suspends all trade — Britain and USSR invade Iran — Germany captures Kiev, Crimea, Kharkov, Smolensk; besieges Leningrad; fails to take Moscow — Japan sinks US fleet at Pearl Harbour; invades Kowloon, Malaya and Thailand — Great Britain and USA declare war on Japan; USA on Germany & Italy — Japan invades Luzon, Malaya, Borneo and Burma; captures Guam, Hong Kong and Wake Island — HMS "Prince of Wales" and "Repulse" sunk — 8th Army relieves Tobruk; drives Rommel back to El Agheila — US/Filipino forces retreat to Bataan Peninsula; Manila made open city — First Washington Conference; Roosevelt and Churchill issue "United Nations" declaration.

THE CRACKING OF THE ITALIAN "EMPIRE": THE CAPTURE OF CYRENAICA.

THE VICTORY AT BARDIA: 30,000 ITALIAN PRISONERS FOR 400 AUSTRALIAN CASUALTIES.

THE BOMBARDMENT IN PROGRESS: A UNIT OF THE BRITISH NAVY FIRES A BROADSIDE INTO BARDIA ON THE LIBYAN COAST, GIVING THE ITALIANS TEN TONS OF METAL AT EACH BURST.

AUSTRALIAN TROOPS ADVANCING AT DAWN ON JANUARY 5 TOWARDS BARDIA. SUPPORTED BY TANKS, THEY LED THE ATTACK.

After the débâcle sustained by the Italian Army in the Battle of Sidi Barrani, and the resultant fall of Sollum and Fort Capuzzo, in which operations 35,949 prisoners were taken, the British encirclement of Bardia was rapidly executed. There the Italians were bottled up, but had prepared formidable fortifications, in a perimeter of about fifteen miles running round the top of a high cliff, with the port of Bardia at the bottom of a five-mile deep wadi. The Italian main defences and the bulk of their forces were situated at the top of the cliff, with machine-gun nests, concrete pillboxes, land-mines and other concealed defences. It was reported that General Berti, in command at Bardia, had intended to evacuate the town and fall back on Tobruk, but was ordered to defend it at all costs. By December 21, the areas to the north-west and west had been cleared by British mechanised units, aided by heavy guns which had been hauled into position up the 400-ft. escarpment into Libya, and the British artillery systematically proceeded to break up the ground, aided by the RAF and the Royal Navy, preparatory to a grand assault by waiting troops, including British, Australian and New Zealanders, and Free French units.

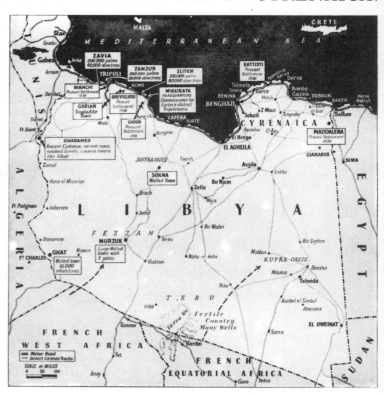

THE ITALIAN COLONY OF LIBYA SHOWN IN ITS ENTIRETY: A BRITISH MILITARY GOVERNORSHIP OF THE PROVINCE OF CYRENAICA HAS NOW BEEN ESTABLISHED.

THE CAPTURE OF BARDIA. A VIEW SHOWING CAPTURED ITALIAN GUNS LYING DERELICT. LARGE QUANTITIES OF WAR MATERIAL WERE TAKEN AND 38,000 PRISONERS, INCLUDING FOUR GENERALS. BRITISH LOSSES WERE SAID TO BE LESS THAN 600.

THE WILL TO LIVE: ITALIAN OFFICERS AND MEN BELONGING TO THE BARDIA GARRISON RACING ACROSS THE OPEN DESERT, WITH HANDS UPRAISED IN TOKEN OF THEIR FULL SURRENDER, TOWARDS THEIR ADVANCING OPPONENTS.

AN EXTRAORDINARY WAR PICTURE, OF ITALIAN PRISONERS FROM THE "INVINCIBLE FASCIST ARMY" IN BARDIA, STREAMING ACROSS THE OPEN DESERT UNATTENDED AND UNGUARDED, ON THEIR WAY TO BRITISH PRISONERS-OF-WAR CLEARING CAMPS.

THE TAKING OF TOBRUK: SCENES OF DEVASTATION AT EL ADEM AERODROME AND THE PORT.

A FREE FRENCH PATROL NEAR BARDIA. FRENCH FORCES CONTRIBUTED THEIR PART TO THE VICTORY.

THE 9232-TON CRUISER "SAN GIORGIO," PREVIOUSLY INCAPACITATED BY BOMBS, A BLAZING DERELICT.

DESOLATION AT EL ADEM. IN RETREAT THE ITALIANS SET FIRE TO ALL THEY COULD, BUT NOT EVERYTHING.

"WAVELL'S WIZARDRY": BENGHAZI FALLS, 230 MILES BEYOND TOBRUK.

The fall of Bardia was the most severe moral as well as military blow to the Italian Fascists, who attached supreme importance to it from a political as well as a strategic point of view. Barely a week before it collapsed to the British assault, General Bergonzoli assured Mussolini that it was impregnable. The outer perimeter defences comprised a very strong barbed-wire fence and a deep trench, the one being torn down by Bangalore Torpedoes, and the other filled in by sappers. The British losses, owing to brilliant generalship and the courage of the attacking forces, were under 600.

By the capture of Tobruk on January 22 the Army of the Nile attained a position of paramount strategic importance in its irresistible advance into Cyrenaica.

Commenting on the third major victory of the Army of the Nile at Tobruk, the military correspondent of the "Daily Telegraph" stated that British forces were then in a position in which two courses were open to them – to push on round the coast and complete the encirclement of Cyrenaica by successive advances from point to point; or to strike inland across to Benghazi and "at one strike cut off what remnants of Italian forces remained in the province." General Wavell, in one of the most brilliant military exploits in history, actually decided on both courses, thus bringing to a culminating point the brilliant series of victories in Libya which, the Prime Minister declared in his inspiring broadcast on February 9, had "broken irretrievably the Italian military power on the African Continent."

AUSTRALIAN INFANTRY MARCH INTO THE TOWN FOR THE HANDING OVER CEREMONY BY THE ITALIAN MAYOR: THE LOCAL INHABITANTS TAKING A KEEN INTEREST IN THE PROCEEDINGS.

THE CRACKING OF THE ITALIAN "EMPIRE": THE INVASION OF ABYSSINIA
UNITED AGAINST A COMMON ENEMY: AFRIKANERS AND BRITISH FROM SOUTH AFRICA.

BRIGADIER D. A. SANFORD, D.S.O., ON AUGUST 12, 1940, ENTERED ABYSSINIA WITH 2000 MARIA THERESA DOLLARS, WITH WHICH TO STIR UP REVOLT AGAINST THE ITALIAN OCCUPIERS.

A CAMEL PATROL OF THE SUDAN DEFENCE FORCE PATROLLING AT AN ADVANCED POSITION ON THE ERITREAN FRONTIER, WELL WITHIN WHICH BRITISH FORCES ARE NOW OPERATING.

GENERAL SMUTS DURING HIS RECENT VISIT TO THE SOUTH AFRICAN FORCES: TAKING BREAKFAST WITH LIEUT.-GEN. ALAN CUNNINGHAM, NEW C.-IN-C. EAST AFRICA.

The Imperial Forces in Kenya have been steadily augmented within recent months; the African Field Force now contains units from seven different British Colonies, as well as those of the Union of South Africa. Hitherto clashes with the Italians have been mainly affairs of outposts, and fighting has been on one side or other of the border of Turkana, with the British outposts strung out across deserts where water is scarce and roads are bad. Numbers of Abyssinian warriors have crossed the border and are undergoing training, hoping to meet the Fascists on the battlefield, having an account of long standing to settle with Marshal Graziani and his armies. The Emperor, Haile Selassie, is meanwhile in the Sudan.

General Jan Smuts who, in December paid a special visit to Kenya to inspect the South African Forces in conjunction with the remainder of the Imperial Troops in Africa, gave a glowing account of the high efficiency of the East Africa Defence Force under their new Commander-in-Chief, Lieut.-General Alan Cunningham, a gunner officer with a high reputation. In a New Year broadcast from South Africa, General Smuts said: "Great Britain, with her own gathering strength and with that of the Empire and the Commonwealth behind her, is much stronger than she was at the beginning of 1940. Hitler's position has definitely deteriorated . . . World opinion no longer regards a German victory as certain or even probable."

THE CAMPAIGN IN ERITREA AND SOMALILAND.

A pincers movement to encircle the Italian forces, from Eritrea in the north to Abyssinia and Italian Somaliland in the south, opened up on January 19 with the recapture of Kassala, occupied by the enemy in July last. The attack coincided with the dramatic news that British military missions had been operating four hundred miles inside the Abyssinian border for the past five months. By the 23rd, 5000 miles of territory had been evacuated by Italy in Eritrea, and simultaneously the South African forces from Kenya had advanced into Southern Abyssinia. From Gallabat, north of Lake Tana, another British advance pressed onward.

BEFORE THE CAPTURE OF KEREN: A STAFF OFFICER, WITH THE HELP OF A SCALE MODEL MADE OUT OF STICKS AND STONES DEMONSTRATES TO AIR-CREWS THE GENERAL PLAN WHICH IS TO BE ADOPTED.

The capture of Mogadishu, the capital and chief port, on February 25 marked a significant step in the conquest of Italian Somaliland, the southern half of the vast pincers which are gradually closing in to meet the corresponding movement from the northern half in Eritrea. To reach Mogadishu, the Empire Forces, under the command of Lieut.-Gen. A. G. Cunningham – who is the brother of Admiral Cunningham – penetrated 370 miles in a month across a country with poor communications and against strongest enemy forces. Mogadishu was an important Italian base in their Abyssinian campaign, and it is doubtless being quickly utilised by General Cunningham to sweep the Italians in Southern Abyssinia towards the coast of the Red Sea. Resistance by the enemy was not intense, but this lightning forced march by a flying column along the swampy, scrub-covered coastal plain is another epic feat by British troops, who, when they entered the town and occupied its white stucco buildings, found it empty of the enemy, who had left everything intact, including armaments, stores and supplies.

Another African Blitz-thrust in the latest approved Cunningham-Wavell fashion was suddenly burst on the Italians on March 17, when, after preliminary bombing by the R.A.F., British forces were landed at Berbera by British warships, whose guns silenced the enemy batteries. R.A.F. fast armoured cars helped to recapture the capital, which showed little resistance. Its capture opens up a direct new route to Addis Ababa, now threatened from thirteen directions.

By March 11 British and patriot forces advancing from the Sudan were only 190 miles, by winding mountain road, from Addis Ababa, while General Cunningham's army, after sweeping through Italian Somaliland, was already at the gates of Negelli and Dagga Bur. In Eritrea, however, our northern forces had met round Keren with the stoutest resistance the Italians had yet offered on any front. With the fall of Keren after weeks of heavy fighting, the operations in Eritrea entered the last phase of the dynamic eastward and southward thrusts by the British Empire and Allied forces under the command of General Platt, commanding the Sudan Forces.

THE PLAN FOR VICTORY: IMPERIAL FORCES PRESSING FORWARD ON SIX DIFFERENT FRONTS.

"THE MILLS OF GOD . . . ": HAILE SELASSIE'S RETURN TO ADDIS ABABA.

THE NEGUS RIDING THROUGH TROPICAL BUSH ON THE LAST STAGE OF A 200-MILE TREK.

THE EMPEROR GREETED BY THE COMMANDER-IN-CHIEF, EAST AFRICAN FORCES, GENERAL SIR ALAN CUNNINGHAM.

THE DUKE OF AOSTA SURRENDERS: AN OFFICIAL PHOTOGRAPH OF THE DUKE, ACCOMPANIED BY BRITISH OFFICERS.

The rapid advance of General Cunningham's South African forces, covering a 700-mile advance in four weeks, through bad country against strong enemy forces and over roads blasted and torn by them in their retreat – a record in military history – resulted on Saturday, April 5, in the sensational withdrawal of the Duke of Aosta's army, and the entry into the capital by advanced South African troops, who occupied the central square in Addis Ababa. After the British crossed the gorge of Awash River, ninety miles from the capital, the course was clear. Aosta retreated to the hills and sent a message to General Cunningham, thanking him for his offer to protect the Italian women and children, of whom there are over 33,000 sheltering in Addis. By this great feat of arms, Abyssinia, except for isolated and broken bodies of Italians, is in our hands.

MR. ROOSEVELT'S HISTORIC DEMAND FOR UNLIMITED AID FOR THE DEMOCRACIES.

AMERICA'S "PRIVATE CITIZEN NO. 1": MR. ROOSEVELT'S LATE ELECTION OPPONENT GETS TO WORK.

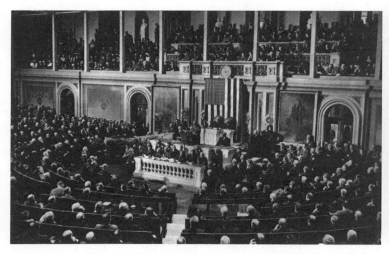

"WE KNOW THAT ENDURING PEACE CANNOT BE BOUGHT AT THE COST OF OTHER PEOPLE'S FREE-DOM" A STIRRING PASSAGE IN MR. ROOSEVELT'S GREAT SPEECH TO CONGRESS.

THE FORMER REPUBLICAN CANDIDATE MEETS BRITAIN'S MINISTER OF LABOUR AND NATIONAL SERVICE: HE IS WARMLY GREETED BY MR. ERNEST BEVIN.

To Congress on January 6, the President emphasised some vital points more strongly than before. "No realistic American," he said, "could expect international generosity, a return of true independence, world disarmament – nor even good business from a dictators' peace." He declared that America would never acquiesce in a peace dictated by aggressors, sponsored by appeasers. "Our most useful rôle," he told Congress "is to act as an arsenal for the democracies as well as for ourselves."

Mr. Wendell Willkie, recently President Roosevelt's spirited election opponent, and now the President's warm supporter in his Aid for Britain policy, arrived in England on January 26. He has come to England to see things for himself and to get all information possible concerning present conditions, and what conditions will be – to quote his own words – "following your victory." He wishes to compare our methods of production with those prevailing in his own country and to see how best they may be co-ordinated.

HOW THE BRITISH NAVY CONTROLS THE MEDITERRANEAN: DIVE-BOMBING ATTACK ON A MEDITERRANEAN CONVOY – GENOA BOMBARDED.

A NAZI REPRESENTATION BOASTS OF "STUKAS" DIVE-BOMBING THE "ILLUSTRIOUS."

STEEL AND ROCKY GUARDIANS OF BRITAIN'S MIGHT. IN THE BACKGROUND IS THE ROCK OF GIBRALTAR AND IN THE FOREGROUND H.M.S. "RENOWN," H.M.S. "MALAYA," AND THE "ARK ROYAL." THE FAMOUS AIRCRAFT-CARRIER IS STILL ON ACTIVE SERVICE, DESPITE HER MANY SINKINGS BY THE GERMAN PRESS.

A VIEW OF GENOA HARBOUR, HEAVI-LY BOMBARDED BY UNITS OF THE BRITISH FLEET ON FEBRUARY 9.

As our War Correspondent, Captain Cyril Falls, says in his article this week, "when Italy entered the war we began by regarding the Mediterranean as virtually closed to our convoys," but the much-vaunted Italian Navy signally failed to live up to the reputation claimed for it in certain quarters, and, although claimed as their "mare nostrum" by the Italians, the Mediterranean has remained under the control of the Royal Navy. On January 10, waves of German "Stukas," attempting to do what the Italian Navy had failed to achieve, launched a heavy and prolonged attack on a large British convoy which was carrying important material assistance to Greece. The Germans lost a number of dive-bombers, while on our side the aircraft-carrier "Illustrious" was struck (but reached port under her own steam), and the cruiser "Southampton," after being abandoned, was sunk by our own forces. Although this German attack continued almost without pause from dawn until dusk the convoy itself escaped injury and reached its destination. From day to day the vital importance of the Mediterranean becomes more apparent and the rout of the Italians by General Wavell in Africa is largely due to Britain's command of the sea, and, therefore, Italy's inability to reinforce her African army with men or materials. Nor have the Germans any means of challenging this British command of the Mediterranean except by attacking with land-based aircraft operating from Sicily or the Italian mainland. In these circumstances the Sicilian Channel becomes a key point in the situation, and the coast of French-occupied Tunisia of paramount importance. The strategic worth of this stretch of French territory (particularly the port of Bizerta) is one of the vital points at issue between Hitler and the Vichy Government. The attack on January 10 has brought into action – and the public eye – once more the Junkers Ju.87(b) aircraft which, following their big successes in Spain during the Civil War, and later against the Poles and the French, met with disaster when tackled by our own "Spitfires" and "Hurricanes." These "Stukas" were withdrawn by the enemy after a large number had been shot down, more particularly when attacking convoys

in the English Channel. The Junkers 87(b) is a sturdily-built machine, designed so that it can be mass-produced, and it is known that the Luftwaffe still has a very large number of the type. They are not particularly fast, nor have they a long flying range, but as dive-bombers pure and simple they are excellent aircraft.

A technique adopted by the Germans against our Army and the French was for the "Stukas" to dive as low as possible and then "hedge-hop" away, remaining only a few feet above the ground. Similar tactics were employed by the German airmen in the Mediterranean on January 10. After dropping their bombs, the "Stukas," flying at about 250 m.p.h., made off, flying less than fifty feet above the sea, and choosing when possible a lane between the convoy and the defending warships so as to blanket the latter and make it impossible for them to use all their guns, for fear of hitting another ship. The number of German 'planes, however, lost and crippled in the Mediterranean action shows that the tactics employed were by no means entirely successful. Nor must it be forgotten that the convoy got through.

At dawn on February 9, under Vice-Admiral Sir James Somerville, H.M.S. "Renown" (32,000-ton battle-cruiser, six 15-in. guns), H.M.S. "Malaya" (31,000-ton battleship, eight 15-in. guns), H.M.S. Cruiser "Sheffield" (9000 tons, 6-in. guns), and other units of the Fleet, appeared off Genoa, Italy's greatest commercial port, and fired over 300 tons of shells on the docks, harbour works, main oil installation and supply ships, among those in harbour, it was reported, being the luxury liner "Rex." The aircraft-carrier "Ark Royal," with the Fleet Air Arm, co-operated. Genoa has been used by the Germans as a port of embarkation for Sicily.

WHERE GERMANS RULE: DEATH DANCE BEFORE POLISH MASS EXECUTION.

REVENGE FOR THE DEATH OF A GERMAN SOLDIER: HANDS TIED BEHIND THEIR HEADS, ONE HUNDRED POLES MARCH THROUGH THE STREETS TO THEIR EXECUTION.

THE LINE OF VICTIMS DIMINISHES AS THE RIFLES CRACK. THE NAZIS PICK OFF THE MEN SEPARATELY, WHILE AN OFFICER NON-CHALANTLY SURVEYS THE SCENE.

UNDER THE EYE OF NAZI SOLDIERS, AND BEFORE THEIR OWN EXECUTION: DOOMED POLES DIG THEIR OWN GRAVES AND THOSE OF OTHERS ALREADY MURDERED.

The above sensational pictures, received from America, are the first published to show the workings of German "justice" in Poland. Showing as they do the cold-blooded and well-nigh incredible brutality of Hitler's New Order, strenuous protests were made by the Germans to prevent their publication once it was known that they had been smuggled through to America. Behind these pictures is a story of cold-blooded horror reminiscent of the Middle Ages. Following the death of a German soldier, one hundred Polish men

were rounded up – amongst them many Jews – and were marched through the streets with their hands tied behind their heads. They were then ordered to dig their own graves and, to gratify the barbaric sadism of the soldiers, forced at the point of the bayonet to perform for the Germans' amusement a "Dance of Death." Methods of execution varied, some of the men being shot, some hanged, and others tied to posts and stoned to death.

GREECE'S TRIUMPH IN ALBANIA: ENEMY TANKS – AND A CAPTIVE COLONEL.

GENERAL JOHN METAXAS, A BRIL-
LIANT LEADER AND FAITHFUL ALLY,
TALKING TO H.M. KING GEORGE II.

A CAPTIVE ITALIAN COLONEL, COMMANDER OF A CRACK ALPINI REGIMENT,
WITH HIS A.D.C., IN THE SIDECAR OF ONE OF THE MILITARY MOTOR-CYCLES
ACQUIRED BY THE GREEK ARMY FROM THE REICH BEFORE THE WAR.

RETREATING ITALIANS DRIVEN BACK BY THEIR OWN WAR MATERIAL: A
FORMATION OF LIGHT TANKS CAPTURED FROM THE ITALIAN ARMY BEING
MANNED BY GREEK M.T. UNITS FOR SUBDUING OBSTINATE ENEMY POSITIONS.

General Metaxas, born in 1870, on Odysseus's island of Ithaka, died on the morning of January 29 at his residence at Kiphissia, near Athens, just three months after his rejection of Mussolini's 3 a.m. ultimatum started the chain of Greek military triumphs over her aggressor, Italy. Prime Minister of Greece and Minister of Foreign Affairs, Education, War, Marine and Air, he assumed dictatorial powers on August 4, 1936, when parliamentary government was suspended owing to political difficulties and the menace of Communism.

Younger people, seeing the photographs of a plump, elderly man, who even when he visited the front in time of war was dressed in an excellently cut lounge suit, knew that John Metaxas was called "General," but can scarcely have realised that he was one of the ablest soldiers produced in recent years by South-East Europe. Few men in the world would be harder to replace at this critical hour. He died in harness, beloved by his country, which will never cease to honour his name.

THE GERMAN THREAT TO THE BALKANS: RUMANIA NOW – BULGARIA NEXT.

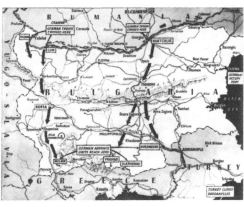

BULGARIA SIGNS AWAY HER INDEPENDENCE: THE BULGARIAN
PREMIER, M. FILOFF (LEFT), IS SEEN SIGNING THE DOCUMENT,
WITH RIBBENTROP (CENTRE) AND CIANO (RIGHT).

THE TWO MAIN LINES OF THE GERMAN ADVANCE THROUGH
BULGARIA. TROOPS NOW STAND AT MANY POINTS ALONG BUL-
GARIA'S SOUTHERN BORDER DIRECTLY THREATENING GREECE.

KING BORIS, THE BULGARIAN PUPPET KING, VISITING FIELD-
MARSHAL LIST AT HIS HEADQUARTERS AT SOFIA WHERE HE
DISCUSSED THE ENTRY OF BULGARIA INTO THE WAR AGAINST
YUGOSLAVIA.

Now that General Antonescu has virtually handed over his country to the Nazis, Britain has had no choice but to sever diplomatic relationships with Rumania. First carved up between Russia and Bulgaria, Rumania is now virtually a German province. In consequence, more than any other of the Balkan Powers, Bulgaria holds the key positions at the present moment. With Greece's forces heavily engaged in Albania, the "back door" into her territory and the approach to Salonika lie through King Boris's domains.

The mountains guarding Greece in the north provide that country with a strong natural barrier against invasion. The possible method of approach to the Struma Valley and the port of Salonika is by way of the Rupel Pass: General Metaxas, foreseeing this possibility, constructed fortification along the whole line in this region with Rupel as a key point, whilst secondary positions cover Demirhassar and Salonika.
The line through the Shipka Pass, to the eastwards, would bring the invader of Bulgaria up to Adrianople: this powerful Turkish strong

point would have to be forced before the enemy's armies could penetrate into Thrace. Turkey stands ready to defend her territory on the Marmara and in Thrace, but she would in all probability be left in peace – at least until Germany had settled with Greece.
On Sunday, February 9, Mr. Churchill, in his broadcast to the nation, solemnly warned Bulgaria of the perils that awaited her if she allowed herself again, as in 1915, to be made a cat's-paw by Germany.

YUGOSLAVIA BETRAYED BY HER POLITICIANS: THE PACT THAT ISN'T.

HITLER AND RIBBENTROP WELCOME THE YUGOSLAVIAN MINIS-
TERS – THE SCENE AT BERCHTESGADEN BEFORE THE SIGNING OF
THE VIENNA PACT, WHICH WILL NOT NOW BE RATIFIED.

PRINCE PAUL OF SERBIA AND KING PETER: AN EXCLUSIVE AND
RECENT PHOTOGRAPH OF THE LATE REGENT OF YUGOSLAVIA
AND THE SEVENTEEN-YEAR-OLD KING.

SOWING THE SEED OF FUTURE BETRAYAL! PRINCE PAUL, REGENT
OF YUGOSLAVIA, IN CLOSE CONVERSATION WITH HITLER AT A
SOIRÉE AT BERLIN IN JUNE 1939.

On February 14 Messrs. Svetkovitch and Cincar-Markovitch (who were then Prime Minister and Foreign Minister of Yugoslavia respectively) arrived at Berchtesgaden for discussions concerning the Tripartite Pact.
Early in March, the Germans began increased pressure on Yugoslavia, which on March 7 led all the Opposition parties in Belgrade to demand a firm policy. It was then known in diplomatic circles that M. Tsvetkovitch was wobbling, and the Regent, Prince Paul, was reported to have met Nazi leaders at his castle in Slovenia. The calling-up of over

a million men led to a belief that Yugoslavia was determined to defend her territories if invaded, but the true intentions of Prince Paul and his Government to surrender under threats were clarified on March 21, when a Cabinet crisis resulted and three pro-Ally Ministers resigned. The German terms revealed the demands to send sealed trains containing war material through Yugoslavia, Axis control of propaganda, and suppression of democratic elements, all inconsistent with neutrality. On Tuesday March 25, after many days' delay, Premier Svetkovitch and his Foreign Minister, Cincar-Markovitch, at length went to Vienna

and signed the Tripartite Pact, sacrificing Yugoslavia's independence. On their return to Belgrade, instead of cheering crowds, the two Ministers had to sneak back into the capital. And then Revolution broke out amongst the angry nation; behind the scenes a military coup d'état had been staged. At 2.30 a.m. on March 27, the two Ministers were arrested, and young King Peter, five months before attaining his eighteenth birthday, issued a stirring manifesto to his people, which announced that he had assumed the full functions of the Throne, to the great delight of his people.

A MESSAGE OF HOPE FOR OPPRESSED NORWAY: THE LOFOTEN RAID.

LOCAL WORKERS WATCH OIL FIRES BURNING AT STANSUND, WHERE AN IMPOR-
TANT OIL-PRODUCING PLANT WAS DESTROYED.

A REMARKABLE OFFICIAL PICTURE SHOWING A NUMBER OF LANDING CRAFT SPEEDING BACK TO THEIR PARENT SHIPS
AFTER THE BRITISH TROOPS HAD COMPLETED THE DESTRUCTION OF THE OIL STORES ACCUMULATED BY THE GERMANS.

The daring raid carried out by British naval and military forces on German objectives on the Norwegian Lofoten Islands on March 4 was a conspicuously successful operation which resulted in the sinking of 18,000 tons of enemy shipping (including the 10,000-ton floating fish-oil factory "Hamburg," from which vessel the majority of the prisoners were taken), the capture of the 215 German prisoners and ten "Quislings," and the bringing off of 300 Norwegian volunteers, including eight women. In addition, fish-oil factories and a power station were destroyed and oil-storage tanks burned. Svolvaer which appears to have been the chief scene of the raid and where an important oil plant was destroyed, is the main trading centre of the islands, lying about 25 miles below the head of the wide Vest Fjord, where a number of narrow fjords open into it, one of which is the Otot Fjord running up to Narvik, the scene of gallant exploits of the British Navy last year. Fine weather favoured the operation, which was marked by perfect organisation and mutual understanding on the part of both the Navy and Army. A number of hand-picked and specially-trained troops took part in the landing, and with them were a number of Norwegian naval ratings and guides, who had been training in Britain.

ITALY'S DEFEAT AND HUMILIATION IN LIBYA: THE NAZIS TAKE OVER.

THE STANDARD OF THE GERMAN AFRI-
KA CORPS SENT TO TRIPOLI TO RE-
TRIEVE THE ITALIAN DÉBÂCLE DIS-
PLAYED ON A MILITARY CAR.

THE GERMANS IN LIBYA. SOLDIERS BUSY UNLOADING FIELD EQUIPMENT FROM A TRANSPORT PLANE, ONE OF THE
METHODS BY WHICH IT WAS POSSIBLE TO BRING LARGE SUPPLIES FROM ITALY.

THE COMMANDER'S FAREWELL TO HIS
FÜHRER: GENERAL ROMMEL, WHO IS IN
COMMAND IN NORTH AFRICA, SAYS
GOOD-BYE TO HITLER.

By air and – as is widely reported – the use of French territorial water, the Germans for a long time past have been landing large supplies of men, munitions and guns in North Africa, despite the vigilance of the Royal Navy. At the same time as German equipment was being transferred by sea and air across the Sicilian Channel, General Wavell's troops were being taken from the African theatre of war to render help to our gallant Greek Allies. On the outcome of the Battle for Greece and the extent of the German penetration in Africa must depend the the success or otherwise of Axis *versus* Allied strategy.

THE BATTLE OF THE TANKS: THE BESIEGED GARRISON OF TOBRUK.

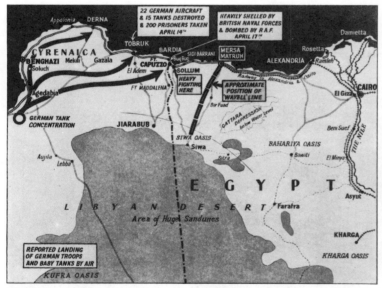

THE SITUATION AT TOBRUK AND AT SOLLUM: HOW THE ATTACK ON CYRENAICA WAS LAUNCHED.

IN TOBRUK TWO DEFENDERS EXAMINE A CAPTURED AND BATTERED GERMAN TANK.

The sudden and unexpected big German advance in Libya, said to include 1400 tanks and over 40,000 men, began on March 24, with the occupation of the lightly held El Agheila, followed on April 3 by the British evacuation of Benghazi, after destroying all military stores. On April 9, Derna was evacuated, with fighting in progress, the British forces retreating to Tobruk. At Mekili, fifty miles south of Derna, heavy fighting took place, and unfortunately three British generals were taken prisoners by an ill chance. On April 13, powerful enemy tank forces occupied Bardia and surrounded Sollum, while in Tobruk a severe tank battle ensued, in which the British were victorious. On April 15 it was reported that the British forces had retired towards Mersa Matruh, their headquarters, from whence they struck their first blow at Italy's army in Sidi Barrani on December 9.

In light of the growing realisation that properly organised columns of tanks can be well-nigh irresistible, it is interesting to gather and study all the available information about that remarkable German drive from Tripoli to Egypt. First and most important, of course, is the question, how did the Germans get to Tripoli (or to that El Agheila on the borders of Cyrenaica whence the drive properly started)? Our aircraft, ships and spies *should* have been able to inform G.H.Q. of what the Germans were doing. Daily our bombers flew across Benghazi to Tripoli, to Malta, to Sicily, to Naples. Our ships were always in the Sicilian Channel, and our intelligence officers were doubtless well distributed in Arab quarters.

But it might well be that fairly comprehensive information about the German activities was delivered to G.H.Q. – and received with considerable anxiety there. This would have been because G.H.Q. also knew about the impending German drive in the Balkans and the necessity of sending more and more troops there. But there is no escaping this fact: Headquarters at Cairo could never have believed that the Germans could be capable of organising Italian material for such a desert thrust as they did eventually deliver. In other words, the potentialities of tanks and Germans were still underrated.

Mention is made of "organising Italian material." The point is worth insisting upon. Too much has been made of miraculous German feats of tank transportation by air. Why should the Germans have adopted that perilous and unsatisfactory method when (1) Graziani's Tripolitanian Army with all its machines and material was still available for employment: and (2) sea-borne material could be brought across to Africa in almost any bulk via Tunisia and through the coastal waters of that colony to Tripoli?

Probably the Germans did bring a certain number of light tanks of motorcycles and of troops by aircraft from Sicily. But the rest of the material, the oil, water, food, ammunition – and several more tanks, lorries and motorcycles – was just waiting to be used in Tripoli.

But we hope and believe that the German has at last made a first-class blunder. His North African tanks may go so far; then our tanks will start off again and retrieve all the territory and positions the Germans have taken. As shown elsewhere, this tank warfare is a game of check and counter-check, with the prize to the stronger. We *should* be, before very long, the stronger in North Africa.

Already two flaws in the plan have been demonstrated. The first was the catastrophic destruction of a whole convoy on its way to North Africa from Sicily – Italian destroyer escorts as well. The second was our landing in Iraq, to checkmate German designs in that country. There may be other shocks in store for the enemy. British and Imperial forces for many weeks have held on to the port of Tobruk, 100 miles west of Sollum, their defence having seriously hampered the Germans' many attempts to advance against General Wavell's army, by making savage sallies, capturing tanks, guns, prisoners and causing heavy casualties. Heavy air raids are frequent, but the garrison remain magnificently spirited and confident in the Formidable defences of the perimeter. Captured Italian guns, manned by Army cooks, camp orderlies and batmen, are even being used.

CHINA STANDS UNDAUNTED AFTER FOUR YEARS' HEROIC RESISTANCE – "BUSINESS AS USUAL": HER DEVASTATED CAPITAL DEFIES AIR-WAR.

PART OF THE DEVASTATED CAPITAL: MANY CLING TO THEIR PARTIALLY-WRECKED HOMES, BUT ALL FIND SAFE CAVE-SHELTERS WHEN BOMBED.

AN AIR-RAID WARNING IN CHUNGKING: TWO RED PAPER BALLS MEAN THAT ENEMY 'PLANES ARE APPROACHING.

THE PHOTOGRAPH WAS TAKEN BY FLASHLIGHT, FOR NORMALLY THE PEOPLE STAND IN THE DARK.

"Chungking," writes the American journal "Life," "is as full of unsung civilian heroes as is London. Bombing has broken the nerve of neither great city. If possible, the people of Chungking do more laughing and joking, make more cheerful noise and are more completely the same under the bombs than even the Londoners." "Business as usual" is the spirited attitude of Western China's capital as it is of London – where notices to such effect are stuck up almost before damaged buildings are free from the ministrations of the fire-fighters. The air-raid shelters of Chungking are remarkable. The city is built over a high backbone of sandstone and the industrious citizens have hacked and dynamited immense numbers of caves, 500 public, 600 private, and 100 for cars and storage, some running 200 ft. underground, many hit repeatedly without a quiver being felt by the troglodyte shelterers. "Life" describes the spectacle of Chungking's entire population of 450,000 going calmly and safely underground long before Japanese planes arrive overhead as "one of the most unpredictable marvels of our time." In London it continues, "perhaps one-sixth of the population uses the shelters, for flat London would find it difficult to build shelters for 6,000,000 people." Day and night workers dig tunnels farther into the rock. Some shelters have four main entrances, several emergency exits, and are furnished with heavy wooden gates at the entrance, narrow wooden benches along the sides, electric lights for the workmen, but not for the people during raids, sometimes a blow ventilating system. "They are damp, stuffy, pitch-dark, crowded, a silent, breathing tomb of humanity. But they are magnificently safe."

BRITAIN'S GROWING AIR POWER: US AEROPLANES FOR THE R.A.F.

A FORMIDABLE BOMBER, THE "BOSTON II." ON AN AERODROME "SOMEWHERE IN ENGLAND." THESE MACHINES WILL PROVE A VALUABLE ADJUNCT TO OUR BOMBER COMMAND.

PILOTS FROM AMERICA TOO: KEEN AMERICAN "EAGLES" OFF ON PATROL.

A GROUP OF AMERICAN "EAGLE" SQUADRON AT A FIGHTER STATION "SOMEWHERE IN ENGLAND": THESE U.S.A. PILOTS ARE NOW DOING BRILLIANT WORK WITH THE R.A.F.

The great workshop of the United States of America is already rendering invaluable aid in providing those tools with which, as the Prime Minister has said, "we will finish the job." Some of the types of aircraft reaching us in ever-increasing quantities from the other side of the Atlantic include a bomber craft, the "Boston II.", and three fighter planes, the "Martlet I.", the "Tomahawk," and the Brewster "Buffalo." All these aeroplanes have high reputations in the country of their manufacture, and although, for obvious reasons, details of these craft cannot be made public, there can be no doubt as to their invaluable worth to the R.A.F.

The founders of the "Eagle" Squadron were United States pilots, all of them volunteers in the fight against Germany. Some joined up with the Air Force of France before that country met with overwhelming disaster, others fought in the great air battle over this country during the summer of 1940.

CAPE MATAPAN: ITALY'S FINALE AS A GREAT NAVAL POWER.

THE NAVAL VICTORY OF CAPE MATAPAN, ON MARCH 23. H.M. DESTROYER "HASTY" LAYING A SMOKE-SCREEN AS SHE STEAMS AT HER FULL SPEED OF 36 KNOTS, WHILE ENEMY SHELLS MAKE NEAR MISSES.

H.M.S. "VALIANT" FIRING A BROADSIDE FROM HER 15-INCH GUNS. IN THE BACKGROUND IS H.M.S. "BARHAM." THESE TWO SHIPS WITH THE FLAGSHIP WIPED OUT THREE ITALIAN CRUISERS.

NIGHT BATTLE SCENE. THE GUNS OF A BRITISH CRUISER FIRING STAR SHELLS IN AN ATTEMPT TO LOCATE THE ENEMY. THE VICTORY OF ADMIRAL CUNNINGHAM'S FLEET WAS WON IN THE DARKNESS.

Out of the first laconic statements issued by the Admiralty on Saturday, March 29, has now emerged a story of the sea seldom equalled in the annals of British naval history. In its briefest form the epic story begins on Thursday, March 27, when British aircraft reported an Italian naval force steaming eastwards from Sicily. Some time after mid-day on March 27 Admiral Sir Andrew Cunningham left Alexandria with the flagship "Warspite" and the battleships "Barham," "Valiant," and the aircraft-carrier "Formidable." Early on the following day Vice-Admiral Pridham-Wippell, commanding a cruiser force in H.M.S. "Orion" established contact with the Italians at 8 a.m., and, as he turned his squadron south-eastward to draw the Italians towards the British battleships, came under the fire of the 15-in. guns of a "Littorio" class battleship. While units of the Greek Navy took up strategic positions to the northward "Orion" immediately sent a message to Sir Andrew Cunningham, then 120 miles away eastward with the main British Fleet, including the battleships "Barham" and "Valiant," as well as the "Warspite." Then, while this powerful force was steaming full speed ahead towards the enemy, the "Orion" proceeded to act as a decoy. "The firing of the Italian battleship was exceptionally good," said Vice-Admiral Pridham-Wippell, "but we, like all the other British ships engaged in the action, escaped without chipping our paint." About noon the Italian battleship was for the first time attacked by aerial torpedoes delivered by aircraft from the "Formidable." Damaged at the outset, she decided to make for port. Steaming westward, she was repeatedly attacked by waves of bombers.

In the afternoon of the same day R.A.F. "Blenheim" bombers also attacked the enemy cruisers "Zara," "Pola" and "Fiume." Day faded to dusk, dusk to night, and at 10 p.m., as the enemy cruisers passed ahead of our destroyer screen, the "Greyhound's" searchlight illuminated the leading ship, which was hit a few seconds later by a broadside from the "Warspite." This was a crushing victory for the Royal Navy, ending with the destruction of the three Italian cruisers, and at least two, and possibly four enemy destroyers, as well as the partial disablement of the battleship.

Admiral Cunningham, said later: "This latest sortie of the Italian Fleet undoubtedly came about through German instigation."

GERMANY'S HAMMER BLOW IN THE BALKANS: YUGOSLAVIA.

YUGOSLAVIA'S PREMIER, GENERAL DUSAN SIMOVITCH, WHO WAS DEPUTED BY KING PETER TO FORM A GOVERNMENT TO MAINTAIN THE INDEPENDENCE OF THE COUNTRY.

THE YUGOSLAV QUISLING: DR. ANTE PAVELITCH, REPUTED CHIEF OF THE CROATIAN USTACHI (A TERRORIST ORGANISATION), WHO IS TO HEAD A NEW "INDEPENDENT" CROAT STATE.

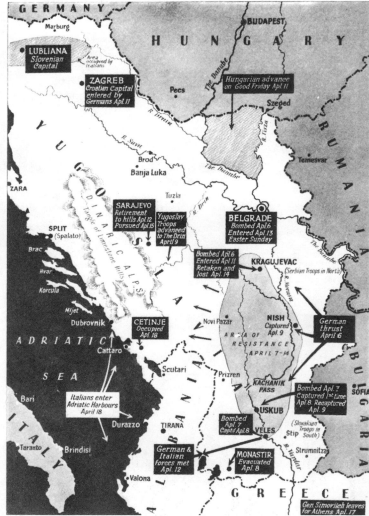

THIS SPECIALLY COMPILED MAP SHOWS WHERE THE MAIN MILITARY RESISTANCE OF THE YUGOSLAV ARMY TOOK PLACE.

After the coup of March 27 came the problem of marshalling the country's armed forces. This was hindered by the Croat demand for a settlement of its autonomy status which occupied several valuable days and was only settled on April 3, Dr. Matche occupying the position of Vice-Premier. Germany vastly chagrined at the nullification of her hopes of a peaceful entry into Yugoslavia, demanded ratification of the pact. General Simovitch answered in terms which were an evident play for time. He had the problem before him of disposing the military forces of the country at strategic positions: no general plan of defence had been discussed with the Allies and the Army was in many ways unprepared for its immediate task though its small but efficient air force appears to have been in a state of readiness for combat. A general exodus of German citizens took place in the next two or three days, Belgrade especially being denuded of these unwelcome guests. After Germany had declared war at 5 a.m. on both Yugoslavia and Greece on the morning of April 6, at 7 a.m. an air attack on the Yugoslavian capital began and was continued with a ferocity which gave evidence of the Führer's intense chagrin at the position into which Yugoslavia had forced him. Although the imminence of an attack by Germany must have been clear to its informed citizens, the great bulk of them appeared to have been taken by surprise, and hundreds died in the streets during the first attack.

It was evident, however, that the battle was on. Almost simultaneous thrusts were made at six points on the eastern frontier of Yugoslavia. At its south-eastern extremity German mechanised forces broke through by way of the Strumitza Valley into the southern tip of Serbia and thence by way of Lake Dorian to Salonika. Further north other forces pushed forward towards Uskub; still further north towards Nish, and to a certain extent towards Kragujevac.

On April 8, Monastir was evacuated by its force of military police, and German forces captured, for the first time, Uskub and Veles. In the meantime the small Yugoslavian air force had made a brilliant onslaught on the German bombers who were attacking Belgrade and while they lasted took a gratifyingly large toll of the enemy bombers.

CLIMAX IN THE BALKANS: THE BATTLE OF GREECE.

A GERMAN TANK ADVANCES ON LARISSA.

"Greece will defend her territory and integrity" was the dignified answer of Prime Minister Alexander Korizis when the brutal notification was made to him at his private residence in Athens at 5.30 a.m. on April 6 by the German Minister of Germany's infamous attack.

On the same day motorised German forces swept in from Bulgaria, by way of the Strumitsa and Vardar Rivers which, by the withdrawal of the Yugoslavs, had left open the road into Greece by Dioran, necessitating a Greek retreat. The Greeks in Macedonia offered heroic resistance, but without sufficient heavy guns had to retreat, leaving the road open to Salonika, which was, however, fully evacuated and all equipment removed. It was occupied on April 9. The Greeks in the Rupel Pass held out valiantly for nearly a week, and the Army retreated to prepared positions with the British Imperial Forces under Lieut.-Gen. Sir Henry Maitland Wilson. By April 20, west of the Pindus the enemy was sweeping down to the Gulf of Corinth by the road through Arta, and Greek resistance was to all intents and purposes at an end. On April 21, in fact, the Greek Government issued the already famous and generous message advising the withdrawal of our forces. This message represented the sentiments of the nation as well as those of its Government. There were no reproaches from this wonderful people.

GERMAN TANKS IN TYPICAL GREEK SCENERY.

THE WAR IN GREECE: A MAP SHOWING THE SUCCESSIVE LINES OF STRATEGIC RETREAT OF THE IMPERIAL FORCES, AS NECESSITATED BY THE COLLAPSE OF YUGOSLAVIA AND THE SUBSEQUENT DESTRUCTION OF THE HEROIC GREEK ARMIES.

THE PASS OF EPIC AND IMMORTAL FIGHTS: THERMOPYLÆ TO-DAY, WHERE FOR FIVE DAYS ANZACS AND BRITISH FORCES FACED THE GERMAN MASSES, INFLICTED ENORMOUS LOSSES, AND RETREATED UNDAUNTED – RECALLING THE HEROIC RESISTANCE OF THE GREEKS TO XERXES IN B.C. 480.

Our picture shows the "Kolonos" mound in honour of the great Spartan General who in B.C. 480, at the head of his 300 Spartans, 700 Thespians, and 400 Thebans, died with his entire force sooner than surrender. Except for the difference in arms and equipment, the stand made by Leonidas and his brave Greeks against the oncoming hordes of the Persian tyrant and dictator of that age, Xerxes, is recalled by the undaunted and fearless stand of the Anzacs and British forces, who for five days, though compelled to retreat slowly, held the pass and inflicted the most sanguinary losses on the Germans, and fought for exactly the same cause as Leonidas – for freedom from oppression. The Pass itself today is more difficult to defend than in Leonidas's day, for whereas it was then a defile of 165 ft between the precipice and the sea, there now extends a flat and partly marshy plain from one and a half to three miles broad.

THE EPIC EVACUATION FROM GREECE: THE VALIANT BRITISH RETREAT.

"SUNDERLAND" FLYING-BOATS PLAYED A BIG PART IN THE EVA-
CUATION: THE R.A.F. AND THE FLEET AIR ARM SHOWED SUPERB
COOLNESS UNDER INCESSANT BOMBING ATTACKS WHILST RES-
CUING THE TROOPS.

AU REVOIR, BUT NOT GOOD-BYE! A CROWDED TRANSPORT MOV-
ING OFF FROM ANCHORAGE. IN THE EVACUATION OF OVER 45,000
MEN ONLY TWO DESTROYERS AND ONE TROOPCARRYING
TRANSPORT WERE LOST.

WINGED INVADERS OF CRETE: THE FIRST MAJOR ATTACK BY AIR-BORNE TROOPS.

LANDING AIR TROOPS: GERMAN GLIDERS OF THE BATTLE OF CRETE.

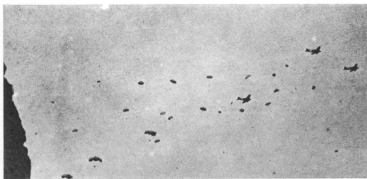

GERMAN PARATROOPS DESCENDING NEAR CANDIA. THE PARACHUTES IN CLUSTERS ARE CARRYING
HEAVY ARTICLES, SUCH AS FIELD GUNS AND SMALL MOTOR-VEHICLES.

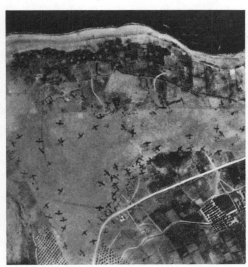

MAX SCHMELING, REPORTED
KILLED, IN PARACHUTIST KIT,
ABOUT TO JUMP FROM A GER-
MAN TROOP-CARRIER

THE CAPTURE OF MALEME AIRFIELD BY MASSED DIVE-BOMBING
AND THE LANDING OF HUNDREDS OF NAZI "JU-52'S" TOWING
GLIDERS: THE FIRST ACTUAL PHOTOGRAPHS OF ENEMY AIR-
CRAFT, MANY BEING ENTIRELY WRECKED.

Max Schmeling, the former German heavyweight boxing cham-
pion, was captured by New Zealand troops in Crete and shot
dead trying to escape.

Air-borne invasion of Crete according to the latest German methods began suddenly, but not unexpectedly, at dawn on Tuesday, May 20. Just before sunrise huge airplanes crossed the 200 miles of sea from Greece and certain Greek islands and unloaded invaders, bringing with them small arms and tommy-guns. All day, at the parts selected by the enemy as principal objectives, "Strukas" first bombed and machine-gunned the area, especially seeking out anti-aircraft defences. Their main target was the airfield of Maleme, about ten miles south-west of Canea, the capital, in the west of the rocky island, but other determined attacks were made on the aerodrome of Heraklion, near Candia, and Retimo, lying half-way between Canea and Candia. Everywhere they were immediately attacked by British, New Zealand, and Greek troops, and on the 21st the Cairo official communiqué reported that "the enemy sustained heavy losses while ours were slight," although the Germans had absolute command of the air. By nightfall on May 20 about 3000 air-borne troops were landed by parachute or gliders round Suda Bay alone, and on the following day, General Freyberg, V.C., Commander-in-Chief Crete, reported that 1800 had been killed or wounded. With few flat spaces for landing, they came down on rugged uplands or undulating olive groves, many being dead before touching earth. Others, dumped by flying-boats, swam or waded ashore and were picked off by our men with tommy-guns. Many baled out in sparsely populated mountains or floated down in gliders to stall on the first flat ground. The battle was scattered over a wide area, in pockets of furiously fighting men, giving and taking no quarter, and with others sniping from olive groves, from behind rocks, or from houses they seized and from which they were blasted out. Paratroops on landing took some ten minutes to recover breath and be quit of their trappings, when Allied marksmen found them easy meat. Over 250 German aircraft were reported destroyed on the beaches and airfields by May 25 and others later added to the total.

Crete is the only battlefield where Hitler could attack with the certainty that his air power could not be challenged. The attack which opened on May 20 was the most hazardous stroke Hitler has attempted, for apart from British defences, Crete is not an island which lends itself easily to the dropping of paratroops. How many men succeeded in landing amid the precipitous mountains, or in the Hades-like ravines, deep in snow, which scarcely see daylight, only time will prove, but many corpses have been found. Maleme Airfield was the main focus of the German air invasion of Crete from May 20, when hordes of enemy divebombers, followed by parachute-carrying aircraft, and then by "Ju-52's" hauling gliders, first began the battle in which the British and Greeks, without adequate air and anti-aircraft support, were finally defeated. On May 28 Cairo estimated that the Nazis had used 1200 "Junkers 52's" to carry troops to the island, and that they were landing at the rate of one per minute. On May 30 the enemy, regardless of their very heavy losses, were putting down troop-carriers as thick and fast as ever at Maleme, the whole campaign being canalised at this airfield. Thousands of troops were landed, mainly by troop-carriers. A Cairo high R.A.F. officer on June 1 put the German losses of aircraft at hundreds, with a high percentage of troop-carriers.

"Crete was won not by the parachute troops but by the bomber, in the absence of air opposition." This asseveration, by the air correspondent of the "Sunday Times," – finds its consoling counterpart in the magnificent achievements of the Royal Navy in decisively smashing every attempt at a corresponding Nazi invasion of the island by sea. The units of the Mediterranean Fleet were given the order by the Commander-in-Chief, Admiral Sir Andrew Cunningham, that "there must be no sea-borne invasion of Crete," and three separate attempts – one at night – to convey fully-armed troops from the mainland and neighbouring islands to the shores of Crete were decisively smashed.

THE PRO-AXIS UPRISING IN IRAQ: THE OIL THAT HITLER COVETS.

THE INFANT KING FEISAL II OF IRAQ, AGED SIX, WITH HIS UNCLE, THE REGENT EMIR ABDUL ILAH.

RASCHID ALI GAILANI, A FORMER PREMIER AND PRO-AXIS POLITICIAN, WHO SEIZED POWER ON APRIL 3.

BRITONS SLEEPING ON THE ROOF OF THE BRITISH EMBASSY, WHERE THEY TOOK REFUGE AFTER THE EVACUATION OF WOMEN AND CHILDREN.

STALWART WARRIORS OF THE ARAB LEGION, WHICH, UNDER ITS FAMOUS COMMANDER, MAJOR GLUBB, HELPED TO QUELL THE IRAQI REVOLT.

That trouble was brewing in Iraq, with which state a 25-years' treaty exists, dating from 1932, was first realised by the seizure of power by Raschid Ali, a pro-Nazi politician, on April 2, who drove out the Regent, Emir Abdul Ilah. On April 6, Raschid declared that Iraq would adhere to the Anglo-Iraqi treaty, and on April 21 British troops arrived at Basra; but when more British troops arrived Raschid, a puppet of the Axis, then showed his hand by massing troops and artillery to threaten Habbaniyeh, the important R.A.F. aerodrome and British base, and after being "requested" to withdraw, on May 2, they suddenly opened fire on the cantonment. At once British forces responded. The Iraqi Air Force lost more than half their 'planes, but at the time of writing appears to hold positions threatening the oil-pipe line from Mosul to Haifa, at Ruta.

On May 4 Sayid Raschid Ali announced that he had suspended work on the British-owned Iraq Petroleum Company's concession. The flow of oil through the pipe-line to Haifa, it was claimed, had been stopped, but "certain refineries," the despatch added, "would continue to work for the benefit of the Iraqi Army." The Iraq oilfield, which is mainly a new one developed since the last war, at present produces about 4,500,000 tons a year. The oil, which is only partially treated at Kirkuk, reaches the Mediterranean by two pipe-lines. That passing through Syria has been cut off since the fall of France; the other, passing through Transjordan, reaches the sea at Haifa, Palestine. Hitler wants that oil, so for the present he does not want to do any considerable damage to any of the plant.

THE HOUSE OF COMMONS, WESTMINSTER ABBEY, HALL AND SCHOOL BOMBED.

THE BOMB-SCARRED FACE OF BIG BEN, 300 FT. ABOVE THE GROUND. BUT THE CLOCK IS STILL CHIMING THE HOURS.

WESTMINSTER ABBEY'S BOMBED ALTAR – NAZI SACRILEGE AT THE HEART OF THE ENGLISH-SPEAKING WORLD.

MR. CHURCHILL SURVEYS THE MOTHER OF PARLIAMENTS, BOMBED ON MAY 10. ON THE RIGHT IS LORD REITH.

Nothing has stirred the civilised world more greatly to anger than the deliberate and wanton attempts to destroy Westminster Abbey. The damage to the venerable Church, built by Edward the Confessor (1042–1066), is, happily, not irreparable, for though the fire destroyed the Lantern, leaving the fabric open to the sky, the edifice is structurally safe, although beneath the Lantern, where English sovereigns have been crowned since Edward the Confessor's time, was a mass of rubble and timber. Irreparable, however, is the loss of the Deanery, in Dean's Yard, with irreplaceable records, its library of thousands of books, and furniture. Westminster Hall's roof has been partially destroyed. The Chamber in which the Commons have met for 89 years was another victim of the fierce German attack.

THE 35,000-TON "BISMARCK," SUNK ON MAY 27 BY AVENGING BRITISH UNITS.

THE PICTURE THAT LED TO THE SINKING OF THE "BISMARCK."

THE "BISMARCK," ARMED WITH EIGHT 15-IN. AND TWELVE 5.9-IN. GUNS, WHICH CARRIED FOUR AEROPLANES, AND WAS CLAIMED BY THE NAZIS TO BE "UNSINKABLE" OWING TO A "HONEYCOMB" OF WATERTIGHT COMPARTMENTS.

THE LAST PICTURE OF H.M.S. "HOOD", IN ACTION AGAINST THE "BISMARCK".

"At the moment when the 'Bismarck' was known to be at sea, the whole apparatus of our Ocean control came into play," said the Prime Minister when describing the fate of the crack German battleship. For 1750 miles the hunted battleship was relentlessly shadowed. From three widely separated points squadrons converged to bring their quarry to the kill. At dawn on the 24th, the battleships H.M.S. "Prince of Wales" and "Hood" intercepted the enemy vessels, and in the ensuing action "Hood" was sunk at about 23,000 yards by a shell which penetrated into one of her magazines, the "Prince of Wales" also sustaining slight damage. The "Bismarck" had also been damaged and on Monday, the 26th, torpedo bombers of the Fleet Air Arm scored a hit, while reconnaissance machines were reporting her movements. On Tuesday, the 27th, visibility was poor, but a "Catalina" flying-boat picked up her position as she went south-west, making for the French coast and leaving a trail of oil. Reconnaissances revealed that the "Bismarck's" speed was greatly reduced and that her steering gear was out of action. Admiral Tovey, on May 27, in poor visibility, engaged the enemy ship and silenced her guns with the main armament of the battleships "King George V." and "Rodney". Then the lean, long cruiser "Dorsetshire" (9975 tons) launched her torpedoes and four minutes later the "Bismarck," with her crew of about 2400, turned over, exposed her keel, cracked in two and sank.

GERMANY'S INFILTRATION TO DAKAR: ITS MENACE TO AMERICA.

THE GROWING MENACE TO THE AMERICAS OF DAKAR, CAPE VERDE ISLANDS, AND THE AZORES EMPHASISED BY PRESIDENT ROOSEVELT IN HIS BROADCAST ON MAY 28.

NAZI PREPARATIONS FOR THE INVASION OF THE AMERICAN CONTINENT: NATIVES CONSTRUCTING A RAILWAY LINE FROM THE MEDITERRANEAN TO DAKAR.

On Tuesday night, May 27, the long-expected broadcast by President Roosevelt reverberated throughout the world, including enemy countries. So intense was the interest taken in the United States that the theatres and cinemas were half-empty owing to people listening in at their homes. The "fireside chat" – which Mr. Malcolm MacDonald, High Commissioner in Canada, quipped later as a "broadside chat" – brought the nation face to face with the necessity of beating Hitlerism, which threatened the security of all America, if Britain were defeated, and met with almost universal support throughout the great Republic. The masses of the U.S.A. hailed its unequivocal determination to uphold the American doctrine of the freedom of the seas with relief and joy. The American Press generally agreed that Mr. Roosevelt spoke for the nation. Throughout the Empire it was welcomed as America's decisive intention to fight.

In his stirring call to the Americas on May 28, President Roosevelt said: "They [Nazis] also have the armed power at any moment to occupy Spain and Portugal, and that threat extends not only to French West Africa but also to the Atlantic fortress of Dakar and to the island outposts of the New World – the Azores and the Cape Verde Islands."
The description of the picture shown above, which has reached us from an American source, states that it shows native block-workers working on the "Trans-Saharan railway now being built by German firms under the nominal direction of a penniless France to span the 1500 miles of desert from the Mediterranean to Dakar." Dakar is only 1900 miles, or eight flying hours, from Brazil, and the line is doubtless intended to carry men and war material for an invasion of the west.

RADIOLOCATION, BRITAIN'S SECRET WEAPON TO BEAT THE NIGHT-BOMBER.

IN A SUBTERRANEAN OPERATIONS ROOM OF FIGHTER COMMAND, SENIOR OFFICERS IN THE GALLERY WATCH INTENTLY THE MOVEMENTS OF AIRCRAFT.

The dramatic use by Britain since the outbreak of war of a device for detecting enemy aircraft, known as radiolocation, "the best-kept secret of the war," was revealed for the first time on June 17 by Mr. Attlee in Parliament, by Lord Beaverbrook broadcasting to North America for more knowledgeable workers, and by the R.A.F. officer who has been in charge of the device for the past eighteen months, Air Chief-Marshal Sir Philip Joubert de la Ferté. The invention, the conception of a Scots scientist, Mr. R. A. Watson Watt, originated with experiments conducted in March 1935 near Daventry. The needs in radiolocator personnel of the three Services in the immediate future are now estimated at a total of some 27,000 effectives. "There's nothing picturesque about me," the inventor said in an interview. "I'm just an ordinary scientist and there are no frills to speak of." He was Meteorologist-in-Charge at the Royal Aircraft Establishment, 1917-21; Superintendent, Radio Department, National Physical Laboratory, 1933-36; and Director of Communications Development, 1938-40.

MR. R. A. WATSON WATT, C.B., F.R.S., M.I.E.E., SCIENTIFIC ADVISER ON TELECOMMUNICATIONS TO THE AIR STAFF SINCE 1940.

Air Chief-Marshal Sir Philip Joubert described radiolocation as Britain's secret weapon against the German bomber. "It is a system," said Sir Philip, "whereby rays which are unaffected by fog or darkness are sent out far beyond the limits of our shores. Any aircraft or ship in the path of this ray immediately reflects back a signal to the detecting station, where people are on watch." At headquarters the radiolocator's message, and those of the Royal Observer Corps, are communicated instantly to R.A.F. Operations Rooms, where they are plotted on large table-maps.

THE FIRST U.S. SHIP TORPEDOED BY GERMANY: ODYSSEY OF THE "ROBIN MOOR'S" SURVIVORS.

ONE OF THE FOUR LIFEBOATS – THREE REACHED CAPE TOWN, AND THE OTHER A BRAZILIAN PORT – WHEN THE "ROBIN MOOR" DISAPPEARED. IN THE TURNED-DOWN HAT IS CAPTAIN E. W. MYERS.

The "Robin Moor," the first United States ship to be torpedoed by the Nazis, was stopped in mid-Atlantic on May 31, while on a voyage to Lorenço Marques, Portuguese East Africa. The commander of the German submarine disregarded the master's protests that his freighter was chartered to a neutral port and was unarmed, and gave the passengers and crew half an hour to leave the ship. He refused to take the ship to a neutral port, but promised to wireless their position. In Washington, news of the deliberate sinking of the "Robin Moor," and the leaving of her passengers and crew to the mercy of the seas, created a tense situation, and largely determined the President's later action to guard the ocean lanes with U.S. warships. A strong protest was made to Germany, accused of violation of the London Naval Treaty she had solemnly subscribed to. On June 16, on the seventeenth day after the U.S. 6887-ton freighter "Robin Moor" had been torpedoed by a German submarine in mid-Atlantic, 28 members of the missing crew and 7 passengers were landed in a British ship, which had rescued them. They had been in three open boats for 13 days, followed by sharks, and lived on tack and such drinking-water as they could collect in their sails when it rained. The passengers included two elderly Britons, two American-born women, and a little American boy of two.

HITLER'S DEPUTY AND "DEAREST FRIEND" ESCAPES TO BRITAIN.

A RARE PICTURE SHOWING HESS (SECOND FROM RIGHT) IN PRISON WITH HITLER (LEFT) AT LANSBERG, AFTER THE NAZI PUTSCH FAILURE AT MUNICH IN 1923.

As we go to press the announcement is made by the B.B.C. that doctors have found Herr Rudolph Hess "fit and sane," and that he has been removed to an unknown destination from the hospital in Glasgow where he had been receiving treatment for an injury to his foot sustained on landing by parachute on May 10 from the Messerschmitt "Me. 110" fighter in which he had made his sensational escape from Germany. The first news of one of the most remarkable incidents of the war was given at midnight on May 12 when a statement was issued from No. 10 Downing Street, revealing that "Rudolf Hess, the Deputy Führer of Germany and party leader of the National Socialist party, has landed in Scotland." The first news that Hitler's "dearest friend," and named by him at the time of the attack on Poland as his successor after Goering, had fled from Germany was broadcast a few hours before the British statement by Nazi radio stations, which declared that he had "either jumped out of his 'plane or has met with an accident" after being "strictly forbidden to embark on any further flying activity as he was suffering from an illness of some years' standing." A Scottish ploughman named David McLean saw Hess land with his parachute and found him lying injured in a field. "He smiled," McLean later told a reporter, and as I assisted him to his feet he thanked me in perfect English".

THE SYRIAN CAMPAIGN: PURGING SYRIA OF VICHY INFLUENCE.

THE CREW OF A BREN-GUN CARRIER HASTILY ALIGHTING ON ARRIVAL AT PALMYRA, SYRIA – SHOWING RUINS OF THE OLD ROMAN COLONNADE.

AUSTRALIAN TROOPS ADVANCING IN SINGLE FILE ALONG A PRECIPITOUS MOUNTAIN PATH TO SEIZE A TACTICAL POSITION, AFTER A RECONNAISSANCE.

CAVALRY IN SYRIA HAVE PLAYED A VERY IMPORTANT PART AS A RECONNAISSANCE FORCE OWING TO THE ROCKY TERRAIN: A PATROL ALONG THE RIVER LITANI.

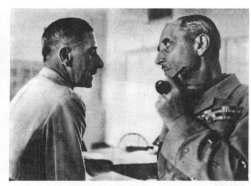

GENERAL CATROUX (RIGHT), THE FREE FRENCH PLENIPOTENTI-ARY, TALKING TO GENERAL DE VERDILLAC, WHO SIGNED THE SYRIAN ARMISTICE ON BEHALF OF THE VICHY FORCES.

CIRCASSIAN NATIVE CAVALRY COMMANDED BY COLONEL COL-LET, WHO LED THE FREE FRENCH VANGUARD INTO SYRIA ON JUNE 8.

For some considerable time the steady penetration of Syria by German aeroplanes and so-called "tourists" caused considerable anxiety in Allied circles. This was relieved when at 2 a.m. on Sunday, June 8, Allied forces under General Sir Henry Maitland Wilson crossed into Syria from four directions, composed of British, Australian, Indian, and Free French troops, the last under the command of General Catroux, who proclaimed the independence of Syria. Marshal Pétain terming it "this unjustifiable aggression," ordered all Frenchmen and Syrians to fight. The R.A.F. have recently bombed the Syrian airfields at Damascus, Aleppo, Palmyra and Rayak.
In a proclamation issued by General Catroux on the eve of the Allied advance into Syria, the head of the Free French in the Middle East called upon *La France au Levant* and the inhabitants of Syria and the Lebanon to rally to the Free French cause. General Catroux promised three million Arab and Lebanese inhabitants of Syria their liberty and independence, also guaranteed on behalf of the British Government by Sir Miles Lampson, British Ambassador in Cairo. As the British and Free French forces, under the command of General Sir Henry Maitland Wilson, crossed the Palestine border squadrons of R.A.F. and Free

French aircraft scattered leaflets over the green valleys of the Lebanon and the desert oases appealing to the French garrison to join the British and Free French in driving the Germans from the Levant.
Partly owing to the desire of the Allies not to regard the advance into Syria as any attempt to wage war with the French unless they resisted, and partly to the considerable difficulties of the terrain, along which the French authorities had built very strong defences, the movement of the British and Allied Forces has been more slow than would have been otherwise the case. Gradually the French fell back, although in places severe fighting took place. On June 12, Merj Uyum, the key strong-point of the Damascus defences, was captured and on the 15th, Sidon, strongly defended, after bombardment by units of the Fleet and bitter hand-to-hand conflict in the streets, with a threat to its flank, also fell, while the coastal advance on Beirut, General Dentz's headquarters, was nearing this important city and port. Marshal Pétain's Government was told by the British Government plainly that the Allies based their action on the facts of the case and not on theoretical considerations, and that the "responsibility for consequences must rest with Marshal Pétain's Government."

FROM "ENTENTE CORDIALE" TO THE FRENCH TRAGEDY OF TO-DAY.

PROOF OF COLLABORATION: THE TAIL OF A GERMAN AIRCRAFT, WITH VICHY MARKINGS PAINTED OVER THE SWASTIKA.

ALLIES PLEDGE THAT NONE WILL CONCLUDE A SEPARATE PEACE.

THE HISTORIC GATHERING OF ALLIED STATESMEN AT ST. JAMES'S PALACE ON JUNE 12, BEING ADDRESSED BY MR. CHURCHILL.

The Prime Minister in a trenchant denunciation of the dictators and their works, pledged the Governments concerned, the Dominions, and Colonies to fight till victory. This historic gathering, the first of such breadth and importance ever held, was also addressed by General Sikorski (Poland), M. Lie (Norway), Dr. Gerbrandy (Netherlands), M.

Pierlot (Belgium), M. Dupong (Luxembourg), Professor Cassin (Free French), M. Masaryk (Czechoslovakia), M. Simopoulos (Greece), M. Soubbotitch (Yugoslavia), and Mr. Eden, all of whom expressed the determination to fight for final victory and to co-operate to the fullest degree in economic and social security after the war.

PIERRE LAVAL, THE JUDAS OF TWENTIETH-CENTURY FRANCE, AND FERNAND DE BRINON, "FRENCH AMBASSADOR IN PARIS!"

Our picture shows two of those who, pretending to represent France, in actual fact are spokesmen for the *soi-disant* Vichy Government. The perfidies of Laval are too well known but it is interesting to recall that as far back as 1933, Fernand de Brinon was claiming notoriety as the first French journalist to be received by Hitler.

"THE GREATEST 'DOUBLE-CROSS' IN HISTORY": HITLER INVADES RUSSIA IN CONTEMPT OF A NON-AGGRESSION PACT OF FRIENDSHIP.

CHIEF ENEMIES OF DEMOCRACY: GOERING, KEITEL, HIMMLER AND HITLER, NOW TURNING TO NON-AGGRESSIVE RUSSIA.

A PHOTOGRAPH FROM THE "BERLINER ILLUSTRIERTE ZEITUNG," THE CAPTION BENEATH WHICH READS: "IN THE GREY DAWN OF THE 22ND JUNE, 1941, BEHIND A FENCE AT THE FRONTIER. WAITING THE ORDER TO ATTACK."

PANZER UNITS PASSING THROUGH A RUSSIAN VILLAGE SET ALIGHT BY THE INHABITANTS BEFORE THEY EVACUATED.

ONE OF THE RUSSIAN TANKS WHICH HAVE SURPRISED THE WORLD AND SHOCKED THE GERMANS.

THE RUSSIAN BATTLEFIELD AFTER A FORTNIGHT OF GERMAN ONSLAUGHT.

"RUSSIAN AIRMEN BOMBED THE FINNISH TOWN": A PICTURE SENT TO AMERICA.

German troops began their attack on Russia in the early hours of June 22. Without hesitation, the armed forces of the U.S.S.R. confronted the invader, and the Red Army, Navy and Air Forces are now locked in combat with the Nazi hordes. On the evening of June 22 Mr. Winston Churchill, in a nation-wide broadcast, stated Great Britain's intention to give every possible support to Russia, and now, as another drama of Germany's perfidy unfolds itself, the world tensely awaits the next developments in the struggle. For years past information concerning the strength of Russia's fighting forces has been scant; little exact knowledge has passed beyond the boundaries of the U.S.S.R., and the field for speculation is wide. It appears, however, that the leaders of the country have by no means neglected those forms of modern warfare which so largely cancel out the value of mere man power: tanks, submarines, aeroplanes and highly-trained paratroops. The Russians were pioneers in the use of paratroops and mass displays were given by Soviet parachutists long before other countries began to develop this form of aerial attack. It is not surprising, therefore, that soon after the Nazi invasion of the U.S.S.R. Soviet troop-carrying aeroplanes were reported at forty different points over German and German-occupied territory. Russia, according to report, has 150 divisions ready and mobilised, 9000 'planes, some 10,000 tanks, and quite a considerable force of cavalry; but perhaps not the least of Russia's weapons lies in her possession of 1,800,000 acres of marshland. As we write, 5000 Nazis are reported captured and 300 enemy tanks destroyed. Russia's first war communiqué, broadcast from Moscow on June 23, stated: "With the dawn of June 22 enemy regular troops attacked our frontier from the Baltic to the Black Sea . . . In the second half of the day the enemy met the first units of our Regular Army, and was repulsed, after violent fighting, with heavy losses . . . Enemy aircraft attacked a number of our aerodromes and localities. They were met by decisive action everywhere . . . " So much for the opening phase of Russia's death struggle with the Nazi hordes.

The sudden and unprovoked attack on Russia by Germany may have been guided by many considerations, but foremost among them is admittedly Hitler's dire necessity to obtain essential supplies on an adequate scale to enable him to attempt to overthrow the concerted preparations of Great Britain and the United States. Primarily his urgent need is oil, although cotton, wheat and other requirements are of first importance, and these were not likely to be forthcoming unless he could smash the Soviet war machine.

BRITAIN AND RUSSIA ALLIED: MOLOTOV SIGNING THE AGREEMENT: STALIN, BEHIND, WITH SIR STAFFORD CRIPPS, CENTRE.

This official picture shows the signing, on July 12 of the Pact of Mutual Assistance between the Governments of the U.S.S.R. and Great Britain in the war against Germany. M. Molotov, Commissar for Foreign Affairs, is shown in the act of signing the agreement on behalf of the Soviet Government, with Stalin standing behind; while Britain's Ambassador to Russia, Sir Stafford Cripps, is on his right. Under the agreement, both Russia and Great Britain undertook that during the war they would neither negotiate nor conclude an armistice or treaty of peace "except by mutual agreement."

VICHY SURRENDERS INDO-CHINA: SAIGON OCCUPIED BY JAPAN ON JULY 27. FORCES DEFENDING AGAINST JAPANESE "CHESS-MOVES" IN THE PACIFIC.

On July 23, under the combined pressure of Germany and Japan, Vichy surrendered to Japan's demands for the grant of bases in Indo-China, required for operations against China and as a potential threat to American, British and Dutch possessions in the Pacific. The most vital bases are those in the south, particularly the important naval base of Camranh Bay, from where attacks could be launched against British territories. Meanwhile a Japanese fleet consisting of seven major warships, three aircraft-carriers, and fifty-five destroyers was reported moving southwards, accompanying thirty Japanese transports. In America the U.S. Navy Secretary said that there was no question that if the Japanese proceeded according to present plans, there would be some action, and that the American Fleet was ready.

On July 28 large numbers of Japanese troops disembarked near Camranh Bay. On July 31 Japanese transports escorted by cruisers entered Saigon Harbour in the south and disembarked troops, in which area the Japanese had completely taken over the military and civil administration. Over 200 bombers and fighters also flew from Hainan Island. In the forced occupation of Indo-China, Japan is in a position to strike north at China, through the Burma Road, west at Burma, through the Shan States at Mandalay, where oil is produced of which Japan is admittedly very short, and south at Singapore, the great British base, either through Thailand or by sea. The aerial position of Japan in seizing Indo-China's airfields threatens all adjoining lands.

This abject capitulation of the Vichy Government, which has enabled Japan to occupy the harbours and airfields of French Indo-China immediately opened up hostilities by land and sea between Britain, Holland and the United States.

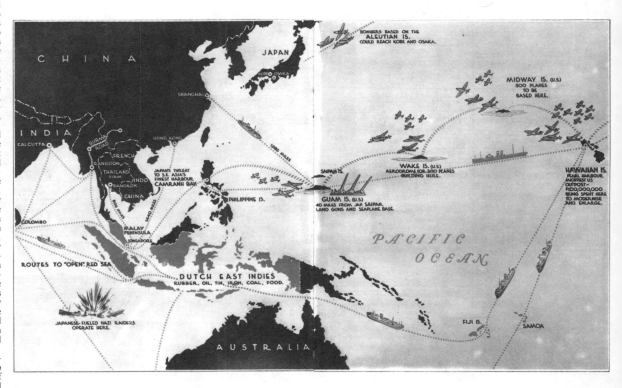

THE AIR AND SEA "LANES" IN THE PACIFIC, US FORTIFIED ISLANDS AND THEIR LINK-UP WITH BRITAIN'S DEFENCES AT SINGAPORE AND THE MALAY STRAITS.

THE DUTCH EAST INDIES FLEET AT WAR PRACTISE OFF JAVA, IN CO-OPERATION WITH THE ISLAND AIR FORCE.

MEMBERS OF THE A.I.F. ON THEIR ARRIVAL AT SINGAPORE STRAITS SETTLEMENTS. MR. HUGHES, AUSTRALIAN NAVY MINISTER, DECLARED ON AUGUST 7 THAT PEACE OR WAR DEPENDED ON JAPAN.

On July 26 Great Britain and America "froze" Japanese assets, and on August 1 the United States banned the shipment of oil to Japan. The suspension of foreign trade transactions between the Netherlands East Indies and Japan and the suspension of the oil agreement between the two countries was announced on July 29. The Dutch Navy is, of course, dispersed, but there is reason to believe that a strong Netherlands naval force based on Sourabaya is co-operating with British and American navies in the Far East. The Royal Navy in the Netherlands Indies includes two light cruisers, one flotilla leader, eight destroyers, fourteen submarines and two gunboats.

The Hong Kong correspondent of "The Times," cabling on August 10, said: "Japan's action in French Indo-China has taken up the last of the slack. The tension, in other words, is so taut now that any move against Thailand, Burma, Singapore, or the Netherlands East Indies is almost certain to result in war in the Pacific." According to the latest estimates, Japan has 50,000 troops in Indo-China, and is moving up in strength to the Thailand border. The Cambodian aerodromes of Pnompenh, Komopongthom, and Siemreap – the last only 250 miles from Bangkok – are in Japanese hands.

Our map is designed to represent the strategic sites in the North Pacific Ocean, stressing especially the American line of naval communications from its base, Pearl Island, Hawaii, to its outlying connections, Wake Island, Guam, to Manilla, Philippine Islands. The strained situation has combined to arouse the worst fears of imminent war, Japan being urged to this policy by the machinations of Germany.

THE TOBRUK GARRISON STILL DEFY ALL ATTEMPTS AT THEIR DISLODGMENT.

THE NEW G.O.C.-IN-C., MIDDLE EAST.

THE HOME GUARD'S FIRST BIRTHDAY: MOUNTING GUARD AT THE PALACE.

HELPING GUNNER OFFICERS TO DO THEIR WORK: THIS RABBIT, ONE OF SEVERAL PETS ADOPTED BY THE TOBRUK GARRISON.

GENERAL SIR CLAUDE AUCHINLECK, G.C.I.E., C.B., C.S.I., D.S.O., A.D.C., WHO ARRIVED IN CAIRO FROM INDIA ON JULY 1 ON EXCHANGING COMMANDS WITH GENERAL WAVELL.

THE KING INSPECTING THE HOME GUARD ON THE FIRST ANNIVERSARY OF THEIR FORMATION.

Life in Tobruk goes on in much the same way from day to day. Our gallant defenders are holding on grimly in the face of repeated attacks by land and air. They are not, however, by any means on the defensive alone; in the last few weeks a series of brilliant raids against enemy positions have been carried out, raids during which the Italians and Germans have suffered severe losses in men and material.

Enunciating the theory that "the enemy must be kept at a distance and attacked wherever he is," General Sir Claude Auchinleck paid a firm tribute to his predecessor in Egypt, General Sir Archibald Wavell. "It will not be fully realised," he added, "until peace is finally restored, what General Wavell and his troops, forsaken by their French allies, have achieved in the past year, and with how little."

The Home Guard, on May 14, the anniversary of their formation, were given the honour of mounting guard at Buckingham Palace, where the King, despite its attentions at the hand of the enemy, remains in residence. Drawn from the 1st County of London (Westminster) Battalion, the men, headed by the band of the Grenadier Guards, marched with the precision of veterans through the gates of the Palace.

IRAN'S SHAH ABDICATES: JOINT BRITISH AND RUSSIAN ACTION.

THE FORMER COSSACK TROOPER WHO ABDICATED ON SEPTEMBER 16: H.I.M. RIZA KHAN PAHLEVI, SHAH SINCE 1926.

THE FAMOUS PEACOCK THRONE, OR *TAKHT-I-TAUS*, IN THE COUNCIL CHAMBER OF THE IMPERIAL PALACE.

THE NEW TWENTY-ONE-YEAR-OLD SHAH OF IRAN – THE FORMER CROWN PRINCE SHAHPOOR MOHAMMED RIZA.

Riza Khan Pahlevi, Shah of Iran, abdicated, ostensibly on the grounds of ill-health, on September 16, after calling the entire Iranian Parliament to the Palace. He is succeeded by his twenty-one-year-old son, Shahpoor Mohammed Riza, who is married to an Egyptian Princess, the beautiful sister of King Farouk.

Starting his career as a Persian Cossack trooper, owing advancement originally to General (now Lord) Ironside, no Oriental ruler has been more pampered by British diplomatists than H.H. Riza Khan, who was elected Shah of Persia in 1925, and has repaid kindness with hostility. A poor country, then the "sick man of Asia," dependent largely upon the big royalties paid by the Anglo-Persian Oil Company, he developed and modernised it, built the trans-Persian railway, schools, roads, an efficient Army, and Europeanised hotels. However, as is now known, for years the Shah has flirted with Germans, allowed their infiltration, until something like 4000 spies, "tourists," and others have occupied vital posts, thus threatening both Britain and Russia, and compelling them to act. On August 25, Russians marched on Tabriz, and the British in three directions, from Basra, Baghdad and Iraq to join the Soviets at Tabriz, and cut off the Nazis.

FAMOUS LONDON BUILDINGS DAMAGED IN RECENT RAIDS.

Further bomb damage to famous London buildings has now been revealed, and many landmarks have succumbed to German ruthlessness. "Nothing else in London," wrote Nathaniel Hawthorne in 1857, after visiting the Temple, "is so like the effect of a spell, as to pass under one of these archways and find yourself transported from the jumble, mob, tumult, uproar, of . . . the present hour, into what seems an eternal Sabbath." His grief would be added to that of countless other lovers of London's ancient haunts of beauty at the havoc wrought by recent Hun air-raid savagery in Inner and Middle Temple, half of which has now been destroyed. The Church of the Knights Templar, the largest and most important of the four remaining Round churches in England, which was consecrated as far back as 1185, is now a charred shell,

THE TEMPLE CHURCH (RIGHT) AND PART OF THE CLOISTERS, AFTER BOMBING.

REMAINS OF ST. MARY-LE-BOW, HOME OF THE FAMOUS BOW BELLS.

and streams of molten lead and sections of steel girders which fell from the roof of the Oblong have burned and pounded into fragments the famous recumbent effigies of thirteenth-century Crusaders. Irreparable damage or disfigurement has likewise been caused by enemy bombs to the quiet Middle Temple Courts; and Crown Office Row, where Charles Lamb was born, has gone altogether.

Further east the church of St. Mary-le-Bow may have to be demolished. This church takes its name from the fact that it was the first church built in England upon arches, or bows, of stone, and Wren rebuilt it at greater cost than most of his others. The famous bells are fortunately safe, having been previously dismantled.

THE G.P.O. CARRIES ON DESPITE HIGH EXPLOSIVE AND FIRE BOMBS.

THIS KIOSK IS NOT WHAT IT WAS BUT IT IS STILL POSSIBLE TO PUT THROUGH A CALL THANKS TO EMERGENCY MEASURES.

WITH THE DESTINATION OF THESE LETTERS RAZED TO THE GROUND, A MEMBER OF THE STAFF COLLECTS THEM.

"THE MAIL MUST GO THROUGH." POSTMEN COLLECTING LETTERS ALMOST BURIED BENEATH MOUNDS OF FALLEN MASONRY.

The telephone wires – the nerve centres of London's commerce – did not escape in the German attempts to set London alight, but such damage as was done was to a large extent negatived by the work of the Post Office engineers. Within a short time improvised telephone services (for the benefit of those whose telephones had been put out of action) were opened at Northgate House, Northgate Street, and Regina House, Cheapside. Meanwhile the collection and delivery of letters continued more or less regularly – even if the mail had sometimes to be rescued from pillar-boxes almost submerged beneath débris and delivered to addresses which had become overnight smouldering heaps of ruins. In the latter case there was sometimes a member of the staff, standing on what had once been a suite of offices, waiting to collect the letters from the postman, or else the mail could be collected from the Post Restante counter at the General Post Office in King Edward Street.

Like many other of London's civic services the G.P.O. has shown its ability to cope with emergencies.

THE RED ARMY BARS THE WAY: WITH FIRE AND STEEL.

THE CROSSING OF THE BERESINA RIVER BY GERMANS ON THE PUSH TO SMOLENSK: THE ENEMY SUFFERED IMMENSE LOSSES AND THE RETREATING RUSSIANS LEFT ONLY "SCORCHED EARTH" BEHIND AS IN THE BLAZING VILLAGE ABOVE.

A NAZI COLUMN THROWN INTO CONFUSION BY A BOMBING ATTACK FROM SOVIET AEROPLANES: MOTORISED UNITS ARE ALL OVER THE ROAD WHILE A TANK HAS SOUGHT COVER ON THE SIDE OF A BANK.

HITLER AND FIELD-MARSHAL VON RUNSTEDT DISCUSS THE EASTERN CAMPAIGN, WHILE THE FÜHRER'S CRINGING ITALIAN LACKEY TRIES TO LOOK AS IF HE WERE NOT BEING TOTALLY IGNORED. EXTREME RIGHT, HERR LOHR, O.C. *LUFTWAFFE*; LEFT, CAVALLERO, ITALIAN AIR CHIEF.

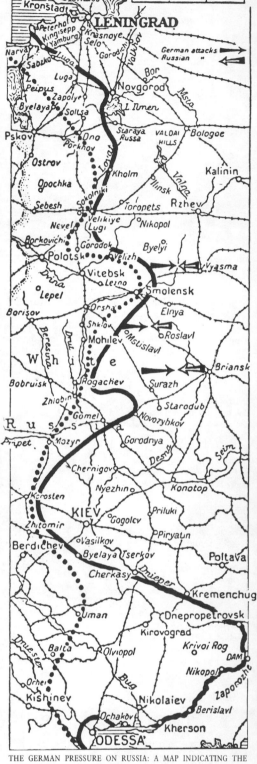

THE GERMAN PRESSURE ON RUSSIA: A MAP INDICATING THE ENEMY POSITION ON AUGUST 12 (DOTTED LINE) AND AS FAR AS ASCERTAINED AT PRESENT (SEPTEMBER 12 – HEAVY BLACK LINE), FROM THE GULF OF FINLAND AND ALONG THE DNIEPER RIVER TO ODESSA.

THE GREAT BATTLE OF LENINGRAD: THE CITY OF CONCEALED FORTIFICATIONS WHICH HAS HELD THE GERMANS AT BAY FOR OVER A MONTH IN NEVER-CEASING GRIM BATTLES, INFLICTING ENORMOUS LOSSES.

The Germans, in a communiqué issued on July 13, claimed new offensives and to have broken through the Stalin line "at all decisive points." It declared that tank divisions were advancing on Leningrad, east of Lake Peipus, on the Russo-Estonian border, while to the south their troops were reported in Vitebsk, eighty miles north-west of Smolensk, and also to be "immediately before Kiev."

Marshal Timoshenko has met the spear-head penetration of enemy Panzer divisions and motorised forces by holding a loose front with deep and mobile defences. These elastic defences, frequently misnamed "guerilla," are the natural reply to the far-ranging effects of tank and aeroplane, whereby, after permitting the advance units to force their way ahead of their infantry supports, the guerillas close in and cut off supplies, seeking shelter in forests and other hidden places. The Germans have posted notices in occupied towns and villages threaten-ing to shoot all who conceal or fail to report the presence of guerillas, but on July 20 the Moscow Radio said not one man has been given up. Stalin's "scorched earth" policy was carried out with thoroughness in the Western Ukraine as Marshal Budenny's forces continued their stubborn withdrawal towards the 600-ft.-wide Dnieper River. The evacuation of Krivoi-Rog, the iron-ore centre ninety miles north-east of Nikolaiev, and the latter great grain port, only resulted after the Germans had suffered losses estimated at 20,000 men. On August 14 the enemy had made a successful thrust 95 miles to the east of Uman, but Budenny's guerilla forces were counter-attacking strongly. The personal movements of Hitler are veiled and conflicting. The Moscow wireless on August 17 stated that the Führer's mental condition was deteriorating, a process which began with the first German set-back on the Russian front.

WITH DESPERATE VALOUR RUSSIANS FIGHT TO THE DEATH.

MARSHAL BUDENNY, ONE OF THE TRIO OF SOVIET MARSHALS WHO HAVE HELD THE GERMAN ATTACKS. A COSSACK, DESCRIBED AS "THE MOST BRILLIANT SOLDIER THE RED ARMY HAS PRODUCED." HE IS IN COMMAND OF THE SOUTH-WEST FRONT.

MARSHAL VOROSHILOV, ONE OF RUSSIA'S "BIG FIVE," APPOINTED TO THE NORTH-WEST COMMAND ON JULY 11. HE HAS SHOWN REMARKABLE RESOURCE IN THE DEFENCE OF LENINGRAD.

MARSHAL TIMOSHENKO, WHO SUCCEEDED VOROSHILOV AS DEFENCE COMMISSAR IN OCTOBER 1940, EQUIVALENT TO COMMANDER-IN-CHIEF ON JULY 11. HE TOOK OVER THE CENTRAL SECTOR OF THE WESTERN FRONT.

BEFORE THE EYES OF A GERMAN OFFICER THE GREAT DNIEPER DAM AT ZAPOROZHE GOES DOWN TO DESTRUCTION.

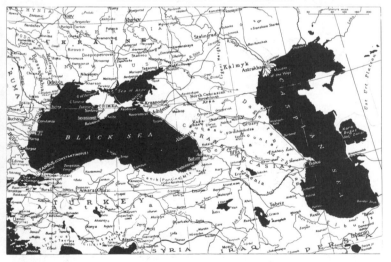

SOVIET WOMEN – WIVES AND DAUGHTERS OF COLLECTIVE FARMERS IN THE VILLAGE OF "N" – WHO ARE FIGHTING WITH THE RUSSIAN GUERILLA BANDS.

THE GIGANTIC BATTLE IN SOUTHERN RUSSIA, THREATENING KHARKOV AND THE DONETZ BASIN TO ROSTOV ON THE DON, WITH THE OILFIELDS OF THE CAUCASUS AS THE GERMAN MAIN OBJECTIVE.

The communiqués last week indicated intensified pressure by the Germans towards Leningrad, claims supported by stirring appeals made by Marshal Voroshilov to the redoubtable people of the former capital, whose fall would release great enemy forces to approach Moscow from the north. The capture of Kingisepp was claimed on August 21, and on the same day Narva and Novgorod. Kingisepp is only 73 miles, and Novgorod 133 miles, from Leningrad, and the advance was threatening. On the other hand, this new offensive has shown none of the impetus of earlier thrusts, and the German losses have been prodigious. The enemy spearhead appears, therefore, to threaten Leningrad from Kingisepp along the line of the Luga River to Norvorod, north of Lake Ilmen. The thrust from Novgorod south to Kholm (about 140 miles) is believed to have been designed to cut off Voroshilov's army from that of Timoshenko, who has counter-attacked strongly.

Marshal Voroshilov, Commander-in-Chief of the Russian Northern Army, has massed, by the third week in August, 1,500,000 men in the Leningrad zones of defence; with the Army is also the people's militia, born of the Marshal's stirring appeal; "Take up your arms and defend the city at all costs! The enemy is attempting to penetrate Leningrad. He will never set foot in our beautiful city. Leningrad never has and never will be in the hands of the enemy." The defences of the city comprise formidable fortifications, built up during the past ten years, when all the Leningrad neighbourhood has been barred to foreigners. Although the countryside for seventy miles round the city is flat and, at first glance, an ideal terrain for Panzer units, the land is seamed with small rivers, marshes, and fells – now swollen with rain – and forests, all of them natural tank obstacles. The concentrated attack upon Leningrad does not stand alone. The Germans have renewed their pressure in the centre, and have made repeated attempts to cross the Dnieper, where the position is still sensitive. Further gains in the Leningrad direction would be followed, in the opinion of military experts, by renewed pressure towards Chernigov, north-east of Kiev, and from the bulge at Gomel the Germans are delivering heavy thrusts towards the important junction of Briansk, which they have claimed. The problem is whether they can deliver such a blow as will shorten their front. Our map shows in dotted outline the approximate German front on August 12, and that of September 12 as far as known.

The situation around Leningrad is obscure at the time of writing. The "storming" of Schlüsselburg, at the mouth of the Neva, on the southern border of Lake Ladoga, was claimed by the Germans on September 8, but not confirmed by the Russians. On September 15, Soviet communications indicated that the city was not surrounded. What is apparent is that Field-Marshal Von Leeb's attempt to seize Leningrad by a *coup de main*

failed owing to the strong counter-attacks of Voroshilov and bad weather, and that the attempt to reduce it by siege has begun. Meanwhile Soviet counter-attacks from the Valdai Hills may change the complexion of this bitter battle. The Russians reported German attempts to enter the sea approaches to Leningrad, and that Russian airmen by heroic self-sacrifice sank five ships loaded with troops. A new and important element is the advent of R.A.F. fighter pilots who are now in action against the Germans on the Leningrad front.

The pictures above, derived from both Russian and enemy sources, mostly radioed from the field of battle, yield some idea of the Titanic conflict now raging over the vast area from the Gulf of Finland to the streets of Odessa, which great port resolutely defends itself, like its sister-city, Leningrad, in the north, and is inflicting unparalleled losses upon the German invaders. It would be idle to deny that the enemy have had very substantial successes. In three months they have overrun a vast area of Soviet territory, including industrial districts of great importance for Russian defence. Leningrad, Kiev and Odessa are all in real danger, and the loss of any one before the winter slows down operations would be a heavy blow to the whole Allied cause. The main strategic aim of the German armies now seems to be to thrust their way to the oil regions of the Caucasus, at Batum and Baku. Baffled at Leningrad and driven back at Smolensk, Marshal von Rundstedt is attempting to batter his way through to the Don Valley and at the time of writing appears to be endeavouring to push on beyond Kiev, even if this means leaving pockets of Soviet troops in his rear. The great naval base of Sevastopol, backed to the east by bases at Novorossik and Batum, and with the harbours of Tuapse and Sukhumi guarantee the Crimea against successful sea-borne attack. The enemy aim is evidently to destroy the Soviet industrial production in the Donetz Basin by the occupation of Kharkov, Stalin and Rostov, then a final sweep from Rostov south and south-east to Batum with its huge oil refineries, and Baku, the nerve-centre of the Caucasian oilfields. But the Germans have 600 miles of difficult country of rivers and lakes and the great barrier of the Caucasus Mountains to overcome – and time is precious.

Armies under the command of Reich Field-Marshal von Reichenau began the final assault on Kiev on September 17, panzer divisions following up an artillery bombardment of ferocious intensity. Fighting side by side with the Red Army, Kiev's citizens put up a desperate resistance. Guerillas, fighting from behind tank barriers, manning machine-gun nests at street corners and in houses, inflicted heavy losses on the enemy. The ancient city of Kiev has fallen after a battle lasting 45 days, but the Russian line still holds, and despite fantastic German claims, it would seem that Marshal Budenny has succeeded in saving a great number of his men from the pincer trap of the enemy.

THE R.A.F. ATTACKS ROTTERDAM: REMARKABLE LOW-LEVEL BOMBING.

HEDGE-HOPPING OVER THE FIELDS AND WINDMILLS OF HOLLAND, THREE "BLENHEIMS" GO IN TO THE ATTACK. OUR BOMBERS FLEW IN "V" FORMATION AND THE DUTCH – PUTTING THEIR OWN INTERPRETATION ON THE SPECTACLE – ENTHUSIASTICALLY WAVED THEM ON TO THE TARGET.

RIGHT AND LEFT OF THE "BLENHEIMS'" TAIL, BOMBS ARE EXPLODING. THIS DARING ATTACK ON ROTTERDAM WAS CARRIED OUT AT A VERY LOW LEVEL IN BROAD DAYLIGHT BY AIRCRAFT OF THE BOMBER COMMAND AND WAS CONCENTRATED ON SHIPPING AND DOCKSIDE WAREHOUSES.

On July 16 an Air Ministry statement told of a daring low-level attack on the docks at Rotterdam. The statement said: "A highly successful daylight raid was carried out this afternoon on enemy shipping in the docks at Rotterdam. Several squadrons of 'Blenheims' of Bomber Command were engaged in the operation, and the attack was pressed home with great daring at very low levels." Direct hits were scored on many ships – including one vessel of over 15,000 tons – and vast damage was done to warehouses and stores. In all, seventeen ships, representing a tonnage of between 90,000 and 100,000, were put out of action. Hedge-hopping over the fields, the aircraft saw Dutch people waving at them everywhere they passed. The attack itself was carried out with supreme brilliance and daring. One pilot found a short cut to the biggest vessel by flying between a wireless aerial on the quayside and the vessel's mast. "I had to bank to port," he said, "to get between them, and then, while still at an angle of 45 deg., we threw our bombs at the ship."

BREST HARBOUR: WHERE THE NAZIS FAILED TO DECEIVE THE R.A.F.

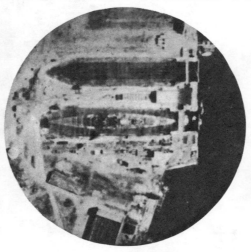

THE R.A.F. DAYLIGHT RAID ON BREST, WHEN THE GERMANS TRIED TO CAMOUFLAGE THE DISAPPEARANCE OF "SCHAR-NHORST." A TANKER PRETENDING TO BE "SCHARNHORST".

"GNEISENAU" IN DRY DOCK: SHE WAS HIT BY SEVEN BOMBS AND REMAINS AT BREST.

THE DISGUISED TANKER: MOORED WITH TWO SMALLER SHIPS, INTENDED TO HOODWINK THE R.A.F BOMBERS BY EXTENDING HER LENGTH.

In an attempt to hoodwink R.A.F. bombers after the dilapidated "Scharnhorst" had been towed from Brest to La Pallice on July 22, the enemy got a long tanker and moored two smaller ships fore and aft. Actually, they were seen placing the boats in position. The daylight attack began at 2 p.m. with great four-engined "Flying Fortresses" and "Halifaxes" arriving over Brest at a fantastic height. A heavy load of bombs was released on the "Gneisenau," she being hit seven times. Then, thousands of feet below the "Fortresses," a tight formation of "Hampdens" swept in over the target, and after they had finished their work, with their guard of fighters, it was the turn of the "Wellingtons." Each attack was timed to the minute. Meanwhile, "Stirlings" glided in to La Pallice to bomb the "Scharnhorst" from about 8000 ft., and later a large force of "Whitleys" attacked her in La Pallice harbour, after which she returned by night to Brest and now occupies the dry dock adjoining the "Gneisenau." Thus the German attempt to hoodwink the R.A.F. proved a costly failure.

THE MOSCOW CONFERENCE: TANKS AND 'PLANES FOR RUSSIA; THE R.A.F. IN RUSSIAN MUD.

THE THREE-POWER CONFERENCE IN MOSCOW: THE ARRIVAL OF LORD BEAVERBROOK AND MR. HARRIMAN.

WITH THE R.A.F. FIGHTER WING IN NORTHERN RUSSIA: A CORNER OF THE IMPROVISED LANDING-GROUND, AFTER RECENT HEAVY RAINS.

The first meeting took place on September 29, M. Molotov, Soviet Commissar for Foreign Affairs, presiding. Britain and the United States agreed that Russia should be granted practically every requirement for which the Soviet civil and military authorities had asked. At the conclusion of the Conference on October 1 Stalin gave a reception for all the delegates in the Kremlin.

On behalf of Great Britain, Lord Beaverbrook promised the Russians every possible assistance, and, on his return to this country, appealed to the workers in the factories to see to it that this pledge was fulfilled. The "Tanks for Russia" drive demonstrated in no uncertain manner that the Soviet appeal was not made in vain.

As an example of the way in which British workers have responded to our hard-pressed ally's call can be cited the case of the Midland factory where 2000 workers were due for a two days' holiday and volunteered to postpone this indefinitely so that the flow of tanks should not only continue unabated, but be increased. At other factories managers have been able to report an output increase of from 10 to 15 per cent.

Fighter Command "Hurricanes" have already given the enemy something to think about on the Russian front, and our picture shows R.A.F. machines and men on a Russian flying field. The Soviet Air Force is working in close co-operation with the R.A.F. units now supporting it.

PRESIDENT AND PREMIER IN THEIR EPOCH-MAKING MEETING: "SOMEWHERE IN THE ATLANTIC".

PRESIDENT ROOSEVELT AND THE PRIME MINISTER DURING DI-
VINE SERVICE ON BOARD H.M.S. "PRINCE OF WALES." THE THREE
OFFICERS STANDING ARE: (L. TO R.) AIR CHIEF-MARSHAL FREE-
MAN, R.A.F., ADMIRAL KING, AND GENERAL MARSHALL. BEHIND
THEM MR. SUMNER WELLES AND MR. HOPKINS.

MEETING OF THE INTER-ALLIED CONFERENCE AT ST. JAMES'S PALACE: A GENERAL VIEW OF THE CONFERENCE IN SESSION PRESIDED
OVER BY MR. EDEN, WITH MR. MAISKY FACING HIM.

A fateful and dramatic meeting in the north Atlantic took place between Mr. Churchill and President Roosevelt on August 9, on board the U.S. cruiser "Augusta" in the battle-riven Atlantic. All the subsequent conferences took place in the "Augusta," the President visiting the British warship only once for Church Service and luncheon. Mr. Roosevelt told his Press conference later that the Service had moved him deeply. "Americans and Britons," he said, "statesmen and sailors, worshipped together in the same spirit of fusion of purpose that marks the eight-point peace aims." The meeting of the two statesmen has profoundly stirred the entire world, friends and foes.

Above, representatives of sixteen nations, express their commitment to the "Atlantic Charter": (l. to r.; back to camera) M. Sertej, M. Nincic (Yugoslavia); M. Bogomolou, M. Maisky (U.S.S.R.); Count Raczynski, M. Strasburger (Poland); M. Lie, Major Sunde (Norway); Dr. Van Kleffens, Dr. Steenberghe, M. Welter (Netherlands); M. Bech (Luxembourg); (L to r.; facing camera) the Rt. Hon. S. M. Bruce, Mr. F. Hudd, Mr. R. Law, Rt. Hon. Lord Moyne, Rt. Hon. L. S. Amery, Rt. Hon. Viscount Cranborne, Rt. Hon. A. Greenwood, Rt. Hon. A. Eden; M. Spaak, M. Gutt (Belgium); M. Masaryk, M. Osusky (Czechoslovakia); M. Cassin, M. Dejean (Free France); M. Tsouderos, M. Varuaressos (Greece).

AMERICAN DESTROYER SUNK; ANOTHER DAMAGED.

THE U.S. DESTROYER "REUBEN JAMES": SUNK BY A TORPEDO WHILE ENGAGED
ON CONVOY DUTY IN THE NORTH ATLANTIC. THE FIRST U.S. WARSHIP TO BE
SUNK IN THE PRESENT WAR.

The "Kearny" was on October 17 some 350 miles south of Iceland when she was badly damaged by a torpedo fired by a U-boat. Despite, however, the large hole in her side, due to a direct hit abreast of the boiler room on the starboard side, she remained afloat, and proceeded under her own power to port.

News of the torpedoing of the U.S. destroyer "Kearny" roused America to a white heat of anger, which was not assuaged when it later transpired that ten Navy men were missing and eleven injured. The "Kearny" was not sunk, but the attack gave added impetus to the demand for the scrapping of the Neutrality Act.

The sinking of the U.S. destroyer "Reuben James" was announced on October 31. She was engaged on convoy duty in the North Atlantic, and, as far as is known at present, 76 of her officers and men are missing. It is, however, fairly certain that she accounted for at least two U-boats before receiving the hit which sent her to the bottom. The loss is the largest sustained by the U.S. since the sinking of the battleship "Maine" in 1898.

THE AMERICAN DESTROYER "KEARNY" (LEFT)
THE DAMAGE INDICATED BY AN ARROW.

BRITAIN SEIZES SPITZBERGEN: THWARTING GERMAN AIMS.

NORWEGIANS WAITING TO BE TAKEN ON BOARD BRITISH VESSELS
AT SPITZBERGEN: AN OFFICIAL PHOTOGRAPH OF PRIME INTEREST
TAKEN DURING THE LANDING OPERATIONS.

The dramatic raid on Spitzbergen by a mixed Canadian, British and Norwegian force, and warships, was officially announced on September 9, with the arrival in Britain of almost the entire Norwegian population of over 700 persons. These consist largely of miners and their families. Most of the men are joining the Norwegian forces or the merchant service. The military force was despatched to prevent the Germans from utilising the Spitzbergen islands and the rich coal-mines for their war purposes, for coal of fine quality has been mined since 1905.

"THE BATTLE OF THE ATLANTIC": A U-BOAT CAPTURED; AN ESCORT LOST.

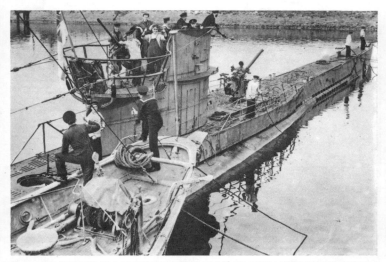

THE U-BOAT CAPTURED BY A "HUDSON" AIRCRAFT IN MID-ATLANTIC LAST MONTH ARRIVES IN A
BRITISH PORT: LIEUT. GEORGE COLVIN (WITH BEARD) AND SOME OF THE PRIZE CREW IN THE
CONNING-TOWER.

BOWS UPWARD, ABOUT TO TAKE HER FINAL PLUNGE: THE 16,644-TON ARMED MERCHANT-CRUISER
"RAJPUTANA" (CAPTAIN F. H. TAYLOR, D.S.C. R.N.) AFTER BEING ATTACKED TWICE BY A U-BOAT. THE
FORMER P. AND O. LINER REMAINED AFLOAT FOR FOUR HOURS AFTER BEING FIRST HIT.

The first U-boat ever captured by aircraft, which surrendered last month in mid-Atlantic to a "Hudson" Coastal Command aircraft, on October 3 slipped silently into a British port, flying the White Ensign and manned by a crew of twenty British naval men under the command of Lieut. George Colvin, R.M., a young, red-bearded officer who comes from London. Of medium size, some 500 or 600 tons, with a length of a little more than 200 ft., the captured enemy U-boat, which came under her own power, carries ordinarily a crew of 40. "It took us about a week to get the hang of her," said Lieut. Colvin, who found her "definitely inferior" to British submarines, although superior in a few details. There was no distinguishing mark upon her, but she has been identified as the "U-570." Her crew are now prisoners of war. Our men found some good Danish hams and butter, and evidence that the crew became panicky.

"The coolness of our men leaving the ship was one of the most amazing things I have ever seen. There wasn't a single man with anything but a normal expression on his face." The words are those of Commander Paul Cross, a senior Canadian officer and a survivor from the armed merchant-cruiser "Rajputana," sunk recently while on patrol duty in the North Atlantic. The first torpedo struck the ship at 5.52 a.m., penetrating to the engine-room and extinguishing the ship's lights. The "Rajputana" listed to port at an angle of 15 deg., and her engines were submerged in ten minutes. At a certain depth, however, the vessel stopped sinking, and there seemed some hope of getting her back to port, but two hours later the submarine attacked again. The ship being struck by another torpedo on the starboard side, the order was given to abandon ship. The survivors were sighted by a "Sunderland" flying-boat, which directed warships to the rescue.

"RUSSIA IS IN DANGER": SCENES FROM THE EASTERN FRONT.

POLINA OSSIPENKO, A SOVIET WOMAN
AIR ACE, NOW FLYING ON THE FRONT.

VALENTINA GRIZODUBOVA, WITH
POLINA OSSIPENKO, AT THE FRONT.

THE UNDERGROUND SHELTERERS OF MOSCOW: THE MAYAKOVSKY STATION DURING AN AIR RAID.

Amongst the many thousands of Russian women to volunteer for the defence of their country, not the least known are two pilots, Valentina Grizodubova and Polina Ossipenko, who together hold the long-distance international record, set up in 1937, between Moscow and California. They are now, according to a statement from the Russian capital, fighting at the front.

With relentless fury, and a complete disregard for the terrible casualties inflicted on them, the German forces continued to batter their way eastward, and the latest and greatest offensive threatened Moscow. With the capture of Orel the Germans succeeded in driving a wedge between armies in the centre and sorely pressed forces in the south.

THE CIVILIANS OF RUSSIA, WOMEN WORKING AS HARD AS MEN, DIG A HUGE ANTI-TANK TRENCH
OUTSIDE MOSCOW.

A FIRE-FIGHTING SQUAD OF A MOSCOW APARTMENT-HOUSE,
WHERE WOMEN ARE TAKING THEIR FULL PART, EXTINGUISHING
FIRES AND INCENDIARY BOMBS.

With the German armies closing in, M. Stalin, in an order of the day on October 19 reiterated Russia's determination. "Moscow," he told his people and the world, "will be defended to the last." In the South whilst Marshal Von Rundstedt's armies, headed by immense numbers of Panzer divisions, are battering their way slowly and suffering tremendous losses in men and material, the Crimea had so far defied every effort of invasion. In his attempts to reach the Donetz Basin, he has by-passed the Peninsula and pressed on to Melitopol, on the Sea of Azov. With the Crimea unconquered, Von Rundstedt is taking considerable risks of a counter-attack on his rear, and is well aware of it, for it is reported that he has prepared a major spearhead attack of three paratroop divisions of 7000 men each and two S.S. divisions, assembled in Rumanian and Bulgarian airfields. But the Soviet High Command, which has already smothered one such attack, is said to be fully prepared to meet the onslaught of more airborne troops.

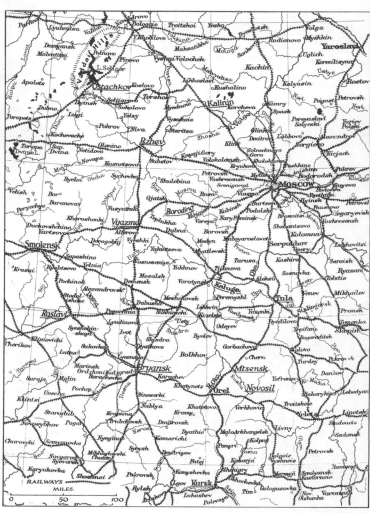

THE VITAL BATTLE OF MOSCOW: THREATENED FROM RZHEV TO MTSENSK, INTO WHICH THE ENEMY
HAS HURLED VAST FORCES REGARDLESS OF LOSSES; THE DEFENCE OF THE CAPITAL BY MARSHAL
TIMOSHENKO'S ARMY HAS BEEN MARKED BY STUBBORN RESISTANCE EVERYWHERE.

The entire army in Odessa, with all guns and equipment, were recently transferred to the Crimea with no loss of men or materials.

As the Russian forces, fighting for every inch of the ground, fall back before the German armies – and draw them ever further away from their sources of supply – everything of worth is destroyed in the path of the enemy. Hitler's forces have indeed penetrated deep into the territory of the U.S.S.R., but they have gained little in the way of material worth. Factories and crops, munition works and laboratories – all have been razed to the ground. Russian soldiers and civilians alike have contributed to the ruthless but vital policy of "scorched earth." Russian Government departments have been moved back to cities on the banks of the Volga, and now have their headquarters at Kuibishev, or, as it is better known abroad, Samara. And even as the civil side of the Soviet war machine has been regrouped, so, too, has the Red Army High Command. This rearrangement of the armies would seem to have been made with the intention of reducing the main sectors of the front from three to two. The northern sector now includes both Leningrad and Moscow, and is under the command of General Zhukov, who recently commanded the Moscow sector alone. Marshal Timoshenko himself has taken over the southern part of the battle-line and is now in charge of the vital Ukrainian front. It

is in the south that the Germans have most to gain, and hour by hour the battle for the riches of the Donets Basin increases in intensity, with Rostov as the main objective.

Marshal Timoshenko has displaced Marshal Budenny as chief of the Ukraine armies, whereas the latter has been charged with the formation of a new army.

With Teutonic disregard for human life, the German armies continue to advance eastward, but they are paying an appalling price in men and material for each yard gained. Latest reports state that the town of Stalino cost the Germans 50,000 men. Along the Ukranian battlefront, the 2,000,000 men and 15,000 tanks of Field-Marshal von Rundstedt are being mercilessly hammered by the soldiers of the Red Army, while the Russians fighting in defence of Moscow are not only obeying with courageous stubborness the order "Not a step back," but launching fierce counter-attacks in many sectors. Whatever the truth concerning German losses in Poland, France, the Low Countries and elsewhere, there is no shadow of doubt about the terrible casualties inflicted on Hitler's men now striving so desparately to obtain a major victory in the East before the Russian winter closes in.

THE RETREAT FROM MOSCOW, 1941: "GENERAL WINTER" CO-OPERATES.

RUSSIA'S LATEST ALLY GENERAL WINTER: LEFT, AN ENEMY PHOTOGRAPH OF GERMAN TROOPS WEARILY PLODDING THROUGH MUD, SLEET AND COLD, HAVING TO LEAD THEIR HORSES. HEAVY SNOWSTORMS AND BITTER COLD HAVE BEEN REPORTED THROUGHOUT RUSSIA, FOR WHICH THE GERMANS ARE SAID TO BE ILL-EQUIPPED. RIGHT, ILL-CLAD GERMAN PRISONERS IN THE RUSSIAN SNOW.

THE SNOWS OF RUSSIA: AN ENEMY PICTURE SHOWING GERMAN SOLDIERS ADVANCING IN CONDITIONS OF GREAT DIFFICULTY; NOW, RETREATING, THEY ARE AT THE MERCY OF THE RED ARMY.

This German propaganda picture was issued to show the difficulties they are meeting in "Stalin's winter." Enemy troops plod wearily through snow, mud, and sleet, leading their horses, as riding is impossible. Leningrad has reported 20 degrees of frost; Moscow, snowstorms and bitterly cold; the Crimea, heavy snowstorms and 30 degrees of frost. This is what Hitler and his generals dreaded beyond all else. The German armies before Moscow are digging in – there are no houses left in the scorched earth – and considerable forces are being withdrawn to winter quarters a long way back. Meanwhile Moscow radio, with fanfares of martial music, announced that Soviet motorised columns were moving forward, and blasting the Germans out of their fortified positions.

Taken from the French (German-controlled) paper "L'Illustration," the above photograph purports to show the advanced mechanised units of a German regiment advancing against the Russians somewhere near Valdai. The caption writer – drawing attention to the obvious – remarks that the advance is made difficult by the morass-like ground and snow. Since this picture was taken the ground has certainly hardened.

COSSACK CAVALRY CHARGING ACROSS THE SNOW: MASSES OF CAVALRY ARE BEING USED AND FORM THE SPEARHEAD OF THE RED ARMY ADVANCE.

A DRAMATIC MOMENT IN ONE OF THE NUMEROUS TANK AND INFANTRY BATTLES WHICH RAGED AROUND TULA BEFORE THE GERMANS WERE HURLED BACK.

It was dive-bombing which cleared the way for the enemy's entry into the Crimea.

According to Russian reports, the Germans prepared a very strong concentration of artillery, brought up a large number of tanks, and put in five divisions, this force being supported by 200 aircraft. The assault on the isthmus lasted several days. The enemy suffered heavy loss, and two more divisions had to be summoned from another part of the front before he could enlarge into a breach the wedge which he had driven into the defensive front. But the Russians do not appear to have offered any further resistance on the spot after the break-through, part of the Russian forces falling back to the hills to defend Sevastopol, while some seem to have withdrawn towards Kertch.

On November 20, under increased pressure from overwhelming German forces, our Russian allies successfully crossed the Kertch Strait under cover of darkness and strong air protection to prepared fortified positions on the Taman Peninsula. Strategically it means that instead of the danger of being driven into the sea, the Soviet defenders can render any attempt at crossing the Strait very hazardous to the enemy.

On December 4, 1941, it was reported that the great German drive towards Moscow appeared to be slackening. It was so. Russian successes against the enemy flanks at Klin and Tula had first hampered and then held the invading armies. From gallant defences the armies of Russia turned to brilliantly timed counter-attacks all along the line, which in turn developed into that great counter-offensive which was to blast the German hopes of a victorious winter campaign on the Eastern front. At Tula the tide of battle had been successfully turned; by December 8 the Germans were admitting that they had abandoned any idea of taking Moscow or Leningrad during the winter; four days later Russian spokesmen claimed that the Moscow offensive had been finally smashed and turned into a rout. In a week's fighting 400 towns and villages were retaken, 30,000 Germans killed, and a vast amount of booty captured or destroyed. The bombastic claims of early victory against the ("already beaten") Russian armies have vanished; Hitler has lost his first battle, and the Russians continue their relentless advance against his demoralised forces. Russian cavalry, supported by ski and sledge divisions, are harrying the enemy, forming an intensely mobile spearhead.

SWAN SONG OF THE "ARK ROYAL": THE END OF A GALLANT CAREER.

Struck by a torpedo on the night of Thursday, November 13, the "Ark Royal" sank in the early hours of the following morning. The loss of this famous ship will be mourned by all those who have followed her vivid and gallant career, but the news that only one man of her complement of 1600 was lost has done much to mitigate the blow. The "Ark Royal" has gone, but in the words of Mr. A. V. Alexander, the First Lord of the Admiralty, she "gave the nation a rich dividend." Sunk again and again by German and Italian propagandists, the famous aircraft carrier was in fact never seriously hit until struck by the torpedo which sank her. She sailed 205,000 miles, and took part in thirty-two war operations.

"THE 'ARK ROYAL' WAS LISTING ALARMINGLY," REPORTED REUTER'S CORRESPONDENT ABOARD, ". . . THEN WE SAW A DESTROYER, WHICH CAME CLOSE UNDER OUR RAILS AND MADE FAST." AIRCRAFT LANDED JUST BEFORE THE SHIP WAS STRUCK.

JAPAN'S NEW PREMIER SWORN IN.

JAPAN'S NEW PRIME MINISTER: GENERAL HIDEKI TOJO.

Reports declare that the new Prime Minister is pro-German. In 1938 he was made Inspector-General of Army Air Training, and has spent much time in Manchuria.

AMERICA SENDS US THE TOOLS, AND THE EIGHTH ARMY ADVANCES.
TOBRUK RELIEVED: EASTERN LIBYA CLEARED OF ALL AXIS TROOPS.

THE PRESENT ADVANCE IS THE MOST FORMIDABLE FORCE BRITAIN HAS YET THROWN AGAINST THE AXIS.

THE NEW LIBYAN OFFENSIVE: THE FAMOUS CUNNINGHAM BROTHERS.

A LONG-RANGE PATROL IN A WELL-ARMED AMERICAN TRUCK. THESE PATROLS OPERATE OVER GREAT DISTANCES.

A BRITISH ANTI-TANK GUN, IN ACTION AGAINST ROMMEL, WHICH PUT THREE ATTACKING ENEMY TANKS OUT OF ACTION.

AMERICAN TANKS MANŒUVRING IN THE DESERT: THESE ARE NOW THE "MOUNTS" OF A FAMOUS CAVALRY REGIMENT.

GENERAL ROMMEL, COMMANDER-IN-CHIEF OF THE GERMAN FORCES IN NORTH AFRICA, PAUSES FOR REFRESHMENT.

THE SUCCESSFUL BRITISH ADVANCE INTO LIBYA: A MAP OF CYRE-NACIA, ITALY'S EASTERN LIBYAN PROVINCE, FROM SOLLUM TO CYRENE, SHOWING THE TERRAIN AND PRINCIPAL SITES NOW AGAIN PROMINENT WITH GENERAL CUNNINGHAM'S OFFENSIVE.

THE COMMONWEALTH IN MICROCOSM: R.A.F. PERSONNEL OPER-ATING AMERICAN BOMBERS IN THE WESTERN DESERT.

BRITISH SOLDIERS GAZE AT THE WADI WHERE THEY WERE KEPT PRISONER.

ARMOURED VEHICLES AND TANKS CAPTURED BY VICTORIOUS IMPERIAL FORCES.

Lieut-General Sir Alan Cunningham's sudden attack on November 18, on a broad front from Sollum to Jarabub, was directed to sweep primarily round Tobruk and to envelop the Axis forces within those areas. The initial phase of the battle was described by Mr. Chester Wilmot, the Australian Broadcasting Commission's commentator, on November 23. "The scene of the battlefield is a huge rectangle," he said, "sixty miles long by forty deep. The northern side is the sea from Tobruk to Bardia. The enemy had a strongly defended eastern wall from Halfaya to Sidi Omar; a covered western wall from Tobruk to Gobi, and their tanks were drawn up deep inside the rectangle, some near Bardia, some near Tobruk. But the southern side was open." "By dark on the first day," continued Mr. Wilmot, "our armoured forces were ranged in three columns from Sidi Omar to Gobi. On the second, Italian tanks at Gobi were mauled, and at Bardia, one column using light American tanks of 11 tons, engaged and drove off big German tanks of 17 to 22 tons. On the third, Rommel threw in his main tank force and cut against our westerly column, now 70 miles inside Libya, heading towards Tobruk. But the column turned back to cut off the retreat of the main German forces, estimated at 180 tanks, attempting to pass between El Adem and Tobruk." The name of Tobruk will ever live in military history, and one of the initial aims of the lightning attack by the Imperial troops in the Western Desert was to link up with its gallant defenders. That junction was early achieved, and General Ritchie, General Auchinleck's Deputy Chief of Staff, who had replaced General Cunningham on Nov 25, went on to drive Rommel's shattered forces all along the coast from Derna to El Agheila, from which he had started on March 24, leaving Banghazi a ruined shell.

"PEARL HARBOUR": THE ACT OF TREACHERY THAT WILL SURELY PROVE TO BE JAPAN'S DEATH WARRANT.

THE BATTLESHIP "NEVADA", COMPLETELY DISABLED AND BEACHED AT HOSPITAL POINT. ALL EIGHT BATTLESHIPS IN HARBOUR WERE HIT.

A TRAGEDY IN TWISTED STEEL: THE 32,600-TON BATTLESHIP "ARIZONA" AS SHE APPEARED AFTER BEING SUNK BY JAPANESE AIRCRAFT.

AT WORK ON THE "ARIZONA," SUNK ON DECEMBER 7, "THE DATE," SAID ROOSEVELT, "WHICH WILL LIVE IN INFAMY."

THE U.S.S. "OKLAHOMA" LYING IN THE MUD AT PEARL HARBOUR, JUST ONE OF THE SHIPS SUNK BY THE JAPANESE.

ALL THAT REMAINS OF THE DESTROYERS "DOWNES" (LEFT) AND "CASSIN." "PENNSYLVANIA" IN THE REAR.

THE U.S. DESTROYER "SHAW" IN FLOATING DRY DOCK. SIX MONTHS LATER SHE WAS BACK IN SERVICE WITH A NEW BOW.

DISREGARDING THE POSSIBILITY OF EXPLOSIONS, AMERICAN SAILORS COME ALONGSIDE THE BURNING "WEST VIRGINIA".

On December 7 Japan declared war on Great Britian and the United States. True to the Axis formula, the declaration was made *after* the attack had begun; Japanese aircraft were bombing Pearl Island at the same moment when Mr. Cordell Hull, United States Secretary of State, was in conference with Japan's "peace negotiators," Mr. Kurusu and Admiral Nomura. In the words of President Roosevelt, December 7, 1941, is "a date that will live in infamy." The attack on Pearl Harbour was as vicious as it was sudden, and very serious damage was done on shore and to American warships lying in the harbour. The "Oklahoma" was sunk; the "Arizona," three destroyers and other ships were lost. Within a space of hours the balance of naval power in the Pacific had been perceptibly altered. Treachery had won the first round and over 3000 of America's soldiers and sailors had been killed.

The sudden, and unprovoked, attack on the U.S. base at Pearl Harbour, Honolulu, decided immediately the entire nation that war with Japan and the Axis Powers was imperative. The first news that the U.S. Pacific Fleet was crippled later transpired to be incorrect. The "Oklahoma" capsized (and can be repaired); the "Arizona," an old battleship, three destroyers, a mine-layer, and an old target-ship were lost. More serious

were the personnel losses; 2729 officers and men killed, and 656 wounded; as well as 168 Army men killed, 223 wounded, and 26 missing. The Japanese lost three submarines, and forty-one aircraft. The Army losses in aircraft were severe. Naval aircraft losses were also heavy, but have been replaced within three weeks. Colonel Knox, Secretary of the Navy, flew to Honolulu, and since his return, the Admiral Commanding the U.S. Fleet, the Chief of the Army Air Corps in Hawaii, and the Chief of the Air Forces have all been relieved of their commands.

It is common knowledge that in the sudden and unprovoked raid the Japanese 'planes showed uncanny knowledge of all U.S. ships and aerodromes. Colonel Knox, Secretary of the U.S. Navy, after investigating matters on the spot, declared that Fifth Columnists had been numerous and busy. A chart of Pearl Harbour was found in a captured Japanese submarine, and the symbols drawn on it indicated the anchorage of ships and details of military establishments around the inner areas of Pearl Harbour. This tell-tale document proves how thoroughly the Japanese secret service had assimilated the exact position of ships and defences in the area. In this matter Pearl Harbour does not stand alone.

THE "KNOCK-OUT BLOW" THAT WAS NO "K.-O."

On the first anniversary of the treacherous Japanese attack on Pearl Harbour, made on December 7, 1941, a report was issued from the Navy Department in Washington which revealed a number of interesting details not before known to the public. It was given out at the time that the battleships "Arizona" and "Oklahoma" had been sunk, but it was not known that three other battleships, the "California," "Nevada" and "West Virginia," were completely disabled and that the remaining three of the eight in harbour, the "Pennsylvania," "Maryland" and "Tennessee," were damaged to an extent that put them out of action. Three out of the seven cruisers present were also put temporarily out of action but these, together with the three last-named battleships, have been back with the Fleet for some time now. It may be added that many of the badly damaged ships are also already in service or under repair, and the total losses have probably been made good

by new construction. Of the twenty-eight destroyers in harbour, only three were sunk.

Of the aircraft in the island of Oahu at the time of the attack, 150 were disabled and 14 blocked from the runways out of a total of 202 naval 'planes. The remaining 52 took to the air. The Army's total, of which even fewer got into action, was 273. Japanese losses numbered about 50 aircraft, or nearly half of those sent in to attack, 28 being shot down by the Navy, 20 or more by Army fighters, and two by machine-gun fire. It is obvious from this account that, apart from the fact that the attack was a complete surprise, the Japanese were in no doubt as to what was their most important target. They concentrated on the battleships, and actually succeeded in putting all eight out of action. The American Fleet has recovered however, and has recently proved beyond doubt that her striking force is as strong as ever.

DECLARING WAR BETWEEN THE U.S. AND THE AXIS.

PRESIDENT ROOSEVELT MAKING HIS DRAMATIC SPEECH TO CON-GRESS ON WAR WITH JAPAN: WITH SPEAKER RAYBURN IN THE BACKGROUND.

"A STATE OF WAR EXISTS BETWEEN THE GOVERNMENT OF GER-MANY AND THE GOVERNMENT AND THE PEOPLE OF THE UNITED STATES." – THE COMPLETED RESOLUTION SIGNED.

PRESIDENT ROOSEVELT SIGNS THE DECLARATION OF WAR WITH (LEFT TO RIGHT) VICE-PRESIDENT WALLACE, SPEAKER RAYBURN, SENATOR AUSTIN AND OTHER WELL-KNOWN SENATORS.

President Roosevelt, in a short, dramatic speech to Congress on December 8, called on the Members to declare "that since the unprovoked and dastardly attack by Japan on Sunday, December 7, a state of war has existed between the United States and the Japanese Empire." The Members having returned to their respective chambers, the resolution was introduced; passed unanimously in the Senate, and with one dissentient in the House. The President was continuously cheered during his speech.

On Thursday, December 11, Germany and Italy declared war on the United States, which replied immediately in the same vein. Shortly afterwards, President Roosevelt, in a special message to Congress, asked that a state of war between the three countries should be recognised, adding: "Never before has there been a greater challenge to life, liberty and civilisation. Delay invites great danger. Rapid and united effort by all peoples of the world who are determined to remain free will insure world victory for the forces of justice and righteousness over the forces of savagery and barbarism." Congress acted immediately, and within half an hour separate resolutions were passed in the House without a debate. In the Senate there was unanimity. In contrast with the wild enthusiasm shown when Congress voted for war against Japan there was an atmosphere of grim resolution and determination when the resolutions were passed and no time was lost in either House in taking the votes and passing on the declaration to President Roosevelt for his signature. One definite result of the entry of America into the war is the second visit by Mr. Churchill to the United States.

THE WAR IN THE PACIFIC: STRATEGIC STRONGHOLDS ATTACKED.

A MAP SHOWING FRENCH INDO-CHINA, THAILAND, AND BURMA, THE JAPANESE ISLANDS OF PARA-CEL, LADRONE, MARSHALL, CAROLINE, AND PELEW ISLES, THE U.S. PHILIPPINE ISLANDS, HER NAVAL AND AIR BASES, AND ALL BRITISH BASES IN FAR-EASTERN WATERS.

MIDWAY ISLAND, A CENTRE OF COMMUNICATIONS BETWEEN ALL AMERICAN PACIFIC BASES.

GUAM, IMPORTANT U.S. NAVAL BASE, 1523 MILES NORTH-EAST OF MANILA.

WAKE ISLAND, HEROICALLY DEFENDED BY A HANDFUL OF U.S. MARINES AND TWO 'PLANES.

On Sunday, December 7, and Monday, the 8th, the Japanese began a widely spread series of attacks across the majestic Pacific Ocean. Pearl Harbour, Honolulu, was the main object of part of the Japanese Fleet, squadrons of bombers appearing out of the sky, attacking the U.S. principal naval and air bases at Pearl Harbour and Hickman Field. Their submarines were reported off California, and to have torpedoed a ship; in the Western Pacific, Guam, an important U.S. naval submarine station, was air-blitzed, and also the Philippines, our Ally's principal naval and air base on the approaches to the Malay Archipelago. Wake Island, a strategic point, between Hawaii and Japan, was invaded. Simultaneously with these attacks on the United States, hostilities commenced against Britain. A gunboat at Shanghai was sunk by shell-fire. Hong Kong and Singapore were bombed. A large Japanese force landed troops at Singora, Thailand (Siam), and proceeded to the Malay Peninsula, where it met our strong Imperial forces. Such, then, were the opening moves in the campaign by sea, air and land, and the sites may be traced in the accompanying comprehensive map of the Pacific, in which the main distances are given. Japan itself is open to long-distance air attacks from the U.S. Aleutian Islands, and more especially from Vladivostok, 700 miles from Tokyo.

Wake Island, a tiny atoll in mid-Pacific with fewer than 400 U.S. Marines, held the Japanese at bay for fourteen days, withstood non-stop raids by air and sea, shot down fourteen enemy 'planes, sank or damaged over a dozen warships or transports, and for most of the time had only two fighter 'planes – her heroic defence an epic of war.

THE DEFENCE OF SINGAPORE: BATTLING IN JUNGLE AND ON BEACH WITH THE JAPANESE IN NORTHERN MALAYA.

AUSTRALIAN TROOPS IN A MALAY JUNGLE: TYPICAL COUNTRY IN WHICH OUR TROOPS NOW FIGHT THE JAPANESE.

NEW THREATS TO SINGAPORE: A MAP INCLUDING THE ISLAND OF SUMATRA, ATTACKED BY JAPANESE PARATROOPS AND BOMBERS.

INDIAN TROOPS CROSSING A LAKE NEAR SINGAPORE: AN EXER- CISE IN WHICH THE DOGRA REGIMENT TOOK PART.

Japan invaded British Malaya by landing troops at Singora, at the southern extremity of Thailand (Siam). Some were reported to have landed on the beach at Padang Jabek and moved south towards the British aerodrome near Kota Bahru, but were driven off by airplanes and machine-guns. The invasion of Thailand was excused by the Japanese in a radio which stated that their troops had entered southern Thailand "to combat British troops from the Malayan border."

It very soon became apparent, after the Japanese had seized the important aerodrome of Kota Bahru on the north-eastern shores of Malay Peninsula, that they would attempt to seize Penang Island, on the opposite shores, through which the only railroad runs to Singapore, whose possession would place them in a strong position to strike at Rangoon, entrance port to the Burma Road, at India, and at Singapore. Japanese troops from Singora, in Thailand, invaded the northern province of Kodah, and bombing raids on Penang followed in quick succession. An attack down the Perak Valley was clearly directed at Penang, as well as the railway, and despite heavy fighting our troops were slowly driven back down by weight of numbers. The great number

of Japanese troops and full equipment which for months past were permitted by the British authorities to enter French Indo-China have been largely transferred through Thailand to the Kra Peninsula, and created a dangerous situation to the safety of both Malaya and Burma.

The situation of Singapore becomes increasingly grim. In Malaya a series of retreats with loss of aerodromes, Japan astride half of Malaya, Penang in its hands, has been followed by further operations against Borneo and Sumatra. Thus the enemy strategy to envelop Singapore and attack it from the mainland, while using Borneo and Sumatra as bases for sea and air attacks, is apparent. On December 29 it was announced that Kuching, the capital of Sarawak, had fallen. On the same date, flying in from Penang, paratroops were dropped on Sumatra near the important Medan airfield, which was heavily attacked by Japanese bombers. Only 60 miles separate Sumatra from Singapore, the width of the Malacca Straits. The activity of the Japanese everywhere is remarkable, from the Philippines to Sumatra, and in the south of this long, volcanic and rich island, across the narrow Strait of Sunda, lies Batavia, the capital of the Dutch East Indies.

THE DESTRUCTION OF H.M.S. "PRINCE OF WALES" AND H.M.S. "REPULSE".

A "WALRUS" AMPHIBIAN BEING HOISTED ABOARD THE MIGHTY "PRINCE OF WALES," NOW REPORTED LOST OFF SINGAPORE.

H.M.S. "REPULSE," LOST ON DECEMBER 10 OFF THE MALAY PENINSULA IN THE SAME ACTION AS H.M.S. "PRINCE OF WALES." OVER 2000 OFFICERS AND MEN WERE SAVED FROM THE TWO SHIPS.

Owing to the presence of Press reporters on board H.M.S. "Repulse," a full account of the disaster suffered by that battle-cruiser and her consort, our latest and finest battleship, H.M.S. "Prince of Wales," was quickly made available. The British fleet, under the command of Admiral Sir Tom Phillips, including the two major ships and a destroyer flotilla, was taken to sea to surprise the Japanese, who had warships and transports along the north coast of Malaya. The Admiral's intention was to effect a surprise attack, but unhappily they scored the surprise on us. At 9.5 p.m. on the night preceding the action, the Admiral, realising that three enemy 'planes were shadowing the fleet, ordered immediate return to Singapore. At dawn the fleet was steaming south. Enemy spotters were seen, but out of range. At 11.15 a.m. "Prince of Wales" suddenly fired at a single aircraft, followed by "Repulse," for about six Japanese aircraft now began an attack. "It was the beginning,"

says Gallagher, "of a superb air attack by the Japanese." Officers had expected some unorthodox flying, of reckless dives straight at the ships. But "it was nothing like that. It was most orthodox. They even came at us in formation flying low and close." They concentrated on the two major warships and left the destroyer screen alone. "Repulse" rocked under a heavy explosion. High above were squadrons of heavy bombers flying at 17,000 ft. and the first bomb scored a direct hit, setting her catapult deck on fire. The enemy shooting was remarkably accurate, whether from high levels or in discharging aerial torpedoes. The outcome, in the absence of supporting fighters, was inevitable, and although the utmost coolness and gallantry were shown by all, in just over an hour both great vessels went to their doom. Admiral Phillips anticipated fighter support from the shore, but only three British fighters appeared, an hour after the tragic encounter.

HONG KONG'S HEROIC RESISTANCE IN FACE OF HEAVY ODDS.

AN INDIAN ARTILLERY UNIT AT HONG KONG TRANSPORTING GUNS ACROSS THE STRAIT TO KOWLOON, TOWARDS WHICH OUR TROOPS HAVE RETREATED.

dive-bombers were broken up by terrific artillery fire. On December 11 our Chinese allies were heavily engaged north and north-west of Canton, attacking along the whole front to relieve the pressure on Hong Kong, in which the Japanese suffered 15,000 casualties.

The capitulation of Hong Kong, after a seige of only seven days, following on the fall of Penang, came as a shattering blow to British prestige in the Far East. Hong Kong has been in the possession of Britain for 100 years, and with its 17 miles of waterfront, its docks, in which the largest battleships could be repaired, is not only the greatest port, but a great business centre. In 1937, General (now Lord) Ironside was sent out to render it as impregnable as possible. Eight Millions sterling were spent on fortifications, and Kowloon, leased in 1898 from China for the sole purpose of defence, possesses high mountains and many advantageous natural defensive positions. The only aerodrome lay on Kowloon, and was reported to have been bombed by the Japanese before hostilities had begun. In their siege the enemy had at least 40,000 men in action, together with a great number of 'planes, and despite the claim that Hong Kong was strongly supplied with anti-aircraft guns, few Japanese air losses were reported. The retreat from Kowloon on the fifth day presaged the fall of Hong Kong. This was necessitated when the Royal Scots at 11 p.m. on the second day lost the Sing Mun Redoubt, which was captured by surprise, as it opened the Castle Peak Road. The enemy used severe pressure on our left flank, in which the Royal Scots suffered severe casualties. The retreat from Kowloon to Hong Kong was safely effected by night, and the Governor, Sir Mark Young, determined to defend it to the last. Once again the Japanese sprang a surprise, and crossed the narrow Lyemun Passage by night and gradually seized one vantage point after another. When they seized the Tytam reservoirs it was inevitable that resistance could not last unless the Chinese from Canton could effect a junction. The 7000 British garrison fought heroically. Brigadier Lawson, commanding the Canadians, was killed in action.

On the night of Christmas Day, when Hong Kong surrendered, a party of eighty-three British and Chinese made a dash for freedom under the

The successful defence of Tobruk decided the military authorities in the Far East to stand fast by Britain's bastion of defence, standing at the mouth of the Canton River. Canadians, with Indians and British troops, were holding Kowloon and the New Territories beyond, leased from China in 1898. At 8 a.m. on Monday, December 8, Japanese 'planes bombed airfields in Hong Kong, and were reported to have machine-gunned British fighters on an aerodrome. Many other raids followed without doing great damage. Attacks on the Kwangtung frontier, where two picked Japanese divisions were said to be stationed, were frustrated, all strategic positions having been blown up. Waves of

HONG KONG SURVIVORS: ADMIRAL CHANCHAK, ON CRUTCHES, WHO LED THE PARTY, AMID ADMIRING CHINESE OFFICERS. NEXT TO HIM IS COMMANDER HUGH MONTAGUE, R.N.

auspices of the Chinese Admiral Chanchak. This little one-legged Admiral (who lost a leg two years ago in the war), although wounded, took command of six naval torpedo-boats which set out from the small harbour of Aberdeen, on Hong Kong Island, in pitch darkness, and the utmost secrecy, because Japanese sentries were within rifle-shot. They made their way towards Canton, losing one boat, sunk with its passengers in a fight with Japanese naval craft outside Hong Kong. On their arrival at Shiukwan, the island town to which they were taken from the point on the coast where they landed, the survivors were entertained by the leading Chinese generals and were given a triumphal reception.

THE ILLUSTRATED LONDON NEWS

THE PRIME MINISTER AND PRESIDENT ROOSEVELT DURING THEIR SECOND HISTORIC MEETING: MR. CHURCHILL ARRIVES AT THE WHITE HOUSE FROM A SECRET AIRPORT.

Mr. Churchill arrived in Washington on December 22 to forge an "over-all unity" in conducting the war for "the defeat of Hitlerism throughout the world." The White House announced on January 2 that the United States, Great Britain, Russia, China, the Netherlands and twenty-one other anti-Axis nations had signed a joint declaration. On December 26 Mr. Winston Churchill addressed a joint Session of the Congress, and moved his audience to deep emotion, laughter and cheers. Never had the kinship between the British and American democracies been better exemplified than on this day.

On December 30 Mr. Churchill addressed a joint session of the Canadian Senate and House of Commons, introduced by Mr. Mackenzie King, the Canadian Prime Minister. Mr. Churchill paid high tribute to the part the Dominion was playing in this war. From Canada he turned to the war situation in general, inferring firstly, the gathering of our strength; secondly, liberation; and thirdly, assault. This great speech ended with these words: "Let us, then, address ourselves to our task, not underrating the difficulties of the task and its perils, but in good heart and sober confidence. . . . God helping us to the end."

1942

Commando raid on Lofoten Islands — U-boat offensive moves to US East coast — Russia gains ground round Moscow and in Ukraine — Rommel breaks out of El Agheila; retakes Benghazi — Japanese drive British and Allies out of Malaya; invade Celebes, New Britain, New Ireland, Bougainville — Singapore falls — Japanese invade Timor, Mindanao and Sumatra — Battle of Java Sea; Japanese occupy Java; capture Rangoon and Mandalay — Bataan Peninsula and Corregidor fall — Japanese invade New Guinea — first US soldiers arrive in Britain — Ste Nazaire raid — Battle of the Coral Sea; Japanese invasion of Port Moresby frustrated — British driven out of Burma — "Baedeker" air raids on Exeter, Bath, Norwich and York — First "1000-bomber" raid on Cologne — Battle of Midway; major Japanese defeat — Rommel takes Tubruk; reaches El Alamein, Egypt — German summer offensive towards Stalingrad and Caucasus begins; Sevastopol falls — "Pedestal" convoy relieves Malta — Disastrous Anglo-Canadian raid on Dieppe — US troops land on Guadalcanal — Battle of Stalingrad begins — British take Madagascar from Vichy French — Battle of El Alamein; Italian Army of Africa captured; Afrika Korps driven back to Tunisia — US/British landings in Morocco and Algeria; Vichy French in North Africa join Allies; German & Italian troops invade Vichy France; French Toulon fleet scuttles itself to avoid capture — German Sixth Army trapped in Stalingrad — first Allied denunciation of German atrocities against Jews.

BOXING DAY RAID ON THE LOFOTEN ISLANDS: THE COMMANDO RAID ON VAAGSO.

WHILST THE COMBINED RAID ON VAAGSO WAS PROCEEDING, THE AERODROME OF HERDLA, 100 MILES ALONG THE COAST, WAS ATTACKED BY "BLENHEIMS" TO DESTROY THE RUNWAYS.

AFTER LANDING: UNDER A SMOKE-SCREEN LAID DOWN BY BOMBERS, THE MEN CREEP CAUTIOUSLY FORWARD THROUGH ACRID FUMES TO THEIR OBJECTIVE.

PRISONERS BEING SENT ON BOARD A BRITISH LANDING BARGE. "IF ANYBODY LIKES TO PLAY ROUGH, WE CAN PLAY ROUGH TOO," AS SAID MR. CHURCHILL.

Last December 27, a combined Navy, Army and R.A.F. raid on islands off the Norwegian coast resulted in the destruction of oil-tanks, enemy ships, munition-dumps, and a radio station. Over 100 Germans were killed, and 95 captured, together with 9 quislings. A strong force of Commandos landed on Vaagso Island, under a smoke-screen laid by the R.A.F. Simultaneously with this attack, another was launched on the island of Herdla, the objective here being the aerodrome, in order to prevent German aircraft assisting the garrison at Vaagso. This attack was carried out by Bomber Command "Blenheims," which, diving as low as 50 ft., unloaded their bombs on the wooden runways, and so prevented the enemy fighters taking off. The whole of this sea, air, and land operation off Norway was carried out with complete success.

"If anybody likes to play rough, we can play rough too," said the Prime Minister in Ottawa, and the dramatic Commando raid on December 27 on the German stronghold of Vaagso proved the truth of Mr. Churchill's words. If British losses were light it was because the attack was beautifully timed, everything worked like clockwork, and the Commandos had been thoroughly trained to their job. Norwegian troops were among those who stormed the German nest of batteries after an initial naval bombardment, and cleaned up the island of Maaloy so thoroughly that not one of its 200 German soldiers got through the net. Vaagso as a German war asset was finished and so were the Huns. With the exception of a few snipers hidden in the trees of the forest, all were either killed or prisoners. The effect of the raid has been a new wave of anti-German feeling.

ROMMEL STRIKES BACK IN THE BATTLE OF THE LIBYAN DESERT.

A TANK WITH CUPOLA GONE AND REPLACED BY A THIN ARMOURED SHIELD: ROMMEL'S "SECRET WEAPON" IN THE BATTLE OF THE LIBYAN DESERT.

GENERAL ROMMEL'S ADVANCE FROM EL AGHEILA, ON JANUARY 23, THROUGH CYRENAICA, IN A NEW ATTEMPT TO ADVANCE ON EGYPT AFTER RECAPTURING AJEDABIA, BENGHAZI, AND DERNA.

THE FORT AT EL AGHEILA, THE FURTHERMOST POINT OF ROMMEL'S RETREAT, 400 MILES FROM TRIPOLI, HELD SUCCESSIVELY BY ITALIANS, BRITISH, AND GERMANS.

Situated on the Gulf of Sirte, the important frontier-post of El Agheila, 400 miles east of Tripoli, constitutes the high-water mark of General Wavell's advance in March 1941, and the subsequent furthest western point of General Rommel's retreat in January of this year. It will be recalled that General Wavell's original advance continued unchecked to Derna, Benghazi, Jedabya, and paused at El Agheila, his campaign, with Tripoli its objective, being held up by the sudden calls to aid Greece. After a short delay, General Rommel, with considerable reinforcements from Tripoli, on March 24, 1941, reoccupied El Agheila and recaptured all General Wavell's gains except for Tobruk. Once again the tide turned when, under General Auchinleck, on December 7, 1941, British armoured forces drove Rommel from place to place, retook every town and site in Cyrenaica and bottled the German General, on January 10, at El Agheila.

On January 22, General Rommel, from El Agheila, sent out three strong columns, for ten miles. It was the prelude to a new and serious enemy offensive towards Egypt. On the 23rd, he reoccupied Ajedabia, and the next day, with powerful and heavily reinforced columns, moved towards the north en route to Benghazi, where

the enemy claimed heavy British losses. On the 26th he advanced in two armoured columns to Msus, where a pitched battle was fought, and the R.A.F. and Australian A.F. caused great damage to his convoys. One column moved rapidly on Benghazi – the other towards Mechile. At the same time Rommel was promoted by Hitler to Oberst-General. The resourcefulness of Rommel seems to have been underrated once more, for, although reinforcements sent him suffered heavy losses, a great many did reach him. The motor transport on the roads from Tripolitania, bombed and machine-gunned by the R.A.F., was described as "black with transport."

On the 30th Benghazi fell after a valiant rearguard by the Indian 7th Brigade. On February 1, he was at Barce, 60 miles north-east of Benghazi, and the next day flung his tank forces on Derna, forty-seven days after he had been chased out in Auchinleck's westward drive. On February 5 he was at Tmimi, 60 miles only from Tobruk, and at the time of writing was halting east of Gazala. There are indications that he anticipates big new reinforcements and will attempt to reach Egypt.

SIRTE: ADMIRAL VIAN'S BOLD ACTION AGAINST ITALIAN WARSHIPS.

A DRAMATIC ACTUAL PHOTOGRAPH SHOWING THE ACTION IN FULL SWING. THE SIX FORWARD 5.25-INCH GUNS OF THE NEAR-BY CRUISER ARE FIRING A BROADSIDE AT THE ENEMY. WHILE BEYOND, ANOTHER CRUISER IS PUTTING OUT A SMOKE-SCREEN TO COVER THE CONVOY'S PASSAGE.

REAR-ADMIRAL P. L. VIAN, AGAIN IN THE NEWS.

A BRITISH DESTROYER EMERGES FROM A SMOKE-SCREEN AS SHE FIRES HER TORPEDOES AT AN ENEMY SHIP. THE CRUISERS AND DESTROYERS, ESCORTING A CONVOY FROM ALEXANDRIA TO MALTA, DODGED IN AND OUT OF THE SMOKE-SCREEN THEY PUT UP, FOR ONE AND A HALF HOURS.

Admiral Vian, who, as Captain of H.M.S. "Cossack," will be remembered for his daring rescue of 300 British seamen from the prison-ship "Altmark," is again in the news. This time the story is told of a naval and air action in the Mediterranean which took place during the passage of an important convoy to Malta.

On the afternoon of March 22, there began a naval action in the Mediterranean in which a British force consisting of no more than a 6-in. gun cruiser, anti-aircraft cruisers, whose heaviest guns were 5¼-in. and a force of destroyers, put to flight an Italian squadron numerically superior in ships, and with far heavier gun-power. The Italian squadron included the 35,000-ton battleship "Littorio," mounting 15-in. guns, as well as two 8-in. gun cruisers, four 6-in. gun cruisers, and destroyers. As a story of a successful, gallant and

brilliantly skilful action against odds, this Mediterranean battle will ever hold a high place in the annals of the Royal Navy. The British squadron was commanded by Rear-Admiral P. N. Vian, who was subsequently awarded the K.C.B.

The Italian objective was the destruction of an important convoy steaming for Malta, but, once the superior enemy forces had been sighted, it was the British ships which immediately went in to the attack, racing towards the Italians until shells from the enemy's long-range guns began kicking up spurts of water round the attacking force. In the running action, the "Littorio" was hit and set on fire. Every British warship returned safely to harbour. Of the Malta convoy, one ship was sunk by bombs.

THE COST HAS BEEN ENORMOUS BUT RUSSIA SWEEPS ON!

A VIVID ACTION PICTURE, TAKEN ON THE FIELD OF BATTLE, SHOWING A CHARGE BY RED ARMY CAVALRY. THESE HORSEMEN ARE THE GUARDS OF GENERAL BELOV, COMMANDER OF THE CAVALRY.

RUSSIAN INFANTRY, DRAWN ON SLEIGHS, GO INTO ACTION BEHIND THE TANKS.

FACTORY WORKERS IN A SOVIET TOWN, ARMED WITH HAND-GRENADES AND MOLOTOV COCKTAILS.

A CONCISE MAP OF THE RUSSIAN ADVANCE TO DATE.

A RUSSIAN BATTLEFIELD: A SCENE OF COMPLETE DESOLATION AS THE BODIES OF MEN AND THE FORMS OF DERELICT TANKS LIE PARTIALLY COVERED BY THE STILL DEEP SNOW. THOUSANDS OF UNBURIED SOLDIERS TURN RUSSIA'S FIELDS INTO ONE HUGE CEMETERY.

On December 25 the Soviet Caucasus forces crossed the Strait of Kerch, supported by the naval arm, and landed at Kerch and Theodosia, cutting off the main line of retreat of General von Manstein's fleeing divisions. The Soviet Information Bureau has since reported that 10,000 Germans were killed, 2000 in Theodosia alone. With the attack developing along the shores of the Sea of Azov, it is probable that the Germans will be compelled to evacuate the Crimea. The importance of this is revealed in "The Times," which says that the capture of Kerch frustrated Hitler's plans for the sudden seizure of Baku, timed for January, and that his entire strategy is dominated by the imperative necessity of replenishing his reserves of fuel oil, the rapid diminution of which is causing the German High Command the utmost concern. The early possession of Baku was an essential need to supplement Germany's rapidly dwindling resources.

General Belov, who has been steadily undermining the German lines south of Moscow, on December 28 threw the enemy out of important strategic positions on the River Oka. Mojaisk, which they occupied at a tremendous price a few weeks ago, was evacuated by the enemy and also Malo Yaroslavets, west and south-west of Moscow. Further north in the Kalinin sector, indifferent German troops broke and ran, and here our allies took masses of equipment. At Tim, 50 miles east of Kursk, the enemy lost over 1000 men and many tanks. An order of the day signed by General Guderian, commanding the Second Tank Army on the Moscow front, after referring bitterly to the Russian winter, exhorts his men to fight valiantly, for "the fate of the German Army is at stake." In the recapture of Kaluga on December 26, the battered, demoralised German forces retreated rapidly on a 100-mile front round the Soviet capital.

Leningrad, like a Gulliver awakening from his sleep, has also begun to throw off the cords by which Nazi Lilliputians had bound it. From the Valdai Hills a flank attack on the entire German position has been made.

THE PHILIPPINES, WHERE GENERAL MACARTHUR HOLDS JAPAN.

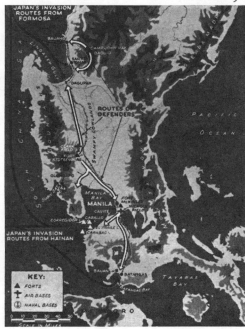

THE INVASION ROUTES OF JAPAN FROM FORMOSA.

GENERAL MACARTHUR, C.-IN-C. OF THE AMERICAN FORCES.

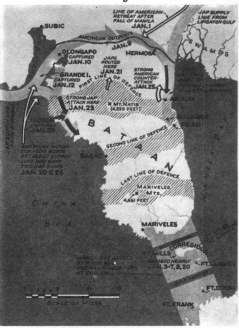

GENERAL MACARTHUR'S LINES OF DEFENCE.

The enormous distance Manila lies from the United States – 6858 miles by ship from San Francisco, via Honolulu, the shortest route – has rendered direct aid to the Philippines from U.S. sources almost impossible, the more so since all the North Pacific Ocean is at present dominated by Japan by sea and air. Added to this, the loss of our two major warships, "Prince of Wales" and "Repulse," has given the enemy temporary command of the China Sea. This is the strategic problem which General Douglas MacArthur, the U.S. Commander-in-Chief in the Far East, has had to face.

MacArthur had been in the Philippines as a young officer in 1898, and no man living was better aware of Japan's ultimate designs. Last July he announced that in the spring of 1942 he would have 125,000 well-trained and equipped Filipino soldiers. He founded at Baguio a military academy modelled on West Point, and had also the nucleus of an air force, turning out 150 fully-trained Filipino pilots. Driven back to Manila by superior Japanese forces, on January 1, General MacArthur, after brilliant defence actions, was forced to evacuate Manila.

SINGAPORE FORCED TO SURRENDER: THE END OF A TRAGIC STRUGGLE.

THE JAPANESE AT SINGAPORE CAUSEWAY: THIS LINK WITH THE MAINLAND WAS PARTLY DESTROYED BY OUR RETIRING TROOPS.

British forces, retreating slowly, but unhappily without being able to make any final stand, on January 31 had to retire from the mainland of Johore and cross to the island of Singapore. For over seven weeks the Japanese, whose seizure of the Kra Isthmus in the first week opened up the west coast to them, entailed the loss of Penang Island, and produced continuous infiltrations in small boats, which we were unable to check effectively, added to their remarkable knowledge of the hitherto "impenetrable" jungles, caused retreat after retreat. With inferior military forces, and with the use of great numbers of tanks by the enemy – which it was said beforehand could not penetrate the jungles – there was no alternative before the British High Command, whose men fought gallantly in thick forests and in crocodile- and serpent-haunted swamps against disguised Japanese. The governing causes of withdrawal were due to loss of command of the sea, which enabled Japan to pour in reinforcements, and, even more particularly, the British weakness in the air, where the enemy held throughout enormous superiority. Not the least cause of defeat was attributed to the under-estimating of the Japanese armed forces and their Air Force.

The story of the last days at Singapore has been told by many of those who got safely away before the island fell. The evacuation of women and children was carried out smoothly and by January 31 7000 Europeans and a great number of women and children of other races had been safely got away. From that date onwards, many other parties were taken off as opportunity offered, the last lot going as late as February 10, when the threat to the city was already acute.

It was on February 4 that orders were given for a general assault on the island, and a four-day barrage by artillery and bombardment by warplanes preceded the night landing on February 8. At 8 a.m. on February 11, Japanese troops swept into Singapore City for the final mopping-up that brought to an end the disastrous Malayan campaign to British arms.

The great naval base is in Japanese hands, and the Allied Fleets must look elsewhere for their re-fuelling and re-fitting.

SINGAPORE FALLS TO THE ENEMY: JAPANESE TROOPS HOIST THEIR FLAG AFTER THE ENFORCED BRITISH SURRENDER.

RANGOON, THE GATEWAY TO THE BURMA ROAD SCORCHED.

RANGOON, THE CAPITAL OF BURMA, EVACUATED ON MARCH 9, BECAME A ROARING INFERNO, SO THOROUGHLY WAS IT "SCORCHED."

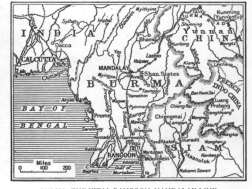

BURMA: THE VITAL RANGOON–MANDALAY LINK.

The military situation in Burma has borne an uncomfortable resemblance to that which existed in Malaya. It has been a series of withdrawals and enemy penetrations, with Japanese strategy directed to the occupation of Rangoon, one of the wealthiest cities in the East, and the port of entry to the Burma Road. Japanese forces first occupied Victoria Point in the extreme south, on December 16, capturing the airfield and effectively dividing the British forces in Burma from those in Malaya. With their Malayan campaign well established, they began to advance northwards into Lower Burma on January 16.

On January 27, after the enemy captured Tavoy and our forces evacuated the port of Mergui, they advanced on Moulmein in three columns. On January 30, fighting took place east of Moulmein, and the official communiqué reported the situation as "well in hand." Next day, the port was evacuated with some difficulty, but the British force held a "rapidly stabilising position" west of the Salween River, which flows under the Burma Road northwards. On February 2 the Japanese were reported across the Salween, and Moulmein was not scorched.

On February 20 the Government evacuated Rangoon and moved to Mandalay. On the 22nd the enemy were reported across the Bilin River, and had bombed Pegu, an important railway centre between Rangoon and Mandalay. It was admitted that he was thrusting strongly toward the Sittang River and Pegu. General Hutton, while claiming to have inflicted heavy casualties on the enemy, and to be receiving air support from the R.A.F. and the American Volunteer Flying Group, appeared unable to stem the enemy advance. Lower Burma was by then entirely a military area and Rangoon little better than a shell. Its big oil refineries at Syriam, of the Burma Oil Co., were expected to be scorched.

After steady retreats and severe fighting, with most of the British forces on the west bank of the Sittang, on March 1, fighting had steadied down, but the Japanese boasted that they had cut the Rangoon–Mandalay railway line. If this proved true, General Hutton's retreat northwards would be difficult. In raids over Rangoon between February 25–26, the enemy lost 51 aircraft to our two. Rangoon was reported to be a city of the dead, lying under a pall of smoke from the many fires left burning when our forces were evacuated.

AMERICA STRIKES BACK: THE U.S. PACIFIC FLEET RAIDS ENEMY BASES.

UNITED STATES AIRCRAFT AND CRUISERS ON THEIR WAY TO ATTACK JAPANESE BASES IN THE MARSHALL AND GILBERT ISLANDS.

Up to the beginning of February, when it was announced that the U.S. Navy had raided seven Japanese-held islands in the Pacific, the course of the war in that area was an almost uninterrupted series of Japanese successes. The news, therefore, of this large-scale attack on the Marshall and Gilbert Islands came as a welcome surprise. Four places in the Marshall Islands, which passed into Japanese hands after the last war, and one in the British Gilbert Islands, recently seized, were attacked by ships and aircraft of the United States Pacific Fleet. Severe damage was done to enemy positions and auxiliary craft, while the Americans suffered a loss of eleven 'planes and minor damage to two ships.

THE BATTLE OF THE JAVA SEA: HEROIC ACTION AGAINST HOPELESS ODDS.

H.M.S. "EXETER'S" LAST FIGHT: THE FAMOUS CRUISER SINKING UNDER SHELL-FIRE WITH HER WHITE ENSIGN STILL FLYING.

On February 27–28 the Japanese, with strong naval forces, conducted a convoy of about forty transports. They were attacked by Dutch, British and American cruisers at 12 miles range and later destroyers closed in. In this action one heavy Japanese cruiser was sunk, another severely damaged and a third, the "Mogami" (8500 tons), set afire. Three Japanese destroyers were left burning or sinking. Eighteen enemy transports and ten smaller ships were sunk or damaged. One Allied destroyer was lost and one cruiser damaged. The Japanese, turned back by this defeat, returned at night, and the Allies, under the order of Admiral Helfrich to "attack regardless of cost," went into action and drove the enemy westwards. Every Allied warship was lost.

JAVA, BALI, THE "ISLE OF BEAUTY" AND SUMATRA FALL TO THE JAPANESE.

OIL WELLS AND REFINERIES AT PALEMBANG, SUMATRA. THE JAPANESE CAPTURED THIS IMPORTANT OIL CENTRE ON FEBRUARY 16, BUT THE RICH PRIZE – MORE THAN HALF OF ALL THE OIL IN THE INDIES – HAD BEEN BLOWN UP AND FIRED BY THE DUTCH.

A YOUNG BALI DANCER. THE BALIS LEARN TO DANCE FROM BABYHOOD. THEY ARE RATHER INDOLENT, BUT GAY, CHARMING AND FRIENDLY.

ONE OF BATAVIA'S MANY CANALS. THE CAPITAL OF JAVA, BUILT ON FLAT AND SWAMPY LAND, AND INTERSECTED BY NUMEROUS CANALS, RESEMBLES MANY TOWNS IN HOLLAND.

Further news of the Axis drive on the Allied oil centres comes from Palembang, Sumatra, captured by the Japanese following an attack by parachutists and landings from the sea. The Dutch, however, determined that this rich area should not fall into enemy hands, have completely destroyed both wells and refineries. This is probably the greatest piece of voluntary destruction the world has ever seen.

Japan's power politics and brutal creed of wholesale destruction have taken the war into the blissful little island of Bali, separated from Java by a mile-wide strait. Bali is best known for the beauty of its women, their artistic taste in dancing, in silk weaving and in decorative work in gold, silver and copper.

Japan's insatiable appetite for conquest led to the bombing of Bali, and on February 23 the airfield of Den Pasar fell into their clutches.

On February 27 the Japanese, with large naval forces, tried to land a convoy on Java, and the Allied Fleet, though greatly outnumbered, struck so hard and successfully that the big convoy drew off northwards. In a second phase the enemy regrouped transports and made coastal landings on the night of February 28, after more severe sea fighting and the loss of all the remaining Allied warships in the squadron in a series of heroic actions. In fierce air fighting, on March 1, large numbers of enemy landing barges were destroyed. The Japanese made, however, three landings, towards Batavia and Bandoing, around Krawang, and at Blora. The Allies put up a violent counter-offensive, and were said to be more than holding their own, with Australian, American, British and Dutch forces in strength. Batavia was evacuated on March 4, and two days later, the Japanese, penetrating from every direction, claimed its capture.

RABAUL AND TIMOR – THREATS TO AUSTRALIA; SUMMARY OF JAPAN'S INVASION DATES.

THE GREAT BARRIER REEF STRETCHES SOUTH ALMOST FROM NEW GUINEA TO 200 MILES NORTH OF BRISBANE. IT IS A MAZE OF COUNTLESS THOUSANDS OF REEFS, AT PLACES 100 MILES ACROSS.

The list of conquests as shown by the numerals is as follows: (1) Kota Bharu, Dec. 10; (2) North Luzon, Philippines, Dec. 10; (3) Guam (U.S.A.), Dec. 11; (4) Southern Burma, Dec. 15; (5) Hong Kong, fell Dec. 25; (6) Miri, Sarawak, Dec. 17; (7) Penang, Dec. 19; (8) Davao, Philippines, Dec. 20; (9) Kuching, Sarawak, Dec. 28; (10) Manila, Jan. 2; (11) British North Borneo, Jan. 3; (12) Tarakan, Jan. 11; (13) Menado, Celebes, Jan. 13; (14) Tavoy, Burma, Jan. 20; (15) Moulmein, Jan. 21; (16) Rabaul, New Britain, Jan. 20; (17) Kieta, Bismarck Archipelago, Jan. 22; (18) Kavieng, Jan. 24; (19) Balik Papan, Dutch Borneo, Jan. 23; (20) Kendari, Celebes, Jan. 25; (21) Singapore, Feb. 15; (22) Amboina, Moluccas, Jan. 31; (23) Pontianak, Dutch Borneo, Jan. 31; (24) Macassar, Celebes, Feb. 10; (25) Gasmata, New Britain, Feb. 11; (26) Martaban,

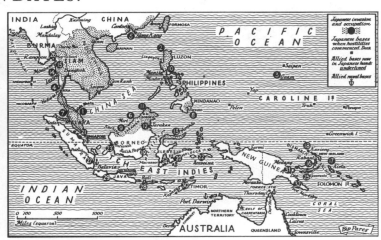

NINETY DAYS OF CONQUEST: ALLIED BASES AND CENTRES, EMBRACING 1,200,000 SQUARE MILES OF TERRITORY, WHICH JAPAN HAS SEIZED IN HER THREE MONTHS' LIGHTNING CAMPAIGN.

Burma, Feb. 11; (27) Palembang, Sumatra, Feb. 15; (28) Bali, landing Feb. 20; (29) Java, Batavia, March 5, Surabaya and other towns also fell; (30) Timor, Feb. 20, still resisting; (31) Lae, New Guinea, March 8; (32) Port Moresby, bombed heavily, March 8; (33) Mindoro Island, Philippines, March 8. In material resources the Japanese have deprived the Allies of 43 per cent. of the world's tin, 89 per cent. of the rubber, 3 per cent. of the oil, and 90 per cent. of the quinine.

The seizure of Rabaul on January 20 opened up possibilities of direct attacks on Australia, only 600 miles distant. The garrison, of mainly Victorian bushmen, retreated to the hills, and on January 26 were superbly resisting 10,000 Japanese.

THE DRAMATIC ESCAPE OF THE THREE GERMAN WARSHIPS FROM BREST.

"GNEISENAU", LIKE "SCHARNHORST", IS OF 26,000 TONS, AND WAS ORIGINALLY DESTINED FOR COMMERCE-RAIDING.

"SCHARNHORST," WHO, WITH HER SISTER-SHIP "GNEISENAU" AND THE "PRINZ EUGEN," ESCAPED FROM BREST ON FEBRUARY 11.

"PRINZ EUGEN," OF 10,000 TONS, A HEAVY CRUISER WITH EIGHT 8-IN. GUNS, WHICH ESCAPED FROM BREST WITH THE OTHER TWO.

A BRITISH MOTOR TORPEDO-BOAT LAUNCHING TORPEDOES WHILE AT HIGH SPEED. EVERY AVAILABLE M.T.B. RACED UP TO THE ENEMY.

A GERMAN PHOTOGRAPH OF THE GERMAN HEAVY SHIPS AND THEIR ESCORT STEAMING THROUGH THE STRAITS OF DOVER: OVERHEAD, AIRCRAFT OF THE *LUFTWAFFE*, UNDER THE COMMAND OF GENERAL FIELD-MARSHAL SPERRLE, FORM A PROTECTIVE AIR SCREEN.

LOADING A SWORDFISH WITH AN AERIAL TORPEDO. NONE OF THE SIX SWORDFISH RETURNED AND ONLY FIVE MEN SURVIVED.

In perfect weather from the German standpoint, with visibility between three and five miles, the two enemy battleships "Scharnhorst" and "Gneisenau," with the 10,000-ton heavy cruiser "Prinz Eugen," left Brest at dusk on February 11 and boldly headed for the Channel. Not until the next morning at approximately 11 a.m. (reports have differed), did R.A.F. aircraft report that the enemy squadron with destroyers, torpedo-boats, E-boats and minesweepers, was approaching the Dover Straits. Bomber Command reports state that the battleships and the cruiser were struck by bombs, but poor visibility made it difficult to ascertain the damage inflicted. So far as is known, all three ships reached harbour safely. Supreme self-sacrifice by the men of the little ships of the Navy and by the pilots and crews of the R.A.F. provided a shining light in an otherwise sombre picture. All the available surface craft which could reach the scene of the action did so, and drove home the attack.

THE BRUNEVAL "TIP-AND-RUN" RAID: A NAVY, ARMY AND R.A.F. SUCCESS.

THE BLAZING FIRES OF LÜBECK.

THE RETURN OF THE VICTORS. FROM THE BRUNEVAL RAID, THE FIGHTING UNITS ARE CHEERED BY THEIR COMPATRIOTS.

AN R.A.F. PHOTOGRAPH TAKEN EARLY IN THE ATTACK ON THIS IMPORTANT GERMAN SEA PORT ON THE BALTIC.

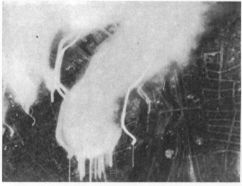

A LATER PHOTOGRAPH – TAKEN AT 12.20 A.M. – SHOWING THE GROWING FIRES IN THE CENTRE OF THE TOWN.

GERMAN PRISONERS BEING SEARCHED. ON THE RIGHT IS A MEMBER OF THE *LUFTWAFFE*, IN THE CENTRE AN INFANTRYMAN.

LÜBECK OBSCURED IN A BLANKET OF WHITE FIRE: A PHOTOGRAPH TAKEN AT THE END OF THE ATTACK.

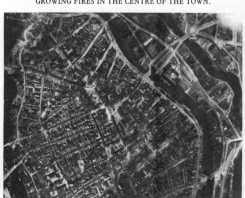

THE CENTRE OF LÜBECK A FORTNIGHT LATER: THE TRAVE CANAL BRIDGE BOTTOM LEFT.

In an operation brilliantly carried out by the three services, a disconcerting blow was struck at the enemy on the night of February 27–28. The objective was an important radio-location unit at Bruneval. British parachute troops made a moonlight descent within easy reach of the objective. A slight mist probably helped to interfere with the accuracy of the concentration of enemy flak. The German defenders put up a stiff fight, but were overcome by the speed and vigour of the parachute troops; the radio-location apparatus was destroyed and heavy casualties inflicted on the enemy. Meanwhile units of the Royal Navy and the Army were ready to carry out the embarkation of the attacking force, at Bruneval beach. Caught between the parachutists at the back of them and confronted by forces landing from the sea, the beach defences were overpowered; and the embarkation proceeded smoothly.

THE R.A.F.'S PARALYSING RAID ON THE CITY OF LÜBECK.

On March 28, the R.A.F. visited Lübeck, and gave the old Hanseatic League capital a very complete hammering. The port, full of accumulated shipping and stores waiting for the Baltic ice to melt, was set ablaze by giant "Stirlings" and "Wellingtons," and the photographs taken early in the attack, at 12.20 a.m., and finally at the end, show what a complete shambles was made of big areas. A large number of heavy bombs exploded with volcanic effect in the midst of the target. The great destruction wrought on the Prussian port was admitted by the Goebbel's radio, which said that over 3000 casualties had resulted, and that we had destroyed ancient buildings but done no military damage. Yet Lübeck was at once closed to inspection!

Our air photograph shows most of the old or inner city situated on a pear-shaped island, bordered by the River Trave (seen in centre with the City Ditch, another arm of the Trave, to the left) with the Trave Canal linking with the main stream in its outlet to the north (seen on right) the waterways being shown in black. Here is the main area of devastation over three-quarters of a mile long, varying from between 200 and 600 yards in width. Row after row of roofless buildings have been left with mere foundations of their walls standing, lining whole streets like open boxes to the sky. Some streets are still choked and impassable, a fortnight after the raid. The white patches over this great area show the damage caused by blast from H.E.-bombs.

INTERESTING NEWS ITEMS FROM BOTH SIDES OF THE ATLANTIC.

GROTESQUE AND ALARMING FLYING "SHARKS," IN REALITY "TOMAHAWK" FIGHTERS CAMOUFLAGED BY AN ARTISTIC MEMBER OF A DESERT SQUADRON OF THE R.A.F.

THE FIRST PEREGRINE FALCON TO BE ENLISTED IN THE U.S. ARMY: NOW UNDERGOING TRAINING, HIS JOB IS TO DESTROY ENEMY CARRIER-PIGEONS.

THE NORMANDIE LYING ON HER SIDE: SHE TOPPLED OVER AS A RESULT OF THE WEIGHT OF WATER POURED INTO HER TO PUT OUT A FIRE, AND WHICH SUBSEQUENTLY FROZE.

Unpleasant as a vision to enemy aircraft at any time, these American "Tomahawks," after being decorated by R.A.F. artists belonging to a desert squadron, must give them an additional feeling of alarm when they see apparently a flying shark, with immense teeth and a cold and glassy eye charging down on them. The "Tomahawk" is a 327-m.p.h. single-seater fighter, a low-wing monoplane with single fin and rudder. It has already given a very good account of itself in desert warfare.

"Thunderbolt," 20 ounces of dive-bombing dynamite, has become the first enemy carrier-pigeon destroyer in the U.S. Army. Mr. Seton Gordon, in "Wild Birds in Britain," says of it: "There is perhaps no other bird that inspires so much fear as the peregrine falcon. . . . Its favourite prey is the carrier-pigeon." To teach "Thunderbolt," perched on the hand of its trainer, to discriminate between enemy and friendly carrier-pigeons is a task likely to require much discretion.

Although the "Normandie" was badly damaged by the blaze which swept the great ship from stem to stern on February 9, her hull and all her lower decks and her machinery are intact and free from water. Top-heavy from ice and from the hundreds of tons of water pumped into her superstructure, she was unable to resist the pull of the rising tide and rolled gently over on her side in 40 ft. of water. The blaze was caused by sparks from a welder's torch.

ONCE A FACTORY FOR FAMOUS RACING AND TOURING CARS, THEN DEVOTED TO TOTAL NAZI WAR PRODUCTION, RENAULT COMES TO ITS SELF-INVITED DESTRUCTION ON MARCH 3. LEFT: OFFICIAL R.A.F. PHOTOGRAPH OF THE WORKS AFTER THE RAID, SHOWING A DAMAGED GAS-HOLDER AND BUILDINGS, INCLUDING A WRECKED TANK-ASSEMBLY SHOP, WITH A NUMBER OF DAMAGED TANKS CLEARLY VISIBLE. RIGHT: A PHOTOGRAPH TAKEN THE NEXT DAY BY A FREE FRENCH AGENT AND SMUGGLED TO LONDON, WHICH PROVIDES DRAMATIC PROOF OF THE R.A.F.'S ACCURACY.

Very serious damage was done to the Renault and Farman aircraft factories and to the Salmson motor factory during the R.A.F.'s raid on the night of March 3 – the first on the enemy-controlled war factories on the outskirts of Paris. Aided by a full moon and clear sky, the R.A.F. crews had no difficulty in finding their targets. The greater part of the Renault works, manufacturing tanks and aero engines for the enemy, is situated on the Ile Seguin, in the middle of the Seine, but it also extends along both river banks. Crews had been given orders to concentrate only on the factories, and should there be any doubt, to bring back their bombs rather than risk the lives and property of civilians. The target, however, was clearly seen in the moonlight. Many large fires were started, which, according to a Vichy report, were still burning the next day. Vichy claimed that 600 persons were killed and about 1000 injured, and German broadcasts emphasised the extent of civilian damage and casualties, hoping, no doubt, to create resentment in the minds of the French people. It has been known for some time that the Renault factory is working for Germany, but certainly not by wish of the French people.

HUSBAND AND WIFE WORK SIDE BY SIDE: MRS. EDITH HARWOOD, WHOSE HUSBAND IS A BURNER, BEING TAUGHT HOW TO DESCALE GUN BARRELS BY MEANS OF INTENSE HEAT.

ALLIES TELL OF NAZI OUTRAGES IN THE OPPRESSED COUNTRIES: A GENERAL VIEW OF THE CONFERENCE AT ST. JAMES'S PALACE ORGANISED BY THE OCCUPIED COUNTRIES THEMSELVES.

THE SAGA OF A "SUNDERLAND": AN AIR, SEA AND DESERT DRAMA. THE CRIPPLED AIRCRAFT BREAKING UP; ALREADY ITS BACK IS BROKEN, AND ITS WINGS TORN AND SHATTERED BY THE WAVES.

As more and more men are leaving to join the Forces, women are playing an ever-increasingly important part in heavy industry. Girls have come forward to take the place of the men and have taken over most of the light labouring work in all departments of Britain's great steel factories. Some of this work, like loading slag and scrap, is heavy, but the women who are doing it are proving most adept and capable. Women are also used as operators, working the controls in the cogging mills, but the most highly skilled job to which women have risen in the steel industry is that of steel examiners.

Representatives of nine Allied countries, overrun or subjugated by Hitler, signed a declaration setting out the punishment of Axis criminals as one of their major war aims. Seated on the left side of the table, and reading from left to right are: M. Bogomolov (U.S.S.R.), Mr. King (China), Mr. Biddle (U.S.A.), Mr. Eden (United Kingdom), Mr. Massey (Canada), Mr. Bruce (Australia), Mr. Jordan (New Zealand), Mr. Waterson (Union of South Africa), and the Duke of Devonshire (India). Poland was the prime mover in this conference, which was organised by the occupied countries themselves.

After a fight with two Messerschmitts, a Sunderland flying-boat carrying twenty men was forced to come down on a rocky beach in the Mediterranean. Hardly had they landed when twenty armed Italian soldiers appeared, the nearest of whom threw away his rifle and advanced with outstretched hands! The Italians explained that they had been left by the Germans to fend for themselves. They proposed that in exchange for help, the Italians should receive favourable treatment if captured. In due course the English and Italian party reached the British lines.

THE HERO OF BATAAN, NOW IN AUSTRALIA, IN SUPREME COMMAND FROM SINGAPORE TO U.S.A.

GENERAL DOUGLAS MACARTHUR (RIGHT), SUPREME C.-IN-C. IN THE SOUTH-WEST PACIFIC, WITH MAJOR-GENERAL JONATHAN WAINWRIGHT, HIS SUCCESSOR IN THE PHILIPPINES COMMAND.

President Roosevelt, on March 17, announcing to the world that General MacArthur had been appointed Commander-in-Chief in Australia at the request of the Australian Government, made it clear that his command includes all the Allied naval, land and air forces between Singapore and America. The General had left Corregidor by speed-boat and then flown from Bataan, leaving behind Major-General Wainwright as his successor. General MacArthur, whose brilliant defence of the Philippines against overwhelming numbers of the enemy has made him a dreaded foe, served in France in the last Great War, was the youngest Chief of Staff of the U.S. Army, and was lent to the Philippines to reorganise the Filipino Army. He is a fighting general, whose motto is "Attack," and his arrival in Australia caused great jubilation.

AUSTRALIA'S OUTER BASTION: PORT MORESBY AND ENVIRONS.

PORT MORESBY, SOUTH NEW GUINEA, AN AUSTRALIAN "TOBRUK," WHICH HAS DEFEATED ALL JAPANESE AIR ATTACKS: A GENERAL VIEW FROM THE PAGU HILL WIRELESS STATION.

The Japanese designs on Australia are frustrated unless they can capture Port Moresby, lying in the south of New Guinea by the Torres Strait. It lies at the base of mountains, strongly protected against attacks by sea and air. On March 25, Port Moresby experienced its nineteenth raid, but only three bombers appeared. No military damage was suffered. It was a significant change from the previous two days, when 40 enemy bombers came over aiming at military objectives, but doing little harm. Desperately anxious to obtain this bastion of Australia's defences, the enemy has attempted to cross the forbidding mountains of New Guinea. Here, jungles unrivalled even in the Amazon are held by grim, Australian bushmen, and the Japs have so far avoided conflict. The defenders believe they can hold any attempt to capture the port by the back door.

A FIGHT TO THE LAST: BATAAN FALLS – CORREGIDOR STANDS DEFIANT.

FOUR MEN OF THE GALLANT PHILIPPINE DEFENCE ARMY DUCK AS JAPANESE SHRAPNEL WHISTLES OVERHEAD.

ONE OF THE BIG 12-IN. GUNS ON FORT MILLS ABLE TO ROTATE TO ANY POINT, AND TO BLOW ANY WARSHIP OUT OF THE SEA.

"I HAVE NEVER KNOWN THE EQUAL OF THOSE 'IGOROTS!' ": NATIVES OF THE PHILIPPINES HIGHLY PRAISED BY MACARTHUR.

After a three-months' magnificent resistance, on April 9 General Wainwright was forced to retreat from Bataan Peninsula to Corregidor Island, the U.S. last Philippine strong-hold. Mr. Stimson, Secretary of War, disclosed that 36,853 gallant men faced capture or death, and added that in their last battle they faced odds of more than six to one. It was reported that General Yamashita had fresh shock troops, amounting to about 135,000 men, new tanks and further air support. No resistance as yet opposed to the Japanese advance is to be compared for tenacity with this, for since Manila fell in the first days of this year, the American and Filipino troops have stood at bay against overwhelming odds. Short of food, sick of malaria, and without hope of reinforcements, they have fought on – and are still fighting on as guerillas – until their capacity to fight was destroyed, and by so doing they have kept occupied some 100,000 of the enemy who would otherwise have been attacking elsewhere. It was General MacArthur who began this heroic stand, and when he was promoted to higher responsibilities, General Wainwright upheld the standard he set. The fighting qualities of the Filipinos are beyond praise, and the way they sat on top of the U.S. tanks to direct them caused General MacArthur to exclaim, "I have never known the equal of those 'Igorots'!" The whole army of Bataan fought as one man, and if they suffered heavy casualties one may be sure that those they inflicted were far greater. The survivors, about 65,000 troops and civilians, are probably prisoners, but General Wainwright is continuing the battle on the island fortress of Corregidor.

THE ANDAMAN ISLANDS SEIZED: COLOMBO AND TRINCOMALEE BOMBED.

SPEARING FISH AND TURTLES WITH LONG BAMBOO HARPOONS, THE ANDAMANESE FISHERMAN LEAPS BODILY FROM THE PROJECTING PLATFORM OF A CANOE, USING HIS WHOLE WEIGHT TO ENSURE SUCCESS.

THE KEY TO INDIA: A MAP OF CEYLON, WHICH ISLAND THE JAPANESE HAVE SEVERAL TIMES RAIDED WITH LONG-DISTANCE BOMBERS AND BEEN REPULSED WITH HEAVY LOSSES.

THE TILTING DECK OF H.M.S. "HERMES" SHORTLY BEFORE SHE SLID UNDER THE SEA. THE "HERMES" WAS SAILING IN THE BAY OF BENGAL WHEN SHE WAS ATTACKED BY JAPANESE DIVE-BOMBERS AND SUNK, WITH THE LOSS OF 304 LIVES.

The Indian Government were compelled to sacrifice the Andaman and Nicobar Islands in the Bay of Bengal owing to the sea command at present held by Japan, and the necessity of concentrating on holding Ceylon, whose ports of Trincomalee, the only naval base left east of Durban, and Colombo must be held at all cost. The Andamans, a group of 204 coral islands, lie in the Bay of Bengal, 120 miles from Burma, 800 miles from Colombo, and 850 from Madras. Port Blair, capital of the archipelago, has a harbour suitable for any naval ships except the largest battleship, and the Japanese aim is undoubtedly directed to the cutting-off of India and China from the Allies. It was announced from New Delhi on March 25 that British forces, women and children, with a number of convicts from the penal settlement, had been evacuated. The Andamans are the home of most primitive aborigines of great interest to anthropologists. They are a race of negroid dwarfs, the men averaging 4 ft 10½ in. and the women 4 ft. 6 in. marked by round-headed, broad-nosed characteristics, with sooty black hair. Physically they are very powerful, using seven-foot-long bows and barbed arrows, tipped with steel, from three to four feet in length, or long harpoons, to shoot or spear the varieties of big fish and turtles swimming fathoms deep below the translucent sea.

On Sunday, April 5, Japan launched her first attack against India's outer defences, Colombo, the capital and port of Ceylon. Using aircraft-carriers, which evidently put out from the recently occupied Andaman Islands, about 75 'planes went into action, concentrating on the harbour and the Ratmalana railway works and airfield, but the attack was a costly one for the enemy as twenty-seven of the raiders were shot down for certain, five others probably shot down, and twenty-five damaged.

On April 9, it was admitted by the Admiralty that in a big Japanese raid on Trincomalee, the enemy lost 18 'planes shot down or damaged. Unfortunately, British losses were severe: the two heavy cruisers H.M.S. "Dorsetshire" (9975 tons) and H.M.S. "Cornwall" (10,000 tons) were destroyed by air attacks and also the 10,850-ton aircraft-carrier "Hermes."

VICE-ADMIRAL LORD LOUIS MOUNTBATTEN, APPOINTED "CHIEF OF COMBINED OPERATIONS."

BRITAIN'S NEW "CHIEF OF COMBINED OPERATIONS," LORD LOUIS MOUNTBATTEN: HIS NEW POSITION CARRIES WITH IT THE ACTING RANK OF VICE-ADMIRAL AND THE HONORARY RANKS OF LT.-GENERAL AND AIR MARSHAL.

Mr. Churchill announced that Captain Lord Louis Mountbatten on March 18 of this year was appointed "Chief of Combined Operations," with the acting rank of Vice-Admiral and the honorary ranks of Lieutenant-General and Air Marshal. Lord Louis was in command of the "Kelly," both during the Channel battle when she was crippled by a torpedo and brought safely to port, and at Crete, when the destroyer was sunk. He was also the hero of another Channel battle in which, by brilliant seamanship, he brought home the destroyer "Javelin."

"A GLOOMY PORTENT FOR MR. HITLER": THE U.S. VANGUARD ARRIVES.

A SOLDIER OF THE U.S.A. IN GREAT BRITAIN, AND A SYMBOL OF UNIFIED DEMOCRATIC STRENGTH.

On January 26 the vanguard of the Second American Expeditionary Force to Europe arrived in Northern Ireland. This force was welcomed, on behalf of the British Government, by Sir Archibald Sinclair, and Mr. Andrews, Prime Minister of Northern Ireland. "Your safe arrival here," said Sir Archibald, "marks a new stage in the world war. It is a gloomy portent for Mr. Hitler." The arrival was a carefully guarded secret. Bandsmen arrived of the Royal Ulster Regiment played the National Anthem and then the "Star-spangled Banner."

LORD BEAVERBROOK, NEWLY APPOINTED MINISTER OF WAR PRODUCTION.

THE MINISTER WHO HUSTLES: LORD BEAVERBROOK, APPOINTED BY MR. CHURCHILL MINISTER OF WAR PRODUCTION TO SUPERVISE ALL WAR NEEDS. HIS SUCCESS AS MINISTER OF SUPPLY MADE HIS SELECTION PRACTICALLY INEVITABLE.

Mr. Churchill promised that a Minister should be appointed with functions comparable to those of Mr. Donald Nelson in the U.S.A., and the selection of Lord Beaverbrook was announced on February 4. Max Aitken, now Lord Beaverbrook, is the son of a Scottish minister, of Newcastle in Canada. As minister of Aircraft Production and Tank Production he was an arch-hustler, and staggered both Washington and Moscow by his activity. Critics have stated that his "powers" will be limited to persuasion and not command.

THE FIRST LAUNCHING OF LAND BOMBERS AT SEA: U.S. RAID JAPAN.

THE U.S. BOMBER RAID ON JAPAN: GENERAL DOOLITTLE FIRST TO TAKE OFF FROM THE U.S. AIRCRAFT-CARRIER "HORNET" 800 MILES FROM TOKYO. OF 16 BOMBERS TAKING PART, ALL MADE FORCED LANDINGS OR CRASHED SUBSEQUENTLY SAVE ONE.

LIEUT.-COLONEL JIMMY DOOLITTLE WIRES A JAPANESE MEDAL TO THE FIN OF A BOMB TO BE "RETURNED WITH INTEREST".

The sensational bombing raid on Tokyo and other cities on April 18 had immediate repercussions on the capital. The raiders flew low enough for the U.S. insignia on their wings to be identified. Tokyo was attacked first, Kobe Japan's largest port, two hours later. Other cities bombed were Yokohama, site of big shipyards, Nagoya, site of the aircraft factories of Kawanishi, Mitsubishi, and others, Wakayama, where are many war factories, Shiga, and Yokkaishi. What damage was suffered is not yet known, but Berlin radio said that the Japanese Government were providing funds for rebuilding factories. There are only three bridges in Tokyo and if these are bombed there is no means of evacuation. The Emperor was said to be "composed, but undoubtedly greatly concerned."

Exactly one month and one day after the raid the identity of the man who led the attack was revealed when President Roosevelt bestowed on Brigadier-General James Doolittle the Congressional Medal of Honour, the

highest American award for valour. The General described the raid as having had a success beyond "our most optimistic expectations." The preparations were made with such secrecy that only six men in Washington knew about it. Each aircraft was assigned a special target, and the objectives began north of Tokyo and extended south. On 20 April 1943 the U.S. War Department disclosed that the aeroplanes were Mitchell medium bombers, which took off from the aircraft-carrier "Hornet." Preparations were started in January 1942, and Doolittle personally selected his crews. The machines were under orders to fly to specified landing-fields in China, but were unable to reach the distance. One landed unharmed on Russian soil and others made forced or crash landings in China or in Chinese waters. Two machines were forced down in Japan and the crews were taken prisoner. The world has been horrified by President Roosevelt's disclosure that some of them were deliberately executed by the Japanese Government.

DRAMATIC ATTACK ON ST. NAZAIRE: H.M.S. "CAMPBELTOWN" RAMS THE LOCK GATES!

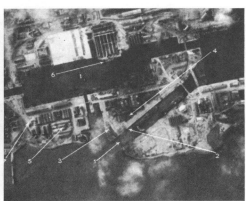

LEFT: *BEFORE* THE COMBINED BRITISH RAID ON ST. NAZAIRE: THE OUTER DOCK GATE (MARKED BY ARROW) BEFORE ITS DESTRUCTION. CENTRE: THE "NORMANDIE" IN THE DRY DOCK AT ST. NAZAIRE BEFORE THE WAR. THE OUTER SLIDING GATE AND THE PUMP-HOUSE ARE SEEN ON THE LEFT. RIGHT: *AFTER* THE RAID ON ST. NAZAIRE; THE OUTER DOCK GATE HAS DISAPPEARED: THE FIGURES REVEAL DAMAGE: (1) OUTER LOCK GATE MISSING; (2) PUMP-HOUSE SEVERELY DAMAGED; (3) MACHINE-HOUSE FOR GATE DAMAGED; (4) TWO SMALL PUMP-HOUSE SHEDS DESTROYED; (5) SECTION OF BUILDING WEST OF HYDRAULIC MACHINE-SHOP PARTLY DESTROYED; (6) DAMAGE TO SUBMARINE PENS; (7) MILITARY BUILDING DAMAGED.

In a brilliant and successful foray at St. Nazaire in the early morning of March 28, the superannuated destroyer H.M.S. "Campbeltown" with her guns blazing, her after-deck cleared of all obstruction, charged at the great 30-ft.-thick dry-dock gates, on her way leaping over a boom obstructing the entrance to the harbour. Behind her followed the commando in motor-launches. On the bridge of the motor gunboat were Lieut.-Colonel A. C. Newman, commander of the commandos, Commander Ryder R.N., in charge of naval operations, and Mr. Holman, a Press correspondent.

The "Campbeltown" well and truly attained her objective. From the M.G.B.s commando troops landed to carry out their tasks while M.T.B.s dashed towards the entrance of the basin to launch torpedoes at the U-boat "hide-out," and the commandos blew up the power plant of the lock gates.

Experts have declared that the gate cannot be replaced under four months, and that the pumping installation will require much longer. The dry dock at St. Nazaire was the only one on the Atlantic coast capable of taking Germany's only surviving battleship, the "Tirpitz", and its destruction will hinder the use of this warship.

OUR CHINESE ALLIES: VICTORY AT CHANGSHA, AID IN BURMA.

CHINESE SOLDIERS COLLECTING JAPANESE ARMS AT CHANGSHA: IN THEIR DISORDERLY RETREAT THE FLEEING JAPANESE THREW AWAY THEIR ARMS.

THE REMARKABLE SOONG SISTERS IN BOMBED CHUNGKING: MADAME KUNG IS ELING (KINDLINESS), MADAME SUN IS CHING-LING (GLORY) AND MADAME CHIANG IS MAYLING (BEAUTY).

CHINA'S RESOLUTE ARMY IN BURMA: WELL-EQUIPPED CHINESE TROOPS ADVANCING IN SINGLE FILE THROUGH TYPICAL BUR-MESE JUNGLE COUNTRY.

The story of the great Chinese victory at Changsha, early in the New Year, makes heartening reading to those who are fighting a desperate battle against huge Japanese forces in the Far East. General Hsueh Yu-eh, a forty-seven-year-old Commander, known in China as "Little Tiger," who was fortunate enough to obtain the attackers' complete plans by raiding a divisional H.Q., succeeded in cutting off the enemy by successive waves of flank attacks, and the Japanese were at no time able to penetrate the city. For the first time since the war started the Chinese had superiority of fire and were able to shell the enemy lines without fear of reprisals, because the Japanese had lost their artillery in the battle of the Milo river.

The Soong sisters are the daughters of "Charlies Jones" Soong, so baptised as a youth after being befriended by an American skipper on whose ship he had stowed away. "Charlie Jones" became a successful business man in America, and a thoroughgoing modernist; he returned to Shanghai to make a fortune, and to print, surreptitiously, revolutionary pamphlets against the Manchu rule; in the course of time, he sent his children to be educated at Christian colleges in America. "Charlie Jones" Soong, was Sun-Yat-Sen's most faithful backer, and his son T. V. Soong, Foreign Minister. His three daughters have always been in the forefront of the fight for freedom and reform, and all married prominent fighters in that cause.

JAPAN'S SUCCESSES IN BURMA: BY INFILTRATION AND LIGHT EQUIPMENT.

JAPANESE TROOPS ENTER MARTABAR, THEIR SUCCESS LARGELY DUE TO TRAVELLING LIGHT AND TO THEIR COMPLETE COMMAND OF THE AIR.

A MAP INDICATING THE JAPANESE ADVANCE BY THE SITTING RIVER.

GENERAL STILWELL, MARCHING THROUGH STEAMY JUNGLE, AFTER RETREAT. FOR THREE WEEKS THE GENERAL AND A SMALL PARTY WERE MISSING.

General Alexander who took over from General Hutton on March 5, was undoubtedly faced with a stiff task in Burma. With a mountain barrier between him and India, crossed by three roads mostly no better than tracks for pack animals, and deprived of Burma's one great port, Rangoon, he was faced with greatly superior forces, treacherous Burmans, a strong enemy air force which commands the air, and Japan's command of the sea. Our map shows the position of the rival armies on March 31, with the defending Chinese army at Toungoo, on the Sittang (on the road leading to Mandalay), and the British/Indian forces on the western road before Paungde and Shwedaung, only ten miles south of Prome, the enemy having also crossed the Irrawaddy. On that day British and Indian regiments cleared the Shwedaung enemy block in a fighting withdrawal, and smashed open the vital Irrawaddy road.

After the separation of the British and Chinese forces in Upper Burma, anxiety was felt as to the fate of General Stilwell, the U.S. Chief of Staff to Marshal Chiang Kai-shek, who was in command of the Chinese Army in Burma. His position at Shwebo was desperate, and a British 'plane was sent to fetch him. He flatly refused to leave his staff and some nineteen Chinese and Burmese nurses. A little party of 200 set out through dense forests for a grim 150-mile trek to Assam. For days they suffered acutely from hunger. Through jungle and river in great heat, bitten by cruel insects, and ever in danger from the enemy, the General, cheerful and unperturbed, led the way, and in three weeks the party reached the Assam border. The nurses belonging to Dr. Segrave's American Harper Memorial Hospital set a fine example of courage. In Delhi the General said: "Our entire Burma campaign was fought blind. We had no air force."

THE BATTLE OF THE CORAL SEA: JAPANESE INVADERS REPULSED.

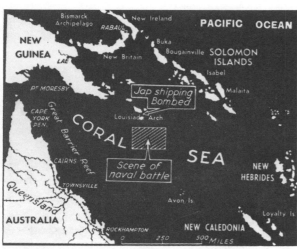

A MAP SHOWING THE SCENE OF THE NAVAL BATTLE OF THE CORAL SEA, BE-TWEEN THE SOLOMON ISLANDS, NEW GUINEA, AND QUEENSLAND.

A FLIGHT OF DOUGLAS "SBD-I" DIVE-BOMBERS. THESE MACHINES ARE IN EXTENSIVE USE WITH THE U.S. NAVY, OPERATING FROM AIRCRAFT-CARRIERS.

THE END OF THE "LEXINGTON": MEMBERS OF THE CREW CAN BE SEEN LEAPING INTO THE WATER WHILST A DESTROYER RACES TO THE RESCUE.

After days of suspense from the first intimation of a big naval battle between Allied naval forces under U.S. command and a Japanese fleet, on May 8, reports were flashed to an advanced Australian base indicating that it had gone in favour of the Allies.
Big Japanese concentrations, apparently making for New Guinea were caught by American dive-bombers, who attacked in waves. The Japanese finally scattered, and their lavish claims to have destroyed many warships and 'planes were largely discounted. All that was known with any certainty was that it marks the biggest naval engagement of the war to date.

The story of the Coral Sea Battle has now been told, a story which proves that the campaign was nothing short of disaster for the Japanese. The enemy lost at least seven warships sunk, and a large number of transports, and at least twenty more ships were severely damaged. The United States, on the other hand, lost only three: a tanker, a destroyer, and the aircraft-carrier "Lexington." It was on May 8 that the "Lexington" was hit by two torpedoes and bombs, but the crew extinguished the fires and recovered the aircraft. Several hours later, after the action was finished, a terrific internal explosion took place, and after fighting the fire for fifteen hours, the crew was obliged to abandon her.

HOW HITLER LOOKS TO-DAY.

FRANCE'S NO. 1 QUISLING BACK IN POWER.

HITLER SEES MUSSOLINI OFF AFTER THE SALZBURG MEETING. HE APPEARS TO BE TAKING LITTLE INTEREST IN HIS PARTNER.

HITLER AS HE LOOKED ON APRIL 4, 1942, DURING HIS ADDRESS TO THE REICHSTAG – HAGGARD AND WEARY AND WITH MUCH OF HIS SELF-CONFIDENCE GONE. EVEN HIS GESTURE OF FAREWELL SHOWS LITTLE OF HIS MUCH-VAUNTED "INDOMITABLE WILL."

PIERRE LAVAL RETURNS AS HEAD OF A RECONSTITUTED VICHY GOVERNMENT.

The pictures above show Hitler as he is to-day; they offer an excellent opportunity for studying the Führer's face after two and a half years of war, and an interesting study it is. Worry and strain have changed it very considerably. In direct contrast to the smiling Hitler of a year ago, we now see a man grave and worried, racked by doubt and with the first signs of a certain defeat dawning in his eyes.

Marshal Pétain, capitulating to a German ultimatum, has gone back on his promise never to have Laval in the Government again, and has agreed to his return as head of the Vichy Government. Born in 1884, Laval has always been completely unscrupulous, mounting the rungs of his political ladder over the bodies of fairer men. His ambitions and policy were made clear from the first, when he said: "I intend by every means to make France into Germany's No. 1 ally – I am governing France to-day, and will continue to govern her when Germany conquers Britain." In France Laval is loathed. America's first reaction to Laval's return is to urge all her nationals living in Unoccupied France to return home as soon as possible. Before making an announcement on any serious question of policy the U.S. is waiting for the new Vichy Cabinet to assume office.

THE "BAEDEKER" RAIDS ON EXETER, BATH, NORWICH AND YORK:
DAMAGED CHURCHES, HISTORIC BUILDINGS AND HOMES.

ST. MARY ARCHES, ONE OF EXETER'S GEMS, OF NORMAN ARCHITECTURE NOW A SHAMBLES. THIS ANCIENT CITY IS RENOWNED FOR ITS CHURCHES.

YORK: A DRAMATIC PICTURE OF THE FAMOUS GUILDHALL ABLAZE. THE FLAMES ARE SEEN REFLECTED IN THE RIVER OUSE.

NORWICH: A MASS OF DÉBRIS WHERE ONCE STOOD THE HOMES OF INOFFENSIVE CITIZENS. ALL PRETENCE OF AIMING AT MILITARY OBJECTIVES HAS BEEN ABANDONED BY THE GERMANS.

The German so-called "Baedeker" raids in April on English towns selected as targets our ancient and venerable monuments, and the Nazi Press went so far as to gloat over the damage done to historic buildings. In Bath, two churches were gutted. The Circus suffered and others of the Beau Nash period. Norwich suffered much devastation. York's historic Guildhall was left a blazing shell.

Exeter was the first victim and the latest, suffering three separate visits, the most destructive being on the third occasion, May 4. Flying low, the raiders dropped high explosive and incendiary bombs and machine-gunned streets. The Cathedral (dating from 1107 to 1369) suffered severely, St. James's Chapel (1257–1280) being destroyed and part of the Choir Aisle, the Bishop's Palace, and also many priceless mediæval stained-glass windows were damaged. Other churches and buildings were also destroyed, including the well-known Town House of the Prior of Plympton.

COLOGNE: BEFORE AND AFTER THE GREAT 1000-BOMBER RAID.

THE KÖLNISCHE GUMMIFADEN FABRIK AT DEUTZ, BEFORE AND AFTER THE RAID: THE MAIN BUILDING HAS BEEN ENTIRELY DESTROYED.

AIR MARSHAL A. T. HARRIS, COMMANDER-IN-CHIEF BOMBER COMMAND. "CITY BY CITY": THE C.-I.-C. BOMBER COMMAND DELIVERS THE FIRST BLOW.

THE KÖLN-NIPPES RAILWAY WORKSHOPS BEFORE AND AFTER THE RAID: THEY HAVE BEEN ALMOST COMPLETELY DESTROYED.

On more than one occasion Air Marshal Arthur Travers "Bomber" Harris, Commander-in-Chief, Bomber Command, said that were it possible to put 1000 bombers over Germany night after night, the war would be over by the autumn. On the night of Saturday, May 30, he directed a raid of over 1000 bombers, with supporting fighters, with Cologne as the main objective. It became immediately clear that R.A.F. Bomber Command had succeeded in delivering one of the heaviest blows of the war.

For several days it was impossible to obtain photographs but as the smoke drifted away the extent of the destruction became apparent. There are six major areas of devastation in the old city – three due west of the Cathedral and the main station, one north-west, one south of the Cathedral, and one near the west station. The cathedral appears to have received but superficial damage – a high tribute to the accuracy of our bomb-aimers. The devastation round the main station is specially pronounced.

THE "BUTCHER OF MORAVIA" IS ACCORDED A STATE FUNERAL: LIDICE'S TRAGEDY.

A VIEW OF THE PEACEFUL MINING VILLAGE OF LIDICE, IN CZECHOSLOVAKIA, BEFORE THE GERMANS OBLITERATED IT AS A REPRISAL FOR THE ASSASSINATION OF HEYDRICH, THE "BUTCHER OF PRAGUE."

"THE BUTCHER OF MORAVIA" SHOT BY A CZECH PATRIOT: REINHARD HEYDRICH (R.) WITH THE GERMAN S.S. AND POLICE CHIEF, HIMMLER.

THE RUINS OF LIDICE, PHOTOGRAPHED ON THE MORNING AFTER THE EXTERMINATION OF THE VILLAGE. THESE PRINTS WERE MADE SECRETLY BY A CZECH PATROL.

Reinhard Heydrich is thirty-eight; he was cashiered from the German Navy in 1931. Himmler, chief of all the police and the S.S., made him his adjutant, in which capacity he organised the Dachau concentration camp, the worst in Germany. Known as "the butcher of Moravia" for his brutality when "Protector" of Bohemia and Moravia, Heydrich has reaped his just deserts. He was shot, and seriously wounded, in Prague on May 27, some accounts say by Nazis. Heydrich died, and had his funeral – in Berlin. Furthermore, his corpse was decorated with the highest degree of the highest German Order by Hitler, for being "one of the best National Socialists" and "one of Germany's martyrs". A ceremony of remembrance was held in the mosaic hall of the Reich Chancellery, and afterwards the coffin was taken under military guard to the Invaliden cemetery, where Udet and Richtofen are buried. As a reprisal for his death, which was presumed to have been brought about by local partisans, the villages of Lidice and Lezaku were obliterated on June 10 and 24 respectively.

JAPANESE DÉBÂCLE OFF MIDWAY ISLAND: U.S. FLEET'S VICTORY.

LEFT: THE "YORKTOWN" RECEIVES A DIRECT HIT DURING THE BATTLE OF MIDWAY ISLAND. RIGHT: DESTROYERS STAND BY TO RESCUE THE CREW OF THE HEAVILY LISTING AIRCRAFT-CARRIER. LATER, SHE WAS TAKEN IN TOW, BUT WAS SUBSEQUENTLY TORPEDOED.

About 9 p.m. on June 3, U.S. Navy air patrols reported a Japanese force about 700 miles west of Midway, steering east. "Flying Fortresses" from Midway attacked and severely damaged a cruiser and transport. At dawn on June 4 other air formations took off from Midway, and despite severe losses, damaged two aircraft-carriers. Later in the day the attacks were renewed, a battleship was hit and believed sunk, and one carrier set on fire. The enemy carrier force was obliged to alter course and began to withdraw to the north-westward. Meanwhile, Japanese carrier-borne 'planes attacked the island in force; at least forty of the attackers were shot down, and although the Midway installation was seriously damaged, it was not disabled. During that same day ship-borne naval air forces came into operation. One flight of fifteen torpedo 'planes, none of which returned, succeeded in making contact and reporting the enemy's whereabouts. Attacks were pressed home and the carriers "Kaga," "Soryu" were set on fire and later sank. Two battleships and one destroyer were hit. It was then that the U.S.S. "Yorktown" was hit by bombs and torpedoes, but her aircraft continued to operate from other carriers. A new Japanese force was then located, and the carrier "Hiryu" was hit and left blazing. By June 5 all the remaining Japanese forces were in full retreat, pursued by the American Fleet, and on June 6 U.S. 'planes attacked and sank the cruisers "Mikuma" and "Mogami" and one destroyer. It was on this day that the American destroyer "Hammann" was torpedoed and sunk, as also was the "Yorktown". Bombed and torpedoed by the Japanese aircraft at the height of the battle on June 4, she was put out of action. Tugs and salvage were sighted by an enemy submarine, which scored two hits with torpedoes amidships. The "Yorktown" remained afloat until the following morning, when she capsized and sank. Japanese losses were severe, including damage to three battleships, two heavy cruisers and several destroyers. America scored a resounding victory.

THE U.S. ALEUTIAN ISLES: JAPANESE BOMB DUTCH HARBOUR, SEIZE ATTU AND KISKA.

JAPANESE BOMBS BURSTING IN THE BAY OF DUTCH HARBOUR, ALEUTIAN ISLES, THE PRINCIPAL U.S. BASE, ON JUNE 3 AND 4.

THE JAPANESE LANDING AT KISKA, ALEUTIAN ISLANDS: U.S. BOMBERS BURNT A TRANSPORT AND DAMAGED A CRUISER.

A BOMBED JAPANESE CRUISER OF THE "MOGAMI" DURING THE BATTLE OFF MIDWAY ISLAND.

The photograph (top) shows the determined Japanese attempt to control the Aleutian Islands from Dutch Harbour, the main U.S. base, off Alaska, to Kiska Harbour (middle picture), towards the extreme west of the archipelago, whose extremity points towards the Japanese islands. Attempts upon Dutch Harbour failed, but on June 6, at Kiska, and Attu Islands (farther west) the enemy established landings. At Kiska they lost a transport, and a cruiser was damaged.

The Japanese raids on June 2–3 upon the Far Northern U.S. naval and air base of Dutch Harbour were thought to indicate the approach of an invasion fleet on Alaska. Admiral Yates Stirling, in New York, however, suggested that Germany may have invited the Japanese to attack the Soviet in the Far East, and as a preliminary the Japs intended to advance on the U.S. Alaskan bases and prevent our Allies from sending aid to the Russians in the Far East. As was later discovered, neither of the explanations offered were correct.

ROMMEL BREAKS OUT: "KNIGHTSBRIDGE", "THE CAULDRON", BIR HAKEIM.

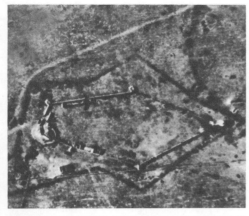

THE FORT OF BIR HAKEIM, SHOWING THE DEFENCES FROM BE-HIND WHICH THE FREE FRENCH HURLED DEFIANCE AT ROM-MEL'S TROOPS FOR NINE GRIM DAYS.

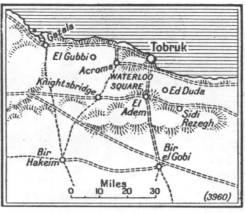

ROMMEL'S NEW LIBYAN OFFENSIVE: THE AREA OF THE BIG TANK BATTLE WHICH CENTRED IN THE "KNIGHTSBRIDGE" SECTOR AND SOUTH OF ACROMA.

INSIDE A "GENERAL GRANT." THE DRIVER'S VIEW AS THESE U.S. 28-TON TANKS GO INTO ACTION IN THE LIBYAN DESERT. THE 75 MM GUNS HAVE OUTRANGED ROMMEL'S PZ IV.S.

Since Rommel on February 8 last reached Gazala, where he has since been anchored until on May 27 he began the new offensive which General Auchinleck was expectantly awaiting, there has been over a three months' lull, in which time both Commanders feverishly acquired supplies, and the British prepared a defensive line from Gazala to Bir Hakeim. The centre of this line was breached in two places in Rommel's initial advance, our forces retiring to the area of the cross-roads known as Knightsbridge.

The biggest struggle that has yet taken place in Libya boiled up on June 5 in the "Cauldron" area between what were the upper and lower gaps which Rommel forced through our minefield, and the new British position at Knightsbridge. An attack launched by Rommel's main armoured forces against Knightsbridge was stopped by our infantry and artillery and the enemy driven westwards. British armoured forces meanwhile reached Harmat which looks as if the bulge which the Germans had made in our forward positions was being shortened. After June 4 the battle centred upon Bir Hakeim, where Free French resisted with the utmost gallantry, for nine glorious days before withdrawing.

Having at long last and at a heavy cost achieved his objective at Bir Hakeim, Rommel then struck swiftly to the north and would seem to have reverted to his original objective – the famous stronghold of Tobruk.

TOBRUK, LIBYA'S HISTORIC LANDMARK, AGAIN IN ROMMEL'S HANDS.

A GENERAL AIR VIEW OF TOBRUK CAPTURED BY GENERAL ROM-MEL AFTER A TWENTY-FOUR-HOUR ASSAULT.

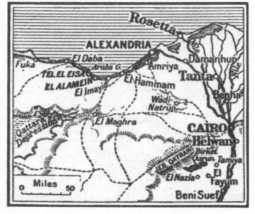

THE EL ALAMEIN FRONT: A MAP SHOWING THE AREA OF OPERA-TIONS BETWEEN TEL EL EISA AND THE QATTARA DEPRESSION, WHERE ROMMEL, IN A TANK ATTACK IN THE CENTRAL SECTOR ON JULY 16, SUFFERED CONSIDERABLE LOSSES.

GENERAL SIR CLAUDE AUCHINLECK WATCHING HIS TROOPS FROM HIS MAP LORRY ON THE RETREAT FROM MERSA MATRUH.

The capitulation of Tobruk to Rommel's forces on the morning of Sunday, June 21, was the crowning disappointment of a campaign that had raised high hopes. The enemy claimed to have occupied the town and to have taken 25,000 prisoners, including several generals, and large quantities of ammunition. The fall of Tobruk was officially confirmed in London at midnight on June 21. However, in reaching Tobruk, General Rommel has not only attained his immediate objective, but has apparently put out of action a large fraction of the forces defending Egypt. Within six days of the fall of Tobruk, Rommel contrived to move his main army and supply columns across 200 miles of desert and to make a supreme bid for a lightning conquest of Egypt.

His objective was to destroy the Eighth Army before it had time to refit or receive major reinforcements. On the same date the Italians claimed to have reached a point 18 miles east of Mersa Matruh; and on June 29 it was known that a great battle was proceeding between the south-west and south-east of Mersa, covering an area of over 400 square miles. On the same day (Monday) both Germans and Italians claimed the fall of Mersa Matruh, later confirmed, which meant that in four weeks Rommel's forces had advanced almost 500 miles from his main base and inflicted a succession of severe defeats upon British arms, leaving Egypt wide open to direct attack, and involving a grave threat to Alexandria and the Suez Canal.

MARTINIQUE WARSHIPS BEING IMMOBILISED.

ONE OF THE FRENCH SHIPS BEING IMMOBILISED IN THE FRENCH WEST INDIES: THE FRENCH AIRCRAFT-CARRIER "BÉARN" (22,146 TONS) IN FORT DE FRANCE HARBOUR, MARTINIQUE.

The French warships at Martinique and Guadaloupe in the French West Indies are being immobilised according to plans agreed on by the French and American naval officials to ensure that no French Caribbean possessions are used to help the Axis. The ships are: the cruiser "Emile Bertin," which conveyed £62,500,000 worth of French gold to Martinique after the Armistice; the aircraft-carrier "Béarn," which took 100 American 'planes to Martinique, bought by France and Belgium before they fell; and the cruiser "Jeanne d'Arc."

THE CRETE BATTLE GOES ON: EMPIRE TROOPS FIGHTING AFTER 11 MONTHS.

BRITISH SOLDIERS AND CRETAN PATRIOTS UNDERGOING EX-AMINATION FOLLOWING THEIR CAPTURE BY ONE OF THE MANY GERMAN SEARCH PARTIES.

Eleven months after the collapse of Crete the Germans have published the dramatic picture shown above, and thus amply confirmed the stories of hundreds of British and Empire troops who are fighting on the island's mountain ranges. Many of our men, trapped after the sea communications had been cut, instead of surrendering to the Germans escaped to the hills to carry on the fight, with the help of Cretan patriots. Information reaching London shows with what success these guerillas and irregulars have carried out raids on the enemy.

MIDGET SUBMARINES: THE SYDNEY HARBOUR RAID.

A JAPANESE MIDGET SUBMARINE, CAPTURED AT PEARL HARBOUR: ITS LENGTH IS 42 FT. IT CARRIES TWO TORPEDOES AND A CREW OF TWO.

Midget submarines of the Japanese Navy – similar to those which took part in the Pearl Harbour action – have been operating against various places on the Australian coastline but with no special success. On May 31 Jap submarines raided Sydney Harbour, but the defences went into action so fast and with such effect that the operation – carried out with daring and cunning – was abortive, save for superficial damage. "The enemy's attack," said the official communiqué, "was completely unsuc-cessful, and damage was confined to one small harbour vessel . . ."

FACETS OF THE WAR ON THE RUSSIAN FRONT: M. MOLOTOV'S HISTORIC FLIGHT.

THE DNIEPER POURS THROUGH THE WIDE CHASM MADE IN THE DAM.

AN HISTORIC MOMENT: MR. EDEN SIGNING THE TWENTY-YEAR TREATY OF ALLIANCE WITH RUSSIA. SEATED (LEFT TO RIGHT), M. MAISKY, M. MOLOTOV AND MR. CHURCHILL.

RUSSIA'S COMMANDER-IN-CHIEF, CENTRAL FRONT: GENERAL GREGORY ZHUKOV, FORTRESS AND DEFENCE-WORK EXPERT.

This photograph comes from a German illustrated paper. It purports to show the way in which the Zaporozhe Dam across the Dnieper is being repaired by German engineers. The German captions beneath the pictures are more eloquent of future hopes than present achievements.

One of the war's best-kept secrets, the journey to Britain and America, in a monster warplane, of M. Molotov, Soviet Commissar for Foreign Affairs, is likely to have unpleasant consequences for the Axis Powers. M. Molotov, who spent six days in London concluded a twenty-year Treaty of Alliance and Mutual Assistance between Great Britain and Soviet Russia, not the least important feature of which is the envisaging of a second front in Europe in 1942. The Treaty was signed on May 26; and M. Molotov then flew across the Atlantic to Washington, where he came to an agreement with President Roosevelt on the extension of the Lease-Lend Act and other matters of strategy.

General Zhukov, who succeeded Marshal Timoshenko in October last, is, under Stalin, responsible for the brilliant advance of the Red Army in the Moscow sector. General Zhukov has seen twenty-six years' military service, beginning as a private. Vice-Commissar for Defence and Chief of the Soviet General Staff he worked in constant close contact with Stalin. He is Russia's greatest fortress and defence-work expert, and was at one time commander at Kiev.

TIME'S WHIRLIGIG – SEBASTOPOL AFTER THE SIEGE OF 1854–55 AND TO-DAY.

SEBASTOPOL TO-DAY. AFTER WITHSTANDING THE SIEGE BY GERMANY FOR EIGHT MONTHS. THE PHOTOGRAPH, VERY SIMILAR TO SIMPSON'S WATERCOLOUR, SHOWS THE SCENE OF DEVASTATION WHICH GREETED THE ENEMY AT HIS ENTRY ON JULY 3.

MARSHAL TIMOSHENKO'S FRONT ON JULY 20: SHOWING THE ENEMY ADVANCE SINCE VON BOCK STARTED HIS BIG OFFENSIVE.

SEBASTOPOL AS IT LOOKED AFTER THE SIEGE OF 1854–1855, AND LAY IN UTTER RUIN UNTIL 1876. THE WOOD-CUT FROM A WATER-COLOUR BY WILLIAM SIMPSON, R.I., WAS PUBLISHED IN "THE ILLUSTRATED LONDON NEWS" OF MAY 29, 1859.

When the Germans at Kerch, in the Crimea, on May 8 launched a sudden big offensive against the Soviet forces in that area, they were evidently unprepared for the immediate counter-blow by Marshal Timoshenko at Kharkov, 300 miles to the north. He waited until the Germans were fully committed and then struck with hurricane force. In their initial attacks the Soviet troops stormed one strongly fortified post after another and threw back von Bock's men to their second line of defences, leaving behind artillery, ammunition and masses of war material in their hurried retreat.

Marshal Timoshenko's sudden offensive on Kharkov between May 12 and 16 advanced to a depth of between 12 and 40 miles, in which German losses were put at 12,000 killed. On the 18th the approximate fighting line

stretched from Bielgorod, 50 miles north of Kharkov, to a line west of Stalino, 125 miles south. In the Kerch Peninsula, the Russians, in fact, only held a bridgehead at Kerch. The German success for which they paid heavily, means that General Kozlov's main force is probably back in the Caucasus area, and while the Russians control the sea a major enemy operation can scarcely be attempted.

Violent attacks on Kharkov and Sebastopol by Generals von Bock and von Manstein, pressed with reckless determination and despite enormous German losses indicated quite plainly that the thrust towards the Caspian and Caucasus had at last begun.

THE ENEMY CROSSING THE DON – ONE OF THE MOST AMAZING AND GRAPHIC BATTLE PICTURES OF THE WAR.

HEAVILY BATTERED, THE ENEMY BATTLE RELENTLESSLY ACROSS THE DON.

This remarkable photograph, depicting war in all its nakedness, was taken on the River Don when the Germans, on July 6, forced two bridgeheads. Here for five hours the German troops were battered heavily by Russian guns, dying in hundreds, until the enemy artillery got the upper hand and covered a forced landing. A flood of German vehicles, men and guns broke through across an improvised bridge, trampling over the bodies of their own dead, and passed on amid the surrounding shambles of vehicles, horses, and men. Even the pictures of the famous Russian painter Basil Verestchagin (Vassili), probably the greatest realist of war's

terrors, could not surpass in crude realism this photograph. Verestchagin proclaimed himself "an apostle of peace and of humanity" who, last century, painted bloody battlefields of the Russo-Turkish War, because he considered it part of his life's mission to disgust mankind in the butchering of their fellow men. In Berlin, in 1882, at a great exhibition of his work, the German Emperor, William I., forbade his Guards to visit it, "lest they should come to regard war not as honourable but as disgusting." It would be well if the wives and sisters of the Axis soldiers could also see war's disgusting reality. Yet it depicts but a very small area in one battle.

MR. CHURCHILL'S SPECTACULAR FLIGHTS TO EGYPT AND MOSCOW: ALLIED CHIEFS CONFER.

IN CAIRO: IN THE BRITISH EMBASSY GARDEN. (BACK ROW; L. TO R.) AIR CHIEF-MARSHAL TEDDER, SIR ALAN BROOKE, ADMIRAL HARWOOD, MR. R. G. CASEY; (FRONT ROW) FD.-MARSHAL SMUTS, THE PREMIER, GENERALS AUCHINLECK AND WAVELL.

NEW COMMANDER-IN-CHIEF, MIDDLE EAST: GENERAL THE HON. SIR HAROLD ALEXANDER SUCCEEDS GENERAL SIR CLAUDE AUCHINLECK.

LIEUT.-GENERAL B. L. MONTGOMERY: HE SUCCEEDS GENERAL N. M. RITCHIE AS COMMANDER OF THE EIGHTH ARMY.

MR. CHURCHILL AND M. STALIN AT THE KREMLIN: THIS HISTORIC PICTURE WAS TAKEN DURING ONE OF THEIR MEETINGS, AND BOTH MR. CHURCHILL AND M. STALIN SIGNED THEIR NAMES ON THE BACK.

Mr. Churchill's recent visits to Egypt and Moscow were of the highest importance. He went first to the Middle East, where the stimulating effect of his presence on the troops and on the whole British community in Egypt was obvious. His talks with such men as Field-Marshal Smuts, Sir Archibald Wavell, General Sir Henry Wilson and Mr. Casey rather point to the fact that the whole of the Middle Eastern area, including India, came under discussion. Mr. Churchill arrived by air in Egypt, flying in a U.S. bomber, piloted by American airmen. His visit had been kept a close secret and he was announced as "Mr. Bullfinch." Very early after his arrival, Mr. Churchill made an excursion to the El Alamein front. During his visit to Cairo a number of changes were made to the Middle East Command structure, General The Hon. Sir Harold Alexander replacing General Sir Claude Auchinleck as Commander-in-Chief, Middle East, and Lt. General Montgomery replacing General Ritchie as Commander of the Eighth Army.

HOW THE TANKER "OHIO" DELIVERED THE FUEL TO MALTA.

A SALVO OF BOMBS FALL HARMLESSLY BETWEEN TWO OF THE MERCHANT SHIPS. THE AXIS LOST 66 'PLANES FOR CERTAIN, AND PROBABLY ABOUT 100. FOR THREE DAYS AND NIGHTS, HOWEVER, THE CONVOY WENT ON AND ON AND ON . . . TO MALTA.

THREE BRITISH AIRCRAFT-CARRIERS, WITH A CRUISER BEYOND, NEAREST IS H.M.S. "EAGLE," WHICH WAS TORPEDOED. IT IS DOUBTFUL IF ANY OTHER INDIVIDUAL SHIP CONTRIBUTED MORE TO THE GALLANT GEORGE CROSS ISLAND'S DEFENCE THAN "EAGLE" IN THE WAR.

In Malta by the end of July 1942 supplies of all kinds were practically exhausted. Submarines could no longer refuel there, ammunition was short and food shorter. A major effort was needed if Malta were not, after all her bravery, to fall to the Axis. An unprecedently large escort was assembled at Gibraltar to accompany the fourteen merchant men available. Everyone concerned knew it meant a desperate task. Early on, the strong naval escort suffered a grievous loss when the aircraft-carrier "Eagle" was torpedoed, though fortunately 930 men – practically all her crew – were saved.

Commander Anthony Kimmins, R.N., broadcasting an eyewitness account, specially alluded to the epic story of the tanker "Ohio," with her valuable cargo of much-needed fuel for beleaguered Malta, which managed to make port. Bombed, torpedoed, and set on fire, the "Ohio" had to be left behind. The other ships continued on their nightmare voyage. The "Ohio" the next morning managed to catch up with the ships, to the surprise of all. A few hours later, once more badly hit, again the convoy had to leave her, but destroyers stood by, for Malta was nearer, when Admiral Burrough signalled the proud compliment, "I am pleased to have met you." At sunset she was again hit and set on fire, but the dauntless crew fought and subdued the flames. Taken in tow, she limped into Valetta Harbour, down by the bows, but triumphant.

THE FLARE-UP IN THE DESERT WAR: ROMMEL SUFFERS A SET-BACK.

A TANK GUNNER EXAMINING ONE OF THE LATEST TYPES OF GERMAN TANKS KNOCKED OUT IN THE RECENT FIGHTING, IN WHICH ROMMEL SUFFERED A SET-BACK.

THIS DESERT SIGNPOST, PUT UP BY THE AUSTRALIANS TO MARK THE EDGE OF NO MAN'S LAND IN THE EL ALAMEIN BATTLE AREA, SPEAKS FOR ITSELF.

THE GREAT SPHINX IN ITS "BIG AND TUCKER": THE GUARDIAN TO THE ENTRANCE OF THE NILE VALLEY PROTECTED BY A WALL AND SANDBAGS FROM POSSIBLE AIR-RAID DAMAGE.

The clash of arms between the Afrika Korps and the Eighth Army of Lieut.-General Montgomery, after a week of severe fighting, on September 7 appeared to be very much "as you were." Rommel chose the time for his offensive, but the dispositions of General Montgomery dictated the place, and to a large extent the conditions, of the engagement. Rommel failed to find the weak spot where he could engage our main armoured forces. He failed to entice us into a trap where he had his batteries of 88-mm. guns, hoping to repeat his manœuvre of last June in the Cauldron area. Although he retreated in a somewhat battered condition, on the other hand, his forces continue to hold nearly all our southern minefield in the area of El Hemeimat, northwards towards the Ruweisat Ridge. They have captured the excellent observation post of El Hemeimat, some five miles east of their former position, from which rocky twin peaks they command a dominating position eastward and southward into the Qattara Depression. They are as yet in control further north of the broken ground of Diers, admirably adapted for cover for guns and tanks. A conservative estimate is that Rommel's armoured losses alone were four times heavier than ours.

FROM THE NEW GUINEA FRONT: A PACIFIC BATTLEFIELD.

AFTER A JAPANESE RAID ON PORT MORESBY: AN AMERICAN "P-39" CIRCLES LOW OVER THE FIELD, LOOKING FOR A SPOT TO LAND AMONGST THE DÉBRIS.

A HUMAN CARAVAN: NATIVES OF NEW GUINEA CARRYING SUPPLIES TO THE ALLIED TROOPS FIGHTING IN THE INTERIOR OF THE COUNTRY.

MOUNTAINS OF THE OWEN STANLEY RANGE IN NEW GUINEA DIVIDE THE JAPANESE AREA ON THE NORTH FROM THE ALLIED TERRITORY AROUND PORT MORESBY AND MILNE BAY.

New Guinea, before the war brought it prominently into the news, was one of the few unknown lands in the world, except for a few parts where the Australians were working the goldfields of the vast mountain ranges, clothed in almost impenetrable jungle, and inhabited by the most savage races of cannibals. The Japanese seized the northern shores of New Guinea, making Buna their base, prepared methodically to invade Port Moresby, which lies only 300 miles from Cape York, Australia, according to the plans they had formulated years before, and on September 9 had succeeded in forcing the "Hell Fire" gap of the Owen Stanley Mountains. This almost impassable range, which runs like a spine down the middle of Papua, climbs to a height of 13,220 ft., and despite the grim resistance of the Australians, the Japs, dodging in and out of the jungle, had advanced 12 miles over the highest point of the divide and were only about 45 miles from the Allied base, Port Moresby. However, on September 11, General MacArthur announced from his headquarters that the Jap advance had been halted, and that plans existed to stabilise the position in New Guinea. The next day, Allied bombers smashed the enemy air base at Buna.

Milne Bay, in the same area, has also proved its strength, the Japanese force which landed there at the end of August having been completely routed. No small part in this Allied success was played by the pilots of civil flying-boats, who, flying in the hours of darkness, transported troops and many tons of urgently required freight to the hidden Allied base there.

GERMAN FEARS OF A SECOND FRONT – REDOUBTS ALONG THE FRENCH COAST.

"BATTERIE TODT": THIS HUGE STRONGHOLD IS BUILT OF STEEL AND CONCRETE WITH STRENGTHENED WALLS AS A PROTECTION AGAINST AIR ATTACK.

MAJOR-GENERAL FRITZ TODT, KILLED IN AN AEROPLANE ACCIDENT LAST FEBRUARY.

ONE OF THE MANY BLOCK-HOUSES AND GUN EMPLACEMENTS IN OCCUPIED FRANCE WHICH THE GERMANS HAVE BUILT ALONG THE CHANNEL SHORES.

For some time Germany has been constructing a powerful defence system along the Channel coast, to meet any threat of an Allied invasion. This consists of block-houses, gun emplacements and searchlight positions forming part of what the Nazis call "a second Westwall." The "Batterie Todt," a gigantic concrete and steel stronghold, described as containing one of the heaviest long-range batteries on the Channel coast, is named after Fritz Todt, builder of the Siegfried Line and Hitler's military roads, who was killed on the Eastern Front. Some of the immense block-houses erected on the Atlantic coast seem to be, as yet, devoid of gun-casemates or guns. The enemy is also known to have built concrete and steel U-boat shelters on this coast. German radio, on July 28, boasted of "thousands of fortifications" in northern France, built in depth. This recent German stressing of these alleged invulnerable defences, widely broadcast, together with Dr. Goebbels' boasts of great numbers of picked German forces taken to the Western Front, is at least curious.

THE RECONQUEST OF THE SOLOMON ISLANDS BY U.S. MARINES: FEROCIOUS HAND-TO-HAND CONFLICTS IN DEEP DUG-OUTS.

U.S. MARINES LANDING ON GUADALCANAL ISLAND IN AMPHIBIAN TANKS, WHICH CAN BE USED AS SEEN ABOVE AND ALSO ON LAND. SAVAGE FIGHTING TOOK PLACE ON THE ISLAND.

AN AMERICAN "JEEP" ON THE NEARLY COMPLETED RUNWAY.

USEFUL LITTLE "JEEPS," RUNABOUTS, WERE LANDED IN THE SANDY BEACH OF GUADALCANAL, BY NEW-TYPE LANDING BARGES. THE ENEMY FOUGHT IN DEEP CAVES AND DUG-OUTS.

One of the most savage and fiercest battles of its kind in the war to date, most of the fighting being of a hand-to-hand character, marked the reconquest of the Solomon Islands by the U.S. Marines, commanded by General Alexander Vandegrift, which resulted in the capture of six of the principal islands of the group. The operations began on August 7, when the Americans seized the islands of Tulagi, the principal island with a fine harbour, Gavutu and Tanamboga, landings being covered by the guns of the U.S. Fleet, the enemy retreating to the interior heights and sniping from all directions. The Japanese retreated in small packets into hundreds of deep caves, the entrances covered by snipers, and to drive them out was difficult and expensive. Volunteers had to crawl to a dug-out and try to destroy it with grenades, after which Marines, armed with sub-machine guns, rifles and bayonets, stormed the cave and wiped out every Jap. Casualties in the ferocious fighting were severe, for the enemy, trapped like rats, fought to the bitter end. By August 10 the Allies had overcome all major opposition. The most deadly fighting occurred on Guadalcanal Island, lying south of Tulagi, where the Japanese had nearly completed a very extensive air-base, to be used against Australia. Great courage and skill were shown by the Marines, whereby, under Lieut.-Colonel Leonard Cresswell, they rounded up and destroyed 750 picked Japs, landed under cover of night by Japanese destroyers, who worked their way through the jungle and tried at 3 a.m. to take the Americans by surprise. Only a handful escaped, but Japanese snipers took a heavy toll. These were carefully camouflaged and some were tied to the tops of trees. They had to be spotted and killed one by one.

The battle of the Solomon Islands may prove a turning-point in the Pacific war. By brilliant "blitz" tactics by sea and air, in which the Japanese are known to have suffered severely, and after ten days of furious fighting, their defences in the Tulagi and Guadalcanal areas, approximately 5000 square miles of the Solomons, were under American control. Vice-Admiral Robert Ghormley's force, augmented by Australian warships, rushed convoys with munitions and supplies to make the islands impregnable to Japanese counter-thrusts, and to carry the offensive of the United Nations further northward and drive them completely out of New Guinea, and Timor beyond.

ARREST OF CONGRESS PARTY LEADERS FOLLOWING BOMBAY RESOLUTION.

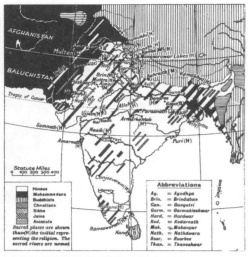

A MAP OF THE MAIN RELIGIOUS AREAS OF INDIA, OF WHICH 68 PER CENT. ARE HINDU, 22 PER CENT. MOSLEM, AND 10 PER CENT. THE "UNTOUCHABLES," OR LOW CASTE, AND OTHER CREEDS, INCLUDING CHRISTIANS.

SIR STAFFORD CRIPPS, P.C., K.C., M.P., LORD PRIVY SEAL AND A MEMBER OF THE WAR CABINET FLEW TO INDIA.

PANDIT JAWAHARLAL NEHRU WHO, AS LEADER OF THE CONGRESS PARTY, REPRESENTS SOME 270,000,000 HINDUS.

JINNAH, PRESIDENT OF THE WORKING COMMITTEE OF THE ALL-INDIA MOSLEM LEAGUE.

GANDHI, AGED CONGRESS LEADER, ARRESTED, AND TAKEN IN "PREVENTATIVE CUSTODY".

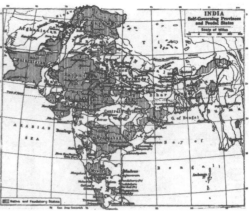

A MAP SHOWING INDIA'S FEUDATORY STATES RULED BY THE PRINCES. THE PRINCES HAVE SHOWN EVERY DESIRE TO MAKE SACRIFICES TO EFFECT UNITY.

No British statesman ever volunteered for a more onerous and delicate mission than Sir Stafford Cripps when he went armed with the War Cabinet's proposals to effect political unity among India's diverse political entities, almost all fundamentally in opposition to one another. Sir Stafford reached New Delhi on March 23, where he immediately interviewed all the Indian leaders. In a broadcast from New Delhi on April 11, he stated that if the British Government accept full responsibility for the naval, military and air defences of India, it must rest in the hands of the C.-in-C. in India, General Wavell, and the War Cabinet. The real cause of the breakdown, he gathered, was that "the temporary form of government envisaged was not such as to enable Indians to join the Government." But, an immediate change of Constitution, raised at the last moment, is "wholly impracticable while war is proceeding"; and, second a "true national government by a Cabinet of Indian leaders untrammelled by any control by the Viceroy or the British Cabinet" would never be accepted by the great minorities in India, nor could his Majesty's Government who have given pledges to these minorities, "consent to their being placed unprotected under possibly inimical rule. It would be a breach of all the pledges we have given." The arrest of Gandhi, Nehru, Azad, and other leaders of the Congress Party at 5 a.m. on Sunday, August 9, was welcomed throughout Britain, the Empire, and the free world as the first breath of wholesomeness after years of futile temporising with irreconcilables, whose threats had become daily more violent. The much-heralded resolution, fathered by the aged Gandhi, and carried at the Congress Conference in Bombay, demanding that the British should quit India forthwith – Gandhi had boasted that he would have us out of India within a month – was so direct a challenge, not merely to British rule, but to the entire war conduct of the Allies, that the Viceroy's Executive Council could no longer remain mere spectators. At the last moment Congress was outlawed and the leaders arrested.

BRITISH AND AMERICAN AIR ATTACKS: ALLIED ACCURACY IN BOMBING.

PART OF MAINZ, NEAR THE MUNICIPAL THEATRE (TOP RIGHT), BEFORE THE HEAVY R.A.F. ATTACKS OF AUGUST 11–12 AND 12–13.

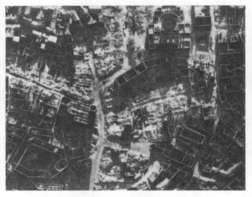

THE SAME PART OF THE CITY OF MAINZ SOME THREE MONTHS AFTER THE RAID.

THE U.S. ARMY AIR FORCE ATTACKS ABBEVILLE AERODROME: "FLYING FORTRESSES" DROPPED THEIR BOMBS.

The fortress city of Mainz, situated on the left bank of the Rhine, and one of Germany's most important industrial cities, was subjected on August 11 and 12 to two exceedingly heavy raids. The story of these raids is told in two of the above photographs, which show (left) a part of the town before the attacks and (centre) the same area afterwards. The damage done to this district near the municipal theatre, was extensive; scores of buildings have been swept away, many more are roofless, and although an attempt has been made to clear away, some of the streets are still blocked by débris. The shattering raids to which Germany is now being subjected by the R.A.F. is part of a plan to destroy completely industries which towns harbour, and which are being used in their all-out war effort against the Allies.

During the Combined Operations raid on Dieppe on August 19, two squadrons of United States Army Air Force "Flying Fortresses," escorted by R.A.F. and Royal Canadian Air Force fighters, made a high-level attack on the German fighter base at Abbeville. The bombing was extremely accurate, high explosives falling on the north-west dispersal area as well as on the runways. Visibility was good, and bursts were seen on many of the buildings round the edge of the aerodrome. Twenty-three bombers dropped their bombs on or near the target and they encountered little opposition from enemy fighters. All the aircraft returned safely, three only being slightly damaged by "flak" splinters. The United States Army Air Force is co-operating more and more with the R.A.F. in raids over the Continent. As soon as the American crews have completed their operational training over here, the enemy will undoubtedly feel the full force of the combined attacks. This will show the German people that the Allies have wrested from the Axis the air supremacy needed to win the war.

THE COMMANDO RAID ON DIEPPE: "THE TOUGHEST JOB WE'VE HAD!"

NAVAL CRAFT FIRE ON THE SHORE DEFENCES AS THE BARGES, CONTAINING TANKS, ARMOURED VEHICLES AND TROOPS, NOSE THEIR WAY TO THE SPECIFIED LANDING POINTS.

LORD LOVAT (LEFT), LEADER OF THE CONTINGENT WHICH SILENCED THE HEAVY GUN BATTERY AT VARANGEVILLE, COMPARING NOTES AFTER THE RAID.

ABANDONED TANKS AND SMOKING BRITISH LANDING CRAFT LEFT BEHIND AFTER THE DIEPPE RAID. CASUALTIES LIE ON THE BEACH BESIDE THE TANK.

The Commando raid on Dieppe, on August 19, the largest operation so far carried out by our forces on the Continent, was completed according to plan when our troops had been nine hours in the town. Re-embarkation of the main forces was begun within six minutes of schedule time. During the raid, British forces destroyed a heavy six-gun battery, ammunition dump, radio-location station, an anti-aircraft battery, and had proved that in spite of German boasts a landing in force was perfectly feasible in the most heavily fortified areas of German-occupied countries. The force consisted mainly of Canadian troops, who suffered somewhat heavy losses. "The battered remnants of the tank force," wrote an official Press correspondent, "fought a rearguard action which Canada can well write into her military history."

In a full Report of the Combined Operations raid on Dieppe, it was claimed that it was a successful demonstration of co-ordination of all three Services. A large military force embarked on board naval vessels and transports, and after negotiating a hazardous sea passage arrived off selected points of the French coast at 4.50 a.m. on August 19. Aircraft covered the landings, the ships and men throughout operations. It became clear during the raid that the enemy had recently brought additional troops and guns to the Dieppe area. Even without this, the Commando raid, on about the stiffest section of Northern France, had been recognised as a supreme test from the first. The men had been told by Vice-Admiral Lord Louis Mountbatten, Chief of Combined Operations: "Your task is most vital. If you don't knock out the German Howitzer battery the whole operation will go wrong. This is the toughest job we've had." They did not fail. The German guns were shattered, their ammunition dump was blown up and the enemy gunners were killed at the bayonet's point in hand-to-hand fighting. Because of that, the seven Canadian regiments were able to land on their beaches, which the howitzers commanded.

PIECES FROM THE JIG-SAW OF THE VAST RUSSIAN WAR FRONT.

THE TENACITY OF RUSSIAN RESISTANCE: GERMAN INFANTRY AND FIELD GUNS IN THE STREETS DURING THE BATTLE FOR RESTOV.

SEATED ON THE BRINK OF THEIR OWN GRAVE, RUSSIAN CIVILIANS ARE SHOT IN THE BACK BY A GERMAN FIRING SQUAD. THIS PICTURE, RADIOED FROM MOSCOW, WAS FOUND ON THE BODY OF A GERMAN OFFICER.

RUSSIAN TROOPS CHARGE INTO ACTION ACROSS A VITAL RAILWAY LINE, WHICH ATTACKING GERMAN FORCES WERE SEEKING TO CUT.

The situation of Marshal Timoshenko's defences, as early as July 26 was described by Moscow as "more and more alarming," when von Bock's forces were gaining a foothold in the Caucasus region. The eclipse of Rostov marked a serious crisis, for this great industrial city lies at the point where the Moscow-Baku railway crosses the Don, is an important centre of distribution for the whole of Southern Russia and is the gateway of the Caucasus. It is true that the enemy held Rostov last October for a short time, but when Von Bock threw in 1000 tanks and 600,000 men on the Rostov section it was a different matter to the tail-end of the previous offensive. The oil and mineral deposits in the flat region lying to the north of the Caucasus lie at the mercy of a victorious enemy advance to the South.

With the continued advance of the German Armies in the Don region, Russia's supply problems have been gravely aggravated by further loss of centres of supply and manufacture. Prudent planning over the past ten years by Stalin has deprived Hitler of the industrial victory he had calculated on when he seized the Ukraine. New factories and new mines in the Urals and beyond can provide arms, although Russian industry is short of machine-tools. As regards cereals, no less than 45 per cent. of Soviet wheat and 41 per cent. of rye were grown in the areas now occupied or menaced, including the Crimea. Oil is increasingly in danger with Von Bock's advance, for Baku provides over 70 per cent. of Soviet needs. Here, too, are the manganese mines which provide more of the ore than the rest of the world together.

THE GERMAN ADVANCE TO THE CAUCASUS: MAIKOP OIL GOES UP IN FLAMES.

THE OILFIELD AT MAIKOP, ON THE EDGE OF THE CAUCASUS MOUNTAINS, SHOWING DERRICKS FOR "BALING" OIL. THE GERMANS HAVE TAKEN THIS OIL CENTRE WHICH THE RUSSIANS "SCORCHED" BEFOREHAND.

WHILE HOUSEWIVES OF MAIKOP TRY TO BEAT OUT THE FLAMES DESTROYING THEIR HOMES, TWO INDIFFERENT YOUNG GERMAN SOLDIERS TURN THEIR BACKS AND GET ON WITH A MEAL.

NORTH OF MAIKOP, A SHEET OF FLAME AND BILLOWING CLOUDS OF SMOKE MARK THE DESTRUCTION OF A GROUP OF OIL TANKS ON THE BANK OF THE RIVER KUBAN, SCENE OF HEAVY FIGHTING.

The Germans are thrusting into the Caucasus in several directions. In the west, at the ports of Novorossisk and Tuapse, they have made headway in valleys which offer few difficulties. South of Krasnodar, where the mountains rise to over 2000 ft., heavy enemy attacks have been launched in different directions, but all were not held. Tanks are being used, and 100 of them were reported to have blasted a way along the valley, but stubborn resistance was put up by Cossacks on a broad front. In the Piatigorsk sector, which covers the Grozny oilfield and also mercury and molybdenum deposits, a further retreat occurred on August 22, and here the fighting was shifting into the mountain gorges, where the Germans fell into several carefully-laid traps. On the mountain military roads, the special mountain divisions of the Army of the Caucasus had taken

up strong positions. The danger at present lies rather along the Black Sea coast road, skirting the Caucasus Mountains, and leading to Batum. Bearing on the situation is the new command of the Tenth Army in Iraq and Persia taken over by General Sir Henry Maitland Wilson, as announced on August 24.
On August 26, when the battle for Stalingrad was in its fiercest phase, the Russian communiqué disclosed that over the past fifteen days General Zhukov had launched an offensive west of Moscow, probably to relieve the strain on Stalingrad, 800 miles to the south-east, that he had killed 45,000 Germans, advanced up to 30 miles, and had broken through the heavily fortified enemy defence lines on a 75-mile front between Rzhev and Vyasma. The Russians also claimed the capture of a vast amount of equipment, including 250 tanks.

"THEY SHALL NOT PASS": BITTER FIGHTING IN AND OUTSIDE STALINGRAD.

USING AN ANTI-TANK RIFLE, RUSSIAN TROOPS SCORE A HIT ON AN APPROACHING GERMAN TANK.

ON SEPTEMBER 27, STALINGRAD STILL STOOD FIRM, HOLDING UP FORTY ENEMY DIVISIONS.

HOUSE-TO-HOUSE FIGHTING IN STALINGRAD: NAZI LIGHT ARTILLERY ENGAGED IN A DUEL AMONGST THE RUINED BUILDINGS.

Day after day at Stalingrad as Von Bock threw in further vast concentrations of Panzers, and although suffering immense losses of men and material, with Stalingrad partly enveloped in an arc stretching from Dubovka to Krasnoarmeisk, it looked as though the great straggling city, already in flames, must succumb. But by September 6 Timoshenko had strongly reinforced his army, though still greatly outnumbered. In the north-west the Germans were thrown from a number of localities. In the south-west he sent his giant tanks sweeping in from the flank, which cut through between the Panzers and the supporting infantry inflicting heavy losses. On September 7 the enemy claimed Novorossisk, the Black Sea naval base, after heavy fighting, but at Mozdok, before the Grozny oilfield, the Germans appeared to be held.
On September 15, after nearly seven weeks of violent assault by Von Bock's troops, including the heaviest aerial bombardment that the *Luftwaffe* could deliver, Stalingrad, focus of the main German drive on the Eastern Front, was reported not only to be holding out, but to have checked any further enemy advance. The

German Press, trying to explain away the slow progress of the assault, says that the Russians defending Stalingrad fight like mad dogs. Actually, they fight cleverly, an instance being their method of counterattacking so swiftly that German 'planes, brought up to support local attacks, are unable to bomb or machine-gun for fear of destroying their own troops. Elsewhere on the front, news from the eastern Caucasus and Volkhov areas continues to be encouraging. Russian forces north-west of Grozny, beyond the line of the River Terek, recently surrounded and destroyed many of the enemy, and recaptured lost ground. In the Leningrad area, enemy strong-points have been captured, and there are reports of activity against the inside of Von Leeb's blockade belt. On the central front, in the Rzhev area, the Russians are still pressing the enemy hard. Reserves now pouring into action against the Germans across the Volga at Stalingrad, and elsewhere, are believed to be the advance guards of the new armies created and organised by Marshal Voroshilov and Marshal Budenny.

THE EPIC OF STALINGRAD: THE CITY OF RUINS STILL DEFIES THE ENEMY.

THE INFERNO OF STALINGRAD: IN A RUINED CITY OF BLAZING BUILDINGS, SHATTERED WALLS AND SMOKE-FILLED SKY, TWO WOMEN IMPERTURBABLY CARRY SUPPLIES TO ITS DEFENDERS.

AN AERIAL VIEW OF THE UNBREAKABLE CITY: CLOUDS OF ACRID SMOKE HANG OVER THE FACTORY AREA, WHICH IS SEEING SOME OF THE BITTEREST FIGHTING OF THIS WAR.

FACTORY WORKERS CAPTURED AT STALINGRAD: THESE MEN FIGHT BY DAY AND TURN OUT GUNS AND AMMUNITION BY NIGHT.

GLAD OF THE SHELTER OF A CRATER IN A STALINGRAD STREET. ANY ADVANCE MADE HAS BEEN AT A COST.

AFTER TERRIFIC ATTACKS BY BOMBERS AND CONTINUOUS SHELLING BY SIEGE GUNS, ALL THAT REMAINED OF THIS STALINGRAD STREET WERE THE BROKEN WALLS WHEN GERMAN TANKS ADVANCED TO SUPPORT THEIR INFANTRY.

TOWARDS ITS TARGET: A GERMAN BOMB RELEASED FALLS IN THE SOUTHERN SECTOR, ALTHOUGH THE DEFENDED FACTORIES ARE MOSTLY IN THE NORTH (SEE KEY IN INSET).

THE DEEP GULLIES, CALLED "BALKAS," WHICH RUN THROUGH THE CITY. ABOVE, ONE SUCH GULLY, LINED WITH CAVERNS WHERE THOUSANDS OF CITIZENS LIVE IN COMPARATIVE SAFETY.

By all accounts Stalingrad should have succumbed to the hammer-blows of von Bock weeks ago. For over two months its undaunted civilian population, at bay, have turned ploughshares into swords, and both men and women have furiously and fearlessly thrown themselves into the fray. The German losses in men and material have been prodigious; alas, among the Russians as well. The city, which straggles along the west bank of the Volga for twenty miles, is no more than a ruined shell, but it fights on. Its resistance is a triumph of morale. In the streets are non-stop tank battles, hand-to-hand fights to the death at street corners and in every house, room by room, in factories turned into improvised forts, while the women with children not evacuated crowd for shelter in caves on the shores of the Volga. The Germans themselves are baffled by this furious resistance. It has long been something of a mystery to many people in the West how thousands of civilians in Stalingrad have been able to continue to live in the heart of a vast ruined city of crumbling ruins, amid raging fires and the never-ending rain of depth-dealing bombs and shells. From an enemy source we obtain an explanation. Through the city run certain notable deep crevices, or eroded gullies, called "Balkas," in which a large number of caverns have been excavated and where thousands are now living. These are particularly prevalent on the banks of the Volga, where, too, are emergency first-aid stations.

MEXICO AND BRAZIL JOIN THE ALLIES.

THE "MINAS GERAIS": ONE OF BRAZIL'S TWO BATTLESHIPS ALTHOUGH SHE IS AN OLD SHIP, SHE WAS RECONSTRUCTED AND MODERNISED IN 1934–39.

Mexico has now joined the Allied nations in their total war against the Axis Powers. She has been since the beginning friendly to Allied war efforts, but stood out against an actual declaration of war until the sinking of three Mexican ships decided her to come in wholeheartedly on the side of justice. President Avila Camacho caused Congress to be called so that he could express verbally the reasons why Mexico should declare war, and his suggestion was accepted unanimously. Brazil too is at war with Germany and Italy! Strategically, Brazil's action is of the greatest importance to the United Nations.

THE DUKE OF KENT KILLED IN AIRCRASH.

THE LATE AIR COMMODORE H.R.H. THE DUKE OF KENT WITH THE DUCHESS.

The news of the tragic death of H.R.H. the Duke of Kent, K.G., B.C., K.T., G.C.M.G., G.C.V.O., was known a little before midnight on Tuesday, August 25, to the deep regret of the nation. On his way to Iceland in the course of R.A.F. duties, the "Sunderland" flying-boat carrying His Royal Highness unhappily crashed in the North of Scotland, all its occupants being killed. Air Commodore Prince George Edward Alexander Edmund, Duke of Kent, was born at The Cottage, Sandringham, on December 20, 1902.

U.S. TROOPS SWIM THROUGH BLAZING OIL.

IN TRAINING AN AMERICAN SOLDIER PREPARES TO LEAP FROM A 20-FT. PLATFORM INTO A FLOATING INFERNO OF BLAZING OIL.

The troop transport is sailing by night. All seems quiet, and the men are turning in. Then, without warning, a crashing thud in the ship's bowels, followed by a muffled explosion, and she settles sluggishly, heeling over on to her side. The lifeboats are smashed, and they must jump for their lives into the blazing oil spreading around the vessel.

THE BRITISH OCCUPATION OF MADAGASCAR: FORESTALLS JAPANESE PLOT.

A VICHY AIRCRAFT HANGAR ALMOST COMPLETELY WRECKED BY BOMBS DROPPED FROM BRITISH AIRCRAFT OPERATING FROM AN AIRCRAFT CARRIER.

MEN OF THE KING'S AFRICAN RIFLES, HEADED BY THEIR BAND, ON A MARCH IN MADAGASCAR. OUR TROOPS THROUGHOUT HAVE SUFFERED VERY LIGHT CASUALTIES.

Madagascar – of which Diego Suarez, the naval base at the extreme northernmost tip, was seized by British naval and military forces on May 5, in view of Japanese machinations with the Laval Government – is the key island controlling the southern gateway to the Persian Gulf and Indian Ocean, as well as being a potential jumping-off mark for an air- and sea-borne invasion of the African continent, the more so since its 980-miles-long coast-line faces Portuguese East Africa, whose neutrality would be little respected by the Japs. South Afirca's east coast cities, like Durban, Natal, are not more than 1000 miles distant from Madagascar. There are some 20,000 French, and 7000 or more French troops on this tropical and volcanic island, most of whom, according to eight recently repatriated British women, are de Gaullist. The island has nine ports and 100 landing-grounds for aircraft. Diego Suarez has been seized purely as necessary protective action. It was hoped that the French Governor-General of the island would then permit the British Command to take the necessary steps in order to deny bases and facilities elsewhere in Madagascar to the Axis Powers. Vichy, however, made it clear that the island would not co-operate peacefully, and so on September 10, further military operations were necessarily begun. The capital fell on the 23rd, where our forces were welcomed with enthusiasm. The British Government has made it clear that it has no territorial designs on Madagascar, which remains French. After initial resistance hostilities ceased at 2 p.m. (local time) on November 5. The armistice terms have been signed and the campaign has been brought to a successful conclusion.

MALTA, "ISLAND FORTRESS OF HEROISM," RECEIVES HER GEORGE CROSS.

THE SCENE IN PALACE SQUARE, VALETTA, ON SEPTEMBER 13, BEFORE THE RUINED PALACE, DURING THE CEREMONY OF PRESENTATION OF THE GEORGE CROSS, RECEIVED FOR THE PEOPLE OF MALTA BY THE CHIEF JUSTICE, WHO SAID: "THIS CHERISHED TREASURE WILL BE HANDED DOWN TO POSTERITY."

THE GEORGE CROSS WITH THE AUTO-GRAPH AWARD IN THE KING'S OWN HANDWRITING.

MALTESE FAMILIES OUTSIDE THEIR ROCK-HEWN SHELTERS: THE ISLAND DE-FENCE IS STILL AS EFFECTIVE AS EVER IN RESISTING AXIS RAIDS.

All Malta queued up on September 13, after the formal presentation of the George Cross, to see it in its case, together with the autograph letter in the King's own handwriting. It lay under the plinth in the centre of Palace Square, placed there by the Chief Justice, Sir George Borg, who received it on the people's behalf from Viscount Gort. Later it will be displayed in other townships of the island. His Majesty's letter read: "The Governor, Malta. To honour the brave people I award the George Cross to the Island Fortress of Malta to bear witness to a heroism and devotion that will long be famous in history. George, R.I. April 15th, 1942." Sir George Borg said that it would be handed down to posterity "as a tangible symbol of Malta's union to the great and invincible nation whose protection is the best guarantee of the safety of our country and religion." Lord Gort, the Governor, brought the George Cross by 'plane from Gibraltar to the Island.

Malta has withstood many hundreds of air attacks and has suffered considerable damage to civilian property, but her magnificent defences, both anti-aircraft and fighter, have turned these persistent attacks into costly failures. Malta boasts the strongest air-raid shelters in Europe: galleries dug deep into a workable island rock are available for the dauntless population, who show such remarkable courage in the face of fierce enemy attacks, and to-day, as earlier in the war, the island defence is still as effective as ever.

THE AXIS POWERS ON THE DEFENCE – ALLIED ACTIVITIES IN NEW GUINEA.

NATIVES OF NEW GUINEA, WHO HAVE BEEN ASSISTING AMERICAN TROOPS, LINE UP FOR THEIR PAY AT THE END OF A DAY'S WORK.

INCREDIBLE DIFFICULTIES OF TRANSPORT IN NEW GUINEA. HAULING A 25-POUNDER GUN THROUGH THE JUNGLE DURING HEAVY RAINS ON THE OWEN STANLEY MOUNTAINS.

Since September 28, when the Australians began their drive up into the Stanley Mountains by blasting their way through the Japanese defences at Oribaiwa, the enemy had apparently performed a "vanishing trick." Efogi, the last jungle post between the Port Moresby side of the Owen Stanley range and Myola on the Buna side, was reoccupied on October 3 and the troops were continuing to advance, with Allied fighters harrying the enemy's line of retreat. They crossed the 6500-ft. ridge without establishing contact with the enemy. Myola is only six miles beyond Efogi, with Kokoda ten miles further, where the Japs must make a stand if they intend to defend the Buna area.

General MacArthur, accompanied by Sir Thomas Blamey, commanding Australian Forces, flew to New

Guinea recently to inspect progress in one of the most baffling of campaigns. A few months ago the Japanese were almost within sight of Port Moresby. Steadily, the Allies have driven them back, inflicted heavy losses, and pinned them to their base at Buna, where they must escape by sea or be exterminated.

Allied troops captured Buna after fierce fighting since November 9, when American and Australian troops closed the pincers on the Japanese. The enemy have made several attempts to reinforce their garrison from the sea, but the result was the loss of several ships and hundreds of men drowned. The capture of Buna means that Papua is now entirely in Allied hands. The difficulties of this campaign cannot be exaggerated. This is the first considerable piece of territory to be won back from the Japanese.

THE BATTLE OF THE SOLOMONS: HEAVY U.S. AND JAPANESE SEA LOSSES.

CLOUDS OF SMOKE ROLL OVER THE OCEAN BATTLEFIELD AS THE UNITED STATES AIRCRAFT-CARRIER "WASP" BLAZES AMIDSHIPS. SHE WAS STRUCK BY TORPEDOES WHILE ESCORTING SUPPLY SHIPS TO THE SOLOMON ISLANDS ON SEPTEMBER 15.

A JAPANESE BOMBER STARTING ON A SUICIDE DIVE WHICH ENDED IN IT CRASHING ON TO THE "HORNET'S" SIGNAL TOWER. THE U.S. AIRCRAFT-CARRIER "HORNET" WAS SO DAMAGED THAT SHE HAD TO BE SUNK BY HER OWN DEMOLITION CREWS.

WORKING, AMIDST SMOKE, FLAMES AND STREWN WRECKAGE AFTER THE JAPANESE BOMBER'S SUICIDE DIVE, FIRE-FIGHTING CREWS ATTEMPT TO SMOTHER THE FIRES ON BOARD THE "HORNET", WHICH SURVIVED TWO ATTACKS.

The U.S. naval forces under Vice-Admiral Halsey, on October 25 have reversed the situation in the Solomon Islands, where, according to American fears, the enemy held the initiative. This anxiety increased when the loss of the U.S. aircraft-carrier "Wasp" on September 15 was announced. The "Wasp" was carrying reinforcements when three torpedoes put paid to her activities. Ninety per cent. of her personnel were saved. Japan's latest defeat has caused her retreat from the Solomon's. Meanwhile, Admiral Halsey is shelling Japanese troops on Guadalcanal, and General MacArthur's Flying Fortresses are creating havoc in the Buin-Faisi area.

Admiral Halsey's victory is undoubtedly the greatest defeat at sea sustained by the Japanese. The American losses were extremely light. The nucleus of the Japanese fleet which failed in the attempt to land fresh troops

on Guadalcanal was four battleships of British design, launched in 1912–13, and since modernised. The appearance of U.S. battleships on the scene directly brought about their ignominious defeat. When the Japanese force withdrew, they had lost two of the four battleships, six heavy cruisers, two light cruisers, six destroyers, eight troop transports, and four cargo vessels. These figures, bring the losses sustained by the Japanese Navy to so high a total that it will be virtually impossible to replace them. The U.S. Navy production and replacement, on the other hand, is increasing daily. The respective aggregate losses of both navies since Pearl Harbour, based on official figures are: (Japanese losses first in each case) battleships 3 to 1, aircraft carriers 6 to 4, cruisers 25 to 6, destroyers 41 to 26, submarines 7 to 4, transports 51 to 4, fleet tankers 19 to 3, gunboats 9 to 4 supply ships 64 to 0, armed auxiliaries 2 to 0, and miscellaneous other craft 23 to 13.

THE COMMANDO RAID ON SARK.

THE EVIDENCE THAT THE GERMANS ARE DEPORTING BRITISH SUBJECTS IN THE CHANNEL ISLANDS TO GERMANY. THE NAZI PROCLAMATION SEIZED BY OUR RAIDING PARTY.

A small-scale raid was recently made on Sark to obtain information about ill-treatment of residents. Suspicions were confirmed by a proclamation signed Knackfuss, Oberst-Feldkommandant, in which it is stated that all male civilians between sixteen and seventy, not born in the Channel Islands, and those not permanently resident there, have been deported to Germany. Retaliatory measures have been forced upon the British and Canadian Governments. This raid had disastrous and unforeseen consequences. As five German prisoners were being escorted to the boats with their hands tied behind their backs they attempted to escape and three of them were shot in the struggle. The discovery of their bodies, still bound in this way, led Hitler to believe that they had been executed in cold blood. He thereupon ordered all prisoners from the Dieppe Raid to be placed in chains, and all commandos taken prisoner to be executed.

DEHYDRATED MILK AND FOOD.

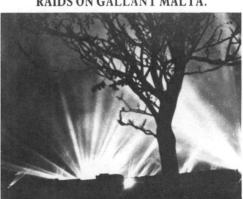

IRISH STEW FOR THREE PERSONS: AN EXAMPLE OF "DEHYDRATED" MEAT WHICH IS 2½ IN. IN DIAMETER BY 1 IN. IN DEPTH AND WEIGHS 2 OZ. COMPARE THE HALFPENNY FOR SIZE.

"Dehydrated" food has been tried and proved a success. The food values, vitamins and the original colour are retained; only the shape is lost. This new process is of enormous value to an army in the field and permits the storing of vegetables and meat which would otherwise perish. For instance, a 2-lb tin of minced meat, the equivalent of 5 lb. of reconstituted meat, will keep for two years; 1 lb. of "dehydrated" carrot or cabbage gives 8 lb. of reconstituted vegetables; and 1 lb. of "dehydrated" potato produces 4½ lb. Carrots, potatoes and meat need soaking in water before cooking, but cabbage can go straight into the saucepan. An interesting point is that these foods require more salt in the cooking than when fresh. It is unlikely that "dehydrated" meat and vegetables will be on sale to householders yet; they are primarily for the Services, and as "The Times" points out: "to the garrisons in Malta and Iceland they will be a boon and a blessing."

THE GEORGE CROSS ISLAND: RENEWED RAIDS ON GALLANT MALTA.

NIGHT RAIDERS OVER MALTA, OUR GEORGE CROSS ISLAND: SEARCHLIGHTS GO INTO ACTION AS THE BOMBERS ARE REPORTED APPROACHING THE ISLAND.

During the month of October Malta's total of destroyed enemy aircraft in one week reached new heights – 114 against 27 Spitfires, and only 13 pilots. During that week, some 1400 sorties were made against the island, proof positive that the enemy realise that the strength of the island's defences has not been seriously impaired. Apart from these defences, which continue almost daily to take heavy toll of German and Italian raiders, our offensive action by Malta-based squadrons is very much in evidence. Our George Cross Island, sometimes referred to as a vast aircraft-carrier, is a bitter pill for the Axis to swallow, for they are totally unable to subjugate it, and unable to prevent supplies from reaching it. As long as Malta stands firm, and she is stronger to-day than ever before, the enemy is debarred from the Eastern Mediterranean, and Rommel can never be certain of getting the reinforcements and supplies he so badly needs.

THE NEW OFFENSIVE IN EGYPT: "BRITISH VICTORY OF THE FIRST ORDER."

INTO VICTORY! AUSTRALIAN TROOPS OF THE EIGHTH ARMY, HELD UP IN THEIR FORWARD SWEEP BY A GERMAN STRONG-POINT, CHARGE THE ENEMY WITH REVOLVER AND BAYONETS.

BRITISH INFANTRY ON OCTOBER 23, AFTER A VIOLENT BARRAGE, RUSH ROMMEL'S ADVANCE POSTS THROUGH SMOKE AND DUST: (A PICTURE WIRED BY RADIO FROM THE BATTLEFIELD).

BRITISH INFANTRYMEN, FIGHTING THEIR WAY INTO ROMMEL'S LINES EARLY IN THE BATTLE, TAKE TEMPORARY SHELTER BEHIND A CRIPPLED ENEMY TANK DURING HEAVY SHELL-FIRE.

AUSTRALIANS STORMING A GERMAN STRONG-POINT. UNDER COVER OF A SMOKE-SCREEN THEY APPROACHED THE STRONG-POINT FROM ALL SIDES.

THE BATTLEGROUND OF EL ALAMEIN: BEFORE THE BATTLE THE AXIS HELD A LINE FROM SIDI ABDELRAHMAN TO QUARET EL HEMEIMAT.

INFANTRY OF THE 51ST ADVANCING TO THE ATTACK: THE HIGHLAND DIVISION IN ACTION FOR THE FIRST TIME SINCE FRANCE FELL.

A few hours before the Eighth Army launched the great new battle of Africa on October 23, General Bernard Montgomery said to the Press "The battle starts to-night . . . For three years we have been trying to plug holes all over the world. Now, thank God, that period is over."

The position on October 31–November 1 was that in overnight heavy fighting our forces in the north broke through near Sidi abd el Rahman, 15 miles west of El Alamein, turned sharp right and extended their corridor to the sea thus bottling up the enemy's 90th Division, Rommel's best infantry.

As the battered remnants of Rommel's army fled to the westward out of Egypt, the main portion of his forces were marching eastward towards the Allied prison camps awaiting them behind our lines. It has been estimated that when Rommel's panic-stricken remnants reached the Libyan frontier they numbered no more than 20,000 men. The Italian army in Egypt has ceased to exist.

"The admirable Shermans," as the Prime Minister described them, "played a recognisable part. indeed, an important part, in General Alexander's battle."

ROMMEL'S TRAIL OF DEFEAT: EL AGHEILA ABANDONED.

TWO OF THE NEW GENERAL SHERMAN TANKS ADVANCING ACROSS THE DESERT. THEIR SPEED AND FIRE-POWER HAVE BEEN A DECISIVE FACTOR IN THE CAMPAIGN.

THE LINE OF ROMMEL'S RETREAT FROM EL AGHEILA TOWARDS TRIPOLI: A MAP OF THE TERRAIN, INDICATING WADIS WHICH MAY OBSTRUCT THE PURSUING EIGHTH ARMY.

THE GERMANS HAD NO TIME TO BURY THEIR DEAD, WHO LITTERED THE ROADSIDE. ONE OF OUR BOFORS A.-A. GUNS IS HURRIED FORWARD TOWARDS THE LIBYAN FRONTIER.

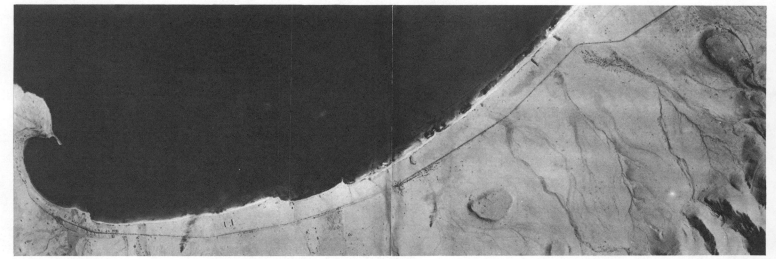

THE WAR'S GREATEST TRAFFIC JAM: THE COAST ROAD FROM SOLLUM ESCARPMENT TO HALFAYA PASS, SHOWING ROMMEL'S PANZER DIVISIONS IN RETREAT WITH VEHICLES BURNING.

The Battle of Egypt is definitely closed. Tobruk is again in our hands. The speed of the pursuit is incredible, our troops recently covering 130 miles in two days, almost twice as fast as Rommel's best move. Our bombers and fighters continue to attack enemy columns retreating westwards, and as our squadrons move their bases further into Cyrenaica the scale of operations increases. Total enemy losses up to date are now estimated at 75,000 Germans and Italians, our casualties at 13,600 officers and men, the majority wounded.

Rommel abandoned his strong strategic positions at El Agheila without a fight, hoping to extricate his Panzer divisions and maintain his retreat towards Tripoli. Buta British column attacked Rommel's flank at the Wadi

Matratin, 60 miles west of El Agheila, thus cutting the enemy's army in two.

With the threat to the enemy's supply ports, Tunis and Tripoli, rapidly increasing in severity, Rommel's situation became more precarious. His chances of escape from the net drawn closely round him have become steadily less. To reach Tripoli he has to cover 490 miles, each one of which brings him nearer the range of the Allies in Tunisia and Malta. At Buerat, a small port about half-way, his supply ships have been shelled by British submarines, and General Montgomery's prediction that "we shall drive the Boche out of Africa" looks uncommonly like being accomplished shortly.

THE BIGGEST NAVAL OPERATION IN HISTORY – THE ALLIES OCCUPY NORTH AFRICA.

LIEUTENANT-GENERAL DWIGHT D. EISENHOWER, COMMANDER-IN-CHIEF.

LIEUT.-GENERAL MARK CLARK, DEPU-TY COMMANDER-IN-CHIEF.

THE WALLS OF THE CONVOY: BRITISH BATTLESHIPS AND AIR-CRAFT-CARRIERS, GUARDING THE ALLIED CONVOY.

A PART OF THE GREAT ALLIED CONVOY PASSING THROUGH THE ATLANTIC EN ROUTE TO NORTH AFRICA.

A GAPING HOLE IN THE SIDE OF THE 35,000-TON FRENCH BATTLESHIP "JEAN BART," BATTERED IN CASABLANCA HARBOUR: WHEN SHE FIRED ON THE ATTACKING FORCES SHE WAS SILENCED BY AMERICAN NAVAL GUNS AND DIVE-BOMBERS.

UNITED STATES TROOPS LANDING AT SURCOUF ON NOVEMBER 8. THE PRODIGIOUS ALLIED OPERA-TIONS WITNESSED MANY SUCH BEACH LANDINGS, MOSTLY UNOPPOSED BY THE FRENCH. ALONG THE COAST OF MOROCCO, THE TWO MAIN OBJECTIVES WERE CASABLANCA AND RABAT.

The vast armada of warships, transports and Anglo-American forces which appeared like a bolt from the blue off various ports in Algeria and French Morocco on the night of November 7–8 concentrated principally off Algiers, and Oran in the Mediterranean. So admirably was it timed and organised, as a military expedition, and supported politically by President Roosevelt and Mr. Churchill, that little resistance was experienced except from some naval and coastal batteries. Algiers capitulated on Sunday evening and was occupied in accordance with the terms laid down, and became at once an open gateway for reinforcements. Admiral Darlan, who by a fortunate chance (for the Allies) happened to be in Algiers at the time, was taken prisoner. Oran, about 250 miles from Gibraltar, and the only port on the Mediterranean coast where any real opposition was encountered, was encircled. Philippeville was the easternmost scene of landings only 60 miles from the

Tunisian frontier. Along the Atlantic coast, Rabat, Casablanca, Safi, Mehdia, Mogador and Agadir were scenes of landings or approaches. Initial resistance by Vichy French warships in Casablanca Harbour was swiftly overcome. Everywhere airfields were seized and rapid infiltrations proceeded. The intention of the Expeditionary Forces was made clear by President Roosevelt's request to the Bey of Tunis to permit Allied forces to pass through Tunisia. Bizerta, the vital French port, the stepping-off mark for any movement against Sicily and Italy, was the obvious aim to prevent further aid to Rommel.

Admiral Darlan has "resumed responsibility for French interests in Africa" with the full approval of the American authorities, and issued a proclamation stating that he has formed a council to conduct all judicial, legislative and executive business in Algiers.

TUNISIA STILL UNCONQUERED.

AIRBORNE GERMAN REINFORCEMENTS ARE SEEN LOADING AN A.-A. GUN IN THE TEBOURBA ZONE, WHERE THE FIRST STRONG ENGAGEMENT TOOK PLACE.

General Anderson, commanding the First Army, in early December made a bold attempt to capture Tunis. For over a week the battle surged first one way and then another, tanks and infantry being hotly engaged, where the enemy held the advantage in the air, using dive-bombers, although gradually the Allies were able to get fighter aircraft in support and meantime heavily bombed enemy positions, and Axis reinforcements coming by sea and air. Finally, the First Army had to retire from positions which could not be held. The German High Command has been able to establish himself from north to south in very strong positions, but a big general move to dislodge him is anticipated shortly, and meanwhile General Montgomery is pursuing Rommel's forces towards Tripoli.

THE ALLIED OPERATIONS IN TUNISIA, WHERE GENERAL ANDER-SON THREATENS THE AXIS ALONG THE MATEUR-DJEDEIDA RAIL-WAY: A CONTOUR MAP OF THE TERRAIN, NOW HEAVILY BOMBED BY ALLIED AIR FORCES.

THE GERMANS OCCUPY VICHY FRANCE.

ITALIANS ALSO SWOOPED INTO MARSEILLES IN THEIR "PROM-ENADE." A MOTORISED DETACHMENT HALT ALONG ONE OF THE SOUTHERN LITTORAL'S TREE-LINED AVENUES.

On November 11 Hitler threw a German Army into Unoccupied France, announcing that, in view of the events in Africa, and to "protect Europe and France," he had decided to occupy Vichy territories. His hopes to do so side-by-side with the French people and the French Army vanished with the dissolving of the French Army and the scuttling of its Fleet. The main German force struck down the Rhone Valley to Marseilles – for the time being sparing Toulon, hoping to acquire the French warships by a trick – and reached it in the night. A curfew was ordered by the French authorities at 8 p.m., a strict black-out. In Paris, the pro-Nazi Vichy representative, Count de Brinon, hoisted the Tricolour over his official residence. Paris remained unmoved. Meantime riots are reported in Toulon and other towns.

WARSHIPS THAT WERE SNATCHED FROM HITLER'S OUTSTRETCHED HAND: THE FRENCH FLEET SCUTTLED IN TOULON HARBOUR.

THE CRUISER "ALGÉRIE," OF 10,000 TONS, COMPLETED IN 1934, AND AT ONE TIME USED AS A FLAGSHIP, SLOWLY TIPS OVER ON HER SIDE.

ADMIRAL DE LA BORDE.
The French Naval C.-in-C. at Toulon, who gave orders to the French Fleet to scuttle after receiving the German Commander's message to hand over his ships. He replied: "I will open fire on anyone endeavouring to enter our ships." He went down with his ship.

THE FRENCH-CRUISER "DUPLEIX," OF 9938 TONS, LISTS AND SINKS AT HER BERTH.

There was a time when the Axis Powers built great hopes on the possibility of luring or seizing the French Fleet for action against the Allies. But those hopes have long since lain shattered among the débris of other Axis plans. Not the least blow dealt to them was the scuttling of an important section of the French Fleet in Toulon Harbour – a diplomatic defeat underlined by this week's announcement of French battleships, cruisers, and other warships which have joined in the fight of the United Nations. It was in the darkness of the early hours of Friday, November 27, that German troops and tanks, bent on the seizure of the main force of the French Navy, swept into the great naval base of Toulon. But they were too late. Even as they clattered into the streets of the town, a series of explosions from the harbour announced that the men of the French Navy were scuttling their ships rather than allow them to fall into German hands. By ten o'clock that morning the great act of self-immolation was completed: more than fifty warships, from auxiliary craft to battle-cruisers, lay smashed at the quaysides or sunk on the bed of the harbour. In a broadcast to the world on Sunday, November 29, Mr. Churchill said that "from the flame and smoke of the explosions at Toulon, France will rise again." France is already rising. Her men are massing in North Africa, and her remaining warships have joined the sea ranks of the Allies.

THE GREAT RUSSIAN OFFENSIVE: THE SEIGE OF STALINGRAD IS LIFTED.

THE GROUND OVER WHICH BITTER BATTLES ARE BEING FOUGHT IN RUSSIA: GERMAN TANKS STRUGGLING THROUGH HALF-FROZEN MUD AS THEY RETREAT BEFORE THE RUSSIAN ADVANCE.

THE GERMANS ARE ROUTED SOUTH-WEST OF STALINGRAD. THE PHOTOGRAPH SHOWS PART OF THE BOOTY WHEN THE RED ARMY DESTROYED FIFTY TANKS AND AN ENTIRE MOTORISED INFANTRY REGIMENT OF THE GERMAN 6TH TANK DIVISION.

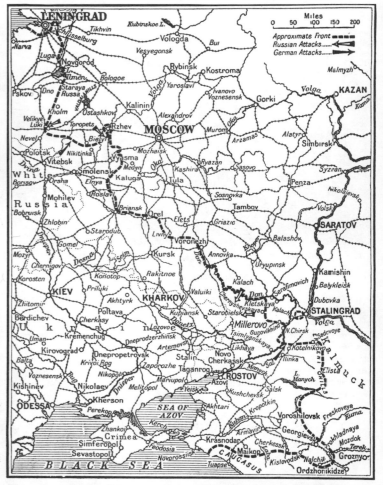

THE GREAT RUSSIAN OFFENSIVE ON THE DON, THREATENING KHARKOV AND ROSTOV, HAVING TRAPPED THE GERMAN FORCES AT STALINGRAD, WHICH WERE ENVELOPED: A MAP SHOWING THE ENTIRE FRONT FROM LENINGRAD TO THE CAUCASUS.

The Russians have wrested the initiative from the Germans in and around Stalingrad and a victory exceeding even the Battle of Egypt is well on the way to becoming a certainty. It was on November 19 that our Allies passed over to the offensive, first in the central Caucasus, ending the danger to the Grozny oilfields, and a few days later to the north, west and south of Stalingrad. Since that date, up to November 29, Russian troops captured 66,000 officers and men, 2000 guns of all calibres, 3935 machine-guns, about 50,000 rifles, 1379 damaged or undamaged tanks, 10,700 horses and 122 dumps with equipment, ammunition and food. The Germans, after this shock of the initial attacks, have managed to a certain extent to regroup their depleted forces; but despite the stiffening of German resistance and stubborn fighting by rearguards attempting to cover the retreat of the main forces, the Russian advance continues. Inside the city of Stalingrad the Russians have also gone over to the offensive and have succeeded in clearing several streets and fortified positions. This was made possible by the joining-up of the forces in the city with the relieving force in the north. Thus, exactly three months after Stalingrad was first assaulted, the defenders have begun to clear the Germans systematically out of their fortresses and cellars. In the Don bend, too, Russian troops have thrown the remnants of enemy units back to the eastern bank of the river, and a powerful new offensive west of Moscow has resulted in the cutting of vital railway lines held by the enemy. The Russians have started their winter offensive, and the Germans have already suffered overwhelming defeat in several sectors.

On December 14 the Germans were pressing on the Russian line south-west of Stalingrad, staging heavy attacks to liberate twenty Axis divisions cut off, and trapped in the town by Marshal Timoshenko's advancing troops. The enemy has recently lost 33 transport 'planes in this zone, giving a clear indication of the scale of Hitler's efforts to feed and reinforce his encircled army. Around Velikye Luki in front of Moscow the Red Army was endeavouring to complete the destruction of more encircled German units. It is not surprising that Berlin has become pessimistic. The Russian successes have been largely assisted by the two-front strategy of the Allies, which throughout has been Hitler's nightmare, and has now come to stay for the duration.

On December 23, which date our map approximately covers, the situation on the Middle Don front was becoming hourly more precarious for the Axis Army. The Red Army offensive was so unexpected and so crushing that it shattered all the plans of the German and Rumanian commands, with the result that enemy troops were falling back rapidly towards the west and south-west. It was sweeping forward along a front of 100 miles, threatening Kharkov. The great Soviet double thrust further south passed Millerovo, cut the railway junction which links the Middle Don with the Donetz basin, and the very important centres of Kharkov, 180 miles north-west, and Rostov, 120 miles south, and reached Nikolskaya, only 80 miles from Rostov. Thus, along a front stretching from Velikye-Luki to Kotelnikovo, the Russians advance like a tide, leaving here and there, as at Rzhev and Stalingrad, enemy divisions stranded by their inexorable forward surge. In Berlin anxiety was the predominant feeling at an increasingly grave situation, for the German army in the Caucasus is also in imminent danger of envelopment. The Russian generals agree that the enemy cannot now extricate himself from the Stalingrad trap and must be destroyed.

The too ambitious plan, conceived by Hitler, of dividing his forces and sending one to Stalingrad and the other south to force the Caucasus, has been foiled, and the enemy reduced to a dangerous pass. Von Paulus' army, arrested half-in and half-out of Stalingrad, is now effectively isolated, and its position is rapidly deteriorating as a result of the Russian advance across the Don bend. Everywhere in this sector, and further south, our Allies are broadening their front, and the figures available up to date reveal that, in the Kotelnikovo sector alone, where the Germans attempted to break back into Stalingrad between December 12 and 28, 17,000 Germans were killed, 60 tanks, 155 guns, and 105 lorries were captured, and 278 aircraft, 427 tanks, 221 guns were destroyed. Kotelnikovo itself was captured on December 29th. The number of prisoners taken reached a total of 3500 while at least sixteen inhabited localities were reoccupied in territory regained during the same period. On the central front, too, the new Russian advance in the Velikye Luki region continues to gain ground. The broadening of the Russian offensive east of Millerovo now threatens Rostov, the town upon which hinges the whole system of communications for the Caucasus army. And so it continues. The enemy still seems to be unable to stem the mighty onrush of the Red Army, and although it would be rash to under-estimate the tactical resources of the enemy, it is certain that his summer campaign has proved a strategical failure, and that the objective of the German Army can be little more than survival until the spring.

FROM ALL QUARTERS: NEWS ITEMS OF INTEREST AT HOME AND ABROAD.

H.M.S. "ONSLOW".

H.M.S. "ONSLOW" RIDDLED WITH SPLINTER HOLES COMES HOME
AFTER HER ENGAGEMENT OFF THE NORTH CAPE.

With her funnel and bridge full of splinter holes, the British destroyer
"Onslow" is home again after the action off the North Cape which
earned her commander, Captain R. St. V. Sherbrooke, the V.C.
"There has been nothing finer in Naval annals," said Mr. Alexander,
First Lord; and, of Captain Sherbrooke: "He led that fight on. He sent
a couple of destroyers against the enemy, and went straight in against
the pocket-battleship and the 8-inch-gun cruiser."

THE FROZEN NORTH.

FROST IS NO RESPECTER OF MIGHT: THE GUNS OF A BRITISH
BATTLESHIP AWAIT THE ICE-CLEARANCE PARTY.

Wintry conditions here persist well into the spring. These pictures give
an idea of the conditions during the "Onslow's" engagement.
Ice is not the least of the troubles which beset our warships in northern
waters and the crews have to fight a constant battle against this natural
enemy. These are the conditions, combined with an almost ceaseless
fight against enemy aircraft, U-boats, and surface raiders, under which
the British Navy delivers supplies to our Russian allies.

RECORD SHIPBUILDING.

IT TOOK JUST OVER 4½ DAYS TO BUILD THIS 10,500-TON CARGO
VESSEL IN AN AMERICAN SHIPYARD.

It was Henry J. Kaiser who set the fashion for rapid shipbuilding in the
United States. The latest news is of the launching of a Kaiser auxiliary
craft 2 days 23 hours 40 minutes after the laying of the keel!
The U.S. Maritime Commission has announced that the shipyards
reached the promised goal of three ships daily, delivering ninety-three
merchantmen with a deadweight tonnage of 1,000,000 tons in September, which equalled the entire production for 1941.

DARLAN ASSASSINATED.

THE TWENTY-YEAR-OLD YOUTH WHO SHOT ADMIRAL DARLAN:
FERNAND BONNIER DE LA CHAPELLE.

On December 24 Bonnier de la Chapelle walked into the Palais d'Eté,
the residence of the French High Commissioner at Algiers; he was
shown into a waiting-room. Darlan passed along the corridor and the
twenty-year-old youth fired five shots at him at a range of about 12 ft.
On Boxing Day he faced a firing squad. General Ciraud was unanimously elected to follow him as High Commissioner – a decision
received with widespread approval throughout the free world.

BEVERIDGE REPORT.

SIR WILLIAM BEVERIDGE IN HIS STUDY.

Sir William Henry Beveridge, whose Report on Social Insurance and
Allied Services has just been published, is Chairman of the Unemploy-
ment Insurance Statutory Committee.

"THE JEWISH PROBLEM".

A GENERAL VIEW OF THE JEWISH "DAY OF MOURNING" SERVICE
IN THE SPANISH AND PORTUGUESE SYNAGOGUE.

The Lord Mayor of London and Lady Joseph (top right) attended the
"day of mourning" service conducted by the Chief Rabbi (bottom left),
who appealed to the United Nations to save European Jews from
Hitler. Synagogues all over Great Britain observed December 13 as a
day of intercession and fast. On December 17 Mr Eden announced that
"the German authorities . . . are now carrying into effect Hitler's oft.
repeated intention to exterminate the Jewish people in Europe."

NAZI ATROCITIES.

THE COMMON GRAVE AT JERNVAAN, WITHOUT CROSSES AND
WITHOUT NAMES, WHERE ABOUT 200 SERBS, SHOT IN COLD
BLOOD BY THE GERMANS, ARE BURIED.

At the beginning of June a large consignment of prisoners from
Yugoslavia arrived in Norway. When they were brought ashore, the
prisoners were kicked and struck with rifle-butts. They were then
driven to the prison camp in Beisfjord. The ill-treatment continued
during the journey. On arrival three or four of the Yugoslavs collapsed
completely. They died later, and their comrades had to bury them.
In the camp, spotted typhus broke out, and many died. On July 17 the
Germans shot all those Serbs who were suffering from typhus. Finally,
the barracks and bodies were burnt.
The remaining prisoners, about 600, were the next day taken to a
deserted mountain range north of Rombaksfjorden, obliged to sit in the
overcrowded barges for forty-eight hours, without water, and with little
food. Eventually they were taken on lorries, to Oevre Jernvann where
they had to lie in the open air in their few clothes. Only after fourteen
days were canvas huts erected.
Prisoners who succumbed to typhus were immediately shot. On the
average, twelve men died every day. The camp at Jernvaan was closed
at the end of August, and the prisoners, then numbering about 350,
were transported back to Beisfjord and Bjoernefjell. At Jernvaan the
local people found huge common graves where it is reckoned about 200
Yugoslavs were buried.

HITLER IN RAVING MOOD.

"PEOPLE ASK WHY WE ARE TAKING SO LONG OVER STALINGRAD?
IT IS BECAUSE WE DO NOT WANT MASS MURDER."

On November 8 Hitler made a speech in the Munich beer hall. He
spoke in excited, vehement tones, raising his voice more than in recent
speeches. Although defiant his blusterings ring hollowly in the ears of
the world. He did not explain Rommel's retreat or the Allied coup in
North Africa. Stalingrad he proclaimed as a victory already won. Much
has happened since then – and the German people must by now realise
that he has put them in a precarious position.

MRS. ROOSEVELT IN LONDON.

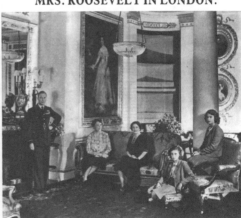

MRS. ROOSEVELT WITH THE ROYAL FAMILY IN THE BOW ROOM AT
BUCKINGHAM PALACE.

The King and Queen were at Paddington Station to welcome Mrs.
Roosevelt when she arrived in London on Friday, October 23. She had
travelled from America by air and for two days was a guest at
Buckingham Palace. Her first day in London opened with a Press
conference, where she said that she had come to Britain to see for
herself how women could help in the business of war. Later in the day
Mrs. Roosevelt, accompanied by the King and Queen, toured the City
and the East End. They visited St. Paul's, and the damaged Guildhall,
and, driving through the bombed areas, stopped at the City A.R.P.
control centre. The tour was continued through Stepney and
Whitechapel, where the party was cheered by large crowds. The King
and Queen and Mrs. Roosevelt finally drove to the Mansion House,
where they had tea with the Lord Mayor and the Lady Mayoress. On
the next day Mrs. Roosevelt visited the Washington Club, where she
was greeted by about 1000 American soldiers, sailors and airmen.

THE ILLUSTRATED LONDON NEWS

THE FRONTIERS GERMANY IS CALLED UPON TO HOLD: AN IMMENSE COASTLINE OF 14,480 MILES, FACING ATTACKS FROM EVERY DIRECTION.

The barriers which Hitler, with his rapid shrinkage of military power, is called upon to-day to defend, have steadily augmented, and since the taking over of hitherto unoccupied France, have yet more largely increased. Carefully prepared estimates show a frontier line altogether of 14,280 miles, to which may be added the Dodecanese making another 200 miles. Starting from Murmansk in the far north, the coast of Norway to Oslo, is 1700 miles; from Northern Denmark to Holland, 550 miles; from Holland to Calais, 350 miles; from thence to Brest, 650 miles; from Brest to the Spanish frontier, 550 miles; from Spain's Mediterranean frontier to Genoa, 450 miles; from Genoa to Messina Straits, 750 miles; Corsica, Sardinia, and Sicily, 1350 miles; from Messina to Trieste, 1200 miles; Trieste to Corfu, 750 miles; Corfu to the Turkish frontier, including Crete, 2530 miles; thence (eliminating the Balkan States) from Odessa, to Novorossisk, 1300 miles; from thence to Stalingrad, 750 miles; thence to Moscow, 850 miles, and on to Leningrad and the Finnish frontier, 550 miles. Along this immense frontier line he must maintain hundreds of divisions of troops, Gestapo, and the *Luftwaffe*. The opening of a new front as in French North Africa compels a drainage of troops from other theatres of war. In addition, throughout Hitler is blockaded by sea and air power.

1943

US/Australians take Buna, New Guinea — Siege of Leningrad lifted — Germans surrender in Stalingrad — Casablanca conference: Churchill and Roosevelt fix priorities for 1943 — Japanese driven out of Papua and Guadalcanal — 8th Army enters Tunisia; links up with Op. Torch forces — Battle of Atlantic reaches climax — British/Indians driven out of Burma again — Axis driven out of North Africa — RAF bomb Mohne and Eder Dams — Allied forces under Wingate and Stillwell operate behind Japanese lines in Burma — Allies take New Georgia — Allies land on Sicily — Bombing of Hamburg begins — Mussolini overthrown and arrested in Italy — Axis cleared from Sicily — New Italian government surrenders — Allies land at Reggio, Salerno and Taranto — Italian Navy surrenders in Malta; Germans occupy Rome and Northern Italy; Mussolini "rescued" by German paratroops — Russians retake Smolensk — Italy declares war on Germany; Allies capture Naples — US marines land on Bougainville — Russians take Kiev; reach Dnieper River — Bombing of Berlin begins — British/Indians launch new attack on Burma — Teheran conference — US forces land in New Britain — Russians attack in Ukraine; cut off German forces in Crimea — Teheran and Cairo conferences consider Post-war boundaries — "Scharnhorst" sunk by Royal Navy.

THE END OF THE PAPUA CAMPAIGN: JAPAN'S ARMY ANNIHILATED.

THE PAPUAN NATIVES HAVE LARGELY ASSISTED THE ALLIED FORCES. CARRYING IN A WOUNDED SOLDIER PAST A HIDDEN MACHINE-GUN POST.

TROOPS CROSSING THE KANUSI RIVER, SWOLLEN BY RAINS, ON FLYING FOXES HASTILY CONSTRUCTED BY ENGINEERS. BEYOND THEM LIES THE UNKNOWN FOREST.

NATIVE STYLE: AMERICAN TROOPS GO CANOEING AS THEY HEAD FOR THE SMALL BOATS WHICH WILL CARRY THEM DOWNSTREAM TO NEW POSITIONS.

The Japanese forces at Burma were cut in two on December 30 by a new Allied drive, which forced a wedge to the sea between the Mission and Giropa Point. Since then the Mission has been occupied and the Giropa Point area is also clear of the enemy, except for snipers who are rapidly being exterminated.

On January 24 it was announced by General MacArthur that the Papua Campaign was completed. It was, he said, a test of a "new form of campaign" which points the way to the ultimate defeat of the enemy. On July 22 last year the Japs landed about 5000 men at Sannanda, and in these twenty-six weeks nothing elsewhere can surpass the simple courage, unconquerable spirit, and resolve of our brothers of British race, battling with a savage and barbarous enemy who had to be exterminated like rats. Men had lived for weeks in the jungle, hunted all the time by the Japanese. Racked with malaria, dysentery, etc., their diet bully beef and dry biscuits, and often little of those, they forged ahead. Their victory is a triumph for Australia.

GUADALCANAL, AMERICA'S NEW GIBRALTAR.

SOME CAPTURED JAPANESE MATERIAL, INCLUDING A SMALL MACHINE-GUN, RIFLES. AND JAPANESE MONEY. NEARLY EVERY CAPTURED KITBAG INCLUDED A JAPANESE FLAG.

The 100-mile-long Solomon island of Guadalcanal was for six months the main Pacific battleground between our American allies and the Japanese. It is as vital in the Pacific as is Gibraltar in the Mediterranean. The Japanese seized it first, but on August 7 American troops landed on several beaches. Three days later, U.S. Marines established themselves on the island; the Jap fleet in an air action were forced to retire, and on the 25th were severely battered in a further sea and air battle. By this time the Marines, after savage in-fighting with sub-machine-guns, grenades and bayonets, had driven the enemy out of the now famous Henderson airfield, which he had almost completed as a take-off base for an intended invasion of Australia.

On October 14 and on succeeding days the Japanese landed many reinforcements, despite heavy losses. On the previous night, in a 30-minutes sea battle, the U.S. sank six Jap warships, including one cruiser, four destroyers and one big troopship, and probably two other warships for the loss of a destroyer. On the 16th a great enemy fleet, including battleships, was observed off Shortland Island, near Rabaul. On the 17th and 18th the enemy landed more troops, and U.S. airmen shot down fourteen bombers and two fighters, also making devastating attacks on warships off Buin in the north-west Solomons.

On October 27 the American troops, who were reported as tired and anxiously awaiting reinforcements, beat off three more fierce attacks from an enemy army estimated to number 30,000 picked Japanese soldiers. The U.S. line was pierced at one point, but they counter-attacked and regained their former positions; the Americans claimed command of the air, and the airfield on Guadalcanal was still operating. Nevertheless, there was a growing pessimism in Washington as to whether relief could reach the sorely-tried troops. But on October 31, a first brief announcement was made that the big Japanese fleet had retreated from the Solomons. Next day it was reported that on October 25 a big sea and air battle had taken place off the Stewart Islands, east of the Solomons, in which Vice-Admiral Halsey was victorious. Even so it required a further three and a half months of some of the bitterest fighting of this war to dislodge the Japanese.

AMERICAN TROOPS WHO TOOK PART IN THE FIGHTING ON GUADALCANAL STAND WITH BOWED HEADS AT THE GRAVESIDES OF THEIR FALLEN COMRADES.

THE SENSATIONAL ALLIED ALL-AIRCRAFT VICTORY IN THE BISMARCK SEA.

FLYING FORTRESSES IN ACTION – PROMINENT IN THE SENSATIONAL BISMARCK SEA BATTLE.

The greatest triumph of air power used singly against warships was recorded last week in the Battle of the Bismarck Sea. The annihilation of a complete armada of warships and twelve transports, without a known survivor, is unexampled in this or any previous war, and for the loss of less than half-a-dozen Allied machines. The critical part of the battle was fought in the Huin Gulf, off Lae, New Guinea. The Allies started the attacks with Havocs upon the landing-grounds near Lae.

Then they attacked the convoy at mast-height. Later, Australian-built Beaufighters, Mitchells and Flying Fortresses, covered overhead by Lightning fighters, attacked. A second raid on the Lae airfield was executed by Kittyhawk fighter-bombers escorted by Lightnings.

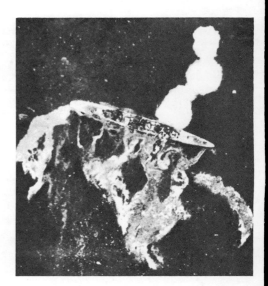

IN THE BATTLE OF THE BISMARCK SEA ON MARCH 2–3: ONE OF JAPAN'S DESTROYERS SINKING, HIT BY ALLIED BOMBERS.

TWELVE WEEKS OF RUSSIAN RECONQUEST.

GERMAN 1942 ADVANCE ---- HALTED NOV.19.
RUSSIAN FRONT MARCH 1943 ———
TERRITORY RECAPTURED BY THE RED ARMY IN 12 WEEKS GIVING DATES OF RE-OCCUPATION

RUSSIA'S WINTER CONQUESTS: AN APPROXIMATE MAP SHOWING THE SOVIET GAINS, WHICH EXCEED IN SIZE ALL GERMANY. (INSET) A MAP OF GERMANY ON THE SAME SCALE FOR COMPARISON.

With the termination of Russia's winter campaign our Soviet allies have published their first map of the war showing a continuous front about 1500 miles long from Leningrad to Taganrog. Features of the Russian map show that the Soviet hold part of the southern shore of the Gulf of Finland, and the gap punched in the Leningrad blockade is 12 miles. From Veliki Luki they advanced west to Novo Sokolniki; and now at the walls of Velizh are under 15 miles from White Russia. Kharkov, recovered by the Russians on February 16, was retaken by the Germans on March 15 after particularly savage fighting.

THE GREAT GERMAN RETREAT.

On January 1 a new Russian offensive developed and proceeded to push northwards. From north, east and south columns are closing in on Rostov. Attention is especially centred in the Northern Caucasus, where, on January 24, the fall of Armavir cut off the German Army trying to get to the Black Sea. Soviet divisions at whirlwind pace were moving on Tikhoretsk, linking Salsk, Armavir, and Krasodar by rail with Rostov. The Germans in Krasnodar were in grave peril.

Rostov was retaken on February 14 after violent fighting. The enemy, dense columns in headlong flight, was pursued by tanks and the Red Air Force. The Russians on February 16 were approaching Mariupol with the object of completely enveloping all Germans in the Donetz Basin. On February 16 fighting reached a pitch of intensity unequalled since the battle of Stalingrad. Hitler threw in a large force but he lost 100 tanks, and the S.S. troops from France were decimated. The enemy forces here were attempting to evacuate the ruined city, but four of the six railroads were in Russian hands, making the retreat a very costly undertaking. The fall of Kharkov was the heaviest strategic defeat yet suffered by the Germans.

The recapture of Kharkov, claimed by enemy forces, is a disappointment and is due to the premature thaw. It has replaced the Germans in the Ukraine virtually where they stood before last summer's offensive. On March 15 the Soviet forces were falling back slowly in the north, but in the south they were hanging on to the actual bank of the Donetz, where the key to the situation was probably Izyum.

The steady advance of the Soviet Army from Vyasma towards Smolensk had been necessarily off-set by the powerful German offensive in the Donetz Basin. Last week the fall of Rzhev was followed by that of Gzhatsk and then Vyasma, the Russians inflicting heavy losses on the retreating enemy. North-west of Vyasma our allies are advancing, and also south, where they are building up a broad front, which is now within 80 miles of Smolensk, the key position in this sector.

THIS WAS THEIR HOME: RUSSIAN PEASANTS, IN THE WAKE OF THE GERMAN RETREAT, SEARCH THE RUINED SITE OF THEIR FORMER VILLAGE.

THE SIEGE OF LENINGRAD LIFTED.

LENINGRAD IS FREED: AFTER 516 DAYS THE SIEGE IS RAISED AND THE RED FLAG FLIES ONCE MORE OVER SCHLUESSELBURG.

A HEAVY GERMAN SIEGE GUN PULLED UP TO THE WALLS OF LENINGRAD: PART OF THE EQUIPMENT CAPTURED BY THE LIBERATING RED ARMY.

After a siege lasting 16 months, Leningrad has been freed. After seven days' heavy fighting the Russians raised the siege of Leningrad. Separate forces, attacking from the Leningrad and Volkhov fronts, had linked up on January 18 and cut the German encirclement. During the early stages of the siege, the 3,000,000 inhabitants of Leningrad suffered fearful privations, considerable numbers dying of starvation. The Russian capture of the southern shore of Lake Ladoga in the autumn of 1941 relieved the strain. This week's great achievement should enable the gallant city to resume its vital role as a major supply base.

LAST DAYS AT STALINGRAD: THE MOST CATASTROPHIC DEFEAT INFLICTED ON THE GERMAN ARMY SINCE 1918.

TWO WOMEN OF STALINGRAD EMERGING FROM THE RUINS TO RESUME LIFE ABOVE GROUND.

The surrender of Marshal Paulus on January 31 put the seal of completeness on the most catastrophic defeat inflicted on the German Army since 1918. This historic battle was won in the first place by the courage and tenacity of the defenders of the city in the face of overwhelming odds; but the tide was finally turned, on January 10, when the relieving forces turned a defensive action into a superb counter-offensive, gradually squeezing the enemy into an ever smaller bag, and eventually cutting his army in two. Many prisoners were taken and great quantities of booty seized. This destroyed or captured army originally numbered no fewer than 330,000 men. Germany went into mourning for three days for Stalingrad, but it will take more than that for the people to forget this, and will do nothing to reassure them as news of fresh Soviet victories comes in daily. The defence of Stalingrad, unsurpassed in military history, will live in the annals of heroic deeds, and already her people pour back to build up her ruins and add her quota to final victory.

PRESIDENT AND PRIME MINISTER DECIDE 1943 STRATEGY AT CASABLANCA CONFERENCE.

PRESIDENT ROOSEVELT AND MR. WINSTON CHURCHILL AT CASABLANCA DURING A CONFERENCE DESCRIBED BY THE PRESIDENT AS THE "UNCONDITIONAL SURRENDER" MEETING.

IN CONFERENCE: (SEATED) ADMIRAL E. J. KING, MR. CHURCHILL AND PRESIDENT ROOSEVELT; (STANDING) MAJOR-GENERAL ISMAY, LORD LOUIS MOUNTBATTEN AND SIR JOHN DILL.

IN THE GARDEN OF THE PRESIDENT'S VILLA, AND IN THE PRESENCE OF MR. ROOSEVELT AND MR. CHURCHILL, GENERAL GIRAUD AND GENERAL DE GAULLE SHAKE HANDS.

On January 27 the world learned that the President of the United States and the Prime Minister of Britain had been in conference at a villa in Casablanca for ten days. It was one of the most momentous conferences of the war – in which all the resources were marshalled for the execution of offensive campaigns in 1943. Complete agreement was reached between the two leaders and between their Chiefs of Staff, who were present throughout the conference, on the steps to be taken to exploit the present favourable turn of events, and Premier Stalin was kept fully informed of all the decisions arrived at. The President and Mr. Churchill made it clear to Press representatives that the war could end only with the unconditional surrender of the Axis Powers. The complete mutual trust between the President and Prime Minister was emphasised by one of the correspondents in Casablanca: "It is obvious," he wrote, "that the greatest friendship exists between the two men." It was an occasion during which, as Mr. Roosevelt put it, "minds have been put in accord on all military operations." The conference was an opportune moment for the much-canvassed meeting between General Giraud, High Commissioner for French North Africa, and General de Gaulle, Leader of the Fighting French Forces, who, after a two-days' conference, issued a statement that they were agreed upon the common objective of "the liberation of France and the triumph of human liberties by the total defeat of the enemy." Both President Roosevelt and Mr. Churchill flew to Casablanca for the conference – the first time in history that a United States President has travelled by air.

PRESIDENTS MEET: ROOSEVELT AND VARGAS – CHURCHILL AND INÖNÜ.

THE HISTORIC MEETING AT ADANA, TURKEY. MR. CHURCHILL AND PRESIDENT INÖNÜ CONFER TOGETHER DURING THEIR RAIL-COACH DISCUSSIONS.

PRESIDENT ROOSEVELT WITH PRESIDENT VARGAS (CENTRE) WHILST ON A TOUR OF INSPECTION OF ARMY, NAVY AND AIR FORCE ESTABLISHMENTS IN BRAZIL.

Two meetings, following on that of historical importance near Casablanca, have recently taken place. President Roosevelt has met and conferred with President Getulio Vargas in Brazil and Mr. Churchill has visited Turkey for talks with President Inönü. Of the former meeting, it is known that it took place at Natal, at the tip of the bulge of Brazil, and although nothing has so far been divulged, it is a fair assumption that it had to do with Brazilian-American co-operation, both naval and air, against enemy submarines and the utilisation of Brazilian merchant shipping in the Allied cause. President Roosevelt is now back in Washington.

Mr. Churchill, who flew from Cairo to Adana and back to Cairo, had important conversations with President Inönü on January 30 and 31, during which the bonds of friendship were confirmed and further strengthened by the frank interchange of policy. Together the statesmen examined the present situation in Europe, and particularly in those regions in which Turkey is directly interested. Agreement was also reached on the aid Great Britain and the U.S.A. would give to Turkey. Turkey has never wavered in her loyalty to the British alliance and has never disguised her resolve to resist aggression.

DAUNTLESS SERB GUERILLAS TIE DOWN AXIS FORCES.

IN THE SERBIAN MOUNTAINS: A COLUMN OF GERMAN PRISONERS BEING MARCHED TO INTERNMENT AFTER THEIR CAPTURE BY YUGOSLAVIAN GUERILLAS.

THE GERMANS SAY THAT THE YUGOSLAV GUERILLAS FIGHT WITH SUPPLIES DROPPED BY PARACHUTE FROM R.A.F. 'PLANES. A GERMAN EXAMINES A SUPPLIES CONTAINER.

A GERMAN MILITARY FORCE IN THE BOSNIAN MOUNTAINS LEAVING A BURNING VILLAGE IN THEIR OPERATIONS AGAINST GENERAL MIHAILOVITCH, THE YUGOSLAV PATRIOT LEADER.

These pictures illustrate the heroic fight against the Axis in unsubjugated Yugoslavia. Serbian guerillas, under the command of the famous General Mihailovitch, have waged a ceaseless war against the invaders, swooping on one strongpoint after another, slaughtering the enemy and taking many prisoners.

The success which has attended General Drazha Mihailovitch and his army of guerilla forces, emerging from their fastnesses in the icy Bosnian mountains, has proved most embarrassing to the Axis Powers. The failure of Italian forces to restrain the patriots, who are said to be well supplied with arms, and whose raids on Italians had been sanguinary and successful, compelled the Germans to divert many of their crack sturm-truppen to wipe out the Yugoslavian guerillas. They have by no means done so in this winter campaign, in which they have burnt down villages and killed men, women and children, for parties have been cut off, slain or taken prisoner by the dauntless Mihailovitch. In January the Germans issued a proclamation against the "rebels" – who, it said, "ignore realities" defying the "legal Serbian Government" – which met with no response. The solidarity of the General's followers has caused the enemy grave concern.

The Nazis are saying that it is the R.A.F. who drop supplies to the guerillas, by parachute, thus enabling them to continue the fight. The container being examined seen in the central photograph above is said to have contained mostly explosives. It was found by German troops, photographed and used in the Axis Press as anti-British propaganda.

TRIPOLI, CITY OF A MILLION PALMS, FALLS TO THE EIGHTH ARMY.

BOOBY-TRAPS WERE USED BY THE GERMANS AND BEFORE ATTEMPTING TO REMOVE A MINE OUR SAPPERS SEARCH ITS UNDER-SIDE WITH THE HELP OF SMALL MIRRORS.

MR. CHURCHILL DRIVING BETWEEN RANKS OF MEN OF THE ROYAL TANK REGIMENT, DRAWN UP IN FRONT OF THEIR TANKS FOR THE TRIPOLI REVIEW.

THE GERMAN SURPRISE WEAPON – THE 88-MM. GUN (LEFT) – AND THE AMERICAN ANSWER – THE M-7 "PRIEST" TANK-DESTROYER, MOUNTING A 105-MM. GUN-HOWITZER.

The pursuit of Rommel's forces went all the way to Tripoli which was entered from both south and east. Our troops quickly took over control of the town, and on January 25, standing in the sun at the Porto Benito cross-roads, just outside the city, General Montgomery officially received the surrender of Tripoli.

As a fitting climax to his historic meetings at Casablanca and in Turkey, Mr. Churchill spent two days with the Eighth Army at Tripoli. Landing on Castel Benito aerodrome on February 3, he drove into Tripoli the next day, where, at a saluting-base in the main square of the town, he reviewed units which had fought Rommel successively out of Egypt, Libya and Tripolitania. The streets of the town were lined with troops,

armoured vehicles and cheering citizens as the Prime Minister, in the first of a line of Staff cars, passed through them. With the fall of Tripoli the chase of Rommel was continued with even added ardour. At the time of writing it is uncertain if he will stand on the Mareth Line, south of Gabes, so strongly fortified before the war by the French. If so, the enemy will have to count on an Allied army operating on his rear. Rommel's broken forces can scarcely strengthen Arnim in Tunisia, when he brings the Eighth Army on his heels. Arnim's strength is already considered unequal to the forces opposed to him. With Tripoli we now have air command over Tunisia within easy distance of light bombers.

WITH THE FIRST ARMY IN TUNISIA: TWO OF THE GREATEST V.C. FEATS OF THE WAR.

BURIED ON THE SCENE OF HIS HEROISM: THE GRAVE OF CAPTAIN THE LORD LYELL, V.C., SCOTS GUARDS WHO SINGLE-HANDEDLY SILENCED A HEAVY MACHINE GUN AND AN 88MM ANTI-TANK GUN IN SEPARATE PITS, IN THE ATTACK ON JEBEL BOU ARADA. WITH GRENADES, BAYONET AND REVOLVER HE KILLED MOST OF THE GUN CREWS AND DIED HIMSELF AS THE ENEMY BROKE AND RAN.

SERGEANT L. P. KENNEALLY, OF THE IRISH GUARDS, IS DECORATED WITH THE V.C. BY GENERAL ALEXANDER: LANCE CORPORAL (AS HE THEN WAS) KENNEALLY CHARGED SINGLE-HANDEDLY A COMPANY OF THE ENEMY WHO WERE FORMING UP FOR A COUNTER ATTACK, FIRING HIS BREN-GUN FROM THE HIP. THEY BROKE IN DISORDER AND THEIR PROJECTED ATTACK WAS ABANDONED.

Mr. Churchill, speaking at a Press conference in Cairo on February 1 said: "We must expect considerable fighting in Tunisia in the next few months, perhaps weeks, but I am confident of the result." The two months that followed saw heavy fighting.

On February 26, General von Arnim launched a general offensive on the northern front in Tunisia, his troops strenghened by recent reinforcements attacking at many points along an 80-mile line between Cap Serrat, on the northern coast, and Jebel Mansour, south of Bou Arada. The enemy thrusts were everywhere held, with heavy casualties in Axis men and materials. Meanwhile, in Central Tunisia, the enemy was reported to be

withdrawing after his thrust in the Kasserine area, and further south the Eighth Army under General Montgomery continued to narrow the gap between its ranks and those of the Allies on the central front. On March 2 the Allies recovered the Kasserine Pass and on 5th had advanced east beyond Sidi Bou Zid. In the north Sejenane was attacked. In the centre the U.S. Fifth Army, driven out of Gafsa on February 17, reoccupied it on March 19, while the Eighth Army was actively occupying Rommel on the Mareth Line. On March 23, with the Battle of Mareth proceeding and the flanking movement at El Hamma underway the U.S. advanced beyond Sened towards the coast.

THE BATTLE FOR THE MARETH LINE, NOW IN BRITISH HANDS.

GURKAS EMERGING FROM A SMOKE-SCREEN AS THEY STORM A HILL. THE DREADED *KUKRI*, THEIR SPECIAL WEAPON, HAS PLAYED AN EFFECTIVE PART IN THE ATTACKS.

On March 6, as the Eighth Army was approaching the Mareth line, Rommel made a sally with 100 tanks near the town of Medenine. Montgomery replied with a mighty artillery barrage, and at least 33 of Rommel's tanks were destroyed. In an order to the Eighth Army on March 10 Montgomery said: "The enemy is caught like a rat in a trap . . . I did not expect for a moment that the enemy would attack us. It seemed absurd . . . We must show him our gratitude in no uncertain way." Rommel's tactics are clearly delaying ones, his object, and that of Von Arnim in the north, being to hold the coastline of Tunisia as long as possible and thus delay the opening of a second front and the command of the Mediterranean.

General Montgomery's advance has been timed to coincide with that of the American General Patton towards Gabes. On March 21 the U.S. forces, including the First Tank Division, who had previously taken El Guettar, captured Sened station, halfway between Gafas and Maknassy,

THE WAR IN TUNISIA: A MAP OUTLINING THE GENERAL LINE OF ATTACK UPON ROMMEL AND THE ALLIED ADVANCE FROM MAKNASSI AND EL HAMMA TO CUT THE CORRIDOR.

A FALLEN BASTION OF THE MARETH LINE: VICTORIOUS SOLDIERS OF MONTGOMERY'S EIGHTH ARMY AFTER CAPTURING AN ENEMY PILL-BOX AMONG THE MARETH FORTIFICATIONS.

50 miles from the coast. It is anticipated that the British force from Ksar Rhilane has also Gabes as its objective. The French are meantime moving eastward on Rommel's west flank. Only in the north has General Anderson's First Army recently been forced back to Tamera. The historic assault on the Mareth Line closed down on the night of March 29, when it was announced that the enemy had been forced to withdraw from the Mareth area and that the Eighth Army had occupied the whole of the strongly organised defences. Rommel was outwitted by Montgomery's flanking manoeuvre of El Hamma and fled – and at the time of writing is still in full flight towards the mountains encompassing Tunis and Bizerta. While the tanks of Montgomery's outflanking force were advancing on El Hamma troops of our frontal assault force were engaged in driving the enemy rearguard out of the Maginot Line-style fortifications. Between them, the two forces took something like 8000 prisoners.

CAMERA OCCASIONS: LAND, SEA AND AIR NEWS FROM MANY FRONTS.

THE "PRESIDENT COOLIDGE" SINKS.

THE LOSS OF THE 21,000-TON "PRESIDENT COOLIDGE" OFF THE SOLOMONS LAST DECEMBER, AFTER STRIKING A MINE.

The majestic liner was making her way slowly through a slate-grey morning off the Solomons when she struck an enemy mine. Captain Henry Nelson rammed a coral reef, and the bow drove well up on it. Her bottom had been torn open, and before long she sank. Fine discipline was shown by all of the 4000 troops on board and there were only two fatalities. Cargo nets were thrown over the side to facilitate descent, and the soldiers wearing lifebelts dropped into the sea.

LONDON RAID SHELTER TRAGEDY.

OFFICIALS MAKING ENQUIRIES AT THE FOOT OF THE SHELTER STEPS WHERE THE ACCIDENT OCCURRED.

On Wednesday, March 3, 178 persons lost their lives and about 60 were injured owing to an accident. There were no bombs and no panic; a woman holding a child tripped and fell on the stairs leading to the tube shelter, and those behind her fell likewise, piling up, one on top of the other, and crushing the life out of those who had preceded them. The Ministry of Pensions immediately set up an emergency office for the payment of special allowance to dependants of the victims.

A SPEECH DELAYED.

THE SPEECH THE R.A.F. DELAYED BY AN HOUR: GOERING TAKES THE SALUTE AT THE AIR MINISTRY, BERLIN, ON JANUARY 30.

On January 30, the tenth anniversary of Hitler's assumption of power, Marshal Goering was to deputise for Hitler in addressing the whole German nation over the radio from the Hall of Honour at the Air Ministry, Berlin. At eleven o'clock precisely, the hour at which he was to speak, R.A.F. Mosquito bombers arrived over the capital – for the first time in daylight – completely disorganising the celebrations, and causing an hour's postponement of the speech.

KINGEE GEORGE'S AEROPLANE.

HOW "KINGEE GEORGE'S AEROPLANE" WAS SAVED BY MERU TRIBESMEN, WHO CARVED A RUNWAY FROM THE RUGGED SLOPES OF MOUNT KENYA, STAMPING IT FLAT WITH THEIR FEET.

When a twin-engined R.A.F. 'plane made a forced landing on the higher slopes of Mount Kenya its pilot led his crew safely through forests, to base and reported a fairly level stretch of moorland about a mile from the aircraft. The position was explained to the Meru tribesmen, 150 of whom promptly volunteered to hack a runway on the mountain slopes. Carrying tools and equipment on their heads, they climbed the mountain, where they filled gullies, bridged crevasses and finally stamped the surface level with their feet. Eventually, amid terrific excitement, the aeroplane was brought up and took off followed by a wildly cheering crowd of tribesmen, who have since told the story of "how Kingee George's aeroplane was saved, and how the Meru were chosen for the task."

MUSSOLINI'S CAIRO MEDAL.

TO COMMEMORATE MUSSOLINI'S "TRIUMPHAL ENTRY" INTO CAIRO. THE MEDAL IS DATED OCTOBER 28, 1942.

This medal, struck by Italy to commemorate Mussolini's triumphal entry into Cairo, is dated October 28, 1942. The Duce's head is shown above the date on the obverse, whilst the words "*Summa audacia et virtus*" are engraved on the reverse. When it was shown to Mr. Churchill on his recent Middle East tour, he remarked that the Italians were then some 1600 miles nearer Cairo.

WASHINGTON'S 211TH ANNIVERSARY.

ON THE 211TH ANNIVERSARY OF THE BIRTH OF GEORGE WASHINGTON. U.S. TROOPS, AND A DETACHMENT OF THE KING'S ROYAL RIFLE CORPS, LAY WREATHS AT SULGRAVE MANOR.

Sulgrave Manor, Northamptonshire, the ancestral home of the Washington family, from whom was directly descended America's historic first President, provides a direct kinship between George Washington and Britain's Prime Minister. It is particularly apposite at this moment, since on February 22 was commemorated the 211th anniversary of Washington's birth, and at Sulgrave Manor U.S. soldiers and Servicewomen laid wreaths before their hero's bust, conducted by Earl Spencer, another kinsman of the Washingtons and Spencer-Churchills. Sulgrave was sold by Robert Washington in 1659, but in 1657 John, great-grandson of Robert, emigrated to Virginia, and became the great-grandfather of George, born at Mount Vernon. The historic house was purchased by Anglo-American subscribers in 1911.

LONDON'S "WINGS FOR VICTORY" WEEK, WITH A TARGET OF £150,000,000.

MISS JEAN BATTEN, THE NEW ZEALAND HEROINE OF MANY SPECTACULAR FLIGHTS, SPEAKING IN TRAFALGAR SQUARE TO A HUGE CROWD AT "WINGS FOR VICTORY" OPENING.

AT THE OPENING CEREMONY IN TRAFALGAR SQUARE ON MARCH 6, LORD KINDERSLEY RELEASED 1300 CARRIER-PIGEONS TO THE 1300 LOCAL SAVINGS COMMITTEES TO DELIVER THEIR MESSAGES.

CROWDS OF PEOPLE PLASTERING TWO 500-LB. BOMB CASES IN TRAFALGAR SQUARE WITH SAVINGS STAMPS. AT THE END OF THE WEEK THEY WILL BE DROPPED ON GERMANY.

London's "Wings for Victory" week, with a £150,000,000 target, had a flying start on Saturday, March 6, when it was announced that over £30,000,000 had already been raised. On Sunday huge and merry crowds – the biggest since the Coronation – turned out to give the campaign their blessing. Trafalgar Square, the scene of the opening ceremony, was packed out, many overflowing into Whitehall, the entrance to the Mall and the Strand. Hundreds hung precariously from every vantage point in the shadow of Nelson's Column, and the lions at the corners of the plinth disappeared almost from sight. They came, not only to see, but to give. They surged forward in an unbroken stream towards the selling booths, and hundreds bought sixpenny Savings Stamps and stuck them on two bombs placed in front of the big Lancaster. The bomb-cases will be inches deep in stamps before the week is ended if the rate is maintained. Many of the stamps are five-shilling stamps cancelled with messages.

ONE OF THE MOST REMARKABLE AND COMPLETE MILITARY VICTORIES OF ALL TIME, AS ALLIED TROOPS SWEEP ONWARDS TO THE DEFEAT OF THE AXIS ARMIES IN TUNISIA.

A WOUNDED TOMMY, PRIVATE S. MAY, OF ST. PANCRAS, SMOKES WITH A WOUNDED GERMAN WHOM HE CAPTURED IN THE MARETH BATTLE.

"WELCOME YOU, LIMEY!" SOUTH-EAST OF GAFSA: SERGEANT BROWN, OF THE DEVON AND THE EIGHTH ARMY MEETS SERGEANT RANDALL, OF IOWA AND THE U.S. SECOND CORPS.

A SHERMAN TANK CREW OF THE FIRST ARMY GREET AN ARMOURED-CAR CREW OF THE EIGHTH ARMY OUTSIDE KAIROUAN.

TWO PRETTY FRENCH GIRLS IN GABES, WAITING TO PRESENT THEIR BOUQUETS TO GENERAL MONTGOMERY.

THE RESULT OF A BET WITH GENERAL EISENHOWER, WHO DID NOT BELIEVE THAT THE EIGHTH ARMY COULD REACH SFAX BY APRIL 15, MONTGOMERY BEAT THIS TARGET BY FOUR DAYS.

THE TUNISIAN PORTS WERE BOMBED TO PIECES BEFORE THE ALLIED ATTACK: ONE OF FERRYVILLE'S SIX DRY DOCKS, WITH A FRENCH DESTROYER LYING DERELICT INSIDE IT.

SUGGESTIVE OF A PREHISTORIC MONSTER WITH WINGS – AN ME.323 SIX-ENGINED GERMAN "POWERED GLIDER" IN FLIGHT: ALL 31 OF A CONVOY OF ME.323S ON ITS WAY TO TUNISIA ON APRIL 22 WERE SHOT DOWN BY KITTYHAWKS AND SPITFIRES. THE ME.323 HAS A WING SPAN ALMOST TWICE THAT OF A LANCASTER BOMBER, AND CAN CARRY 10 TONS OF EQUIPMENT OR 100 FULLY ARMED MEN, BUT HAS A TOPSPEED OF ONLY 170 MPH.

INFANTRYMEN DASH UP TO A KNOCKED-OUT GERMAN POSITION FROM WHICH THE ENEMY HAD BEEN TRYING TO HOLD UP THE ALLIED ADVANCE WITH A NEBELWERFER SIX-MANNED MORTAR, THE DAY BEFORE TUNIS AND BIZERTA FELL.

A CAPTURE OF PRISONERS FROM A NAZI ARTILLERY REGIMENT ON APRIL 24. THEY SURRENDERED DURING THE FIRST ARMY'S ATTACK NORTH-EAST OF MED-JEZ EL BAB, AND ARE LED IN BY A BRITISH "TOMMY" WITH A WHITE "FLAG" CARRIED ON HIS BAYONET END.

GENERAL VON ARNIM, ERSTWHILE LEADER OF THE GERMAN ARMIES IN TUNISIA, IS POLITELY ESCORTED BY OFFICERS INTO THE BARBED-WIRE ENCLOSURE SURROUNDING HIS NEW QUARTERS – IN ENGLAND.

CONGESTED PRISONER CAMPS: THE SCENE ABOVE, TYPICAL OF MANY, SHOWS VAST CROWDS OF APPARENTLY CHEERFUL PRISONERS, NONE OF WHOM HAS THE SLIGHTEST DESIRE TO ESCAPE. THEY ARE GENUINELY RELIEVED TO BE DONE WITH MORE FIGHTING!

General Montgomery must surely be the first officer to have been presented by an ally with a heavy bomber as a private taxi – and as the result of a bet. Montgomery promised a group of American generals he would take Sfax by April 15. General Eisenhower is reported to have bet him a private Flying Fortress, complete with crew for the duration that he wouldn't. The Eighth Army entered Sfax on April 11. The Flying Fortress was delivered six days later. On April 12, Rommel's army joined von Arnim's in "the Box," the last corner of African soil left to the Axis. On Tuesday, April 20, General Montgomery started the new phase of his offensive on a line from Enfidaville for a distance of 45 miles inland.

On April 30 Von Arnim's forces began a series of repeated counter-attacks, notably north and north-east of Mejez el Bab, and strong points changed hands repeatedly. On May 3 the general situation was dramatically changed by a surprise thrust carried out by the U.S. forces under General Patton, in which they captured Mateur the vital junction 20 miles south-west of Bizerta, after a 15-mile advance. The French to the north also advanced 7 miles. This outstanding triumph for American arms enabled an advance southwards towards Jedeida to outflank the enemy who had checked the First Army's progress towards Tebourba. The advance also hastened activities by the Eighth Army in the south.

Tunis fell to the First Army, with certain units of the Eighth, at 3.40 p.m., May 7, in pouring rain but with cheering crowds welcoming their rescuers. General Alexander, driving a jeep, accompanied by Air Marshal Coningham, in command of Tactical Air Forces, drove almost unrecognised through the streets.

Fifteen minutes later, Bizerta was seized by Americans and French when Ferryville capitulated. The rapidity of General Alexander's advance on Tunis was such that the enemy army was cut in two and left dazed and demoralised. Strong defensive nests were by-passed and surrounded like a flood. Large numbers of Axis troops endeavoured to reach Cape Bon, with no escape possible, as the sea was held by Admiral Cunningham. These surrendered on May 13. General Alexander reported to Mr. Churchill on May 15: "Prime Minister, – Sir, – it is my duty to report that the Tunisian campaign is over. All enemy resistance has ceased. We are masters of the North African shores." Mr. Churchill reported to the House of Commons that nearly 250,000 prisoners had been taken since the fall of the Mareth Line, the majority German. "There have also been lost to the enemy," he said, 6200 guns, 2550 tanks and 70,000 trucks, which is the American name for lorry and which, I understand, has been adopted by the combined staffs in North-West Africa in exchange for the use of the word petrol in the place of gasolene."

A TITANIC BLOW AT GERMANY: R.A.F. SMASH EUROPE'S DAMS.

TAKEN BEFORE THE ATTACK, THIS PICTURE OF THE MOHNE DAM, WHICH HELD BACK 70 PER CENT. OF THE REQUIREMENTS OF THE RUHR INDUSTRIAL BASIN, SHOWS THE TORPEDO NETS INSIDE WHICH OUR CREWS PLACED THEIR 1500-LB. MINES.

THE MOHNE DAM A FEW HOURS AFTER IT HAD BEEN ATTACKED. WATER ROARING THROUGH THE BREACH IS SWEEPING DOWN THE VALLEY IN A RAGING TORRENT, DESTROYING POWER STATIONS, FACTORIES AND EVERYTHING THAT LIES IN ITS PATH.

THE 202,000,000 TONS OF WATER IN THE EDER RESERVOIR BEGIN TO POUR THROUGH THE BREACH MINED IN THE GREAT DAM BY OUR LANCASTER CREWS. IT SWEPT TOWARDS KASSEL IN A 30-FT.-HIGH TIDAL WAVE.

Bomber Command, in breaching the Mohne and Eder Dams, has achieved in one night more disruption of Germany's war potential than could be achieved by weeks of bombing. Working on the suggestion of a German-Jewish refugee Air Chief-Marshal Sir Arthur Harris, C.-in-C. Bomber Command, drew up a plan of attack on the dams, and a "task force" of specially selected Lancaster crews went into intensive training in complete secrecy. The leadership of this vital operation was entrusted to Wing Commander Guy Penrose Gibson, D.S.O., and Bar, D.F.C. and Bar, who at twenty-five years of age is regarded as one of the outstanding bomber pilots of the war. In the early morning hours of Monday last, May 17, when the conditions of weather and light were exactly right, Wing-Commander Gibson led his men to their objectives, personally heading the attack on the Mohne Dam. After he had dropped his mines, he flew up and down the dam, drawing and returning the fire of its defenders so as to give the following bombers an easier task. It was after the fourth load had been dropped that the dam burst, hurtling out a cascade of water horizontally for at least 200 ft. Reports brought in by reconnaissance pilots during Monday and Tuesday told a story of a mounting catastrophe as 134,000,000 tons of water roared down the Ruhr Valley, sweeping away power stations, factories, whole villages and built-up areas that lay in its path.

THE FATE OF ITALY'S LAST TWO HEAVY CRUISERS, "TRIESTE" AND "GORIZIA."

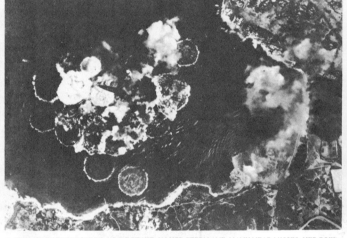

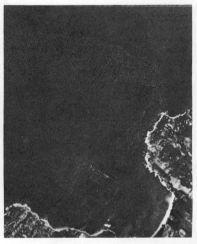

1. THE "TRIESTE" LIES (TOP RIGHT) PROTECTED BY ANTI-TORPEDO NETS.

2. THE "TRIESTE" RECEIVES A DIRECT HIT ON HER STERN AND MANY NEAR MISSES. HER BOWS SHOOT HIGH OUT OF THE WATER.

3. THE CRUISER "TRIESTE" HAS DISAPPEARED: THE TORPEDO NETS MARK HER POSITION.

On April 10 one of the largest formations of United States Army Flying Fortresses ever put into the air took off from their bases in North Africa. Their objective was the naval base of La Maddalena, on the southern coast of Sardinia, and there they attacked two of Italy's heavy cruisers, the "Trieste" and the "Gorizia," as they lay at anchor. The "Trieste" was sunk and the "Gorizia" merely damaged. These photographs show the various stages in the sinking of the "Trieste." The direct hits she received on her stern caused her bows to shoot up out of the water before she finally went to the bottom. The anti-torpedo nets and spreading oil were all that were left to mark her position. The "Gorizia," which also received a direct hit, remained afloat, although in a very badly damaged condition. It seems probable that she will be out of action for some considerable time. The sinking of the "Trieste" and the damaging of the "Gorizia" have deprived Italy of the use of her last 8-in.-gun cruisers. She entered the war with seven, all of about 10,000 tons. Three, "Fiume," "Pola" and "Zara," were sunk in the Battle of Cape Matapan, and two others by our submarines. As far as is known, no new ships of this type have been built during the war.

THE NEW VICEROY OF INDIA.

WASHINGTON CONFERENCE ENDED.

WOMEN SHARE THE DANGERS AT SEA.

FIELD-MARSHAL SIR ARCHIBALD WAVELL, WHO SUCCEEDS THE MARQUESS OF LINLITHGOW AS VICEROY OF INDIA.

THE PRIME MINISTER WITH MR. ROOSEVELT AND MR. MACKENZIE KING AT THE MEETING OF THE PACIFIC WAR COUNCIL.

MARGARET BOURKE-WHITE HAS A HOT DRINK ON BOARD WITH LORD DAVID HERBERT, TRANSPORT RADIO OFFICER.

Field-Marshal Wavell is the first professional soldier to be appointed Viceroy of India, and the importance of the choice lies in the new Viceroy's wide experience of India, his remarkable organising and administrative capabilities and his exceptional knowledge of Indian government. In July 1941 he became C.-in-C., India, his work there being interrupted in January and February 1942, when he became supreme military and naval commander in the Pacific.

On May 12 Mr. Churchill was met by President Roosevelt on arrival in Washington. It was their fifth meeting since the war. The President and Prime Minister began their conferences immediately, and parallel talks went on between the Chiefs of Staffs and Commanders of the two nations, including Field-Marshal Wavell, called from India. The Prime Minister pledged that Britain would wage war against Japan, side by side with the United States.

In an article, illustrated with photographs taken by herself, Miss Margaret Bourke-White tells the story of the torpedoing of an Africa-bound troopship, and her adventures in a lifeboat before being picked up by a destroyer. Miss Bourke-White was last year assigned by "Life" to the U.S. Air Forces as the first woman photographer ever so accredited. Her story is really of the women, nursing sisters and others, and of their cheerfulness and courage in the open boats.

MR. CHURCHILL, WITH ALLIED CHIEFS IN ALGIERS, DISCUSSES EVENTS FOR WHICH THE WORLD HAS WAITED.

THE PRIME MINISTER, SEATED AT A TABLE AT ALLIED FORCE HEADQUARTERS IN ALGIERS, TALKS STRATEGY TO THE SERVICE CHIEFS GROUPED ABOUT HIM. (LEFT TO RIGHT) MR. ANTHONY EDEN, SIR ALAN BROOKE, AIR CHIEF-MARSHAL TEDDER, ADMIRAL SIR ANDREW CUNNINGHAM, GENERAL SIR H. ALEXANDER, GENERAL MARSHALL (U.S.A.), GENERAL EISENHOWER, AND GENERAL MONTGOMERY.

Mr. Churchill summoned his Foreign Minister, Mr. Anthony Eden, to Algiers for a conference with Service Chiefs of the Allied Nations, the first part of which the Prime Minister had already concluded in Washington. The results of these conferences are expected to decide world destiny, and their purpose will unfold as the months go by. General Marshall, Chief of Staff of the U.S. Army, spoke of "continuity of offensives" at the conclusion of the Algiers meetings – offensives for which the whole world is on tiptoe and waiting. Time alone will show just where the Allied blows will fall, but it is safe to assume that what has come to be known, in Mr. Churchill's own phrase, as "the soft under-belly of the Axis," formed part of the discussions. Germany's nervousness on this point is reflected in articles in the German Army's periodical, "Die Wehrmacht," in which the admission is made that "an Anglo-American force might perhaps succeed in crossing the Mediterranean and in landing somewhere in Southern Europe." The conferences just concluded form part of a carefully prepared long-term strategy of which Mr. Churchill spoke in guarded terms as far back as October of last year. "We make this wide encircling movement in the Mediterranean," he told the House of Commons, "having for its primary object the recovery of the command of that vital sea, but also having for its object the exposure of the under-belly of the Axis, especially Italy, to heavy attack." Mr. Churchill, in the same speech, gave one more broad hint. "The establishment of a Mediterranean as well as an Atlantic or Channel front," he said dryly, "would obviously give us wide freedom of manœuvre."

A FULL-DRESS REHEARSAL FOR A LARGER-SCALE INVASION: COMBINED OPERATIONS' SYNCHRONISED ASSAULT ON PANTELLARIA.

R.A.F. BOSTON BOMBERS ATTACKING LAMPEDUSA, WHICH DIS-PLAYED A WHITE FLAG OF SURRENDER ON JUNE 12: A BOMBER'S VIEW OF LAMPEDUSA ISLAND DURING ITS "SOFTENING."

Strategic Air Force bombing of the islands of Sicily, Sardinia and Pantellaria. Air Chief-Marshal Tedder's "carpet," or the softening-up process, has placed enemy airfields out of action, damaged ports and installations, and made transport between Italy and her dependencies precarious in the extreme. Pantellaria was so plastered by bombs and the shells of the Navy that her value as an attacking centre was negligible a week ago, thus opening up the entire Mediterranean to the British Fleet. Pantellaria, defended by 10,000 Italians, offered an ideal site for a rehearsal of an opposed landing before a more serious target was attempted.

For a month it had been subjected to terrific bombardment. Its little town of Pantellaria had been utterly laid waste by raiders and by the shells from British warships, yet the garrison held out with great tenacity and courage. The island, only some 31 miles in extent had been a prominent seaplane and airplane base, and held up our complete command of the Southern Mediterranean.

Two columns of infantry landing craft moved in on the port at 11.45 a.m. on June 10, led by their "flagship" – a motor-launch. Preceding these in the distance were the smaller assault craft. To right and left of the landing craft were escorting destroyers of "Tribal" and "L" class, minesweepers, motor torpedo-boats, etc. Overhead, Fortress forma-tions pulverised enemy resistance by concentrated bombing, and above also our fighters were engaging enemy aircraft attempting to interfere. In the event it was found that the bombers had already done the landing party's work for it and only a few sporadic shots greeted its arrival. Pantellaria's formal unconditional surrender was received on June 11 and that of its small neighbour Lampedusa, with a garrison of a further 3000, on June 12.

OUR LANDING PARTIES FOUND A SCENE OF UTTER RUIN, WITH ENEMY INVASION BARGES PILED UP AGAINST THE QUAYS.

OUR SOLDIERS SEARCHING THE BROKEN RUINS OF PANTELLARIA DURING THE ROUNDING-UP OF THE ENEMY GARRISON.

A QUISLING IN THE CHAIR: IN BERLIN. ON THE OCCASION OF THE INDIAN DAY OF INDEPENDENCE, THE LEADER OF THE "FREE INDIANS," SUBHAS CHANDRA BOSE, MADE A SPEECH IN WHICH HE GAVE HIS VIEW OF THE WILL OF THE INDIAN PEOPLE FOR INDEPENDENCE.

MEMBERS OF BRIGADIER WINGATE'S JUNGLE COMMANDO FORCE, THE CHINDITS, FORDING A RIVER IN RUBBER BOATS AT THE START OF AN EPIC THREE-MONTHS FORAY BEHIND THE JAPANESE LINES IN THE JUNGLES OF BURMA.

BRIGADIER ORDE CHARLES WINGATE, LEADER OF THE EXPEDITION. HIS REMARKABLE PERSONALITY HAS BEEN STRESSED BY NEWSPAPER CORRESPONDENTS IN BURMA.

Led by Brigadier Orde Charles Wingate a long-range commando force recently emerged from the Burmese jungle into which it had plunged more than three months ago. It has wrecked Japanese posts, cut their communications, drawn the best part of a Japanese division on itself, and thrown the enemy intelligence network into confusion. Throughout these operations, the Chindits were kept going with supplies dropped by R.A.F. pilots, in itself an amazing story of perfect timing and navigation. Some of the columns marched upwards of a thousand miles during the three months – an almost incredible feat in the mountainous jungle country of Burma. Throughout the expedition, Brigadier Wingate controlled his columns by radio, and proved the value of long-range columns operating independently in a general offensive. The confusion the Chindits caused had its repercussions all over Burma, and the information they have brought back with them is invaluable. Brigadier Wingate is a remarkable leader. "He dreams things – do you know what I mean? He dreams a thing and then makes it come true." That is the opinion of one of his companions, Major Michael Calvert. Another view is that of the Burmese. To them, he was known as the Lord Protector of the Pagodas, for he had introduced his jungle columns as "mysterious men who have come among you, who can summon great air power, and who will rid you of the fierce, scowling Japanese."

"FAITH," LAST OF A FAMOUS TRIO OF GLADIATORS, PRESENTED TO MALTA.

UNLOADING BY ARC-LIGHT IN MALTA DURING A RESPITE FROM BOMBING.

THE KING VISITS MALTA: A TRIBUTE TO THE MEN AND WOMEN OF THE GEORGE CROSS ISLAND.

THE PEOPLE OF MALTA CROWD AROUND THE FUSELAGE OF "FAITH," ONLY SURVIVOR OF THE FAMOUS TRIO, "FAITH," "HOPE," AND "CHARITY," THE ISLAND'S ORIGINAL DEFENDERS.

A NEW UNITED NATIONS CONVOY GETS THROUGH TO MALTA AND UNLOADS THROUGHOUT THE NIGHT BY ARC-LIGHT.

THE KING SALUTES HIS GEORGE CROSS ISLAND: HIS MAJESTY ON THE BRIDGE OF THE CRUISER "AURORA," AS SHE ENTERS VALETTA HARBOUR ON THE OCCASION OF HIS RECENT VISIT.

"Faith," now reposes in the Armoury at the Palace of the Knights of St. John of Jerusalem, in Valetta. Air Vice-Marshal Sir Keith Park, presenting the historic aircraft to the Island, recalled that in May 1940 Malta possessed no fighter defences, but the R.A.F. obtained the three Gladiators from the Fleet Air Arm's store. During the first five months of the war, "Faith," "Hope," and "Charity," with the assistance of a handful of Hurricanes, intercepted seventy-two enemy formations and destroyed or damaged thirty-seven enemy machines.

Thanks to the Eighth Army's victorious advance, a series of convoys carrying supplies to Malta have enjoyed fighter protection. Some got through entirely unmolested, and all arrived unscathed. This fighter protection must have been more than welcome to the gallant men who, for so many months, have had little but their own guns to protect them. Blacked out Malta, the most bombed place in the world has now become floodlit to welcome her convoys, the arrival of which is the best news the people can have.

Unparalleled scenes of enthusiasm marked the King's visit to Malta. He arrived at the George Cross Island on the morning of Sunday, June 20, in the cruiser "Aurora," flying the Royal Standard and escorted by destroyers. The fact that he had travelled by sea within 60 miles of Sicily, with its enemy aerodromes and ports, aroused special delight among the citizens. Field-Marshal Lord Gort, V.C., the Governor, went aboard the "Aurora" to welcome his Majesty who later presented him with his Field-Marshal's bâton.

THINNING THE WOLF PACKS: MORE U-BOATS MEET THEIR FATE.

BROUGHT TO THE SURFACE BY DEPTH CHARGES FROM THE U.S. COASTGUARD CUTTER "SPENCER", THE U-BOAT IS IMMEDIATELY ASSAILED WITH A RAKING FIRE FROM THE CUTTER'S GUNS. HER CONNING-TOWER IS BLASTED OPEN BY A DIRECT HIT.

THE AMPHIBIOUS HELICOPTER, ITS PILOT NONCHALANTLY WEARING HIS HAT, RISES VERTICALLY FROM A CAR PARK WITHOUT DISTURBING ITS CO-PARKERS: THE VOUGHT SIKORSKY HELICOPTER CAN OPERATE FROM WATER WITHOUT A SPLASH.

A DOOMED ENEMY SUBMARINE A FEW SECONDS BEFORE SHE SANK, THROWING HER CREW INTO THE WATER. SHE HAD BEEN ATTACKED BY A LIBERATOR, WHICH SWEPT OVER HER AT LOW LEVEL.

German submarine crews are finding life in the Atlantic somewhat hectic in these days, when the Allies, with their new-anti U-boat devices, are causing them acute anxiety. On June 14 the naval correspondent of "Volkischer Beobachter" admitted increasing losses, and a few days earlier, Admiral Gadow, the German naval expert, made the significant admission that the Battle of the Atlantic was going against Germany. Just before this admission, Mr. Churchill had announced that the first week of June was a record one for the Allies. It is believed that Doenitz's system of "wolf-packs" is breaking down. It was devised to enable the skill of the few experienced U-boat "aces" to operate for the benefit of large numbers of officers and men by leading them in attack. With mass-produced U-boats and unskilled conscript crews, a "wolf-pack" system is essential – and it is failing because when the pack loses its leader, the tyros are in dire difficulties.

The announcement by Captain Balfour, Parliamentary Under-Secretary for Air, that Britain is acquiring a number of helicopters for the protection of shipping, heralds the closing of the gap in mid-Atlantic in which U-boat packs can operate beyond the reach of shorebased bombers. Now, they will have to contend with the helicopter, which may prove to be one of the most important anti-submarine weapons. The Vought-Sikorsky machine – the product of the Russian-American designer, Ivan Sikorsky – is almost certainly the one referred to by Captain Balfour. The U.S. naval authorities have recently decided to use it as an anti-submarine weapon. It has many advantages for the purpose, one of the most outstanding being its ability to rise vertically from and return to the deck of a ship, thus enabling it to operate in any part of the ocean. Also, it can unload depth-charges on a submarine with faultless accuracy, as it is able to hover directly above its prey.

The story of how aircraft of Coastal Command, and aircraft of the U.S. Navy operating with Coastal Command, in an eight-day battle attacked fifteen U-boats, sinking six of them for certain, has recently been told. The enemy submarines attempted to attack three Transatlantic convoys. The first of the six was sunk on the second day by a Ventura of the U.S. Navy, followed two hours later by a "kill" made by a Liberator. Early on the third day a Hudson got the third, and on the sixth day Liberators and a Sunderland sank three more. The Coastal Command aircraft which took part in these actions were from R.A.F. squadrons commanded by Wing-Commander R. M. Longmore; Wing-Commander J. Riley; Wing-Commander P. A. Gilchrist; and Wing-Commander H. R. A. Edwards. Aircraft of R.C.A.F. squadrons also took part in the battle. In these fiercely fought engagements Coastal Command has scored a decisive victory in the anti-U-boat offensive.

GENERAL SIKORSKI KILLED IN AN AIR CRASH.

GENERAL SIKORSKI SEEN HERE WITH HIS DAUGTER IN CAIRO, KILLED NEAR GIBRALTAR ON JULY 4.

By a lamentable accident, General Wladyslaw Sikorski, G.B.E., Prime Minister and Commander-in-Chief of Poland, was killed by a Liberator crashing shortly after leaving Gibraltar for England. With him was his daugher, Mme.-Sophia Lesniowska, and on board, besides his Chief of Staff, Major-General Klimecki and other Polish officers, was Colonel Victor Cazalet, M.P. for Chippenham, all of whom suffered the same fate, the pilot alone surviving, although badly injured. The General was returning from a tour of the Middle East.

"JUST WHERE WE WANTED OUR BOMBS TO FALL".

RESCUERS TOILING IN THE RUINS OF THE SCHOOL DEMOLISHED IN A RECENT GERMAN DAYLIGHT RAID ON LONDON, LED BY CAPTAIN SCHUMANN.

Earlier this year, Captain Schumann, who the previous day had led a force of *Luftwaffe* bombers in a daylight raid on civilian property in London, broadcast to the German people a boast that all his planes had reached their objectives. "They dropped their bombs just where we wanted them to fall," he said. One of the objectives of Captain Schumann's force was the school at which this picture was taken. When the bombers arrived the children, all between the ages of five and fourteen, were having their lunch. When the bombers left, there was a pile of smoking wreckage in which Civil Defence workers, frantic parents, and passers-by dug with every tool they could lay their hands on. They were still digging there by the light of flares, thirty-six hours later, while Captain Schumann was gleefully telling the German people about the exploit. "It was a most interesting raid," he said. "You might call it a special treat." Forty eight died, including six teachers. Sixty-two other victims were taken to hospital injured. Captain Schumann may well be proud of his achievement!

AN ANCIENT CUSTOM STILL OBSERVED IN MODERN MALTA.

A 400-YEAR-OLD MALTESE CUSTOM: THE HARBINGER OF DEATH WALKS THROUGH THE STREETS.

For three days prior to an execution, hooded figures of the Archconfraternity of Mercy appear in the streets of Malta – harbingers of death. They collect money for spiritual assistance for the condemned man. Only members of the Maltese nobility, legal and medical professions, and the clergy may join this society, which was founded in Spain in 1512 and came to Malta with the Knights of St. John of Jerusalem in 1530. It was originally instituted to take care of the dead bodies of hanged criminals, and it performs the same service today.

BOMBING THE ENEMY'S WAR POTENTIAL: SCHEINFURT, PLOESTI AND HAMBURG.

LIBERATORS SWEEP IN LOW ON PLOESTI'S TARGETS AGAINST A BACKCLOTH OF SMOKE AND FLAMES. THE DAMAGE DONE WAS REPORTED TO BE IMMENSE.

On August 2 nearly 200 Liberators of the U.S. Ninth Air Force roared in at 500 ft. over the Ploesti oil refineries in Rumania and launched a devastating attack on Hitler's most vital single target. Specialists in oil-refining, commanding their knowledge and worked for months to perfect the attack by 2000 airmen, which later results showed to have been most successful. Production has been seriously crippled. 54 American bombers were lost.

AN ME. 110 GOES DOWN IN FLAMES UNDER THE GUNS OF FLYING FORTRESSES DURING THE AIR BATTLE WHICH ACCOMPANIED THE RAID ON SCHWEINFURT.

A record total of 307 enemy fighters destroyed in a single day's air battle was claimed on August 29, when U.S. headquarters in Europe announced the final official figures for the August 17 attacks by Flying Fortresses and Thunderbolts on the Messerschmitt factory at Regensburg and the ball and rollerbearing plant at Schweinfurt where 147 fighters were destroyed by Fortresses. Thunderbolts accounted for 20 more. The Fortresses at Regensburg shot down 140.

A SMALL FRACTION OF THE VAST AREA OF DEVASTATION RESULTING FROM R.A.F. AND U.S.A.A.F. BOMBER ONSLAUGHTS ON HAMBURG IN JULY AND AUGUST.

Further evidence of the terrific battering Hamburg received from R.A.F. and U.S.A.A.F. bombers in July and August of this year is provided by this ground photograph. Aerial reconnaissance pictures had already established beyond doubt that the greater part of the city was practically obliterated, but the above, taken from eye-level by someone in Hamburg at the time of the raids, bring home with even greater force the vast extent of the devastation.

WONDERFUL U.S. PRECISION BOMBING: THE F.W. FACTORY AT MARIENBURG.

NOT A BOMB MISSED ITS MARK: PRECISION BOMBING IN EXCELSIS: AMERICAN FORTRESSES UNLOAD EVERY BOMB PLUMB ON THE TARGET TO OBLITERATE THE FOCKE-WULF FACTORY AT MARIENBURG IN A RAID INVOLVING A ROUND FLIGHT OF 1800 MILES

"We have demonstrated to every German that no part of his Fatherland is safe," said Brig.-General F. L. Anderson, commanding the U.S. Eighth Air Force Bomber Command, after the crippling blow dealt at German fighter output when American Fortresses and Liberators on Saturday, October 9, bombed the Focke-Wulf Aircraft factory at Marienburg, in East Prussia, 200 miles beyond Berlin. This factory, which assembled about half of all Germany's F.W. 190s, was virtually obliterated. Comparison of the central picture with the close-up aerial view of the plant before and after bombing, will indicate the complete pattern bombing of the target. The bombing of the Focke-Wulf Factory in daylight was remarkable and outstanding in two particulars: firstly, the target meant a round flight of about 1800 miles, and, secondly, the brilliant precision work of the bomb-aimers, whereby, as 2nd-Lieut. Gordon H. Wharton on his return said, "not a bomb missed its mark, and a lot of F.W.s died at birth." Another U.S. officer present said: "This was the most perfect pattern of bombing I have ever seen." That it has completely wiped out the plant is proved by the reconnaissance photograph showing the concentrated bomb-pitted site after the raid.

A PORTENT OF VICTORY: THE INVASION OF SICILY.

ALLIED SHOCK TROOPS APPROACHING THE SHORES OF SICILY WHERE THE TROOPS ESTABLISHED FIRM BRIDGEHEADS FOR THE SUBSEQUENT ADVANCE AND OCCUPATION.

SICILY NOW INVADED, SEPARATED FROM ITALY ONLY BY THE NARROW MESSINA STRAITS: A CONTOUR MAP OF THE TERRAIN.

THE FIRST WAVE OF OUR INVASION ARMY IS HACKING OUT ROUGH BEACH ROADS; MEN IN THE WATER FORM A SUPPLY CHAIN; AND BREN CARRIERS DRIVE THROUGH THE SURF.

Suddenly, on Saturday, July 10, a brief communiqué announced that Sicily had been invaded. Later it was known that paratroops and glider-borne forces had landed some four hours before the main invasion forces began to land on the beaches at 3 a.m., consisting of British, Canadians and U.S troops. Behind an enormous naval and air bombardment, the Allied forces met with little determined resistance, and the Canadians – obtaining their first chance of active warfare, except for the Dieppe operation – established a bridgehead at Pachino, on the south-east tip of the island, meeting some stubborn resistance, and taking many prisoners. The U.S. troops, at Gela, also experienced determined resistance, but captured two airfields, the third taken on the first day being Pachino. On July 12 a battle was raging at Ragusa, which lies between Gela and Pachino, a town of about 40,000 inhabitants, noted for its asphalt mines. On July 12 it was announced that British troops had captured Syracuse, a famous port and aerial base. The naval forces were under the personal command of Sir Andrew Cunningham, 2000 vessels being used in the landings, perfectly timed throughout. Immediately the Allied Forces had a bridgehead. General Montgomery, commanding the Eighth Army and the Canadians, made for Syracuse, which fell at night after severe street fighting, followed about twenty-four hours later by Augusta. These two important harbours were both captured practically intact.

ROME'S MARSHALLING YARDS BOMBED; AND DAMAGE TO SAN LORENZO BASILICA.

AN INTERIOR VIEW OF SAN LORENZO *EXTRA MUROS*, WITH THE HIGH ALTAR.

SAN LORENZO BASILICA IS NUMBERED 1, THE CEMETERY 2, MARSHALLING YARDS 3, AND THE RAILWAY STATION 4.

SAN LORENZO WAS NOT COMPLETELY DESTROYED. AS CAN BE SEEN, THE MAIN STRUCTURE HAS SURVIVED.

The central photograph of the raid on the marshalling yards of San Lorenzo, Rome, bombed by U.S. Fortresses and Liberators on July 19 reveals clearly the proximity of the ancient Basilica of San Lorenzo to this very vital military target. Most careful preparation was taken to avoid damaging Rome's ancient monuments, selected precision bombardiers being used and the raid held in broad daylight. Unfortunately, the ancient Basilica, erected on the site of the Emperor Constantine's Church of the Martyrs in 330, was damaged. The Axis raised a furore and distorted expressions used by the Pope. His Holiness, in a letter to the Vicar-General, did not say (as some reported) that the Basilica was completely destroyed. He said that a very great part was destroyed. The front part (composed of two churches) is destroyed, and the high altar has suffered serious damage, which, reports state, can be repaired. The photographs make it clear, however, that the marshalling yards which control the whole mainline traffic were hit by careful precision bombing.

FIGHTING DURING THE RAPID ALLIED ADVANCE ACROSS THE ISLAND.

INFANTRYMEN FIRE ON A RAILWAY STATION STRONG-POINT: THE ALLIED SOLDIERS ADVANCED FROM A DISUSED RAIL CUTTING, TAKING ADVANTAGE OF WHATEVER COVER OFFERED.

THE KEY POINT IN THE BATTLE OF CATANIA: THE GAUNT IRON BRIDGE OF GORNALUNGA, ORIGINALLY CAPTURED BY BRITISH PARATROOPS AND RETAKEN, NOW AGAIN IN OUR HANDS.

The capture and loss of Gornalunga Bridge rivals any deed of heroism performed by the Eighth Army in North Africa. Amid orange groves and blackened fields, the brunt of the fighting was supported by Paratroops with orders to capture and hold the bridge. Whilst some dropped behind the enemy lines and rounded up Italian prisoners, others held the bridge, like "brave Horatius." They held it for nearly 24 hours, though shelled, mortared, machine-gunned from the air, and attacked by seven Italian battalions. Fewer than two hundred resisted stubbornly, knowing that behind them our infantry were fighting furiously to come to their aid. When our troops could advance from Lentini they were too late. The paratroops, reduced to their last four rounds, had been forced to retreat. Subsequently our men seized a bridgehead, throwing off violent enemy counter-attacks, and once more the iron bridge lay in our hands. German losses were considerable.

Such, in brief, was the Battle of Gornalunga Bridge, adding further laurels to Montgomery's Eighth Army. On July 16, after much braggadocio by Mussolini, by Italian broadcasters and the Press, Pavolini, former Fascist Minister of Popular Culture, in "Messagero" told the brutal truth. The Italians were to expect the loss of Sicily and the invasion of Italy. The German Press went all silent. The situation was further dramatised by the fact that not only the Sicilians but the Italian soldiery were surrendering wholesale and breathing revenge, not against the invaders, but the Germans, who had, they declared, betrayed them. The capture of Lentini opened up the Catania plain and put railroad communications to Catania and the interior into our hands. North of Catania, any large-scale resistance to the advance along the coastal road to Messina became improbable, as the Allies completely dominated the air and the British Fleet could shell every defence post.

SICILIAN SIDELIGHTS: ASPECTS OF THE STORY OF INVASION.

WITH SMILING FACES AND LUGGAGE READY PACKED, ITALIAN SOLDIERS MARCH TO THE BEACH AFTER SURRENDERING TO THE 51ST HIGHLAND DIVISION.

CHEERS, FLOWERS AND SMILING FACES GREET OUR TROOPS AS THEY ENTER CATANIA. THERE WAS NO DOUBT OF THE GENUINE WELCOME AFFORDED THE ALLIES BY THE CATANIANS.

BRITISH SAPPERS SWEEPING THE ROAD TO RANDAZZO OF GERMAN MINES, SOME OF WHICH ARE SEEN. MINES AND DEMOLITION BECAME THE PRINCIPAL MEANS OF GERMAN RESISTANCE.

Since the landing a fortnight ago Sicily is in Allied hands, except for the mountainous triangle in the north-east with, south and southwest of Etna, a narrow strip of plain-land. This area is being stubbornly held by the enemy, both Germans and Italians, not, obviously, with any hope of maintaining it permanently, but in order to delay any projected Allied invasion of the Italian mainland. An important stage was reached in the conquest of the whole island when the American Seventh Army entered Palermo on July 22; with its capture the western end of Sicily was cut off, and the mopping up of such forces that remained has been both rapid and easy, and with the fall of Marsala and Trapani it is, to all intents and purposes, complete. Now the Americans are pushing on well beyond Palermo, and a join-up with the Canadians in the centre may be expected. The Germans in the north-east have been receiving reinforcements, but a good deal of damage has been done to their transport by our air forces, and this Allied air supremacy, combined with the complete control of the surrounding seas, must, before very long, dispose even of the natural defences of Mount Etna. Prisoners taken during the Sicilian fighting must now exceed 70,000. The Italians captured seem pleased at their fate, and in many cases it was not unexpected as is shown by the fact that they had their suit cases ready packed. The civil population in the west was as welcoming as in the south-east, and have, in most cases, co-operated freely with the Allies. The Italian people are, like the Sicilians, thoroughly sick of war. There were reports of Italian forces fighting the hated Germans.

THE FALL OF BENITO MUSSOLINI: BADOGLIO FORMS NEW GOVERNMENT.

KING VICTOR EMMANUEL III., WHO SUCCEEDED HIS FATHER UMBERTO. HE WILL BE SEVENTY-FOUR ON NOVEMBER 11, A PUPPET KING.

HIS FINEST HOUR: MUSSOLINI, ACCOMPANIED BY GENERALS DE BONO AND BALBO, AFTER THE MARCH ON ROME AND *COUP D'ÉTAT* OF 1922. KING VICTOR EMMANUEL AGREED TO A FASCIST GOVERNMENT, REFUSING BADOGLIO'S REQUEST TO FIRE ON THE FASCISTS.

MARSHAL BADOGLIO, AGED SEVENTY-TWO, THE KING'S FRIEND, IS NOW PRIME MINISTER IN MUSSOLINI'S PLACE, HOPING TO SAVE THE THRONE.

The sudden resignation of Mussolini, dramatically broadcast by Rome Radio at 10.52 p.m. on Sunday night, was the sequel of his abortive meeting the previous week with Hitler. Mussolini's fall was doubtless directly affected by the Roosevelt-Churchill message of July 16, which said, "The time has come for you to decide whether Italians shall die for Mussolini and Hitler – or live for Italy and Civilisation."
Benito Mussolini came to power in October 1922, when his Blackshirts made their march on Rome, and were suffered to effect a *coup d'état* by King Victor Emmanuel. The Duce himself was not then at the head of his Blackshirts. He followed discreetly twenty-four hours later by sleeping-car, after learning that the King refused the plea of Badoglio to machine-gun the rebels. What was Mussolini? He was short, corpulent and bald-headed, a man of many parts, and of superficial knowledge. He was a braggadocio, a "hot-gospeller" politician, a *poseur*, a "pinchbeck Cæsar," as Mr. Churchill has described him. Yet he represents a well-defined phase of world history, when political gangsters believed that by trickery and force they could for ever smash the principles of democracy and freedom, and establish an era of absolute tyranny, ruling by the sword. He was Hitler's mentor, and set the pace when the Austrian painter was a down-and-out. He succeeded in imposing himself upon the easy-going Italians, with the imprisonment and murder of political opponents. Fascism started as a corrective to the anarchy into which Italy was falling after the last war, when Communists seized factories and chaos reigned. Mussolini has been taken to the island of Ponza.

THE SICILIAN CAMPAIGN: THE END COMES WITH THE FALL OF MESSINA.

AN HISTORIC ENCOUNTER – THE ROAD JUNCTION OUTSIDE RANDAZZO, WHERE THE U.S. AND BRITISH SEVENTH AND EIGHTH ARMIES MET. BOTH THEN JOINED HANDS AND SWEPT ONWARD.

A SUNKEN TRAIN-FERRY SHIP BESIDE THE SLIPWAY AT THE MESSINA FERRY TERMINUS – A PRIORITY TARGET FROM THE EARLIEST PREPARATIONS FOR THE CAMPAIGN.

TROOPS OF THE AMERICAN SEVENTH ARMY PASS THROUGH SOME BADLY DAMAGED STREETS IN MESSINA – JUST THIRTY-NINE DAYS AFTER THE INVASION OF SICILY.

The position in Sicily towards the end of the lull, when Montgomery had opened up a tremendous barrage on the German positions before Catania, was that the centre was held by the Eighth Army, with the Canadians in action between it and the U.S. Seventh Army. Our official line then ran for 82 miles, from Cefalu, on Sicily's picturesque north coast, down to Catania on the east, with the great Mount Etna occupying 470 square miles in between. By August 3 the Eighth Army had crossed the three rivers which presented so formidable a barrier to Catania; in the north General Patton's U.S. Seventh Army, after taking Nicosia and San Stefano, were moving to Messina, 80 miles distant. With the fall of Regalbuto to the Canadians, commanding the road round Etna, Catania became untenable. The Germans, who had three divisions, with three Italian divisions, smothered by the Allied air forces, could not adequately hold so long a line as from San Stefano to Catania. When Nicosia fell the line was broken in two, and the exit of the enemy became inevitable, only a question of how many could escape the pincers. The powerful Allied air forces and the growing difficulty of the Germans to obtain supplies, pointed to a near repetition of Cape Bon Peninsula or El Alamein.
The Sicilian campaign lasted thirty-eight days; coming to an end when the American Seventh Army entered the "ferry" port town of Messina on August 17. Joined later by the Eighth Army the Allied Forces now stand only 3½ miles from the Italian mainland. The town of Messina suffered as the result of intensive Allied bombing, but the really bad damage was done to the port and installations, used, right up to the last minute, as an evacuation point by the Germans. Official figures of casualties have not yet come in, but General Alexander has said that up to August 17, those of the Allies were: Eighth Army, 11,835; Seventh Army, 7400; whereas the total Axis losses were about 200,000. Furthermore the enemy has lost a large number of aircraft, ships, tanks and guns. Another great victory has been achieved by the forces of Democracy.

JAPANESE NOW DRIVEN ENTIRELY FROM POSSESSION OF THE ALEUTIAN ISLANDS.

U.S. AND CANADIAN LANDING BARGES DRIVING ASHORE ON THE BEACHES OF KISKA ISLAND, LAST OF THE ALEUTIAN CHAIN RECAPTURED FROM THE JAPANESE.

WEARING THICK CAMOUFLAGED CLOTHING, FIGHTING IN CONTINUOUS FOG, THE U.S. TROOPS FIRING ON JAPS FROM COVER ON ATTU.

The Japanese have held possession of the island of Attu since June 11 last year; this spring their garrison there began to feel the weight of American bombardment from the air, followed, at the beginning of May by bombardment from the sea, under cover of which American troops, on May 11, landed simultaneously at Holtz Bay on the northeast coast and Massacre Bay on the southeast. These two places are on either side of Chicagof Harbour, separated by a ridge of hills. Seven days after landing, the Americans had joined hands across the pass and had penned the enemy into a small area round the village at the head of the harbour. With the capture of Attu Island, nearest of the Aleutians to Japan – about 1200 miles from the Kurile Isles –

the U.S. forces creep nearer to bombing distance of Tokyo, from which Attu is 1778 miles. Fighting here had been bitter and without quarter for eighteen days, but on May 29 the enemy, after a last desperate assault on the floor of Chicagof Valley, was annihilated, a garrison of some 3000. Tokyo broadcast claimed that the wounded or sick committed hari-kari.

The announcement that the Japanese had been driven from Kiska Island was issued in Quebec on August 21 over the signatures of President Roosevelt and Mr. Mackenzie King. The Japanese fled from the island, under cover of fog, after a strong force of U.S. and Canadian troops occupied Kiska.

BLASTING OUT JAPANESE IN SAVAGE JUNGLE WARFARE IN THE SOLOMON ISLANDS.

THE LANDING ON RENDOVA ISLAND, SPRINGBOARD FOR ATTACKS ON THE JAPANESE IN THE SOLOMONS. U.S. TROOPS CREEP ASHORE TO MOP UP THE ENEMY DEFENDERS.

A U.S. GUN CREW, USING A 155-MM. GUN, MAKES READY TO SHELL MUNDA AIRFIELD, FIVE MILES AWAY, FROM THEIR POSITION ON RENDOVA ISLAND. IT FELL ON AUGUST 6 TO ASSAULT.

ROYAL NEW ZEALAND AIR FORCE WARHAWK FIGHTERS TAKING OFF FROM AN OPERATIONAL STRIP ON GAUDALCANAL, THE BASE OF SEVERAL OF THE NEW ZEALAND AIR SQUADRONS.

On June 30, General MacArthur, who is himself directing operations from a forward H.Q., started a new offensive from Guadalcanal Island, directed against the big Japanese base at Rabaul. Rendova Island, south of New Georgia, 160 miles north-west of Guadalcanal, was occupied with little resistance. In four hours of fighting, on Rendova Island, two Barracuda companies killed sixty-five Japanese, losing only four casualties. They drove the remainder of the enemy, about 300 men, into the wild jungle of the interior. The Barracudas are spearhead assault units of infantry, specially trained to operate with naval amphibious forces.

U.S. Troops also landed at Viru Harbour in the south of New Georgia, which they captured after thirty-six hours' hard fighting. Trobriand and Woodlark Islands were also seized without resistance, and Nassau Bay, from which they were in sight of Rabaul. Australian troops coming overland from Port Moresby via Mudo were threatening this stronghold and Lae. The strategy appears as a pincers movement centring on Rabaul.

Only a few hours after landing on Rendova Island U.S. forces were pouring shells into the Japanese air base at Munda, on New Georgia. An attack by sixty Japanese dive-bombers and fighters on American positions in the harbour of Rendova and on nearby islands cost the enemy six aircraft and caused negligible damage. Japanese warships attempted to run between the islands of Kolombangara and Vella Lavella. The attempt was a failure as the American Navy sank a cruiser and two destroyers and damaged a third destroyer, without loss. Munda fell on August 6, and in the final assault U.S. troops literally burnt the Japs out of their positions with the use of flame-throwers in conjunction with tanks. Japanese air and sea losses have been very heavy.

Once Munda was captured further assaults were made by American and New Zealand forces on Kolombangara and Vella Lavella on August 13 and 15.

They are now preparing to drive the enemy out of Rabaul, the principal Japanese South-West Pacific base.

BERLIN IS THEIR OBJECTIVE: SOVIET AIRMEN PREPARE FOR A RAID.

CHECKING AND PREPARING BOMBS TO BE DROPPED ON THE GERMAN CAPITAL, BERLIN.

Perhaps more than any others, Russian airmen are familiar with difficult flying conditions, for many of them have flown for years through the terrible Arctic regions, where the eternal ice and freezing cold are more dreadful than the worst anti-aircraft fire. As for landings, they are equally impossible in Germany and the Arctic. Each 'plane makes a long distance bombing flight independently, the pilot using his own judgment. The itinerary is, of course, determined on the ground, and, in the case of a raid on Berlin, is very simple, as the flight is a direct one, there and back. Describing one such flight, a Soviet airman says: "The front line is crossed at night; the flight over the enemy's rear being carried out at such an altitude that the crew can seldom take off their oxygen-masks. Berlin 'raises a curtain' of anti-aircraft fire; a heavy shock is felt; the bombs have been dropped." Twice more this manœuvre is repeated, and then the aircraft turns for home.

THE CONTINUOUS BATTLE TO KEEP BRITAIN'S SEA-LANES CLEAR.

"WIMPEY'S WEDDING RING": CLOSE-UP VIEW OF THE 2½-TON ELECTRIFIED METAL RING CARRIED BY WELLINGTONS TO EXPLODE ENEMY MAGNETIC MINES.

It is now three years since the men of a special Wellington squadron began flying modified versions of their aircraft, popularly known as "Wedding Ring Wimpeys," for the purpose of exploding enemy magnetic mines. This picture gives an impression of the cumbersome 2½-ton 50-ft. electrified circle of metal, suspended from nose, wings and fuselage, which necessitates an extra-long take-off run. The high-voltage current running is supplied by a V-8 auxiliary motor.

THE GERMAN FAILURE IN THE OREL-BIELGOROD FRONT.

RED ARMY TANKS ON THEIR WAY UP TO THE FRONT LINE: SPEEDING ALONG A GULLY BETWEEN TWO GRASS-COVERED SLOPES.

THE KURSK SALIENT AT THE START OF OPERATION ZITADELLE.

A GERMAN PHOTOGRAPH OF THE PROKOROVKA BATTLEFIELD, WITH PANZERS ADVANCING IN CLOSE FORMATION AGAINST A HEAVY RUSSIAN BARRAGE.

In the summer of 1943 the Germans launched no big offensive in Russia. Instead on July 5 a limited operation (Zitadelle) began with attacks south from Orel and north from Bielgorod along the two railway lines to Kursk with the intention of pinching out the Kursk salient.

Only a limited advance was made in the north, but in the Bielgorod area von Manstein, overcoming the Russian Sixth Army advanced some 20 miles to Prokhorovka where the biggest tank battle of the war took place as he encountered the Russian reserves. At first the Germans had a limited success but on July 12 the Russians launched their own offensives to the north and the east of Orel. The news also came through of the extent of the United Nations landings in Sicily, and the German offensives had to be abandoned.

Hitler's *non possumus* to Mussolini's desperate plea for aid, on July 19 resulting in his sudden downfall, was a necessary sequel to the powerful counter-offensive of the Russians at Orel. The German summer offensive fizzled out with heavy losses in men and equipment and a further drain on their reserves, which they can ill afford. With Bolkhov and thirty other places in their hands on July 26, they had closed steadily on Orel. Significant of the future was the fact that the rôles between the belligerent armies have now been reversed, for it is not only a Russian summer offensive, but the Soviet Army is superior in personnel and equipment to the Germans, whose first-line troops are very nearly exhausted. Other Russian thrusts from the Donetz, and perhaps from Leningrad, threaten grave danger, from end to end of the Russian line.

SOVIET VICTORIES FOLLOW IN SUCCESSION OF A 1000-MILE FRONT.

A RUSSIAN BATTLEFIELD ON THE SOUTHERN FRONT: RED ARMY TROOPS MAKING ADVANCE RUSHES AGAINST THE ENEMY, WHO IS USING FOREST LAND AS COVER. THE RED ARMY, WHICH CAPTURED TAGANROG BY STORM ON AUGUST 30, ON SEPTEMBER 3 WERE APPROACHING STALINO, AND THREATENING THE RETREAT OF A GREAT GERMAN ARMY.

The fall of Orel – immediately followed by that of Bielgorod – was a bitter pill for the Germans. The Soviet communiqué of midnight on August 5 announced that the Red Army was in this important strategic city, whose capture opens the road to Briansk and eventually Smolensk. The attack was so fierce that the Germans, who had lined up large numbers of tanks to counter-attack, were overwhelmed. The Soviet thrusts from three sides caused the defences to crumble within less than 42 hours. Yet the defences of Orel were as formidable as any the enemy have ever built on the Eastern Front. They had nearly two years to turn the Orel position into a fortress, and they had worked hard. There were three powerful defensive belts manned by Germany's finest troops. Its storming by the Russians is a triumph of far-seeing generalship and its repercussions stretch far.

On August 23 the Red Army, who had encircled Kharkov to one narrow sector, announced its capture, after a furious offensive which began on August 4. By the 13th our Allies were within one mile of the north-eastern suburbs of Kharkov and had recaptured Chuguyev, their old bridgehead over the Donetz to the east. They then suffered their first setback of the summer, the Germans counter-attacking with great force and recklessness. On August 22 the Russians advanced again, and having captured the key junction of Merefa, to the south of Kharkov, so vital to the enemy, it was enveloped. Our Allies, advancing along a 60-mile front, on August 23 were progressing steadily towards Poltava, with the Ukraine before their eyes, and Kiev lying beyond. The Germans have used minefields on an unprecedented scale, as they did in Tunisia and Sicily.

THE RUSSIAN ARMIES PRESS WESTWARDS FROM NORTH TO SOUTH.

A SOVIET ANTI-TANK CREW ADVANCING UNDER A SMOKE-SCREEN, TOWARDS THE GERMAN POSITIONS TO INTERCEPT ENEMY TANKS.

THE APPROXIMATE FRONT LINE AT THE END OF THE THIRD WEEK OF SEPTEMBER 1943.

THE GERMAN FOG-THROWER IN ACTION IN RUSSIA: ONE OF THE CURIOUS NEW WEAPONS PRODUCED BY THE NAZIS.

"DUCK" SHOOTING ON THE KUBAN FRONT. RED ARMY SHARPSHOOTERS IN RUBBER RINGS MOVING THROUGH SWAMPS TO ATTACK.

RUSSIAN SOLDIERS ENTERTAINING ONE ANOTHER DURING AN INTERVAL OF LEISURE ON THE EASTERN FRONT.

After the fall of Kharkov on August 23, it became obvious that the whole of the advanced German armies between the Donetz and the Sea of Azov were in danger of being cut off. Thus the enemy was compelled to pivot at all costs south-west of Kharkov, but his withdrawal from Taganrog led to the fall of Stalino and Mariupol, our allies moving from Stalino, through Chaplino, threatening both Dnepropetrovsk and Zaporozhe, both on the Dnieper, and on September 12 were within 40 miles of these important points. Another westward thrust lies further north through Konotop and Bakhmach, towards Kiev. Further north

yet, the Red Army, by capturing Byelev, were only 12 miles east of Briansk which fell on September 17. The Russians recaptured Smolensk on September 25, and by the end of the month the great natural barrier of the Dnieper had been reached by the Red Army from Zaporozhe to Kiev and at various points further north. At the southern end of the long front, the great battle for the gateway to the Crimea is still raging, a titanic struggle for the Melitopol-Zaporozhe railway and for the towns themselves, whilst on the Caucasian mainland, an even smaller foothold has been left to the enemy.

DENMARK AT BOILING-PITCH – IN GERMANY'S "MODEL PROTECTORATE."

THE FORUM HALL IN COPENHAGEN, DAMAGED BY SABOTEURS' EXPLOSIVES ON AUGUST 24 AFTER THE GERMANS HAD REQUISITIONED IT FOR QUARTERING TROOPS.

DENMARK'S "TOULON": THE "PEDER SKRAM," SECOND LARGEST VESSEL OF THE DANISH FLEET, SCUTTLED BY HER CREW DURING THE REVOLT.

HAVING STOPPED A VAN AND RESCUED PATRIOT PRISONERS, CITIZENS OF ODENSE, IGNORING A POLICEMAN, SUCCEED IN OVERTURNING IT, WHILE A CROWD GATHERS IN THE DISTANCE.

The Danish temper has been slowly rising to boiling-point for a long time, and now it seems that it has "blown the lid off" what Germany once boasted was her model protectorate. Martial law, declared at 4 a.m. on Sunday, August 29, failed to stem the rising tide of sabotage, and was followed by fighting in which both sides suffered casualties. The Danes are reported to have demolished all defences except part of the fortress outside Copenhagen, to have blown up docks and set dumps ablaze. Part of the Danish Navy escaped to Sweden in two destroyers, six torpedo-boats, a mine-sweeper and numerous other craft, and sailors are reported to have scuttled some forty-five warships in Copenhagen Harbour and elsewhere. Copenhagen has now been re-occupied by the Germans and the Danish Army disarmed. King Christian is confined to his palace.

QUEBEC'S CONFERENCE.

THE QUEBEC CONFERENCE OF 14 TO 24 AUGUST WHERE VITAL WAR DECISIONS HAVE BEEN TAKEN. PRESIDENT ROOSEVELT, MR. CHURCHILL, AND MR. MACKENZIE KING, WITH THEIR MILITARY ADVISERS, ON THE TERRACE OF THE CITADEL. IN THE BACKGROUND IS THE HOTEL CHATEAU FRONTENAC.

Front row: Mr. Mackenzie King, President Roosevelt, and Mr. Churchill. (Back row, left to right; General Arnold, U.S. Commander-in-Chief, Air Chief-Marshal Sir Charles Portal, General Sir Alan Brooke, Admiral King, Field-Marshal Sir John Dill, General Marshall, Admiral Sir Dudley Pound, and Admiral Leahy.

THE "TIRPITZ" CRIPPLED BY H.M. MIDGET SUBMARINES IN ALTEN FIORD.

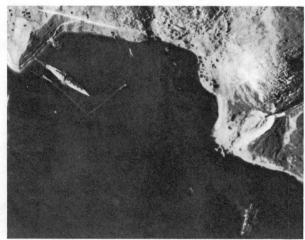

BEFORE THE ATTACK BY OUR MIDGET SUBMARINES: THE GERMAN BATTLESHIP "TIRPITZ" "SAFE" AT HER ANCHORAGE IN ALTEN FIORD, NORWAY, 1000 MILES FROM THE NEAREST BRITISH BASE.

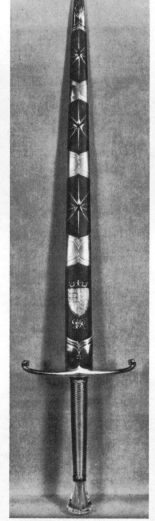

THE SWORD IN ITS SCABBARD.

THE POSITION OF THE "TIRPITZ" WHEN SHE WAS ATTACKED.

STALINGRAD'S SWORD.

STALINGRAD'S SWORD OF HONOUR COMPLETED: EXPERTS WHO CO-OPERATED IN ITS MANUFACTURE EXAMINE THE SWORD AND SCABBARD.

Stalingrad's Sword of Honour, presented to the heroic city by the King, has been finished and will be on exhibition to the public at the Victoria and Albert Museum from October 9–11, before going on a tour of the provinces. In Westminster Abbey from October 29–31. Engraved in English and Russian, on either side of the blade, are the words: "To the steel-hearted citizens of Stalingrad – the gift of King George VI – in token of the homage of the British people."

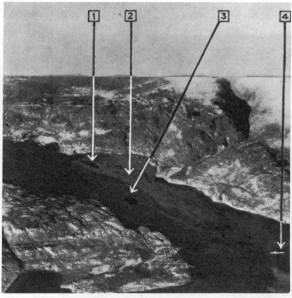

AFTER THE ATTACK: 1. THE DAMAGED BATTLESHIP, WITH A NUMBER OF SMALL, UNIDENTIFIED CRAFT ALONGSIDE. 2. THICK OIL COVERS THE VICINITY OF THE "TIRPITZ'S" ANCHORAGE AND EXTENDS FOR MORE THAN TWO MILES.

"A very gallant enterprise," and one which will rank amongst the greatest of the war, has been carried out by his Majesty's midget submarines. Involving hazards of the first order, they carried out an attack on main units of the German battle fleet in their heavily protected anchorage in Alten Fiord, Northern Norway, inflicting underwater damage on the battleship "Tirpitz." The attack was highly successful, and the photograph shows the "Tirpitz" surrounded by thick oil, which extends over a distance of more than two miles from her berth. Giving some idea of the magnitude and difficulties of this remarkable achievement, the official Admiralty communiqué says: "It must be remembered that Alten Fiord, in which the "Tirpitz" lay, was 1000 miles from the nearest British base. The midget submarines . . . had to pass through the minefields guarding the approaches to the anchorage, and after negotiating the intricate fiords, always vigilantly patrolled by the enemy, they had to carry out an attack in the strongly protected and confined waters where the ships were moored." Alten Fiord lies about 100 miles south-west of the North Cape and is more than 200 miles within the Arctic Circle. Entry to the position where the "Tirpitz" was lying is through a channel less than a mile wide under the shadow of high, overhanging cliffs, and outside the effective range of Allied bombers. Flak batteries commanded the narrow, twisting fiord, 50 miles from the outer sea; destroyers and flak-ships screened the "Tirpitz" and cruisers, with their torpedo nets. Three of our midget submarines did not return.

SECOND U.S. RAID ON SCHWEINFURT.

BOMB BURST COVERING THE FOUR MAIN FACTORIES PRODUCING BALL-BEARINGS AND AIRCRAFT COMPONENTS AT SCHWEINFURT: (1) KUGELFISCHER WERKE; (2) V.K.F. WERKE NO. 11; (3) W.K.P. WERKE NO. 1; AND (4) FICHTEL AND SACHS.

The picture above shows the huge Schweinfurt ball- and roller-bearings factory area blanketed by bombs by Flying Fortresses during the great daylight raid of October 14, the results of which are shown to be even more effective than was at first supposed. Formerly accounting for more than half the entire Axis output of ball-bearings, the Schweinfurt factories, in the heart of Germany, are now stated to be completely inactive. One report says that Germany urgently placed large orders with ball-bearing factories in Switzerland. Sixty Fortresses failed to return from the raid, but official opinion is that the results achieved more than compensate for this heavy loss.

THE MOMENTOUS SECOND MOSCOW CONFERENCE.

WHERE GREAT DECISIONS WERE TAKEN: THE THREE-POWER CONFERENCE IN SESSION AT MOSCOW, WHERE COMPLETE ACCORD WAS REACHED.

The decisions taken at the Moscow conference by the Foreign Ministers of Britain, the United States and the Soviet Union covered every aspect of collaboration and laid the foundations of full and permanent consultation and co-operation during and after the war. The main results so far published deal with close Allied military collaboration; a three-Power Committee for London; the restoring of Austrian freedom; the punishment of war criminals; and post-war security. Our picture shows the delegates seated: (From the right clockwise) M. Molotov, Soviet Foreign Secretary; Marshal K. E. Voroshilov, Marshal of the Soviet Union; Lt.-Gen. Sir Hastings Ismay; Sir Archibald Clark Kerr, British Ambassador to the U.S.S.R.; Mr. Anthony Eden, British Foreign Secretary; Mr. William Strang; Major-Gen. John R. Deane, U.S. Army; Mr. James Dunn (not visible); Mr. Averell Harriman, U.S. Ambassador to the U.S.S.R.; Mr. Cordell Hull, U.S. Foreign Secretary; Mr. Green Hackworth; M. Litvinov, Deputy Commissar for Foreign Affairs; and M. A. Y. Vyshinski.

MAKING SPIDERS HELP IN THE WAR.

A VENOMOUS BLACK WIDOW SPIDER IS INDUCED TO WIND ITS WEB ON A COAT-HANGER FRAME AS IT DANGLES IN THE AIR.

THE SPIDER'S THREADS, AS CROSS HAIRS, MOUNTED ON A DIAPHRAGM READY FOR FITTING IN A TRANSIT INSTRUMENT.

Spiders' webs are used by the Allied armies in the construction of precision-sighting instruments, on which so many modern war weapons depend. About one-fifth the diameter of a human hair, the spider's silk weaves into delicate and often nearly invisible snares. Tougher than steel or platinum wire of the same diameter, it can outlast the writhings of victims many times the spider's size. These same qualities make spider webbing the ideal material for the cross hairs that frame the objectives of telescopes, microscopes, surveyors' transits, bomb-sights, range-finders, and other precision instruments. Once pulled taut, its elasticity and strength keep it strung in a perfect straight line. In the past, for the normal requirements of precision optics, webbing has been extracted from the various garden species of spider. To meet the quantity demands of war production, however, the U.S. Army Quartermaster Corps has had to take on strength the big and venomous Black Widow. The spiders are stabled in glass coffee jars, fed two live flies per week, and put on a strict routine of production. Every two days, each spider is lured out of her lair for de-webbing. The thread is wound on a spindle bent from a wire coat-hanger. Production varies between 100 and 180 ft. of usable thread per spider per week. None of the handlers has yet been bitten.

WHY BERLIN IS THE FOCUS POINT OF R.A.F. BOMBING.

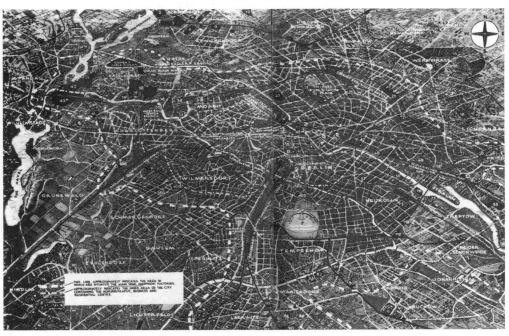

THE MAIN WAR INDUSTRIES, TRANSPORT CENTRES AND POWER STATIONS OF GERMANY'S CAPITAL.

Nothing less than the elimination of Berlin as the main focus of the German war effort is the declared objective of Air Marshal Sir Arthur Harris, Chief of Bomber Command. It is not being laid low for any other reason than that it is the most important war potential centre in Germany. Its size is half that of Greater London, its population being about 4½ millions, of whom 25 per cent., are directly or indirectly employed in the manufacture of war materials. It has hundreds of factories employing 10 per cent. of the Reich's workers, and it is the very heart of transport, being the greatest railway centre in Central Europe, with fourteen main lines radiating from it.

THE ALLIED INVASION OF ITALY: FIRST LANDINGS BY THE EIGHTH ARMY.

PRELIMINARY TO INVASION: PART OF THE NIGHT BARRAGE PUT UP BY ALLIED ARTILLERY FROM SICILY BEFORE THE FIRST LANDINGS ON THE ITALIAN MAINLAND AT DAWN ON SEPTEMBER 3.

"MONTY" WATCHES HIS TROOPS: GENERAL MONTGOMERY, COMMANDER OF THE EIGHTH ARMY, STANDS UP TO SEE HIS MEN PASS THROUGH A STREET IN REGGIO, CALABRIA.

CANADIAN TROOPS ROLL ASHORE NEAR REGGIO IN AMPHIBIOUS "DUCKS." FROM SHORE BASE TO SHORE BASE THEY NEVER CHANGED THEIR VEHICLES.

"To the Eighth Army is given the great honour of being the first troops of the Allied armies to land on the mainland of the Continent of Europe. . . . There can only be one end to this next battle – another success." These words were included in General Montgomery's message to his men before they attacked in the early hours of September 3. That same day an armistice was signed, secretly, between the Allies and Italy, but it did not come into force until September 8, when the invasion was well under way. The landings, made across the Straits of Messina, were preceded by a very heavy artillery barrage from our batteries, as the result of which enemy guns on the Calabrian coast were silenced. Then, at 4.30 a.m., British and Canadian troops began the invasion, with Spitfires providing a continuous cover. There was a haze over the ground at the time, but the sea was covered with hundreds of craft. This new phase in the Mediterranean campaign followed after a lull of only seventeen days since the termination of the fighting in Sicily. The fortress of Europe is menaced; the Allies are already at one of its gateways, and they will go on hammering until the time is ripe to blast their way in. Step by step they are nearing Germany, the very heart of the Axis stronghold.

SECRET ARMISTICE SIGNED WITH ITALY.

THE SIGNING OF THE ITALIAN ARMISTICE: THE GROUP OF AMERICAN, BRITISH AND ITALIAN OFFICIALS WHO WITNESSED THE UNCONDITIONAL SURRENDER OF GERMANY'S PARTNER.

Italy has surrendered unconditionally to the Allies; General Eisenhower made the announcement at 5.30 p.m. on September 8, and all hostilities between the armed forces of the United Nations and those of Italy ceased at once. The actual signing of the Armistice took place on September 3 – four years to the day after the British peoples had taken up the fight, and the very day of the first invasion of the continent of Europe – but the Allies declared that they would choose the time most favourable to them for when it would come into force, which was when the main invasion was well under way. The secret was well maintained.

THE ITALIAN FLEET SURRENDERS AT MALTA.

A GENERAL VIEW OUTSIDE THE GRAND HARBOUR AT VALETTA, SHOWING ITALIAN BATTLESHIPS AND CRUISERS AFTER THEY HAD STEAMED FROM SPEZIA TO SURRENDER.

"The Italian battle fleet is now anchored under the guns of Malta." With this terse official statement on the morning of September 11, Admiral Cunningham summarised one of the most spectacular events in naval history – the crossing over of a powerful Navy from one belligerent to another. The most impressive convoy was the one which started from Spezia and included three battleships, five cruisers and four destroyers. Of these, the battleship "Roma" (35,000 tons) was sunk during an attack by the *Luftwaffe* when the convoy was off the Straits dividing Corsica and Sardinia and before we had provided it with air cover.

THE BATTLE OF SALERNO: ALLIED LANDINGS AGAINST STRONG DEFENCES.

GENERAL ALEXANDER (LEFT) JOINS A BRIGADIER IN AN *AL FRESCO* LUNCH DURING A VISIT TO THE INVASION BRIDGEHEAD.

THE "WARSPITE'S" GUNS, WHICH, WITH THOSE OF THE "VALLIANT," SENT SALVO AFTER SALVO OF 15-IN. SHELLS INTO GERMAN POSITIONS BEYOND THE SALERNO BRIDGEHEAD.

THE GERMAN GENERAL VON LÜDERITZ RECEIVING A REPORT OF THE BATTLE. HIS AIDE-DE-CAMP LOOKS BOTHERED.

THE LATEST TYPE OF FLAT-BOTTOMED INVASION SHIP LANDING MEN AND VEHICLES AT SALERNO. THE GREAT DOORS IN THE BOWS ARE OPENED, AND DISGORGE THEIR CARGO.

While Marshal Badoglio was yet broadcasting the "cease fire" to the Italian forces on the night of September 8, a huge Allied Armada was steaming up the west coast of Italy, with Salerno its destination. Tens of thousands of highly-trained British and American soldiers in the ships heard the astounding news from the B.B.C. that they were about to land in territory with which we were no longer at war! Approximately 1000 square miles was swarming with the invasion fleet, varying in size from assault barges to warships. All knew that the operation ahead was one of the biggest gambles of the war. They knew that the Gulf of Salerno, although 180 miles from our nearest fighter aerodromes in Sicily, was, in fact, the only possible choice, for the west coast of Italy from Reggio to Salerno offers nothing but high mountains and rugged cliffs, impossible terrain for a landing and subsequent operations. They were equally aware that the enemy was similarly wise to the fact, and had made preparations for a warm reception accordingly.

THE GERMAN OCCUPATION OF NORTHERN ITALY: FROM LOMBARDY TO ROME.

ARMED S.S. UNITS BEFORE THE GATES OF PARMA, IN LOMBARDY, WHERE THEY DISARMED THE ITALIAN GARRISON AFTER THE SHORT RESISTANCE.

A HEAVY GERMAN GUN IN A STREET IN THE SUBURBS OF PAVIA, NEAR MILAN, WHERE ARE LARGE IRON FOUNDARIES AND A CONSIDERABLE INDUSTRIAL POPULATION.

ROME: GERMAN PARATROOPS TAKING UP POSITION BEFORE THE ROME MINIS-TRY OF INNER AFFAIRS. THE PICTURE COMES FROM AN ENEMY SOURCE.

The Germans reacted extremely swiftly to the news of the Italian Armistice. Italian troops were everywhere disarmed and Italy treated as an occupied country.

The above pictures throw a certain light on what is happening in the parts of Northern Italy which, at present, are occupied by the Germans. The true state of affairs since Rommel's troops established their control there is obscure; that there has been some resistance is indisputable, and the Germans themselves admit it, but what is clear is that the threat of resistance and sabotage is grave enough to be a factor in the military situation. In Rome, the Germans found an accomplice in the person of General Count Calvi di Bergolo, the commandant of the garrison, but in the north all orders are given by the German generals themselves, or by the German Consul-General in Milan. One thing is quite certain, however: nowhere, throughout the length and breadth of Italy, are the Germans welcome, and the attempt to resurrect Fascism has been a fiasco.

RESCUE OF MUSSOLINI FROM HIS MOUNTAIN HOTEL PRISON NORTH OF ROME.

A RADIOED PICTURE OF MUSSOLINI, SAID TO HAVE BEEN TAKEN AS HE LEFT THE GRAN SASSO HOTEL.

A special announcement from Hitler's H.Q., broadcast by Berlin radio on the night of September 12, gave to the world the news that German parachutists had rescued Mussolini from his mountain prison. Subsequent German reports filled in the outlines of the story. According to them, Mussolini had been imprisoned in an hotel on the 9000-ft. Gran Sasso peak in the Abruzzi Mountains, north of Rome, and was rescued by parachutists, who overpowered the forces guarding the hotel.

BADOGLIO SIGNS LONG-TERM ARMISTICE: ITALY DECLARES WAR ON GERMANY.

GENERAL EISENHOWER (SECOND FROM RIGHT) MEETS MARSHAL BADOGLIO (THIRD FROM LEFT) AFTER THE CONFERENCE ON BOARD H.M. BATTLESHIP "NELSON."

On September 30, 1943, General Eisenhower received Marshal Badoglio for a conference on board the battleship "Nelson," during which the Armistice of September 3 was confirmed and extended.

In this picture we see (left to right) Lord Gort, Air Marshal Tedder, Marshal Badoglio, Lieut.-General Mason Macfarlane, Governor and C.-in-C., Gibraltar, General Eisenhower and General Alexander. On October 13 the Royal Italian Government declared war on Germany, as a co-belligerent with the Allied Powers.

THE WAR IN ITALY: ADVANCE OVER MOUNTAIN FASTNESSES TO NAPLES.

AN AMERICAN RANGER PATROL SCRAMBLING UP A HILLSIDE UNDER COVER OF SMOKE DURING THEIR ADVANCE INTO THE HILLS OVERLOOK-ING THE PLAIN OF NAPLES.

A CONTOUR MAP OF THE SCENE OF THE ALLIED OFFENSIVE.

NEW WORLD TROOPS IN ANCIENT GREEK SURROUNDINGS: AMERICAN TROOPS PASSING THE RUINS OF THE TEMPLE OF POSEIDON AND THE BASILICA AT PÆSTUM, FORMERLY POSEIDONIA.

The Allied advance in Italy – of which almost a quarter of its length is now in our hands – is mainly by the two coastal corridors, east and west, separated by the shin-bone of the rocky Apennines. The Fifth and Eighth Armies, having linked up from Salerno to Potenza and Bari, were advancing on the next lateral link through Avelino and Ariano. On September 27, the Eighth Army whose territory stretches from the Apennines to the Adriatic were racing for Foggia, near the east coast, sweeping rapidly across the plains. With its main aerodrome of Gino Lisa and its twelve satellite landing-grounds, Foggia has been one of the main Axis bases in Southern Italy, and its possession will open up wide air command of the Adriatic shores and the Balkans. The advance from the Salerno bridgehead towards Naples has been one of the slowest of our recent campaigns, partly due to the nature of the terrain and partly to the fact that here the Germans are fighting one of the most stubborn of all their delaying actions. On this west coast the Fifth Army is finding that it has to reduce German strong-points one by one. Fighting takes place among terraced slopes covered with olives and fig-trees, orange groves and vineyards, and on hilltops covered with scrub, much as in Tunisia.

THE SAVAGE AMPHIBIOUS BATTLE OF THE VOLTURNO RIVER – ASSAULT BOATS FOUGHT IN MAIN STREAM AND MEN SWAM TO THE ATTACK.

ALLIES BRIDGE THE VOLTURNO: BRITISH TROOPS CROSSING A PONTOON BRIDGE BUILT BY U.S. ENGINEERS AS THE FIFTH ARMY POURS MASSES OF MEN AND MATERIAL OVER THE RIVER.

FIFTH ARMY TROOPS WHO TOOK PART IN THE CAPTURE OF CANCELLO CHARGED ACROSS THE VOLTURNO BY WAY OF THE REMNANTS OF A WRECKED BRIDGE.

A SHERMAN TANK OF A BRITISH REGIMENT, HAVING FORDED THE RIVER THROUGH SIX FEET OF WATER, EMERGES ON THE NORTH BANK TO ENGAGE THE ENEMY.

The Battle of the Volturno River – the first big river battle of the European war – took place amidst marshes and dykes, with the Volturno the main obstacle to the Fifth Army, under General Mark Clark. The river itself was swollen with the waters of heavy rains, and on the northern bank are a series of dykes about 10 ft. wide and with about 5 ft. of water, every one being a tank obstacle, with canals in addition. The enemy had laid mines on the beach at Castello Volturno, while they had powerful guns and mortars everywhere. At dawn on October 13 the attack went in. The main attack was on the coast and fighting raged up and down the river. British landing craft, full of tanks, put out to sea and cleverly navigated round the river's mouth, scraped the sand-bars and landed on the northern shore. The infantry swam, waded, and paddled their journey across in the face of furious German fire, and in some cases four petrol tins lashed to a wooden ramp got the lads across. It was a fantastic battle, with men swimming into the assault, boats and dinghies fighting in mid-stream, tanks creeping over the sand-bars to the shore, and wetness everywhere. Nevertheless, the enemy was worsted, we established first one bridgehead, then several, and after a thirty-hours battle in mud, water, and sand the Germans beat a hasty retreat. A leapfrog landing from the sea, under cover of naval guns, taking the enemy in the rear, completed his defeat as this attack on his flank threatened all his advance forces.

NAPLES HARBOUR AGAIN IN USE.

REINFORCEMENTS ARRIVE IN NAPLES. DAMAGE IN THE DOCK AREA WAS NOT SO COMPLETE AS THE GERMANS BOASTED: GANGS REMOVED DÉBRIS, AND THE HARBOUR IS NOW OUR SUPPLY BASE.

Berlin boasted, a day or two before Kesselring's forces evacuated Naples, that the city and harbour had lost their importance. Not speaking of their own demolitions, the Germans said that British and American bombing had already made it impossible to consider Naples worthwhile from either a military or maritime standpoint. The third largest city in Italy is not needed as a military centre since the Allies are advancing not retreating, but as a maritime base. Allied repair parties set to work as they did at Bizerta, and within a few days had made the harbour fully workable. Then entered the first large Allied convoy.

FRENCH RECOVERY OF CORSICA.

FRENCH TROOPS, HEAVILY EQUIPPED, LAND AT AJACCIO FROM A FRENCH DESTROYER. THE CORSICANS GREETED THEIR LIBERATORS WITH JOY THROUGHOUT THE ISLAND.

Fighting French operations in Corsica, which led to the final extinction of the German forces on October 4, give some idea of the way General Giraud's men set to work. It was the first opportunity given our French Allies to carry out an independent task in their own island. Their arrival at Ajaccio was described by Sub-Lieut. Adrian de Wael, R.N.V.R., who shared liaison duties in a French destroyer with another British naval officer: "It was like a Mexican fiesta or the arrival of a stage-coach in some Western cowpunchers' village. The jetty was jammed with people firing revolvers into the air and yelling and dancing."

ISLANDS OF THE DODECANESE, A SCENE OF BITTER STRUGGLE.

OPERATIONS IN THE DODECANESE: SYMI, NORTH-WEST OF RHODES, IN BRITISH HANDS. HERE, ON OCTOBER 8, A GERMAN ATTACK WAS REPELLED WITH HEAVY ENEMY LOSSES.

THE GERMAN ATTACK ON LEROS ISLAND, WHICH THE ENEMY CAPTURED ON NOVEMBER 16: BOMBS SPRINKLING THE AREA WHERE THE BRITISH GARRISON HAD SOUGHT SHELTER IN CAVES, ACCORDING TO PRESS REPORTS.

GERMAN TROOPS LANDING FROM BARGES ON THE ISLAND OF COS, IN THE DODECANESE, DURING DETERMINED ENEMY ASSAULTS TO RECAPTURE THE ISLAND.

It will be recalled that the islands of the Dodecanese off the Turkish coast were captured from Turkey by Italy in 1912, and that in this war they have been garrisoned by Italians with a number of Germans on the larger islands, since the occupation of Greece.
The little mountainous island of Symi is typical of the isles. The situation is at the moment somewhat unfortunate. We have seen Rhodes and Cos ours for the taking after the Italian armistice and we have witnessed the heroic episode of Cos end at present in misfortune. Disappointed of Rhodes, owing to the surrender of 30,000 Italian troops to 7000 Germans before we could reach it, we occupied smaller islands of the group, Cos being far and away the most important because it contained a good airfield, and with the absence of fighter cover our seizure of this base was of great importance. We landed about 1000 British troops on September 15 and appear to have relied on 3000 Italian troops, who promptly surrendered when the Germans attacked on October 3. The island of Leros, occupied by British troops with Cos and Samos, was also captured by the Germans on November 16, who claimed to have taken 3700 British prisoners. With the loss of Cos and its airfield, Leros became untenable, the Germans keeping up non-stop Stuka dive-bombing attacks on the small garrison who were driven to a large cave at the summit of a mountain, according to Press reports. Why the garrison was not withdrawn, as was done subsequently at Samos, is as yet unexplained. Mr. Attlee, Deputy Prime Minister, told the Commons on November 24, that while "the loss of Leros and its gallant defenders is a matter of profound regret," the operation contained superior forces at a critical period of our invasion of Italy and inflicted severe losses on the enemy. He estimated that 4000 Germans were drowned.

THE SLOW ADVANCE IN ITALY: DEMOLITIONS, RAIN, SNOW AND MUD.

THE ROUTE TO ISERNIA, NOW IN BRITISH HANDS. NEAR S. ELENA, GERMAN DEMOLITION SQUADS DESTROYED THIS ROAD. THE EIGHTH ARMY SECURED ISERNIA BY AN ALTERNATE ROUTE.

WITH THE EIGHTH ARMY: BRITISH TROOPS AT THE TOP OF THE MOUNTAIN TRACK LEADING TO THE SUMMIT OF MOUNT CAMINO, EXPERIENCING HEAVY RAIN.

CHANGING THE GUN EMPLACEMENT: A D-6 TRACTOR PULLS A 5.5-IN. GUN OUT OF THE THICK GLUTINOUS MUCK TO A NEW AND MORE SUITABLE POSITION.

Our pictures give some idea of the sort of obstacles the Fifth and Eighth Armies are meeting in their advance to Rome. Apart from the stubborn defence put up by the enemy in his retreat, the troops are facing the forces of nature in the shape of huge quagmires and swamps of thick, glutinous mud, into which men wallow well over the ankles and even the lightest vehicles are bogged over their axles. Guns have to be hauled by the invaluable bulldozers, churning up the liquid mire, a route previously made worse by the enemy. Aircraft have had to take off from and land on airfields which have often more resembled shallow lakes. When our men escape the mud, high in the rocky mountains they encounter heavy snow blocking the passes.

Rivers and mud present the greatest difficulties in the advance towards Rome. Almost three weeks have passed since the present offensive was launched. The Eighth, after its success at the Sangro River, has since crossed the Moro, but has to tackle five more rivers before reaching the Pescara River, twelve miles northward. Long before it can reach either Rome or Terni it must face the great gorge which confines the Pescara River north-east of Popoli. The Fifth Army have been engaged in bitter fighting in extraordinarily difficult mountain country, in clearing the approaches to the Cassino gap on the inland road to Rome. The slowness of our progress has enabled the enemy to move divisions to Russia.

BARI RAIDED IN SURPRISE ATTACK BY GERMAN BOMBERS.

THE ALLIES LOST SEVENTEEN SUPPLY SHIPS IN THE GERMAN RAID ON BARI ON DECEMBER 2: ALLIED CARGO VESSELS BURN FIERCELY IN THE PORT.

About thirty German bombers, which raided the Italian Adriatic port of Bari on December 2, sank seventeen United Nations merchant ships within a few minutes. The raiders flew over at dawn, very low and fast, taking the defences by surprise. So far as could be established, the raid had no extremely disruptive effect on Allied strategy, although the Eighth Army suffered badly in the matter of supplies for two or three days. Mr. Stimson, U.S. Secretary of War, said that five American ships were destroyed when bombs hit two ammunition ships which exploded. Fires damaged harbour facilities. Casualties were estimated at 1000, but most of the ships had discharged their cargo before the attack.

ALL ROADS LEAD TO ROME – AND MOST OF THEM ARE MINED, SAYS ALEXANDER.

A RELIEF MAP SHOWING THE COUNTRY OF CENTRAL ITALY WITH COMMUNICATIONS CONVERGING ON ROME, INCLUDING ROADS, RAILWAYS AND TOWNS ALONG THE LINE OF THE ALLIED ADVANCE.

By December 5, British and American troops of the Fifth Army blasted the enemy by bayonet charges out of their positions on Monte Camino, which towers 2800 ft. above the road near Mignano, and opened a deep breach into the enemy line. American troops advanced on the bleak sides of Monte Maggiore, 1500 ft. high, which dominates the railway and road between Mignano and Cassino. In the east the Eighth Army are advancing steadily on a 20-mile front towards Pescara, on the coast. The Germans are fighting savagely along a 100-mile front, with nine divisions in action, five opposing the Fifth, and four the Eighth Army, with at least two others in reserve. Rommel's plan is to fight delaying actions right up the peninsula.

THE GRIM BATTLE OF ORTONA: CANADIANS *VERSUS* ENEMY PARATROOPS.

HOW THE ENEMY WAS EXPELLED HOUSE BY HOUSE: TANKS READY TO FIRE ON A SNIPER'S NEST. THE OFFICER DIRECTING OPERATIONS IS ON THE EXTREME RIGHT.

A TOUGH-LOOKING GERMAN PARATROOPS WARRANT OFFICER WITH IRON CROSS: ONE OF A BUNCH OF PRISONERS CAPTURED SINGLEHANDED BY A CANADIAN PRIVATE.

CANADIAN INFANTRY, WHO FOUGHT WITH GREAT GALLANTRY THROUGHOUT, PICKING THEIR WAY AMIDST RUBBLE AND RUIN, WHERE EVERY STREET WAS STRONGLY MINED.

In the early hours before dawn on Tuesday, December 28, Canadian infantrymen of the Eighth Army, who for eight days had been fighting their way into Ortona, ferreting out German snipers house by house and street by street, bombed the last Germans from the last houses of the town. The fighting for possession of this important Italian port has been described as the hardest and bloodiest of the whole Italian campaign. Ordered to hold up the Eighth Army so as to permit the preparation of defence positions between the town and Pescara to the north, the Germans charged with the defence of Ortona made nearly every house a sniper's nest, and the streets and buildings a mass of death-traps. Property continually collapsed to the explosion of time bombs, and at one street crossing alone sappers removed sixty-seven telemines.

The Canadians fought most gallantly against what were no less than hundreds of strongly fortified posts, with tanks concealed in basements firing along the streets, machine-gun nests and snipers in solidly-built house after house, the enemy being only dislodged by massed guns and finally extinguished by the bayonet. The Germans clung desperately to the northern fringe of the town even after the rest of it was in the hands of the Eighth Army. The enemy was using selected tough paratroops for the defence, and all the Germans killed were these tough paratroops.

Once Ortona had fallen, the Canadians lost no time in pushing on north of the town. The native Italians mostly fled to the mountains and returned to find once-beautiful Ortona in rack and ruin.

THE PACIFIC WAR: PICTURES FROM THE NEW GUINEA FRONT.

LANDING CRAFT APPROACHING THE JAPANESE-HELD FINSCHAFEN, NEW GUINEA, WITH TROOPS AND SUPPLIES, FOR JUNGLE FIGHTING. THIS LAST IMPORTANT JAPANESE ANCHORAGE WAS CAPTURED ON OCTOBER 2.

"FUZZYWUZZY ANGELS": NEW GUINEA NATIVES WHO CARRY ALLIED WOUNDED THROUGH THE JUNGLE TO SAFETY.

PRIMITIVE AND MODERN: A PAPUAN SOLDIER WITH A BREN GUN, WHICH HE USED TO ATTACK JAPANESE BARGES IN NEW GUINEA. INSET MAP SHOWS THE AREA IN WHICH ALLIED RECENT SUCCESSES HAVE BEEN GAINED.

After the capture of Salamaua on September 12, and Lae on September 16 following a parachute drop from the largest air fleet ever assembled in the South-West Pacific, Finschafen, Japan's last important anchorage in New Guinea, sixty miles north-east of Lae, was taken, after desperate fighting by men of the 9th Australian Division, on October 2. After concentrated blasting of enemy dug-outs and machine-gun nests by Australian dive bombers and U.S. Bostons and Havocs, Australian troops on mortar and machine gun posts on the top of a ridge sealed the fate of the Japs guarding Finschafen. Dragging mortars and Vickers guns, the attackers climbed a jungle ridge so wild and steep that the enemy, who had considered their positions impregnable, were taken by surprise, and were annihilated. General MacArthur said that the capture of this strategic site eliminated all defensive value of enemy-held centres as far as Madang. An outstanding feature of the Finschafen operations was the dovetailing of Australian and American effort, in obtaining air superiority. A fleet of barges, as seen above, was operated by the amphibious engineers of the U.S. Army, which in landing operations were supported by units of the U.S. Navy. To American production the Australian Army is indebted for much mechanical equipment, as in these landing craft, of which one is shown approaching the shores of Finschafen, with the jungle in the background. For two months the Australians' progress towards Madang was barred by Jap sharp-shooters at what is known as "Green Snipers' Pimple." It stands, a sheer 100 ft. ridge, over the northern end of Shaggy Ridge, 5600 ft. above sea-level. Following one of the biggest and most sustained artillery and dive-bombing barrages of the South-West Pacific war, Australian infantrymen literally clawed their way through fire to the crest of the crag on December 29. They captured it in two hours. The Japs are almost entirely expelled now from New Guinea, except for one site on the coast, and are cut off from supplies.

U.S. BOMBERS RAID RABAUL.

THE CLIMAX TO JAPAN'S ASCENDANCY IN THE SOUTH-WEST PACIFIC: THE JAP FLEET FLEEING FROM RABAUL HARBOUR, NEW BRITAIN.

The rape of Pearl Harbour was avenged on November 11 at Rabaul, New Britain, the enemy's main base in the South-West Pacific. Avenger torpedo-bombers and Dauntless dive-bombers caused havoc by prolonged raids, torpedo bombs smashing into five heavy cruisers and a light cruiser, another also being damaged. As a result, and with the Japanese inferiority in the air, the Jap Fleet fled precipitately, deserting the base, in an attempt to evade the bombers.

NEW ZEALANDERS IN SOLOMONS ASSAULT.

AN EARLY-MORNING SCENE ON SEPTEMBER 17. NEW ZEALAND TROOPS, BROUGHT ASHORE AT VELLA LAVELLA BY LANDING CRAFT, WHICH CARRIED THEM FROM TRANSPORTS, MOVE FORWARD INTO THE JUNGLE OF THE ISLAND OF BAKA BAKA, DURING OPERATIONS AGAINST THE JAPANESE IN THE SOLOMON ISLANDS.

Parallel to the operations in New Guinea the drive to clear the Solomon Islands continues. A feint attack on Choiseul on 28 October by paratroops, who were successfully withdrawn on November 3, was followed by a full-scale attack on Bougainville where the U.S. Third Marine Division landed in Empress Augusta Bay on November 1. Although there are believed to be upwards of 50,000 Japanese on Bougainville, the landing was only lightly opposed, and our Allies' beach-head is now well established.

U.S. MARINES WIN A GREAT VICTORY ON TARAWA AND MAKIN ATOLLS.

U.S. MARINES IN ACTION AGAINST THE JAPS, THEIR TRENCHES LYING ONLY A FEW YARDS BEYOND: A GRAPHIC SCENE ON TARAWA, WHERE THE MEN CROUCH UNDER COVER AS GRENADES ARE TOSSED OVER.

ON THE BEACHES DEAD JAPANESE SOLDIERS AND HEAPS OF JUNK TESTIFY TO THE BITTER STRUGGLE FOR TARAWA ATOLL: ANOTHER OF THE DRAMATIC PHOTOGRAPHS WHICH DEPICT THE WAR IN ITS UGLIEST ASPECT.

THE CAPTURE OF MAKIN ATOLL, IN THE GILBERTS: U.S. TROOPS OF THE 165TH INFANTRY, FORMERLY THE "FIGHTING 69TH OF NEW YORK," ADVANCE ON BUTARITARI BEACH. THE ISLAND IS ALREADY ABLAZE FROM NAVAL BOMBARDMENTS.

The American landings in the Gilbert Islands were the beginning of a new campaign to open a more direct route to Japan – across the Central Pacific. On November 23 U.S. Marines and soldiers took the Gilbert Islands in the bloodiest battle of the war in the Pacific. In seventy-six hours of fighting, Marine casualties were 1025 killed and 2557 wounded. Six thousand Japanese were slain. It was American Army troops who took Makin Atoll, the northernmost of the Gilbert Islands, and U.S. Marines captured Tarawa Atoll which, by now, has become an effective U.S. base, bringing the Allies another important step closer to defeat of the enemy in the Pacific. The Tarawa invasion was commanded by Rear-Admiral Harry W. Hill and Major-General Julian C. Smith, of the U.S. Marines. It was a magnificent feat.

HISTORIC MEETINGS IN TEHERAN AND CAIRO: ALLIED LEADERS AND THEIR ENTOURAGE.

MR. CHURCHILL, PRESIDENT ROOSEVELT AND PRESIDENT ISMET INÜNÜ, OF TURKEY, DURING THEIR "MOST FRUITFUL" TALKS AT MENA, NEAR CAIRO, ON DECEMBER 4–6.

THE TEHERAN CONFERENCE, FROM NOVEMBER 28 TO 30: MARSHAL STALIN, PRESIDENT ROOSEVELT, AND MR CHURCHILL ENJOY A JOKE.

MARSHAL CHIANG-KAI-SHEK, MR. ROOSEVELT, MR. CHURCHILL, AND MME. CHIANG, WITH THEIR DIPLOMATIC ADVISERS, IN "NORTH AFRICA", ON NOVEMBER 22–26.

It was first announced in Great Britain on December 2 that Mr. Roosevelt, Marshal Chiang Kai-shek, and Mr. Churchill had met, for the first time, in a vitally important conference "somewhere" in North Africa. War moves in the Far East were fully discussed and a declaration was issued that Manchuria and Formoas would be restored to China, that Korea would obtain here independence and that Japan would be stripped of all the Pacific Isles she has occupied or seized since 1914. The three great Allies expressed their resolve to bring unrelenting pressure against their brutal enemies by sea, land and air.
The triangular Conference, with Marshal Chiang Kai-shek, and his indomitable wife to translate proceedings to him, sat from November 22 to 26, when Marshal Chiang and Mme. Chiang flew back to China. The President and Mr. Churchill flew to unrevealed destinations, but it was late confirmed that the three Allied leaders, Mr. Churchill, President Roosevelt and Marshal Stalin, had held a four-days meeting at Teheran. There they "shaped and confirmed" their common policy, expressing their determination that the three Nations would "work together in war and in the peace that will follow." During the following week Mr. Churchill, President Roosevelt and M. Ismet Inönü, President of Turkey, held a three-day Conference in Cairo on December 4–6.

RUSSIA'S MIGHTY VICTORIES AGAINST GERMANY – MILESTONES IN THE WAR.

WHILST RED ARMY MACHINE-GUNNERS AND RIFLEMEN ENGAGE THE RETREATING GERMANS, A NURSE TENDS A WOUNDED MAN. RUSSIAN NURSES ADVANCE WITH THE TROOPS, GIVING FIRST AID WHERE THEY FALL.

The world is witnessing in Russia at the present moment one of the most stupendous spectacles of all time. In the fall of Stalingrad on January 31 of this year and its resultant sweep, which took the Russians to the gates of Orel in the north, and the expulsion of the hated enemy from the Caucasus, except for a small area of the Kuban, the United Nations saw the writing on the wall. Then, after a short lull, in which the Germans vainly strove to collect a stable front, the vast Russian military machine rumbled forward again, and, as it moved onward, gaining added impetus, by a succession of giant blows, the Germans were beaten back farther and farther; so perished the Nazi visions of

A MAP SHOWING THE GERMAN HIGH TIDE OF ADVANCE IN RUSSIA IN 1941–42, AND OUR ALLY'S MIGHTY VICTORIES FROM NOVEMBER 19, 1942, TO THE DNIEPER OF TO-DAY.

AFTER THE BATTLE IS OVER: ENEMY GUNS AND OTHER WAR MATERIAL LITTER THE OREL-BRYANSK HIGHWAY. THE GERMAN LOSSES, BOTH IN MEN AND MATERIAL, HAVE BEEN COLOSSAL DURING THE GREAT SUMMER RETREAT.

victory and conquest in mighty Russia. They were flung completely out of industrial Dombas. City after city fell to Russian arms and brilliant strategy. At the end of October they found themselves hurled back towards the Soviet boundaries, with no prospect of being able to stabilise their position, and we watch now the supreme drama of the Dnieper, with the Crimea cut off. General Tolbukhin's left wing on November 1 by-passed Perekop and the Battle of the Tauride Steppe will pass down in history as one of Germany's most disastrous defeats, a scene of frightful slaughter. Our map denotes the various milestones in Hitler's ill-begotten war on Russia.

"SCHARNHORST," 26,000 TONS, TRAPPED AND SUNK IN AN ARCTIC BATTLE.

THE GERMAN BATTLESHIP, A BRITISH CONVOY HER DESTINED VICTIM, IS INTERCEPTED BY THE HOME FLEET.

Latest details of the brilliant action in which the "Scharnhorst" was sunk make it clear that she was completely outmanœuvred by the units of the Home Fleet. Emerging from her lair in Alten Fiord she was sighted in the half-light of the Arctic dawn, by cruisers of an escorting squadron, which opened fire. The matter then became an affair of nursing the 'Scharnhorst' towards the H.M.S. 'Duke of York.' At 4.49

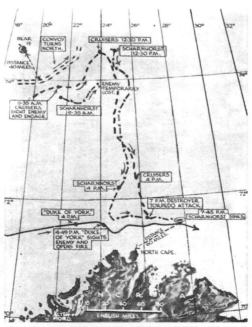

THE APPROXIMATE PLAN OF THE ACTION, SHOWING MOVEMENTS OF "DUKE OF YORK," THE CRUISERS "BELFAST," "NORFOLK," AND "SHEFFIELD" SYNCHRONISING WITH THE COURSE OF "SCHARNHORST".

p.m. the "Duke of York" sighted the enemy battleship fine on her port bow, and altered course to bring her broadside of ten 14-in. guns to bear on the target. Several hits were registered, and then four

H.M.S. "DUKE OF YORK," LEADER OF THE HOME FLEET FORCE, FIRING A SALVO FROM HER AFTER 14-INCH TURRET.

destroyers delivered a successful torpedo attack. The British battleship closed to 10,000 yards and scored repeated hits. By this stage the "Scharnhorst's" hull appeared to be a black mass of shattered metal from our gunfire. She was burning, listing and nearly stopped when the Admiral sent the cruiser "Jamaica" speeding in to the kill. Only thirty-six survivors were picked up.

THE ILLUSTRATED LONDON NEWS

MORE REMINISCENT OF SWISS ALPINE HEIGHTS THAN OF SUNNY ITALY: AFTER LONG WEEKS OF VIOLENT STORMS AND BLIZZARDS, THE SUN CASTS HIS WELCOME RAYS ON THE SNOW-MANTLED APENNINES.

The weather in Italy is beginning to clear. After many weeks during which the Allied advance has been held up by drenching, unceasing rain, roads of deep mire, where mechanical vehicles became hopelessly bogged, or delayed by heavy falls of snow, there are indications of the coming spring. The sun is beginning to shine, and before long our patient Armies may greet sunny Italy, where, happily, spring starts early.

1944

Russians relieve Leningrad — Allied advance held at Monte Cassino — Allies land at Anzio — US Marines land in Marshall Islands — capture Admiralty and Saint Matthias Islands — Japanese Invasion of Assam held at Imphal and Kohima — Russians retake Odessa and Crimea — Stillwell's US/Chinese Army re-enters Burma — takes Myitkyina — Monte Cassino falls — Allies enter Rome — D-Day landings in Normandy — V1 raids on Britain begin — US invade Mariana Islands — Battle of the Philippine Sea — Russians retake Minsk — US forces take Cherbourg — Russians retake Vilna and Lvov; reach suburbs of Warsaw — Poles rise but are crushed — US troops drive south from Avranches — Seal off Brittany and swing East — Canadians close Falaise Pocket but 40,000 Germans escape — Allies land in South of France — Russians begin Balkan Campaign; enter Rumania — US and Free French enter Paris — Russia takes Bucharest; invades Bulgaria — Allies liberate Northern France and Belgium — First V2s fall on London — Russians enter Sofia — US and British Airborne Troops take Nijmegen; fail to hold Arnhem — Russians enter Yugoslavia, Hungary and Czechoslovakia — British land in Greece — Russians take Riga, and Petsamo in Northern Finland — US troops land on Leyte — Battle of Leyte Gulf — Tito's Partisans liberate Belgrade — Roosevelt elected to fourth term — Port of Antwerp opened — German counter-attack in Ardennes halted.

THE RELIEF OF LENINGRAD: THE END OF THIRTY MONTHS OF A TRAGIC SIEGE.

After a three-point Russian assault on the Leningrad salient, thousands of Germans south of Leningrad were trapped and wiped out. It was with real jubilation that Moscow learned of the break-through. It means that the German 10-mile corridor, which ran up to the Gulf of Finland and to the outskirts of Leningrad, has been cut off – and trapped. The dominating feeling in Leningrad is one of immense relief that the terrible two-and-a-half-year ordeal is over. The memories of this siege are bitter indeed. It has caused the death of hundreds of thousands through sheer starvation and many more by enemy shells; and the city's beautiful surroundings with their historic palaces have been turned into a vast waste-land.

THE GREAT IMPERIAL PALACE OF PETERHOF, SHOWING HOW NOTHING BUT THE OUTER WALLS REMAIN. COSSACKS OF THE RED ARMY ADVANCE GUARDS STAND IN FRONT OF THE PALACE AFTER ITS RECAPTURE.

THEY MARCH THROUGH LENINGRAD, PRISONERS NOT CONQUERORS: GERMAN SOLDIERS, LED BY A RED ARMY GUNNER.

REORGANISATION OF THE USSR: THE NEW SOVIET COMMONWEALTH.

A MAP SHOWING THE SIXTEENTH FEDERAL REPUBLICS (INCLUDING RUSSIA HERSELF WITH SIBERIA) FORMING THE NEW SOVIET COMMONWEALTH ANNOUNCED BY M. MOLOTOV ON FEBRUARY 2. EACH WILL HAVE THE RIGHT TO INDEPENDENT DIPLOMATIC REPRESENTATION, ITS OWN ARMY, AND THE RIGHT TO SECEDE FROM THE U.S.S.R.

M. Molotov, Russian Foreign Commissar, on February 2 laid before the Supreme Soviet Assembly proposals that each of the sixteen Republics of the Soviet Union should be empowered: (1) to create its own independent army units; (2) to initiate direct relations with foreign Powers; and (3) to sever relations with the Soviet Union if so desired. "The enemies of the Soviet Union need not doubt," said M. Molotov, "that the outcome of the new measures will be a further strengthening of the State." Our map shows the sixteen Federal Republics, among which, Lithuania, Latvia, Estonia, Moldavia and the Karelo-Finnish Republic are as yet in enemy hands.

THE "GOLIATH" THAT FAILED: THE RADIO-CONTROLLED MIDGET TANK.

HITLER'S "SECRET WEAPON," THE RADIO-CONTROLLED MIDGET TANK. HERE THE DETONATOR IS FIXED INTO THE LOADED MIDGET TANK, WHICH IS DRIVEN BY DUAL ELECTRIC MOTORS CONTROLLED BY RADIO IMPULSES.

The German nickname of "Goliath," accorded to their radio-controlled midget tank, can be explained as a satirical reference to the pretentious claims of Hitler's "secret weapon." A demonstration was given before specially paraded German troops. The tanks advanced, the wheels went round, but the machines obstinately stopped. Allied gunners had a heyday and destroyed fourteen.

ON THE UKRAINE FRONT: THE GREAT GERMAN RETREAT FROM RUSSIAN SOIL.

SWIFT-MOVING SLEIGHS – PROPELLER DRIVEN – CARRY RED ARMY SHOCK TROOPS, IN WINTER CAMOUFLAGE, ACROSS THE FROZEN MARSHLAND.

In the Ukraine the fighting had been fluctuating in character. As far back as mid-November the Germans began a strong armoured counter-offensive against the Kiev salient. But by the end of 1943 the German

ZHUKOV'S BREAK-THROUGH IN THE WESTERN UKRAINE: A MAP SHOWING THE GREAT NEW DRIVE SOUTH OF TARNOPOL AND SHEPYETOVKA, TO THE ODESSA-LVOV-BERLIN RAILWAY, MANSTEIN'S SOLE LIFELINE OF 500,000 GERMANS TO THE EAST.

effort came to an end. Then, in early January, the Russians resumed their advance, smashed a way into Berdichev, thrust out a long arm towards Vinnitsa. Now the German salient touching the Dnieper at Kanyev had become more acute than ever.
The natural thing seemed to be the abandonment of the Kanyev salient, but the enemy hung on to it. Powerful Russian armoured forces struck across the salient through Smyela and Zvenigordka, joined hands, and

MOVING UP TO THE FRONT LINE NORTH-WEST OF KIROVOGRAD: A LONG LINE OF GERMAN TROOPS AND TRANSPORT PLOD THROUGH THE SNOW.

trapped the defenders. The Russians carried through the operation with great skill, boldness and determination, but it would certainly seem that the Germans played into their hands.

THE ALLIED ASSAULT ON THE GERMAN STRONGHOLD AT MT. CASSINO
USED AS A FORTRESS BY THE ENEMY – MT. CASSINO'S HISTORIC MONASTERY.

AN AERIAL VIEW OF THE MONASTERY. FIRST FOUNDED BY ST BENEDICT IN 529 AD, ITS ARCHIVES CONTAIN PRICELESS TREASURES.

THE MASSIVE WALLS OF THE BENEDICTINE MONASTERY OF MT. CASSINO, WHICH THE GERMANS HAVE USED AS A FORTRESS AND FOR FIRE-CONTROL.

GUN-FLASHES PIERCE THE ITALIAN NIGHT AS ALLIED FORCES OPEN UP IN ONE OF THE HEAVIEST CONCENTRATIONS OF SHELLING IN THE WAR IN ITALY.

As was first announced on February 13, the Germans were using the Benedictine Monastery on the summit of Mt. Cassino as a fire-control tower from which they could direct the full weight of their artillery against any point at a moment's notice, and in addition its massive walls were lined with mortars and machine-guns. The Vatican had specifically asked that this historic monastery, founded by St. Benedict more than 1400 years ago, the cradle of the Benedictine Order, and a centre of education and science, should be spared, the same request having been made to the enemy. But it had become a gigantic pill-box in the heart of the battle area, and German bad faith has already led to many casualties which otherwise would have been avoided. The enemy could not be expelled from Mount Cassino until the monastery fortress was liquidated and the road to Rome opened up. The gun-flashes which stand out so sharply against the blackness of the night in our bottom picture were taken as U.S. Army artillery units opened up in a furious attack against the Germans.

NEW CHIEFS FOR THE LIBERATION OF EUROPE.

GENERAL MONTGOMERY, SEEN WITH LT.-GEN. LEESE, WHO TAKES OVER EIGHTH ARMY, HAS JOINED GENERAL EISENHOWER IN ENGLAND TO HELP PLAN THE INVASION OF EUROPE.

THE US EIGHTH AIR FORCE'S GREATEST DAYLIGHT RAID OVER EUROPE.

The launching of the U.S. Eighth Air Force's greatest daylight attack over Europe on January 11 "drew" the biggest force of German fighters yet engaged in the defence of the Reich. This force employed a variety of methods, including towed aerial mines, and the use of rocket shells fired in "broadsides" by line-abreast fighters. Describing the attack, Lieut.-Colonel Thorup said: "In the distance we saw a line of more than twenty Messerschmitt 110s. They got around to one side of us, and then turned into line-abreast head-on to our formation and let go a broadside of rockets that seemed to burst into a great line of red and yellow fire." Most of this first salvo missed, apparently, and the Me. 110s then fired another salvo of two rockets apiece, indicating that each fighter carried four rockets. This double bombardment was the beginning of an aerial battle which lasted for an hour and a half as the formation of Fortresses fought its way home across Europe. Of the total raiding force of Fortresses and Liberators, sixty were lost, but official statements claim the destruction of at least 152 German fighters. It is also known that the raid so panicked the Germans that they disclosed the existence of an entirely new fighter – the 210R "destroyer."

A FAMOUS FORTRESS ESCORT – THE NEW SUPER-RANGE VERSION OF THE P-38 LIGHTNING FIGHTER.

ALLIED LANDINGS IN THE NETTUNO-ANZIO AREA: SCENES ON LAND AND SEA.

A THREE-TON LORRY COMES TO GRIEF DURING THE LANDING OPERATIONS IN THE NETTUNO-ANZIO AREA. THE ROUGH SEAS MADE THINGS DIFFICULT FOR OUR TROOPS.

THE ROYAL NAVY SUPPORTS THE FIFTH ARMY'S LANDINGS AT ANZIO: A CRUISER BOMBARDS THE ENEMY SHORE POSITIONS AS LANDING CRAFT (SEEN BEYOND THE WARSHIP) WAIT THEIR TURN.

Following the successful Allied landings on the coast south of Rome in the district round Nettuno and Anzio – on January 22, 1944 – Allied forces are pushing inland, fighting off strong counter-attacks. The enemy has brought up fresh troops to this area and heavy fighting is reported in the beachhead sector, especially along the line of the British advance, where our forces are consolidating their positions.

THE FIFTH ARMY COMES ASHORE IN ITALY: DUCKS ON THEIR WAY INLAND NEAR NETTUNO DURING THE LANDING OPERATIONS SOUTH OF ROME.

THE FIFTH ARMY IN ACTION ON THE MT. CASSINO AND ANZIO FRONTS.

THE ANCIENT BENEDICTINE MONASTERY – A BULWARK OF EARLY CHRISTIANITY.

"THE MOST SACRED SHRINE ON EARTH": THE MONASTERY HOUSES PRICELESS TREASURES.

A NEW ALL-OUT ASSAULT LAUNCHED BY THE FIFTH ARMY: ARTILLERY POUNDING THE MONASTERY.

THE INTERIOR OF THE BASILICA, SHOWING MARBLE, WITH MOSAICS AND FRESCOES.

On February 15 the Fifth Army surrounding Cassino was compelled to shell and bomb the ancient and historic monastery of St. Benedict, used as a fortress and a gun-direction tower by the enemy in defiance of the Pope's appeal. Within a short time waves of Fortresses, Mitchells and Marauders and heavy artillery had left it little more than a ruined shell. It is understood that the removable treasures, consisting of 1200 MSS. and 80,000 volumes, were evacuated to safer keeping in Vatican City in January. A new all-out assault on Cassino and Monastery Hill was launched by the Fifth Army at dawn on February 18.

THE BENEDICTINE MONASTERY, USED BY THE GERMANS, DURING A BOMBING ATTACK BY U.S. FORTRESSES.

A QUIET CORNER OF THE CLOISTERS REFLECTING THE PEACE OF THE ANCIENT MONASTERY BEFORE THE INEVITABLE ATTACK.

THE GERMAN COUNTER-ATTACK ON THE ANZIO BEACH-HEAD.

ESCAPE FROM AMIENS: A MIRACLE OF PRECISION BOMBING.

On February 18, 1944, a Mosquito wing of the R.A.F. Second Tactical Air Force carried out an attack on the prison at Amiens in an attempt to assist over 100 prisoners to escape, the prisoners being French patriots condemned to death for assisting the Allies. To obtain the required accuracy it was necessary to bomb from "deck level." The prison wall was breached, the ends of the building smashed, and prisoners were seen running out. Group Captain Pickard, leader, was shot down.

TROOPS OF A GERMAN ARTILLERY UNIT OPERATING A RANGE-FINDER DURING THE SHELLING OF ALLIED POSITIONS IN THE ANZIO BEACH HEAD.

On the Anzio beachhead, Kesselring, attacking with some 50,000 infantry supported by tanks and big artillery concentrations, achieved a small advance not exceeding 3,000 yards in the Carroceto area, suffering very heavy losses, but subsequently lost ground was practically recovered by a succession of brilliant counter-attacks, in which Allied tanks and infantry pushed nearly two miles ahead in double-quick time.

A CLOSE-UP OF THE BREACH BLASTED IN THE SOUTH SIDE OF THE OUTER WALL OF AMIENS PRISON: A MIRACLE OF PRECISION BOMBING.

RENEWED ATTACK ON MONTE CASSINO: EVERY BUILDING REDUCED TO RUBBLE.

This might be the picture of an ancient deserted city, ravaged by centuries of storms and neglect. But most of its ravaging was packed into one day of intense bombardment when, on March 15, Allied aircraft rained down 1400 tons of bombs on a target area of less than one square mile – the smallest area ever to receive so great a weight of bombs in such a short space of time. Constant shelling has also contributed to the result seen in the above picture of Cassino, in which not a single building remains whole. It was hoped that this "softening-up" attack, unprecedented in warfare, would leave the way clear for the Fifth Army to advance past Cassino, whose stubborn resistance had held them up for so long, but in fact it defeated its own object, smashing up the town to such an extent that tanks and infantry were unable to pour into the defences. The Germans were thus able to bring up reinforcements.

Our pictures, taken in Cassino after it had been smashed by bombs and shells, show how the utter destruction of this Italian town was in fact more of a liability than a victory. The very scope of the devastation made it impossible for armoured columns or massed infantry to advance into the blocked streets, but left enough overhead cover in the ruins to create a snipers' paradise. That is why the New Zealanders were forced to kill the Germans one by one.

TENSE MOMENTS AS A NEW ZEALANDER SMASHES IN A DOOR CONCEALING GERMAN SNIPERS, WHILE HIS COMRADES STAND READY FOR ANY EMERGENCY.

THIS WAS A TOWN! AN AERIAL PHOTOGRAPH OF ALL THAT WAS LEFT OF CASSINO AFTER THE TOWN HAD BEEN BLANKETED BY BOMBS AND SHELLS. NOT A SINGLE BUILDING REMAINS WHOLE.

THE RUINS OF CASSINO HALT THE ARMOURED COLUMNS, BUT GIVE REFUGE TO THE SNIPERS.

ALLIED ADVANCE IN THE PACIFIC: SMASHING JAPANESE STRONGHOLDS.

LANDINGS IN NEW BRITAIN: U.S. MARINES ASHORE AT CAPE GLOUCESTER.

A BUSY SCENE ON CAPE GLOUCESTER AS U.S. MARINES WADE ASHORE. IN THE CENTRE IS A MARINE ALLIGATOR CARRYING STRETCHERS WHILE ANOTHER CAN BE SPIED AMONG THE TREES (LEFT BACKGROUND). THE MARINES THREW BACK THE ENEMY, USING FLAME-THROWERS AND ARTILLERY AGAINST PILL-BOXES.

On December 30, U.S. Marines formed a bridgehead at Cape Gloucester, in the island of New Britain. Here the Japs had dug themselves in and had numbers of pill-boxes from which it was difficult to dislodge them. To defeat these the marines used flame-throwers and artillery. From then onwards the Japs were steadily beaten back until on January 12, the enemy attempted to send in reinforcements and to land large numbers at Cape Gloucester. In this effort they failed, the U.S. Air Force sinking forty-three enemy barges, many loaded with troops.

ONE OF SEVENTEEN AIR RAIDS ON RABAUL HARBOUR SINCE OCTOBER.

U.S. AIR FORCE BOMBERS' RAID ON RABAUL, WITH SHIPS SINKING OR ABLAZE, THE TOWN IN FLAMES.

U.S. aircraft raided Rabaul, and sank two ships in the harbour. Japs occupying this British-owned port have seen their town blown sky-high in a way they little expected. Seventeen times Allied 'planes have blasted all Japanese shipping, smashed warehouses, and destroyed 'planes at nearby Vuna Kanau, Rapopo, and Tobera airfields. 141 Jap ships and nearly 700 'planes have been destroyed. Our picture shows one of these occasions. The whole of this area is intensely volcanic and two islands, Natupi and Vulcan, are active volcanoes.

HARDSHIPS FACED AND CONQUERED BY AUSTRALIAN SOLDIERS IN NEW GUINEA.

WOUNDED AUSTRALIANS RECEIVING FIRST-AID TREATMENT BEFORE TRANSFER TO DRESSING-STATIONS – A PHOTOGRAPH TAKEN LESS THAN 100 YARDS FROM JAP LINES.

This picture conveys something of the wild jungle atmosphere in which the New Guinea campaign is being fought out, and of the unbeatable spirit of the Australian infantrymen, who are achieving near-miracles in their constant combat against an unyielding foe. The battle discipline is second to none. The jungle is one of the dirtiest places to fight in, but it is a rarity to see a soldier with more than one day's growth of beard; every stream in their path is regarded not only as another obstacle to cross but as an opportunity for a guard to bath!

A MAP OF PACIFIC CAMPAIGNS.

THE NEW ALLIED ADVANCE IN THE PACIFIC, ONLY 1400 MILES SOUTH OF TOKYO: A MAP OF THE WESTERN PACIFIC, WITH MARIANA ISLANDS CENTRE, HEAVILY BOMBED BY THE U.S. TANK FORCE.

The official statement from Washington on the heavy U.S. attack on Truk, Japan's Central Pacific bastion, announced that "The Pacific Fleet has returned in Truk the visit made by the Japanese Fleet [to Pearl Harbour] on December 7, 1941, and has effected a partial settlement of the debt." Hundreds of American carrier-based 'planes blasted the islands sinking twenty-three ships and doing tremendous damage to the air base on Eten Island, enemy installations on Dublon Island and the landing-strip on Umam Island.

JAPANESE BASES BLASTED.

TINIAN ISLAND IS BOMBED BY AMERICAN BOMBERS: PILLARS OF SMOKE RISE FROM THE AIRFIELD.

U.S. NAVAL 'PLANES BLAST A JAPANESE TANKER IN THE JAPANESE NAVAL BASE IN THE CAROLINES.

CONQUEST IN THE PACIFIC: THE US CAPTURE THE MARSHALL ISLANDS.

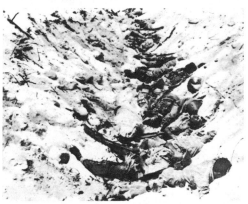

JAPANESE INSTALLATIONS ON NAMUR GO UP IN SMOKE AS U.S. DEMOLITION SQUADS GO INTO ACTION. IN THE FOREGROUND, AMERICAN SNIPERS RETURN ENEMY FIRE.

The American task force in the Pacific, by striking at Japan and Tinian, in the Marianna group, north of Guam (the U.S. base captured by the Japanese soon after war was declared), offers a formidable challenge to the enemy. On February 22, several hundred 'planes from a carrier task force raided these two islands. They lie in the innermost ring of Japan's island defences, only 1400 miles south of Tokyo, 1000 miles nearer Tokyo than is Truk, and only 1500 miles from the Philippine Islands. In just over three weeks American task forces in strength have attacked the Marshalls, the Eniwetok Atoll, and Truk. They threaten Japan's communications, and have cut off supplies to the enemy garrisons in New Guinea, Rabaul, and Bougainville.

The interesting fact in relation to the American capture of the Marshall Islands, which has since given the Tokyo Government a headache, was that the Japs were taken by surprise and most of them were dazed by the tremendous bombardment they suffered from sea, air and land. As always in these island battles, they fought on fanatically, sniping in the daytime, trying to infiltrate into the U.S. lines at night, and often allowing the patrols to pass them in their hiding-places so as to attack them from the rear. Again and again the U.S. soldiers were forced to advance to the very doors of blockhouses to clear them of enemy snipers. The Japanese losses in the Marshall Islands were exceedingly heavy, having regard to the size of the atolls. Kwajalein, one of the largest, is only 2½ miles long, and on February 3 the Japs had lost 1250 out of a garrison of 2000, whereas the American losses were 27 killed, 9 missing and 190 wounded. The enemy are believed to have lost over 20,000 altogether in the Marshall Islands.

JAPANESE DEAD LIE IN A TRENCH OF NAMUR ISLAND IN THE KWAJALEIN ATOLL FOLLOWING AERIAL AND SEA BOMBARDMENTS WHICH PRECEDED THE U.S. INVASION.

ALLIED VICTORIES IN BURMA: ON THE ARAKAN FRONT – THE ANGLO-INDIAN ADVANCE.

JUNGLE SCOUTS IN BURMA: THEIR FACES PROTECTED BY MOSQUITO NETTING, THEY STALK THE JAPANESE THROUGH THE JUNGLE.

MAJOR-GENERAL F. MESSERVY, COMMANDER, 7TH INDIAN DIVISION.

BATTLE OF THE NGAKYEDAUK PASS. TROOPS IN AN OBSERVATION POST IN THE JUNGLE.

The first serious defeat inflicted by British and Indian forces on the Japanese land Army has taken place in Burma. An enemy force of 6000 men which attacked the rear of the 7th Indian Division has been almost liquidated. Our success has been attributed to two main factors: first, the high morale and good training and equipment of the British and Indian troops; and secondly, the tactics by which the 7th Indian Division was made to accept encirclement and to act as a pivot of manœuvres for the destruction of the enemy force by the men inside the "trap" and reinforcements descending from the north. During the whole twenty-one days of fighting, the 7th Indian Division, under General Messervy, was supplied entirely by aircraft, only one of which was lost. The Battle of the Ngakyedauk Pass continued for over a month, and will go down in the annals as an epic. Though on a relatively small scale, it was all the more intense, in which the Japanese plans to segregate and decimate the Fourteenth Army were defeated with immense enemy losses.

THE JAPANESE MOVE TO INFILTRATE TO THE ASSAM-BENGAL RAILWAY, CUT THE MANIPUR ROAD AND ENVELOP IMPHAL.

The new Ledo Road, under construction since December 1942, is being pushed to completion from Assam, across Northern Burma to China's old Burma Road. United States Army engineers were told the job "couldn't be done," but, in spite of the conditions, the task is being completed.

BUILDING THE LEDO ROAD – LIFELINE FROM INDIA TO CHINA.

THE WIVES AND MOTHERS OF NATIVE TRIBESMEN WORKING ON THE LEDO ROAD BRING GIFTS OF FRUIT AND VEGETABLES TO THE WORKMEN.

AN AIRFIELD IS BUILT IN THE REAR OF THE ENEMY: A BURMA FEAT.

WITH THE AIRFIELD COMPLETED, ALLIED AIRCRAFT PROMPTLY STRAFED JAP SUPPLIES.

One of the outstanding feats of the campaign in Burma was the capture by airborne troops of an area hundreds of miles behind the Japanese lines, and its subsequent transformation into an airfield from which Allied fighters and bombers are busily engaged in strafing enemy supply bases and troop concentrations. The original "invasion" was made by ground troops of the famous jungle force commanded by Major-General O. C. Wingate, who was subsequently killed in an air crash. The gliders carrying these troops were commanded by Colonel Philip Cochran, leader of the first Air Commando Force, U.S.A.A.F., whose men also took part in the operation.

In the first landings, some made in darkness, a number of gliders cracked up. But the invading force established their hold on the field and rapidly constructed emergency airstrips on which following troop transports were able to land. The field was held against enemy snipers, and the runways built in the face of Japanese machine-gun nests. Rapid work soon produced a finished airfield.

ONE OF THE LAST PICTURES TAKEN OF MAJOR-GENERAL WINGATE BEFORE HIS DEATH.

SAVAGE COMBATS IN THE JUNGLE FASTNESSES OF MANIPUR.

NEAR KOHIMA, ON THE WAY TO IMPHAL.

On April 1, small parties of Japanese penetrated to the road between Imphal, capital of Manipur State, and Kohima, which road connects Imphal with the railhead at Manipur Road, Assam. Some days previously they had inflicted a defeat on our troops at Ukhrul, in the Manipur Hills. For months the defences of Imphal have been built, and have been ready since the Japs began their movements across the Chindwin River and through the Chin Hills. Imphal, their avowed objective, lies in a plain about 50 miles long by 20 miles wide, and to approach nearer than 10 miles they will have to come to an open battle. The enemy strength is being bled as they move forward: in six weeks they are estimated to have lost 2600 dead. Their later movements between Tiddim and Dimapur suggest an attempt to by-pass Imphal and strike towards the Assam-Bengal railway – main supply route to General Stilwell's Chinese troops.

THE LOOK-OUT OF A NAGA VILLAGE, OVERLOOKING KOHIMA.

RUSSIA'S HURRICANE TRIUMPH IN THE CRIMEA.

BY SPEED AND GENERALSHIP GENERAL MALINOVSKY RETAKES ODESSA.

THE RED ARMY STORM SEVASTOPOL, "HERO CITY".

THE RECAPTURE OF ODESSA BY GENERAL MALINOVSKY: AN OVATION TO SOVIET SOLDIERS BY THE POPULATION, WHO HAD MAINLY LIVED IN THE CATACOMBS.

SEVASTOPOL, THE FAMOUS BLACK SEA PORT, AS IT WAS BEFORE THE GERMAN INVASION. FINALLY EVACUATED IN JULY 1942, THE GREAT BASE WAS STORMED AND RETAKEN BY TOLBUKHIN'S TROOPS ON MAY 10, AFTER A THREE WEEKS' SIEGE.

SEVASTOPOL CITY OF DESOLATION: HOW THE GERMANS FOUND IT AFTER THEIR ENTRY ON JULY 1, 1942. SCARCELY A ROOF REMAINED.

By the overwhelming speed of the Russian blow which took Odessa simultaneously from east and west, many thousands of Germans were trapped in the city and many more thousands killed as they made desperate attempts to escape across the Dniester estuary.

The great naval base of Sevastopol, the last German stronghold in the Crimea, was stormed by the Red Army shortly before midnight of May 9–10, after it had been under siege for three weeks and under direct assault for three days. In 1942, when the Russians were besieged by the Germans, the port held out for eight months and cost the Germans and Rumanians 300,000 casualties. Sevastopol cost Hitler another 112,000 men before it fell to General Tolbukhin's gallant forces. The losses incurred by the enemy were enormous, and thousands who escaped in ships were beaten up and destroyed by the Russian Black Sea Fleet. A few days later smoke still overhung Sevastopol and ruins were smouldering, but remnants of buildings in the centre were decorated here and there with red flags. The last hours were marked by extraordinary scenes of panic on the part of the enemy, who threw down arms and deserted their officers on a basis of *sauve qui peut*. Those who tried to sail away did so vainly. Sixty-nine transports were sunk, fifty-six landing barges, and seventy-three other vessels.

DEVASTATING DAYLIGHT BOMBING ON BERLIN: NOW SAID TO BE ONE VAST RUIN.

FORTRESSES PASSING OVER BERLIN IN THE FIRST MAJOR DAY AIR BATTLE OF MARCH 6: ON MARCH 9, NOT ONE ENEMY FIGHTER CHALLENGED THE U.S. AIR FORCE.

"WE GREET THE FIRST WORKER OF GERMANY – ADOLF HITLER": A SLOGAN DECORATING THE FAÇADE OF A GUTTED FACTORY ON HITLER'S BIRTHDAY.

THE EMPTY SHELL OF LARGE BUILDINGS AND A MASS OF RUBBLE (LEFT) MARK THE CORNER OF BISMARCK STREET AND BERLINER STREET, BERLIN.

The sequence of U.S. daylight raids on Berlin on March 6, 8 and 9, when bomb after bomb rained down through a layer of clouds on the heart of Berlin, had a remarkable sequel in the enemy fighter defences. On the first visit the Eighth Air Force was furiously attacked by German fighters. The U.S. lost sixty-eight bombers and eleven fighters, but they shot down 176 of the enemy. On Wednesday, 8th, fewer German fighters were encountered, though the raiders were more numerous. On March 9 not one enemy fighter was seen. The long-range escort-fighter is the key to the disaster which confronts Germany.

These revealing pictures by radio from a neutral source give a good idea of the really severe bomb damage in Berlin following the many heavy raids carried out by R.A.F. and American bombers. Present-day Berlin presents a very different face to her inhabitants than that familiar to the world in 1939. Whole districts in the heart of the city, as well as in the outlying factory areas, have been razed to the ground.
The great new Air Ministry is severely damaged. On Hitler's birthday Berlin was decorated with swastikas and slogans as usual, but this time they flew over ruins and heaps of débris.

PUTTING UP A "MAGNIFICENT RESISTANCE" – THE FRENCH AND YUGOSLAV PARTISANS.

THE MEN WHOM MR. CHURCHILL PRAISED.

AN OUTSTANDING LEADER.

THE MAQUIS-GUERILLAS OF FRANCE.

GENERAL TITO. THE COMMANDER-IN-CHIEF OF THE YUGOSLAV PARTISANS, NOW RAISED TO THE STATUS OF A FULL ALLIED COMMANDER.

YUGOSLAV PARTISANS UNDER MARSHAL TITO ARE WAGING STRONG GUERILLA WARFARE IN THEIR MOUNTAINS AGAINST THE GERMANS: A PATROL ADVANCES.

A PATROL GROUP OF YOUNG FRENCH PATRIOTS SET OUT THROUGH THE SNOW. MOST WEAR CIVILIAN CLOTHES, BUT SOME RETAIN FORMER UNIFORMS.

The Partisan Army in Yugoslavia, led by Marshal Tito, has been supplied with war material by the Allies as far as militarily possible. Partisan operations have on numerous occasions been supported by our air forces and close liaison has been maintained by Allied officers with Tito. This guerilla army, fighting with desperate courage in its mountains, has engaged up to fifteen German divisions, the principal fighting being in Eastern Bosnia and the Sanjak. In Dalmatia and Croatia the Partisans have also well held their own and inflicted many sanguinary defeats on the Germans as well as sabotaging their lines of communication. Both in Italy and in the Middle East numbers of women and children have been evacuated to rest camps, including also combatant women, many of whom have thrown themselves into the fight with desperate indifference to risks.

This picture is a still from a film made at one of the secret bases of the Maquis – the French guerillas who are fighting in the Savoy mountain region of the Maquis. The film was smuggled out of France to London, and shows the routine life of these young patriots before Darnand, the Himmler of France, launched his main attack on them early in February. Their resistance against Vichy and the Germans – who are obliged to hold about 6000 troops in the district ready to go into action if necessary – is more than a matter of "thorn in the flesh" sabotage, for these guerillas are laying a solid foundation for offensive aid for the Allied expeditionary forces when the time comes to set about the liberation of France. A dramatic appeal was re-broadcast recently by the B.B.C. to France on behalf of this patriot army, asking Frenchmen to join the Maquis.

THE BRILLIANT ONWARD SURGE OVER THE GUSTAV LINE.

SHAFTS OF SUNLIGHT PIERCING A HEAVY SMOKE-SCREEN LAID DOWN WHEN NEW ZEALAND TROOPS FOUGHT THEIR WAY INTO CASSINO. SMOKE IS BEING USED ON A LARGE SCALE TO SCREEN TROOP MOVEMENTS IN THE ITALIAN CAMPAIGN.

INFANTRYMEN OF A CANADIAN DIVISION ON THE EIGHTH ARMY FRONT MOVING UP TO TAKE OVER POSITIONS CAPTURED BY INDIAN TROOPS.

General Alexander's new offensive in Italy opened on May 11. His intention seems to be to break the Gustav Line where it follows the Rapido across our second sector, to break the Adolf Hitler Line where it runs five to nine miles in the rear, and to move up the corridor of the Sacco, to reach Frosinone. On May 14, Kesselring was pulling his guns out of the hills flanking the southern edge of the valley, while British tanks were smashing enemy strong-points at point-blank range. The war of to-day is thick with smoke laid down to screen bridges and to baffle the enemy, who, in turn, uses smoke against the attacker. In the full-scale Allied assault aimed at breaking the Gustav Line, it was by smoke that observers were able to mark the places at which our forces had established bridges across the Rapido and Gari Rivers.

WHAT REMAINS OF THE HISTORIC MONASTERY OF MONTE CASSINO.

CASSINO MONASTERY TO-DAY, AN OBJECT LESSON IN THE TERRIBLE EFFECTS OF MODERN WARFARE: UNRECOGNISABLE RUINS JUTTING UP LIKE MOUNTAIN CRAGS, NOT LONG AGO A HISTORIC CENTRE OF CHRISTIANITY AND EDUCATION, WHICH THE GERMANS MADE INTO A FORTRESS.

Monte Cassino Monastery is a mass of ruins; only the north-west wall remains completely intact, and underneath it a few parts of the original building, including one small chapel, are standing. The long struggle is at last over, and high above the shattered town of Cassino, one of the world's most publicised battlefields, the Monastery stands like jagged spikes of rock on a hill-top.
General Alexander, having ascertained that the Germans were employing the historic Monastery of St. Benedict as a fire-control tower, was reluctantly compelled to commence a siege of it on February 18 last. On May 18, as the British stormed the town below, the Poles, creeping up the steep hill along what they call "The Lane of the Dead Men," because of their heavy losses, captured the grim shell of the monastery after desperate fighting.

THE BEACH-HEAD TROOPS LINK UP WITH THE FIFTH ARMY.

THE HISTORIC FIRST MOMENT OF MEETING BETWEEN PATROLS OF THE FIFTH ARMY AND THE ANZIO BEACH-HEAD FORCE AT BORGO GRAPPA. IN THE DISTANCE, AN ANZIO SERGEANT ADVANCES CAUTIOUSLY TO MEET AN AMERICAN SERGEANT.

After a comparative lull on the Anzio beach-head for the last three months, on May 23 it suddenly burst into life from the American sector overlooking the flat country towards Cisterna. On the 24th – Empire Day – as the U.S. troops of the Fifth Army occupied Terracina along the coast and advanced towards the Pontine Marshes, the Beach-head Force had crossed the Appian Way, threatening the Germans in their retreat. In the meantime British tanks had crossed the River Moletta, on the left flank of the beach-head, and advanced to the north-east, towards Campoleone. Allied and enemy tanks clashed in one of the bitterest tank battles on the Beach-head Front. The Allies captured many hundreds of prisoners, and overran hundreds of German strong-points. In the early hours of May 25 the Fifth Army's main front contacted patrols from the Beach-head Force, thus bringing to a climax the spectacular advance of more than 60 miles in only 14 days.

STEPS ON THE ROAD TO ROME – THE GREAT ALLIED OFFENSIVE.

Fifth Army forward troops cleared German rearguards from Rome about 8 o'clock on the evening of June 4 and obtained control of the city. The next day Rome was in holiday mood; shops were closed and the population thronged the streets, acclaiming the Allied troops with tremendous enthusiasm. Bunches of flowers were hurled into passing cars, and any soldier who stopped for even a moment was immediately the centre of a crowd eager to show him welcome.

As soon as it was known that the Allied commanders were holding a conference on Capitoline Hill, a procession of several hundred persons marched with flags up the Corso to greet the C.-in-C. of the Army of Liberation. There was no questioning the genuineness of the Romans' hatred for the Germans. The Pope appeared on the balcony of St. Peter's, and addressing the vast crowd, including men of the Fifth Army assembled in the Piazza, gave thanks to God that Rome had been saved the horrors of war. His Holiness also invited Allied war correspondents and cameramen to a conference in the Throne Room of the Vatican shortly after its liberation.

CROSSING THE MELFA RIVER: ADVANCING FROM AQUINO, FIFTH ARMY TROOPS FOUND THIS BRIDGE "BLOWN," SO THE INFANTRY WADED ACROSS.

PART OF THE HUGE CROWD IN ST. PETER'S SQUARE WHEN, ON JUNE 5, THE POPE THANKED THE ALLIES FOR SPARING ROME THE HORRORS OF BOMBARDMENT.

CAMERA OCCASIONS: NEWS ITEMS OF GENERAL INTEREST AT HOME AND ABROAD.

THE TOWN OF OYONNAX IS TAKEN OVER BY THE MEN OF THE "MAQUIS": FRENCH PATRIOTS MARCH THROUGH THE TOWN.

November 11, 1943, will long be remembered in Oyonnax, for on that day the town was taken over by the men of the "Maquis," while they held their Armistice Service and placed a wreath on the War Memorial.

ROCKET GUN BEING MANIPULATED. HOME GUARDS MAN MANY ROCKET BATTERIES.

Anti-aircraft rocket guns have been used against night raiders since 1941, most manned by the Home Guard.

VESUVIUS AT NIGHT: AN AWE-INSPIRING SPECTACLE TO WATCH AS THE GLOWING LAVA SPREADS.

The recent eruption of Mount Vesuvius has been the worst since 1906. Two small towns, San Sebastiano and Massa di Somma, were engulfed by the lava stream, whilst clouds of steam hung over the whole area.

AT THE SWEARING-IN CEREMONY OF THE NEW BADOGLIO GOVERNMENT: COUNT SFORZA AND BENEDETTO CROCE (RIGHT).

Marshal Badoglio recently announced the constitution of the new National Government of Liberated Italy, in which all six democratic parties are now represented.

THE DOMINION PREMIERS IN LONDON FOR THE IMPERIAL CONFERENCE: (L. TO R.) MR. MACKENZIE KING (CANADA), GEN. SMUTS (S. AFRICA), MR. PETER FRASER (NEW ZEALAND), MR. JOHN CURTIN (AUSTRALIA) – WITH MR. CHURCHILL.

The welcome arrival in London of the four Dominion Premiers was followed by an inaugural meeting where Mr. Churchill greeted the nation's distinguished guests.

ANOTHER HITLER-MUSSOLINI MEETING, BUT THIS TIME THERE IS ONLY ONE DICTATOR. MUSSOLINI IS REPORTED ILL.

Hitler and Mussolini have met once more, presumably to discuss the coming Allied invasion of Europe, but Mussolini is no longer of any importance for his rule is finished in Italy.

SCENE OF THE TRAGIC SHOOTINGS OF 47 OFFICERS: A COMPOUND AT STALAG LUFT III.; SHOWING PRISONERS' HUTS.

His Majesty's Government was profoundly shocked to hear that forty-seven officers of the Royal Air Force, Dominion, and Air Forces had been shot by the Germans after a mass escape from Stalag Luft III.

THE SECOND EXPLOSION SHAKES BOMBAY: THE WHITE TRACERY IS CAUSED BY SMOKE TRAILING FROM BURSTING PARTICLES.

On April 14 an accidental fire broke out in a ship in Bombay Docks, spread to some ammunition and caused the violent explosions and clouds of smoke and flame shown in our photograph.

AS ALLIED FORCES LANDED ON THE ISLAND OF ELBA, TROOPS STREAMED ASHORE NEAR MARINA DE CAMPO.

The capture of the island of Elba by French forces was announced on June 20 after twenty-four hours of stubborn resistance by the Germans. The capital, Porto Ferraio, was wrecked beyond belief.

PART OF THE BEATRIX POTTER GIFT: HIGH YEWDALE FARM, CONISTON, LANCASHIRE. THE BEQUESTS ALSO INCLUDE A SUM OF £5000.

MISS BEATRIX POTTER, FAMOUS AUTHOR, DIED ON DEC 22.

THE WEDDING OF H.M. KING PETER OF YUGOSLAVIA AND PRINCESS ALEXANDRA OF GREECE: KING PETER WITH HIS BRIDE AFTER THE CEREMONY.

Beatrix Potter, famous author of books for children and the originator of the Peter Rabbit books, died on December 22. For several years she designed Queen Mary's Christmas-cards. Under the will of the late Mrs. William Heelis – Beatrix Potter – the National Trust will acquire the many properties she owned in the Lake District. During her lifetime Beatrix Potter did much to conserve the beauties of the Lake District, by gifts to the Trust, and by her practical example as a farmer and breeder of Herdwick sheep.

The wedding of King Peter of Yugoslavia and Princess Alexandra of Greece took place at the Yugoslav Embassy, Upper Grosvenor Street, on Monday, March 20.
Earlier this year it was reported that controversy between King Peter's Government in Cairo and General Tito, Commander-in-Chief of the Yugoslav partisans, was taking on disagreeable proportions, and the King's Government was facing what Reuter terms "the gravest crisis of its career."

THE FIRST WAVE OF THE SEABORNE ASSAULT HITS THE NORMANDY BEACHES.

THE FIRST WAVE OF THE ASSAULT HITS ONE OF THE BEACHES. TROOPS ARE SEEN FOLLOWING THE FIRST TANKS PLUNGING THROUGH THE WATER TO THE SHORE IN THE BACKGROUND, WHILE OTHERS, TAKING COVER BEHIND OBSTACLES RETURN THE ENEMY'S FIRE.

LANDING, FORMING UP, AND MARCHING OFF: BRITISH TROOPS WITH A FORMIDABLE ARRAY OF LANDING CRAFT.

In the early hours of D-Day, Tuesday, June 6, 1944, the first wave of the Allied seaborne assault troops stormed up the beaches of Normandy. Long stretches of the beaches were covered by a withering cross-fire from German pill-boxes. Over 4,000 ships were involved, with thousands of smaller craft, and 11,000 front-line aircraft were available for operations.

The success of the landings was made possible by three outstanding factors. The first was the brilliant co-ordination of the Allied Air Forces, which provided an air umbrella of unequalled protection, and the absence of any challenge of note. The second was the powerful support of the great guns of the Fleet, including the battleships "Nelson" (16-in. guns), "Warspite" (15-in.), "Ramillies" (15-in.), U.S. "Nevada" (14-in.), U.S. "Arkansas" (12-in.), and U.S. "Texas" (14-in.), which pulverised coastal guns within reach. The third was the brilliant manœuvres of Allied paratroops.

PRE-INVASION BOMBING: DAY AND NIGHT PRECISION.

ALLIED RAIDS SMASH VITAL WESTERN RAIL LINKS IN EUROPE.

PINPOINT PRECISION: "BEFORE AND AFTER" VIEWS.

A LUFTWAFFE SIGNALS EQUIPMENT DEPÔT AT ST. CYR, NEAR VERSAILLES, BEFORE IT WAS VISITED BY LANCASTERS OF R.A.F. BOMBER COMMAND...

ACCURATELY PLACED CLUSTERS OF BOMBS BURSTING ON THE IMPORTANT RAILROAD MARSHALLING-YARDS AT HIRSON, 120 MILES INLAND IN FRANCE, DURING A RAID BY US MARAUDERS ON MARCH 25.

...AND THE SAME TARGET AFTER PRECISION BOMBING BY THE LANCASTERS ON THE NIGHT OF APRIL 10. THE DEPÔT HAS BEEN VIRTUALLY OBLITERATED.

It was General H. H. Arnold, Commanding General of the U.S. Army Air Forces, who said that Allied bombing attacks on Europe "are by no means merely preliminaries to invasion. They *are* invasion." General Arnold was speaking at Washington on March 28, and he pointed out that the continued bombing of Europe was in fact defeating the enemy in advance. The pictures reproduced here grimly illustrate the General's remarks. They show the tremendous confusion caused to communication lines on which the enemy can no longer depend for moving his armies and supplies to meet the coming Allied invasion in the west. These attacks on key railway centres are carried out with "pinpoint" precision.

THE BATTLE OF NORMANDY: SCENES OF SHARP COMBAT WITH FIGHTING IN PROGRESS.

INCIDENTS ON THE NORMAN FRONT: SHERMAN TANKS ON THE WAY TO TILLY-SUR-SEULLES.

A LARGE GERMAN COAST-DEFENCE GUN ON THE CHERBOURG PENINSULA, WITH ITS DEAD CREW.

The first week's operation on the coast of Normandy saw a bridgehead firmly established of some sixty miles in length and steadily increasing in depth, on the Cherbourg Peninsula. Caen, desperately defended, still stood at bay. Carentan fell, and American troops were steadily closing in. In this area there are (apart from fishing harbours) only two ports, Cherbourg, and Caen, linked to the sea by a ten-mile ship canal, of immense value for an invading army.

Generally speaking, the country is favourable to mobile manœuvre and resembles Southern England. The rivers are small, the hills low and undulating, the roads many. Some twenty miles inland it is largely forested, which could constitute large tank obstacles. Some of the bitterest fighing of the war has been the lot of our troops since the first landing was made but the bridge heads are already almost safe and the phase of consolidation is well on the way.

THE BRITISH PRESS ONTO CAEN: THE AMERICANS CUT OFF THE CHERBOURG PENINSULA.

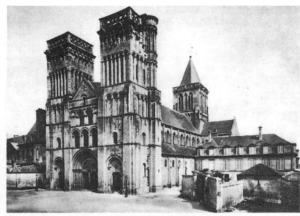

THE ABBAYE-AUX DAMES OF CAEN OR THE CHURCH OF TRINITY, FOUNDED BY MATILDA, WIFE OF WILLIAM THE CONQUEROR, IN 1062.

HIS MAJESTY ARRIVES ON FRENCH SOIL: MET BY GENERAL MONTGOMERY, THEY ARE SEEN WALKING IN THE BRITISH SECTOR.

PONT L'ABBÉ TAKEN BY AMERICAN TROOPS AFTER BITTER FIGHTING. IN THE FOREGROUND IS A WRECKED GERMAN ANTI-TANK GUN.

Caen, towards which the Allied armies of liberation are drawing steadily nearer, is the chief town of the department of Calvados. Situated on the Orne, about 9 miles from the coast, it is connected with the sea by a canal. Caen first rose to importance in the time of William the Conqueror, whose beautiful churches are still the chief ornaments of the town. In 1346 Caen, at that time "a city greater than any in England save London," was taken and pillaged by Edward III. of England; and Henry V. again captured it in 1417. France did not succeed in finally wresting it from the English until 1450.

His Majesty the King went to Normandy on June 16 for a conference at General Montgomery's H.Q., where he decorated a number of officers and other ranks now serving in France. In Tierceville and Courseulles, groups of French men, women, and children gathered at the corners to wave and cheer as the King drove past. The last time his Majesty was in France was in 1939, when he toured the Maginot Line, and there could be no more convincing proof of the solid foothold that has been secured on French soil than this royal surprise visit within a few days of the Allied landing.

Neither coastal defences nor inland flooding have prevented the steady Allied advance in Normandy, and the Cherbourg Peninsula is now cut and the wedge widened and strengthened. The outstanding incident of the fighting on June 18 was the reduction of a German underground position at Douvres near the sea, which had been holding out ever since the landings. In view of its great strength, it had been by-passed, but the garrison, living in concrete chambers deep down, had become a nuisance. Tanks and a detachment of a Royal Marines commando stormed the position and took the surviving garrison prisoner.

THE FINAL ASSAULT ON THE PORT OF CHERBOURG.

THE DUST AND HEAT OF WAR HANG OVER THE NORMANDY COUNTRYSIDE AS AMERICAN ANTI-TANK GUNNERS GO INTO ACTION IN THE BATTLE OF THE CHERBOURG PENINSULA.

"MULBERRY", THE PREFABRICATED PORT OF THE NORMANDY BRIDGEHEADS.

ONE OF SEVERAL LONG RUNWAYS ON FLOATING PIERS, WHERE THE PARTS FIT LIKE MECCANO PIECES, MOORED TO HEAVY RAMPS AND "SPUD" PIERHEADS.

A mighty feat of engineering is pictured in these views of "Mulberry," or "Port Winston," as the Merchant Navy call it – a feat that has revolutionised amphibious warfare. Clamped off the inhospitable shores of Arromanches Beaches, in Normandy, is to-day a great harbour able to vie with that of Gibraltar, all pre-fabricated in Britain and towed out in sections when the D-Day landings had established a provisional beach-head.

THIS GREAT TUNNEL IN FORT DU ROULE, THIRD STOREY UNDERGROUND, CONTAINED TORPEDOES, OTHER NAVAL STORES, AND HUNDREDS OF CASES OF COGNAC.

The great port of Cherbourg fell to the arms of the U.S. forces under Lieut.-General Omar Bradley, after a brilliant advance up the Cotentin Peninsula and a brief but violent siege lasting only six days. On June 21 the Germans were forced to withdraw into the town's inner defences. On June 23 almost all the heights commanding the town were in American hands. It was then a doomed town, but the Germans refused an offer to surrender. On Sunday, June 25 the stronghold was entered from the west and street-fighting began. Meanwhile, a task force of warships, commanded by Rear-Admiral Morton L. Deyo, U.S.N. engaged the German heavy guns from 15,000 yards.

On June 26, while the huge guns of Fort du Roule at Cherbourg were still firing, U.S. infantry blasted their way three storeys underground, blowing out the Germans. Many enemy were killed, but hundreds walked out with their hands up, including 200 from a great tunnel packed with naval stores ranging from torpedoes to hundreds of cases of cognac. From this fortress the German C.-in-C., Lieut.-General von Schlieben, emerged and surrendered.

THE WAR IN BURMA: THE CLEARING OF THE KOHIMA-IMPHAL ROAD.

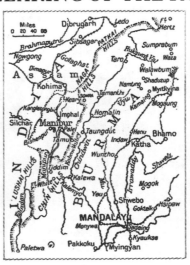

SECTIONS OF A MOUNTAIN GUN CARRIED BY INDIAN TROOPS ON THE IMPHAL FRONT TO THEIR POSITION IN ONE OF THE BRITISH "BOXES". THE ENEMY LOST OVER 25,000 KILLED AND WOUNDED IN FIVE MONTHS' CAMPAIGNING.

THE ADVANCING FRONT IN BURMA: GENERAL LENTAIGNE'S FORCE AND CHINESE ENTERED MOGAUNG. JAPS SUFFERED HEAVY DEFEAT.

AUXILIARY FUEL TANKS IN A TRANSPORT 'PLANE. R.A.F. TRANS- PORT COMMAND HAVE DROPPED EVERY FORM OF SUPPLY TO ISOLATED UNITS, ENABLING THEM TO CARRY ON THE WAR.

The South-East Asia Command communiqué on June 23 announced that British troops on the previous day had cleared the last of the Japanese forces from the Kohima-Imphal road in Burma. The longdrawn battle for this 90-mile road on the frontier of India and Burma began when, late in March, it was cut by the Japanese, thus isolating our forces in the British-held base of Imphal. The Imphal garrison thereafter had to be supplied mainly by air, while ground forces began a tenacious fight for the recovery of the road.

The keynote of the operations leading to the expulsion of the Japanese has been the perfect co-operation among all departments of the Services. The patient tactics and fighting ability of the troops of several nations are bringing their reward in the shape of a heavy defeat of the Japanese forces committed to the defence of Northern Burma. Ukhrul, some 35 miles north-east of Imphal, is now in Allied hands. Japanese casualties in dead alone on the Burma front are about 40,000.

THE GROWING MIGHT OF AMERICA'S SEA AND AIRFLEETS IN THE PACIFIC.

BATTLE OF THE PHILIPPINE SEA: ANOTHER US VICTORY.

BOMBING OF TOKYO FROM BASES IN CHINA.

WHILST A PALL OF SMOKE HANGS OVER TWO JAPANESE WARSHIPS (RIGHT), A BOMB IS SEEN EXPLODING NEAR AN ENEMY CRUISER (RIGHT FOREGROUND) DURING THE BATTLE OF THE PHILIPPINE SEA, WHICH EVENTUATED INTO A GREAT U.S. VICTORY.

THE SIZE OF THE SUPER-FORTRESS MAY BE ESTIMATED FROM THIS PHOTOGRAPH OF WORKMEN BESIDE A VERTICAL FIN.

In a surprise attack on a strong Japanese fleet on the afternoon of June 19, U.S. carrier-based aircraft sank four, or possibly five, of its ships, damaged nine or ten others, some of them severely, and shot down fifteen to twenty enemy aircraft, all for the loss of forty-nine U.S. aircraft. An unofficial summary of Japanese shipping losses so far states that 2468 ships have been sunk or damaged, 641 of them warships. The strength of the

American Fleet has been reliably described as "reaching staggering proportions," and by the end of this year it will have no fewer than 100 aircraft-carriers. In the air, the most interesting news is that the new giant Super-Fortress bombers attacked Tokyo on June 15. They are powered by four Wright Cyclone sixteen-cylinder radial engines rated at 2200 h.p. Bristling with guns they will be used on a world scale.

THE CAPTURE OF THE MARIANAS ISLANDS: SAIPAN, GUAM AND TINIAN.

UNITED STATES MARINES WADING ASHORE AT TINIAN ISLAND, IN THE PACIFIC, TO REINFORCE AMERICAN ASSAULT TROOPS FIGHTING INLAND.

A ROW OF HOUSES, INHABITED BY NATIVES IN AGANA, CAPITAL OF GUAM.

AMERICAN TROOPS ADVANCING ALONG THE BEACH AT SAIPAN AFTER DIS- EMBARKING FROM AMPHIBIOUS TRACTORS AND OTHER VEHICLES.

Saipan, whose reduction by the U.S. was effected on July 10, denoted a major victory of the Pacific war, and was quickly reflected by the downfall of Tojo. It was a most important Japanese base in the Marianas, with good and well-developed airfields, and in the hands of the Allies will be able to give shore-based cover to naval task forces and amphibious operations over practically the whole of the great triangle enclosing the Marianas

and Carolines. It will facilitate the future invasion of Japan, for it lies only 1400 miles distant from Tokyo, in the centre of the Japanese mainland.

On July 20 U.S. Marines and Infantry began their expected invasion of the much-battered Guam Island, landing under cover of a heavy bombardment from carrier aircraft and warships.

THE BATTLE OF THE FLYING BOMB: HITLER'S LATEST ATTACK ON ENGLAND.

THE FLASH OF A FLYING BOMB BLOWN UP BY GUNFIRE. A.-A. GUNNERS HAVE TAKEN A HEAVY TOLL OF THESE ROBOTS.

Germany's latest "secret weapon," was launched indiscriminately against southern England in an attempted terror attack. Measures were swiftly taken against the flying bomb, resulting in a high proportion being shot down. It is now generally accepted that these robots are jet-propelled by means of a unit mounted above the main fuselage. The launching is said to be from inclined rails, and the take-off may be assisted by either catapult or rocket installation. Once launched, and having reached the required height, its flight is automatically controlled on a straight course by means of a "gyro pilot." The size of the flying bomb has been officially estimated at 25 ft. 4½ in. long, with a wing-span of sixteen ft., and it reaches a speed probably in the region of 350 m.p.h. A bright light is usually visible in the tail, and when this goes out and the noise of propulsion ceases, the robot goes into a dive, exploding within five to fifteen seconds.

Mr. Herbert Morrison, in a speech in London on September 6, announcing that the Battle of London against the flying bombs had been won, referred to the "immense resources" which Germany employed on this weapon, even to the detriment of her own fighting troops. Of more than 8000 flying bombs launched, 2300 got through into the London region; in the first week of attack about 33 per cent. of the bombs launched were brought down, the same proportion reaching London; in the last week of the attack some 75 per cent. were being brought down, with only 9 per cent. reaching London, and on the best day, August 28, out of 101 bombs approaching the coast of England 97 were destroyed, only four getting through our defences.

GUNNERS EXHIBITING THE COMPRESSED AIR CONTAINER WHICH DRIVES THE GYROSCOPE OF A FLYING BOMB.

AN UNDERGROUND TOWN IMPERVIOUS TO FLYING BOMBS.

A SCHOOL CLASS DURING SHELLING OF DOVER: IT TAKES LESS THAN A MINUTE TO GET FROM CLASS-ROOM TO SHELTER.

Here in Southern England, nature has provided safe shelters for the residents – deep caves in which they sleep soundly, oblivious to the flying bombs. Many amenities have been provided, and the cave-dwellers have organised their own social life underground.

LONDON'S MAMMOUTH SHELTERS 100 FT UNDERGROUND.

A PARTY OF LONDONERS, ON THEIR WAY TO THEIR LIVING QUARTERS UNDERGROUND, WALKING ALONG ONE OF THE APPROACH TUNNELS OF A DEEP SHELTER.

London's mammoth deep shelters were made accessible to the public during the attack. The shelters are built 100 ft. underground, air-conditioned, brightly lit by "daylight" bulbs, and are provided with a canteen each, a hospital, and other amenities. Dormitories hold tiers of bunks divided into sections to house complete families in privacy. Those using the new shelters were delighted with them. Said one, "There's no noise, and all you can hear is the rumble of tube trains in the distance. They are selling sandwiches and buns at the canteen and there is a place for the kiddies to play."

LIVING THE LIVES OF TROGLODYTES FAR UNDERGROUND.

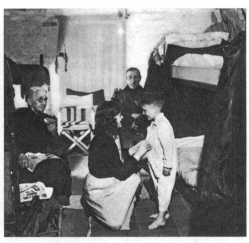

BEDTIME FOR THIS LITTLE BOY: HE CANNOT REMEMBER ANY OTHER BED, FOR HE IS ONLY FIVE YEARS OLD.

The cave shown here is one of the Athol Terrace caves, long ago hewn out of the chalk cliffs of Dover for their lime. In these caves of Britain's "front-line" city live a handful of Dover citizens who have made the caves their permanent home.

THE SYSTEMATIC PARALYSING OF GERMANY'S COMMUNICATIONS BY LAND AND SEA.

THE ALLIED AIR FORCES WHITTLING AWAY GERMANY'S RESOURCES: A BOMB HIT ON A NAZI TRAIN HAULING SUPPLIES TO ENEMY LINES.

BOMBING THE LOIRE BRIDGES AND CUTTING GERMAN COMMUNICATIONS.

WAR ON U-BOATS: A SUNDERLAND, HAVING SIGHTED A U-BOAT HAS ATTACKED AT LOW LEVEL. A MINUTE LATER SHE SANK.

While Herr Hitler is stringing up generals in his Wehrmacht *putsch*, his armies east, west and south are being rapidly denuded of necessary supplies in every direction by the Allied Air Forces of U.S.A. and Britain. Outstanding, perhaps, is the concerted attack on his oil supplies, whether refineries or dumps. In France the shortage of oil supplies prevents any elasticity in the German retreat. Berlin's war industries have been bombed now almost to extinction, and Berlin is to-day very nearly valueless to the Germans so far as war production goes. Another target for the Strategic Air Forces are railway trains, and especially engines, of which hundreds have been destroyed, again striking very vitally at enemy communications. At sea, too, his merchant ships and escort vessels are suffering heavily.

THE EASTERN FRONT: THE RED ARMY'S GREAT ADVANCE.

CITIZENS OF MINSK WATCHING THEIR HOMES BEING BURNED BY THE GERMANS BEFORE THE LIBERATING RUSSIAN TROOPS DROVE OUT THE ENEMY.

A STRIKING ILLUSTRATION OF THE SPEED WITH WHICH THE RED ARMY ADVANCES. ARTILLERY AND TANKS ARE SEEN FORCING A RIVER CROSSING IN AN ADVANCE TOWARDS LVOV.

Less than three weeks from the launching of their great offensive on June 23, the Red Army had at some points advanced 250 miles, and the momentum of their forward sweep showed no signs of slackening. In the first week of the offensive the Germans were reported to have lost upwards of 80,000 killed alone, with uncounted thousands wounded, trapped or prisoners of war. By July 7 the Red Army was surging forward on a front of 400 miles from northern White Russia to south of Kovel, and by July 10 were reported to have reached the Latvian border. On the same day it was announced that the vital railway junction of Lida had been captured, and that the Russian flood was within 70 miles of the borders of East Prussia. The great advance still continued unchecked.

A BID FOR POLISH UNITY.

FINLAND TO MAKE PEACE WITH RUSSIA?

THE PRIME MOVER IN A BID FOR POLISH UNITY: H.E. THE PREMIER OF THE POLISH REPUBLIC, M. STANISLAW MIKOLAJCZYK. A PORTRAIT OF KARSH.

THE RUSSIAN FRONTS IN WHITE RUSSIA AND FINLAND, ON JUNE 26 WHEN VITEBSK FELL.

FIELD-MARSHAL MANNERHEIM. PRESIDENT RYTI RESIGNED ON AUGUST 1 AND MANNERHEIM AGREED TO ACCEPT THE PRESIDENCY.

M. Stanislaw Mikolajczyk, Polish Prime Minister, visited Moscow for discussions with Soviet leaders and with Polish members of the Committee of National Liberation recently in a bid to bring together all substantial Polish forces.

A new Russian offensive against Finland began on June 9, and by June 20 the important Finnish town of Viipuri (Viborg) had fallen to the Red Army. The Finnish President, Ryti, resigned suddenly on August 1 and Marshal Mannerheim agreed to accept the Presidency. The upheaval almost certainly means that Finland is making a final attempt to conclude peace with Russia before a German collapse.

RUSSIA'S IRRESISTIBLE ADVANCE: ROKOSSOVSKY REACHES THE VISTULA.

ON THE WAY TO RIGA: HEAVY SOVIET SELF-PROPELLED GUNS CROSSING A RIVER IN LATVIA AS THE RED ARMY RACES TOWARDS THE LATVIAN CAPITAL, CAPTURING MANY PLACES ON THE WAY.

THE EASTERN FRONT ON AUGUST 3, AS THE RED ARMY APPROACHED WARSAW, AND CUT OFF THE GERMAN FORCES IN ESTONIA AND LATVIA BY REACHING THE GULF OF RIGA.

On August 3, the Germans were in sorry plight. They had thrown in more reserves to stem if possible the Russian advance towards the East Prussian border, but had been beaten back with large losses. Rokossovsky had Warsaw in his grip, Koniev was advancing on Cracow, and in the North, the Russian forces had reached the Gulf of Riga, hence cutting off the many German divisions in Estonia and Latvia. Praga, the Warsaw suburb on the eastern bank of the River Vistula, has been liberated by Marshal Rokossovsky's joint Soviet-Polish forces after more than five weeks of the bitterest fighting of the summer offensive.

MASS EXTERMINATION OF PRISONERS AT MAJDANEK CAMP.

THE GAS CELLS INTO WHICH THE PRISONERS WERE PACKED SO TIGHTLY THAT THEY DIED ON THEIR FEET AS THE POISON GAS WAS PUMPED IN.

SOME OF THE PASSPORTS AND IDENTITY CARDS BELONGING TO THE VICTIMS OF NAZI BRUTALITY AT MAJDANEK CAMP.

The Majdanek camp was called by the Germans themselves "the camp of annihilation"; built over an area of 20 square kilometres it was never intended to provide permanent accommodation for the inmates. In ferro-concrete gas cells victims were packed so tightly that they died on their feet as the gas was pumped in. Fifteen minutes later the executioners removed the dead. In the centre of the camp stands a huge stone building – the world's biggest crematorium. In this crematorium are five large ovens, where five furnaces were never allowed to go out. Day and night, pillars of black smoke belched from the chimneys, as the bodies of the prisoners were dragged from the gas chambers and burnt. One thousand four hundred corpses were so disposed of every twenty-four hours, and the ashes sent to Germany as fertiliser for Nazi kitchen gardens.

POLISH HEROISM: THE UNDERGROUND ARMY AND THE WARSAW REVOLT.

NO. 9 UNIT IN ACTION NEAR ZAMOSC: THE HELMETS AND GUNS ARE POLISH, HIDDEN IN 1939. THEY ARE AGAIN IN USE AGAINST THE COMMON ENEMY.

A UNIT OF THE POLISH UNDERGROUND ARMY IN THE VILNO DISTRICT RECEIVING LAST ORDERS BEFORE AN ATTACK. NOTE THE WHITE CAMOUFLAGE CAPES.

The Polish underground army, as well as the underground movement as a whole, is magnificently organised, despite a woeful lack of arms, and the Germans suffer no illusions about its strength; they can gauge it from the precision with which simultaneous attacks are made on railways or mills, or particular sets of offices, in different parts of Poland. The various units of the underground army, for the most part, train in the huge forests which cover vast tracts of land in Poland. Since the Red Army has appeared over the Polish border, the underground forces have intensified their struggle against the enemy.

BRAVE FIGHTERS IN A PREMATURE UPRISING.

THIS WOMAN, FOUND SUFFERING FROM A HIGH FEVER IN A WARSAW CELLAR, IS BEINT CARRIED IN A DECK CHAIR TO THE ROUND-UP OF CIVILIANS FOR A GERMAN CAMP.

It was on August 1 that the Polish Patriot Army in Warsaw rose in an effort to seize the capital from the German troops in occupation. Two months of heroic fighting followed, until, having been without water for some days, and facing literal starvation, the patriots surrendered.

STARVED CIVILIANS SURRENDER.

A RADIOED PICTURE OF A STREET SCENE IN WARSAW AFTER THE SURRENDER, SHOWING STARVED AND WEARY CIVILIANS HERDED TOGETHER FOR REMOVAL BY GERMANS.

The announcement of their capitulation was contained in the following official message from the Commander of the Polish Home Army: "Warsaw has fallen, after having exhausted all means of fighting and all food supplies, on the sixty-third day of her heroic struggle against the overwhelming superiority of the enemy. On October 2, at 22.00 hours, the defenders of Warsaw fired the last shots." Thus ended a prolonged

WARSAW HAS FALLEN AFTER BITTER RESISTANCE.

WARSAW WAS FORCED TO SURRENDER THROUGH LACK OF SUP-PLIES: (L. TO R.) DR. BARTOSZEWSKI, COUNTESS TARNOWSKA, AND TWO OTHER POLISH PATRIOTS, SEEKING A TRUCE.

struggle in which untold miseries and privations overtook the patriot troops and the civilians of Warsaw, many of whom lived and died in cellars and drain-pipes during the battle. Their Commander, General Bor, was subsequently reported to be in German hands.

ON THE NORMANDY FRONT: THE BATTLE FOR CAEN: ARMOURED AND INFANTRY FORCES GO INTO ACTION.

THE FIRST ENTRY OF THE CANADIANS INTO CAEN: TROOPS MOVING CAUTIOUSLY IN SEARCH OF ENEMY SNIPERS.

Caen, capital of Calvados, fell to British and Canadian forces of the Second Army on July 9, after one of the most massive assaults from air, sea, and land Rommel has ever had to face in the war. The victory was won against fierce German resistance, both at the approaches to the town and in the suburbs themselves. The Germans fought back into the streets over open ridges and cornfields, through the woods and valleys, in which defensive works formed a ring of steel round the place. "The Times" Special Correspondent says of Caen today: "Words fail to describe the anguish of Caen, a broken, shattered town . . . Happily, some of its fine historical monuments, such as the Abbaye aux Dames . . . have survived." The whole of Caen as far as the River Orne is now ours, though the Germans still hold the Eastern suburb of Vaucelles beyond the blown bridges.

Both British and Canadian troops, who have borne the brunt of the fighting, had the honour of first entering the city where the welcome was tremendous.

CITIZENS OF CAEN "KEEPING HOUSE" IN THEIR FAMOUS CATHEDRAL, WHERE MANY CIVILIANS SOUGHT REFUGE DURING THE BATTLE FOR POSSESSION OF THE TOWN.

THE PROMINENT ANTI-NAZI, VON RUNDSTEDT, DISMISSED.

GERMANY'S MOST APPALLING CRIME: THE GHASTLY MASSACRE OF ORADOUR.

FIELD-MARSHAL VON RUNDSTEDT, RETIRED BY HITLER.

Field-Marshal von Rundstedt is of an independent turn of mind, and has never been fond of the Nazi party. In the German Army he is regarded as the most prominent anti-Nazi among the senior officers. Hitler's reason for superseding him as Supreme C.-in-C. in the West has not been stated.

Of all appalling and motiveless crimes perpetrated by the Germans in this war, in which their barbarities are unequalled in history, that of Oradour-sur-Glane stands out as a monument of ghastly cruelty. Oradour, a peaceful rural village, some 16 miles from Limoges, was visited on June 10 by lorries bringing S.S. troops of the Führer Division. The Mayor was ordered to assemble the whole population on the fair-ground, men, women and children. The men, in batches of twenty, were taken into a barn and shot on the spot, without any explanation. The women and children, tiny babies, and the old and infirm, crying and wailing, were pushed into the church, where children were preparing for their first communication. The assassins then fired the church and burnt all inside indiscriminately. From this shocking mass-murder, only seven persons escaped. The German Commandant's sole explanation was that "it was the wrong village" he had massacred. Thus is another Lidice.

CORPSES OF WOMEN AND CHILDREN AFTER THE HOLOCAUST.

THE BATTLE OF THE HEDGEROWS.

AT THE ENTRANCE TO THIS GERMAN DUG-OUT IN A HEDGE BANK STANDS AN OLD WARDROBE PACKED WITH EARTH AS A PROTECTIVE WALL. THE DUG-OUT PROVIDES A FIRST-CLASS LOOK-OUT.

AN AMERICAN SOLDIER INSIDE A GERMAN FOXHOLE TUNNELLED IN THE EARTH OF A HEDGE BANK, WITH A LOOK-OUT HOLE COVERING FORMER ALLIED POSITIONS.

Veterans of the first World War, now in Normandy, have described the fighting conditions there as worse than the trench warfare they experienced, because the countryside offers such perfect concealment for the defending army. The Normandy countryside, indeed, is even more "compact than the English, the lanes being narrower and with bigger hedges, the stretches of woodland thicker, and the fields smaller. It almost calls for the type of jungle tactics which have been developed in the Pacific zone of operations, with advance by infiltration rather than by massive frontal assault. Our pictures show various ways in which the Germans have taken advantage of these conditions, with foxholes, trenches, dug-outs and strong-points sited in hedgerows and woodlands, which additionally often carry stretches of concealed barbed wire, and in any case provide first-class observation posts. Nevertheless, by July 18, American forces had succeeded in capturing St. Lô and are at last entering more open country.

OPERATION GOODWOOD: MONTGOMERY'S GREAT DRIVE INTO NORMANDY.

CANADIAN INFANTRYMEN AWAITING THE ORDER TO ATTACK COLOMBELLES, IN THE OUTSKIRTS OF CAEN, IN THE WAKE OF THE WAR'S GREATEST AERIAL BOMBARDMENT.

THE PRIME MINISTER'S VISIT TO THE CAEN AREA: MR. CHURCHILL, WITH MONTGOMERY AND DEMPSEY (IN REAR OF CAR), PASSING OVER "WINSTON BRIDGE."

As dawn broke on July 18, after the greatest assembly of air power ever known had poured down a colossal weight of more than 7000 tons of bombs on the German divisions beyond the Orne, hundreds of British and Canadian tanks moved across the bridges. In a few hours they crashed through the German front east of the river and burst out into the open plain beyond. By 12.30 a.m. on July 20 the breach in the enemy defences had been widened and Allied troops had occupied the villages of Touffreville, Demenville and Giberville.

The Prime Minister spent three days touring the Normandy battlefront last week, accompanied by General Ismay. His tour covered Caen, Cherbourg, flying-bomb sites and the beaches. He had several conferences with General Montgomery and General Dempsey, C.-in-C. of the Second Army. Wearing a yachting cap and a short grey mackintosh over a blue suit, he received a hearty welcome from the troops. He remarked, summing up the situation in an informal talk to the Canadians, "The Germans are not very happy."

ROMMEL DISAPPEARS.

GERMANY'S INTERNAL CRISIS: DISSIDENCE AMONG THE GENERALS.

ROMMEL (AHEAD) DURING ONE OF HIS LAST APPEARANCES ON THE NORMANDY BATTLEFRONT BEFORE THE CAR ACCIDENT FOLLOWING AN ALLIED RAID.

GENERAL BECK, FORMER CHIEF OF STAFF, THE MOVING SPIRIT IN THE REVOLT.

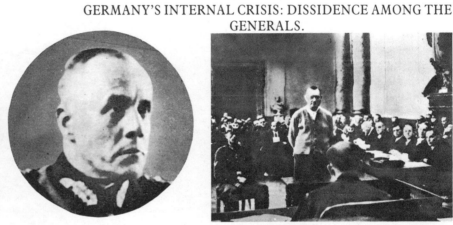

COLONEL-GENERAL HOEPPNER, AWAITING HIS TRIAL BEFORE THE NAZIS' "PEOPLE'S COURT" IN BERLIN. HE WAS HANGED.

The mystery of what exactly happened to Rommel was partly solved when the German news agency announced that he had met with a car accident as the result of an air raid in France on July 17. "He suffered injuries and concussion. His condition is satisfactory and his life is not in danger." Rommel was first reported to have been wounded and later was said to have died.

The startling rumour began to circulate on July 20 to the effect that there had been an attempt to assassinate Hitler – locality not given – by a cabal of German generals, particularly those in Russia. A bomb had been thrown by Colonel Klaus von Stauffenberg, who, according to later news, was shot by a firing-squad. A number of Hitler's colleagues were seriously injured, one was killed, but he was unhurt.

OPERATION COBRA: THE LONG-AWAITED BREAK-OUT FROM CAUMONT TO AVRANCHES.

TANKS ARE SEEN MOVING UP FOR THE ATTACK LAUNCHED AT DAWN ON JULY 30 FROM THE CAUMONT AREA.

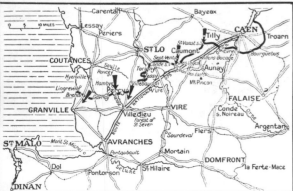

A MAP OF THE OPERATIONS IN NORMANDY: THE NEW BRITISH ATTACK SOUTH FROM CAUMONT APPEARS TO BE LINKED WITH THE U.S. OFFENSIVE IN A DRIVE TO SEIZE ROUTE NATIONALE 175, FROM AVRANCHES TO CAEN.

THE AMERICANS IN THIS TANK ON THE OUTSKIRTS OF AVRANCHES MAY HAVE BEEN "BATTLING" EARLIER THIS YEAR IN SOUTH DEVON. PASSING THEM TO THE REAR IS A LONG LINE OF GERMAN PRISONERS.

The Americans have speeded up their drive south-west of St. Lô, Coutances having fallen, and an armoured column having entered Avranches, some 25 miles to the south. Meanwhile, the British Second Army are steadily advancing southward into the Normandy hills, having captured nearly a dozen towns and villages in the first twenty-four hours of the offensive. On July 30, the Allied Forces under General Bradley, sweeping southward with impetuous speed had captured Coutances, and were across the base of Cherbourg Peninsula from Avranches to Caen. On July 31, an American column entered Avranches and cut the Granville-Paris railroad. This advance has rolled up Rommel's western Flank, offering great possibilities.

THE ALLIED BREAKTHROUGH AT AVRANCHES: GERMANS SURROUNDED AT FALAISE.

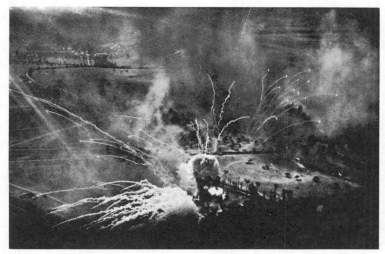

AN ENEMY AMMUNITION DUMP EXPLODING, SHOWERING BURNING PARTICLES OVER THE COUNTRY-SIDE. A DIRECT HIT DURING A MASS DAYLIGHT ATTACK NEAR FALAISE.

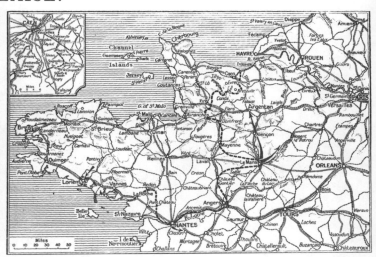

THE BATTLE OF FRANCE: A MAP SHOWING THE ALLIED FRONT AS ON AUGUST 13, ON WHICH DATE THE AMERICANS WERE AT ALENÇON, AND ON THE 14TH REPORTED TO BE BEYOND ARGENTAN.

Hitting out in all directions, the American hustle of General Omar Bradley's Army marks an historical record for speed and completeness unsurpassed even in Russia's big strides. Tearing southwards on July 27 from Periers and Lessay through Coutances and Avranches almost before the bewildered Germans knew what was happening his powerful armoured columns swarmed into Brittany. On August 3 their spearheads were at Rennes, and heading for Brest while his main forces advanced to Nantes, and then East to Le Mans, leaving villages wild with excitement. From Le Mans, the hurricane advance proceeded north to Alençon and on the 13th held Argentan, with Falaise, twelve miles beyond, held by the Canadians, only a narrow gap remains for 100,000 retreating Germans after this great encircling drive on August 14.

FIRST ALLIED LANDINGS IN SOUTHERN FRANCE.

WAVING CHEERILY TO THEIR COUNTRYMEN AND ALLIES, THIS FRENCH TANK CREW IS SEEN BRINGING THEIR TANK ASHORE SOMEWHERE IN FRANCE.

MANY THOUSANDS OF ALLIED VEHICLES READY TO ROLL FORWARD ON THE EVER-SHORTENING ROAD TO BERLIN.

General Sir Henry Maitland Wilson's invasion of Southern France in the early hours of August 15, under the immediate command of Lieut. General Alexander Patch, of the U.S. Seventh Army, achieved remarkable success. Resistance was described as "fantastically light" and airborne troops had gained all first objectives. By Sunday night, the 20th, they had occupied 1000 square miles of French territory, Aix-en-Provence, an important road junction on the main road from Paris to the Riviera, was in their hands, and forces were advancing on Toulon and Marseilles, as well as pressing on towards Avignon. Over 12,000 prisoners had been taken at the time of writing. Inland, as a result, the French population was rising everywhere, and the Maquis were showing the most brilliant co-operation, as the Allies advanced along the Rhône Valley.

CLOSING THE FALAISE GAP: GERMAN SEVENTH ARMY ENTRAPPED.

AN HISTORIC *RENCONTRE* BETWEEN FALAISE AND ARGENTAN: THE ALLIES, TRIUMPHANT, HAVE MET FOR THE FIRST TIME ON THE ROAD FROM ARGENTAN, AND CONSEQUENTLY CONGRATULATIONS ARE MUTUAL WITH HEARTY HANDSHAKES.

A GERMAN GENERAL IN A US HELMET: LIEUT.-GENERAL KARL SPANG, CAPTURED NEAR BREST, WAITING TO BE DRIVEN OFF TO CAPTIVITY.

The Falaise gap has been effectively sealed off by a rapidly thickening screen of armour and infantry swung across it to the east in the vicinity of Trun and Chambois, and those formations that passed through the jaws beteeen Argentan and Falaise, fighting rearguard actions as best they can, are in retreat all along a wavering line from the coast, where British troops, under General Crerar's Canadian command, are within striking distance of Cabourg, while armour is established on the River Vie at Liverot on the broad *route nationale* that runs north to Lisieux and Trouville. It was the Canadians who first entered Falaise, and they hold Trun. British formations, on the other hand, have cut the Germans' escape corridor in many places. These formations are bearing down from the north to link up with the American forces in the south.

THE RACE FOR THE SEINE: THE ALLIES CLOSE ON THE ENEMY RETREAT.

THE BRITISH CAPTURE A SEINE FERRY TERMINUS: THE QUAYSIDE AT QUILLEBEUF, SHOWING ABANDONED ENEMY 88-MM. HORSE-DRAWN GUNS.

A COMPLETED BAILEY BRIDGE ACROSS A WIDE STRETCH OF THE SEINE (LEFT), WITH TROOPS AND VEHICLES PASSING OVER A PONTOON BRIDGE (RIGHT).

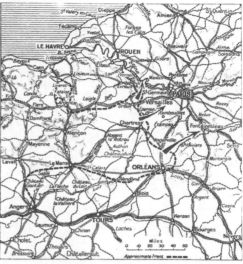

THE ADVANCE TOWARDS PARIS: A MAP SHOWING THE POSITION OF GENERAL BRADLEY'S U.S. FORCES ON AUGUST 20: ARMOURED SPEARHEADS ARE EDGING ROUND THE SUBURBS OF THE CAPITAL, SUGGESTING AN ENVELOPING MOVEMENT.

Writing on August 24, when the beaten German Army was making all haste back across the Seine, a "Daily Telegraph" special correspondent with the British Second Army said: "We have the problem of building and repairing bridges." That problem was quickly solved by the building of Bailey and pontoon bridges at various chosen positions along the Seine, and our troops and vehicles were pouring over the river with scarcely a halt, to catch up with, and cut off, further large forces of retreating Germans. The speed with which the Seine was bridged and crossed is an outstanding achievement. It is interesting to note that the 88-mm. guns shown abandoned on the quayside at Quillebeuf (top left) are horse-drawn, surely an indication of the acute shortage of petrol now being felt by the enemy armies in the West.

SCENES FROM THE GREAT LIBERATION OF PARIS.

GENDARMES INDICATING MARKS MADE ON AN ABESTOS WALL BY CIVILIAN VICTIMS IN THEIR EFFORTS TO CLIMB FROM FLAMES.

GENERAL DE GAULLE, AFTER SALUTING THE TOMB OF THE UN-KNOWN WARRIOR, LEADS THE WAY TOWARDS NOTRE DAME.

A CAPTURED GERMAN BEING CONFRONTED WITH THE BULLET-CHIPPED POSTS TO WHICH HOSTAGES WERE TIED AND SHOT.

A TRULY PARISIAN RECEPTION FROM ALWAYS GAY PARIS. "OH, WE HAVE WAITED SO LONG, SO IMPATIENTLY," CRIED THE PARISIENNES, AS THEY EMBRACED THE SOLDIERS WHO LIBERATED THEM.

The liberation of Paris began on August 19, when French police took over the Prefecture. Next day members of the Resistance, now renamed the "French Forces of the Interior", or "F.F.I.," seized the Hotel de Ville. By August 23 the remaining Germans had been bottled up in strong points scattered through the city, and General Eisenhower, who had so far kept all troops out of the city, to avoid a battle, following a long standing promise that French forces should be the first to enter Paris, ordered General Leclerc's Second Armoured Division to advance. The Germans, except for a few isolated snipers, surrendered to General Leclerc on Friday, August 25, who with General de Gaulle entered the capital in triumph at seven o'clock that evening.

The General spoke to the people of Paris the same night from the Prefecture of Police, and said, "France will take her place among the great nations which will organise the peace." Telling of the Allied entry into Paris, Mr. Alan Moorehead, of the "Daily Express," says that machine-guns began firing again. "Young boys, with armbands marked "F.F.I.," were rushing about with Sten guns, and cars seemed to be dashing around for no reason at all." Three days later, at General de Gaulle's request, the American divisions were deployed through the city in a show of force designed to impress the many armed collaborators still at large, and to restore the confidence of the public.

THE ALLIED ADVANCE: FROM ROME TO THE GOTHIC LINE.

THE DUOMO (CATHEDRAL) OF FLORENCE. BRITISH TROOPS MARCHING PAST IT.

THE PRESENT FRONT IN ITALY: KESSELRING'S COSTLY ATTEMPTS TO GAIN TIME, FOR STRENGTHENING A NEW DEFENCE LINE, HAVE FAILED HIM. HE HOPES TO HOLD A LINE PISA-RIMINI WITH TWELVE DEFEATED DIVISIONS.

Alexander's great Italian offensive, now in full swing, has driven Kesselring's powerful forces from the Gustav and Adolf Hitler Lines in Italy, out of Rome, and sent them in headlong rout northward through Italy. General Alexander's troops are pursuing the disorganised German divisions towards Florence. The Allied Armies, racing on the enemy's heels were nearly 70 miles north of Rome on June 12. They have already inflicted upwards of 70,000 casualties since the opening of the offensive on May 12.

On July 3, the French entered Sienna but only paused long enough to raise triumphantly the Tricolour with the Cross of Lorraine, and passed grimly on in pursuit. They were given a great welcome, heartier than that in Rome. Kesselring's retreating army, on July 7 took a stand before Leghorn to Anzona in order to complete his Gothic Line with its 6000-ft-high peaks. On Friday, August 11, the Germans evacuated Florence, leaving behind them many snipers, who are being dealt with by both our own troops in the city and by Italian patriots. The population of this famous city is in serious need of food and the Allied Military Government is now feeding three-quarters of the city's population. South of the Arno 80,000 Italians are being fed, and north of the river 250,000 are being supplied. Italian patriots, civilians, and former soldiers are doing everything they can to help, and the patriots, in particular, have worked courageously, running the risk of reprisals.

THE PRIME MINISTER IN ROME MEETS THE ITALIAN PRIME MINISTER.

THE PRIME MINISTER WITH MARSHAL BADOGLIO (LEFT) AND SIGNOR BONOMI MEETING MR. CHURCHILL AT THE BRITISH EMBASSY DURING HIS VISIT TO ROME.

It was after his visit to the armies in Italy that Mr. Churchill went to Rome and began to devote a closer attention to Italian affairs. He had an interview at the British Embassy with Signor Bonomi, the Prime Minister, which lasted more than an hour. Signor Bonomi remained to luncheon at the Embassy, Marshal Badoglio being another guest. Mr. Churchill, it is reported, found the Italian situation absorbing and he gave it his fullest attention.

THE KING IN ITALY AWARDS HONOURS AND DECORATIONS.

SIR OLIVER LEESE, C.-IN-C. EIGHTH ARMY, KNEELING TO RECEIVE THE ACCOLADE OF KNIGHTHOOD DURING THE KING'S VISIT.

His Majesty during his recent tour of the Italian front held an investiture outside his caravan on a hill within close range and sound of German gunfire. He gave the accolade to Lieut.-General Leese.

THE ARDEATINO CAVES: SCENE OF A GERMAN MASSACRE.

PREMIER BONOMI AND MEMBERS OF THE ITALIAN GOVERNMENT LEAVING THE ARDEATINO CAVES, THE SCENE OF A GERMAN MASSACRE OF ROMAN CITIZENS.

During the Allied advance on Rome earlier this year, a German military column was bombed on its way through the Italian capital. The reply of the Germans was a ruthless reprisal, in which they were reported to have dragged 320 Roman citizens to the caves at Ardeatino, and there to have massacred them. Allied officials have since appointed a committee to examine the bodies and remains in the caves, to check the identity of the victims, and to verify other details of the atrocity charge.

THE ALLIES BREACH THE GOTHIC LINE, THREATENING THE GREAT NORTHERN PLAINS.

A BRITISH SELF-PROPELLED 25-POUNDER SEXTON GUN ABOUT TO FORD THE RIVER FOGLIA, THE FIRST OBSTACLE IN THE ADRIATIC SECTOR.

USED AS A STATIC ANTI-TANK GUN: A GERMAN MARK IV. TANK BACKED INTO THE ROOM OF A HOUSE NORTH OF THE RIVER MARANO.

ALEXANDER'S BREACH OF THE GOTHIC LINE, SEIZING PISA AND CROSSING THE ARNO.

Our advance in Italy is gathering strength; the Gothic Line is completely gone on the eastern side, and the last of the big ridges has been passed. On September 1, General Alexander, by a superb ruse of secretly transferring the main strength of the Eighth Army to the Adriatic area, surprised the Germans in Pesaro, and further inland crossed the River Foglia. Establishing a strong bridgehead, threatening Rimini, the Gothic Line was turned and the Allies are advancing into the Po Valley. On the West, the Fifth Army captured Pisa and crossed the Arno. Meanwhile all North Italy behind the Gothic Line is in a fement. In the whole sector, our advance is spreading into the plains, but the enemy is still fighting hard and has not yet begun his withdrawal tactics.

GERMANY MENACED FROM THE WEST: LUXEMBOURG, FRANCE AND BELGIUM LIBERATED.

THE LIBERATION OF BRUSSELS ON SEPTEMBER 3: DELIRIOUS EXCITEMENT AS BRITISH TROOPS IN AMERICAN TANKS TRAVERSE THE BELGIAN CAPITAL.

ALLIED VICTORY IN THE MAKING: (L. TO R.) LT.-GEN. BRADLEY (U.S.), GEN. MONTGOMERY, LT.-GEN. DEMPSEY, AND MAJ.-GEN. HODGES (U.S.).

General Eisenhower on August 31 reported more than 400,000 German losses in the first 81 days of the Allied onslaught on Northern France. On September 1, the enemy front had been split open and the retreat in Belgium was turning into a rout. U.S. troops were on the borders of Belgium. British forces were racing on beyond Amiens with less than 45 miles to go to the frontier and in the south the Germans were in headlong retreat. Arras, Amiens and Abbeville were captured by the lightning advances of the Allies now heading for Berlin. The liberation of Dieppe on September 1 was achieved by the Canadians.

The British reached Brussels towards sunset on September 3, having advanced 73 miles since sunrise. As they entered, a red glare showed them the Palais de Justice in flames, and although most of the enemy had left in

BRITISH INFANTRY DASHING ACROSS A BRIDGE IN ANTWERP'S DOCK AREA, COVERED BY A BREN GUN. ANTWERP WAS CAPTURED INTACT ON SEPTEMBER 4.

ON SEPTEMBER 13, GENERAL HODGES' U.S. FIRST ARMY MADE HISTORY BY FIRST CROSSING INTO GERMAN TERRITORY: ABOVE, THEY ARE PASSING THROUGH AACHEN FOREST.

disorder, a few pockets of them were left. The stutter of enemy machine-guns was met by the deep slam of our tank guns. For hours after the exodus of the Germans, the Brussels citizens thronged the streets and cheered, and burnt Hitler in effigy. British and U.S. Armies raced for the German border. In Rouen, the devastation was very great. Heavier fighting took place on the left wing, Le Havre falling on the 12, Boulogne on the 22

and Calais on the 25 September. On the right wing Patton's Third Army made contact with the U.S. and French troops advancing from the south of France on September 11. On September 13, the U.S. First Army, under General Hodges, was the first to assault the Siegfried Line. It is believed that the enemy have neither the men nor material to defend the Siegfried Line to any depth.

THE SURRENDER OF A GERMAN ARMY TO 20 U.S. SOLDIERS.

SECRET AID TO THE MAQUIS.

ANY AND EVERY FORM OF TRANSPORT WAS REQUISITIONED FOR THE FOOTSORE, DEFEATED ARMY FROM THE BORDEAUX REGION, HAMMERED BY FIGHTER-BOMBERS AND THE MAQUIS.

THE SPECIAL AIR SERVICE – A BRITISH UNIT OF PARACHUTISTS WHOSE IDENTITY WAS HITHERTO KEPT SECRET: COLONEL STIRLING WITH A PATROL IN THE MIDDLE EAST.

One of the most astonishing stories of the war is how Lieutenant Samuel Magill, of Ohio, induced 20,000 German Marines, Wehrmacht, and Luftwaffe, to lay down their arms to his twenty men. The German commander, Major-General Erich Elster, agreed to surrender unconditionally at the Loire if his troops were permitted to carry arms for protection against the Maquis. Magill suddenly had 20,000 Germans on his hands.

The disorganisation of German resistance in depth in France was not due only to the work of the Maquis but to that of a British unit of parachutists known as the Special Air Service. The S.A.S. was conceived and created by two young officers, Lieut. David Stirling and Lieut. Jock Lewis, who started a school in the desert called "Stirling's Rest Camp," where the first seventy-three volunteers were trained.

THE RUSSIAN CAMPAIGN IN THE BALKANS:
RUMANIA'S SUDDEN CHANGE OF POLICY.

THE FIRST GERMANS TO SURRENDER TO THE RUMANIAN ARMY BURN THEIR ARCHIVES PRIOR TO GIVING THEMSELVES UP.

H.M. MICHAEL I., KING OF THE RUMANIANS.

On August 23 King Michael of Rumania took the future of his country into his own hands and issued a proclamation whereby all hostilities with the United Nations were to cease immediately. As a result, King Michael entrusted the forming of a new Government to General C. Senatescu, with M. Niculescu-Buzesti as Foreign Minister. The Pro-German M. Antonescu was arrested. When Rumania finally decided to throw off the German yoke damage was done to two of the Bucharest's principal buildings by German bombing raids.

These raids were dictated by revenge, and owing to the lack of defences, the capital and her inhabitants were at the mercy of the bombers. All the Palace area and most of the main shopping centre have been smashed virtually beyond repair. In a 35-mile advance from Ploesti, captured the previous day, the Red Army entered Bucharest on August 31, relieving the capital from a German threat from the north. An armistice between Russia, Great Britain and the United States and Rumania was signed on September 13.

THE THIRD MOSCOW CONFERENCE: POLAND'S FUTURE BOUNDARIES.

No State in the world has experienced such vicissitudes as Poland from the tenth century to the present day. After the First World War, Poland participated in the Versailles Peace Conference and agreed that the Allied Powers should settle the vexed question of future frontiers, as a result of which the Curzon Line of demarcations was drawn up. In the meantime, the Poles had complicated matters by marching into White Russia and the Ukraine beyond the Curzon Line. The Russians counter-attacked and drove the Poles back to the gates of Warsaw. This war led to the Treaty of Riga in 1921, and established the Riga Line (see map 1) as the boundary, which was in effect the frontier between Poland and Russia prior to the present war. After the Polish collapse in 1939, Russia moved rapidly west and established a new boundary on a line slightly to the west of the Curzon Line. Such, then, is the history of the boundary delimitation now of urgency in view of the recent Soviet suggestion that the Curzon Line should become the basis of frontier negotiations. Of considerable importance is the question of race divergencies in the territories east of the Curzon Line. Here the Poles are in a

THE LAST PARTITION OF POLAND: AS GERMAN OVERRAN POLAND IN 1939, RUSSIA INVADED HER FROM THE EAST.

distinct minority, although in certain cities, like Vilna and Lwow, they form the majority. From the Polish standpoint it is natural that she is reluctant to desert her people of pure Polish blood living east of the Curzon Line. Russia has suggested that in return Poland should be "compensated" with German territories implying Upper Silesia and part of Eastern Prussia, which would ensure her a Baltic sea-board.

At the Third Moscow Conference during October, slight improvement was made with this vexed issue. The Poles were willing to accept the Curzon Line "as a line of demarcation between Russia and Poland," while the Russians maintained that the Curzon Line should form the "basis of frontier between Russia and Poland." Neither side would give way at this point. However, later talks on October 22 between Churchill, Stalin and Mikolajczyk were more hopeful. Mikolajczyk promised to form a government friendly to the Russians, and to urge the case for the Curzon Line, including Lvov, for the Russians.

A MAP OF PRE-WAR POLAND, SHOWING THE CURZON LINE AS SUGGESTED DURING THE VERSAILLES PEACE CONFERENCE OF 1919.

CHURCHILL MEETS TITO, THE YUGOSLAV LEADER.

TITO'S PARTISANS, WITH BRITISH GUNNERS AND R.A.F., SCORE IN YUGOSLAVIA.

MR. CHURCHILL IN ITALY GREETS MARSHAL TITO, THE YUGOSLAV LEADER.

Mr. Churchill recently had meetings in Italy with Marshal Tito and with the Yugoslav Prime Minister, M. Subasic, at which political and military questions were discussed. Marshal Tito's National Liberation Committee has been fully recognised as the *de facto* administrative and military authority in Yugoslavia.

TROOPS OF MARSHAL TITO'S ARMY ENTERING BELGRADE, CAPITAL OF YUGOSLAVIA, WHICH, IN CONJUNCTION WITH THE RED ARMY, THEY LIBERATED ON OCTOBER 20.

On October 20 an Order of the Day by Marshal Stalin was addressed to Marshal Tolbukhin, announcing that troops of the Third Ukrainian front, in conjunction with Marshal Tito's National Army of Liberation, had liberated Belgrade after stubborn fighting. This fighting has gone on all the previous night in the north-western part of

AT LEDENICE WERE TWO 105-MM. GUNS, ONE KNOCKED OUT BY BRITISH GUNNERY, THE OTHER TAKEN INTACT: BRITISH GUNNERS EXAMINING THE DAMAGED GUN.

the capital, where remnants of the German garrison, S.S., and police troops made their final stand. The end came when the German morale broke, large groups surrendering. Marshal Tito's Partisans advancing in Croatia, were actively supported by British gunners and the R.A.F., all being in fraternal accord.

THE JUNGLE ROAD TO MANDALAY: FIGHTING DURING THE MONSOON.

MOVING AN ENTIRE DIVISION IN BURMA BY AIR: THE FIFTH INDIAN DIVISION WAS FLOWN 300 MILES TO THE IMPHAL PLAIN, INCLUDING BULLOCKS, AS SEEN IN THE PICTURE ABOVE.

GENERAL STILWELL.
The leader of a United Nations force of Chinese, Indian and American troops in Burma, General Stilwell has been relieved of his command in South-East Asia and recalled to Washington. He speaks many languages and a great many Chinese dialects.

"WE WILL FIGHT ON THROUGH THE MONSOON," SAID LORD LOUIS MOUNTBATTEN, C.-IN-C.: JEEPS SEEN BRINGING ESSENTIAL SUPPLIES UP THE "CHOCOLATE STAIRCASE" ON THE TIDDIM ROAD.

Troops of the 5th Indian Division captured Tiddim on October 19, enemy resistance collapsing and giving the Fourteenth Army complete control of the 100-mile-long road between it and Imphal. On December 3, after ten days of bitter fighting, Kalewa was captured by the 11th East Africa Division from Kenya and Uganda, under British officers. Before the Fourteenth Army could advance every ton of armour had to be man-handled across a mountain range and scrub jungle country. In the first six months of this year the Fourteenth Army sustained 237,000 cases of sickness, which had to be evacuated over long, difficult communications.

THE SECOND QUEBEC CONFERENCE, 1944.

THE SECOND QUEBEC CONFERENCE: MR. CHURCHILL SPEAKING TO THE PRESS. HE TOLD THEM THAT THE DISCUSSIONS HAD BEEN HELD "IN A BLAZE OF UNITY."

In a joint statement Mr Churchill and President Roosevelt said: "The most serious difficulty with which the Quebec Conference has been confronted has been to find room and opportunity for the marshalling against Japan of the massive forces which each and all of the nations concerned are ardent to engage against the enemy."

V-2 ROCKET BOMBS: A GERMAN "REVENGE WEAPON."

THE ROCKET PASSES INTO THE STRATOSPHERE, AND IT CONTINUES TO A HEIGHT OF MORE THAN SIXTY MILES. THE TREMENDOUS ENERGY NEEDED MAKES IT A VERY DANGEROUS WEAPON TO LAUNCH.

The V2 has been stated to be approximately 47 ft. in length and about 5 ft. in diameter. It is a long, slender projectile, with a pointed nose, and its tail is provided with stabilising fins. The weapon is obviously remotely controlled as there are wireless sets inside it and control surfaces attached to the fins. The propulsion is by liquid fuel, and the method employed is that of the true rocket with a continuous flow of energy. V2s began to fall on London on September 8.

JET-PROPULSION EXPLAINED: A SYSTEM NOW IN ITS PRACTICAL STAGE.

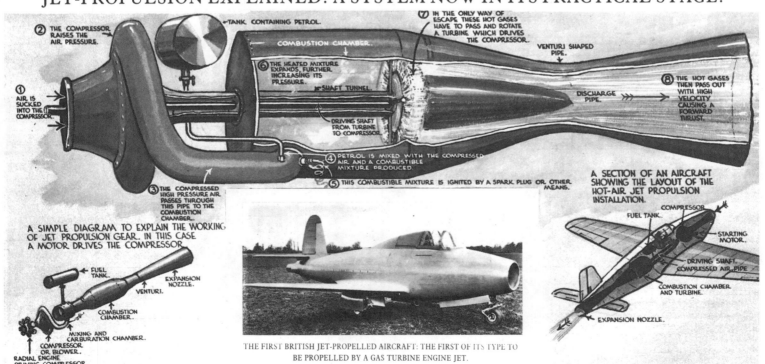

THE FIRST BRITISH JET-PROPELLED AIRCRAFT: THE FIRST OF ITS TYPE TO BE PROPELLED BY A GAS TURBINE ENGINE JET.

Jet-propelled fighter aircraft have successfully passed tests and will soon be in production for the Allies. Our drawings explain the basic principles of the system. In brief, air is first sucked in by the rotation of an air compressor and its pressure raised. The compressed air, passing along a pipe, is blended with oil fuel to create a combustible mixture. The fire mixture, expanding in the combustion chamber, still further increases its own pressure, and finally streams out through a nozzle at the rear of the aircraft to create a forward thrust. It is continuous forward thrust which keeps the aircraft in flight.

THE GREATEST OF AIRBORNE OPS – THE INVASION OF HOLLAND.

GLIDERS WHICH CARRIED THE ALLIED AIRBORNE FORCES ARE SEEN "PARKED" AT THE ENDS OF THEIR TRACKS.

The outstanding episode of the latest phase in the whole war against Germany has been the airborne operation in Holland, on September 17, followed immediately by the advance of the British Second Army to the lower branches of the Rhine. The plan was daring and imaginative: four stepping-stones were to be provided for the land forces, each formed by an airborne force. The first was at Eindhoven, some twenty-odd miles from the previous front; the second at Grave, on the Maas; the third at Nijmegen, on the left bank of the Waal; the fourth at Arnhem, north of the Lek. The airborne landings at Eindhoven, Grave and Nijmegen were American, while that at Arnhem was British. The landings were brilliantly organised and successfully carried out. The initial advance of the Second Army, with strong air support, was extremely rapid. Eindhoven and Grave were reached without great difficulty, and the Maas was passed. At Nijmegen there was hard and bitter fighting, but the Americans had done their work finely and saved the road bridge. The second water barrier, the Waal, was also passed.

R.A.F. HALIFAXES TOWING BRITISH HORSA GLIDERS OVER THE RHINE AS THE VAST AIRBORNE ARMY WAS FLOWN FORWARD INTO HOLLAND.

NIJMEGEN BRIDGE TAKEN INTACT: A MONUMENT TO U.S. GALLANTRY.

BRITISH ARMOUR CROSSING NIJMEGEN BRIDGE, GATEWAY INTO NORTHERN GERMANY, AFTER ITS CAPTURE INTACT BY THE GALLANTRY OF AMERICAN INFANTRY, WHO CROSSED THE RIVER IN DAYLIGHT UNDER SEVERE ENEMY FIRE. THE U.S. TROOPS, FIGHTING ALL NIGHT, FORCED A BRIDGEHEAD, AND BRITISH ARMOUR FROM THE SOUTH CHARGED POINT-BLANK THE ENEMY GUNS.

A BRITISH SENTRY KEEPING THE WATCH ON THE RHINE, FROM A COMMAND POST ON THE NIJMEGEN BRIDGE; NEAR HIM IS A BEAMING PORTRAIT OF HITLER.

The capture of Nijmegen Bridge, intact, was an achievement of the first order. To seize it, U.S. paratroops crossed the river on September 20, in rubber boats, two miles west of the bridge and fought their way along the far bank. Simultaneously British armour and infantry forced a path through the town and joined up with the paratroops the same evening. Before dark they had thrown an infantry battalion with Recce troops and tanks across the river, followed by a strong armoured force on the 21st.

One of the most daring enemy acts of the war was an attempt to blow up the Nijmegen railway and road bridges. But the men selected for the task made the mistake of swimming back upcurrent. After covering 6¼ miles exhaustion forced them to rest in the shallows. British soldiers saw them and fired, killing two. The remainder surrendered. The first charge exploded by the road bridge, doing little damage, the second was heroically rendered harmless by a naval lieutenant who dived under the bridge.

HEROES OF ARNHEM: BRITISH TROOPS WIN THE ADMIRATION OF THE WORLD.

AIRBORNE TROOPS ENGAGING THE ENEMY. OUR MEN HELD ON AGAINST HEAVY ODDS FOR MORE THAN A WEEK.

BRITISH TROOPS OF THE HEROIC AIRBORNE DIVISION MARCHING FORWARD TOWARDS ARNHEM WITH THE GUNS AND EQUIPMENT DROPPED WITH THEM: THE DIVISION LANDED IN OPEN COUNTRY SOME SIX MILES WEST OF THE TOWN AND ITS BRIDGES.

The Germans had by now recognised that the British airborne division at Arnhem was the most easily assailable link in the Allied chain. Resigning themselves to the loss of the other stepping-stones, they hurled themselves from all sides against the British island and claimed that they were wiping out the isolated airborne division. On Friday last they claimed at one moment to have destroyed it entirely, though later they admitted that "elements" were still resisting.

These splendid troops, some of the best we have ever had, put up a nine-day fight which will never be forgotten, but were forced to surrender before the relieving force could reach them. Of the ten thousand men who landed north of the Rhine over eleven hundred were killed, and six thousand, more than half of them wounded, were captured. Montgomery's heroic gamble to by-pass the Siegfried line had not come off, and it would be seven months before British troops returned to Arnhem.

WINNING A JUMPING-OFF AREA FOR THE PHILIPPINES: THE PALAU ISLANDS INVADED.

THE CONQUEST OF THE PALAU ISLANDS, KEY AREA TO THE PHILIPPINES, ONLY 450 MILES DISTANT: U.S. TROOPS SMOKING OUT JAPS SHELTERING IN CAVES.

In some respects the conquest of the Palau Islands, which flank the south-eastern shores of the Philippines, only 450 miles distant, has proved the most difficult operation yet encountered in the Pacific. They are a group of twenty-six islands of various sizes, of which Angaur and Peleliu are among the largest and most important, and here the Japanese, after Admiral Halsey's Third Fleet had bombed and shelled them, sought shelter in fortified caves, from which they were ousted with difficulty by hand grenades, rifle grenades and "Molotoff Cocktails." Outside, U.S. Marines awaited them and shot them down like rats as they were forced to emerge. The Japanese, who acquired a mandate for this group, lying inside a largely extended coral reef, had fortified them strongly. By October 1 over 10,000 of the enemy had been killed, mainly in Peleliu.

At one point during the battle, an American tank-landing ship discovered seven barges, each capable of holding about 100 soldiers, trying to reinforce Peleliu from Ngesebus Island, half a mile to the north. It sank one of them, and a cruiser and aircraft drove the others ashore, where they were destroyed. The U.S. Marines who made the initial landings on the island fought for nine days and nights before relief troops took their place. The Japanese garrison on Peleliu suffered very heavy casualties; by far the heaviest, in fact, of the whole group of Palau Islands, seized one by one by the Americans. The importance of these islands, apart from the gradual liquidation of all enemy forces in the Pacific, lies in their situation between the Western Carolines and the Philippines, now the scene of a new Allied invasion.

A CRUSHING ROUT OF THE JAPANESE NAVY IN BATTLE FOR THE PHILIPPINES.

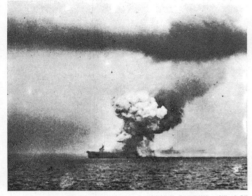

THE END OF THE UNITED STATES ESCORT CARRIER "ST. LO" DURING THE BATTLE OF THE PHILIPPINE SEA: THE CARRIER IS SEEN, A MASS OF FLAMES AND SMOKE.

HARD-PRESSED BY U.S. BOMBING 'PLANES, A JAPANESE COMBINED BATTLESHIP-CARRIER IS SEEN STEAMING FULL SPEED AHEAD TO SAFETY. SHE WAS DAMAGED.

THE DEATH OF A JAPANESE CRUISER OF THE "NACHI" CLASS: THREE TORPEDOES, LAUNCHED BY U.S. CARRIER-BASED AIRCRAFT, STREAKING THROUGH THE WATER.

On October 21 and in the following days began a major and portentous sea-battle between Allied and Japanese warships involving sea-air power, which resulted in an overwhelming Allied victory and the utter rout of the enemy. Extending in three separate engagements, in over 1000 miles of the Philippine waters, the Third Fleet under Admiral

Halsey, and the Seventh under Vice-Admiral Kinkaid, sank or heavily damaged fifty-eight Japanese warships, including twenty-four sunk (four carriers and two battleships), thirteen severely damaged believed sunk, twenty-one damaged, and 171 'planes. U.S. losses were six, including two carriers.

The great naval victory of Leyte Gulf in the Philippine Sea not only made possible the continued supply of men and munitions to General MacArthur's successful invasion forces on Leyte, but by its magnitude can conservatively be said to have greatly reduced future casualties in both men and waterborne equipment.

FIRST STEPS IN THE LIBERATION OF THE PHILIPPINES: U.S. TROOPS INVADE LEYTE.

THE FIRST WAVE GOING ASHORE ON LEYTE: PLUNGING INTO THE SEA FROM THE OPEN BOWS OF LANDING CRAFT, AMERICAN TROOPS AND TANK (BACKGROUND) ARE SEEN HEADING FOR THE SHORE TO BEGIN THE LIBERATION OF THE PHILIPPINES. SMOKE IS HOVERING OVER THE PALMS.

FIGHTING THROUGH A WRECKED VILLAGE: WORMING THEIR WAY FORWARD, U.S. SOLDIERS OF THE NINETY-SIXTH DIVISION CAN BE SEEN ENGAGING THE ENEMY WITH RIFLE FIRE FROM BEHIND DÉBRIS AND THICK BRUSH.

In the greatest amphibious operation in the Pacific, American forces, under General MacArthur, landed on Leyte Island on Friday, October 20. By evening two major beach-heads had been established on the east coast while tanks and infantry, advancing on the capital, Tacloban, had captured its airfield. Three days prior, American Rangers went ashore on three islands covering the approaches to the Gulf of Leyte, and warships

and aircraft began plastering the invasion coast, whilst minesweepers cleared a passage. Then, a vast armada of 600 warships and transports swept into the Gulf, and under cover, hundreds of landing craft rushed the beaches. U.S. assault troops quickly overran the pill-boxes and machine-gun nests. Less than two weeks after the initial landings, American troops had gained control of two-thirds of Leyte.

MOPPING-UP IN BRITTANY: ST MALO, CEZEMBRE, BREST CAPTURED.

THE GERMAN COMMANDER OF ST. MALO, VON AULOCH – THE "MAD COLONEL," CARRYING HIS OWN BAGGAGE AS HE SURRENDERS TO THE AMERICANS.

On August 16 the German High Command admitted the surrender of the St. Malo garrison, after the town itself had been in American hands for some time. The German commander, Colonel von Auloch, led 605 men from the depths of the fortress 60 ft. below ground, and all their holding out has done is to cause the almost complete destruction of the picturesque old town of St. Malo. The Isle de Cezembre, commanding the entrance to the Gulf of St. Malo, held out for three weeks longer, and thus prevented the Allies using the harbour. It was brought to its knees by continued and heavy bombing, finally surrendering on September 2. The Allied siege of Brest, the important port and U-boat base, was reported, on September 14, to be nearly over. The investing U.S. troops were then closing in around the battered U-boat pens, where some Germans were making a last, desperate stand. Two days previously, an eye-witness had described Brest as a sea of flame and smoke under a pitiless bombardment from the air and from the ground, under which the town appeared to be visibly crumbling away. The commander of the German garrison, Major-General Bernard Ramcke, had refused repeated calls to surrender, and the German radio announced that in consequence he had been honoured by promotion to the rank of Parachute General. Brest surrendered on September 18.

AN EXAMPLE OF THE DEVASTATING RESULTS OBTAINED BY R.A.F. BOMBING ATTACKS ON THIS FORMER GERMAN U-BOAT BASE AT BREST. A HUGE 40-FT. HOLE IS TORN IN THE ROOF.

GENERAL BRADLEY HONOURED.

HIS MAJESTY THE KING ENJOYING A JOKE WITH GENERAL EISENHOWER, LT.-GEN. O. BRADLEY AND LT.-GEN C. HODGES.

During his Majesty's recent visit to his troops on the Belgian-Dutch front, he motored 200 miles to confer the K.C.B. on Lieut.-General Omar Bradley, Commander of the U.S. 12th Army Group (seen standing behind the King). His tour had been kept a close secret, and it was not until later, when he was driving through Holland, that crowds of Dutch people recognised him and shouted, in their own language, "Long live the King of England!"

STATE FUNERAL FOR ROMMEL.

GENERAL FIELD-MARSHAL ROMMEL.

The death of Field-Marshal Rommel, who met with a car accident has been announced from Berlin. It was later reported that he died by his own hand, preferring suicide to execution.

"HOME GUARD" FOR GERMANY.

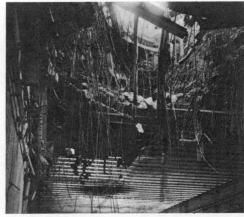

MEN OF THE *VOLKSSTURM* ON PARADE BEFORE BEING SENT TO THE FRONT. THEIR ONLY UNIFORM IS A WHITE ARM-BAND.

On October 18 Hitler issued a proclamation conscripting German men between the ages of sixteen and sixty to form a *Volkssturm* for the defence of German soil, announcing that: "to strengthen the active forces, to wage a ruthless war at any point where the enemy enters German soil I call upon German men able to carry a weapon to make themselves ready for the fight." The new organisation's only uniform is a white arm-band bearing the German eagle.

BRITISH TROOPS LAND IN GREECE: ATHENS LIBERATED.

GREEK GIRLS CARRYING THE NATIONAL FLAG TO THE ACROPOLIS AT A CEREMONY ATTENDED BY THE GREEK PRIME MINISTER.

TRIUMPHAL PROGRESS: A BRITISH JEEP RECEIVING A GREAT WELCOME IN A FLOWER-STREWN STREET ON THE ROAD TO CORINTH.

It was announced on October 5 that Allied forces had landed on the Greek mainland and had entered Patras. A few days before the landings, R.A.F. Spitfires of the Balkan Air Force had come down on the Greek mainland, where partisans and citizens immediately came forward as volunteers to help in the construction of emergency landing-strips. Parachute troops were also dropped in daylight, and were followed by transport aircraft bringing airfield personnel. Naval forces landed infantry, commando troops, and engineers. Landings were also made on Greek islands and in Albania. By October 9 it was reported that the Allies, advancing eastward from Patras, were on the outskirts of Corinth, and that the Germans were preparing to leave Athens.

The news that Athens had been liberated came on October 13. Paratroops who landed near the city were welcomed by crowds of civilians. There was a great welcome, too, for the British troops who arrived in the port by sea, and for others travelling by road. The people of Athens themselves were jubilantly happy. One of their greatest moments was the raising of the Greek Flag above the Parthenon in the Acropolis on Oct. 18. This ceremony was attended by members of the newly-returned Greek Government. Naxos, one of the few remaining islands held by the enemy in the Ægean, surrendered on October 15. Since that date Allied sea and air domination of the Ægean has been completed; many islands, such as Leuitha, Santorin, Lemnos, Scarpanto and Chios, have been reoccupied. Various specially trained units, including Earl Jellicoe's Royal Marine Commandos, and the Greek Sacred Squadron, were taken in little boats from a secret base at Casteloriso to visit practically every island. Over 100,000 tons of enemy shipping has also been sunk.

THE GREEK PRIME MINISTER, M. GEORGE PAPANDREOU, WITH GENERAL SCOBIE CLIMBING THE STEPS OF THE ACROPOLIS.

RUSSIA LIBERATES NORTHERN FINLAND AND NORWAY.

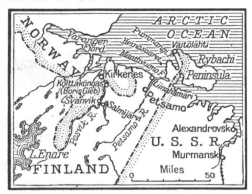

NORWAY'S PROUD MOMENT: WITH THEIR FLAG CARRIED ALOFT, THE FIRST NORWEGIAN TROOPS MARCHING INTO LIBERATED KIRKENES WITHIN FORTY-EIGHT HOURS OF ITS CAPTURE, THANKS TO RUSSIAN COOPERATION.

PETSAMO, THE ICE-FREE FINNISH NAVAL BASE AND NICKEL PORT WHICH FELL TO A COMBINED SOVIET SEA AND LAND ASSAULT ON OCTOBER 15.

Finland signed a treaty with Russia on August 19, one of the effects of which was to free Russian troops, who had been confronting the Finns in the south of Finland, to attack the Germans in the north.

On October 15 Russian troops from the Karelian front broke through the German defence zone north-west of Murmansk, and captured Petsamo, strongly fortified by the enemy. Its capture cuts the only sea-escape route for the German troops trapped in the north of Finland. An Order of the Day from Marshal Stalin on the night of October 25 announced that that day the Red Army had crossed the frontier of German-occupied Norway, and that troops of General Meretskov's forces had captured Kirkenes, the chief German naval and transport base above the Arctic Circle.

FLIGHTS OF FANCY IN CAMOUFLAGE FOR ENEMY AND ALLIED DEFENCES.

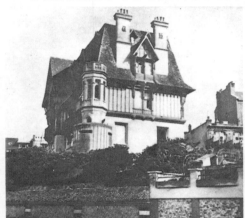

OVERLOOKING THE HARBOUR AT LE HAVRE, THIS GERMAN PILL-BOX, ONE OF MANY CONSTRUCTED TO MERGE INTO THEIR BACK-GROUNDS, WAS BUILT INTO THE CORNER OF A VILLA.

THE BOOKSTALL THAT WASN'T A BOOKSTALL! THE CLEVERLY-CAMOUFLAGED CONCRETE MACHINE-GUN POST BUILT IN PARLIA-MENT SQUARE WHEN INVASION WAS FEARED.

A "TEA KIOSK" WHICH HAS DECEIVED MANY; IN REALITY, A PILL-BOX ON THE APPROACH TO THE KINGSTON BY-PASS.

Although well-known for their clever tricks of deceptions, the Germans do not have a monopoly of inventive camouflage. The defences of the London District included an outer ring of forts with a 100-mile anti-tank ditch, and two inner rings of pill-boxes, as well as those in the West End, such as the Enquiry Bureau at the top of Whitehall and 'Smith's bookstall' at the other end of the same street. The best camouflage results were usually obtained by disguise rather than by any attempt to hide the actual post. It would not be surprising, for instance, to find a chapter-house next to a chapel, or a somewhat similar erection by the Fulham Church at the end of Putney Bridge. The "tea kiosk" (shown above) deceived many. The loopholes in the pill-boxes were covered with metal gauze, painted on the outside to match the adjoining material, which would enable the men of the garrison to see attackers approaching whilst themselves remaining invisible. With their weapons levelled in readiness, all the defenders had to do was to unmask the loopholes by releasing a string, when the covers, hinged at the bottom, fell outwards. The officer responsible was Captain G. V. Myer, F.R.I.B.A., the architect who designed Broadcasting House.

ON THE EASTERN FRONT: THE GREAT SOVIET DRIVE ACROSS HUNGARY.

SOVIET ARTILLERY UNITS CROSSING A BRIDGE OVER THE RIVER TISZA EN ROUTE TO THE DANUBE, WHICH WAS SUBSEQUENTLY FORCED ON A WIDE FRONT.

THE FATE OF BUDAPEST: A MAP OF THE RUSSIAN FRONT IN HUNGARY, WITH THE CAPITAL COMPLETELY ENCIRCLED.

On November 30 this year it was announced that Soviet troops had smashed through the German defence lines on the Danube and were driving towards Lake Balaton and the Austrian frontier. A week later the Russian High Command reported that their troops had entirely cleared the southern shore of Lake Balaton of the enemy. Meanwhile, on their right flank, other Soviet armies were steadily out-flanking the Hungarian capital, Budapest, and on December 10 were reported to be closing in on the city from north, east and south. On December 30, Red Army emissaries were murdered as they proposed terms of capitulation. The final battle for Budapest was expected to be the bitterest the East Front has seen. It was expected that the beautiful city on the Danube would suffer gravely.

ANTWERP: THE OPENING OF A GREAT SUPPLY PORT FOR THE WESTERN FRONT.

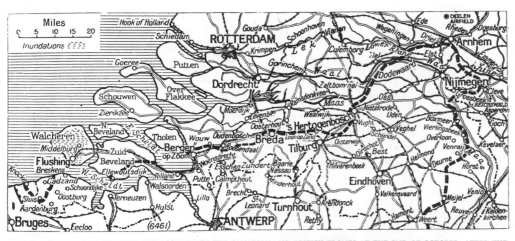

SOUTH-WEST HOLLAND, SHOWING THE POSITION OF THE CANADIAN AND BRITISH FRONTS AT THE END OF OCTOBER: AFTER THE CLEARING OF THE SCHELDT ESTUARY AND THE EXPULSION OF THE GERMANS FROM THE DUTCH MAINLAND SOUTH OF THE MAAS, GENERAL DEMPSEY WAS REPORTED TO BE PREPARING TO BREAK OPEN THE DUTCH GATEWAY INTO GERMANY.

Having narrowly failed to break through at Arnhem in September, the British and Canadian Armies in Holland turned their attention to strengthening their hold over the gains made by the "Market Garden" thrust and in clearing the Scheldt Estuary in order to allow fresh supplies to come in through the port of Antwerp. By the end of October the Eindhoven-Nijmegen corridor had been expanded to a salient as can be seen in our map, and operations north and west of Antwerp were well in hand. Breskens, the chief port of the pocket held by the Germans on the south bank of the Scheldt Estuary and from which they were operating big railway guns commanding the Estuary, fell to troops of the Canadian First Army on October 22. At the same time, other Canadian forces entered Fort Frederik Hendrik, a mile west of Breskens, where the Germans had coastal batteries dominating the Scheldt gateway to Antwerp. As the Allied forces drove the Germans back on Breskens, the garrison there attempted to assemble an escape fleet of small boats in which to cross to Flushing, but this was largely smashed up by Allied bombing.

By then the Canadians were already across the escape neck of the Beveland peninsula, and the British were threatening Hertogenbosch, an important junction on the railway running from the north to Tilburg and Bergen-op-Zoom, and then to Flushing.

Royal Marine Commandos landed in their amphibious fighting vehicles at Westkapelle, Walcheren Island, on November 1. From this bridgehead they pushed north and south along the dyke to Domburg and Zoutelande, and gradually silenced the big guns which controlled the Scheldt estuary to Antwerp. The landing on Walcheren was to have been covered, as on the beaches of Normandy, by an air attack on the

BRITISH MARINE COMMANDOS LANDING AT WESTKAPELLE, WALCHEREN ISLAND, IN THE FACE OF HEAVY ENEMY FIRE: THE SCENE ON THE BEACH-HEAD AS THE INVADING FORCE WERE DRIVING AMPHIBIOUS FIGHTING VEHICLES ASHORE AFTER LANDING AT DAWN.

A HUSBAND AND WIFE PADDLING SALVAGED FURNITURE FROM THEIR MAROONED HOME ON WALCHEREN ISLAND TO DRY LAND AND NEW ACCOMMODATION.

concrete emplacements of the German 250-mm. guns, but unfortunately the weather prevented air operations and the assaulting forces were thus exposed to the full brunt of the enemy batteries. They went in to the beaches at Westkapelle under withering enemy gunfire, which sank many of their landing craft, and defeated the German garrison against what at first seemed almost impossible odds. Upwards of 80 per cent. of our support craft were reported to have been lost. Except for a few districts, Walcheren Island is almost completely under water, and its capture was only made possible by the landings in the west and south, which followed an assault across the causeway from South Beveland. The most severe fighting was in Flushing, where British infantry waded waist-high in water to capture the H.Q. of Flushing's German garrison. When it fell, hundreds of German prisoners trooped out from pill-boxes and underground tunnels, with their commander in tears.

On November 6, General Dempsey's Second Army was along the line of the Maas, thus practically freeing all the Dutch mainland south of that river. On Walcheren Island, except beyond Domburg and Middelburg, which was surrounded, the enemy was defeated, thus opening the vital port of Antwerp to the Allied Armies. After minesweepers and divers had cleared a channel through the minefields and obstructions the port of Antwerp was opened to traffic on November 26.

THE FIRST COASTER ENTERING ANTWERP. THE PORT HAS WET BASINS COVERING NEARLY 26 MILES OF DOCK FRONTAGE, AND THREE MILES OF RIVERSIDE QUAYS.

BREENDONCK AND 'S-HERTOGENBOSCH.

A BELGIAN WIFE CUTTING A SLIVER OF WOOD FROM THE STAKE AGAINST WHICH HER HUSBAND STOOD BEFORE A FIRING-SQUAD IN THE COURTYARD OF BREENDONCK.

The fort of Breendonck, between Brussels and Antwerp, was the scene of some of the ugliest of German atrocities in Belgium. One of the rooms contains branding-irons, heated on a small stove in sight of victims strapped to a table; in another are steel rods used for whipping men and women for hours on end; a third contains a pulley from which victims were slung by their ankles and jerked up and down: a fourth has inlet pipes which played alternate blasts of fiery-hot and ice-cold air on naked prisoners; a fifth is a gas chamber. There are other rooms – and all of them have peepholes through which the Germans could watch the struggles and agonies of their victims. Outside the fort are gallows with a low drop on which victims strangled slowly to death in the nooses, and rows of stakes against which the tortured victims were finally shot. Belgium intends to preserve Breendonck intact. As our troops move on into Holland a further chapter has been added to the horrible story of Nazi concentration camps, by the capture of 's-Hertogenbosch. It is called the "hygienic hell," and 13,000 people died at the camp, their bodies burnt in the three large ovens provided for the purpose. Unlike Lublin, and other camps we have illustrated, gallows were used at 's-Hertogenbosch, "on the slightest provocation," as British soldiers were told by Dutch inhabitants of the locality.

GERMAN TORTURE CENTRES.

THE CAMP WHERE 13,000 DIED – 'S-HERTOGENBOSCH CONCENTRATION CAMP. ONE OF THE THREE OVENS USED FOR THE CREMATION OF THE VICTIMS.

THE WESTERN FRONT: ADVANCES ALL ALONG THE ALLIED LINE.

The Siegfried Line – Hitler's "unbreakable" West Wall – has been pierced and Allied troops hold a bridgehead through it between Merkstein and Geilenkirchen, to the north of Aachen. As we write, comes news of a new assault east of Aachen, in a north-west direction, by General Hodges's First Army, in a bid to join with the American troops holding the bridgehead. Already the gap between the two pincer arms on Aachen has almost closed on October 9, and the possibility of the German garrison of 1500 S.S. troops, inside the town, escaping has become slight.

Aachen has fallen. Ten days after the "surrender or die" ultimatum to the garrison, the end came on the evening of Friday, October 20. The city we have won, of immense stategic importance, is little but a skeleton, a city of ruins where not a building has escaped damage. Dead Germans are everywhere, piled against sand-bagged basement windows which have been machine-gun nests, or sprawling in shattered doorways.

On November 16, General Eisenhower suddenly threw the secret U.S. Ninth Army, under General William Hood Simpson, into a violent offensive preceded by an earth-shaking barrage of shells and overhead bombers. Its location, to deceive the enemy, was in liaison with Dempsey's Second British Army on its north, and Hodges' First U.S.

THE "V-13" – AN AACHEN TRAMCAR BEING FILLED WITH GERMAN AMMUNITION BY U.S. ENGINEERS AND FITTED WITH A TIME-FUSE PRIOR TO ITS BEING ROLLED DOWNHILL INTO THE CITY.

A LEAF FROM THEIR OWN BOOK: GERMAN CIVILIANS LEARN WHAT IT IS TO LOSE HOME AND POSSESSIONS IN THE FACE OF AN ADVANCING ARMY.

A BRITISH A.V.R.E. TANK, OF THE TYPE USED FOR SMASHING FORTIFICATIONS, ENTERING GEILENKIRCHEN, WHICH WAS HEAVILY DEFENDED BY CONCRETE STRONGHOLDS.

TWO AMERICAN SOLDIERS EXAMINING THE BATTERED REMAINS OF A FORT DRIANT WALL. THE STRONGHOLD WAS THE SCENE OF FURIOUS FIGHTING IN UNDERGROUND TUNNELS.

STRASBOURG, CAPITAL OF ALSACE-LORRAINE, WAS FREED ON NOVEMBER 23: A FRENCH HALF-TRACK AND CREW (PLUS LOCAL BOY) CARRY HITLER'S PORTRAIT AS A TROPHY.

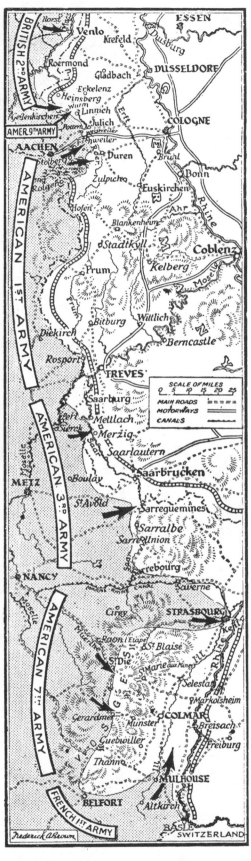

THE WESTERN FRONT: A MAP SHOWING THE POSITION OF SIX OF THE SEVEN ALLIED ARMIES, FROM THE BRITISH SECOND ARMY IN THE NORTH TO THE FRENCH FIRST ARMY IN THE SOUTH. THE CANADIAN FIRST ARMY IS OF COURSE TO THE NORTH AND WEST OF THE BRITISH.

Army on its south. It advanced, without great opposition, on an average of 1000 yards on a nine-mile front, between Geilenkirchen and Eschweiler. Several towns were overrun and left behind in flames, giving the German population a taste of what they had given others. Further south, the Germans were in general retreat along the whole of the American Third Army front; their convoys moving steadily east. This retreat came just twelve days after the opening of General Patton's attack and with the fortress of Metz – the main German defensive position this side of the Maginot Line – still the scene of bitter street-fighting. All organised resistance ceased during the evening of November 20th.

Fort Driant, west of Merz, finally fell to the 5th Infantry Division of the U.S. Third Army on December 8. Its capture left only one remaining Metz fort holding out – Fort Jeanne d'Arc – and this fell five days later, on the morning of December 13, when 520 prisoners were taken. Its last teeth drawn, Metz presents no further menace to our lines of communication.

Meanwhile the French Forces, under the direct command of General Leclerc, advanced rapidly on Mulhouse and then on Strasbourg. French tanks, with the aid of infantry of the U.S. Seventh Army, freed this important strategic city on November 23, and endeavoured to seize three bridges crossing the Rhine from it, which the enemy had mined but not yet destroyed. On November 24, U.S. and French reconnaissance units crossed the Rhine for the first time.

The news is good from all along the Allied line on the Western Front, with Berlin reporting a "tremendous" Allied concentration of tanks and men massed before the Siegfried Line. Meanwhile General Patton's U.S. Third Army troops have fought their way against tough opposition into the Saar basin, and General Hodge's U.S. First Army has pressed on to only a short distance from Duren, capturing Echiz and D'Horn. The enemy is clearly struggling desperately to hold on to every yard of German soil in the hope that something will happen to turn the remorseless tide of war, but while he still hopes, the whole line moves doggedly into position, and there has not been a day since the offensive opened when one or other of the Allied armies has not made some advance to the east.

ROOSEVELT'S FOURTH TERM.

THE DEMOCRATIC CANDIDATE FOR THE 1944 PRESIDENTIAL ELEC-
TIONS, FRANKLIN D. ROOSEVELT, PRESIDENT OF THE UNITED
STATES OF AMERICA SINCE 1933.

President Roosevelt, who has been President of the United States of America since 1933, was re-elected for a fourth term on November 7. His Vice-President is Harry S. Truman, former chairman of the committee charged with investigating defence expenditure, which is said to have saved the American tax payer more than one billion dollars.

DRAMATIC END OF THE TIRPITZ.

THE "TIRPITZ" AFTER BEING SUNK BY R.A.F. BOMBER COMMAND.

The "Tirpitz" has been sunk. Germany's great 45,000-ton battleship has been sent to the bottom of Tromsö Fjord by direct hits from 12,000-lb. bombs dropped by twenty-nine Lancasters of R.A.F. Bomber Command led by Wing-Commander J. B. Tait and Squadron-Leader A. G. Williams on the morning of Sunday, November 12.

ARMISTICE DAY IN PARIS.

ALLIED FLAGS, SYMBOL OF UNITY, FORM A BACKGROUND AS TWO OF THE WORLD'S GREAT LEADERS, MR CHURCHILL AND GENERAL DE GAULLE, STAND AT THE SALUTING BASE IN PARIS.

The reunion of the people of Paris and the Prime Minister was one of the most moving experiences in the liberation of France. As in the past, an immense Tricolor hung from the vault of the Arc de Triomphe at the Tomb of the Unknown Soldier on November 11, and Mr. Churchill and General de Gaulle each laid a wreath on the Tomb.

ALLIED PARTISANS IN ITALY: MUTUAL HELP IN THE MOUNTAIN WAR.

PARTISANS BEHIND THE BRITISH LINES FOR RE-EQUIPMENT AND REST: (LEFT) THE PRIEST OF SAN VALENTINO, WITH THE PARTISAN LEADER AND ADHERENTS.

In a proclamation to Italian patriots, quoted by Rome radio on the night of November 12, General Alexander said: "The summer campaign in Italy is over, and the winter campaign is about to begin." Almost simultaneous with this announcement came the news from Allied H.Q. in Italy that British troops of the Eighth Army, advancing beyond Forli, which they captured on November 9, had forced a bridgehead across the Canale Nuovo, north-west of the town, against bitter opposition. Snow is reported to have fallen in all the mountainous areas of the Italian front, and to a depth of 9 ins. in the higher Apennines.
The quality of Italian patriotic resistance groups has greatly advanced since the Allies entered Tuscany. The patriots were entrusted with the task of taking over the administration of Florence since the Germans evacuated it as an open city – although they committed characteristic demolitions. In Leghorn (Livorno), Arezzo, Ancona, and, reports say, Ravenna, partisans took up arms against the enemy to prevent him from wanton destruction. The partisans, who have been appealed to more than once by Field-Marshal Alexander, have rendered great assistance by carrying out large-scale sabotage and guerrilla warfare. They have been

THE LAST PARADE OF A STEADFAST FORCE: THE PASSING OF THE HOME GUARD.

THE HOME GUARD STAND-DOWN PARADE IN LONDON: CONTINGENTS GIVING THE "EYES LEFT" TO THEIR ROYAL COLONEL-IN-CHIEF, THE KING.

extremely useful also in pointing out to the Allied forces where German mines are laid. Many of the patriot bands were formed long ago, during the Fascist régime, to keep alive Italy's true traditions.
The capture of Ravenna on December 5 and Faenza on December 16 were important milestones in the Eighth Army's advance on the extreme right of the Allied front in Italy. Since the assault on the Gustav Line last winter Allied troops have fought their way against thirty German divisions, 56,000 being taken prisoner, 34,000 killed, and 104,000 wounded.
"The Home Guard has reached the end of its long tour of duty under arms. But I know that your devotion to our land, your comradeship, your power to work your hardest at the end of the longest day, will discover new outlets for patriotic service in time of peace . . ."
These words come in the King's message to the Home Guard on the occasion of the Home Guard's official Stand Down. To mark this event, parades were held all over the country, and notably in London, where about 7100 representative members paraded before the King.

GENERAL RONALD SCOBIE, BRITISH O.C. GREECE, MEETING THE TWO GREEK RIVAL MILITARY LEADERS, BEFORE THE OUTBREAK OF VIOLENCE: (LEFT) GENERAL SARAFIS, COMMANDING E.L.A.S., AND (RIGHT) GENERAL ZERVAS, COMMANDING E.D.E.S.

MR CHURCHILL, WITH ARCHBISHOP DAMASKINOS AND A BODY-GUARD, PHOTOGRAPHED IN ATHENS DURING THE PRIME MINIS-TER'S CHRISTMAS MISSION TO GREECE. THE ARCHBISHOP HAS SINCE BEEN APPOINTED REGENT.

STREET-FIGHTING IN ATHENS: BRITISH PARATROOPS, SUPPORTED BY TANKS AND UNDER CONSTANT SNIPING, ADVANCING AT THE DOUBLE INTO EURIPIDHOU STREET. THEIR JOB WAS TO SEARCH BUILDINGS. WITH THEM WENT GREEK POLICE.

On December 2, the Greek E.L.A.S. formations, the military wing of E.A.M., under Communist leaders, began violent action in Athens and the Piræus to overthrow the Government of M. Papandreou to create a *coup d'état* and seize power. The trouble arose originally owing to the agreed disbandment of the armed E.L.A.S., which resulted in violent denunciations of the Premier, the calling of a general strike, and street-fighting. Anarchy became so alarming that General Scobie, in order to maintain order, was forced to employ British forces, including tanks, armoured cars, paratroops and naval aid, and incurred British casualties. M. Papandreou, head of the Provisional Government of Greece, offered to resign, but the British Government, deeming it essential to maintain the existing régime at the moment, until the Greeks could elect their Government, objected.
On December 12, Mr. Harold Macmillan and Field-Marshal Alexander were despatched to deal with the situation in Athens to the best of their ability, to bring about a reconciliation between the Government of M. Papandreou and E.L.A.S., or at least an agreement to stop further partisan guerrilla warfare. On December 16, fighting in the streets of Athens was severe; now, fighting is still going on, and savage encounters are taking place north-east and north-west of Omonia Square as picked British detachments carry on with their

difficult task of clearing street by street. The fighting, however, is moving towards the outskirts.
Mr. Churchill and Mr. Eden, who had flown to Athens late on Christmas Eve returned to London on Friday afternoon, December 29, and reported immediately to the War Cabinet. After the Cabinet meeting the King of the Hellenes called on Mr. Churchill, and this consultation was followed by several important and hopeful developments during the week-end. The first of them was a declaration by the King of the Hellenes, on December 30, appointing Archbishop Damaskinos as Regent of Greece – a popular and wise decision, as the Archbishop has the trust and respect of the great majority of Greeks at home and overseas. The declaration also stated the resolve of the King of the Hellenes "not to return to Greece unless summoned by a free and fair expression of the national will." Other developments in the situation included a memorandum from the Central Committee of E.A.M. addressed to Mr. Churchill, announcing that the basic points of General Scobie's memorandum had been accepted; General Scobie's reply, which sought a clarification of this alleged acceptance of "basic points" and foreshadowed the cessation of hostilities; and the resignation of the Greek Government under M. Papandreou on December 31, to permit the formation of a new Cabinet under the Regency of Archbishop Damaskinos.

THE ENEMY BREAK-THROUGH IN BELGIUM: VON RUNDSTEDT'S OFFENSIVE IN THE WEST.

FIELD-MARSHAL KARL VON RUNDSTEDT (RIGHT), THE LEADER OF THE PRESENT GERMAN OFFENSIVE AGAINST THE AMERICAN FIRST ARMY, STUDYING A MAP IN THE FIELD.

THIS PICTURE FROM A CAPTURED GERMAN FILM IS DESCRIBED AS SHOWING AN ENEMY SOLDIER GIVING A HAND SIGNAL TO ADVANCE.

GERMAN TROOPS PASSING A ROAD SIGN ON THE WAY TO ST. VITH, A HOTLY CONTESTED POINT IN THE EARLY STAGES OF THE ENEMY ADVANCE INTO BELGIUM.

When Field Marshal von Rundstedt opened his new offensive at dawn on December 16, against the American First Army he threw in fifteen divisions, representing from 150,000 to 225,000 men. On December 20, the Americans were bringing up big reserves and holding the enemy in various places, but between Montjoie (Monschau) which the Americans have recovered after heavy fighting, and St. Vith, he seems to have driven a gap of 25 miles in the U.S. front. In this area, Malmedy and Stavelot were claimed by the enemy. More disconcerting was the German claim that they had captured Verviers, only 15½ miles from Liége. Further south a strong drive was reported on Bastogne, while another proceeding from Trier (Treves) *via* Echternach was on the highway to Luxembourg. Jet-propelled German aircraft were reported to be bombing and strafing Allied positions in the opening stages of von Rundstedt's full-scale counter-offensive and at least one jet-propelled Me.262 was shot down on the first day. German losses in this push have been very heavy, and

AT STAVELOT GERMAN S.S. TROOPS SHOT WOMEN AND CHILDREN IN COLD BLOOD: A U.S. OFFICER LOOKING AT A DEAD BOY OF ABOUT SIX.

WHERE UNITS OF THE 101ST U.S. AIRBORNE DIVISION SUCCESSFULLY WITHSTOOD ALL NAZI ATTEMPTS AT A BREAK-THROUGH – BASTOGNE, BELGIUM, SHOWING A GROUP OF REFUGEES PLODDING THROUGH THE CENTRE OF THE TOWN.

the grave accusation has been made against von Rundstedt that many U.S. prisoners have been shot after surrender. Field-Marshal Karl von Rundstedt possesses all the traditional qualities of the Prussian general. Militarily he has a record of success which no German general has approached since Moltke.

On December 18 there were no effective American fighting troops within forty miles of the important communications centre of Bologne, apart from isolated units retreating from the shattered front line and von Lüttwitz panzers were within fifteen miles of its outskirts. Nevertheless it was the American 101st Airborne Division, supported by elements of the 10th Armoured Division, which won the race to the town during the night of December 19–20 and gallantly defended Bastogne during a seven-day siege. Under their commander, Brig.-General A. C. McAuliffe, the garrison made an epic stand, repulsing all attacks and inflicting losses in tanks and men. Contact was made, on December 27, from the south and by the 4th Armoured Division of

DROPPING SUPPLIES BY PARACHUTE TO THE BASTOGNE DEFENDERS: DOZENS OF PARACHUTES, CARRYING AMMUNITION AND FOOD, MAY BE SEEN IN THE AIR.

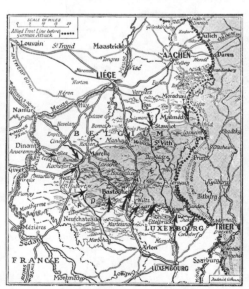

THE GERMAN BULGE IN BELGIUM: A MAP SHOWING GENERAL PATTON'S OFFENSIVE THRUST NORTHWARD ON DECEMBER 31, WHILE THE ENEMY WAS FIRMLY HELD IN THE NORTH AND WEST.

AMERICAN SOLDIERS BRUSHING THE SNOW FROM THE BODIES OF 130 COMRADES WHO, AS PRISONERS, HAD BEEN MASSACRED IN COLD BLOOD BY VON RUNDSTEDT'S TROOPS.

General Patton's Third Army. On the Nazis' own admission, Patton's lightning drive slowed down and eventually checked the advances by Rundstedt's southern columns. By December 27 also the Allied command's new dispositions had been made, and the German drive slowed down. From then on, the initiative slipped from Rundstedt's grasp into the hands of the Allies, whose air forces in clearer weather were able to make a decisive contribution to the halting of the enemy offensive. As usual, the Germans have shown their cold-blooded and murderous tactics. One of several instances was when two German tanks poured a hail of machine-gun bullets into 130 defenceless American prisoners, including Red Cross men, after stripping them of all their possessions. At Stavelot, as one of our pictures bears grim witness, are the huddled bodies of Belgian civilians in the courtyard of a house where, during the hand-to-hand fighting, the Germans shot mothers and children in cold blood.

At the turn of the year it was believed in the highest military circles that von Rundstedt's great offensive had failed. He gained much territory and committed much damage, but he appeared to have got himself into an impossible position. Just before midnight of New Year's eve, General Patton's Third Army launched a new full-scale offensive against the southern flank of the German salient in the Ardennes.

THE ILLUSTRATED LONDON NEWS

GEN. GEORGE MARSHALL: CHIEF OF STAFF OF U.S. ARMY. 1939–1945.

The man who virtually created the new United States Army, General George Catlett Marshall, was appointed Chief of Staff in the autumn of 1939, when President Roosevelt and Secretary of War Henry L. Stimson lifted him, then a brigadier, over the heads of twenty major-generals and fourteen brigadiers to the highest military post in America. Since his appointment General Marshall has achieved the stupendous task of building an American Army completely new in concept from top to bottom, and designed specifically for its present task.

As Secretary of State (1947–1949) under President Truman he devised and carried through the European Recovery Programme, better known as the "Marshall Plan" under which the U.S.A. supplied economic aid for the post-war reconstruction of Europe. For this he was awarded a Nobel Peace Prize in 1953.

1945

Communist uprising in Greece quelled — Russians take Warsaw, liberate Auschwitz, and cross Oder 50 miles from Berlin — Burma Road cleared — Yalta Conference — Dresden bombed — Western Allies advance to and cross Rhine — US/Chinese take Lashio; British take Mandalay — US takes Iwo Jima — Allies surround Ruhr, trapping more than 300,000 German troops — Advance concentrated on Southern Germany, leaving Berlin to Russians — US invades Okinawa — Kamikaze attacks begin — Battle of Vienna — Battle of East China Sea — Roosevelt dies; Vice President Truman takes over — Buchenwald and Belsen liberated by Allies — US lands on Mindanao — US and Russian troops meet on Elbe — San Francisco Conference completes UN Charter — Mussolini captured and killed by partisans — German army in Italy surrenders — Hitler and Goebbels commit suicide — Berlin surrenders to Russians — British take Hamburg and Rangoon — German armies in Europe surrender — German High Command and Provisional Government arrested — Burma cleared; Australians land in Borneo — Okinawa falls to US — 50 nations sign UN Charter — Churchill loses General Election in Britain — Philippines declared liberated — Atomic bomb tested — Potsdam Conference; Attlee replaces Churchill; division of Germany agreed — Atomic bombs dropped on Hiroshima and Nagasaki — Russia invades Manchuria — Japan surrenders.

WITH THE U.S. 7TH ARMY ON THE ALSACE FRONT – ALLIED VICTORY AT COLMAR.

WOMEN AND CHILDREN, WEARING THE NATIONAL COSTUMES OF ALSACE, WALK-ING IN THE VICTORY PROCESSION THROUGH THE CITY SQUARE OF COLMAR, LIBERATED BY FRENCH AND AMERICAN TROOPS UNDER GENERAL DE LATTRE DE TASSIGNY.

U.S. TROOPS TAKING COVER FROM AN ENORMOUS EXPLOSION AS A SEVEN-ROOMED GERMAN PILL-BOX, BLOWN UP BY SAPPERS, RAINS CONCRETE OVER A WIDE AREA.

AMERCIAN M-10 TANK-DESTROYERS, OPERATING AS ARTILLERY, LIGHT UP THE SNOW-COVERED BATTLEFIELD IN A NIGHT BARRAGE ON ENEMY POSITIONS. THE BLIZZARDS HAVE BEEN AL-MOST CONTINUAL ON THE ALSACE FRONT.

On New Year's Day a two-pronged German attack on Strasbourg was launched south from the Saarland and north from the Colmar Pocket by forces under the direct control of Heinrich Himmler, who on November 26 had been put in charge of all German troops and aircraft on the Upper Rhine.

Although the pace of the operations north of Strasbourg has temporarily slackened, it is becoming clear that the enemy is throwing in some of his best troops. Making the most of bad flying weather – an almost continual blizzard is in progress on the Alsace front – large reinforcements of armour and infantry have been ferried across the Rhine into the bridgehead between Gambsheim and Selz.

Meantime, operations in Alsace have taken a new turn, with a series of strong attacks launched against German troops in the Colmar pocket by forces of General de Lattre de Tassigny's French Army who claim to have written the German Nineteenth Army off the strength of the Wehrmacht. With the British advance towards the Roer and the steady ironing out of the Ardennes salient, this attack shows that the Allies are regaining the initiative in the west.

ALLIED COUNTER-OFFENSIVES ON VON RUNDSTEDT'S FLANKS: IRONING OUT THE GERMAN BULGE.

TWO ARMIES MEET IN HOUFFALIZE: A HALF-TRACK OF THE 2ND ARMOURED DIVISION, FIRST U.S. ARMY, CROSSING THE OURTHE TO LINK UP WITH THE THIRD ARMY.

On January 16, armoured forces of the United States Third Army, approaching from the west, entered Houffalize and there met men of the 2nd Armoured Division of the First Army, who had got in from the north the previous night. Patrols which entered the town at midnight found that it had been hurriedly abandoned, and the meeting of these two American armies meant the virtual writing-off of the deep salient thrust into the Ardennes by the Germans a month ago.

THE NEW "LUNGS" OF THE U-BOAT: THE SCHNORKEL BREATHING SYSTEM REVIVES THEIR THREAT.

THE EXHAUST AND FRESH-AIR "PERISCOPE" WHICH ENABLES U-BOATS TO REMAIN UNDER WATER FOR LONG PERIODS.

A joint statement by President Roosevelt and Mr Churchill on December 9 gave first warning of a new device which enables U-boats to remain submerged for long periods, and thus to penetrate into areas denied to them for three years. The Germans claim that the new device, necessitated by our Ceaselers anti-U-boat campaign which has made it almost suicidal for a U-boat to surface by day or by night, and known as the Schnorkel Spirall, enables a submarine to take in fresh air without surfacing.

THE BRITISH SECOND ARMY CLEAR THE ROER SALIENT.

A "TWO-GOAT-POWER" VEHICLE USED BY BRITISH TROOPS FOR FETCHING RATIONS FROM THE COMPANY COOKHOUSE TO FORWARD TROOPS.

An attack by the British Second Army northward from Sittard on the morning of January 16 was aimed at the German salient between Roermond, on the north, and Geilenkirchen, on the south. The attack, which opened in fog, has continued in wintry weather, which has not prevented the Second Army troops pushing steadily into Germany. The village of Dieteren was captured on the opening day and on the following day our troops took Susteren and the little town and road junction of Echt, in Holland. This success was followed by the capture of Hongen, across the border inside Germany. On January 21 the British were reported to have captured the German village of Bocket, to have reached Waldfeucht to the north, and to be engaged in clearing the Echter woods. By January 26 the salient had been eliminated and the Germans driven back to the Roer river.

A GERMAN SNIPER'S "CROW'S NEST" IN A TREE-TOP FOUND BY BRITISH SECOND ARMY TROOPS WHEN THEY ENTERED THE GER-MAN TOWN OF SAEFFEINE.

THE WINTER CAMPAIGN OF THE RED ARMY: WARSAW LIBERATED.

TROOPS OF THE RED ARMY AND THE POLES SERVING UNDER THE LUBLIN GOVERNMENT PASSING THROUGH THE STREETS OF WARSAW. IN THE BACKGROUND A SCENE OF UTTER DESOLATION AND DESTRUCTION.

THE LIBERATION OF WARSAW: UNITS OF THE POLISH ARMY PASSING THROUGH WARSAW SQUARE.

On January 14, Marshal Koniev launched a big new offensive in Poland, and cut the railway from Kielce to Cracow, the great industrial centre and German base. A second new offensive was reported on the River Narew sector, moving to encircle Warsaw and outflank East Prussia from the south. A third offensive was also reported in East Prussia, with fifteen divisions and tank formations between Eydtkuhnen and Schlossberg, west of Insterburg. From East Prussia to Budapest the Russians had thrown in vast armies. In the main attack the fall of Kielce and 400 other places was followed by many other strategic centres, so that on January 18 Koniev was on the borders of German Silesia. Meanwhile Marshal Zhukov was advancing on a line towards Berlin, and Marshal Rokossovsky threatened East Prussia from the South. Warsaw, encircled by Marshal Zhukov's troops from the south, fell on January 17. Meantime, Marshal Rokossovsky, had entered the Junker territories on a front of 50 miles, while General Cherniakovsky was assailing East Prussia from the north.

THE RUSSIAN HURRICANE OFFENSIVE INTO GERMANY: THE ODER CROSSED.

INFANTRYMEN OF THE RED ARMY MARCHING THROUGH THE STREETS OF CRACOW, SECOND CITY IN POLAND, WHOSE LIBERATION PRECEDED KONIEV'S SILESIAN DRIVE.

THE BATTLE OF GERMANY: SHOWING EAST PRUSSIA'S ENCIRCLEMENT AND THE DRIVE FOR BERLIN.

RUSSIAN SELF-PROPELLED GUNS, WITH TOMMY-GUNNERS ON BOARD, DRIVING ON TOWARDS GERMAN DEFENCE POSITIONS DURING THE RED ARMY'S ADVANCE INTO GERMANY.

The Russian steamroller advance into the Reich itself may lead to more spectacular events in the near future. As our map shows, East Prussia and Latvia, is sufficiently momentous. General Bagramyan captured Memel, and completed the liberation of Lithuania. Rokossovsky, on January 28, was blocking the German retreat from East Prussia and advancing on Zhukov's right while Marshal Zhukov had his spearheads thrust forward into Brandenburg. In Silesia Koniev, once he consolidated his crossings of the Oder, was free to advance along its left bank and loosen the German hold opposite Zhukov, in the Middle Oder.

Marshal Zhukov's men are still pushing ahead. On February 3 they captured Sonnenburg and the fall of Reppen severed the last lateral railway and main road connecting the Brandenburg battlefield with Pomerania. From East Prussia and the central Oder sectors heavy fighting is reported and General Cherniakovsky is bringing his full strength to bear on Königsberg. In the last few day forces under Marshals Zhukov and Rokossovsky have reached the Baltic at two places in the Kolberg area, trapping all German troops in Eastern Pomerania.

THE CRIMEA CONFERENCE WHICH SOUNDED THE DEATH KNELL OF NAZISM.

A VIEW OF THE LIVADIA PALACE, YALTA, WHERE THE THREE-POWER CONFERENCE TOOK PLACE OVER EIGHT DAYS.

The conference of Mr. Churchill, President Roosevelt, and Marshal Stalin, held at Yalta has drawn up military plans for the final defeat of Germany. The conference has also agreed on plans for enforcing the "no surrender" terms but these terms will not be made known until German armed resistance has been crushed. The forces of the three Powers will each occupy a separate zone of Germany, with a central control commission H.Q. in Berlin. The Crimea conference was held at the Livadia Palace from February 4 to 11.

The results have been greeted everywhere with whole-hearted approval, and the meeting has laid the foundation-stone for the creation of a long and durable peace.

THREE GREAT LEADERS: (L.-R.) MR. CHURCHILL, WEARING A COSSACK CAP; PRESIDENT ROOSEVELT; AND MARSHALL STALIN, IN THE GROUNDS OF THE LIVADIA PALACE.

DRESDEN: BOMBED BY THE ALLIES IN SUPPORT OF THE RED ARMY.

A VIEW OF THE BAROQUE-STYLE ZWINGER, WHICH, WITH THE MUSEUM, CONTAINED DRESDEN'S MOST FAMOUS PICTURES.

FIRES BURNING IN DRESDEN DURING THE ATTACK BY LANCASTERS OF R.A.F. BOMBER COMMAND ON THE NIGHT OF FEBRUARY 13–14.

After the attack by R.A.F. Lancasters on February 13–14 the city lay in ruins, with fires everywhere. Among other famous buildings totally destroyed in the attacks, regrettably but necessarily, since the Nazis use every German city as a fortress, were reported by German wireless: the Opera House, famed for Richard Strauss's operas, first produced there; the Zwinger, a baroque edifice of the eighteenth century; the Royal Palace; the picture gallery; the Academy of Arts, and the two town halls. The raids produced panic in the city. 39,773 persons were classed as "officially identified dead". Most of these were asphyxiated in shelters or cellars as the resulting "fire storm" sucked all oxygen from the city. At least another 20,000 are believed to have died, buried in the rubble, or too badly burned to be identified.

THE ALLIED CAMPAIGN IN BURMA: SCENES OF THE JUNGLE ADVANCE.

LIEUT.-GENERAL DAN SULTAN (CENTRE), WHO TOOK OVER GENERAL STILWELL'S COMMAND IN S.E.A.C., WITH MAJOR-GENERAL FESTING (LEFT), COMMANDER OF THE 36TH DIVISION.

In the fighting in Upper Burma both British and American services are intensifying their efforts to bring guerrilla forces to the rear of the Japanese. The Airborne Chindit forces have weakened the enemy hold on the thickest jungle and forest country. These operations have one great strategic aim, the reopening of the old Burma Road into China. In addition a pipe-line is being driven 1800 miles into China – a remarkable engineering feat, performed under great difficulties. Meanwhile, troops of Lieut.-General Sir W. F. Slim's Fourteenth Army on January 8 were within a few miles of Shwebo, the key town for the defence of Mandalay. The battle of Shwebo is the first major engagement to be fought on the flat country outside the jungle area of Burma.

At the same time on the west coast Akyab fell to British and Indian troops early in January without a battle. Possession of the island gives the Allied Command a very needed strategic site for further operations.

A TRIUMPH OF ROAD-MAKING: THE FIRST ALLIED CONVOY TO CHINA TO BREAK THE JAPANESE BLOCKADE, SEEN ON A CAUSEWAY OF THE LEDO ROAD, *EN ROUTE* TO THE REOPENED BURMA.

LEDO ROAD NOW OPEN – THE HIGHWAY FROM INDIA VIA BURMA REACHES CHINA.

THE ROUTE FROM LEDO TO BHAMO EFFECTING A JUNCTION WITH THE OLD BURMA ROAD.

A SECTOR UNDER CONSTRUCTION: A U.S. CATERPILLAR TRACTOR HAULING A LORRY ON AN AWKWARD STRETCH. CONVOYS MOVE UP AS SOON AS A STRETCH IS CLEARED.

In early 1942, the Japanese seized the Burma Road from Kunming to Lashio, 705 miles through mountainous country. Under the U.S. General Stilwell, the building of the Ledo Road from the railhead of the Bengal-Assam railway was begun. It climbs the Patkai Bum to Shingbwiyang, crosses the Upper Chindwin, mounts the Hukawang Valley and descends into the Mogaung Valley and finally links up with the Burma Road from Lashio. Admiral Lord Louis Mountbatten stated: "From Ledo through Myitkyina and Bhamo the new road now sweeps south to join the old Burma Road, and land communication to China is open." On February 15 it was reported that the first convoy had gone up into China from Myitkyina. American and Chinese troops were driving on Lashio, the Southern terminus of the Burma Road, forcing the Japanese out of the Shan States. The first convoy was cheered by enormous crowds, and a brass band blaring out military marches preceded it to the capital in triumph.

AGREEMENT WITH E.L.A.S. SIGNED: ATHENS REGAINS CONFIDENCE.

GENERAL SCOBIE, C.-IN-C. GREECE, SIGNING THE TRUCE WITH E.L.A.S. WHICH CAME INTO OPERA-TION AFTER MIDNIGHT ON JANUARY 14. STANDING ARE TWO OF THE E.L.A.S. DELEGATES.

A VAST UNION JACK CARRIED IN PROCESSION ON JANUARY 14, TO CELEBRATE THE TRUCE SIGNED BY LIEUT.-GENERAL SCOBIE. PLACARDS READ: "ENGLISHMEN, GREEKS ARE GRATEFUL TO YOU."

At midnight on Sunday, January 14, the truce General Scobie signed with E.L.A.S. came into operation, compelling E.L.A.S. forces to withdraw from the whole south-east corner of Greece. It released all prisoners except civilian hostages. The Regent was "profoundly shocked with the E.L.A.S. representatives' refusal to release the hostages," while Downing Street said that no truce can ripen into peace unless or until the hostages have been effectually safeguarded and released. Meantime Athens was recovering her poise. Food remained scarce, but soup kitchens were feeding many.

Enthusiastic scenes took place simultaneously in Athens and the Piræus, where Korai Square was renamed after Mr. Churchill, with a plaque, saying, "In recognition of the British Liberation and Britain's leader."

GENERAL MACARTHUR'S GREATEST HOUR: MANILA LIBERATED AFTER THREE YEARS.

HUNTING SNIPERS IN MANILA: TWO U.S. INFANTRYMEN ON THE LOOK-OUT FOR ENEMY TROOPS WHO MAY BE HIDING IN THE RUINED BUILDINGS.

GENERAL MACARTHUR VISITING A JAPANESE MONUMENT AT DAMORTIS, WHICH THE ENEMY ERECTED TO COMMEMORATE HIS FORCES WHO ENTERED LUZON THERE IN DECEMBER 1941.

THE BOMBING OF CLARK FIELD, MANILA'S GREATEST AIRFIELD, BY U.S. MITCHELL MEDIUM BOMBERS. SCORES OF PARACHUTE BOMBS DROPPED ON THE AIRFIELD.

When General MacArthur was forced to quit the Philippines in 1942 he said grimly, "I will return." On January 9 a vast U.S. force under his supreme command landed in the north of Luzon Island, shattering Japanese resistance, and now, only twenty-six days since his army landed Manila is again in his hands. U.S. losses have been comparatively light, those of the enemy extremely heavy. In the three-weeks' battle the Japanese seem never to have expected to hold the city and the action has taken the form of a slow, viciously destructive retreat. The landing followed that on Bataan Peninsula on February 15.

THE INVASION OF IWOJIMA: COSTLIEST ACTION OF THE PACIFIC WAR.

SMALL INVASION CRAFT SPEEDING TOWARDS THE IWOJIMA BEACHES AS THE FIRST ATTACK TOOK PLACE.

These scenes reflect the fierceness of the fighting on this little island which, within fighter-range of Tokyo, was fanatically defended by its Japanese garrison. American Marines first landed on Iwojima on February 19, and rapidly established a firm beach-head. Resistance was very stiff; the invasion was described by the Marines as the toughest fight in their history. The U.S. Navy Department described the battle for Iwojima as "the costliest single action of the Pacific War." The Marines suffered 19,938 casualties, of whom more than 4000 were killed. The Japanese suffered more than 21,000 casualties most killed.

AN HISTORIC MOMENT: MARINES WHO HAD FOUGHT UP THE SLOPES OF MOUNT SURIBACHI PLANTING THE STARS AND STRIPES ON ITS SUMMIT.

THE REICHSWALD OFFENSIVE: THE LAST GREAT BATTLE WEST OF THE RHINE.

ON A MUDDY ROAD IN THE AREA OF THE ALLIED OFFENSIVE IN THE REICHSWALD, BRITISH INFANTRY ARE PASSING ANTI-TANK GUNS AND THEIR CREWS ON THEIR WAY TO THE FRONT.

OUR "INLAND NAVY" INFANTRY, IN BUFFALOES, CROSSING THE FLOODED COUNTRY BETWEEN NIJMEGEN AND CLEVE WITH SUPPLIES FOR GENERAL CRERAR'S TROOPS ADVANCING INTO GERMANY.

As part of the bid by XXI Army Group under Montgomery to clear the west bank of the Rhine from Dusseldorf to the confluence of the Maas, on February 8, British and Canadian troops of the Canadian First Army renewed their land offensive against Germany with the launching of an attack from the area just south-east of Nijmegen. The offensive was opened with a tremendous barrage by massed Canadian artillery which continued for eleven hours, and, throughout air support in great weight was given by bombers of the

Ninth Tactical Air Force and by fighter-bombers. The front of the attack was about five miles, and flail tanks and armoured flame throwers preceded the infantry. On the left flank in particular, where the Germans released big floods in the path of our advance by breaching the banks of the Rhine, the Canadians have been fighting an amphibious operation which at times has almost amounted to a minor naval engagement. In spite of the conditions the Canadians advanced to and have held a ten-mile stretch of the Rhine.

THE RUINS OF CLEVE: THE BATTLE OF THE ROER DAMS.

The assault on Cleve opened on February 7, when it was a key target for a fleet of 700 heavy bombers of R.A.F. Bomber Command, whose attack using high explosive instead of the requested incendiary bombs was so concentrated that scarcely a single house had been left habitable. The rubble in the streets also seriously impeded our troops's advance and although Allied forces reached the town on February 9, it was not completely cleared until the 11th, by which time the Germans had been able to bring up reinforcements behind it. Montgomery's plan for XXI Army Group included an advance by the US 9th Army across the Roer at Jülich to join up with the Canadian thrust from the north, but first the dams above Düren had to be captured. Reports on February 9 placed troops of the American First Army within a mile of the Roerstausee, most important of the series of dams by means of which the Germans have held control over the Roer Valley and have been in a position to release a devastating flood down the Roer Valley at will, submerging it to a depth of 5–6 feet. This system of dams has thus been the dominating tactical factor in the battle to force the line of the Middle and Lower Roer. Having proved impervious to bombing, they became a priority objective of the American First Army, whose attacks, interrupted by Rundstadt's Christmas offensive in that area, have since been resumed. On February 9 the Germans of the main dams released the expected flood, but of course removing at the same time any future threat. The British and Canadians were left to press on alone on the east bank of the Roer.

A GUTTED CORNER OF CLEVE. A HEAVY NIGHT ATTACK BY R.A.F. BOMBER COMMAND LAID THIS GERMAN TOWN IN RUINS BEFORE THE LAUNCHING OF MONTGOMERY'S LAND OFFENSIVE.

NORTH EASTERN SECTOR OF THE ALLIED LINE. MONTGOMERY'S OBJECTIVE IS THE TRIANGLE BETWEEN THE MAAS AND THE RHINE.

CAPTURED COLOGNE: THE AMERICAN ADVANCE INTO GERMANY.

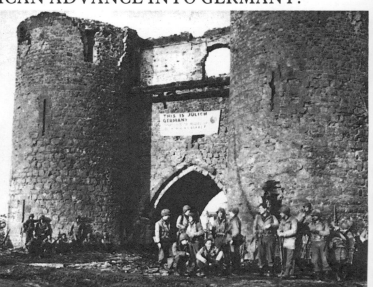

A DRAMATIC ILLUSTRATION OF THE DEVASTATION WROUGHT IN COLOGNE, THE FOURTH LARGEST CITY OF THE REICH, CAPTURED BY THE U.S. 1ST ARMY ON MARCH 7.

"THIS IS JÜLICH, GERMANY," SAYS THE SIGN ABOVE THE GATE TO THE CITADEL, CAPTURED BY U.S NINTH ARMY TROOPS. "SORRY IT IS SO MESSED UP, BUT WE WERE IN A *HURRY!*"

The offensive launched on February 23, by the American First and Ninth Armies started well. Jülich and Düren fell into their hands. To the north, General Crear's Canadians began a new attack south of Calcar and to the south the American Third Army burst across the Prum River and hit in strength through a 32-mile Siegfried breach. General Eisenhower has declared that the immediate object of the Allies is the destruction of the enemy's armies west of the Rhine, and undoubtedly that destruction, in the form of a full-scale offensive has begun. On February 26 the Ninth and First U.S. Armies were only 13 miles from Cologne.

At the time of writing, the Allies straddle the Rhine from Cologne to the North Sea and the Anglo-Canadian Army has linked up with General Simpson's Ninth Army and together some 50,000 prisoners. On the night of March 4, British, Canadian and U.S. troops were closing on the last escape bridges left to the Germans north of Cologne. On the southern flank, bridgehead advance guards of the Ninth Army reached Homberg, opposite Duisburg, the great inland port. Cologne itself fell with little resistance on March 7, von Runstedt having taken the decision to withdraw and not to try and hold the city.

THE FIRST RHINE CROSSING: U.S. FIRST ARMY TROOPS CAPTURE THE BRIDGE AT REMAGEN.

TROOPS OF THE 9TH ARMOURED DIVISION OF THE U.S. FIRST ARMY ADVANCING ON TO THE LUDENDORFF BRIDGE FROM REMAGEN TO MAKE THE HISTORIC FIRST CROSSING OF THE RHINE ON THE AFTERNOON OF MARCH 7.

U.S. TROOPS AMONG THE REMAINS OF THE EASTERN SPAN OF THE LUDENDORFF BRIDGE, PULLED DOWN BY THE COLLAPSE OF THE CENTRAL SPAN.

The battle for the Rhine bridges has begun in earnest; at Cologne, the western end of the Hohenzollern railway bridge had been blocked by the collapse of the superstructure and both it and the Deutz suspension road bridge had been destroyed blocking the river. At Homberg, American infantry seized the western approaches to the railway and road bridges. At Düsseldorf the Allies reached the Rhine and American tanks lunged through to the Südbrücke only to see this fall into the water in front of them. At Verdingen American tanks were actually on the bridge before the charges went off. Finally at Remagen the Ludendorff bridge was left intact, according to the Germans "by accident of chance." The American First Army was still battling fiercely to enlarge the bridgehead, but it had advanced to cut the Ruhr-Frankfort motor road in at least two places, and troops were holding six miles of the highway; and at 3.15 p.m. on Saturday, March 17, the bridge at Remagen collapsed into the Rhine. On March 20, Major-General C. R. Moore, Chief Engineer, European Theatre of Operations, stated that it was now unnecessary to reconstruct it as we now had a number of emergency bridges over the Rhine in this area.

THE U.S. THIRD AND SEVENTH ARMIES CLEAR THE RHINELAND IN A COMBINED OFFENSIVE.

HANGING OUT HIS WASHING ON THE SIEGFRIED LINE! AN AMERICAN SOLDIER, LIKE THE POPULAR SONG, DRIES HIS WASHING BY THE SIEGFRIED LINE NEAR PRUM.

THE DIMINISHING GAP BETWEEN THE EASTERN AND WESTERN FRONTS: A MAP SHOWING THE TERRAIN IN GERMANY PROPER, THE FIRST U.S. ARMY 280 MILES FROM BERLIN.

MEN OF GENERAL PATTON'S THIRD ARMY CROSSING THE RIVER MOSELLE IN ASSAULT CRAFT PRIOR TO STORMING INTO THE GREAT RHINE CITADEL OF COBLENZ.

Further south, Patton, smashed the German pocket west of the River Prum, crossed it, and breached the Siegfried Line on a 25-mile front while his right flank fought its way down the Moselle Valley to Coblenz. On Saturday, March 17, turning right to drive southward to the Saar, it stormed into the great Rhine citadel of Coblenz. For ten days American artillery had subjected this city of originally 60,000 inhabitants to continuous shelling. The last German defenders surrendered on March 19. With an advance southwards on March 20 the Third Army next captured Worms. On the night of March 22–23 elements of Patton's Third Army stiffed across the Rhone almost unnoticed near Oppenheim, south of Mainz, and by the evening of the 23rd had established a bridgehead seven miles wide and six miles deep on the eastern shore.

MONTGOMERY'S CROSSING OF THE RHINE WITH 21ST ARMY GROUP.

WITH THE U.S. NINTH ARMY AS IT CROSSED THE RHINE: AN ALLIGATOR, UNDER COVER OF A SMOKE-SCREEN, TAKING TO THE WATER.

THE PRIME MINISTER, WITH FIELD-MARSHAL MONTGOMERY AND GENERAL SIMPSON, CROSSING THE RHINE IN AN AMERICAN L.C.V.P.

Within a matter of hours the battle moved east of the Rhine, where Allied forces are striking at the industrial heart of Germany. The news of General Patton's crossing came first, followed by Field-Marshal Montgomery's assault and four major landings under General Dempsey and General Simpson between Roes and Wesel. On March 25 Mr. Churchill and Field-Marshal Montgomery made a trip across the Rhine to visit troops in areas which, thirty-six hours previously were in German hands.

The Battle of the Rhine was heralded and followed by an enormous influx of German prisoners, with German troops surrendering at an average rate of 10,000 a day. The German Army seemed to lose central control. German officers over the whole area of the front took decisions into their own hands and surrendered their forces piecemeal to the advancing Allies. Reports from the front speak of the majority of German prisoners as suffering from exhaustion and a complete loss of morale.

NEARING THE END IN GERMANY: THE ADVANCE IN THE WEST.

ON APRIL 15 THE MEN OF ARNHEM WERE AVENGED, WHEN THE CITY WAS TAKEN BY STORM: BRITISH TROOPS WITH THE FIRST CANADIAN ARMY IN LANDING CRAFT PREPARATORY TO THE ASSAULT.

By the time that the Allied armies crossed the Rhine they had between them taken more than 300,000 German prisoners in the battles of the West bank, over 100,000 of them falling to the US 3rd and 7th Armies in the last 10 days of the campaign. The Allied command, particularly Generals Eisenhower and Montgomery, have been criticised for not crossing sooner but these West bank battles represented, between enemy dead, wounded and captured, well over half a million men less to oppose the crossings when they came. Montgomery too has been singled out for his refusal to allow the US 9th Army under his control to cross in the Dusseldorf area when it first reached the Rhine. Time however proved Montgomery right. Instead of losing itself in the heavily defended wasteland of the Rhur this Army, drawn reluctantly to the north to join in the British crossing, was able to form the northern aim of the pincers movement – with the US 1st Army as the southern – that cut off the German Army Group B in the Ruhr area, and effectively removed at a stroke twenty one divisions from the centre of the German line.

THE SIXTH GUARDS TANK BRIGADE'S CAPTURE OF MUNSTER, CAPITAL OF WESTPHALLIA: BRITISH GUARDSMEN AND INFANTRY OF THE U.S. 17TH AIRBORNE DIVISION CONFERRING IN THE HEART OF THE CITY DURING PATROL.

The speed with which the Allies have advanced across Northern Germany has surprised the most optimistic observers in both countries. The prime cause is, however, simple. It is the destruction or envelopment of the main body of the enemy opposed to the Allies on this front. Practically the whole of the surviving forces of the German Central Army Group – Army Group B – has been penned into the pocket of which the northern flank is composed of the industrial area of the Ruhr. This created a yawning gap in the German array. The colossal losses suffered by the enemy have drained away the sources of man-power. The isolated bodies of defenders have had no chance against the mobility and striking power of the Allies. Where a core of resistance has been found hard enough to be troublesome it has regularly been outflanked.

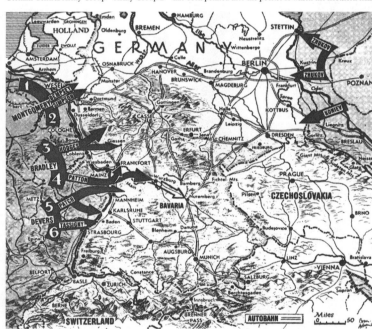

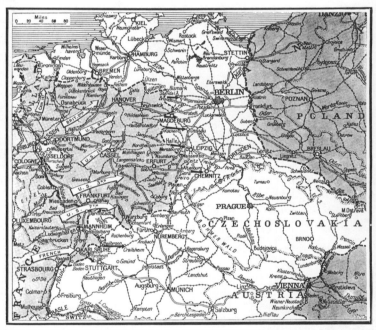

THE TWO FRONTS – EAST AND WEST. LEFT: ON MARCH 27, MONTGOMERY'S NEAREST POINT TO THE GERMAN CAPITAL WAS APPROXIMATELY 280 MILES, WITH ZHUKOV 44 MILES DISTANT ON THE EASTERN FRONT. BRADLEY'S SPEARHEAD NORTH OF GEISSEN WAS ONLY 260 MILES FROM BERLIN. RIGHT: BY APRIL 16, WHEN THE FINAL RUSSIAN DRIVE FOR BERLIN BEGAN THE U.S. FIRST ARMY HAD REACHED THE ELBE AT MAGDEBURG. PATTON WAS ABOUT TO CAPTURE NUREMBERG, MONTGOMERY WAS PRESSING ON TOWARDS HAMBURG, AND THE CANADIANS HAD REACHED THE NORTH SEA.

The one serious danger has been that of a shortage of supplies, but the country which the Allies are penetrating is served by one of the best road systems in the world purely for military purposes. Again, there are airfields which the enemy cannot defend, and which have enabled the Allies to transport supplies, especially petrol. With their complete dominance of the air and their great resources in aircraft, they have also been enabled to drop supplies by parachute or land them in gliders. Finally, we know that the Rhine is spanned by at least one railway bridge, and may surmise that a second is likely to be open by now.

On the Allied right flank the German forces had not been disintegrated or destroyed to the same extent. The country is also better suited to defence, especially on the French front in the Black Forest. There resistance has been somewhat stronger, but it has not prevented progress which would have been remarkable in other circumstances. On the left, the enemy has been endeavouring to form a line covering Hamburg, Bremen and Emden. It may well be that his U-boats have been ordered to use the Ems, the Weser and the Elbe up to the last possible minute, and, in any case, the denial of the ports to the Allies would be in

THE EAGLE'S NEST: BUILDINGS OF HITLER'S FORMER H.Q. AT BAD NAUHEIM, CAMOUFLAGED WITH NETTING AND "GARNISH."

EISENHOWER AND GENERAL PATTON IN HIGH SPIRITS – JUSTIFIED BY THE SUCCESSFUL CROSSINGS OF THE RHINE.

A SMALL SECTION OF A GROUP OF 82,000 GERMAN PRISONERS TAKEN BY THE EIGHTEENTH AIRBORNE CORPS DURING THE CLEANING UP OF THE RUHR POCKET.

accordance with his general policy. But the clearance of this coast should be an easy matter by comparison with the final clearance of Holland, the hard task allotted to the Canadian First Army. Resistance has already collapsed in the country east and north of the Zuider Zee, but the provinces of North Holland, South Holland, and even part of Utrecht will present greater difficulties. Unfortunately, too, it is these provinces in which the population is heaviest and starvation most universal. Gelderland and Overijssel are agricultural and contain food enough for their people, especially since it has become impossible to move food from one province to another. But the western provinces are enduring the greatest misery of any district in Europe, and one cannot see an immediate end to their sufferings.

LEST WE FORGET! SOME EXAMPLES OF GERMAN SADISTIC INHUMANITY.
OHRDRUF, BUCHENWALD AND NORDHAUSEN: RECORDED HORRORS OF THE TORTURE CAMPS.

NORDHAUSEN CAMP, WITH EVIDENCE OF COLD-BLOODED ATROCITY: IN THE FOREGROUND ARE THE PITIFUL CORPSES OF A CHILD AND A BABY. SEVEN THOUSAND DIED IN THIS CAMP.

Accounts of German atrocities continue to mount during the advance of the Allies, not only of cruelty towards enemy aliens, but towards their own people, as witness the shooting of German civilians at Wehoff, when from a slag-mine shelter they raised a white flag and the public hanging of soldiers who "betrayed the Führer." The brutalities of Nordhausen are as harrowing and terrible as any. At this camp there was a series of long sheds with wooden racks reaching to the ceiling. On these were laid hundreds of men, shrunken with starvation, only waiting to die. The death-rate at Nordhasen at one recent period was 900 a day. The camp was designed to hold 8000, but 59,000 were thrown in there. Germans living near these camps said they had no idea such cruelties were being done, but at Nordhausen civilians, out walking with their girls, cracked jokes at the "extermination centre."

Nothing that Dante could conceive of the Inferno we term Hell can exceed in agony the ghastly scenes at Belsen concentration camp, near Bremen, which was taken over on April 17 by General Dempsey's Second Army. Thus huge camp, which had contained some 60,000 civilians, was little more than a mass of dead and dying, mainly from starvation, typhus, and typhoid. The camp was declared a neutral area and the Allied military authorities stood by to reach it at the earliest possible moment, for it was known that the living had been without food and water for over six days. It was found to be littered with dead and dying, and huts capable of housing only thirty persons were crowded with as many as 500. So terrible was the situation that the prison doctors told General Dempsey's senior medical officer that cannibalism was going on. Food sent by the Red Cross to Jewish inmates had not been distributed. The revelations of Belsen and the other camps have horrified the entire civilised world.

THE USUALLY GENIAL GENERAL EISENHOWER SHOWS BY HIS GRIM ASPECT HIS HORROR OF GERMAN BRUTALITY: VICTIMS MURDERED BY S.S. GUARDS AT OHRDRUF CAMP.

A DORÉ DRAWING OF DANTE'S INFERNO: SCENES IN BELSEN AND LANGENSTEIN.

HUMAN WRECKS IN THE PRISON HOSPITAL AT LANGENSTEIN, ONE OF THE GERMAN TORTURE CAMPS OVERRUN BY THE ALLIED ADVANCE. THIS CAMP, WHERE THE DYING SHARED BUNKS WITH THE DEAD, WAS FREED BY ADVANCE TROOPS OF THE U.S. NINTH ARMY.

MORE TERRIBLE THAN EVEN THE IMAGINATION OF A DANTE COULD CONCEIVE IN HIS "INFERNO": ONE OF THE GHASTLY COMMUNAL GRAVES OF GERMANY'S HELPLESS VICTIMS IN BELSEN CONCENTRATION CAMP, NEAR BREMEN, LIBERATED BY THE BRITISH SECOND ARMY.

S.S. MEN AND WOMEN OF THE CAMP GARRISON WHERE PRISONERS WERE SCIENTIFICALLY EXTERMINATED.

THESE FEMALE FIENDS, WELL-NOURISHED AT BELSEN, WIELDED THE LASH WITH EQUAL VIOLENCE AS S.S. MEN. THEY SHOWED ABSOLUTELY NO REMORSE WHEN ARRESTED.

THE COMMANDANT OF THE BELSEN CAMP, S.S. HAUPTSTURMFÜHRER JOSEF KRAMER, NOW UNDER CLOSE ARREST. HE WAS QUITE UNASHAMED OF HIS GHOULISH DEEDS.

THE HUN IS ALWAYS THE HUN! AT LIPPSTADT, WHEN THE GERMAN POLICE FLED, THE PEOPLE IMMEDIATELY LOOTED SHOPS, INCLUDING WINE STORES.

CONVERGING MOVEMENTS IN BURMA: THE RELIEF OF PAGAN, LASHIO AND MANDALAY.

BRITISH TROOPS ADVANCING ALONG THE ROAD TO MANDALAY PAST THE DEAD BODIES OF JAPANESE, WHICH LITTERED THE APPROACHES TO THE CITY'S OUTSKIRTS.

A SECTION OF FORT DUFFERIN'S 30-FT.-HIGH BRICK-FACED RAMPART OF EARTH AND ROCK WHICH WITHSTOOD FIFTY SHELLS FROM A 5.5-IN. GUN FIRED AT POINT-BLANK RANGE.

Thrusts into the Japanese-held area are going in at so many points that the campaign is decidedly difficult to follow. In the north, by mid-February U.S. and Chinese troops were driving on Lashio, the southern terminus of the Burma Road, and were slowly but surely forcing the Japanese out of the Shan States. Further south the British Thirty-sixth Division was closing in on Mongmit and the ruby mines of Moyok.

On the Burma Road front Lashio and its main airfield were captured by General Sultan's Chinese First Army, and on March 9 the entire Burma Road had been cleared of the enemy. After forced marches, Mandalay was surrounded on March 6 by men of the Fourteenth Army, headed by British and Indian troops of the 19th Indian ("Dagger") Division, and fell to them on March 20.

THE ALLIED CAMPAIGN OF GERMANY'S SYNTHETIC OIL PLANTS: THE WORKS AT ZEITZ.

THE ZEITZ SYNTHETIC OIL PLANT NEAR LEIPZIG, BEFORE BEING BOMBED TO EXTINCTION BY R.A.F. BOMBER COMMAND MACHINES ON JANUARY 16.

ZEITZ, AFTER THE R.A.F. BOMBING: A PHOTOGRAPH TAKEN A MONTH AFTER THE R.A.F. ATTACK. THE PLANT SHOWS A MASS OF DÉBRIS AMONG A CONCENTRATION OF CRATERS.

The recent concentration of Allied bombing on German synthetic oil plants is well exemplified in these two pictures of Zeitz, near Leipzig, before it was visited by R.A.F. Bomber Command on January 16, and afterwards, from a reconnoitre a month later. The Zeitz plant employed some 5000 hands and its output equalled that of some of the largest plants in the Ruhr. The plant is a mass of débris amongst a dense concentration of craters. In addition, there is no sign of any attempt at repair work or of activity of any kind.

In a joint statement issued by the Air Ministry and the U.S. Strategic Air Forces in Europe on February 15, it was stated that Germany's oil output had been reduced through air attacks and by the Red Army to a potential of less than one-fifth of the amount before the bombing offensive against oil plants began last April. When the full story of the Allied air forces' systematic campaign can be told, it will prove to have been one of the most decisive factors in forcing a German collapse. It has limited enemy mobility on all fronts.

EVENTS IN THE BALKANS: PEOPLE IN THE PUBLIC EYE.

MEMBERS OF THE HUNGARIAN PROVISIONAL GOVERNMENT: THE PRIME MINISTER, GENERAL BELA MIKLOS (EXTREME LEFT), WITH DR. BELA JEDENI, PRESIDENT, STANDING NEXT TO HIM.

DR. SUBASITCH (LEFT, HOLDING BLOTTER) AT THE SWEARING-IN OF THE YUGOSLAV REGENTS: (L. TO R., SEATED), DR. MANDITCH, DR. BUDISAVLJEVITCH AND M. SERNEC.

EXECUTED AS WAR CRIMINALS – THE THREE FORMER REGENTS OF BULGARIA: (LEFT TO RIGHT) PROFESSOR FILOV; PRINCE CYRIL, AND GENERAL MIKHOV.

The Hungarian Provisional Government, set up in the liberated area of the country, is remarkably widely based. The Prime Minister was at one time Horthy's A.D.C. The Minister of Defence is also a general. Altogether, three of the Ministers belong to the Smallholders Party, two are Communists, three or four are Socialists or Social Democrats, and three are Generals.

Dr. Subasitch, the Yugoslav Prime Minister in London, recently handed his own resignation, and that of his Government, to King Peter. The three members of the new Regency Council of Yugoslavia, in the composition of which Marshal Tito and Dr. Subasitch reached full agreement, were sworn in on March 6. The following day Marshal Tito formed the first United Yugoslav Government.

The three former Regents of Bulgaria, Prince Cyril, brother of the late King Boris, Professor Filov, a former Prime Minister, and General Mikhov, once War Minister, were executed on Thursday night, February 1. They were among 101 Bulgarians sentenced to death in the great trial of war criminals in the People's Court in Sofia. In addition, twenty-seven persons were sentenced to hard labour for life.

ON THE EASTERN FRONT: INSIDE BRESLAU, AND LIBERATED POZNAN.

TANKS IN THE WRECKAGE-STREWN STREETS OF POZNAN, WHICH WAS LIBERATED AFTER A MONTH-LONG SIEGE INVOLVING SOME BITTER STREET-FIGHTING.

BRITISH TROOPS, FREED BY OUR SOVIET ALLIES FROM A GERMAN CONCENTRATION CAMP NEAR POZNAN, POLAND, BEFORE LEAVING FOR A REPATRIATION CENTRE.

On February 23 the Red Army celebrated its twenty-seventh birthday in a continuance of their offensive and the capture of the Polish city of Poznan. Almost within an hour of Poznan's liberation, ceaseless streams of military traffic began to pour westward through the city on the main roads leading to Zhukov's front more than 100 miles nearer Berlin. During nearly four years of heavy fighting the Red Army has achieved resounding victories which have driven the German invaders across more than a thousand miles of territory and inflicted stupendous losses on the Wehrmacht. In their last great offensive alone, they had, within the first forty days, ejected the enemy from 300 towns, seized more than 9000 miles of railways, killed upwards of 800,000 Germans, and taken more than 350,000 prisoners.

WITH THE GERMAN FORCES AS THE RED ARMY DRIVES TOWARDS BERLIN.

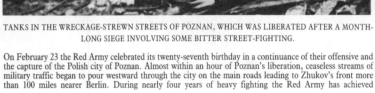

THE CAPTION ON THIS PICTURE RADIOED FROM SWITZERLAND DESCRIBES VON RIBBENTROP AS WATCHING THE ODER FRONT FROM A TRENCH OUTSIDE BERLIN.

HITLER AT AN EASTERN FRONT H.Q. IN THE RIVER ODER AREA: HE IS SEEN CONFERRING WITH MEMBERS OF THE GERMAN HIGH COMMAND.

The most interesting news from the Eastern Front in late March came from the Danzig area, where Russian troops advancing with great dash were converging on Danzig and Gdynia, which the Germans are believed to be holding in great strength. The spectacular deterioration of the enemy position about Danzig was attributable to the feat of Russian generalship which caused the German commander to switch elements of two Panzer and one infantry divisions from the sector south-west of the city to north Pomerania, thus leaving the Polish corridor poorly defended. At 0500 on April 16 Zhukov launched his long awaited assault on Berlin from his bridgeheads round Kustrin-on-Oder. Seventy five minutes later Konev attacked across the Neisse at Triebel some sixty miles to the south.

WAR'S RAVAGES IN TWO FAMOUS CAPITALS – BUDAPEST AND VIENNA.

RED ARMY MEN IN STREET-TO-STREET FIGHTING IN BUDAPEST: SOVIET TROOPS, ENSCONCED ON HIGH GROUND, FIRING AT AN ENEMY STRONG-POINT.

RED ARMY HEROES IN THE FIGHTING FOR VIENNA: THE ACTUAL FIGHTING IN THE STREETS LASTED LESS THAN A WEEK AND THE RUSSIANS CREDITED THE VIENNESE WITH AIDING THEM.

Budapest was bombed and shelled by the Russians when the Germans decided to defend it house by house. It was encircled by Soviet troops on December 23, and by December 27 it was being slowly pounded to submission by Red Army shock troops led by tanks. By January 18 the enemy had retained only a small part of Buda. The city fell on February 13. In the course of the seven-weeks siege, it was reported that the enemy lost 49,000 killed and 110,000 captured. Vienna, capital of Austria, was liberated on April 13 by Red Army forces under Marshal Tolbukhin whose men broke into the city from the south, acting in co-operation with Marshal Malinovsky's troops, who attacked from the east. Tolbukhin's advance on Vienna began a month before the capture but the actual fighting in the city's streets lasted less than a week, with the result that most of this famous city has been saved from destruction. First steps were taken to feed the famished people. Porridge was ladled out to children in the city squares. Vienna stands at the centre of one of Europe's most important communications networks. During the battles for Vienna, Marshal Tolbulkin's troops took more than 130,000 prisoners; and destroyed or captured 1345 tanks and self-propelled guns.

PRESIDENT ROOSEVELT DIES: VICE-PRESIDENT TRUMAN TAKES OVER.

THE SIXTY-YEAR-OLD EX-FARMER AND VICE-PRESIDENT WHO SUCCEEDS PRESI-
DENT ROOSEVELT AT THE WHITE HOUSE.

THE LATE PRESIDENT FRANKLIN DELANO ROOSEVELT, WHOSE SUDDEN DEATH ON APRIL 12 CAME AS A SHOCK TO THE
ENTIRE CIVILISED WORLD.

The sudden death of President Roosevelt on April 12 was received everywhere with profound sorrow and sympathy for the American people thus robbed of their great leader, and with scarcely less concern by the British nation, which had long looked upon him as one of its dearest and most confident of friends all through the black days of 1940. He is doubtless destined to live in history as one of the greatest of United States Presidents. Within a few hours, Senator Harry S. Truman was sworn in as thirty-third President of the United States. After being sworn in, the new President stated: "It will be my effort to carry on as I believe the President would have done. To that end, I have asked the Cabinet to stay on with me."

U.S.S.R. SIGNS TREATY WITH POLAND.

MARSHAL STALIN SIGNING AT THE KREMLIN THE TREATY OF FRIENDSHIP AND COLLABORATION
BETWEEN THE SOVIET UNION AND THE POLISH REPUBLIC.

On April 21, a twenty-year friendship pact between Russia and the Lublin Polish Government was concluded, after a conference between Marshal Stalin and M. Bierut, President of the Lublin Government and M. Osubka Morawski, the Prime Minister. It was described by Marshal Stalin as marking a radical turning-point in the relations between the Soviet Union and Poland, and forming a solid basis for friendship and alliance.

U.S. NAVAL VICTORY OFF OKINAWA.

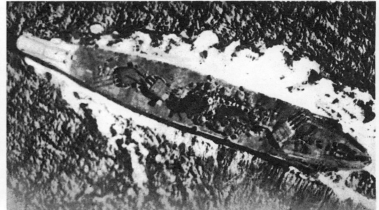

THE LAST OF JAPAN'S SUPER-DREADNOUGHTS, THE "YAMATO," SUNK, WITH CRUISER AND THREE
DESTROYERS, IN MAJOR NAVAL BATTLE OFF OKINAWA ON APRIL 7.

On April 7 the Japanese Fleet, forced into the open by the U.S. seizure of Okinawa Island, advanced from the Inland Sea and was attacked by a fast carrier force under Vice-Admiral Marc Mitscher. The enemy was annihilated, the "Yamato" sunk, a light cruiser, three destroyers sunk, and three others left burning. "Yamato" had a believed displacement of 46,000 tons, overall length of 870 ft., and carried nine 16-in. guns.

MUSSOLINI MEETS HIS DESERTS: INCIDENTS IN HIS CAREER.

Mussolini with his mistress, Clara Petacci, and twelve members of his Cabinet were executed by Partisans in a village on Lake Como on Sunday. April 29. The bodies were taken to Milan, whence he first rose to power, and in the working-class quarter of Lereto were heaped together in the square where a year ago fifteen partisans had been shot by Fascists. The Milanese mob fired bullets into the body of the man once their Dictator. They kicked it and spat on it. The end of "the Bullfrog of the Pontine Marshes," the man who inspired Hitler to his Nazi terrorism, came with terrible swiftness. Within twenty-four hours he was arrested, tried, sentenced, shot in the back and flung to the Milan mob. Mussolini's worst enemies could not have selected a more humiliating end to his bombastic, boastful and brutal career, one responsible for the death and ruin of untold millions. In July 1943, after more than twenty-one years of arbitrary rule, he was overthrown by the votes of the Fascist Grand Council, previously his puppets. His great ambition to found a new Roman Empire, with himself as Cæsar, had fallen in ruins and he died mourned by none.

AT TRIPOLI IN 1937 ARAB CHIEFS PRESENTED HIM WITH THE TWO-HANDED SWORD OF ISLAM HE IS ARROGANTLY HOLDING.

IL DUCE, RADIATING SELF-CONFIDENCE, MAK-ING AN IMPROMPTU OUTDOOR SPEECH TO A CHEERING MOB.

AFTER HIS DECLINE AND FALL IN 1943: HITLER GREETING HIM AT NAZI HEADQUARTERS AFTER HIS ESCAPE FROM THE ALLIES.

EAST AND WEST MEET; THE BREAKDOWN OF GERMAN RESISTANCE.

CELEBRATING HITLER'S BIRTHDAY! TROOPS OF THE SEVENTH ARMY RAISING THE STARS AND STRIPES OVER THE NAZI SWASTIKA AT HITLER'S STADIUM IN NUREMBERG, THE SCENE OF MANY NAZI PARTY MEETINGS.

THE COLLAPSE OF GERMANY: A MAP SHOWING THE VESTIGES OF THE THIRD REICH, THE NORTH ISOLATED FROM THE SOUTH, AND THE REMAINING NAZI TERRITORIES, AT THE BEGINNING OF MAY IN PROCESS OF FINAL EXTINCTION.

This map, showing the position of the Allies in shaded tint, reveals the situation of the Third Reich in its last gasp. A tidal wave of the Allied armies was sweeping onward with the impetuosity of the ocean. Berlin, in its expiring gasps, Frankfurt-on-Oder, Stettin and Potsdam – all had fallen to the Russians. Farther south Bradley's 12th Army Group and Koniev's Russians had linked up while Munich had capitulated to the 42nd Infantry and 12th Armoured Division of Patch's troops. The Wehrmacht, in a state of dissolution, was confined to little more than pockets of resistance and it was expected at any moment that the Allies would receive an offer of unconditional surrender. Thus collapses Hitler's Empire which he boasted would last a thousand years and expires, unhonoured and unsung, after thirteen years.

SOVIET AND AMERICAN OFFICERS HAVING A FRIENDLY CHAT OVER THE BONNET OF A JEEP AFTER THE FIRST CONTACT OF U.S. AND RUSSIAN TROOPS AT 4.40 P.M. ON APRIL 25.

THE BURGOMEISTER OF LEIPZIG AND HIS WIFE (IN ARMCHAIR) AND DAUGHTER (ON SETTEE), FOUND DEAD IN THE CITY HALL, WHERE THEY HAD COMMITTED SUICIDE.

On April 20, the 3rd Division of the Seventh Army raised the Stars and Stripes over the ruins of the Adolf Hitler Platz, in the centre of Nuremberg, the town of the Nazi party meetings. Only four hours previously the Platz had echoed to the rattle of small-arms fire and the crash of bazookas. The beautiful old town has suffered badly from bombing and shelling, made necessary by the fanatic resistance put up by the S.S. defenders. A few hours before organised resistance ended in Nuremberg, the city of Leipzig finally fell to General Hodges' First Army, after armour had reduced the last enemy strong-points, manned mostly by S.S. troops. An end, too, was made of the strenuous resistance in Halle, north-west of Leipzig and forces of the American Seventh Army entered Munich, where no organised resistance was met.

MEN OF THE US SEVENTH ARMY MARCHING UNCONCERNEDLY PAST THE ENTRANCE TO THE NOTORIOUS BÜRGER-BRÄU-KELLER.

REFLECTIONS ON THE NEWS OF THE WAR.
BY CYRIL FALLS.

It is to be expected that the overthrow of the main German armies is something to be measured by days. There is, however, no great disposition to believe that this will bring about a speedy ending of the war. Some still talk of a huge mountain area in the mountains of Austria and Bavaria into which Hitler will withdraw the remains of his forces in Germany and to which he will recall the majority of his divisions in Italy. A few observers seem to envisage the last stand being made on both sides of the Alps; but the enemy in Italy would find it no easy matter to continue a full-scale resistance if he were driven away from the Italian munition factories which he has been using. The other school foresees resistance in a number of centres of limited size in the same region, and in any others in which defence can be maintained. In this scheme there would be no large formations with their complicated paraphernalia, no heavy artillery, and few if any, tanks. Small bodies of desperate men would fight it out, mainly with light weapons, having at hand rock shelters in which they could defy bombardment from land or air, and perhaps secret hiding-places. That seems to me nearer the mark, and possibly the more troublesome alternative from the Allied point of view.

BERCHTESGADEN IN FLAMES AS AN AMERICAN SOLDIER APPROACHES HITLER'S HOME IN THE BAVARIAN MOUNTAINS.

A TRIUMPHANT END TO THE LONG AND ARDUOUS CAMPAIGN IN ITALY.

GEN. MARK CLARK (CENTRE), LT.-GEN. MCCREARY (RIGHT), AND AIR VICE-MARSHAL FOSTER WATCHING THE AERIAL BOMBARD-MENT WHICH OPENED THE SPRING OFFENSIVE OF THE EIGHTH ARMY FROM THE TOP OF MONTGOMERY'S OLD TANK.

IN LIBERATED BOLOGNA: THE U.S. 34TH DIVISION RESTING IN REPUBLIC SQUARE AFTER THE CITY HAD FALLEN TO THE FORCES OF THE FIFTH AND EIGHTH ARMIES.

One of the heaviest bombing assaults yet witnessed in the Italian theatre heralded the opening of the Allied spring offensive on April 9. Within three days Eighth Army troops were reported to have crossed the River Santerno in strength. On April 21, forces of the Eighth and Fifth Armies entered Bologna, in the morning, and by the evening other columns were reported to be 20 miles beyond the city. The Allied advance swept rapidly across the north of Italy liberating Bergamo, Brescia, Vicenza and Padua. The 56th (London) Division, entered Venice, the 2nd New Zealand Division reached the Piave River, and the Fifth Army entered Milan. Patriot-controlled broadcasting stations assert that by April 26 most of the area west of the line Como-Milan-Genoa was under patriot control.

TRIESTE: THE EIGHTH ARMY'S ARRIVAL WELCOMED BY PARTISANS.

YUGOSLAV PARTISANS, CARRYING BANNERS, GREETING ARMOURED CARS OF THE 12TH LANCERS, WHO SPEAR-HEADED THE DRIVE ON TRIESTE.

It was on May 1 that troops of the Second New Zealand Division of the Eighth Army linked up with Marshal Tito's Partisans near Trieste after crossing the River Isonzo. On the following day the New Zealanders occupied Trieste, whose German garrison surrendered to General Freyberg. Subsequently, a difficult situation arose when Marshal Tito set up a Yugoslav administration in Trieste, in contradiction to his agreement with Field-Marshal Alexander at their meeting in Belgrade in February. Under this agreement, the western part of the province of Venezia Giulia, including the important port of Trieste, and the towns of Gorizia and Monfalcone, were to come under the undisputed authority of Alexander, as Allied Supreme Commander, in order that lines of communication into Austria should remain unimpeded. Marshal Tito excused his action on the grounds that the situation had changed since his meeting with Alexander, but the British and American Governments did not agree, and dispatched Notes to Marshal Tito, asking his Government to observe the general principle that any territorial adjustments must be made by an orderly process and not by conquest in advance of the Peace Conference. Following the dispatch of these Notes, the situation was somewhat eased by the withdrawal of Yugoslav troops to the eastern bank of the Isonzo River, but at the time of writing no final settlement had been reached.

A MAP OF VENEZIA GIULIA, THE DISPUTED TERRITORY, TEMPORARILY TO BE ADMINISTERED BY FIELD-MARSHAL ALEXANDER.

THE UNCONDITIONAL SURRENDER OF THE GERMAN FORCES IN ITALY ON MAY 2.

THE CROWNING TRIUMPH OF ALEXANDER'S ITALIAN CAMPAIGN: (BOTTOM.) GEN. MORGAN SIGNING THE DOCUMENT ON HIS BEHALF.

LIKE A PLAGUE OF LOCUSTS: MASSED PRISONERS AWAITING A SOLUTION TO THE PROBLEM OF WHERE TO PUT THEM.

The unconditional surrender of the German armies in Italy to Field-Marshal Sir Harold Alexander, Allied Supreme Commander, Mediterranean, was publicly announced on May 2. This, prior to the capitulation of the Twenty-First Army Group to Field-Marshal Montgomery on May 4, was the greatest unconditional surrender in military history.
The swift advance of the Allied Armies in Italy – ending in the surrender of nearly a million men – and in

Western and Central Europe – where further millions of Germans are in our hands – has set the Allies many major problems, not the least among which is the question of what to do with the prisoners of war. These beaten Germans have been housed in vast camps behind the lines in former German prison camps, or, in the case of small numbers, in their own barracks. But these must, of necessity, be temporary measures only, and what will be the ultimate fate of these men remains a very great problem at the present time.

THE BATTLE FOR BERLIN: SCENES FROM THE DYING REICH CAPITAL.

A SOVIET TANK-BORNE PATROL MOVING THROUGH THE BATTERED STREETS OF THE CONQUERED REICH CAPITAL. BEHIND IS THE BRANDENBURG GATE, WITH ITS QUADRIGA OF VICTORY.

THE RED FLAG FLYING FROM THE TOWER OF THE REICHSTAG – A SYMBOL OF RUSSIAN VICTORY. THIS PHOTOGRAPH WAS TAKEN AT THE MOMENT OF THE SURRENDER OF THE GERMAN GARRISON.

After a ferocious and unceasing battle, lasting seventeen days, Berlin fell to the Russians at 3 p.m. on May 2, 1945. This great news was made known in an order of the day by Marshall Stalin, addressed to the Red Army and the Red Navy, and announcing that troops under the command of Marshals Zhukov and Koniev, after stubborn street battles, had "completed the rout of the Berlin garrison and captured the city of Berlin, the capital of Germany, the centre of German imperialism, and the heart of German aggression." By 9 o'clock the same evening, Soviet troops in Berlin had taken more than 70,000 prisoners, and later reports stated the total captured in the capital during the day as 100,700. All through the night, in the glare of searchlights, and well into the following morning, long columns of prisoners were streaming from the centre of conquered Berlin towards P.O.W. camps on the outskirts. Most of them were described as half-crazed by the ordeal of shelling and bombing, which had reduced many parts of the Reich capital to unrecognisable scenes of wreckage.

WHERE HITLER DIED? LIGHT ON A HITLER MYSTERY.

THOUGHT TO BE THE SCENE OF THE DEATH OF HITLER AND EVA BRAUN: THE OFFICE IN HITLER'S SHELTER IN THE CHANCELLERY.

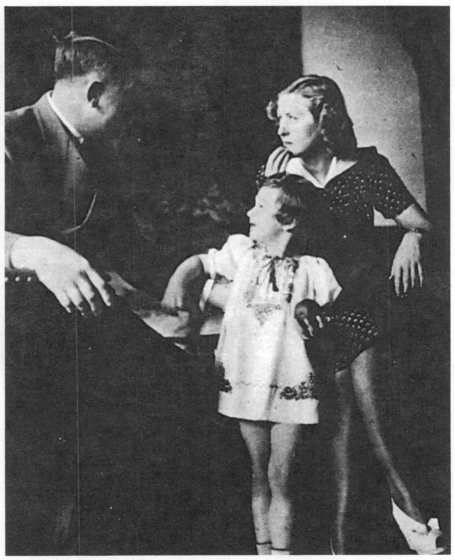

THE FÜHRER POSES AT HOME: HITLER WITH EVA BRAUN AND USCHI, WHO IS RUMOURED TO BE THEIR DAUGHTER AND APPEARS FREQUENTLY IN THE FAMILY ALBUM.

Rumours abound about the fate of Adolf Hitler. Circumstantial but unofficial reports speak of Hitler, a dying man, directing the final struggle from the heart of the capital. In any case, he could have had little left to direct, for in the closing stages of the battle the city was described as in a state of complete chaos.

Marshal Zhukov, while stating that Hitler's body had not yet been found and that escape by air from Central Berlin was feasible, disclosed that he possessed evidence showing that two days before Berlin fell Hitler married Eva Braun. Prior to 1932 she was secretary to Hitler's photographer, Heinrich Hoffman, and stories of her close association with Hitler have been reported.

With the recent arrival of British personnel in Berlin, fresh light has been thrown on the reports of Hitler's death. It will be remembered that it was stated that Hitler and Eva Braun died in the shelter at the Chancellery, Hitler's last stronghold in Berlin, and that their bodies were thrown into a shallow grave and attempts made to burn them with petrol. It is now revealed that Frau Heusermann, assistant to Dr. Blashke, Hitler's regular dentist, was treating the Führer within a few days of the end and indeed took refuge in the Chancellery. It is said that she stated that Hitler took poison and then shot Eva Braun and himself. She did not see the bodies, but heard that they had been burnt. Later, at Russian headquarters, she confidently identified from the dental work an upper and lower jawbone as Hitler's; and with less certainty identified some bridge-work as Eva Braun's. Frau Heusermann is apparently still in Russian custody.

The United States Counter-Intelligence Corps recently made an interesting discovery in Bavaria, which may throw some light on Hitler's private life and the mystery of his marriage to Eva Braun. They found a number of chests containing many personal possessions belonging to Eva Braun, including the uniform of black trousers and field-grey coat which Hitler is thought to have worn at the time of the bomb attempt on his life last year. The garments were bloodstained and torn to shreds and had apparently been cut off him.

Apart from Eva Braun's diary and extracts from her letters to Hitler, the most interesting human document is a photograph album showing Hitler with Eva Braun in "family" poses. In many of these a little girl called Uschi appears, and it is rumoured that she is Hitler's daughter, though another suggestion is that she may be the child of one of Eva's sisters. The investigators also found a quantity of silver, jewellery and other articles which probably represent Eva's share of the loot, particularly as the silver bears the emblem of the Polish crown.

THE HISTORIC CLIMAX TO MONTGOMERY'S VICTORIOUS CAMPAIGN.

THE GERMANS AT MONTGOMERY'S H.Q. ON MAY 3, ASKING FOR TERMS OF SURRENDER: GENERAL-ADMIRAL VON FRIEDEBURG (C.-IN-C. GERMAN NAVY), GENERAL KIENZEL AND REAR-ADMIRAL WAGNER.

THE "INSTRUMENT OF SURRENDER OF ALL GERMAN ARMED FORCES IN HOLLAND, IN NORTH-WEST GERMANY INCLUDING ALL ISLANDS, AND IN DENMARK."

THE SCENE AT AN HOTEL AT WAGENINGEN, NEAR ARNHEM, SHOWING LIEUT.-GENERAL FOULKES LEANING FORWARD TO READ THE SURRENDER INSTRUCTIONS TO BLASKOWITZ.

On a wild stretch of Luneberg Heath, Field-Marshal Montgomery signed the instrument of unconditional surrender of all German armed forces in Holland, North-West Germany, and Denmark at 6.25 p.m. on Friday, May 4, in his Army tent. This was the culminating act of the big German surrender of over a million men, freeing Holland and Denmark, following the historic victory of British arms. On May 5 Colonel-General Blaskowitz, unconditionally surrendered himself and his army to Lieut.-General Foulkes, Commander of the Canadian First Corps, signing the instrument of surrender.

THE TASK ACCOMPLISHED: THE GENERAL UNCONDITIONAL GERMAN SURRENDER SIGNED AT RHEIMS ON MAY 7.

THE SETTING FOR THE SIGNING OF THE ACT OF UNCONDITIONAL SURRENDER BY THE GERMANS: GENERAL EISENHOWER'S ADVANCED H.Q. IN RHEIMS, WITH THE THREE REPRESENTATIVES OF GERMANY. AND THOSE OF THE ALLIED NATIONS, INCLUDING GENERAL SEVEZ; GENERAL BEDELL SMITH; AND GENERAL SUSLOPAROV.

The end of the long journey came at Rheims, at General Eisenhower's advanced H.Q., where, in the early hours of May 7, emissaries of Admiral Doenitz tendered the unconditional surrender of Germany's beaten military forces wherever they might still be fighting in the scattered pockets of Europe. General Jodl, the Nazi Chief of Staff, signed for the German High Command, and General Bedell Smith, Chief of Staff of the Allied Expeditionary Force, and General François Sevez signed on behalf of the Supreme Commander of the Allied Expeditionary Force, and General Susloparov signed on behalf of the Russian High Command.

The act of signing was recorded as 2.41 a.m. on May 7. So, in almost exactly 11 months, this tremendous campaign from the Normandy beaches to the banks of the Elbe has ended in overwhelming victory.

JOURNEY'S END: THE LAST ACT OF SURRENDER RATIFIED IN BERLIN.

THE TENSE MOMENT BEFORE THE SIGNING AT RED ARMY'S H.Q. IN BERLIN: THE THREE GERMAN REPRESENTATIVES OF THE THREE ARMED FORCES.

THE RATIFICATION OF THE ACT OF UNCONDITIONAL SURRENDER TOOK PLACE IN BERLIN: MARSHAL G. ZHUKOV SIGNING ON BEHALF OF THE RUSSIAN ARMY.

For the second time within 48 hours the unconditional surrender of all German armed forces to the Allied Expeditionary Force and the Russian High Command was signed on May 9 – this time in Berlin. What General Jodl did at Rheims, Field-Marshal Keitel, Admiral Friedeburg, and Air Colonel-General Stumpf repeated at 16 minutes past midnight on Wednesday morning, May 9. This final act of surrender was signed before Marshal Zhukov, representing the Russian High Command, and Air Chief-Marshal Tedder, Deputy Supreme Commander of the Allied Expeditionary Force. General Spaatz, of the U.S. Air Forces, and General de Lattre de Tassigny, of the French First Army, signed as witnesses. After the Germans had left Air Chief-Marshal Tedder and Marshal Zhukov shook hands, and there were congratulations all round.

THE LIBERATION OF HOLLAND, DENMARK AND NORWAY.

ROTTERDAM AFTER FIVE YEARS OF MISERY: DELIGHTED CROWDS RUNNING TO GREET A CANADIAN COLUMN BRINGING FOOD TO THE STARVING PEOPLE.

ONE OF THE GERMAN CRUISERS WHICH CAME UNDER THE GUNS OF THE ROYAL NAVY IN COPENHAGEN HARBOUR – THE 10,000 TON "PRINZ EUGEN" UNDER DANISH GUARD.

IMMENSE CROWDS DELIRIOUS WITH DELIGHT, AS THE BRITISH FIRST ARRIVED: THE GERMANS DID NOT INTERFERE.

After the final ratification in Berlin of Germany's unconditional surrender, and since Holland and Denmark had been surrendered unconditionally to Field-Marshal Montgomery on May 4, the reoccupation of Norway completed the liberation of the three countries at the hands of the British. The Dutch in The Hague, Utrecht, Rotterdam, and Amsterdam, who had feared the destruction of the dams and whose lack of foodstuffs threatened them with utter starvation until the R.A.F. dropped supplies, received their rescuers, the Canadians, with wide-open arms, relief and joy being such that the usually phlegmatic Dutch threw off all reserve. The Danes, too, from the moment advance British forces crossed the frontier, let themselves go in a delirium of joy. The surrender was effective from 8 a.m. on May 5, but the demonstrations began on the previous day, when Danish police began to free political prisoners and internees, and officials of the resistance movement began rounding up collaborators, of whom they had prepared a list of 15,000. The first British soldiers of the Armies of Liberation to cross the Danish border on May 5 were troops of Montgomery's famous "Desert Rats," who were given a tumultuous welcome. In Norway a single Dakota-load of British officers from Copenhagen landed before the airport building. German airmen stood rooted to the spot and when the tubby General appeared, the tall British air commodore requested that the British party should be driven in Luftwaffe staff cars to Oslo. At first the Norwegians stood amazed. Then a crowd, listening to the B.B.C. realised what was happening, and cheering spread along the streets like a forest fire.

VE-DAY CELEBRATIONS: "WE HAVE NEVER SEEN A GREATER DAY THAN THIS."

THE TUMULTUOUS PUBLIC OVATION TO THE PRIME MINISTER ON VE-DAY: MR. CHURCHILL ACCLAIMED BY AN EXCITED AND CHEERING CROWD IN WHITEHALL.

GREETING THEIR VICTORIOUS PEOPLE: THE KING AND QUEEN, WITH PRINCESS ELIZABETH, PRINCESS MARGARET, AND THE PRIME MINISTER, ACKNOWLEDGING THE CHEERS OF A VAST CROWD FROM THE BALCONY OF BUCKINGHAM PALACE.

THE BRIGHT LIGHTS OF VICTORY SHINING ON CROWDS IN TIMES SQUARE, NEW YORK, DURING VE-DAY CELEBRATIONS ON THE NIGHT OF MAY 8.

A DRUMHEAD THANKSGIVING SERVICE IN FRONT OF THE GUARDS' CHAPEL, WELLINGTON BARRACKS, WHICH WAS DESTROYED BY A FLYING BOMB LAST YEAR, WITH GREAT LOSS OF LIFE.

The two main centres to which flocked the vast crowds who came to London to celebrate victory on VE-Day were Buckingham Palace and Parliament Square. The scenes outside the Palace surpassed even those of the Coronation. From morning onwards, the people streamed steadily from all directions to converge on the open space around the Victoria Memorial and by the time Big Ben sounded the three notes which heralded the Prime Minister's announcement of Victory, the throng numbered many thousands. Mr. Churchill began with a plain recital of facts which grew in emotion as it proceeded to its fine climax, "Advance, Britannia!" After Mr. Churchill's announcement, the crowd roared for the King and Queen, whose appearance on the balcony was the signal for tumultuous cheering and the waving of innumerable flags in a kaleidoscope of red, white and blue. When the Prime Minister joined the King and Queen on the balcony soon after five o'clock, the roar of welcome continued for at least five minutes. Across the Channel Gay Paris of pre-war years showed herself true to her reputation on VE-Day. Parisians did not wait for the official announcement, and the usual boulevard crowds, swollen by thousands of newcomers, gave vent to the wildest enthusiasm. General de Gaulle, who took part in singing the Marseillaise amid a vast concourse, sent a message to Mr. Churchill, to whom he addressed his "sincere greetings, full of friendship and admiration." The celebrations in Paris continued for several days. America too forgot her cares and worries on May 8 to join in the celebrations of VE-Day, crowds in the cities and towns and parties in the villages sharing the country's joy.

THE MASS ARREST OF THE GERMAN HIGH COMMAND AT FLENSBURG.
HIMMLER COMMITS SUICIDE, "LORD HAW-HAW" IS WOUNDED.

WILLIAM JOYCE ("LORD HAW-HAW") BEING CARRIED ON A STRETCHER INTO A BRITISH SECOND ARMY H.Q. HOSPITAL AT LÜNEBURG.

HENRICH HIMMLER, DRAWN BY OUR WAR ARTIST, CAPTAIN BRYAN DE GRINEAU.

THE FINAL SCENE ON BOARD THE SHAEF SHIP "PATRIA": DOENITZ (CENTRE, RIGHT) IS BEING CURTLY INFORMED THAT HIS GOVERNMENT AND THE GERMAN HIGH COMMAND ARE AT AN END.

The final scene in the life of Grand-Admiral Karl Doenitz's self-styled Government and the German High Command was played out on board the Shaef mission ship "Patria," moored off Doenitz's headquarters at Flensburg, on the morning of Wednesday, May 23. At 10 a.m., in accordance with a prearranged plan, Doenitz, whom Hitler, shortly before his suicide, had appointed as his successor, accompanied by Admiral-General Hans von Friedeburg, and Colonel-General Jodl, went on board the "Patria" and were shown into the lounge bar. Major-General Lowell W. Rooks, of the U.S. Army, entered the room accompanied by Brigadier E. J. Foord, of the British Army, and Major-General Trusov, representing the Russian High Command. The subsequent scene occupied only four minutes. General Rooks curtly informed Doenitz that his Government had come to an end and that the German High Command was under arrest.

General Rooks then rose to his feet, and the Germans were dismissed under escort. Only one of them escaped – Friedeburg, who while collecting clothing from his home had locked himself in a bathroom and taken a dose of poison from which he died within a minute. Himmler, the former head of the Gestapo, the S.S., and the whole of the police machinery of the Reich, and the most sinister figure in Germany, is also dead. He committed suicide by taking poison, just after 11 p.m. on May 23 at the British Second Army H.Q. at Lüneburg. On May 28, the notorious William Joyce, who broadcast for the Germans and won the sobriquet of "Lord Haw-Haw," accosted two English officers. They were suspicious of him, and on challenge he admitted his identity. He made a movement as if to draw a pistol, and one of the officers shot him in the thigh and took him into custody.

BRITAIN'S NEW LABOUR GOVERNMENT: THE SOCIALISTS VICTORIOUS.

MR. ERNEST BEVIN, SECRETARY OF STATE FOR FOREIGN AFFAIRS.

SIR STAFFORD CRIPPS, PRESIDENT OF THE BOARD OF TRADE.

MR. C. R. ATTLEE: "IT WILL ENABLE US TO IMPLEMENT THE POLICY OF THE SOCIALIST PARTY."

MR. HERBERT MORRISON, LORD PRESIDENT OF THE COUNCIL.

MR. HUGH DALTON, CHANCELLOR OF THE EXCHEQUER.

Probably the most outstanding difference between this and preceding General Elections was the radical change in the geographical distribution of the electorate. This was due not only to the movements of population directed to war factories far removed from their homes, but to the incidence of evacuation, which transferred many thousands of women voters and Civil Servants to new districts. Thus London lost almost exactly one-third of its electorate, while voters in South-West England, one of the main evacuation areas, increased by 34 per cent. Many of these latter votes were, however, ineffective, for thousands of electors who returned to London since VE-Day were too late for re-registration.

At 7 p.m. on July 26, Mr. Winston Churchill, who had led Britain through five of the most critical and trying years of her history, drove to Buckingham Palace and tendered to the King his resignation. By the

early afternoon of that day, it had become clear that Labour had gained a sweeping victory in the General Election, and Mr. Attlee's immediate comment was: "It will enable us to implement the policy of the Socialist Party." Within a few minutes of Mr. Churchill leaving the Palace, the King received Mr. Attlee and invited him to form a new Government. Britain's new Premier, the Rt. Hon. Clement Richard Attlee, was born on January 3, 1883. Educated at Haileybury College and University College, Oxford, he has been a Socialist all his life. He served throughout the first World War, in the South Lancashire Regiment and Tank Corps, retiring as Major in 1919. Mr. Attlee was Deputy Prime Minister in Mr. Churchill's Coalition Government from 1942. These four leading Ministers in Mr. Attlee's new Government all served in prominent posts under Mr. Churchill during the Coalition, and all have long political records in the ranks of the Labour Party. Mr.

Ernest Bevin, who now becomes Secretary of State for Foreign Affairs, will be remembered as the forceful Minister of Labour and National Service who, under Mr. Churchill, organised Britain's man-power and woman-power for war. He is sixty-four years of age. – Sir Stafford Cripps, the new President of the Board of Trade, spent the first two years of the war as Britain's Ambassador to Moscow, and on his return to this country in 1942 became Minister of Aircraft Production. He is fifty-six years of age. Mr. Hugh Dalton, now Chancellor of the Exchequer, served Mr. Churchill's Coalition first as Minister of Economic Warfare and then as President of the Board of Trade. He was chairman of the National Executive of the Labour Party in 1936-37. His age is fifty-eight. – Mr. Herbert Morrison, now Lord President of the Council, will be remembered for his war services as Home Secretary and Minister of Home Security.

POTSDAM: THE VENUE OF THE LATEST "BIG THREE" CONFERENCE.

A MOMENTOUS CONFERENCE: THE FIRST MEETING OF THE BIG THREE AT POTSDAM.
CLOCKWISE FROM MR. CHURCHILL (CENTRE): MAJOR A. H. BIRSE (INTERPRETER); BEHIND HIM SIR A. CLARK KERR (BRITISH AMBASSADOR IN MOSCOW); MR. ATTLEE; NEXT BUT ONE, M. MOLOTOV (SOVIET FOREIGN MINISTER); BEHIND HIM, M. GUSEV (RUSSIAN AMBASSADOR IN LONDON); GENERALISSIMO STALIN; FIFTH FROM STALIN, PRESIDENT TRUMAN; THIRD ON HIS LEFT, SIR ALEXANDER CADOGAN (PERMANENT UNDER-SECRETARY OF STATE FOR FOREIGN AFFAIRS); MR. ANTHONY EDEN.

THE PREMIER AT THE SALUTING-BASE FOR THE VICTORY PARADE AT BERLIN. ON EITHER SIDE OF HIM, FIELD-MARSHALS MONTGOMERY AND ALEXANDER. RIGHT, MR. ANTHONY EDEN.

THE BERLIN CONFERENCE IN SESSION: PRESIDENT TRUMAN (LEFT), MR. ATTLEE AND MR. BEVIN (CENTRE), AND GENERALISSIMO STALIN (STANDING, RIGHT).

The first official conference of the heads of Government of the United Kingdom, United States and the Soviet Union took place at Potsdam on the afternoon of July 17 at 5 o'clock. By invitation of his two colleagues, President Truman presided at all meetings of the conference. The official announcement states that a preliminary exchange of views took place on matters requiring decision by the three Allied leaders, and that it was decided that the three Foreign Secretaries should hold regular meetings to prepare the work of the conference. On July 21 struck one of the finest hours of the Prime Minister's life, the hour, he said, which he had lived for, the hour in which he took the salute of the great parade of the British Armed Forces in Berlin, and in which perhaps most astonishing of all he received the spontaneous plaudits of the population of Berlin. Leading the parade was the 7th Armoured Division. The Potsdam Conference has ended, and it has imposed rules on Germany

which are stern and drastic, but are framed to allow the German people, after a long period of supervision and gradual political development, to take their place among the free peoples of the world. Germany is to be completely disarmed and demilitarised. On July 27, Mr. Clement Richard Attlee, Britain's new Prime Minister, succeeded Mr. Churchill. On being invited by the King to form a new Government, Mr. Attlee made some key appointments and then returned to Berlin, accompanied by Mr. Bevin, the new Foreign Secretary, to resume work at Potsdam. Within a short time of his arrival by air, the two ministers had made formal calls on President Truman and Mr. Byrnes and Generalissimo Stalin and M. Molotov at their still secret places of residence, and a full meeting of the three heads of government was held later in the evening. Mr. Churchill's wisdom in associating Mr. Attlee with the work of the Conference from the start is now obvious.

WHAT THE GERMANS HAVE TO THANK HITLER FOR: LIFE IN GERMANY TO-DAY.

ORPHANED CHILDREN, BEING MOVED FROM ONE AREA OF BERLIN TO ANOTHER ARE HALTED TO RECEIVE CHOCOLATE GIVEN THEM BY ALLIED SERVICEMEN.

FULL CIRCLE: GERMANS, WHO ENTERED CZECHOSLOVAKIA AS CONQUERORS TO COLONISE THE "GREATER GERMAN REICH," LEAVING A LIBERATED CZECHOSLOVAKIA AS REFUGEES.

THREE GERMANS, ENEMIES OF THE NAZI RÉGIME WHO HAD SPENT TEN YEARS IN CONCENTRATION CAMPS, WALKING WITH THEIR BELONGINGS ALONG A ROAD TO LIBERTY.

However much they cheered when Hitler's armies were overrunning Europe, rarely in history can people have paid a more fearful price for the crimes of their leaders than the Germans. They are paying for the war in terms of human misery, and few will deny that that payment is but just retribution for the suffering inflicted on others. Berlin is the focal point of all the complex problems that are going to arise in the occupation of Germany, for whatever the conclusions reached in council and whatever the rations may be on paper, there is no doubt that the mass of Berliners are facing starvation. The Berlin winter is normally severe, and with the lack of water and soap, the shortage of food, drugs, and medicaments, the city is liable to become a focus of disease. Dysentery and typhoid are the worst menaces, outbreaks of both having already been reported, and with many Berliners suffering from semi-starvation now, the future outlook is grim. Berlin is still numb from the cataclysm that swept over it – the capital received more bombs than any other German city – and the people who remained there, mostly women and children and old men, are merely existing, their lined faces and staring eyes, and the unfamiliar leanness of their bodies bearing testimony to their long ordeal.

"ALADDIN'S CAVES" OF LOOT: PRICELESS TREASURES HIDDEN IN GERMANY.

A CAPTURED REICHSBANK OFFICIAL HELPING U.S. EXPERTS TO CHECK STACKS OF FOREIGN CURRENCY IN A MINE GALLERY.

DESTINED FOR HITLER'S PROJECTED HOUSE OF GERMAN ART AT LINZ, "A GARDEN SCENE," BY WATTEAU.

SOME OF THE 10,000 BELLS STOLEN BY THE GERMANS FROM CHURCHES IN EUROPE AS A METAL RESERVE FOR ARMAMENTS.

Two German women in search of a midwife are said to have given away the secret hiding-place of the bulk of Germany's gold reserve and looted art treasures. The women, of the small village of Merkers, told American military policemen: "Down there in that mine is all the gold in Germany." Investigation of this hiding-place – a salt mine – uncovered some 100 tons of gold bullion, together with probably the greatest collection of priceless paintings, sculpture and tapestries ever hidden away. It includes pictures by Raphael, Van Dyck, Rembrandt, and Dürer, and manuscripts and relics of Goethe. Kesselring is reported to have personally assured Reichsbank directors that General Patton's troops would not get to the salt-mine, but officials sent from Berlin had only just arrived when infantry of the US Third Army over-ran the mine. Pending discussions by the Allies, this great hoard of treasure is to remain in the custody of the US Army.

It was announced on May 14 that the Allies had found on the Loser Plateau, in Austria, hidden in a saltmine, a huge collection of art treasures, including the Rothschild Collections obtained from Paris during the occupation. Recent examination of Hitler's library at Berchtesgaden has revealed certain portfolios which contain superb reproductions of the pictures concerned. Many were allotted to Vienna, but perhaps the cream were earmarked for the "Gaumuseum, Linz." This "District Museum" was not the museum which already exists in Linz, the nearest big Austrian town to Hitler's birth place, but was a grandiose affair, a "House of German Art", a project of Hitler's own, a "Führer Galerie", a collection of German and Foreign Art to be parallel to the "House of German Art" at Munich. It was intended that this collection should be of European importance and its foundations were to be laid by the Führer's "purchases" from private collections.

Near Hamburg there lies a huge dump of metal stolen by the Germans and placed there as a metal reserve for the production of armaments. In it are upwards of 10,000 church bells looted from practically every church, convent and chapel in German-occupied territory, and thousands of statues collected from all over Europe. Fortunately, the bells and many of the statues were never melted down, and the Allied Military Governments of Germany are now engaged in sorting out these stolen treasures and returning them to their rightful places.
Most of the bells had cast on them the places of their dedication, and the Fine Arts Branch of the Military Governments is classifying, as far as possible, the unidentified objects. The first shipload of the bells left Hamburg for Holland and Belgium on October 2nd, containing about 700 bells stolen from Belgium, and about the same number from Holland. Many of the statues come from Germany itself.

THEIR COUNTRYMEN PASS JUDGEMENT ON THOSE WHO AIDED HITLER.

THE DEFENDANT IN ONE OF THE GREATEST POLITICAL TRIALS IN HISTORY: MARSHAL PÉTAIN IN COURT.

The trial of Philippe Pétain, eighty-nine-years-old Marshal of France, on charges of plotting against the internal security of France and of intelligence with the enemy opened in Paris on July 23.
Marshal Pétain was sentenced to death on August 14. The sentence was later commuted to life imprisonment.

ABRAHAM VIDKUN QUISLING, WHOSE NAME HAS BECOME A SYNONYM FOR "TRAITOR."

Quisling standing to hear the verdict of guilty of many crimes, from treason downwards, and the death sentence pronounced by the judge at Oslo on September 10. He was executed by firing squad on October 24.

ANTON MUSSERT, THE DUTCH QUISLING, IN GAOL AWAITING HIS TRIAL.

The trial of the Dutch Nazi "Führer," Anton Mussert, is due to start shortly. Mussert was Hitler's puppet "ruler." Charged with many murders and acts of cruelty, he was hanged at The Hague on May 7, 1946.

A TRIAL THAT HAS LITTLE IN COMMON WITH BRITISH METHODS: PIERRE LAVAL.

The trial of Pierre Laval, formerly Prime Minister of the Vichy Government, opened on October 4 in the Paris High Court. Laval was condemned to death on October 9. He was found guilty on all the main charges. After an unsuccessful attempt to commit suicide by poison, he was executed by shooting on October 15, in a field outside the prison.

THE INGENUITY OF GERMAN SCIENTISTS APPLIED TO WAR AT SEA.

DIAGRAMMATIC DRAWINGS ILLUSTRATING MARITIME INVENTIONS AND TACTICS INTRODUCED BY THE GERMANS DURING THE WAR.

On this and the following pages our artist has depicted some of the scientific methods and inventions which the Germans introduced and exploited in the war. "The Times" Military Correspondent stated on June 29: "The more that is learnt of German preparations and progress with new weapons, the more apparent is it that the Allies ended the war with Germany only just in time," and proceeds to give a list of the formidable secret weapons, still in the experimental or prototype stage, which have been discovered by the British investigating authorities.

We are not here concerned with these weapons, but only with those which have been in actual use – at sea (shown on this page) and on land and in the air (which are illustrated on the following three pages, from page 181 to 183). The devices we illustrate above are mainly concerned with submarines, mines, and torpedoes. Germany relied at sea mainly on her submarines, her methods of U-boatwarfare being immensely improved as the war proceeded, notably by using underwater boats in "packs." In the early stages, cargo-carrying submarines were much used to supply the fighting craft. Later, when our aerial attacks forced their craft under water, they were able to answer with Schnorkel apparatus. In mines, also, extensive use was made of magnetic, acoustic and "antennæ" versions. In torpedoes, electrical propulsion was a great advance, as the electric torpedo leaves no tell-tale trail of bubbles; and the acoustic torpedo, which followed the beat of a ship's screw, was a particularly ingenious weapon.

THE INGENUITY OF GERMAN SCIENTISTS APPLIED TO WAR ON LAND.

DIAGRAMMATIC DRAWINGS SHOWING THE EXPLOITATION MADE BY THE GERMAN ARMY OF SCIENTIFIC AND TECHNICAL INVENTIONS.

The strategy and tactics of the Wehrmacht being from the very beginning based on the "Blitzkrieg," with its reliance on rapidly-moving armour, it is not surprising that Germany entered the war with large numbers of excellently designed tanks. As the war proceeded, they introduced many developments, notable among which were the Tiger and later the Royal Tiger, probably the most powerful tank used in the war, its special features being its 88-mm. gun, its heavy armour, and its wide and massive tracks; the Panther, smaller but fast, with a 75-mm. gun, perhaps their most successful design; tanks mounted with special weapons, such as A.-A. guns, rockets and mortars; and self-propelled guns of several types. Unsuccessful developments were the small tanks with explosive charges, the V-4, driven part of the way and then radio-controlled, which dropped its charge and returned to base; and the "Goliath," nicknamed the "Beetle" by our men, electrically controlled on a long cable, which exploded with its charge. Enormous numbers of land-mines were used by the Germans, and of these the non-metallic, designed to defeat our detecting devices, are perhaps the most interesting. Of the various types of artillery produced, the well-known "88" was probably the best. In addition, some remarkable long-range guns were produced. In artillery also extensive use was made of improved muzzle brakes, designed to restrict recoil and also effective in reducing "gun flash." Many developments of rocket-guns and mortars were also made; and camouflage and the extensive use of concrete were fully exploited.

THE INGENUITY OF GERMAN SCIENTISTS APPLIED TO WAR IN THE AIR.

METHODS AND MACHINES EXPLOITED AND USED BY THE GERMANS IN THE AIR WAR: DIAGRAMMATIC DRAWINGS.

Although concentration on the production of new and extraordinarily interesting air developments by German scientists tended to restrict construction of more orthodox fighter aircraft and so, in the opinion of some authorities, lost Germany the control of the air, nevertheless, as we have indicated on a previous page, had the enemy been permitted to develop his new inventions at leisure, there is no doubt that Allied territory, particularly the British Isles, would have been placed in a very serious position. As regards the actual use of air power, we show two developments of tactics: first, the technique of the dive-bomber, a battle-winning weapon during the early stages of the war, in Poland, France and Russia; and secondly, the dropping of parachute troops from very low altitudes by the employment of the device we illustrate, whereby the

parachute was instantly opened – the tactic whereby Crete was seized despite British control of the sea. Other technical inventions of great interest included in our drawings, besides the notorious V-1 and V-2, are a very large troop transport, a radio-controlled bomb, a composite fighter-plus-explosive-bomber, and various types of jet- and rocket-propelled aircraft.

The helicopter kite we illustrate is an ingenious development of the man-carrying kite. When towed, for example, by a ship, the blades of the helicopter rotate and cause the kite to climb aloft without any engine power whatever, thus enabling short-range reconnaissance to be made. It is also of interest to recall that it was the Luftwaffe which introduced the cannon as a fighter weapon in this war.

HOW ALLIED SCIENCE AND INGENUITY CONTRIBUTED TO GERMANY'S DEFEAT.

A FEW OF THE MANY WEAPONS AND DEVICES WITH WHICH THE ALLIES FIRST COUNTERED THE ENEMY AND LATER DROVE HOME THE GRAND ASSAULT.

On earlier pages we gave examples of German scientific and mechanical ingenuity. While we are still at war with Japan, security reasons prevent the publication of details of many weapons used with great effect against Germany. Others have, however, been removed from the secret list. Antidotes to the magnetic and acoustic mine were rapidly discovered, while in 1942 a corps of "frogmen" was formed, whose most spectacular achievement was the clearing of a path for our landing-craft through the "impenetrable" belt of underwater obstructions off the invasion beaches of Normandy. Within weeks of D-day fuel for the Allied armies was being pumped through underwater pipelines, from the Isle of Wight, where they were connected to an underground system stretching back to the Mersey, to Cherbourg, and later to Boulogne as soon as it was captured. Meanwhile our skies were increasingly protected by Radar, developed secretly since 1935, and substantially complete by the time of the Battle of Britain, which located invading aircraft and the acoustic shell which destroyed them, while "Fido" kept our airfields clear of fog for long enough to allow our own returning bombers to land. But most ingenious of all were the various devices designed to confront an invading army with a "wall of fire", at sea, on the beaches and inland, of which the rumours did much to influence German plans in the summer of 1940.

JAPANESE PILOTS' "SUICIDE" TACTICS AGAINST ALLIED WARSHIPS.

SEVEN JAP SUICIDE PILOTS WERE REPORTED AS HAVING CRASHED ON BRITISH WARSHIPS, INCLUDING TWO AIRCRAFT-CARRIERS, BUT NONE WAS LONG PUT OUT OF ACTION.

THE JAPANESE "SUICIDE" PLANE – THE "BAKA": SIMILAR TO THE GERMAN FLYING BOMB IN DESIGN, IT IS FLOWN BY A SUICIDE PILOT, WHO THROWS IT INTO A DIVE ON THE TARGET.

THE FLIGHT-DECK OF THE "BUNKER HILL" AFTER TWO SUICIDE AIRCRAFT HAD CRASHED ON HER AND SCATTERING HER 'PLANES LIKE NINEPINS, SETTING OFF BOMBS AND ROCKETS.

The chief threat to the Allied Navies operating in Japanese waters of recent weeks has undoubtedly been the "suicide 'plane" tactic. In this a fighter or medium bomber is loaded to its manœuvrable limit with explosives, and "crash-landed" on its target by the pilot, who perishes in the explosion. The latest method, however, is to employ a specially designed piloted flying bomb. These are not unlike the V1, being in the form of a stubby-winged monoplane, with a warhead in front and a rocket-propulsion unit behind, with the great difference, however, that a pilot is carried. The Americans have christened it "Baka," the Japanese word for "Fool." This "Baka" is carried underneath a Mitsubishi bomber, the pilots of the bomber and the flying bomb being linked by telephone. Once the target is sighted the "Baka" is released and the bomber turns away. At first the "Baka" glides; then, as he approaches, the pilot switches on his rockets; reaching a speed in the neighbourhood of 500 m.p.h., he aims himself and his 'plane at the most vulnerable point of his target.

THE FINAL CONQUEST OF OKINAWA: THE STRATEGIC KEY TO JAPAN.

THE STIFFEST FIGHTING THE U.S. TROOPS ENCOUNTERED WAS AT SHURI, THE OLD CAPITAL: THE DÉBRIS OF THE CASTLE AND THE RUINS OF A CHURCH.

MEN OF THE U.S. TENTH ARMY USING A LANDING-NET AS A SCALING-LADDER.

THE TERRAIN OF OKINAWA ISLAND MADE ADVANCE DIFFICULT: A FLAME-THROWING TANK ON THE WAY TO NAHA.

In the largest Pacific amphibious operation to date, men of the U.S. Tenth Army landed on Okinawa, a vital stepping-stone in the Allied advance to Japan; only 325 miles south-west of Kyushu, the southernmost major island of Japan, from Okinawa all Japan is vulnerable from the air. The conquest of this long and narrow island has not been an easy job, for large Japanese forces defend it from rocky heights and caves, but by May 17 its capital Naha had fallen to General Buchner's soldiers and marines. The battle for Okinawa is vital, the most vital, so far, in the Pacific, both for the Allies and for Japan, hence her desperate resistance. If this is an example of what will have to be faced eventually in Japan itself the Ikinawa campaign will have to be studied very carefully. On June 21, eighty-two days after the U.S. Marines first went ashore the bloodiest, most protracted, and most critical major battle of the Pacific came to a close. It is said that Okinawa has cost little short of one American killed or wounded to every Jap encountered. Already in the United States, certain military commentators have levelled fierce criticism at the generalship shown. But, by June 27, General Buchner was dead, and his place taken by General "Vinegar Joe" Stilwell, the veteran of Burma.

FINAL VICTORY IN BURMA: AUSTRALIAN LANDINGS IN BORNEO.

MEN OF THE R.A.F. REGIMENT MANHANDLING LIGHT 20-MM. ACK-ACK GUNS ACROSS THE SEA OF MUD TO WHICH THE MONSOON HAD TRANSFORMED THE LANDING BEACHES AT RANGOON.

BRUNEI, THE IMPORTANT PORT IN NORTH BORNEO CAPTURED BY AUSTRALIAN TROOPS. THE TOWN IS BUILT UPON PILES IN A GREAT LAGOON FORMED BY THE LIMBANG RIVER.

AUSTRALIAN INFANTRYMEN MOVING THROUGH THE ROYAL DUTCH SHELL OIL REFINERY, NEAR BALIKPAPAN, WHILST OIL BURNS IN THE BACKGROUND.

Rangoon fell on May 3. Prior to the arrival of troops of the Fourteenth Army in the Burmese capital, a successful invasion landing was made by men of the R.A.F. Regiment in the Rangoon River, in spite of the fact that the monsoon, breaking a week earlier than had been expected, had turned the beach-heads into a mass of mud. Since the fall of Rangoon, R.A.F. Liberators of the Strategic Air Force, Eastern Air Command, have concentrated on cutting all lines of communication of the Japanese troops retreating from South-East Burma. On July 27 the British Twelfth Army, under General Stopford, despite monsoon difficulties, trapped the remnants of the Twenty-eighth Japanese Army on the Sittang River, in their endeavour to escape into Siam. At the same time, while the British Fleet was forcing the entrance into the Straits of Malacca, a British force was reported to have landed on the island of Puket, with the intention of cutting the narrow Isthmus of Kra, thus isolating the Malay Peninsula and Japanese forces within it. Captain Falls suggests that the British plan, as the enemy claims, has the intention of freeing Malaya and consequently Singapore, as also the Dutch East Indies.

The invasion of Tarakan Island, off the north-east of Borneo, which was made by Australian infantry, and a small Netherlands Indies force, covered by mainly American naval forces, has proceeded well from its start at the beginning of last month, and, despite fanatical resistance by the Japanese it was reported on May 24 that mopping-up was in progress and that a quarter of the Japanese force had been wiped out. Tarakan, with its oilfields, is a rich prize and the largest field, Pamosian, fell early into Australian hands and was little damaged. Major-General Casey, commanding the U.S. Engineer Corps in the South-West Pacific, has stated that the oil-wells captured on Tarakan could furnish much oil for the final drive against Japan.

A communiqué from General MacArthur's H.Q. on June 9 reported air assaults and bombardment of the small island of Labuan, adjoining British North Borneo, formerly a naval port. Tokyo reports were of an Allied armada of 100 warships, including battleships, cruisers, destroyers, etc.

After seizing Labuan Island, on June 10, the Allies tightened their stranglehold on Japan's stolen Pacific Empire by making four simultaneous landings in the Brunel Bay area of N.W. Borneo. Watched by General MacArthur, C.-in-C. Land Forces in the Pacific, assault troops of the Australian Ninth Division, veterans of Tobruk and El Alamein, quickly established beach heads against little enemy resistance. Bombardments by warships of the U.S. Seventh Fleet and the Royal Australian Navy and U.S. 'planes prepared the way by levelling the beach defences. General MacArthur who went ashore on Labuan shortly after the initial assault, said, "Rarely is such a strategic prize obtained at such a low cost in life."

The Balikpapan landing, in South-Eastern Borneo, was made on July 1 by the Australian 7th Division after a heavy naval and air bombardment by U.S. forces. General MacArthur was in personal command. Four days later, after a whirlwind assault, Australian troops had occupied most of Balikpapan's battered ruins. The town's great industrial area is now mainly scrap-iron, and only air-raid shelters were untouched by the devastating air and naval bombardment which was necessary to oust the Japanese from this oil centre and one of the greatest Japanese strongholds in the Far East. The Pandan Sari oilfields and refinery in the northern section of Balikpapan are some of the richest in Borneo, and their loss is a serious blow to the enemy. It is announced as we go to press that Australian troops have made a new landing on the Borneo coast at Tempadeong, 14 miles north-west of Balikpapan. This is the fourth major operation in Borneo.

CIVILISATION LETS OUT THE ATOMIC GENIE:
WILL IT BE POSSIBLE TO CONTROL IT IN THE FUTURE?

A VIEW OF THE SHOPPING QUARTER OF HIROSHIMA, FORMERLY A CITY OF OVER 240,000 PEOPLE. TOKYO REPORTS SAID THAT BUILDINGS WERE CRUSHED OR WIPED OUT, AND THE POPULATION KILLED BY BLAST FROM THE ATOMIC BOMB, RELEASED UPON IT ON AUGUST 6.

THE HARBOUR OF NAGASAKI, AN IMPORTANT NAVAL BASE: IT LIES AT THE HEAD OF A BEAUTIFUL INLET. TARGET OF THE SECOND ATOMIC BOMB ON AUGUST 9. THE CITY OF 255,000 PEOPLE IS BELIEVED TO HAVE BEEN OBLITERATED.

The Allies disclosed on August 6 that they had used the most terrible device of war yet produced – the atomic bomb. It was dropped on the Japanese port and Army base of Hiroshima, 90 miles west of Kobe. The city was blotted out by clouds of dust and smoke, but the crew of the Super-Fortress who dropped the bomb reported that there was reason to believe that Hiroshima no longer exists. Within a few hours Tokyo broadcast to the world the horror of this city of 244,000 people, in which every living creature had been "seared to death".

On August 9, three days after Hiroshima had been obliterated by the first atomic bomb, a second was released on the famous port of Nagasaki, with a population of 255,000 people. Within a few hours of the dropping of this bomb, and following a broadcast by President Truman that "we will atom-bomb Japan until she surrenders," the Japanese Government made overtures to end the war, agreeing to accept the unconditional surrender terms of the Potsdam ultimatum, subject to the condition that Hirohito remained the Emperor.

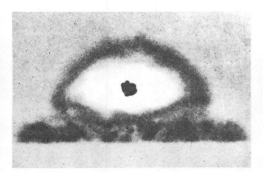

THE BEGINNING OF THE EXPLOSION: THE CENTRAL BLACK AREA, INTENSER THAN THE SUN, SHOWS REVERSED IN THE NEGATIVE.

LIKE A STEEL HELMET: THE FORM TAKEN AT ONE STAGE BY WHAT APPEARS TO BE WHITE-HOT AIR.

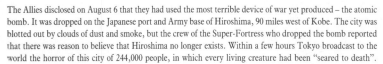

THE BLINDING FLASH, WHICH LIGHTED UP THE WHOLE AREA, AT THE MOMENT OF EXPLOSION, WITH THICK CLOUDS OF SMOKE BEGINNING TO RISE.

THE HUGE MUSHROOM-SHAPED CLOUD OF SMOKE AND DUST, REPORTED TO HAVE RISEN TO 50,000 FT., THAT FOLLOWED THE DROPPING OF THE ATOMIC BOMB ON THE JAPANESE PORT OF NAGASAKI.

THE BASE BEGINNING TO SPREAD AS AIR IS FLUNG OUTWARD IN AN OVERWHELMING BLAST FROM THE CENTRAL POINT OF THE EXPLOSION.

The world's reaction to the releasing of the force of the atom is much that of Sindbad and other characters of fable, who have released gigantic uncontrollable genii from small bottles: How on earth can we put back the genie into the bottle and cork him securely in his prison? The immensity of the genie released is graphically described by Group Captain G. L. Cheshire, V.C., who watched the dropping of an atomic bomb on Nagasaki on the morning of August 9, 1945. He spoke of the towering pillar of smoke and flame brooding over the stricken city as "a wicked sight – a sort of yellow, and luminous and foul." The flash was so vivid that its glare completely dimmed the sunlight and his first impression thereafter was a great ball of fire of so intense a heat that its temperature has been estimated at 10,000,000 degrees. Then, with incredible speed, a great pillar of grey smoke lifting a fiery ball of flame on its summit climbed up into the clear sky, whirling and seething with a terrifying impression of life. At its foot, vast fires blazed up and spread rapidly outward. Twenty minutes after the explosion the pillar, now 60,000 ft. tall, began to lose its solid outlines and, as it formed a huge cloud, its luminous fiery top broke clear and whirled upward to dissipate in the upper air.

THE DESOLATION OF HIROSHIMA: THE CIRCLE OF DESTRUCTION, FOUR MILES IN DIAMETER.

THE DISINTEGRATION OF A GREAT CITY: NAGASAKI AFTER THE BLAST OF AN ATOM BOMB.

The recent pictures of Hiroshima, such as that shown above left, provide an awful warning for civilisation; and the appalling and, it would appear, incalculable results of this most recent of science's achievements form a terrible commentary on modern war. On September 8 the Japanese Domei agency stated that 126,000 persons had been killed by the single atomic bomb which fell on Hiroshima on August 6. The details of the list were given as follows: instantly killed, 66,000; died of injuries, 60,000; missing and believed dead, 10,000; seriously injured, 14,000; slightly injured, 104,000. European eye-witnesses state that Hiroshima is utterly destroyed and that from the centre of the city complete desolation stretches for two miles in every direction. In addition, it has been claimed that the radio-active after-effects of the bomb are in themselves lethal; and that even those who were only slightly injured are nevertheless doomed. These lethal effects are thought to be produced by gamma-rays, the same sort of activity as that used in radium treatment of cancer. Above right we show the first ground-level photograph of the desolation of Nagasaki. Taken by a Japanese photographer after the smoke and dust of the atom-bomb explosion had settled, it illustrates graphically the complete disintegration of a once-teeming city, whose buildings have vanished as if swept away by a giant broom. Observers flying over the site of the Japanese city have spoken of the "horrifying" absence of rubble and craters. Describing the scene, they said: "It was as though a giant typhoon had swept Nagasaki into the bay leaving no trace of where the streets once stood. Nagasaki looks like a bone picked clean."

WHY JAPAN WAS AT THE END OF ITS TETHER BEFORE THE ATOMIC BOMB.

LILLIPUTIAN CITIES BUILT UP IN MINIATURE: TRAINING FOR PRECISION BOMBING OVER JAP CITIES.

To ensure the accuracy of their precision bombing, whole Japanese cities have been reconstructed by the American Air Force, at a scale of one foot to the mile, using the latest reconnaissance photographs. These Lilliputian cities are then filmed and copies distributed to the bomber units. This system was also employed at Hiroshima and Nagasaki. The picture of Tokyo gives some idea of the resulting terrible effects of the concentrated air raids which were directed upon the chief cities of Japan before the atom bombs were dropped. In an interview after the war Admiral Suzuki, who was Japanese Premier from April 7 to August 15, is said to have stated that peace feelers were made as long ago as the

RUSSIA INVADES MANCHURIA.

RUSSIAN SAILORS AT PORT ARTHUR CHEERING AS THE SOVIET FLAG IS HOISTED ON AUGUST 25, FORTY YEARS AFTER THE PORT HAD BEEN WRESTED FROM RUSSIA BY THE JAPANESE.

Mr. Molotov informed the Japanese Ambassador in Moscow, on August 8, of Russia's decision to declare war on Japan.
The first report of Soviet troops in Manchuria came on August 22, when the Soviet High Command announced that airborne troops had landed at Port Arthur. Four days later the Soviet Pacific Squadron was reported at anchor in the harbour, where, forty years previously, the Japanese had attacked the Pacific Squadron of Tsarist Russia and thus begun the Russo-Japanese War. Marshal Stalin, on September 2, said: "We men of the older generation have waited forty years for this day."

ONE OF 60,000 LEAFLETS DROPPED BY U.S. 'PLANES ON ELEVEN JAPANESE CITIES, EACH NAMED IN A CIRCLE, WARNING THEM THEY WILL BE DESTROYED.

JAPAN SUES FOR PEACE.

HIS IMPERIAL MAJESTY THE EMPEROR HIROHITO OF JAPAN.

On August 10, the Japanese Government was then ready to accept the terms enumerated in the Joint Declaration issued at Potsdam, with the understanding that that declaration did not comprise any demand which prejudices the prerogatives of the Emperor as a sovereign ruler. The Allied reply was that "From the moment of surrender the authority of the Emperor and the Japanese Government to rule the State shall be subject to the Supreme Commander of the Allied Powers."
At noon, Japanese time, on August 15 the Emperor himself announced that he had ordered his Government to accept these provisions.

THE REAL THING: THE RUBBLE AND DÉBRIS OF TOKYO, SHOWING THE EFFECTS OF ALLIED MASS RAIDS.

San Francisco Conference in June and that the Russians were then asked to negotiate with the Allies. The only answer received to this offer was Russia's declaration of war two months later. The claim was made in the same interview that the militarists were fully determined to drag their country into annihilation rather than surrender and that earlier disasters had been hidden from the people and the Emperor. It would appear, that it has only been the terrible effects of saturation and atomic bombing that have brought home alike to the Emperor and to the Japanese man in the street the extent of their losses and the pit of annihilation which was opening before them.

U.S.S. "INDIANAPOLIS" LOST.

THE U.S. HEAVY CRUISER "INDIANAPOLIS" RECENTLY LOST BY ENEMY ACTION IN THE PHILIPPINE SEA, AFTER CARRYING ATOMIC BOMB MATERIAL TO GUAM.

Two minutes before the announcement of the Japanese surrender, the U.S. Navy Department revealed that the heavy cruiser "Indianapolis", whose last mission was to carry essential atomic bomb material from San Francisco to Guam, had been recently lost in the Philippine Sea. Later a figure of 883 deaths was given, 484 of them from drowning or sharks during the three days that more than 800 men who had survived the initial torpedoing had spent in the water before a search was organised. This is the greatest single disaster in the history of the United States Navy.

CELEBRATING VE-DAY – AND NIGHT – IN LONDON AND PEARL HARBOUR.

THE HUGE CROWD WHICH GATHERED BEFORE BUCKINGHAM PALACE TO GREET THE ROYAL FAMILY ON VICTORY DAY: A PANORAMA TAKEN FROM THE ROOF OF THE PALACE, SHOWING THE THRONGS WHICH CONTINUED DAY AND NIGHT. WHILE IN PEARL HARBOUR WORKERS CELEBRATED THE JAPANESE SURRENDER BY BURNING AN EFFIGY OF THE EMPEROR HIROHITO.

Many thousands of Londoners and Allied Servicemen and women disregarded the official request that the reported Japanese surrender should be treated with reserve and decided to make merry after the news broke last Friday, August 10. As on VE-Day, Piccadilly Circus was the hub of the preliminary victory celebrations, a large crowd soon assembling round the base of the Eros statue. Dancing soon became general, but later had to be abandoned for lack of space.
On the night of Victory Day itself, August 15, the King in his broadcast to his peoples said: "The war is over.

You know that those four words have for the Queen and myself the same significance, simple yet immense, that they have for you. Our hearts are full to overflowing, as are your own." This sharing of rejoicing and thanksgiving were overwhelmingly shown by the feelings of the thousands who flocked during Victory Day to the heart of London and demonstrated their happiness and their loyalty. London was a centre of contagious happiness. In Honolulu, the US Navy at Pearl Harbour celebrated the final collapse and downfall of Japan by a great firework display and by the burning in effigy of the Emperor Horohito.

JAPANESE EMISSARIES IN MANILA: FIRST U.S. LANDINGS IN JAPAN.

THE JAPANESE ENVOYS FOR THE MANILA CONFERENCE: LIEUT.-GENERAL TAKASHIRO KAWABE, WITH GRIM-FACED DELEGATES, ARRIVING AT IE SHIMA.

GENERAL MACARTHUR ARRIVES AT ATSUGI AIRFIELD ON AUGUST 30. WITH GENERAL KENNEY, COMMANDING FAR EASTERN A.F., AND GENERAL SPAATZ, COMMANDING STRATEGIC A.F.

The first surrender talks started in Manila at 9 p.m. on August 19 and lasted five hours, after many delays. MacArthur had forced the Japanese emissaries to fly to the Philippines to obtain preliminary conditions and used "Bataan" as the password, because he knew the ignominy the locale implied to the would-be dictators of Asia, whose noses must be rubbed in the dirt. Led by Lieut.-General Takashiro Kawabe, Vice-Chief of the Japanese General Staff, and sixteen other envoys, they were received frigidly by Lieut.-General R. K. Sutherland, General MacArthur's Chief of Staff. Kawabe, a diminutive little man of 5 ft. 4 in., was four days late, a Japanese attempt, it was said, to save "face" which failed. They were told these were only preliminary talks, and were called upon to give full details of airfields, harbours and troops emplacements.

U.S. occupation troops began landing in Japan on August 23. A few days later General MacArthur triumphantly landed at Atsugi Airfield, near Yokohama, soon after 2 p.m. on August 30, and proclaimed "This looks like the pay-off." Greeted by a dozen of his subordinate generals, he found the occupation plans "going splendidly." The picture of the General was taken just after his arrival, where he smoked his corncob pipe and was photographed and filmed. Begged to say something for world consumption at this historic epoch, he remarked, "From Melbourne to Tokyo is a long road – a long road and a hard road. The surrender plans are going splendidly." He then drove with a small escort from Atsugi airport to Yokohama along a route lined by more than 30,000 Japanese soldiers with bayonets fixed.

SIGNING THE INSTRUMENT OF SURRENDER ON BOARD THE U.S. BATTLESHIP "MISSOURI."

JAPAN'S FINAL SURRENDER: SHIGEMITSU, THE JAPANESE FOREIGN MINISTER, SIGNING THE SURRENDER DOCUMENT, WHILE GENERAL MACARTHUR (LEFT) WATCHES NONCHALANTLY.

THE HISTORIC DOCUMENT OF JAPAN'S SURRENDER, SIGNED BY THE ENEMY ENVOYS AND THE ALLIED CHIEFS.

THE JAPANESE EMISSARIES, WITH GRIM EXPRESSIONS, WAITING TO SIGN THE SURRENDER PAPERS: MAMORU SHIGEMITSU, FOREIGN MINISTER; (RIGHT) GENERAL YOSHI UMEZU.

With Battle Ensign flying, Admiral Halsey's fleet of 112 British and U.S. warships sailed into its anchorage in Sagami Bay, just outside the entrance to Tokyo Bay, at 5.30 a.m., B.S.T. on August 27 – the first act in the occupation of Japan. The Allied ships were led by Japanese pilots, who met the U.S. battleship "Missouri," Admiral Halsey's flagship, 20 miles out at sea. The British ships in the fleet included the battleships "Duke of York" and "King George V." On Sunday, September 2, Japan signed the historic 400 words of final surrender accepting the Potsdam Declaration and the authority of General MacArthur in the U.S. battleship "Missouri" in Tokyo Bay. Eleven Japanese emissaries, four frock-coated and top-hatted diplomats, four soldiers minus swords or sabres, and three sailors who had lost their ships, stood uneasily on the deck of the battleship while the official ceremony of their surrender was carried out. Before them, wearing no decorations, stood General Douglas MacArthur, watching as Shigemitsu, Japan's Foreign Minister, signed his name. The surrender docu-

ments – one set in English for the Allies bound in gold the other set in Japanese for the enemy bound in black – had been placed on a long table covered with green baize. MacArthur then said: "Will General Wainwright and General Percival accompany me while I sign?" Lieut.-General Wainwright, "Defender of Corregidor," and Lieut.-General Percival, former C.-in-C., Malaya, who was forced to surrender Singapore in 1942, were both recently freed from prison camps. During the ceremony a fleet of 450 Super-Fortresses roared over Tokyo Bay and Tokyo itself. In a moving speech, General MacArthur said it was for us, both victors and vanquished, to rise to that higher dignity which alone benefited the sacred purposes they were about to serve. "It is my earnest hope," he said, "and, indeed the hope of all mankind, that from this solemn occasion a better world shall emerge out of the blood and carnage of the past – a world founded upon faith and understanding, a world dedicated to the dignity of man and the fulfilment of his most cherished wish for freedom, tolerance, and justice."

JAPANESE SURRENDER SCENES: INCIDENTS IN VARIOUS THEATRES OF WAR.

THE SURRENDER AT SINGAPORE OF JAPANESE FORCES: SEATED AT THE DESK IS LORD LOUIS, ADDRESSING JAPANESE ENVOYS.

CAMP STANLEY, HONG KONG: SOME 2400 INTERNEES WERE LIBERATED.

PU-YI, PUPPET EMPEROR OF MANCHURIA, ENTERING THE 'PLANE IN WHICH HE WAS TAKEN TO THE RUSSIAN HEADQUATERS.

The official surrender of Japanese forces in South-East Asia took place in Singapore on September 12. Admiral Lord Louis Mountbatten promised to support the firmest measures against any attempt at evasion, impudence or obstinacy. The principal official Japanese representatives were General Itagaki and Lieut.-General Numata (Chief of Staff to Count Terauchi, the enemy Supreme Commander). A message from General MacArthur to the Japanese Imperial Headquarters, said that the Japanese forces in Hong Kong will

surrender to Rear-Admiral Harcourt, Royal Navy, at a time subsequent to August 31 and in accordance with arrangements made directly by Admiral Harcourt." Seventeen days after the arrival of the first British warships in Hong Kong Harbour, the surrender of the Japanese took place. The liberation of several thousand prisoners was delayed by Japanese obstruction, but when the Admiral said he had come with all speed, the prisoners, mostly skin and bone, laughed and cheered.

THE TRIAL AT LUNEBERG OF BELSEN AND AUSCHWITZ GAOLERS.

ON THE LEFT IS THE NOTORIOUS JOSEF KRAMER, TERMED "THE BEAST OF BELSEN," FORMER COMMANDANT OF THE CAMP, TALKING TO HIS COUNSEL, MAJOR WINWOOD.

SOME OF THE ACCUSED IN THE DOCK AT LUNEBERG COURT TRIAL. IN FRONT ARE (LEFT TO RIGHT) HERBA EHLERT (8), IRMA GRESE (9), AND ELSE LOTHE (10).

BODIES DISCOVERED IN A PINE FOREST NEAR LUNEBURG, WHERE 243 PRISONERS WERE MURDERED AND FLUNG INTO PITS BY GERMAN GUARDS.

The trial of Kramer, commandant at Belsen, and forty-four others, charged with the most ghastly crimes at Belsen and previously at Auschwitz, opened at Luneberg on September 17. Colonel Backhouse, chief prosecuting officer, declared that 13,000 corpses were found when British troops occupied the camp. Another 13,000 died within six weeks after that. The average life of a man in Block 18 was twelve days from the time of his arrival. Some of the twenty accused women, previously at Auschwitz, were said to have regularly amused themselves by setting hounds on women prisoners, who were torn to pieces. The Jewish witness, Dr. Ada Bimko, whose father, mother, brother, and little son were murdered at Auschwitz, accused Charlotte Klein of sending persons into the incinerating chamber, giving revolting details. Dr. Bimko, telling of Auschwitz, alleged that she saw healthy persons lined up for the gas chamber. One girl she knew, who cut a blanket to put around her shoulders one cold day, was sent promptly to the gas chamber. Terrible details at Belsen were also revealed by Le Druilleneg, a Jersey man, who in only nine days at Belsen, was beaten, ill-treated, and starved, and when released weighed only 7 stone, against a normal thirteen.

"OF SUPREME IMPORTANCE TO MILLIONS OF PEOPLE": THE INTERNATIONAL TRIAL, NUREMBERG – JUDGES AND DEFENDANTS.

UNIQUE IN THE ANNALS OF THE WORLD'S HISTORY: THE INTERNATIONAL TRIBUNAL IN SESSION IN THE PALACE OF JUSTICE AT NUREMBERG, SHOWING, LEFT, THE JUDGES BACKED BY THE FLAGS OF THE UNITED NATIONS AND, RIGHT, IN THE DOCK BACKED BY AMERICAN MILITARY POLICE, THE DEFENDANTS: FRONT ROW (L. TO R.) GÖRING, HESS, VON RIBBENTROP, KEITEL, ROSENBERG, FRANK, FRICK, STREICHER, FUNK AND SCHACHT; BACK ROW (L. TO R.) DÖNITZ, RAEDER, VON SCHIRACH, SAUCKEL, JODL, VON PAPEN, SEYSS-INQUART, SPEER, VON NEURATH, FRITZSCHE.

On November 20 the trial of the major Nazi war criminals opened at Nuremberg before the International Tribunal. Of the twenty-four Nazi leaders indicted, only twenty were present in court. Robert Ley committed suicide in his cell on October 26; Martin Bormann has not yet been found, and is being tried in his absence; while Ernst Kaltenbrunner and Gustav Krupp von Bohlen und Halbach were too ill to be present. Only three of the accused wore uniform in court – Göring, Keitel and Jodl – and these had been stripped of insignia. They are all charged with conspiracy, crimes against peace, war crimes, and crimes against Humanity. The Permanent President, Lord Justice Lawrence, said: "The trial which is now about to begin is unique in the history of the jurisprudence of the world, and it is of supreme importance to millions of people all over the globe. For this reason there is laid upon everybody who takes any part in this trial the solemn responsibility to discharge his duties without fear or favour in accordance with the sacred principles of law and justice." The indictment is a document of some 24,000 words, and was read to the defendants. They all made a plea of "Not guilty". The case for the prosecution was put forward by Justice Jackson, who described the prisoners as "Reproached by the humiliation of those they have led almost as bitterly as by the desolation of those they attacked, their personal capacity for evil is forever past."

THE NUREMBERG TRIAL: ASPECTS OF THE PROCEEDINGS AGAINST THE WAR CRIMINALS.

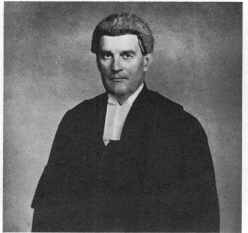

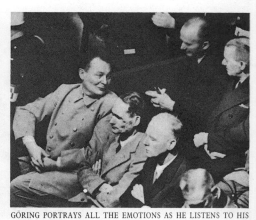

"CROWCASS" CLERKS CHECKING INCOMING P.O.W. CAMP INFORMATION SHEETS AGAINST THE CLASSIFIED DETAILS OF "WANTED" CRIMINALS IN THEIR OWN BOOKS.

LORD JUSTICE LAWRENCE, PRESIDENT OF THE INTERNATIONAL MILITARY TRIBUNAL.

GÖRING PORTRAYS ALL THE EMOTIONS AS HE LISTENS TO HIS ACCUSERS: THE "PLAYBOY" OF THE NAZI PARTY IN THE DOCK WITH HESS AND RIBBENTROP AT THE NUREMBERG TRIAL.

The elaborate interior of 53, Rue des Mathurins, Paris, the "Crowcass" organisation – the Central Registry of War Criminals and Security Suspects. The files which "Crowcass" has assembled contain exhaustive details of upwards of 7,500,000 German prisoners of war and civilians, and are recorded on cards by a system of punched holes similar to that used by our War Office for the demobilisation scheme.

Lord Justice Lawrence is the British President of the Military Tribunal now sitting at Nuremberg to try major war criminals. He is assisted by a panel of seven judges, one British, and two each from the U.S.A., Russia and France.

During the opening days of the trial of the Nazi leaders at Nuremberg much attention has been paid to the behaviour of the prisoners in court. Known formerly as the "playboy" of the Party, Göring's attitudes and expression provide a pictorial commentary on the trial, showing in turn amusement, boredom, anger, concentration and anxiety. Beside him sits Hess, who usually maintains an attitude of complete detachment.

THE RELEASE OF PRISONERS AFTER THE FINAL DEFEAT OF JAPAN.

TERRIBLY EMACIATED, BUT FREE AGAIN AND SMILING, TWO OF
THE PRISONERS RECENTLY LIBERATED.

THE "LUXURIOUS" HOME OF TWO INTERNEES: LIKE OTHERS,
THEIR SPIRIT REMAINED UNBROKEN TO THE END.

FREED AT LAST! BRITISH AND AMERICAN P.O.W.'S, HALF-NAKED,
BUT CHEERING, SHOUTING AND LAUGHING, GREET THE ALLIES.

After the British capitulation at Singapore in February 1942, civilians were rounded up, herded into a series of prison camps in conditions of indescribable filth and misery – one example is that latrine buckets and garbage tins had to be used for cooking and distributing food – or crammed into Changi Criminal Jail. Into this jail, built in 1936 to accommodate 600 prisoners, the Japanese packed more than 3000 internees, including 650 women and children. Among the countless discomforts of the internees, the jail was infested with bed bugs, the great majority of the prisoners were grossly deficient in even the barest necessities of life, and the food was so poor in quality and minute in quantity that the internees became progressively more and more emaciated.

Under such conditions illness and disease were, of course, a grave problem aggravated by an acute shortage of medical supplies which the Japanese made no attempt to alleviate. Among psychological cruelties practised by the Japanese – apart from many examples of physical ill-treatment and torturing of internees, often resulting in agonising deaths – was the complete separation of husbands from wives, and of parents from their children. These and other inhuman cruelties produced an atmosphere of dark terrorism in which the internees lived with the constant fear that such little restraint as was exercised by their guards might at any moment be completely cast aside, with results too horrible to contemplate.

A TRIAL IN MANILA.

GENERAL YAMASHITA, LEAVING THE COURT-ROOM AT MANILA,
DURING HIS TRIAL AS WAR CRIMINAL, BETWEEN HIS COUNSEL,
COLONEL CLARKE (LEFT) AND CAPTAIN REEL (RIGHT).

During the trial of General Yamashita, the Japanese commander in the Philippines, on charges of being a war criminal, a tale of ghastly atrocities by the Japanese under his command has been unfolded by witnesses. This ghastly record was directly linked with Yamashita by a witness who reported hearing the Japanese General maintain that the Filipinos were enemies of Japan and giving orders that they should be wiped out. Yamashita was found "guilty" of condoning crimes, and was hanged in Los Banos, Philippines, on February 23, 1946.

THE EMPEROR OF JAPAN INFORMS HIS ANCESTORS THAT THE WAR IS ENDED.

THE EMPEROR PAYING HOMAGE AT THE IMPERIAL TOMB OF HIS
ANCESTORS DURING HIS RITUAL VISIT TO INFORM THEM OF THE
END OF THE WAR.

The Emperor of Japan travelled recently by private train to the Imperial Tomb for the ritual purpose of informing his ancestors of the ending of the war. The Japanese State religion of Shinto, combining the ancient cult of ancestor-worship, reaches its culmination in the form of Emperor-worship. There is only one higher degree – the worship of the Emperor himself by his divine ancestors, in the pursuit of which he made this journey to the shrine of his forbears to bring them news of the downfall of their people.

JAPANESE ARMS DESTROYED.

THE FUNERAL PYRE OF JAPANESE "SUICIDE" AIRCRAFT: PART OF
THE HUGE DUMP OF KAMIKAZE 'PLANES WHICH WAS SET ON FIRE
BY FLAME-THROWING TANKS AT SASEBO.

Following the U.S. policy of destroying Japanese equipment, large quantities of guns and other weapons have been carried out to sea and pushed overboard or burnt, less portable weapons have been sprayed with petrol and burnt, while units of the Japanese navy, notably the battleship "Nagato" are to be used in tests of the effectiveness of atomic bombs against surface vessels to discover if the bomb will cause the destruction of such a vessel; what it will do to a fleet; and what effect it will have on the sea.

THE "YANKS" GO HOME.

PASSENGERS ON BOARD THE LINER "QUEEN ELIZABETH" – ANNO
DOMINI 1945.

The passengers seen crowding the "Queen Elizabeth" – the world's largest and fastest liner – are part of a contingent of about 14,000 American soldiers returning home after the end of the war in Europe. Both the "Queen Elizabeth" and the "Queen Mary" are being used in the repatriation of U.S. and Canadian troops.

ANGRY "G.I." WIVES.

A GROUP OF "G.I." WIVES, WITH THEIR BABIES, IN A QUEUE
HOPING TO ENTER CAXTON HALL FOR THE MEETING DEMANDING
PASSAGES TO AMERICA.

On October 11 over 1500 mainly young British brides surged up and down the roads outside Caxton Hall, Westminster, one and all concentrated on the same object – to get transport to take them to the States to their soldier husbands. Out of the 1500 women from all parts, only 150 were able to obtain entrance into Caxton Hall, owing to limited accommodation. Some of them had waited five hours outside. Dark-haired Mrs. Frances Rhodes, of Manchester, presided, and there were several stormy scenes interspersed with laughter. Commander Agar, of the U.S. Embassy, told the wives they were not "forgotten," but they would have to wait until accommodation could be provided. The wives who were unable to obtain entrance held indignation meetings in the street while others marched along Whitehall, obtaining sympathy and cheers from "G.I.s."

FROM WARPLANES TO SAUCEPANS.

FULL CIRCLE: ALUMINIUM PROPELLERS BEING LOADED INTO A
FURNACE DURING RECONVERSION TO SAUCEPANS.

This war-to-peace reconversion scene was photographed in a factory in the London area at which propellers from fighters and bombers of the Royal Air Force are being melted down and recast into the saucepans which Britain's housewives so gallantly sacrificed in the dangerous days of our aircraft shortage.

THE ILLUSTRATED LONDON NEWS

A BRITISH-FIRED V-2 ROCKET BOMB STREAKING UP FROM AN EXPERIMENTAL LAUNCHING-STATION IN GERMANY: ITS TARGET WAS 150 MILES DISTANT – IN THE NORTH SEA.

The first V-2 rocket-bombs launched by British experts recently streaked into the air from Cuxhaven, in Germany, aimed at a target area 150 miles out in the North Sea. One of them fell within three miles of the target point. These launchings followed intensive research and preparation based on such parts of V-2 weapons as were available after the collapse of Germany, together with statements of German rocket technicians on the methods they employed. No launching-site was available, and Royal Engineers constructed one in six weeks, with large buildings for the testing and assembly of the rockets. The work has been carried out by scientific experts of the B.A.O.R. and technicians from the Ministry of Supply. These V-2s incorporated improvements designed by British brains, and their launching was greatly assisted by newly-designed guiding devices. They are said to be the first launched since the last of more than a thousand hit Southern England.

INDEX